SHAKESPEARE SURVEY

ADVISORY BOARD

Aspects of *Macbeth*
Aspects of *Othello*
Aspects of *Hamlet*
Aspects of *King Lear*
Aspects of Shakespeare's 'Problem Plays'

SHAKESPEARE SURVEY

62

Close Encounters with Shakespeare's Text

EDITED BY

PETER HOLLAND

CAMBRIDGE
UNIVERSITY PRESS

CAMBRIDGE UNIVERSITY PRESS
Cambridge, New York, Melbourne, Madrid, Cape Town, Singapore, São Paulo, Delhi

Cambridge University Press
The Edinburgh Building, Cambridge CB2 8RU, UK

Published in the United States of America by Cambridge University Press, New York

www.cambridge.org
Information on this title: www.cambridge.org/9780521111034

First published 2009

Printed in the United Kingdom at the University Press, Cambridge

A catalogue record for this publication is available from the British Library

ISBN 978-0-521-11103-4 hardback

EDITOR'S NOTE

Volume 63, on 'Shakespeare's English Histories and their Afterlives', will be at press by the time this volume appears. The theme of Volume 64 will be 'Shakespeare as Cultural Catalyst' and of Volume 65 will be '*A Midsummer Night's Dream*'.

Submissions should be addressed to the Editor at The Shakespeare Institute, Church Street, Stratford-upon-Avon, Warwickshire CV37 6HP, to arrive at the latest by 1 September 2010 for Volume 64 and 1 September 2011 for Volume 65. Pressures on space are heavy and priority is given to articles related to the theme of a particular volume. Please send a copy you do not wish to be returned. Submissions may also be made as attachments to e-mail to pholland@nd.edu. All articles submitted are read by the Editor and at least one member of the Advisory Board, whose indispensable assistance the Editor gratefully acknowledges.

Unless otherwise indicated, Shakespeare quotations and references are keyed to *The Complete Works*, ed. Stanley Wells, Gary Taylor, John Jowett and William Montgomery, 2nd edition (Oxford, 2005).

Review copies should be addressed to the Editor as above. In attempting to survey the ever-increasing bulk of Shakespeare publications our reviewers inevitably have to exercise some selection. We are pleased to receive offprints of articles which help to draw our reviewers' attention to relevant material.

P.D.H.

CONTRIBUTORS

ROBERTA BARKER, *Dalhousie University*
JUDITH BUCHANAN, *University of York*
ROB CONKIE, *La Trobe University*
NATASHA DISTILLER, *University of Cape Town*
PAUL EDMONDSON, *Shakespeare Birthplace Trust*
LUKAS ERNE, *University of Geneva*
ANDREW JAMES HARTLEY, *University of North Carolina, Charlotte*
DAVID HILLMAN, *University of Cambridge*
TON HOENSELAARS, *Utrecht University*
GRAHAM HOLDERNESS, *University of Hertfordshire*
PETER HOLLAND, *University of Notre Dame*
SHOICHIRO KAWAI, *University of Tokyo*
ALYSIA KOLENTSIS, *University of Toronto*
HESTER LEES-JEFFRIES, *University of Cambridge*
LYNNE MAGNUSSON, *University of Toronto*
SONIA MASSAI, *King's College, London*
CARY M. MAZER, *University of Pennsylvania*
MICHAEL NEILL, *University of Auckland*
REIKO OYA, *Keio University*
ROBERT B. PIERCE, *Oberlin College*
ERIC RASMUSSEN, *University of Nevada, Reno*
THOMAS RIST, *University of Aberdeen*
CAROL CHILLINGTON RUTTER, *University of Warwick*
JULIE SANDERS, *University of Nottingham*
HANNA SCOLNICOV, *Tel Aviv University*
ROBERT SHAUGHNESSY, *University of Kent*
JAMES SHAW, *University of Oxford*
STUART SILLARS, *University of Bergen*
CATHERINE SILVERSTONE, *Queen Mary, University of London*
EMMA SMITH, *University of Oxford*
PAUL WERSTINE, *University of Western Ontario*
YONG LI LAN, *National University of Singapore*

CONTENTS

vii

CONTENTS

ILLUSTRATIONS AND TABLES

ILLUSTRATIONS AND TABLES

ILLUSTRATIONS AND TABLES

ILLUSTRATIONS AND TABLES

SHAKESPEARE, TEXT AND PARATEXT

SONIA MASSAI

'Reader, . . . Introth you are a stranger to me; why should I Write to you? you neuer writ to mee.'
(Nathaniel Field, *A Woman is a Weather-Cock*, STC 10854, 1612, A3ᵛ)

'To the onely rewarder, and most iust poiser of vertuous merits, the most honorably renowned No-body, bounteous Mecænas of Poetry, and Lord Protector of oppressed innocence.'
(John Marston, *Antonio and Mellida*, STC 17473, 1602, A2)

The early modern dramatic paratext is a rich and varied repository of tributes to patrons and readers, where dramatists negotiated or parodied their attitudes towards dramatic publication and their reliance on the medium of print as a source of income and literary reputation. However, the lack of signed dedications or addresses to the reader in the early editions of Shakespeare's plays has deflected critical and editorial attention from early modern dramatic paratexts and from the significance of other paratextual features in Shakespeare, including title-pages, head titles, running titles and act and scene divisions. This article shows that a close analysis of some of these features and a contrastive analysis of Shakespearian and non-Shakespearian early modern playbooks lend fresh insight into what we mean by 'Shakespeare' and 'text' and how the texts of Shakespeare's plays are edited and re-presented to the modern reader.

Critical and editorial neglect of paratextual features in the early editions of Shakespeare's plays is also due to the enduring legacy of the New Bib-liography. One crucial aspect of this legacy is the common tendency to identify the printer's copy rather than the printed text as the ultimate source of textual authority. As a result, all those features that were added to the printer's copy as the dramatic manuscript was transmitted into print and transformed into a reading text tend to be over-looked. The paradox of course is that no dramatic manuscripts used as printer's copy to set up early modern playbooks have survived.[1] Scholars interested in Shakespeare and performance often criticize the 'tyranny of print'.[2] Ironically, the study of Shakespeare in print has also been deeply affected by the 'tyranny of the lost manuscript'. This understanding of the printed text as a misrepresentation of the printer's copy, combined with the absence of any address or dedication signed by Shakespeare, has in turn led to a near-universal misconception of the paratext as marginal, dispensable, occasional, fundamentally different and ultimately detachable from the text.

Even the more familiar types of theatrical paratexts, such as prologues, epilogues, presenters and choruses, are regarded as inherently different and separate from the main body of the dramatic

---

[1] No dramatic manuscripts or printed editions were for example identified as printer's copies used to set up extant early modern playbooks by J. K. Moore in *Primary Materials Relating to Copy and Print in English Books of the Sixteenth and Seventeenth Centuries* (Oxford, 1992).

[2] See, for example, Margaret Jane Kidnie, 'Where is *Hamlet*? Text, Performance, and Adaptation', in Barbara Hodgdon and W. B. Worthen, eds., *A Companion to Shakespeare and Performance* (Oxford, 2005), pp. 101–20; p. 104.

dialogue, or the *text* of the play. Early modern theatrical paratexts may indeed have been detachable from the plays in performance. According to Tiffany Stern, prologues and epilogues were meant 'for new plays and, more specifically, for new plays before their benefit performance'.[3] But prologues and epilogues, along with title-pages, dedications, addresses, dedicatory poems, lists of dramatis personae and errata, postscripts and colophons, were certainly not detachable, nor were they meant to be detached from the printed playbooks which originally included them. It is certainly true that preliminaries were often printed last and on independent units or sub-units of paper. This practice was, however, driven by the practical challenge of casting-off the printer's copy before the presswork started rather than by any difference in the perceived status of prefatory materials when compared to the rest of the text. And it is certainly true that early modern playwrights occasionally maximized their chances to secure patronage by adding dedications only to presentation copies[4] or by using the same edition to woo different patrons.[5] But the presence or absence of a dedication or any other paratextual feature has a significant impact on how the playbook presents itself to the reader. Well known is the alternative presentation of *Troilus and Cressida* '*As it was acted by the Kings Maiesties* seruants at the Globe' or as '*a new play, neuer stal'd with the Stage, neuer clapper-clawd with the palmes of the vulger*' (¶2) in the two issues of the 1609 edition. As John Jowett has most recently put it, the two issues of *Troilus and Cressida* turn the play into 'a cultural object that exists in relation to posited readers . . . the regular purchaser of plays from the Globe [and] the coterie readership that the reset preliminaries seem to court'.[6]

Even more crucially, early modern theatrical paratexts cannot always be disentangled from the text. In *Summers Last Will and Testament* (STC 18376, 1600), the opening stage direction reads as follows: '*Enter Will Summers in his fooles coate but halfe on, comming out*' (B1). The actor is half-dressed and not quite ready to play Tudor jester Will Sommers. The actor is also reluctant to play his role

as presenter, or prologue: 'Other stately pac't *Prologues* vse to attire themselues within: I that haue a toy in my head, more then ordinary, and vse to goe without money, without garters, without girdle, without a hat-band, without poynts to my hose, without a knife to my dinner, and make so much vse of this word *without*, in euery thing, will here dresse me with-out' (B1). The actor is most obviously 'without' the fictive world of Nashe's masque when he, 'a foole by nature', playing Will Sommers, a fool 'by arte', proclaims to be speaking to the audience '*in the person* of the Idiot our Playmaker' (my emphasis, B1) The actor continues to stay 'without' the masque by acting as a disparaging commentator – he calls the masque a 'dry sport' (D1) and confesses half way through that 'I was almost asleep; I thought I had bene at a Sermon' (C1ᵛ). But he also interacts with the characters, most memorably when Bacchus forces him to drink and knights him by dubbing him with his '*black Iacke*' (D2). Will Sommers is simultaneously within and without Nashe's masque, he is simultaneously text and paratext.

Drawing a distinction between text and paratext is just as difficult in plays written for the commercial stage. The Chorus in the First Folio edition

---

[3] Tiffany Stern, '"A small-beer health to his second day": Playwrights, Prologues, and First Performances in the Early Modern Theatre', in *Studies in Philology*, 101 (2004), 172–99; p. 174.

[4] A dedication to the 'intire friends to the familie of the Sherleys', signed by John Day, William Rowley and John Wilkins, was, for example, added to only a few copies of the 1607 edition of *The Travels of the Three English Brothers* (STC 6417). Interestingly, the dedication attempts to reconcile the tension between the wide circulation ensured by print and the authors' wish to present their play only to friends of the family: '*wee wish all to peruse, and yet none but friends, because wee wish all should be friends to worth and desert*' (A1).

[5] An autograph epistle 'To my Honorable Freinde Sʳ Francis Foliambe knight and Baronet', signed by Philip Massinger, was inscribed on X2v in one copy of the 1623 quarto edition of *The Duke of Milan* (STC 17634), although all extant copies already include a printed dedication 'To the Right Honourable and much esteemed . . . Lady Katherine Stanhope'.

[6] John Jowett, *Shakespeare and Text*, Oxford Shakespeare Topics (Oxford, 2007), pp. 61, 64.

of Shakespeare's *Henry V*, for example, fulfils both textual and paratextual functions. Conventionally paratextual is the classical trope of the authorial invocation of divine inspiration in its opening lines: 'O For a Muse of Fire, that would ascend / The brightest Heauen of Inuention'. Similarly paratextual is the Chorus's prologue-like appeal to the audience – 'let vs, Cyphers to this great Accompt, / On your imaginarie Forces worke' – and the explicit instruction to 'Suppose within the Girdles of these Walls / Are now confin'd two mightie Monarchies' (STC 22273, h1). As in Nashe's masque, the Chorus in *Henry V* functions as prologue, presenter, actor, authorial persona but also as a character. After Act 1, for example, the Chorus echoes Harry's parting lines – 'omit no happy howre, / That may giue furth'rance to our Expedition: / For we haue now no thought in vs but France' – as Harry is leaving the stage: 'Now all the Youth of England are on fire, . . . For now sits Expectation in the Ayre' (h2ᵛ). The Chorus of course used to be a character in Greek tragedy, where it originated, and it is still primarily a character in plays like *Gorboduc*, which self-consciously imitates classical models. The Chorus in *Henry V* is similarly a character, but it is also actor and authorial persona, prologue, epilogue and presenter.

One further feature of Nashe's masque seems enlightening when thinking about 'Shakespeare', 'text' and 'paratext'. Towards the end of his first speech, Will Sommers delivers the following lesson to the actors:

Actors, you Rogues, come away, cleare your throats, blowe your noses, and wype your mouthes e're you enter, that you may take no occasion to spit or to cough, when you are *non plus*. And this I barre ouer and besides, That none of you stroake your beardes, to make action, play with your cod-piece poynts, or städ fumbling on your buttons, when you know not how to bestow your fingers (B2).

This lesson to the actors is delivered by a presenter-epilogue-authorial persona-character in the opening speech of Nashe's masque. Hamlet's lesson to the actors – 'Speake the speech I pray you as I pronoun'd [sic] it to you, trippingly on the tongue'

(Q2, G3ᵛ, STC 22276)[7] – is delivered in character and half-way through the play. However, both distinctions – within or without the fictive world of the play, within or without the printed text of the play – are often unhelpful.

Our readiness to endorse these distinctions is intimately connected to the etymology of the very word we use to describe the paratext. The etymology of the word 'paratext' implies a spatial dislocation, meaning 'next to, by the side of, beside' (*OED*) the text. Gérard Genette's influential definition of paratext as a 'threshold, or "vestibule" that offers the world at large the possibility of either stepping inside or turning back', or as a 'transitional zone between text and beyond text',[8] reinforces distinctions that are quite simply inadequate and counterproductive when applied to early modern printed playbooks.[9] As much as early modern

---

7 'Pronounce me this speech trippingly a the tongue' Q1, F2, STC 22275; 'Speake the Speech I pray you, as I pronounc'd it to you trippingly on the Tongue', F1, Oo5ᵛ STC 22273.

8 Gérard Genette, *Paratexts: Thresholds of Interpretation*, trans. by Jane E. Lewin, foreword by Richard Macksey (Cambridge, 1997), pp. 2, 407.

9 Genette's definition is neither misleading nor anachronistic in relation to other types of early modern paratexts. According to Wendy Wall, for example, the shift from manuscript to print for the circulation of sixteenth-century sonnet sequences and poetic miscellanies often led their predominantly male authors to 'convey a sense of social scandal by naming publication in terms of spatial metaphors' and their publications 'as ladies lavishly displayed to a public audience' (*The Imprint of Gender: Authorship and Publication in the English Renaissance* (Ithaca, NY and London, 1993), pp. 180–1). The sense of disclosure and voyeuristic exposure of intimate spaces and bodies to the gaze of the reader would certainly seem to be in keeping with the wider circulation which was suddenly afforded by print to texts which were previously reserved for the eyes of a few select readers. Spatial metaphors – the threshold or the vestibule – therefore work well to describe the sense of 'social scandal' brought about by the printing of this type of texts for a multitude of anonymous readers. The publication of commercial drama evoked quite an opposite set of anxieties, as scholars of Jonson, Chapman and Webster, among others, know full well. The trajectory of dramatic publication of plays originally performed in the London open theatres started from a public, commercial space open to anybody who cared to attend a show and aimed to reach a much smaller and select group of discerning readers.

drama is intrinsically metadramatic, early modern printed playbooks are self-consciously meta- rather than para-textual, meta- meaning both 'next to, by the side of, beside' *and* 'denoting change and transformation' (*OED*), as in 'metamorphosis'. The presence of what we improperly call paratext in early modern playbooks is genuinely and thoroughly transformative. Detaching metatextual features from early modern playbooks is as foolish as attempting to draw a distinction between Hamlet's soliloquies and his lesson to the actors, between drama and metadrama. By contrast, regarding as *text* all the different parts of early modern printed playbooks, including paratextual features such as title-pages, head-titles, running titles, and act and scene divisions, which are normally excluded from or normalized in modern critical editions of Shakespeare's plays, can be extremely beneficial, because it forces us to rethink what we mean by 'Shakespeare' and 'text' and how we edit Shakespeare for the modern reader.

The recent re-definition of 'Shakespeare' as 'literary dramatist', for example, has been useful in refocusing critical and editorial attention on the printed text. However, this definition is somewhat qualified by a closer look at Shakespeare's text, if by text we mean anything and everything included (or not included) in the early playbooks. A glaring anomaly for a playwright supposedly committed to dramatic publication is the lack of any signed or unsigned dedication, address or postscript in the early editions of plays published during Shakespeare's lifetime. Worth pointing out is that Ben Jonson,[10] John Marston[11] and Thomas Dekker[12] wrote addresses to their readers and occasionally signed them, starting from the early 1600s. Also problematic is the drop in the number of first editions of Shakespeare's plays after 1602 and the fact that only two Jacobean plays – *King Lear* (STC 22292, 1608) and *Pericles* (STC 22334–5, 1609) – reached the press after 1603.[13] Theories advanced so far to explain the drop in the number of new Shakespearian editions after 1602–3 are fundamentally unsatisfactory. In his book *Shakespeare as Literary Dramatist*, Lukas Erne discusses and only partly

endorses two popular theories, '[a] temporary glut in the playbooks market and the resurrection of the children's companies'.[14] However, other playwrights published plays written for the commercial stage at regular intervals during the first decade of the seventeenth century. Nine of Thomas Dekker's plays were for example published between 1600 and 1612, and only two of them had been written for the same children's company, the Children of Paul's.[15] The alternative theory endorsed by Erne and shared by others is that Shakespeare and the King's Men, inspired by Jonson's example, were already planning a collected edition.[16] Once again, this explanation is highly problematic, considering that Jonson went on to publish eighteen plays and masques at regular intervals between the early 1600s

---

10 Ben Jonson, *Cynthia's Revels* (STC 14773, 1601), unsigned; *Sejanus, His Fall* (STC 14782, 1605), signed.

11 John Marston, *Antonio and Mellida* (STC 17473, 1602), signed.

12 Thomas Dekker [with John Marston?], *Satiromastix* (STC 6520.7, 1602), unsigned.

13 Two Elizabethan plays were printed after Elizabeth's death: *Hamlet* was entered in the Stationers' Register on 26 July 1602 but it was published (after 19 May) 1603, see Greg, *A Bibliography of the English Printed Drama to the Restoration* (Oxford, 1939–1959), p. 309; *Troilus and Cressida* was entered in the Stationers' Register on 7 February 1603 but was not printed until 1609.

14 Lukas Erne, *Shakespeare as Literary Dramatist* (Cambridge, 2003), p. 107.

15 *Satiromastix* (STC 6520.7, 1602) was exceptionally performed by the Chamberlain's Men and by the Children of Paul's. Erne does stress that the 'glut in the playbooks market' may only provide a partial explanation for the lack of new Shakespearian plays in print in the first half of the 1600s, because 'the four-year period from 1605 to 1608 saw the publication of no fewer than fifty-two plays written for the commercial stage, more than in any other four-year period during Shakespeare's lifetime' (p. 109). Also worth noting is the fact that new plays published in the first decade of the seventeenth century are attributed to 'W. S.' or to 'W. Shakespeare'. These are *Thomas Lord Cromwell* (STC 21532, 1602), *The Puritan* (STC 21531, 1607), and *The Yorkshire Tragedy* (STC 22340, 1609). The Shakespearian plays that do get published in the 1600s also include Shakespeare's name on the title-page, sometimes foregrounding it by placing it first, as in the first quarto of *King Lear* (STC 22292, 1608).

16 Erne, *Shakespeare as Literary Dramatist*, p. 110.

and 1612, and that all of these plays and masques were then included in the 1616 Folio, except for *The Case is Altered* (STC 14757, 1609) and, unsurprisingly, *Eastward Ho!* (STC 4970–3, 1605). The likelihood that Shakespeare's popularity was on the wane is also remote, given the sheer number of apocryphal plays attributed either to 'W.S' or to 'W. Shakespeare' in the first decade of the seventeenth century and the prominence accorded to Shakespeare's name and reputation in all the Jacobean editions of his plays and poems.[17]

A different explanation for the drastic drop in the number of new editions of Shakespeare's plays printed after 1603 can be found on the title-pages of the early playbooks. If the impulse to commit Shakespeare's plays to print had come primarily from Shakespeare or his company, Shakespeare's name would have featured consistently on title-pages starting from 1598, when, as Erne puts it, '"Shakespeare", the author of dramatic texts, was born.'[18] However, Shakespeare's name is absent not only from the title-page of two 'bad' quartos, namely the first and second editions of *Henry V* (STC 22289, 1600; STC 22290, 1602), but also from the second edition of *Romeo and Juliet*, where the title-page goes as far as advertising the text as 'Newly corrected, augmented, and amended' (STC 22323, 1599), but does not mention Shakespeare. What is strikingly consistent is the correlation between some stationers and the inclusion or exclusion of Shakespeare's name on title-pages. For example, Thomas Millington, bookseller in London between 1593 and 1603,[19] acted as publisher or retailing bookseller of Shakespeare's plays both before and after 1598,[20] but none of the plays published or retailed by Millington included Shakespeare's name on their title-pages. Cuthbert Burby, stationer in London between 1592 and 1607,[21] also published Shakespeare's plays both before and after 1598, but while the title-page of his 1598 edition of *Love's Labour's Lost* identifies Shakespeare as corrector and reviser of an earlier version of the play,[22] possibly an earlier printed edition which is no longer extant,[23] the title-page of his 1599 edition of *Romeo and*

Juliet fails to identify Shakespeare as the corrector and reviser of the first quarto edition printed and published by John Danter in 1597.[24] By contrast,

---

[17] The fact that Shakespeare's name is printed in large-sized letters at the top of the title-page of the first quarto edition of *King Lear* (STC 22292, 1608) has often been discussed by editors and textual scholars. See, most recently: Douglas Brooks, '*King Lear* (1608) and the Typography of Literary Ambition', in Jeffrey Masten and Wendy Wall, eds., *Institutions of the Text, Renaissance Drama*, 30 (2001), pp. 133–59. Also 'sensational' is the title-page in Thomas Thorpe's 1609 collection of poems: 'SHAKE-SPEARES SONNETS. Neuer before Imprinted', set, once again, in large, capital letters at the top of the title-page. Thorpe's initials also feature at the end of a dedication which addresses Shakespeare as 'OVR.EVERLIVING.POET' (STC 22353, 1609). The address to the reader added to the second issue of *Troilus and Cressida* similarly mentions Shakespeare's popularity as a writer of witty, conceited comedies comparable to Terence and Plautus and predicts a time 'when hee is gone, and his Commedies out of sale, [the readers] will scramble for them, and set vp a new English Inquisition' (STC 22332, 1609, A2v).

[18] Erne, *Shakespeare as Literary Dramatist*, p. 63.

[19] R. B. McKerrow, *A Dictionary of Printers and Booksellers in England, Scotland and Ireland, and of Foreign Printers of English Books, 1557–1640* (London, 1910), pp. 193–4.

[20] Thomas Millington was the publisher of the first and second quarto editions of *2 Henry VI*, printed by Thomas Creede in 1594 (STC 26099) and by Valentine Simmes in 1600 (STC 26100), and of the first and second editions of *3 Henry VI*, printed by Peter Short in 1595 (STC 21006) and by William White in 1600 (STC 21006a). Millington also acted as retailing bookseller of the first quarto edition of *Titus Andronicus* in 1594 (STC 22328) and as co-publisher with John Busby of the first quarto edition of *Henry V* in 1600 (STC 22289).

[21] McKerrow, *A Dictionary*, p. 55.

[22] 'Newly corrected and augmented | By W. Shakespere' (STC 22294).

[23] See, for example, Arthur Freeman and Paul Grinke, 'Four New Shakespeare Quartos' in *The Times Literary Supplement*, 5 April 2002, which offers fresh external evidence to prove that an earlier edition did exist and that it was dated 1597, as shown by the library catalogue of Edward, 2nd Viscount Conway.

[24] The title-page of Burby's second quarto edition of *Romeo and Juliet* (STC 22323) goes as far as drawing the reader's attention to the fact that the text of Danter's first quarto edition (STC 22322) had been 'Newly corrected, augmented, and | amended', but does not attribute the correction and revision to Shakespeare. Burby was also the publisher of the

starting from 1598, Andrew Wise's editions of *Richard II*, *Richard III*, *1 Henry IV* and *Much Ado About Nothing* include authorial attributions on their title-pages.[25]

The title-pages of Wise's editions highlight another interesting correlation between Shakespeare's name and the name of his patron. The Lord Chamberlain's name features on thirteen title-pages of plays printed in the late 1590s/early 1600s and ten of these plays are by Shakespeare and nine were published by Wise.[26] Furthermore, as I have established elsewhere, Andrew Wise published the work of two other main authors beside Shakespeare, viz. Thomas Nashe and Thomas Playfere, and all three of them were under the direct patronage and protection of George Carey, Lord Chamberlain between 1597 and 1603.[27] So far, royal and aristocratic patronage has been identified as having a beneficial influence on the development of early English drama *in performance*.[28] The early editions of Shakespeare's plays show that royal and aristocratic patronage had a similarly beneficial influence on the development of early English drama *in print*. This conclusion would seem to tally with David Bergeron's observation that dedications to royal and aristocratic patrons increased in printed playbooks in the 1630s, when dramatic publication was most buoyant.[29] Ironically, 'the change of reign and patron',[30] the one explanation rejected by Erne as 'far-fetched', seems to me entirely plausible. The evidence provided by paratextual features in early playbooks supports what we have known for a long time: that the thrifty Elizabeth made plays rather than masques the staple feature of Court entertainments;[31] that Elizabeth introduced a conventional 'reward' for the actors on top of the standard payment, a custom which was no longer observed by members of James's family, who watched plays at the standard rate;[32] that George Carey was a patron of the arts, but that Thomas Howard, Lord Chamberlain from 1603, never took the slightest interest in the actors; and that the deficit the Chamber Treasury routinely ran under James very nearly wiped the Revels Office out of existence in 1607.[33] The frequency of new editions up to 1602–3 and the connection

between the emergence of Shakespeare's name in print and aristocratic patronage would therefore seem to suggest that Shakespeare regarded dramatic publication targeted at a relatively small number of select readers as an extension of his services to his patron and the small number of select spectators who, by the sheer act of watching his plays, turned them from popular to courtly entertainment.

Shakespeare was no Jonson. Positing a Shakespeare who saw the stage and the page as opportunities directly related to his position as a company man, as a Lord Chamberlain's Man, makes more sense than positing a Shakespeare who single-mindedly willed his plays into print. In turn, understanding Shakespeare as a company man, as

---

first and second quarto editions of *Edward III* (STC 7501, 1596; STC 7502, 1599).

25 The only exception is the first quarto edition of *1 Henry IV* (STC 22280, 1598; this edition was preceded by an earlier edition, generally referred to as Q0, of which only quire C is extant, STC 22279a), which was entered in *The Stationers' Register* on 25 February 1598 and may have preceded the printing and publication also in 1598 of the second and third editions of *Richard II* (STC 22308 and STC 22309) and the second edition of *Richard III* (STC 22315).

26 The only two exceptions are the first and second quarto editions of *1 Henry IV* (STC 22280, 1598 and STC 22281, 1599).

27 See Sonia Massai, *Shakespeare and the Rise of the Editor* (Cambridge, 2007), pp. 91–105.

28 See, for example, Richard Dutton, *The Mastering of the Revels: The Regulation and Censorship of English Renaissance Drama* (Basingstoke, 1991), or, more recently, Andrew Gurr, *The Shakespeare Company, 1594–1642* (Cambridge, 2004).

29 David M. Bergeron, *Textual Patronage in English Drama, 1570–1640* (Aldershot, 2006), pp. 20ff.

30 Erne, *Shakespeare as Literary Dramatist*, p. 109.

31 John Pitcher, *Jacobean and Caroline Revels Accounts, 1603–1642*, *Malone Society Collections* 13 (1986), p. xviii.

32 W. W. Greg, *Dramatic Records in the Declared Accounts of the Treasurer of the Chamber, 1558–1642*, *Malone Society Collections* 6 (1961 [1962]), p. xxv.

33 The Revels Office, traditionally housed in the priory of St John of Jerusalem in Clerkenwell, was made homeless, destitute and hardly in a position to remain operative from 9 May 1607, when James gave the Priory to his cousin Esmé Stuart, Lord Aubigny. For further details, see Greg, *Dramatic Records*, p. xi; Pitcher, *Revels Accounts*, pp. xiii–xiv.

opposed to 'Shakespeare as Literary Dramatist', does make a difference in terms of how we read Shakespeare and what we regard as 'Shakespeare'. More specifically, reading Shakespeare's histories, the most popular of Shakespeare's histories, as performed *and* printed under the patronage of the Lord Chamberlain has important implications for the type of writer we think Shakespeare was and for what we think he may or may not have written.

The Lamentable Tragedie of Locrine is a good case in point. *Locrine*, printed in 1595, was an older play, written possibly by George Peele, or, more probably by Robert Greene, and, as the title-page tells us, it was 'Newly set foorth, ouerseene and corrected, *By W. S.*' (STC 21528). By far the most sensible theory about the identity of '*W.S.*' was put forward by C. F. Tucker Brooke in 1908, who argued that 'there is . . . no shadow of a reason why we should not accept as absolute truth the statement of the title-page'. Tucker Brooke also believed that out of all the known potential candidates 'possessed of those initials'[34] – namely William Smith, son-neteer, William Stanley, Earl of Derby and patron of actors, Wentworth Smith, jobbing dramatist in the early 1600s, William Smyght and William Sheppard, actors – William Shakespeare is the most likely candidate.[35]

What interests me, of course, is the epilogue and why this interesting specimen of theatrical paratext seems to have been all but forgotten.

> Lo here the end of lawlesse trecherie,
> Of vsurpation and ambitious pride,
> And they that for their priuate amours dare
> Turmoile our land, and see their broiles abroach,
> Let them be warned by these premisses,
> And as a woman was the onely cause
> That ciuill discord was then stirred vp,
> So let vs pray for that renowned mayd,
> That eight and thirtie yeares the scepter swayd,
> In quiet peace and sweet felicitie,
> And euery wight that seekes her graces smart,
> wold that this sword wer pierced in his hart.

This epilogue, a tribute to the Queen universally ascribed to the reviser '*W.S.*', was very possibly written for a revival of the play at Court by the Queen's Men, with whom Shakespeare is likely to have been connected before he became a Lord Chamberlain's Man. I again agree with Tucker Brooke when he claims that 'there is no question connected with *Locrine* which is less worth the settling' than whether Shakespeare wrote this epilogue.[36] What is crucial is not the authenticity of this epilogue, but the fact that it was ascribed to '*W. S.*', that contemporary readers would have associated those initials with William Shakespeare more readily than with any other known play-wrights or writers in the mid-1590s, and that we do not seem to take the slightest interest in the significance of this attribution. This blind spot may be due to our expectation of what Shakespeare's debut in print should have looked like: '*W. S.*' is not a literary dramatist self-consciously using the medium of print for the sole purpose of shaping his literary reputation; '*W. S.*' is a popular dramatist whose name is for the first time deemed attractive enough to entice readers to buy the edition of an older play. '*W. S.*' is also connected to the one section of the text that draws attention to the 'here and now', to the time of publication, by eulogizing the 'eight and thirty years' of Elizabeth's reign. In other words, this '*W. S.*' is interestingly in keeping with the William Shakespeare who as a company man would continue to regard the stage and the page as extensions of his service to his patron, possibly as a member of the Queen's Men

---

34 C. F. Tucker Brooke, *The Shakespeare Apocrypha* (Oxford, 1908), p. xx.

35 See also Jane Lytton Gooch, ed., *The Lamentable Tragedy of Locrine, A Critical Edition* (New York and London: Garland, 1981), p. 29. I would add that while the use of the initials on title-pages of apocryphal plays in the early seventeenth century can be explained as a marketing ploy exploiting Shakespeare's by then well-established reputation in print, Shakespeare's name had not as yet appeared on the title-pages of any of the editions of plays now attributed to Shakespeare. And yet Shakespeare was already a popular dramatist by 1595, certainly popular at Court, since his name is, for example, explicitly mentioned in the 'Declared Accounts of the Treasurer of the Chamber' in 1595 (Greg, *Dramatic Records*, p. 29).

36 Tucker Brooke, *The Shakespeare Apocrypha*, p. xx.

first and then more prominently as a member of the Chamberlain's Men.

Paying attention to one other paratextual feature, which is often acritically adopted and reproduced by modern editors of Shakespeare, namely act and scene divisions, does not only challenge the simplistic distinction between 'text' and 'paratext' or what we think we mean by Shakespeare – literary dramatist versus company man – but also how we edit Shakespeare for the modern reader. Positing that Shakespeare was a company man rather than a literary dramatist does not mean that the texts of the plays preserved in the early playbooks necessarily reflect theatrical practice. Act and scene divisions, for example, need to be carefully reconsidered as being the product of printing house, rather than playhouse, practices.

In 'The Structure of Performance: Act-Intervals in the London Theatres, 1576–1642', Gary Taylor established that children's companies started using intervals from at least 1599 and that all adult companies had also adopted this convention by roughly 1616,[37] and some of them from as early as 1607–10.[38] Taylor reached this conclusion by arguing that, since all children's plays printed after 1599 and all plays printed after 1616 include act divisions, act divisions in these plays must reflect theatrical practice rather than a more gradual change in the social and literary status of playbooks or a change in printing conventions.[39] According to Taylor it was 'the first acquisition of a private theatre by an adult company', the King's Men acquiring the Blackfriars in 1608, that prompted the adult companies to abandon continuous playing in favour of 'the more academic Renaissance convention of a formal division into five acts'.[40] Taylor also specified that '[o]f plays written in 1642 or before, but first printed in 1616 or after, only nine are printed without a division into five Acts'.[41] Interestingly seven of the nine exceptions are Folio plays in the second half of the volume: 2 and 3 Henry VI, Romeo and Juliet, Hamlet, Troilus and Cressida, Timon of Athens, and Antony and Cleopatra.[42] Erratic division in plays in the first half of the volume, including Shrew and Henry V, also suggests editorial intervention aimed at imposing a formal structure onto plays meant for continu-

ous performance. More generally, act divisions in the Folio suggest potential editorial intervention at least as far as the middle of the Histories section. Every play included in the Comedies section, for example, is divided despite the fact that twelve of them predate the acquisition of the Blackfriars. Taylor is confident that most comedies 'were set from late transcripts, or from quartos which had been annotated with reference to a prompt-book' and that 'their divisions are, at least presumptively, theatrical in origin'.[43] I have argued elsewhere that changes in the text of the dialogue, speech prefixes and stage directions in at least two Folio comedies – Love's Labour's Lost and Much Ado About Nothing – reflect the typical pattern of local changes introduced by light annotation of the printer's copy for the press rather than consultation of a theatrical manuscript.[44] I would now like to suggest that act and scene divisions in some Folio comedies may also reflect editorial rather than theatrical practice.

Andrew Gurr has argued that only The Tempest, the first play grouped with the other 'comedies' in the Folio, 'shows unequivocal evidence that it was conceived with act breaks in mind'. According to Gurr,

Some . . . pause, at least for music, must have been designed to intervene between Acts 4 and 5 . . . . Prospero and Ariel leave the stage together at the end of Act 4 and enter together again to open Act 5 . . . . He has the same characters leaving and re-entering like this in none of his other plays. For that reason if no other it is clear that he had the Blackfriars in mind, not the Globe, when he wrote The Tempest.[45]

---

[37] Gary Taylor, 'The Structure of Performance: Act-Intervals in the London Theatres, 1576–1642', in Gary Taylor and John Jowett, Shakespeare Reshaped, 1606–1623 (Oxford, 1993), pp. 4–8.

[38] Taylor, 'Structure of Performance', p. 25.

[39] Taylor, 'Structure of Performance', p. 17.

[40] Taylor, 'Structure of Performance', pp. 30–1.

[41] Taylor, 'Structure of Performance', p. 18.

[42] Hamlet is divided up to Act 2, scene 2, but division is abandoned thereafter.

[43] Taylor, 'Structure of Performance', pp. 44–5.

[44] Sonia Massai, Rise of the Editor, pp. 136–58.

[45] Andrew Gurr, 'The Tempest's Tempest at Blackfriars', Shakespeare Survey 41 (Cambridge, 1989), p. 93.

Other Folio comedies may reflect the use of act breaks in later revivals of plays originally conceived for continuous performance. The text preserved in the first and second quarto editions of *A Midsummer Night's Dream* (STC 22302, 1600; STC 22303, 1600 [1619]), for example, has no act divisions. By contrast, the Folio text introduces act divisions whose origin in a later revival of the play is suggested by at least one additional stage direction at the end of Act 3, which specifies that 'They [the lovers] sleepe all the Act' (STC 22273, 1623, O1), where 'Act' is taken to mean 'Act-interval'.[46] However, in other Folio comedies act breaks are neither in keeping with the structure of the play nor obviously related to later revivals which may have prompted the introduction of act breaks in a play meant for continuous performance.

Act and scene divisions in *As You Like It*, for example, would seem fairly straightforward. A new scene starts every time the stage is cleared, and at least the shifts to Acts 2 and 3 are marked by the first scene set in the Forest of Arden (2.1) and a short scene back at the Court of Duke Frederick (3.1). However, continuous action, or what Jonathan Bate and Eric Rasmussen conveniently describe as a 'running scene' in their recent edition of Shakespeare's *Complete Works*,[47] overlaps twice with the act divisions preserved in the Folio. The first meeting between Rosalind disguised as Ganymede and Orlando in the forest opens a long sequence which spans five scenes and one act break in the Folio text. These five scenes are both thematically and temporally intertwined: they focus on young lovers who are being taught how to woo (Rosalind and Orlando in 3.2 and 4.1 and Silvius and Phoebe in 3.5) and how to wed (Touchstone and Audrey in 3.3), with Rosalind and Celia constantly onstage except for a short intermission in 3.3. The brief hunting scene and song in 4.2 are followed by another long sequence of interrelated strands of the plot involving the lovers. This sequence is divided into four scenes spanning across Acts 4 and 5, but is thematically and temporally distinctive as a unit. Once again, Rosalind and Celia are the main focus of the action as they make arrangements for their own weddings and for Silvius and Phoebe's

wedding in the final scene, marked in the Folio as 5.4. Touchstone and Audrey provide two short intermissions, which are thematically related to the rest of the sequence, as Touchstone and Audrey also prepare to get married in 5.4.

Act divisions in the Folio text of *As You Like It* run against the grain of the dramatic action at least twice in the second half of the play. More generally, *As You Like It* has no five-act structure. There are, for example, few significant and clear-cut temporal breaks shaping plot and character development. Oliver's question to Charles in 1.1 – 'What, you wrastle to morrow before the new Duke' (STC 22273, 1623, Q3ᵛ) – provides the first temporal break after the opening scene. The next significant temporal break falls between Rosalind and Celia's preparations to leave Frederick's Court in 1.3, and Celia's attendants finding her bed 'vntreasur'd' of its mistress early the next morning in 2.2 (Q5ᵛ). Once all characters have resettled in the forest, temporal breaks become blurry. When Orlando is late for his appointment with Rosalind, and Rosalind complains – 'But why did hee sweare hee would come this morning, and comes not?' (R4) – we are given no clues to establish what morning this might be (later on the same morning of Rosalind and Celia's arrival in the forest, or Orlando's arrival, or one other morning after their arrival in the forest). The only other temporal break clearly signalled in the dialogue separates Rosalind's promise that every Jack will have his Jill in 5.2 and Hymen's celebration of four weddings in the final scene. What is remarkable about the continuous quality of the action in the forest is that Shakespeare makes it a central motif in his rewriting of pastoral tropes. When Rosalind disguised as Ganymede is looking for a pretext to start a conversation with Orlando, she rather awkwardly asks, 'what i'st a clocke?' Orlando's point – 'there's no clocke in the Forrest' (R3) – has wonderful resonance. Jaques

---

46 Harold F. Brooks, *A Midsummer's Night Dream*, The Arden Shakespeare, 2nd series (London, 1979), p. xxxii.

47 Jonathan Bate and Eric Rasmussen, eds., *William Shakespeare: Complete Works*, The Royal Shakespeare Company (Basingstoke, 2007).

memorably makes fun of Touchstone's meditations upon a dial: "'Tis but an houre agoe, since it was nine, / And after one houre more, 'twill be eleuen' (R1). Measuring time makes little sense in the Forest of Arden. As Rosalind puts it, time 'ambles', 'trots', 'gallops' and 'stands still', which is a variant of Jaques's description of the seven ages of man, with the schoolboy 'creeping like snaile / Vnwillingly to schoole', with the soldier 'sodaine, and quicke in quarrell', with the 'sixt age shift[ing] / Into the leane and slipper'd Pantaloone' and the 'Last Scene of all', 'meere obliuion', when time stands still again (R1ᵛ). Touchstone's meditations upon a dial and the passing of time 'And so from houre to houre we ripe and ripe, / And then from houre to houre we rot and rot' (R1) reminds us of the experiential quality of time in a play where time refuses to be measured. Tempting in this respect is to read 'As the Dial Hand Tells O'er', a poem discovered by William Ringler and Steven May and tentatively identified as an occasional epilogue written by Shakespeare for a 1599 court performance of *As You Like It*, as a celebration of Elizabeth's triumph over time, metonymically evoked by another dial.[48]

The thematic emphasis on the experiential quality of time in the Forest of Arden and the organization of the play into long sequences which refuse to fall into a five-act structure suggest that the act division introduced in the Folio originated in editorial, rather than dramatic or theatrical, practices. This view is reinforced by textual and bibliographical evidence which has recently been used to attribute the act divisions in this play to Ralph Crane, the scribe hired by the King's Men from the late 1610s and responsible for preparing the printer's copy of several Folio plays.[49] It is therefore all the more surprising that, given the increasing amount of evidence to suggest that act division in *As You Like It* originated as part of the process whereby the text of some Folio comedies was prepared for the press, recent editors retain it and describe it as befitting the play's structure.[50]

Act and scene divisions in other Folio comedies deserve careful reconsideration, and especially in those comedies that were set up from copies

prepared by Ralph Crane. *The Merry Wives of Windsor*, for example, would seem to be shackled with divisions which artificially break up the flow of the action. As one of its recent editors has noted, '*The Merry Wives of Windsor* is a comedy so loosely structured that it must have undergone, more than most plays produced at the time, constant changes, omission or additions during its stage career.'[51] Act and scene divisions in this play might once again be the by-product of Crane's editorial intervention. Particularly noticeable is the frequent use of divisions and massed entries in Act 5, in light of the fact that massed entries are typical of Crane's scribal practices. The Act division falls awkwardly in the middle of a sequence set at the Garter Inn and is followed by a massed entry, '*Enter Falstoffe, Quickly, and Ford*' (E5ᵛ), with Ford actually entering and speaking eight lines later. The last sequence in the play starts at 5.2 and is marked by the entrance of the first of the several parties of characters meeting in Windsor Great Park at night to play one final trick on Falstaff. The impulse to divide the text each time one group of characters exits (or moves to a different area on the stage) produces three short scenes, 5.4 consisting of a mere entry direction and four lines of dialogue spoken by one character. Rather than reflecting theatrical practice, act and scene divisions in *The Merry Wives of Windsor* would seem to be the product of the idiosyncratic scribal changes routinely introduced by Crane as he prepared the printer's copies of several Folio plays for the press.

Having started this essay by pleading for the paratext to be considered as integral to and coextensive with the text, I am now going to end by

---

[48] Attribution of this poem to Shakespeare has been persuasively disputed by Michael Hattaway in his essay 'Dating *As You Like It*, Epilogues and Prayers, and the Problems of "As the Dial Hand Tells O'er"' (forthcoming in *Shakespeare Quarterly*).

[49] James Hirsch, 'Act Divisions in the Shakespeare First Folio', *Publications of the Bibliographical Society of America*, 96 (2002), pp. 219–56.

[50] See, for example, Juliet Dusinberre, ed., *As You Like It*, The Arden Shakespeare, 3rd series (London, 2006), p. 126.

[51] Giorgio Melchiori, ed., *The Merry Wives of Windsor*, The Arden Shakespeare, 3rd series (London, 1999), p. 109.

stressing that the paratext should be edited as carefully as the text, and, when necessary, emended. Retaining Folio act divisions when act divisions are clearly imposed on a play that has no five-act structure is no less preposterous than retaining the scene locators imposed by Nicholas Rowe on plays written for the pre-Restoration platform stage, although the use of act breaks in plays written for public amphitheatres did start as Shakespeare was reaching the end of his playwriting career and did affect the way in which Shakespeare conceived and structured at least one of his late plays, as mentioned above. However, the vast majority of Shakespeare's plays were conceived and written for continuous performance and while some were set in print from copies which reflect the use of act breaks in later revivals, others acquired act divisions as they were prepared for inclusion in the First Folio. Paradoxically, while the accuracy of the texts preserved in the early editions of Shakespeare plays is meticu-lously weighed against the possibility of error arising from the transmission of these texts as scripts on the stage and as printer's copies in the printing house, the viability of act divisions introduced in Folio plays which clearly have no five-act structure has so far had no impact on editorial practice.

In short, early modern dramatic paratexts and even paratextual features in the early editions of Shakespeare's plays are still being overlooked or taken for granted. As a result, current theories about what constitutes an early modern play text, or what we mean by 'Shakespeare' and 'text', are severely lopsided. As this essay has shown, the first step towards achieving a more balanced understanding of the relationship between textual and paratextual features in early modern playbooks is to depart from Genette's definition of paratext as a marginal element of the text and to conceive it as metatext, or, more simply and more radically, as text.

THE POPULARITY OF SHAKESPEARE IN PRINT

LUKAS ERNE

This article assesses the scope of Shakespeare's bibliographic presence in the early modern period. We have long known that approximately half of Shakespeare's plays were published during his lifetime, that some were reprinted early on, and that thirty-six of them were gathered in the First Folio in 1623. Many companions to Shakespeare contain a chapter on the early editions: 'Shakespeare Published', 'Shakespeare's Plays in Print', 'Shakespeare Writ Small: Early Single Editions of Shakespeare's Plays', 'Shakespeare in Print, 1593–1640', and so on.[1] The early chapters of David Scott Kastan's *Shakespeare and the Book* cover similar ground, and Andrew Murphy's *Shakespeare in Print* also devotes a chapter to 'The early quartos'.[2] What these chapters, useful though they are, do not examine in any detail is the comparative popularity of Shakespeare in print: how present was Shakespeare as 'a man in print' compared to contemporary writers, in particular contemporary playwrights? Did Shakespeare sell well? Were his playbooks more or less popular than, say, Jonson's or Fletcher's? By how much? Judging by his presence as a man in print, what kind of authorial status did Shakespeare have in early modern England? These are some of the questions this article proposes to investigate.

It may be useful to start by taking a snapshot of the presence of Shakespeare's writings in the London book trade. Let us briefly look at a single year: 1600. It is true that this is an extraordinary year for Shakespeare, with more publications than in any other year during his life, yet the year's total book production, with approximately 300 titles produced and published in London, is

also of unprecedented scope.[3] The subject matter to which the greatest part of these titles was devoted is religion, which accounted for over a third of the total output. A fair number of other books dealt with historical and political subjects (about

The research project from which the present article results is funded by the Swiss National Science Foundation. I would like to thank Sarah Van der Laan and Louise Wilson for their assistance in the preparation of my typescript.

[1] Laurie Maguire, 'Shakespeare Published', in Stanley Wells and Lena Cowen Orlin, eds., *Shakespeare: An Oxford Guide* (Oxford, 2003), pp. 582–94; Russ McDonald, 'Shakespeare's Plays in Print', in McDonald, *The Bedford Companion to Shakespeare: An Introduction with Documents* (Boston, 2001), pp. 201–6; Thomas L. Berger, 'Shakespeare Writ Small: Early Single Editions of Shakespeare's Plays', in Andrew Murphy, ed., *A Concise Companion to Shakespeare and the Text* (Oxford, 2007), pp. 57–70; Thomas L. Berger and Jesse M. Lander, 'Shakespeare in Print, 1593–1640', in David Scott Kastan, ed., *A Companion to Shakespeare* (Oxford, 1999), pp. 395–413.

[2] David Scott Kastan, *Shakespeare and the Book* (Cambridge, 2001), pp. 14–49; Andrew Murphy, *Shakespeare in Print: A History and Chronology of Shakespeare Publishing* (Cambridge, 2004), pp. 15–35.

[3] Mark Bland writes that 'the Short-Title Catalogue lists 342 books published either during 1600 or in a few cases approximately dated to that year'. After deducting variant imprints and items printed outside London, he arrives at '262 items . . . printed in London': 'The London Book-Trade in 1600', in Kastan, *Companion to Shakespeare*, pp. 450–63, 457. John Barnard and Maureen Bell's statistical tables mention 298 items produced in London in 1600: 'Appendix 1: Statistical Tables', in John Barnard and D. F. McKenzie, eds., and Maureen Bell, assistant ed., *The Cambridge History of the Book in Britain, Vol. IV: 1557–1695* (Cambridge, 2002), pp. 779–93, 782. See also Maureen Bell and John Barnard, 'Provisional Count of STC Titles 1475–1640', *Publishing History*, 31 (1992), 48–64.

ten per cent each) and a smaller number (about five per cent) to science or to what we might call sociological subjects (commerce, education, good conduct, tobacco pamphlets, and so on). A handful of books concerned the arts (music and the fine arts) and sports. Finally, quite a considerable segment of the year's book production, approximately thirty per cent of the titles published, was devoted to what we now call 'literature', a category under which a surprising range of texts appeared, including translations from Latin (Ovid's *Heroides*, translated by George Tuberville) and from vernacular languages (e.g. Edward Fairfax's rendering of Tasso's *Jerusalem Delivered*), romances (the anonymous *Heroicall Adventures of the Knight of the Sea*), plays (Thomas Dekker's *Shoemaker's Holiday*), prose fiction (Thomas Deloney's *The Gentle Craft*), collections of tales (Robert Armin's *Fool upon Fool*), lengthy narrative poems (*The Legend of Humphrey Duke of Glocester*, by Christopher Middleton), verse satires (*Pasquil's Mad-Cap*, by Nicholas Breton), allegorical poems (Cyril Tourneur's *The Transformed Metamorphosis*), epyllia (Christopher Marlowe's *Hero and Leander*), elegies (*An Italian's Dead Body, Stuck with English Flowers*, by Joseph Hall and others), religious poetry (Robert Southwell's *Saint Peter's Complaint*), epigrams (Thomas Rowlands's *The Letting of Humour's Blood in the Head-Vein*), poetic miscellanies (*The Paradise of Dainty Devices*), anthologies (*England's Parnassus, or the Choicest Flowers of Our Modern Poets*), single-sheet verse ('As Pleasant a Ditty As Your Heart Can Wish'), and ballads (Thomas Deloney's 'Most Pleasant Ballad of Patient Grissell').[4]

Given the breadth of the bibliographic production, Shakespeare made a remarkable contribution to the year's output: the first editions, all in quarto, of *Henry V*, *Much Ado about Nothing*, *2 Henry IV*, *A Midsummer Night's Dream* and *The Merchant of Venice*; the second editions, also in quarto, of *The First Part of the Contention (2 Henry VI)* and *The True Tragedy of Richard, Duke of York (3 Henry VI)*; and the fourth and fifth editions (the second and third in octavo) of *The Rape of Lucrece*. In other words, no fewer than nine books published in 1600 were by Shakespeare. Moreover, two commonplace books

(*Englands Parnassus: or the Choysest Flowers of our Moderne Poets* and *Bel-vedére, or, The Garden of the Muses*) and a poetical anthology (*England's Helicon*) were published the same year with excerpts from Shakespeare's writings. If we add these to Shakespeare's plays and poem published in 1600, we arrive at a total of twelve books – about four per cent of the year's output – which contain writings by Shakespeare. It seems fair to say that Shakespeare had a remarkable presence in the London book trade at the turn of the seventeenth century.

I. SHAKESPEARE, POET AND DRAMATIST

Shakespeare is mostly remembered today as a playwright, but his debut in print took the form not of a play but of a narrative poem, *Venus and Adonis*, published in 1593. It remained very popular, receiving a second edition in 1594, another eight before the end of Shakespeare's life. With a total of ten editions, *Venus and Adonis* is Shakespeare's most successful publication during his lifetime, well ahead of the most popular playbook, *1 Henry IV*, with six editions. *The Rape of Lucrece*, Shakespeare's second narrative poem, was also popular: it reached

---

4 For the approximate percentages in the preceding division of subjects, see Edith L. Klotz, 'A Subject Analysis of English Imprints for Every Tenth Year from 1480 to 1640', *Huntington Library Quarterly*, 1 (1937–38), 417–19. H. S. Bennett divides up the book production in similar fashion: 'Religion', 'Law', 'Education', 'Medicine', 'Information', 'Arithmetic, astronomy and popular science', 'Geography', 'History', 'News', and 'Literature' (*English Books and Readers, 1558–1603* (Cambridge, 1965), pp. 112–258). The Early English Booktrade Database (Project Director: David L. Gants), in 'A Discussion of Project Methods', proposes the following subject division: '1. Information, including works on language, business training and skills, education, husbandry, popular science and medicine. 2. Ephemera, including ballads, almanacs, catalogues and news pamphlets. 3. History, both popular and scholarly. 4. Law & Politics, including law books and non-religious polemics. 5. Literature, including belles lettres and popular, classical and travel works. 6. Official Documents, including forms, and proclamations. 7. Religion, including sermons, bibles, prayer books, instruction and commentary along with controversial and devotional works' (www.lib.unb.ca/Texts/Gants/EEBD/methods.html, accessed 10 October 2008).

print in 1594 and was reprinted five times in the course of Shakespeare's life. It received three more editions by 1655 and *Venus and Adonis* six more by 1636.

The popularity of Shakespeare's narrative poems has led Roger Chartier and Peter Stallybrass to argue, in an essay published in 2007, that 'The "authorial" Shakespeare was above all Shakespeare the poet, not Shakespeare the dramatist.'[5] Before we agree with this statement, we need to take a closer look at the evidence. 'Shakespeare the poet' had of course more publications to his credit than the two narrative poems: in 1609, Shakespeare's *Sonnets* (with 'A Lover's Complaint' appended to them) were published in quarto format. They proved strangely unpopular and were not reprinted until the Benson edition of 1640, more than three decades later. In addition, 'Shakespeare the poet' found his way into print in the form of *The Passionate Pilgrim*, a miscellaneous collection of twenty poems, which appeared in 1599.[6] Only five poems in *The Passionate Pilgrim* are now confidently assigned to Shakespeare, although the early title-pages attribute to him the collection as a whole.[7] With three editions in Shakespeare's lifetime, *The Passionate Pilgrim* was reasonably successful, yet without approaching the popularity of *Venus and Adonis* or even that of the most popular plays, *1 Henry IV*, *Richard II* or *Richard III*. The picture that emerges of the popularity of Shakespeare the poet in his own lifetime is thus rather complex: an extremely popular early narrative poem, a second very popular early narrative poem, a reasonably popular collection published approximately half-way through Shakespeare's career, and a distinctly unpopular collection of sonnets published late in his career.[8] This picture does not conform to what Chartier and Stallybrass may be taken to suggest, namely that Shakespeare the poet, contrary to Shakespeare the dramatist, was consistently popular in print.

Nor is it true that the bibliographic presence of Shakespeare the dramatist pales in comparison with that of Shakespeare the poet. On the contrary. During Shakespeare's lifetime, forty-five editions of his plays appeared in print, as opposed to twenty editions of his poems. It is true that many of these playbooks did not advertise Shakespeare's authorship, but twenty-six of them did, which is still more than the total number of poetry editions.[9] Chartier and Stallybrass argue that 'Before 1623, the name of Shakespeare as a published writer was above all connected to the two narrative poems that he had written in the 1590s',[10] but in fact more than two-thirds of the editions of Shakespeare's writings published during his lifetime were playbooks, and so were almost 60 per cent of the editions which identify him as the writer, on the title page or – as

---

5 Peter Stallybrass and Roger Chartier, 'Reading and Authorship: The Circulation of Shakespeare 1590–1619', in Murphy, *Concise Companion to Shakespeare and the Text*, pp. 35–56, 39.

6 For *The Passionate Pilgrim*, see Katherine Duncan-Jones and Henry Woudhuysen, eds., *Shakespeare's Poems*, The Arden Shakespeare (London, 2007), pp. 82–91; Colin Burrow, ed., *Complete Sonnets and Poems*, The Oxford Shakespeare (Oxford, 2002), pp. 74–82; and Hyder Edward Rollins, ed., *The Poems*, A New Variorum Edition (Philadelphia, 1938). See also Patrick Cheney, *Shakespeare, National Poet-Playwright* (Cambridge, 2004), pp. 151–71; James P. Bednarz, 'The Passionate Pilgrim and "The Phoenix and Turtle"', in Patrick Cheney, ed., *The Cambridge Companion to Shakespeare's Poetry* (Cambridge, 2007), pp. 108–24; and Bednarz, 'Canonizing Shakespeare: *The Passionate Pilgrim*, *England's Helicon*, and the Question of Authenticity', *Shakespeare Survey 60* (Cambridge, 2007), pp. 252–67.

7 The earliest edition of *The Passionate Pilgrim* is extant in a single copy of which the title-page is lost. For the third edition, two title-pages appear to have been printed, one with and one without Shakespeare's name on it, probably due to discontent (by Shakespeare or Thomas Heywood or both) over the inclusion of material by Heywood in a volume ascribed to Shakespeare (see Burrow, *Complete Sonnets and Poems*, pp. 77–9).

8 See Lukas Erne, 'Print and Manuscript', in Cheney, *Cambridge Companion to Shakespeare's Poetry*, pp. 54–71. Shakespeare's 67-line 'The Phoenix and Turtle' appeared in 1601 among a group of poems appended to the long narrative poem, *Love's Martyr*, by Robert Chester. Given that I am interested in Shakespeare *books* in this essay and that *Love's Martyr* is in no conceivable sense a Shakespeare book, I do not include it in the present survey of the bibliographic popularity of Shakespeare, the poet.

9 Note that two apocryphal plays, *The London Prodigal* (1605) and *A Yorkshire Tragedy* (1608), were also ascribed to Shakespeare during his lifetime.

10 Stallybrass and Chartier, 'Reading and Authorship', p. 39.

is the case with *Venus and Adonis* and *The Rape of Lucrece* – in the dedicatory epistle.

Chartier and Stallybrass find support for their belief that '"authorial" Shakespeare' was associated with his poetry rather than his drama by turning their attention to a collection, constituted by an early reader, which binds together *Venus and Adonis* (the edition of 1599), *Lucrece* (1600) and *The Passionate Pilgrim* (1599) with Thomas Middleton's narrative poem *The Ghost of Lucrece* (1600) and *Emaricdulfe. Sonnets written by E.C. Esquier* (1595). Given that only three of the collection's five books are attributed to Shakespeare, it is perhaps rather strained to call the collection 'quasi-Shakespearean'.[11] If this gathering of early editions can be said to make for a 'quasi-Shakespearean' volume, then so, surely, could one of the volumes of plays which was assembled by Sir John Harington (1561–1612): it contains thirteen plays, including *Richard III*, *1* and *2 Henry IV*, *The Merchant of Venice*, *Hamlet*, *King Lear*, *The London Prodigal*, wrongly attributed to 'William Shakespeare' on the title-page of the 1605 quarto, and *Locrine* ('By W. S.' according to the 1595 title-page). The volume contains four more plays, all non-Shakespearian, including *King Leir* (1605), which Harington marks as 'old' so as to distinguish it from 'King Leyr' by 'W. Sh.'. Yet Chartier and Stallybrass, though aware of the Harington volume, argue that 'authorship played no role in the organization of his collection' and thus oppose the poetry, associated with the '"authorial" Shakespeare' as suggested by the quasi-Shakespearian volume, to the plays, for which the authorial association remained allegedly unimportant during Shakespeare's lifetime.[12] Accordingly, they argue that the Pavier quartos, the nonce collection of Shakespeare playbooks of 1619, constituted 'the first serious attempt to materialize Shakespeare as a dramatic author in the form of a bound book'.[13]

Yet, in fact, such a collection existed considerably earlier, long before Shakespeare's death; and contrary to the volume of poetry mentioned above, it is genuinely made up of writings by Shakespeare. According to a 1627 inventory in EL 6495 (part of the Ellesmere MSS collection at the Huntington Library), the remarkable library of Lady Frances Egerton, first Countess of Bridgewater, contained a set of eight bound volumes of plays, and the first one on the inventory list is called 'Diuers Playes by Shakespeare 1602'. The other playbook volumes feature no authorial designation but are simply referred to as 'Diuerse playes'. Approximately halfway through Shakespeare's career, even before the publication of *Hamlet*, a collection of playbooks – not of poems – thus existed which was authorial, genuinely the first attempt, as far as we know, 'to materialize Shakespeare as a dramatic author in the form of a bound book'.[14] This fact confirms what the number of playbooks as compared to the number of poetry books suggests, namely that in terms of his appearance in print, Shakespeare, during his lifetime, was first and foremost a dramatist.

2. THE POPULARITY OF SHAKESPEARE'S PLAYS IN PRINT, 1594–1642/1660: NUMBERS OF EDITIONS

How then does the bibliographic presence of Shakespeare, the dramatist, compare to that of his contemporary playwrights? The question of the popularity of playbooks has received sustained scholarly attention in recent years, most notably by Alan Farmer, Zachary Lesser and Peter Blayney.[15]

---

[11] Stallybrass and Chartier, 'Reading and Authorship', p. 40.
[12] Stallybrass and Chartier, 'Reading and Authorship', p. 41.
[13] Stallybrass and Chartier, 'Reading and Authorship', p. 42.
[14] Stallybrass and Chartier, 'Reading and Authorship', p. 42. See Heidi Brayman Hackel, '"Rowme" of Its Own: Printed Drama in Early Libraries', in John D. Cox and David Scott Kastan, eds., *A New History of Early English Drama* (New York, 1997), p. 125. The Countess of Bridgewater's playbook collection is analysed in detail in Lawrence Manley's unpublished article, 'Shakespeare and the Countess of Bridgewater: Playing, Patronage, and the Biography of Books', presented to the theatre history seminar at the conference of the Shakespeare Association of America in San Diego, April 2007.
[15] Peter W. M. Blayney, 'The Publication of Playbooks', in Cox and Kastan, *New History of Early English Drama*, pp. 383–422, and 'The Alleged Popularity of Playbooks', *Shakespeare Quarterly*, 56 (2005), 33–50; Alan B. Farmer and Zachary Lesser, 'The Popularity of Playbooks Revisited', *Shakespeare*

Yet despite the fact that their debate has come to a head in the journal *Shakespeare Quarterly*, in three articles published in 2005, their work, including Blayney's seminal 1997 article on 'The Publication of Playbooks', shows little interest in the specific case of Shakespeare. Indeed, a reader could easily come away from reading Blayney's 1997 article thinking that Shakespeare playbooks were not particularly popular. Blayney compiles a best-seller list with eleven plays, of which only three are by Shakespeare, and with none of them appearing at the top of the list. Blayney adds that if he had included 'closet and academic plays', this 'would have pushed Shakespeare firmly out of the top five', adding that 'Shakespeare's best-selling work, *Venus and Adonis*, outsold his best-selling play by four editions'.[16] None of this is wrong, but the effect of Blayney's influential essay, to the extent that it focuses on dramatic authors, is to suggest that Shakespeare's playbooks were relatively unpopular.

My aim here is not to make a contribution to the debate over whether playbooks constituted a significant share of the book trade in early modern England.[17] Rather, my chief objective is to arrive at a better sense of Shakespeare's authorial presence in print, with which I hope to contribute to a re-evaluation of Shakespeare's authorial standing in his own time, in which a variety of scholars have recently participated, including Richard Dutton, James Bednarz, Brian Vickers, Patrick Cheney, Henry Woudhuysen, Jeffrey Knapp and MacDonald P. Jackson.[18]

The point is sometimes made that Shakespeare, from early on, outshone his contemporaries not only as a playwright writing for the stage but also as a dramatist in print. John Jowett, for instance, in *Shakespeare and Text* (2007) writes that 'By 1600 Shakespeare had become the most regularly published dramatist.'[19] Other critics, however, seem more inclined to stress the radical difference between Shakespeare's authorial standing in the eighteenth century and that before. In *The Cambridge History of the Book in Britain, 1557–1695*, in a chapter devoted to 'Literature, the Playhouse, and the Public', John Pitcher writes that 'The modern dispute about who the seventeenth century regarded as its pre-eminent dramatist – Shakespeare or Jonson or Beaumont and Fletcher – is not yet concluded, because literary historians are properly concerned not to project back into this earlier period the reputation Shakespeare subsequently enjoyed.'[20] We might be tempted, Pitcher seems to be saying, to consider Shakespeare the seventeenth century's pre-eminent dramatist because of the eminence he later came to acquire, but we should beware of jumping to such a conclusion without good evidence. Others have even categorically contested that Shakespeare was the most popular dramatist during his active life and the decades immediately following it. Gerald Eades Bentley devoted a two-volume study to answering the question of Shakespeare and Jonson's

---

Quarterly, 56 (2005), 1–32, and 'Structures of Popularity in the Early Modern Book Trade', *Shakespeare Quarterly*, 56 (2005), 206–13.

[16] Blayney, 'The Publication of Playbooks', p. 388.

[17] I argued in 2003 that 'printed playbooks became a conspicuous presence in St Paul's Churchyard' (*Shakespeare as Literary Dramatist* (Cambridge, 2007), p. 16) in Shakespeare's time, a view for which I find confirmation in the work by Farmer and Lesser.

[18] Richard Dutton, 'Shakespeare: The Birth of the Author', *Licensing, Censorship and Authorship in Early Modern England: Buggeswords* (Basingstoke, 2000), pp. 90–113; James P. Bednarz, *Shakespeare and the Poets' War* (New York, 2001); Brian Vickers, *Shakespeare, Co-Author: A Historical Study of Five Collaborative Plays* (Oxford, 2002); Patrick Cheney, *Shakespeare, National Poet-Playwright* (Cambridge, 2004), and *Shakespeare's Literary Authorship* (Cambridge, 2008); H. R. Woudhuysen, 'The Foundations of Shakespeare's Text', in *Proceedings of the British Academy: 2003 Lectures* (Oxford, 2004), pp. 69–100; Jeffrey Knapp, 'What Is a Co-Author', *Representations*, 89 (2005), 1–29; and MacDonald P. Jackson, 'Francis Meres and the Cultural Contexts of Shakespeare's Rival Poet Sonnets', *The Review of English Studies*, 56 (2005), 224–46, and 'Shakespeare's Sonnet CXI and John Davies of Hereford's *Microcosmos* (1603)', *Modern Language Review*, 102 (2007), 1–10. See also Richard Meek, Jane Rickard and Richard Wilson, eds., *Shakespeare's Book: Essays in Reading, Writing and Reception* (Manchester, 2008), and the forum on Shakespearean authorship in the 2008 volume of *Shakespeare Studies*.

[19] John Jowett, *Shakespeare and Text*, Oxford Shakespeare Topics (Oxford, 2007), p. 8.

[20] John Pitcher, 'Literature, the Playhouse, and the Public', in Barnard and McKenzie, *Cambridge History of the Book in Britain, Vol. IV* pp. 351–75, 373.

relative popularity, concluding that 'throughout the [seventeenth] century until the last decade Jonson was more popular in England than Shakespeare', adding that 'Clearly, Jonson, and not Shakespeare, was the dramatist of the seventeenth century' and that 'Jonson's general popularity was greater than Shakespeare's from the beginning of the century to 1690.'[21] The instances of Jowett, Pitcher and Bentley suggest that no scholarly consensus has emerged so far, and a closer investigation may therefore seem desirable.

A fairly basic way of investigating the bibliographic presence of Shakespeare, the dramatist, compared to that of his contemporaries is to count the number of editions in which their playbooks appeared. Yet as soon as one starts undertaking such a count, various methodological questions arise: what kinds of plays should be included or excluded? How about closet drama or university drama or drama translated from other languages? What about plays which were written in co-authorship, such as *Titus Andronicus*? And what about collections containing several plays, such as the Shakespeare First Folio, which contains thirty-six plays, the Jonson First Folio, with nine professional plays, or the 1590 octavo edition of the two parts of *Tamburlaine*? The first figures I present here include all plays written in sole or co-authorship (so *The Two Noble Kinsmen* is counted not only as one of Shakespeare's but also as one of Fletcher's plays); in addition, I concentrate in the first stage on play*books* rather than play-*texts*, meaning the number of times a publisher invested in a playwright, be it in the form of a collection or a single play. Finally, I focus throughout the rest of this essay on what Farmer and Lesser call 'professional plays', plays, that is, that were written for adult or boys' companies performing them in front of paying audiences.[22]

The result of this first count is that for the whole period from the beginning of the publication of professional plays to 1642, when public performances ceased, Shakespeare, with 73 editions of playbooks, out-publishes all his contemporaries by more than 50 per cent. The second most published playwright is not Jonson, who has only 22 editions

of playbooks to his credit by 1642, nor Middleton, whose total is 25, nor Beaumont or Fletcher, for whom I count 26 and 34 editions respectively, but Thomas Heywood, with 49 editions, which is 15 more than Fletcher, and over 20 editions ahead of everyone else.

Table 1 lists the number of editions of playbooks, per dramatist, for the period up to 1642, and includes all playwrights with at least 15 playbook editions to their credit. Even though public performances stopped in 1642, the publication of playbooks did not, so 1642 may seem an arbitrary end point and 1660 a valid alternative, all the more so as this may do better justice to playwrights who, contrary to Shakespeare, were still active during the Caroline period. In Table 2, with the period extended to 1660, Shakespeare still comes first with 75 editions. Only two of Shakespeare's plays were reprinted between 1642 and 1660, *King Lear* and *Othello*, both in 1655. Yet Shakespeare's number of playbooks up to 1660 is still almost one and a half times that of Heywood, almost twice that of Fletcher, and twice or more that of everyone else. Shakespeare exceeds Jonson's number of playbooks by a factor of more than three. Heywood's prominence in print is easily overlooked. For instance, David Kastan, in *Shakespeare and the Book*, writes that 'in his own age more editions of [Shakespeare's] plays circulated than of any other contemporary playwright', adding that 'Eventually the prolific Beaumont and Fletcher would close the gap'.[23] According to my count, Beaumont and Fletcher never came close to rivalling Shakespeare, and the playwright who came closest to doing so was Thomas Heywood.

A few words of caution before I proceed: reduced into simple figures and tables, my statistics look more straightforward than they are, and this for more than one reason. First of all, collaborative plays are so common that they cannot be ignored,

---

[21] Gerald Eades Bentley, *Shakespeare and Jonson: Their Reputations in the Seventeenth Century Compared*, 2 vols. (Chicago, 1945), vol. 1, pp. 133, 139, 138.

[22] See Farmer and Lesser, 'Popularity', p. 6, in particular note 24.

[23] Kastan, *Shakespeare and the Book*, p. 21.

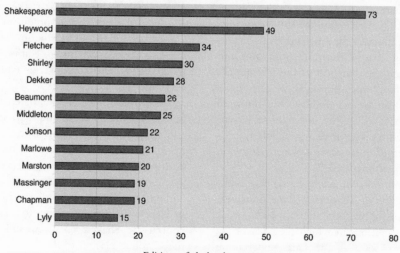

1. Editions of playbooks to 1642.

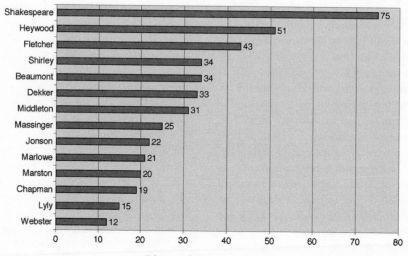

2. Editions of playbooks to 1660.

yet their inclusion inevitably distorts the evidence. *Eastward Ho!*, for example, a collaborative play by Jonson, Marston and Chapman, received three editions, all dated 1605. In my count, the play appears under all three playwrights, adding three editions to their totals, even though each of them wrote no more than a part of the play. My figures for playwrights who often wrote collaboratively thus exaggerate the amount of their dramatic writing that was available in print. Shakespeare, even though

he collaborated on a number of plays, did so much less than many of his contemporaries; so what this means for my figures is that Shakespeare's superiority in terms of the bibliographic presence of his dramatic writings may have been even greater than my tables suggest.

A further problem is that the authorship of many collaborative plays is a matter of ongoing scholarly discussion and may never be known with certainty. *The Spanish Gypsy*, for instance, was ascribed to

Thomas Middleton and William Rowley on the title page of the first quarto (1653), but a number of scholars, including David J. Lake, argue that it was written by Thomas Dekker and John Ford, whereas Gary Taylor, in *Thomas Middleton: The Collected Works* contends that all four contributed to the play.[24] In a situation like this, I adhere to the argument I find most convincing – meaning that presented in the Middleton *Collected Works* in the case of *The Spanish Gypsy* – but it is clear that the authorship of many early modern plays, and in particular of collaborative plays, will remain a matter of debate and that, therefore, figures such as those presented here cannot be considered definitive.[25]

3. THE POPULARITY OF SHAKESPEARE'S PLAYS IN PRINT, 1594–1642/1660: NUMBERS OF REPRINTS

The preceding statistics give us a sense of the number of editions of dramatic writings by Shakespeare and his contemporaries that were published in the early modern period, but they fail to distinguish between simple quarto playbooks and collections, including large Folio collections, and therefore do not assess how many play-*texts* and editions thereof were available in print. Clearly, the totals of dramatists whose plays were published in large collections (such as Shakespeare, Jonson, and Fletcher) are affected if we take into account the individual plays these collections included rather than only the collection as a whole. Whereas the statistics for playbooks inform us of the number of commercial ventures publishers undertook, the figures for play-texts are more apt to convey the availability in print of the full breadth of the playwrights' dramatic output.

Such an examination documents with even greater clarity Shakespeare's predominance as a published playwright in early modern England, as Table 3 makes clear. In the period up to 1642, the texts of Shakespeare's 39 published plays – meaning the 36 plays in the First Folio plus *Edward III*,

Pericles, and *The Two Noble Kinsmen* – appeared in a total of 144 editions, almost 90 more than Heywood, with 55. Due to the nine plays in the 1616 Folio, Jonson comes third, but remains over a hundred play-text editions behind Shakespeare. (Playwrights with fewer than fifteen editions are again not recorded.) If the period is extended to 1660 (Table 4), Fletcher, thanks to the Folio of 1647, overtakes Heywood and gets somewhat closer to Shakespeare but, with 146 editions of play texts as opposed to Fletcher's 77, Shakespeare still out-publishes Fletcher by a factor of almost two to one, with the number of Heywood's editions being approximately 40 per cent and Shirley, Jonson, Massinger and Beaumont's fewer than 30 per cent of Shakespeare's.

The preceding figures give us a sense of the total number of editions in which the plays appeared, but they tell us little about how well Shakespeare's or other dramatists' plays sold once they were in print. The total number of editions conveys how often stationers decided to invest in plays by certain authors but, if we are interested in knowing whether these investments proved worthwhile, then – as Farmer and Lesser have insisted – we need to focus on reprint

---

[24] David J. Lake, *The Canon of Thomas Middleton's Plays: Internal Evidence for the Major Problems of Authorship* (Cambridge, 1975), pp. 215–30. Gary Taylor and John Lavagnino, eds., *Thomas Middleton and Early Modern Textual Culture: A Companion to the Collected Works* (Oxford, 2007), pp. 433–7.

[25] I have drawn on various sources in trying to determine the exact corpus of the various playwrights, including the electronic *English Short-Title Catalogue*, or *ESTC* (http://estc.bl.uk), the online *Database of Early English Playbooks* (*DEEP*) compiled by Alan B. Farmer and Zachary Lesser (http://deep.sas.upenn.edu/), or recent authoritative editions such as the Oxford *Collected Works of Thomas Middleton* (2007; Gary Taylor and John Lavagnino, gen. eds.) and the Cambridge edition of *The Works of John Webster* (1995–2007; David Gunby, David Carnegie *et al.*, eds.). In the particularly thorny case of the 'Beaumont and Fletcher' canon, I have consulted the work of Cyrus Hoy, 'The Shares of Fletcher and His Collaborators in the Beaumont and Fletcher Canon', *Studies in Bibliography*, 8 (1956), 129–46; 9 (1957), 143–62; 11 (1958), 85–106; 12 (1959), 91–116; 13 (1960), 77–108; 14 (1961), 45–67; and 15 (1962), 71–90, but have only adhered to it when more recent scholarship presents no good evidence that contradicts Hoy's arguments.

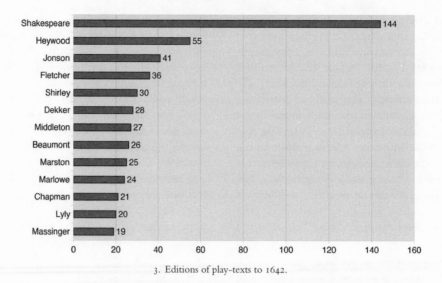

3. Editions of play-texts to 1642.

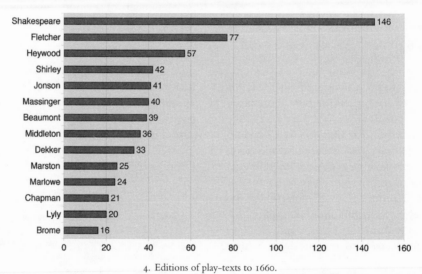

4. Editions of play-texts to 1660.

rates.[26] A reprint means that an edition had sold out, or was on the point of selling out, and that the publisher anticipated enough of a demand for a second edition to pay for its production. Since expenses for a reprint were considerably lower than for a first edition, reprints tended to be considerably more profitable than first editions. Of course, on a purely textual level, reprints are often less interesting than so-called substantive editions, insofar as they simply copy the text of an earlier edition. E. K. Chambers's view may be repre-

sentative of how little value was long attached to reprints: 'several of the plays had been reprinted from time to time', Chambers wrote, adding that 'there is not much to be said about the reprints'.[27] More recently, however, Sonia Massai's study of *Shakespeare and the Rise of the Editor* has warned us against underestimating the textual importance of

---

[26] See Farmer and Lesser, 'Popularity', pp. 5–6.
[27] E. K. Chambers, *William Shakespeare: A Study of Facts and Problems* (Oxford, 1939), vol. 1, p. 133.

reprints, showing that many of them contain local, but important, editorial interventions.[28] Independently of the question of the textual importance of reprints, bibliographically they are crucial witnesses to a book's popularity.[29]

Blayney's article, 'The Publication of Playbooks', led the way in establishing the importance of reprints. He counted the professional plays published between 1583 and 1642 and their reprints, showing that 'Fewer than 21 per cent of the plays published in the sixty years under discussion reached a second edition inside nine years' (p. 389). This allows for an instructive comparison with Shakespeare: 13 out of Shakespeare's 22 plays published separately in quarto or octavo format – that is the 19 published during Shakespeare's lifetime plus *Othello* (1622), *The Taming of the Shrew* (1631) and *The Two Noble Kinsmen* (1634) – received at least a second edition inside nine years, that is almost 60 per cent, as opposed to the 20 per cent for all professional plays, meaning almost three times as many. Since comparatively few plays first published during the Caroline period reached a second edition – what Farmer and Lesser call 'The Caroline Paradox'[30] – it may be more pertinent to focus on an earlier, shorter period. Blayney writes that 'Of the 96 plays first published in 1583–1602, only 46 (just under 48 per cent) were reprinted inside twenty-five years. The percentage is slightly higher for the plays of 1603–1622 (58 out of 115, or just over 50 per cent).'[31] If we add up Blayney's figures, then 104 of the 211 plays published between 1583 and 1622, or not quite 50 per cent, reached a second edition within 25 years. As for Shakespeare, 20 of his plays were first published during the same years and only three of them, *2 Henry IV*, *Much Ado About Nothing*, and *Troilus and Cressida*, did not receive a second edition within 25 years; so the rate of plays that reached at least one reprint within a quarter century is an astounding 85 per cent, as opposed to the not-quite 50 per cent for playbooks in general. Of the 17 Shakespeare plays that were reprinted at least once, seven received two editions, four went through three editions, three through four, *Richard II* through five, *Richard III* through six, and *1 Henry IV* through seven edi-

tions. On average, the twenty Shakespeare plays published between 1594 and 1622 received 2.95 editions (59 editions for the 20 plays), or almost three editions per play, within 25 years of original publication. If we consider *The Whole Contention* as a separate playbook rather than as a reprint of *The First Part of the Contention* and *True Tragedy*, and if we add *The Taming of the Shrew* (1631) and *The Two Noble Kinsmen* (1634), which received no reprints, and the 1623 Folio (reprinted in 1632), then the average number of editions drops slightly but remains high at 2.6.

This frequency of reprints and the scarcity of Shakespeare playbooks that did not reach a second edition are even more remarkable if we now look at some of Shakespeare's contemporaries. Only three of John Lyly's nine playbooks published between 1584 and 1632 received at least a second edition, one of them going through three, and one through four editions within 25 years. Five of George Peele's plays reached print between 1584 and 1599, of which only *Edward I* reached a second edition. The only play to which Peele contributed which was even more successful is the mostly Shakespearian *Titus Andronicus* of which Peele seems to have written Act 1 and two or three additional scenes,[32] which went through three editions within 25 years. Robert Greene contributed to a commercial hit, *A Looking Glass for London and England*, co-authored with Thomas Lodge, which went through five editions within 25 years. Yet of the five plays Greene seems to have written in sole authorship, only one received a second edition, whereas the other four did not.

[28] See Sonia Massai, *Shakespeare and the Rise of the Editor* (Cambridge, 2007).

[29] For 'second-plus editions', see Farmer and Lesser, 'Popularity'.

[30] Farmer and Lesser, 'Popularity', pp. 27–8. See also Alan B. Farmer and Zachary Lesser, 'Canons and Classics: Publishing Drama in Caroline England', in Alan B. Farmer and Adam Zucker, eds., *Localizing Caroline Drama: Politics and Economics of the Early Modern English Stage, 1625–1642* (New York, 2006), pp. 17–41.

[31] Blayney, 'The Publication of Playbooks', p. 387.

[32] See Brian Vickers, *Shakespeare, Co-Author*, pp. 148–243.

As for Shakespeare's later contemporaries, 23 of Thomas Heywood's playbooks appeared between 1599 and 1656, of which 15, or more than 65 per cent, failed to reach a second edition within 25 years. Some of Heywood's early plays were genuinely popular, though without rivalling the popularity of Shakespeare's playbooks: in Shakespeare's lifetime, ten of Heywood's plays appeared in print, of which two received a single reprint, one two, one three, two four, and one even five editions within 25 years, with the remaining three failing to receive a second edition.

While Heywood's popularity as a print-published dramatist, judging by the number of reprints, was clearly inferior to Shakespeare's, it was distinctly superior to that of many others. Fourteen of Chapman's playbooks found their way into print between 1598 and 1639, and only two of them received at least a second edition within 25 years. *The Conspiracy and Tragedy of Charles Duke of Byron* was reprinted 17 years after the first edition, and only the collaborative *Eastward Ho!* had considerable commercial success, with three editions. Similarly, 21 of Thomas Dekker's plays were published between 1600 and 1658, of which 16, or 75 per cent, were never reprinted, while three plays received a second and two a fourth edition within 25 years. As for John Marston's 12 playbooks published between 1601 and 1633, three of them went through three editions, and two of them through two, but as many as seven plays were not reprinted within a quarter century of original publication. Thomas Middleton, now rightly considered as one of the greatest Renaissance dramatists since the Oxford *Collected Works* has established the full scope of his dramatic oeuvre, was no more popular in print judging by the rate of reprints. Twenty of his playbooks appeared between 1604 and 1657, of which six received a second edition, and only two a third within 25 years, whereas 12 remained without a reprint inside 25 years. Of William Rowley's ten (mostly collaborative) playbooks which appeared between 1607 and 1660, seven remained without reprint and three reached a second but none a third edition.

As for Ben Jonson, 11 quarto playbooks were published between 1600 and 1620, of which eight failed to receive a reprint within 25 years, and the three that were reprinted include the collaborative *Eastward Ho!*. Jonson's First Folio reached a second edition after 24 years, but the Second Folio of 1641, which partly built on the abortive 1631 Folio, failed to receive a second edition within 25 years, as did *The New Inn*, published in octavo in 1631.

Of Shakespeare's Jacobean and Caroline successors, 17 of Philip Massinger's playbooks were published prior to 1660, of which only five reached a second edition and none a third within a quarter century.[33] Eight plays, or play collections, by Richard Brome were published prior to 1660, and only two of them reached a second edition within 25 years. Finally, 11 of Ford's plays were published in quarto between 1629 and 1660, and only one of them received a reprint, while 31 playbooks by James Shirley were published between 1629 and 1657, of which 27 remained without a reprint inside a quarter century.

What all of the dramatists I have just mentioned have in common is that the majority, and often the vast majority, of their playbooks failed to reach a second edition within 25 years. In fact, apart from Shakespeare, there appear to be only four exceptions to this rule: Marlowe, Webster, Beaumont and Fletcher. Seven of Marlowe's plays reached print between 1590 and 1633. Three of them were not reprinted within 25 years, but the others were, going through four editions (the *Tamburlaine* plays and *Edward II*) or even eight editions (*Doctor Faustus*) within 25 years of original publication.[34] As for John Webster, seven playbooks reached print

---

[33] In addition, the 1647 'Beaumont and Fletcher' Folio (not reprinted, with additions, until 1679) contains so many plays to which Massinger contributed that it deserves being considered as not only a Beaumont and Fletcher but also a Massinger playbook.

[34] Note that the *Tamburlaine* plays appeared as a two-play collection in 1590, which was reprinted twice in 1593 and 1597, before the plays were published separately in 1605 (*Part I*) and 1606 (*Part II*). Since I am counting playbooks and distinguish collections from single plays, the 1605 and 1606 editions do not qualify as reprints.

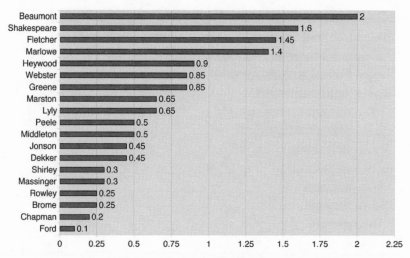

5. Average number of reprints within 25 years of playbook's original publication (1).

before 1660, of which four received at least a second edition (including *The Duchess of Malfi* and *The White Devil*). Of the eight plays Beaumont wrote alone or in co-authorship, and which were published in quarto between 1607 and 1621, only two received not a single reprint within a quarter of a century, while three received as many as four reprints. As for John Fletcher, 14 of his plays were published in quarto format between 1610 and 1640. Of these, four were not reprinted within 25 years, but four received a second, two a third, one a fourth, and three even a fifth edition within the same period.

To sum up, if we calculate the average number of reprints per play by author (Table 5), then Beaumont heads the table, with exactly two reprints, followed by Shakespeare (1.6), Fletcher (1.45), and Marlowe (1.4). Since the number of first editions of playbooks is small in the cases of Marlowe (eight) and Beaumont (nine), their averages may not be very representative. For Marlowe, for instance, the average greatly depends on *Doctor Faustus*, with its eight editions. If we calculate the average number of reprints of Marlowe and Shakespeare without taking into consideration their most popular plays, *Faustus* for Marlowe and *1 Henry IV* for Shakespeare, then the average rate of reprints drops

sharply, from 1.4 to 0.85, in the case of Marlowe, but only slightly, from 1.6 to 1.4, in that of Shakespeare. The representative table may thus be the one which confines itself to those playwrights with a solid corpus of at least ten different plays (Table 6). The noteworthy point about this table is not so much that Shakespeare, followed by Fletcher, heads the table, but that Shakespeare's reprint rate is massively superior to the playwrights in the lower half of the table, starting with Jonson and Dekker. The average number of reprints of a Shakespeare playbook is eight times that of a Chapman and almost four times that of a Jonson playbook.

If we calculate the average number of reprints within ten years of original publication, the popularity of Shakespeare's printed plays emerges with even greater clarity (Table 7). With almost one reprint per play on average, Shakespeare is ahead of everyone else by about a third or more. Lyly, much in vogue for a limited time, comes second, level with Marlowe. Beaumont and Fletcher figure considerably lower in Table 7 (reprints within ten years) than Table 6 (reprints within 25 years), suggesting that their popularity in print grew steadily and took some time to establish itself. If we again restrict the table to the playwrights with a representative corpus of at least ten different playbooks

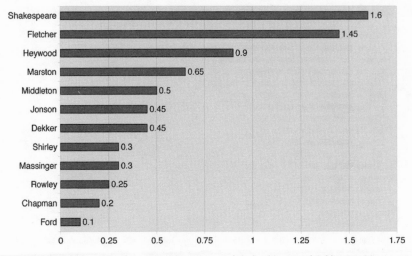

6. Average number of reprints within 25 years of playbook's original publication (2).

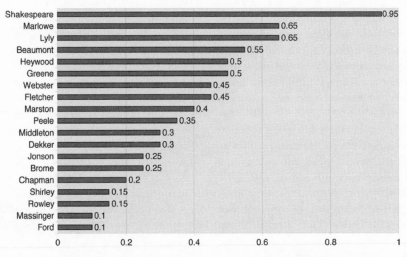

7. Average number of reprints within 10 years of playbook's original publication (1).

(Table 8), then the difference between Shakespeare and the others is even starker. Shakespeare's average number of reprints again exceeds Jonson's by a factor of almost four to one, and even Fletcher's by two to one.[35]

With these figures in mind, we may now wish to return to the question of Jonson and Shakespeare's comparative popularity. We remember that Bentley, in his two-volume study, argued that 'Jon-son's general popularity was greater than Shakespeare's from the beginning of the century to

[35] Note that, like Alan Farmer and Zachary Lesser, but unlike Peter Blayney, I include in the count editions published in the tenth or twenty-fifth year after the year of original publication (see Farmer and Lesser, 'Popularity', p. 31; and Blayney, 'The Publication of Playbooks'). So a 1608 edition of a play originally published in 1598 is considered as having been reprinted inside ten years.

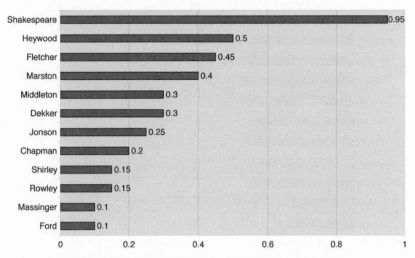

8. Average number of reprints within 10 years of playbook's original publication (2).

1690.'[36] However, the number of editions of Shakespeare playbooks up to 1660 is 76 as compared to 22 for Jonson, and the number of editions of play-texts for the same period is 146 for Shakespeare and only 41 for Jonson. In addition, and perhaps most eloquently as a comment on popularity, Shakespeare's reprint rate, both within ten and 25 years, is almost four times that of Jonson. It is true, of course, that there are other ways of judging the popularity of playwrights than the scope of their bibliographic presence. But I would argue that the print publications do provide important indications, and that book history has a contribution to make to the kind of research Bentley undertook in the mid-twentieth century. Bentley arrived at his very different conclusions by counting not editions but allusions to and quotations from the playwrights and their plays. What this suggests is that while Jonson may have been the writers' writer, who was endlessly drawn upon and pointed to, Shakespeare was the readers' writer, whose popularity called for a steady supply of new editions. Despite his literary ambitions, Shakespeare appears to have been popular in more than one sense, not only widely read but equally enjoyed by a less elite readership, unlike Jonson, who pleased not the million.

4. THE POPULARITY OF SHAKESPEARE, DRAMATIST, IN PRINT UP TO 1616

My analysis has so far focused on the period up to 1642 or 1660, but it seems important to examine also the number of publications during Shakespeare's lifetime. If we consider the period from 1584, when Lyly's and Peele's earliest playbooks were published, to the year of Shakespeare's death, then, as shown in Table 9, Shakespeare again comes out top with 45 editions, Heywood follows behind with about half that number, and Marston, third with 18, is followed by Dekker, Jonson, Chapman and Lyly, whose number of editions constitutes approximately one third of Shakespeare's.

The advantage of looking at playbook publication from this angle is that it can provide us with a sense of how Shakespeare's exact contemporary playwrights, and Shakespeare himself, may have experienced the success of their plays in printed form. During the time of his active career, Shakespeare was not only the most published playwright, but his bibliographic presence compared to that

---

[36] Bentley, *Shakespeare and Jonson*, vol. 1, p. 138.

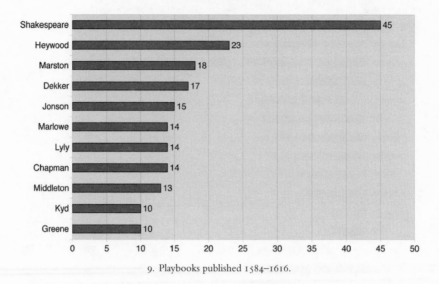

9. Playbooks published 1584–1616.

10. Playbooks published 1584–1600.

of his contemporaries was massive. No two playwrights together saw as many editions of their plays reach print as Shakespeare did alone. Nor did Shakespeare have to wait until the end of his career to become the most published playwright: until 1597, this distinction had gone to John Lyly, who was in print with 12 playbook editions, but by the end of 1598, Shakespeare's total had risen to 14, Lyly's only to 13. By the end of 1600, Shakespeare had taken a commanding lead with 25 editions

(Table 10), which he had further consolidated by the end of the year in which Queen Elizabeth died (Table 11).

It is true that many of Shakespeare's early playbooks were published without authorship attribution. In the 1590s, the majority of playbooks were published anonymously, although ascriptions were becoming increasingly common towards the turn of the century, and, as early as the first decade of the seventeenth century, the majority

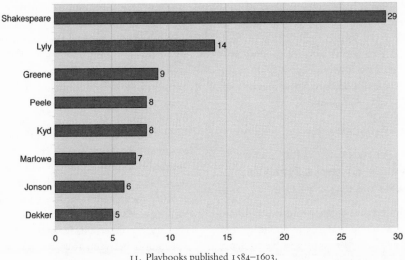

11. Playbooks published 1584–1603.

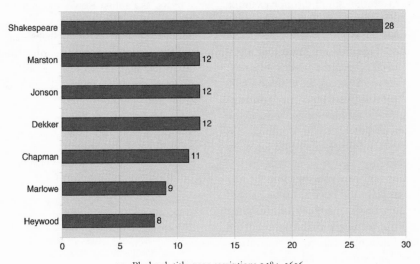

12. Playbook title-page ascriptions 1584–1616.

of playbooks mentioned the author on the cover.[37] Shakespeare's plays participated in this trend, and his number of title-page mentions soon surpassed that of his contemporaries. His name first appears on a title-page in 1598, in the second and third quartos of *Richard II*, the second quarto of *Richard III*, and the first extant (though in fact the second) edition of *Love's Labour's Lost*. With four title-page ascriptions, Shakespeare catches up at once with Greene, who also has four editions of playbooks with his name on the title page by 1598.

Shakespeare takes the lead the following year, with a fifth attribution on the title-page of *1 Henry IV*, and distances Greene and everyone else in 1600, by the end of which Shakespeare's name figures on the title pages of no fewer than nine playbook editions. By the end of Shakespeare's life (Table 12), the number of his title-page mentions totals 28

37 See the chapter devoted to 'The legitimation of printed playbooks in Shakespeare's time' in Erne, *Shakespeare as Literary Dramatist*, pp. 31–55.

(including the apocryphal *London Prodigal* of 1605 and *A Yorkshire Tragedy* of 1608), far ahead of Marston, Dekker and Jonson with 12 and Chapman with 11.[38] Shakespeare's advance over his contemporaries is thus no less impressive than in the earlier tables. Clearly, not only Shakespeare sold, but so too did Shakespeare's name.

5. IMPLICATIONS OF THE EARLY POPULARITY OF SHAKESPEARE, DRAMATIST, IN PRINT

It was long believed that Shakespeare was indifferent towards, or even opposed to, the publication of his plays in print, a belief I find impossible to share, for reasons I fully explained in *Shakespeare as Literary Dramatist*. My earlier study did not examine the publication of playbooks from the angle of the London book trade the way I have proposed to do here, yet I find confirmation for my earlier argument in the evidence presented in this article: if we go on believing in a Shakespeare with no interest in his plays in print, we would have to imagine an artist who was so single-mindedly theatrical that he was unaffected by his rise to dominance as playwright in print, and this while being intensely interested in books more generally, as both the fiction of his works and the wide reading he did before writing his plays and poems, makes clear.[39] A Shakespeare thus mythographically constructed would seem more in keeping with the notion of the romantic genius, floating loftily above the material concerns of his own time and place, refined out of existence, paring his fingernails, than with the competitiveness of Shakespeare and his professional world, as suggested by Greene, Heywood and other early commentators.[40] The present article thus adds to the argument advanced in my earlier book by suggesting that Shakespeare not only had the ambition of being a successful literary dramatist but that he really became one. The earlier study maintained that Shakespeare wanted to be published, bought and read; the present article argues that indeed he was all those things, and this on a scale unrivalled by any other early modern dramatist. Shakespeare's massive bibliographic presence in his own time which this article has established suggests that there was nothing fanciful about the ambition for which *Shakespeare as Literary Dramatist* argued. On the contrary, Shakespeare cannot have helped noticing that, thanks to the book trade, his ambition was fulfilled during his own lifetime.

The other chief purpose of this article has been to suggest that Shakespeare's texts, and in particular his playbooks, had a bibliographic presence of considerable scope in the first half of the seventeenth century more generally. Insofar as the question of Shakespeare's relative popularity in the seventeenth century is concerned, it makes sense, I believe, to distinguish between the first and the second half of the century. If we focus on the second half, it appears, as Paulina Kewes has argued, that Shakespeare's later pre-eminence was still very much in doubt.[41] Yet if we focus on Shakespeare's own time, and the early seventeenth century, then it emerges, this article suggests, that Shakespeare was considerably more popular, judging by how often his plays

---

38 The totals include the abbreviated 'Ch. Marl.' or 'Ch. Mar.' on the title pages of *Doctor Faustus*, but not simple initials, such as 'B. I.' on the title pages of Jonson's *Every Man Out of His Humour* (three editions in 1600), or 'W. S.' on *Locrine* (1595), *Thomas Lord Cromwell* (1602 and 1613) and *The Puritan* (1607), nor 'W. Sh.' on the second quarto of *The Troublesome Reign of King John* (1612).

39 For Shakespeare's interest in books in the fiction of his plays, see Cheney, *Shakespeare's Literary Authorship*, and Charlotte Scott, *Shakespeare and the Idea of the Book* (Oxford, 2007); for the books Shakespeare must have read before writing his plays, see Geoffrey Bullough, ed., *Narrative and Dramatic Sources of Shakespeare*, 8 vols. (London, 1957–75) and Leonard Barkan, 'What Did Shakespeare Read?', in Margreta de Grazia and Stanley Wells, eds., *The Cambridge Companion to Shakespeare* (Cambridge, 2001), pp. 31–47.

40 See Erne, *Shakespeare as Literary Dramatist*, pp. 1–5.

41 Paulina Kewes, 'Between the "Triumvirate of wit" and the Bard: The English Dramatic Canon, 1660–1720', in Cedric C. Brown and Arthur F. Marotti, eds., *Texts and Cultural Change in Early Modern England* (Basingstoke, 1997), pp. 200–24. See also Gary Taylor's comments on the general 'failure to remember much of Shakespeare' by 1660, in *Reinventing Shakespeare: A Cultural History from the Restoration to the Present* (London, 1989), p. 10.

were printed, than his contemporaries. What this implies is that the question of whether playbooks were popular or not may have depended importantly on the identity of the playwrights: whereas the publication of the playbooks of many of Shakespeare's contemporaries seems to have constituted mostly unprofitable commercial ventures, that of Shakespeare's playbooks was mostly profitable, in fact several times more profitable, on average, than that of Jonson, Chapman and other contemporaries and successors. To a surprising extent, Shakespeare's popularity as a printed dramatist in his own time anticipated his authorial pre-eminence in later centuries.

THE CONTINUING IMPORTANCE OF NEW BIBLIOGRAPHICAL METHOD

PAUL WERSTINE

This essay focuses on New Bibliographical method[1] and on its application to analysis of the particular texts – those of John Fletcher's play *Bonduca* – on which Sir Walter Wilson Greg depended for his influential conception of 'foul papers'. New Bibliographical method, in large part Greg's own creation, requires us to attend to what separates us as readers from our authors. As Greg once put it, New Bibliographical method concerns 'how a number of steps often intervene between the work as it formed itself in the author's mind and as it reaches modern readers'. For example, Greg went on, the New Bibliographer will 'describe the conditions under which manuscripts were . . . copied, the kinds of mistake that scribes habitually made, [and] the extent of corruption to be expected.' And Greg issued a dire warning to editors who fail to employ his method: 'Everywhere the editor suffers from not being a bibliographer; he gives himself all sorts of unnecessary trouble and arrives at all sorts of impossible results.'[2]

My object is to demonstrate that in the essay where Greg developed his conception of 'foul papers', he himself did not employ New Bibliographical method, and as a consequence he arrived at impossible results. These have vitiated much editorial work on early modern drama during the period when his paradigm has been in force, despite formidable challenges to it by such comparable luminaries as R. B. McKerrow[3] and Fredson Bowers.[4] For most of that period it was not possible to identify Greg's crucial mistake because the essay in which he made it lay unpublished. Instead, in book after book including *The Shakespeare First Folio* (1955), Greg's massive authority carried the day as he asserted his theory of 'foul papers'.[5] According to his theory, dramatists submitted their plays to theatrical companies as manuscripts too messy to be used to guide production, with the result that the companies had to have the plays copied in order to perform them. The companies, he argued, retained the authorial 'foul papers' and often provided them to the stationers who published plays. Cruces in these printed texts, on Greg's theory, are to be resolved with reference to putative authorial sloppiness in the printer's copy. The demonstration of his theory did not turn up until almost twenty years ago when his essay titled

---

[1] My title alludes to Giorgio Melchiori's essay titled 'The Continuing Importance of New Bibliography', in Ann Thompson and Gordon McMullan, eds., *In Arden: Editing Shakespeare: Essays in Honour of Richard Proudfoot* (London, 2003), pp. 17–30, an essay that reasserts some New Bibliographers' conclusions without regard to whether such conclusions were founded on New Bibliographical method.

[2] 'What is Bibliography?', in J. C. Maxwell, ed., *W. W. Greg: Collected Papers* (Oxford, 1966), pp. 85, 83.

[3] *Prolegomena for the Oxford Shakespeare: A Study in Editorial Method* (Oxford, 1939), pp. 6–7. See my 'Editing Shakespeare and Editing Without Shakespeare: Wilson, McKerrow, Greg, Bowers, Tanselle, and Copy-Text Editing', *TEXT*, 13 (2000), 27–54.

[4] *On Editing Shakespeare* (Charlottesville, 1966), pp. 14–16.

[5] *Dramatic Documents from the Elizabethan Playhouses* (Oxford, 1931), vol. I, pp. 195–6; *The Editorial Problem in Shakespeare: A Survey of the Foundations of the Text* (1942; 3rd edn Oxford, 1954), pp. 33–4; *The Shakespeare First Folio: Its Bibliographical and Textual History* (Oxford, 1955), pp. 106–11. It's to be noted that in 1955 Greg's conception of 'foul papers' still depended exclusively on his reading of the *Bonduca* texts.

'*The Final Revision of Bonduca*', a 1927 manuscript written in his own hand, was found in the Huntington Library, to which it had been donated by Greg's widow.[6] A summary of and excerpts from it were published,[7] but it has been subjected to no critical scrutiny. The present essay is based on Greg's own manuscript,[8] not the summary and excerpts.

John Fletcher's play *Bonduca* exists in two texts, one printed in the 1647 Beaumont and Fletcher First Folio, the other an undated transcript made by Edward Knight, book-keeper for the King's Men in the 1620s and 30s.[9] It was in Knight's transcript of *Bonduca* that Greg first discovered the term 'foul papers'. As Knight was copying out *Bonduca* apparently for a prospective patron, he found when he arrived at the fifth act that his exemplar lacked some scenes that he remembered from production. He offered this explanation for the absence of these scenes: '*the occasion. why these are wanting here. the booke where* [*it*] *by it was first Acted from is lost: and this hath beene transcrib'd from the fowle papers of the Authors w*f*h were found.*'[10]

Greg set about in his unpublished essay to discover the meaning of Knight's term 'foul papers'. To do so, he analysed the variants between Knight's transcript and the First Folio text, which was evidently typeset from some manuscript other than the one Knight called 'foul papers', since the Folio contains the two-plus scenes identified by Knight as absent from his copy. Comparing the two texts, Greg discovered that, besides lacking these scenes, Knight's transcript of Fletcher's 'foul papers' also sports twenty-two lacunae in the play's dialogue.[11] That is, in almost two dozen places, Knight has left blank spaces where the Folio prints meaningful words or phrases. Greg, setting aside New Bibliographical method, inferred from the lacunae that Knight was so scrupulous a transcriber that he left blanks whenever he was unsure exactly what Fletcher had written, rather than risk mistranscribing his author's words.[12] From this inference Greg concluded that Knight could be trusted to copy the 'foul papers' as well as they could be copied. In making this inference and accepting its implications, Greg forgot to factor in the impact

of the scribe's own practices and forgot about describing the conditions under which the transcript was being copied. Instead, with the exception of Knight's obvious errors (of which there are many), Greg assigned deficiencies in Knight's transcript entirely to alleged shortcomings in the 'foul papers' themselves, having been so bold in an earlier published article as to declare that the missing two and half scenes from the beginning of Act 5 had originally been part of the 'foul papers', but that the two foolscap sheets or eight pages on which Fletcher had written them had gone missing somehow before Knight took up the 'foul papers' to copy them.[13]

In comparing the two texts of *Bonduca*, Greg noted many examples of a peculiar species of variant: namely, the relocation of a line or passage of

---

[6] Greg does not date his MS. The date '1927' ('25.vii.1927') is found in a letter from A. W. Pollard, editor of *The Library*, now accompanying the MS. In it Pollard refuses Greg's essay, at least in its present form, for publication.

[7] Grace Ioppolo, '"The Final Revision of *Bonduca*": An Unpublished Essay by W. W. Greg', *Studies in Bibliography*, 43 (1990), 62–80.

[8] MS RB112111 PF, Huntington Library.

[9] The handwriting in this MS was identified as Knight's by J. Gerritsen, ed., *The Honest Mans Fortune: A Critical Edition of MS Dyce 9 (1625)* (Groningen, 1952), pp. xxi–vi. As Gerritsen notes, Knight seems to have joined the King's Men sometime between 1619 and 1624.

[10] John Fletcher, 'Bonduca Queene of Brittaine:' Additional MS. 36758, fol. 23ª, British Library. See also W. W. Greg, ed., *Bonduca by John Fletcher,* Malone Society Reprints (London, 1951), a diplomatic transcript of this MS. Square brackets within the quotation indicate deletion.

[11] The count is R. C. Bald's (*Bibliographical Studies in the Beaumont & Fletcher Folio of 1647* [London, 1938], p. 58).

[12] '*Final Revision*', pp. 5–8.

[13] 'Prompt-Copies, Private Transcripts, and the "Playhouse Scrivener"', *The Library*, ser. 4, 6 (1925), 148–56. Greg may have been led into such speculation in part because the first line of the 'foul papers" fifth act is metrically defective, containing only eight syllables, and is completed by the addition of two further syllables in the half-line that precedes it only in F. However, many scenes in Fletcher's plays begin with metrically defective lines: *Monsieur Thomas*, said to be of undisputed Fletcher authorship, alone shows a half-dozen examples: 2.3.1, 3.3.1, 4.4.1, 4.5.1, 5.4.1, 5.5.1 (ed. Hans Walter Gabler, *The Dramatic Works in the Beaumont and Fletcher Canon*, gen. ed. Fredson Bowers (Cambridge, 1979), vol. IV, pp. 415–540).

dialogue from one place to another, sometimes several lines away, but with little or no change in wording. He observed that the passages or lines that shifted usually made at least some sense in each of the different positions they occupied, but the transcript's placement of the passages frequently impaired metre. One representative example involves an exchange between the Roman soldiers Junius and Petillius. The half-line 'what a spirit', which I have put in bold, is part of Petillius's first speech in the Folio; this half-line shifts down three lines to its position in his second speech in Knight's transcript:

FOLIO

Petill.   – take it,[14]
        a love-mange grown upon me? **what, a**
           spirit?
Iun.   I am glad of this, I have found ye.
Petill.   In my belly,
        O how it tumbles?
Iun.   Ye good gods, I thank ye.

                       (4.4.156–9)[15]

TRANSCRIPT

petill: pox take it. a loue mange growes vpon me.
Iuni: I am glad of this. I have found ye.
petill: In my belly.
        oh how it tumbles.
        what a spirit
Iuni: ye good godℓ I thanke ye.

                       (2361–6)[16]

As Greg says, 'the position [of 'what a spirit'] is, of course, quite indifferent so far as sense is concerned, but the metre is decisive' in proving that the Folio position is the correct one[17]; in the Folio, the words in question complete a pentameter, while in the transcript they separate two part-lines that together form a pentameter. To account for how such lines as these came to be misplaced in Knight's transcript, Greg tries to imagine where these movable lines appeared in the 'foul papers'. He concludes that 'there [must] have been additions to the text as originally written and . . . there was some doubt as to the exact place to which they belonged.'[18] However, he does not describe how the 'foul papers' must have looked so as to give rise to such doubts. R.C. Bald, who happily

accepted Greg's reasoning here, confessed that, in some cases, it is not possible 'to visualize the foul papers in order to explain exactly how the confusion has arisen'.[19]

A larger example of the same sort occurs at the end of Act 2, which reads in the Folio

Iud.   **Arm, arm, Bullyes;**
        all's right again and straight; and which is
           more,
        more wine, more wine: Awake ye men of
           Memphis,
        be sober and discreet, we have much to do boyes.

                       (2.4.91–4)

The lines are in quite a different order in Knight's transcript and two words have been added to the end of the speech:

Iud: more wine. more wine. awake you men of
        Memphis.
        be sober and discrete. wee have much to doe
        boyes.
        arme arme bullyes. all's right agen. &
        straight.
        and wch is more Iust *Decius.*

                       (1199–1202)

According to Greg, 'metre and sense show F. to be correct, and MS. cannot possibly be anything but corrupt, but there must have been considerable confusion in the copy so to mislead our scribe'.[20] Greg's judgement of the metre is incontestable. The part-line that begins the Folio speech links to the part-line that immediately precedes it in both texts, a link destroyed in the transcript. Yet there seems

---

[14] In the Folio text of this play, censored words and phrases are replaced by dashes.

[15] Act-scene-line numbering is from Cyrus Hoy, ed., *Bonduca*, in *Beaumont and Fletcher*, gen. ed. Fredson Bowers, vol. IV, pp. 149–259.

[16] Line numbering is from Greg's Malone Society Reprint.

[17] '*Final Revision*', p. 11.

[18] '*Final Revision*', p. 14.

[19] *Bibliographical Studies*, p. 84. In his Preface Bald indicated how closely he worked with Greg and therefore how he could have had access to Greg's unpublished account of *Bonduca*: 'Dr. W. W. Greg . . . read and criticized the manuscript [of my book] at various stages' (p. vi).

[20] '*Final Revision*', p. 9.

little to choose between the two versions in regard to sense: 'all's right again and straight and, which is more, just, Decius', however redundant it may be, does not defy our making sense of it. Again Greg offers no conjecture about what the 'foul papers' must have looked like in order to 'mislead our scribe' as they are said to have done. Especially hard to explain according to Greg's theory of 'confusion in the copy' is the scribe's addition of the words 'Iust *Decius*', which have no parallel in the Folio.

Nonetheless, Greg was confident that these variants arose from the putatively confused condition of Fletcher's 'foul papers' that served Knight as copy. Such confidence led Greg to the meaning for the term 'foul papers' that he would employ throughout his writing: 'a copy representing the play more or less as the author intended it to stand, but not itself clear or tidy enough to serve as a prompt-book', *prompt-book* being Greg's anachronistic term for a theatrical manuscript used to guide production.[21] 'Foul papers', Greg said, were 'at times illegible [as well as] full of deletions, corrections, and alterations.'[22] Greg's 1927 story of *Bonduca* is then as follows: Fletcher gave the King's Men a sloppy copy or 'foul papers' of his play, but one that included all three scenes that were eventually printed in the Folio's last act. Then Fletcher himself produced a transcription of the 'foul papers' that would provide the text later printed in the Folio, whether or not this authorial transcript actually served as printer's copy for the Folio. Greg felt that Fletcher alone could have made the transcription because only Fletcher could have made sense of his own 'foul papers'.[23] Fletcher's transcription, Greg argued, was also a revision – hence the title of the unpublished essay '*The Final Revision of Bonduca*'. In that 1927 essay, Greg offered in support of his theory of revision three differences between Knight's transcription of the 'foul papers' and the printed Folio text: (1) single-word variants in the Folio that were introduced 'with taste and judgement, having regard to the context', and that therefore 'speak strongly of the hand of the author';[24] (2) a number of other examples of relocated passages of precisely the same kind as those I have

already quoted;[25] (3) some Folio-only additions (4.3.33–51 [1973–83], 4.3.73–141 [2008–57], and 5.3.196–201 [2598 +]). In Greg's story, then, long after Fletcher produced this revised copy, Knight came upon the 'foul papers', from which had disappeared about eight pages of Act 5, and he attempted the transcription we now have. As Grace Ioppolo has observed, Greg's theory of this text, taken as a whole, anticipates to some extent, although only in relation to this single play, E.A.J. Honigmann's contention that dramatists in this period produced both 'foul papers' and fair copies of their plays.[26] This argument was left to Honigmann to make because Greg never published '*The Final Revision of Bonduca*'; Pollard rejected it for publication in *The Library*, and Greg himself does not seem to have been satisfied with some of his own arguments, writing in the essay's margins 'rot' (twice) and 'wrong'.[27]

By 1951, when he returned to close study of the *Bonduca* texts in preparing his Malone Society Reprint of the manuscript, Greg began to entertain serious doubts about Fletcher's possible

---

[21] *Shakespeare First Folio*, p. 106. William B. Long pointed out that Greg's use of *prompt-book* was anachronistic in 'Stage Directions: A Misinterpreted Factor in Determining Textual Provenance', *Text: Transactions of the Society for Textual Scholarship*, 2 (1985), 124–5. Long uses *playbook* instead.

[22] '*Final Revision*', pp. 4, 3. As the foregoing indicates, Greg arrives empirically (through the examination of particular documents) at his textual category 'foul papers'. Thus the category can be validated or invalidated with reference to these documents and others; Greg's category of 'foul papers' is not, as Edward Pechter has mistakenly asserted, an heuristic rather than an empirical category ('Crisis in Editing?', *Shakespeare Survey 59* (Cambridge, 2006), 33).

[23] '*Final Revision*', p. 20.

[24] '*Final Revision*', p. 44.

[25] Initially Greg had copied out exactly a dozen passages as evidence of Fletcher's revision, but then he must have noticed that he had already used one of these as evidence of Fletcher's confused alteration of his 'foul papers' that had led the scribe into misplacing a passage in transcribing it. Greg then crossed out his second transcription of this twice-used passage ('*Final Revision*', pp. 48, 49).

[26] Ioppolo, 'Unpublished Essay', pp. 67, 78 n.16. She refers to E. A. J. Honigmann, *The Stability of Shakespeare's Text* (London, 1965).

[27] '*Final Revision*', pp. 7, 18, 33.

revision of *Bonduca* between the 'foul papers' and the Folio version. In editing the *Bonduca* transcript Greg again compared it to the Folio, and decided that a number of individual Folio readings he had in 1927 thought were superior authorial revisions of those in the transcript were improvements only because the transcript's readings were obvious scribal errors; he noted such errors in the Malone Society Reprint by marking them with '*sic*'.[28] Re-examination of the *Bonduca* texts also led Greg in 1951 to conclude that none of the relocated passages could be construed as evidence of revision; all pointed only, in Greg's new opinion, to Knight's 'uncertainty regarding the intended position of marginal additions of the nature of alterations made in the foul papers'.[29] Finally, Greg preferred to leave undetermined the agency behind the substantial changes to 4.3 and 5.3: 'Whether these alterations and additions were the work of Fletcher himself or of the scribe who prepared the prompt-book is one of the critical problems of the play, but lies beyond the present discussion.'[30] By 1955 Greg's opinion had shifted even further in the direction of non-authorial alteration of the play, or at least of its ending; he then wrote that Fletcher 'had left one strand of the plot in the air, to be tucked in perhaps by a different hand'.[31] Yet Greg never altered his 1927 narrative to take into account his well-founded doubts that Fletcher had revised his 'foul papers' to produce the version printed in the Folio.

To arrive at a coherent story about the *Bonduca* texts, we need Greg's New Bibliographical method, the very method he himself neglected in this case; we need, that is, to consider 'how a number of steps often intervene between the work as it formed itself in the author's mind and as it reaches modern readers'. In the case of the Folio *Bonduca* text published in the 1647 Folio, that method reveals three intervening steps: first, theatrical adaptation of Fletcher's 'foul papers'; second, one or more scribal transcriptions of this adaptation, and, third, of course, typesetting of the Folio. Greg paid attention only to the third in his 1927 essay,[32] but in the note that Knight included in his transcript of the 'foul papers', we have good con-

temporary witness to theatrical adaptation of the play and to subsequent transcription of that adaptation. In the case of the other surviving *Bonduca* text, Knight's own extant transcript of Fletcher's version, what intervenes is Knight himself, of whom more shortly.

First, though, I'd like to consider the Folio version, the version that alone contains, among other unique features, those two and a half scenes from the fifth act. Knight tells us where these scenes come from and therefore where the Folio version comes from: '*the occasion. why these* [the two and a half scenes] *are wanting here. the booke where by it was first Acted from is lost: and this hath beene transcrib'd from the fowle papers of the Authors u^{f}h were found.*' Some of what Knight tells us here is that he could not find the whole play that was performed; all he could find was the part written by the author. His note assumes a knowledgeable reader – one sufficiently familiar with the playhouse to know that the play as staged, especially in revival, might not be entirely its author's work.[33] Some of what is staged might be the work of a playhouse adapter. That such an agent is at work here becomes clearer when we appreciate that the 'foul papers' version of Fletcher's play as Knight copied it seems in itself a perfectly coherent piece; Knight could never have been able to perceive a gap in its Act 5 unless he had seen the play performed or had at least read and remembered '*the booke where by it was first*

28 113, 1.1.99; 426, 1.2.165; 598, 2.1.28; 1880, 4.2.53; 2203, 4.4.44. See '*Final Revision*', pp. 39, 42–3. In including 426, 598, 2203 in this list, I am following Ioppolo's interpretation of Greg's argument in '*Final Revision*', even though it is not certain if Greg's text can necessarily bear that interpretation. See Ioppolo, '*Unpublished Essay*', pp. 66–7, where '2203' is misprinted '2320'.

29 Greg, ed., *Bonduca*, p. xii.

30 Greg, ed., *Bonduca*, pp. xii–xiii.

31 *Shakespeare First Folio*, p. 111.

32 '*Final Revision*', pp. 20–31.

33 According to G. E. Bentley, *The Profession of Dramatist in Shakespeare's Time, 1590–1642* (Princeton, 1971), p. 263, 'the refurbishing of old plays in the repertory seems to have been universal practice in the London theatres from 1590 to 1642'. The refurbisher, says Bentley, could be the dramatist who first wrote the play, or another employed by the acting company.

Acted from'. Indeed, it's fairly obvious that the 'foul papers' version of *Bonduca* is much more coherent than the stage version with the additional scenes as printed in the Folio.

Fletcher's play is chiefly about Boadicea's or Bonduca's defeat by the Romans and her subsequent death. In the first act the Britons are prevailing and the Romans starving. Nonetheless, the Roman general Swetonius is determined to fight a pitched battle, and orders Penyus, general of the other Roman army in Britain, to bring up his troops. Although Penyus refuses to join the battle, by the third act Swetonius's army is victorious. Swetonius sends an officer to dissuade the now desperate Penyus from suicide, but Penyus kills himself anyway. Act 4 concludes with the suicides of the defeated Bonduca and her daughters. Of the royal Britons, only two remain alive, the heir to the throne, the boy Hengo, and his protector, Caratach, who has been firmly established as a great admirer of the Romans. But in Act 4 this pair, already hungry, are being tracked by Swetonius's soldiers and, if Hengo's life is to be saved, they must find a refuge instead of satisfying their hunger. Fletcher's – that is, the 'foul papers'' – fifth act opens with Swetonius's officers moving in to attack Hengo and Caratach in their refuge. While it is hard to envision exactly how the scene might have been staged, the dialogue depicts this refuge as a hole in a cliff, with acting space above the hole. The two Britons remain, as in Act 4, under surveillance by Roman soldiers who, afraid to confront Caratach, are now trying to lure him or Hengo into the open so as to slay them from above. The soldiers dangle food in front of the cave; Hengo stretches down to reach it; a soldier kills the boy. Caratach surrenders. The end.

To this story, the Folio adds two scenes and part of a third, only the first of which I here consider. It opens with Caratach and Hengo already starving in their refuge when the army of the dead Roman general Penyus marches by in funeral procession. Caratach begs the Romans to halt so that he and Hengo can join them in their grief. The Romans recognize Caratach and allow the two Britons to participate in their ritual. Caratach eulogizes

Penyus and presents the Romans with hatchments or ensigns armorial to lay on the general's hearse. Before moving on, the Romans praise Caratach in return – at which point the Britons return to their refuge to starve because they cannot leave it to seek food. If they show themselves to the Romans who have them pinned down, they will be killed instantly, for the Folio text, despite its additions, concludes exactly as the 'foul papers' version does: as soon as Hengo exposes himself to reach for the dangling food, he's slaughtered.

Because this Folio-only scene makes nonsense of the play's concluding action, it is hard to conceive that Fletcher was the one who added it or the other parts of the fifth act that are unique to the Folio version. If this inference is granted, it follows that someone besides Fletcher transcribed the 'foul papers' and included the playhouse adaptations like these additional Act 5 scenes. The resulting, no longer extant, transcription would have been what Knight calls *'the booke where by it was first Acted from'*, the manuscript that later would, directly or indirectly, provide the Folio its text of the play. Since Fletcher's 'foul papers' therefore lie behind not only Knight's extant transcript but also the printer's copy for the very good Folio text, the 'foul papers' cannot have been the sloppy manuscript that Greg took them to be. Instead, the term *foul papers* seems to be used by Knight in his note with its well-known historical meaning. The term *foul papers* referred to a MS that is to be or is being or has been fair-copied. Knight calls Fletcher's own copy 'foul papers' simply as a way of noting that it had been copied in the preparation of *'the booke where by [Bonduca] was first Acted from'*, or the fair copy.

However, such an account of *Bonduca* leaves us with the question why Knight's extant transcript is so bad if his exemplar, the foul papers, was so good. To answer this question, we need to apply New Bibliographical method and look at Knight himself, who intervenes between Fletcher and our reading of the extant transcript. More specifically, we need to look at Knight's scribal practices, which reveal themselves clearly in his transcript of another play, *The Honest Mans Fortune* (*HMF*), superbly

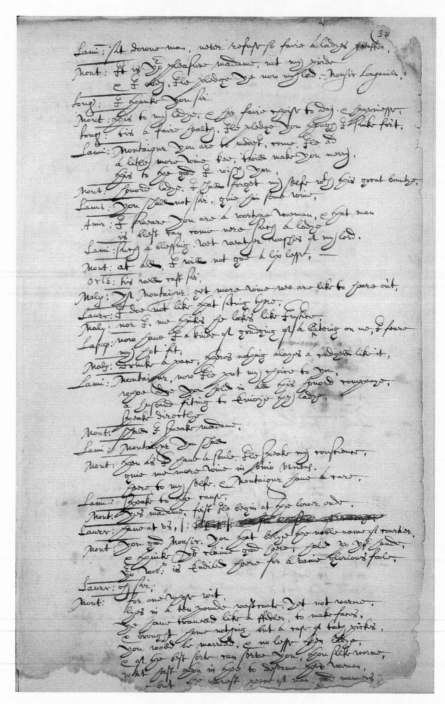

13. *The Honest Mans Fortune*, fol. 32ᵃ.

edited in 1952 by Johann Gerritsen. Here we can compare the transcription directly with the play's Folio text, which, scholars have generally agreed, was printed from the same manuscript that Knight transcribed or one very like it.[34] It is also generally agreed that Knight's *HMF* transcript is a theatrical manuscript written to guide performance; it bears at its end the licence of the Master of the Revels, Sir Henry Herbert. It shows Knight as a scribe preparing a copy for the censor and the acting company, a scribal situation in which, for Knight, the aesthetic appearance of his work was unimportant – as you can see from the page of it reproduced as Illustration 13. Knight seems to have depended on the fact that he could correct his copying as necessary, and seems therefore not to have trained himself to attend meticulously to his exemplar; instead, he allows his eye to skip about or his attention to wander and then, when he notices his mistake, he fixes it. In *HMF* Knight's eye demonstrably skipped from 'I wil' in 2.2.148 to 'I wolld' in line 149, which would have stood just below 'I will'; had he not noticed the error (homœoteleuton) immediately and corrected it, he would have lost the intervening line:

> yf it
> be assurd to you: I will gladly deale in it;
> that portion I haue I wolld not hazard. . . .

Nine other times in *HMF*, Knight's eye and pen leapt from a letter or word earlier in a line to the same letter or word later in the line or the next line, omitting the intervening text, but in seven of these cases he repaired the omissions.[35] Another time his eye dropped, in Gerritsen's words, 'to the corresponding place in the next line', even though this time it did not skip to the same letter, and a line was lost (1.3.79–80).[36] Knight almost made a similar mistake at 5.4.33 (the top line in Illustration 13) when his eye went from the last word in the line ('offer') to the last word in the next line ('pride'), there now being a 'pr' deleted before 'offer'. Other full lines were lost as Knight's eye slipped from the beginning of a speech to the beginning of one below it, although in none of these cases did the speeches in question begin with the same letter (4.1.192[b]). According to Gerritsen, Knight once apparently omitted two speeches and then copied them both on the same line as the speech that preceded them (5.4.17[b]–18), and, again according to Gerritsen, he did the same with another speech that he had at first omitted at line 63[a] in the same scene. Then, still in the same scene, he left out two other speeches and failed to notice his error (line 95); they can now be recovered only from the Folio version of *HMF*. It seems clear that Knight was often guilty of eye-skip and that he often compensated for his errors by correcting them. Altogether, in *HMF* Knight fixed about ninety of his mistakes; he left standing only about forty errors that are obvious from their violation of either sense or metre.

Knight's *Bonduca* transcript contrasts with his *HMF* transcript in both infrequency of correction and frequency of uncorrected errors. In *Bonduca* we find only 31 corrections of errors, and 115 obvious errors left unrepaired – that is, three times fewer corrections and almost three times as many uncorrected obvious errors as in *HMF*. Furthermore, in *Bonduca* such correction of error as we find is far less immediately visible than in *HMF*. About half the time in *Bonduca* Knight did not cross out or blot his errors in correcting them. Instead, he rectified errors by boxing the word in question and writing the correct word above. Illustration 14 provides an example of this kind of correction in its twenty-second line. Reluctance to correct or even to appear to correct contributes to the beautiful appearance of Knight's *Bonduca* transcript, which was apparently to be a reading text for a patron, not a MS for playhouse use. The visual attractiveness of the *Bonduca* transcript, as Illustration 14 indicates, distinguishes it from Knight's usual work

34 Greg, *Dramatic Documents*, vol. II, p. 290; Gerritsen, ed., *Honest Mans Fortune,* pp. xlvi–lii; Bald, *Bibliographical Studies*, pp. 56–7; Cyrus Hoy, ed., *The Honest Mans Fortune*, in *Beaumont and Fletcher*, gen. ed. Fredson Bowers, vol. X, p. 5.

35 Corrected: 1.1.32; 1.3.52; 2.4.2, 29; 3.3.22; 4.2.33; 5.4.148[c]; uncorrected: 3.2.73; 5.4.227[c].

36 Gerritsen, ed., *Honest Mans Fortune*, p. 139.

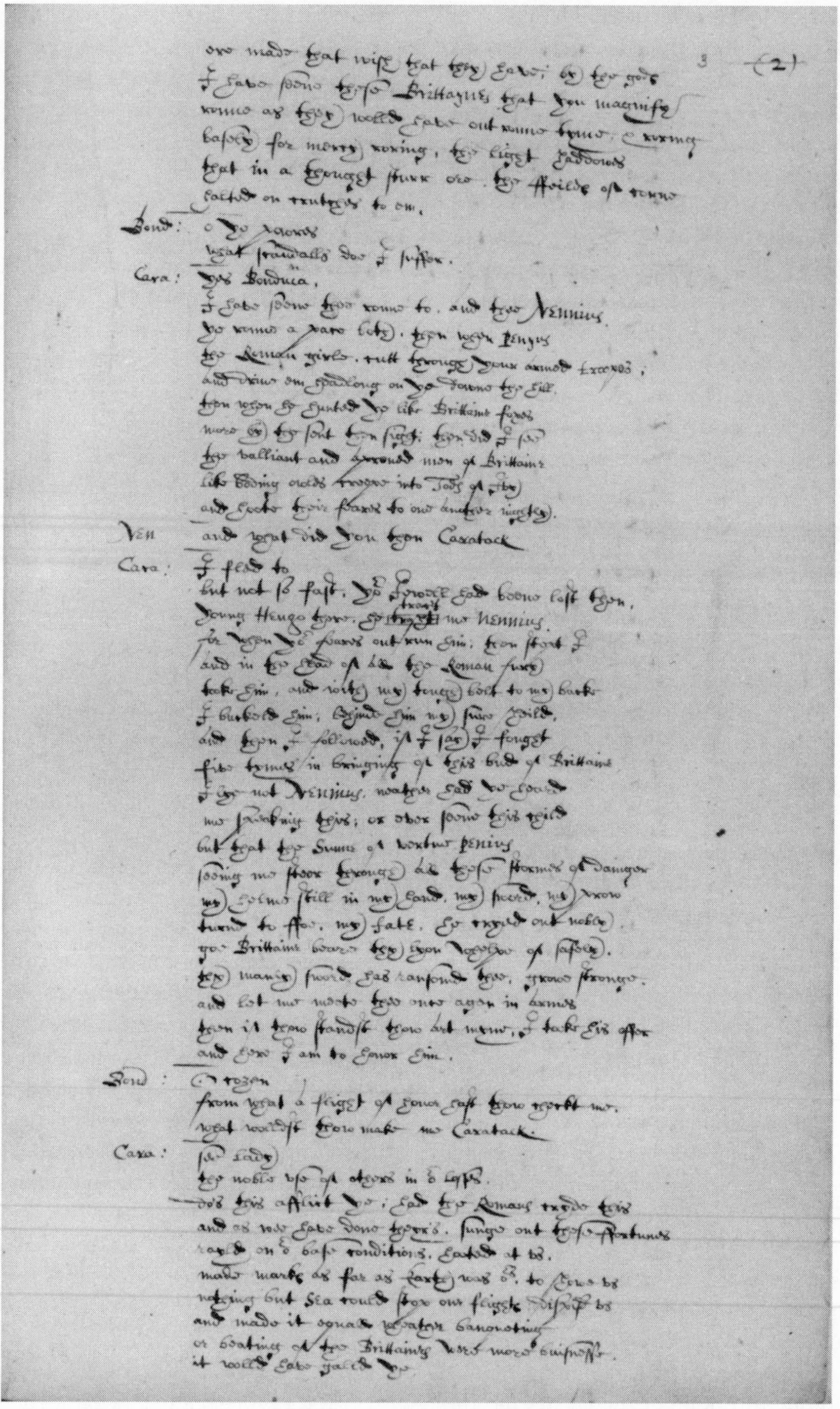

14. *Bonduca*, fol. 2ª, Additional MS. 36758.

as evidenced by *HMF.* The *Bonduca* transcript has been described as 'an unusually large folio' comprising paper of 'excellent' quality, its text 'not exactly calligraphic', but 'very carefully and neatly written'.[37] 'The lines never stray very far from the level.'[38] From comparison of *The Honest Mans Fortune* transcript with the *Bonduca* transcript we may surmise that Knight was reluctant to correct *Bonduca* so as not to detract from the beauty of his work. We are now in a position to see how he dealt with his eye-skips in *Bonduca.* Knight's eye skipped the Folio line from *Bonduca* that I have printed in boldface below; as a result, the line 'I have robb'd ye of your vertues: Justice, seek me,' was lost from his *Bonduca* transcript. Here it is impossible to say if his eye went from the *I* of '**I have robb'd**' to the *I* of 'I have broke' (homœoteleuton), or from 'souldiers, seek me,' to '**Justice, seek me,**' (haplography):

FOLIO

> Come, souldiers, seek me,
> **I have robb'd ye of your vertues: Justice,**
> **seek me,**
> I have broke my fair obedience, lost: shame take
> me,
> take me, and swallow me, make ballads of me . . . .
> (4.3.20–3)

TRANSCRIPT

> come soldiers seeke me.
> I have broke my faire obedience. lost shame take
> me.
> take me and swallow me. make ballettℓ of me.
> (1956–8)

Elsewhere in comparable situations, the results were somewhat different. In the passage quoted below, Knight skipped over the first line that I have marked in boldface in the Folio and went straight to the second boldface line; however, this time he must have noticed his error. Had he not, the line would have been lost from his transcript as was the line from the last example. But, noticing his error, he chose not to correct it and mar his beautiful page. Instead, he simply added it after the line his eye had skipped to, thus transposing lines.

FOLIO

> and still to try these *Romanes,* whom I found
> **(and if I lye, my wounds be henceforth**
> **backward,**
> **and be you witnesse, gods, and all my**
> **dangers)**
> as ready, and as full of that I brought . . . .
> (1.1.74–7)

TRANSCRIPT

> and still to try these *Romans.* whome I found
> **and be you wittness godℓ. and all my dangers**
> **and if I lye my woundℓ be hence forth**
> **backward**
> as ready. and as full of that I brought . . . .
> (84–7)

Over and over again in *Bonduca* Knight resorted to the same dodge when he had missed a line – but only when the lines as he transposed them would make at least some sense.[39] This observation needs to be combined with the one already made above: namely, that in *HMF* Knight can be shown to have accidentally omitted lines and speeches even when simple eye-skip involving the repetition of the same letter or word is not in question. Together, these two observations give us reason to suspect that when his *Bonduca* transcript differs from the Folio through the shifting of passages such as those quoted near the beginning of this essay, it was Knight who is responsible, and not, as Greg thought, the sloppy state of the foul papers from which Knight was working.

What though of the twenty-two lacunae in Knight's *Bonduca* transcript that Greg interpreted as proof of Knight's scrupulous fidelity to his copy? Greg thought Knight left these gaps in his transcription because he found Fletcher's hand in the foul papers occasionally illegible and, as an honest scribe, preferred to write nothing rather than misrepresent Fletcher's text. Greg's case is

---

37 Greg, ed., *Bonduca*, p. v.
38 Gerritsen, ed., *Honest Mans Fortune*, p. xxxii.
39 See 4.2.62–5, 1893–6; 4.3.9–12, 1944–7; once he compromised the beauty of his transcript by writing a line he had left out into the margin; evidently there was no place later in the dialogue into which he could insert the omitted line without destroying the sense of his text (line 2219).

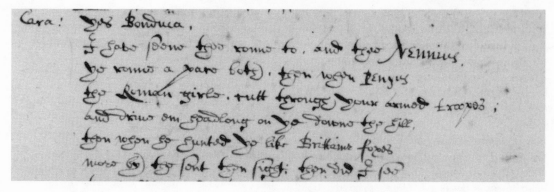

15. From *Bonduca*, fol. 2ª, Additional MS. 36758.

questionable in three ways. First, Knight seems to have placed greater value on the appearance of his transcription than on its accuracy, at a certain cost to his honesty or scrupulousness as a scribe. Second, the words that Knight omitted are not likely to have been illegible in the form in which Fletcher originally wrote them. What Knight left out of his transcript seems to have been correctly copied the first time the foul papers were transcribed by someone other than Fletcher, after the play was adapted, in the creation of '*the booke where by it* [i.e., *Bonduca*] *was first Acted from*', which contains the Folio text. Third, we can identify in Knight's transcript of the foul papers one place where he left a gap at the end of the line and then returned to complete it with a word that was much less novel in context than the one Fletcher used. Perhaps Greg was right to claim that whenever Knight could not read Fletcher's word, he left a lacuna but, whether he could read the foul papers or not, Knight demonstrated, contrary to Greg's expectation, a willingness to insert in place of Fletcher's word one of his own choice. Knight can also be shown to have done the same thing on other occasions in his transcription when lacunae are not in question. Furthermore, a majority of the lacunae in Knight's transcript are filled in the Folio by words and phrasing that challenge then-conventional expectations for the use of language. These lacunae therefore belong to the same class as the single lacuna that we find Knight filling with his own choice of word.

This single lacuna appears in Illustration 15. The line in question is the fourth one, which reads 'the *Roman* girle. cutt through your armed troopes' (line 113). It is clear that the last word 'troopes' has been written in later – first, because it angles up toward the right, while the other words in the line tend to angle down, and, second, because the initial *t* of 'troopes' is italic, unlike the secretary 's found earlier in the line in 'the' and 'through'.[40] In his Malone Society Reprint of *Bonduca*, Greg properly identified 'troopes' as an obvious scribal error. Here the Folio reads 'armed Carts', an expression invented by Fletcher and used by him

---

[40] In reproducing Knight's transcript of *Bonduca* for the Malone Society, Greg failed to notice that Knight had not written 'troopes' when he wrote the rest of the line. In filling another lacuna with the word *fate* (135, 1.1.119: Folio: 'face'), Knight used his italic hand, just as he did when he began to write *troopes* in the lacuna under discussion. Bald noted that Knight came back to fill in another gap with the word 'henceforth' (86, 1.1.75, where the Folio reading is the same), as is obvious from the word's inscription in a lighter brown ink in a context where the ink is a blacker brown (Bald, *Bibliographical Studies*, p. 58). If I read him correctly, Bald also indicated his belief that lines 849–58, filling in the bottom of fol. 8ᵛ, were added later. However, it seems to me that instead the scribe mended his pen after 'but that*ℓ*' in line 848 and then continued, with fol. 9ʳ resembling his writing after line 848. Bald's evidence in this regard would indicate Knight's care early in the process of transcribing to go back and fill in lacunae where he could, something he later gave up – hence the unaddressed absence of the speech prefixes on fol. 18ʳ. I believe that the word 'since' at line 343 may possibly have been added later.

repeatedly in *Bonduca* to refer to the Britons' scythe-bearing war-chariots. As far as I can tell from the database Literature Online, the expression 'armed carts' is not recorded as appearing before *Bonduca* and therefore would have been unfamiliar to Knight. 'Armed troopes' appears many times before *Bonduca*. This 'troopes' / 'Carts' variant is not the only one that arises from Knight's substitution of familiar phrasing for Fletcher's new expressions. On the same page (in the twenty-second line of illustration 14), Knight first correctly transcribed Fletcher's word 'trasht' in the context 'young *Hengo* there. he trasht me *Nennius*', but then boxed 'trasht' to indicate its deletion and interlined 'trac't' above it. 'Trasht', which is also to be found in the Folio, means 'encumbered', as the need to save the boy Hengo encumbered the speaker Caratach's retreat from the Romans, and is therefore doubtless the correct reading. 'Trac't', which can mean 'followed', seems in the limited context of the line itself a possible reading, but turns out to be an obvious error once Caratach goes on to describe how he used his belt to buckle the boy behind him. *Trash* as a verb is just entering the language at the beginning of the seventeenth century, and it seems that Knight, in the way of scribes, has preferred a reading more familiar to him. Such practice is consistent with Knight's transcription of *HMF*. There he preferred the common word 'crownes' for 'Cardekues' (that is, the coins called 'quarts d' écu', 3.2.63). Knight's practice therefore encourages development of a hypothesis different from Greg's about the lacunae in *Bonduca*: rather than being so scrupulous that he left lacunae only when Fletcher's hand was illegible, Knight, when not initially satisfied with Fletcher's choice of word, may have left a gap rather than copy a word he might later want to change at the cost of the beauty of his transcript, which he was forced to compromise when he changed 'trasht' to 'trac't'.

This hypothesis is supported by the observation that a number of the other lacunae signal omission of unusual words and expressions that, like 'trasht', 'Cardekues' and 'armed Carts', can reasonably be assumed to lie outside Knight's linguistic experience. Knight declined to copy such then-recent coinages as 'touchie' (274) and 'Falanx' (1085, especially unfamiliar in this, the Folio spelling), the rare word 'nesh' (1733), and the place name '*mona*' (419, later added in another hand). He also left out common words that were being used with new or rare meanings: 'hound' (i.e. incite 1436), 'doubt' (i.e. fear 1210), and 'trim' (i.e. fine, used ironically 1771). Sometimes Knight seems to have been put off by Fletcher's extraordinarily involved syntax – he left out 'shall' in 'that must or shall can carrie' (695) – and some of the dramatist's extravagant figuration: Knight omitted 'timber they' and 'mud with' from the hyperbolic 'timber they can digest and fight vpon't, / old matt*l* and mud with spoons' (348–9); 'destruction' from the metaphor 'o love [i.e., Cupid] / thow prowdly blind destruction' (390–1); 'hourly' from the again hyperbolic 'as I weare these stones wth hourly weeping' (1252), and 'burning' from 'burning vallors' (1392).

However, several other words and phrases that Knight deliberately left out of his transcript seem in their contexts unremarkable, as, for example, 'to shame 'em' (18), 'forc'd' (505), 'likelihood' (1311), and 'sledges' (1679). Yet these examples need not drive us back to Greg's hypothesis about illegibility because elsewhere in his transcript Knight was capable of altering the ordinary, as well as the extraordinary, language of the foul papers. He transcribed a speech from Junius to Petillius as follows:

> know sir
> the *Regiment* was given me. but till time
> calld ye to doe some worthy deed might stop
> the peoples Ill thought*l* of ye for lord *penius*
> I meane his death. how soone this *Iunius* comes to ye.
>
> (2416–20, 5.3.61–5)

In the Folio the last line quoted ends 'How soon this time's come to ye'. The obviously erroneous substitution of '*Iunius* comes' for 'time's come' seems to have been deliberately made by Knight, who, Greg thought he could observe, initially followed copy and transcribed the 't' of 'time's', but then altered it to the '*I*' of '*Iunius*'.[41] Very similar is Knight's apparently coming upon the Folio 'due

---

[41] '*Final Revision*', p. 9.

to' in his copy and beginning to transcribe it with a 'd' that he then very lightly hatched out in order to write instead 'vnto' (1212, 3.1.6). Since Knight was sometimes inclined to substitute his own diction for Fletcher's even when the dramatist's language was pedestrian, it follows Knight could have left lacunae for virtually any words. He was apparently always sitting in judgement on Fletcher's diction, ready to avail himself of the opportunity to change it, and sometimes leaving this option open by declining to transcribe some quite unremarkable words, even when he could not immediately think of alternatives.

Greg's fundamental error, then, was ignoring the role of the scribe and attributing to the foul papers the numerous problems found in the transcript. His most influential error, though, was to raise up his misreading of the *Bonduca* case as a paradigm for the transmission from author through the playhouse and into print of much early modern drama – this despite the fact that A. W. Pollard, in declining Greg's unpublished essay for the 1927 volume of *The Library*, wisely observed that Greg's reading of these texts did not seem to have any 'wider applicability'.[42] Actually, Greg's paradigm has no applicability at all to the transmission into print of early modern drama. Fredson Bowers was correct when he wrote, after studying the documents that survive from Philip Henslowe's papers and Diary,

There is no evidence whatever here or elsewhere in Henslowe that an author ever submitted for payment anything but a fair copy, or that the company required a dramatist to turn over his original foul sheets along with the fair copy. That this last was ever required is sheer guesswork on our part without a shred of substantiating evidence; and in fact the various occasions when playwrights independently printed their plays would appear to negate any such general assumption.[43]

I do not want to make the same mistake as did Greg with my rather different reading of the same texts. In all of Shakespeare's large canon, for instance, Knight's well-known hand has been located only behind the 1634 quarto of the collaborative *Two Noble Kinsmen*. That quarto contains some unmistakable production notes that would

indicate Knight worked on it in his regular capacity as book-keeper[44] and, in this capacity, as his transcript of *The Honest Mans Fortune* for the stage shows, Knight was far truer to his exemplar, thanks to his many corrections of his own mistranscriptions, than when he was preparing beautiful fair copy for a patron. So what Knight did to *Bonduca* does not necessarily apply to anything by Shakespeare.

Nonetheless, Knight's scribal practice with *Bonduca* has wider applicability to the editing of early modern English plays. He stands as an example of a book-keeper working for a prominent London professional company – the kind of man such a company employed for this function – and knowledge of his attitudes, as these reveal themselves in his work, is useful chiefly in putting the brakes on some generalizations that have been running away with us lately. One of these may be Honigmann's revision hypothesis. We have three texts of *Hamlet*, and two of *Othello* and of *King Lear*, to take the most prized Shakespearian examples, and no contemporary witness to how these came to differ from each other. With *Bonduca* we have Knight to tell us that his transcript provides the author's foul papers; Knight also by implication identifies the Folio text as at least very close to the adapted playhouse version. Yet none of the agents producing the differences between these texts can be identified as Fletcher revising his play. Instead the principal agents are a theatrical adapter and, in Knight, a scribe altering Fletcher's text to avoid marring his beautifully written copy with corrections. Usually when Knight fiddled Fletcher's text, he provided an intelligible reading. Thus Greg, who was nobody's fool, could at first in 1927 mistake Knight's

---

42 See n. 6.

43 *On Editing Shakespeare*, pp. 15–16. Recently Bowers's case, stated so succinctly here, has been made again at length with reference to the same documents, although without reference to Bowers. See Grace Ioppolo, *Dramatists and their Manuscripts in the Age of Shakespeare, Jonson, Middleton, and Heywood* (London, 2006).

44 See, for example, my 'On the Compositors of *The Two Noble Kinsmen*', in Charles H. Frey, ed., *Shakespeare, Fletcher, and The Two Noble Kinsmen* (Columbia, MO, 1989), pp. 6–30.

readings for Fletcher's. Knight's desire to have his own text make sense is something we might keep in mind when we compare, say, the two texts of *King Lear* and find that sometimes, when they differ, they both make sense. Such differences, the *Bonduca* texts inform us, need not arise only through the agency of the author. We need to raise the bar for the identification of authorial revision; it is not enough simply to recognize variant readings as both somehow intelligible in order to attribute the variation to authorial revision.

We have also been encouraged to regard successful theatrical adaptation as compatible with literary revision and indeed sometimes the product of the same revising hand.[45] However, in the *Bonduca* case, the adapter's intervention is ruinous to Fletcher's play as a dramatic work of art while, at the same time, essential to successful performance of the play within the conventions of the Jacobean and Caroline playhouses. Fletcher's fifth act for *Bonduca* is the shortest last act he ever wrote for a play;[46] it is only 167 verse lines. Because of the introduction early in Fletcher's career of intervals between acts of King's Men's plays, its brevity would be an intractable problem in performance; an audience would have been obliged to return their attention to the stage only to find the play almost immediately over. Theatrical personnel, and particularly Edward Knight himself, demonstrate a persistent concern with the location of act breaks and intervals, and especially with the lengths of final acts. Those who annotated the following playhouse texts all noted at least some act breaks: *Believe as You List* (annotated by Knight),[47] *The Captives*,[48] *Edmond Ironside*,[49] *The Two Noble Ladies*,[50] *The Soddered Citizen* (annotated by Knight),[51] *The Wasp*,[52] *Thomas of Woodstock*,[53] and *The Fleire* (which, unlike the foregoing, is not a MS but an annotated printed quarto).[54] In the case of *The Wasp*, the theatrical reviser cut a substantial scene from the second act and then moved the act breaks preceding each of the last three acts one scene later. Having thus shortened the last act by a scene, he reversed his decision in part and restored to Act 5 the scene he had initially cut, thereby returning the last act to its original length.

Knight intervened in *The Soddered Citizen* again to adjust the length of the fifth act, this time cutting it by a scene, which he moved to the fourth act. In transcribing *The Honest Mans Fortune* the only scene Knight cut was from the last act. As these examples show, arriving at a final act of suitable duration was an important theatrical concern, one that was met by the adapter of *Bonduca* through his addition of more than two scenes to the play's fifth act. And through his additions, the play's performance gains spectacle with the adapter providing for a lavish military procession, like the one that Michael Neill has argued stood at the centre of performances of Shakespeare's *Antony and Cleopatra*.[55] On the whole, however, adaptation of *Bonduca* indicates how success on the stage is not always compatible with success on the page.

Another current narrative the *Bonduca* case bears on is the one about maximal and minimal texts. According to this narrative, playwrights, especially Shakespeare, wrote plays that were far too long to be staged. From these maximal versions, the playhouse crafted various shorter, so-called minimal versions for production. This narrative entitles us to assume then that when there are two versions of a play, say the 1600 quarto and the 1623 Folio versions of *Henry V*, the longer Folio version is the authorial one, and the shorter quarto version the playhouse text. And oddly it is on the

45 See, for example, Gary Taylor, 'General Introduction', in *William Shakespeare: A Textual Companion* (Oxford, 1987), p. 19; Stanley Wells, 'Introduction: The Once and Future King Lear', in *The Division of the Kingdoms: Shakespeare's Two Versions of* King Lear (Oxford, 1983), pp. 19–20.

46 It is not the shortest by all that wide a margin, however. *The Humorous Lieutenant* has a fifth act of only 283 verse lines, and *The Chances'* last act is only 271 verse lines.

47 British Library (BL) Egerton MS 2828.

48 BL Egerton 1994 (3).

49 BL Egerton 1994 (5).

50 BL Egerton 1994 (11).

51 Wiltshire and Swindon Record Office MS 865/502/2 (as renumbered in 2006).

52 Alnick Castle MS 507.

53 BL Egerton 1994 (8).

54 BL 11773 c.8.

55 Michael Neill, ed., *The Tragedy of Anthony and Cleopatra*, The Oxford Shakespeare (Oxford, 1994), p. 219.

variant *Henry V* texts that this narrative is built.[56] However, we do not actually know how the *Henry V* versions came to differ, but we do know how the *Bonduca* versions did, and we know that the much longer version of *Bonduca* is the one for the stage, the shorter one from the author's foul papers.

We've also recently been encouraged to think that printed playtexts are almost never the versions that were staged,[57] while we've at the same time been encouraged to believe by Peter W. M. Blayney, I think quite rightly, that it was the acting companies that usually sold manuscripts of plays to stationers in a bid to advertise the companies' wares.[58] However, Knight's attitude to the *Bonduca* texts indicates that as a member of an acting company he thought the only version of a play worthy of transmission was the acting version, the one that did eventually get published in the 1647 Beaumont and Fletcher First Folio. Apparently, when Knight discovered in copying *Bonduca* that his exemplar lacked scenes from the theatrical version, he did not even complete his transcript, abandoning it with most of its lacunae unfilled. In general, then, it would seem that when stationers got their printer's copy from acting companies, playhouse manuscripts would have been what they got because, insofar as we can generalize from Knight's evident attitude, the only thing worth having was the play as performed.

From the point of view of editorial theory, the hoped-for consequence of recognizing Greg's mistake in characterizing *foul papers* will be the use of the term in its proper historical sense. As I noted above, historically, *foul papers* is a term used in relation to the term 'fair copy'; that is, *foul papers* refers to a MS that is to be or is being or has been fair-copied. Contrary to Greg's assumption, *foul papers* need not refer exclusively to authorial drafts, whether these are messy or not; the term simply describes papers that, for whatever reason, are to be or have already been transcribed. In other words, papers that come to be called *foul papers* may once have been an author's or scribe's fair copy of a play that has been censored or, like *Bonduca*, adapted after it has gone to the playhouse and is thus in need

of transcription. Richard Fanshaw in his translation of the poem titled *The Lusiad*, published in 1655, uses the terms *foul* and *fair* in opposition to each other in their broad and relatively straightforward historical sense in connection with MSS when he writes simply '(transcribed *faire* / From that *foule*) Copy.'[59] However, the terms are not simply relational and therefore neutral; *foul papers* has a pejorative sense, referring to a MS set in opposition to another, somehow superior MS, the 'fair copy'. Both the relational and pejorative senses of *foul papers* are brought out in a scene in John Webster's *The Devil's Law Case*, which provides a context very similar to the one in which Knight uses the term. Sanitonella, a law clerk, finds his brief torn up and declares that he 'must make shift / With the foul copy'.[60] To 'make shift' is 'to do one's best *with* (inferior means)' (*OED n.* 6d). Webster's context therefore brings out the pejorative as well as the relational sense of 'foul copy'; but this pejorative sense does not extend to the legibility of the 'foul copy', for Contilupo, the lawyer to whom it is given, says he can read it 'exceeding well, very, very exceeding well' and compliments Sanitonella on the quality of his hand: 'you write a pretty secretary' (4.1.85, 93). Knight too appears to employ *foul*

[56] Andrew Gurr, 'Maximal and Minimal Texts: Shakespeare v. the Globe', *Shakespeare Survey 52* (Cambridge, 1999), 68–87.

[57] Andrew Gurr, *The Shakespeare Company, 1594–1642* (Cambridge, 2004), pp. 120–4.

[58] 'The Publication of Playbooks', in John D. Cox and David Scott Kastan, eds., *A New History of Early English Drama* (New York, 1997), p. 386.

[59] *The Lusiad, or Portugals Historicall Poem . . . by Luis de Camoens; and Now newly put into ENGLISH BY RICHARD FANSHAW Esq.* (London, 1655), sig. Q3ᵛ. No one has yet discovered Early Modern usage that refers to the same document as simultaneously *foul papers* and *fair copy*. Definition of the terms that leads to identification of a single MS as both one and the other cannot then be supported by reference to Early Modern usage. Such anti-historical definition occurs in Ioppolo, *Dramatists and their Manuscripts*, where, for example, the extant holograph of Massinger's *Believe as You List* is presented as both foul papers and fair copy (p. 136).

[60] John Webster, *The Devil's Law-Case*, ed. Frances A. Shirley, Regents Renaissance Drama (Lincoln, 1972), 4.1.80–1. Honigmann was the first to draw attention to this Webster passage in connection with *foul papers*. See *The Texts of 'Othello' and Shakespearian Revision* (London, 1996), p. 150.

papers by way of indicating that, in comparison to the 'fair copy' or 'booke', which he cannot locate, his original provides 'inferior means' by which to copy *Bonduca* because – and only because – it lacks scenes from the performed version.

It's a shame that Pollard never published Greg's 1927 essay on *Bonduca* when Greg gave it to him. Had he done so, Greg's mistake in attributing to Fletcher's foul papers the consequences of Edward Knight's scribal habits might well have been recog-nized a long time ago. Many subsequent schol-ars would not thus have been so badly misled. Nonetheless, it is Greg's triumph to have pro-vided us with a method – the New Bibliographical method – that would allow us to discover his mis-take, now that his work on *Bonduca* has finally come to light.

---

* My sincere thanks to Barbara A. Mowat for her advice about this article.

'HONOUR THE REAL THING': SHAKESPEARE, TRAUMA AND *TITUS ANDRONICUS* IN SOUTH AFRICA

CATHERINE SILVERSTONE

The turn to the traumatic has gained considerable currency in a range of humanities' disciplines over the last fifteen years, alongside an increased popular usage of the term following the inclusion of Post-traumatic Stress Disorder (PTSD) in the *Diagnostic and Statistical Manual of Mental Disorders* of the American Psychiatric Association in 1980.[1] Trauma, which derives from the Greek $\tau\rho\alpha\acute{\upsilon}\mu\alpha$, literally meaning 'wound', denotes both a 'wound, or external bodily injury in general' (*OED* 1), and, in the context of developments in psychoanalysis and psychiatry, it emerges in the late nineteenth century as a 'psychic injury, esp. one caused by emotional shock the memory of which is repressed and remains unhealed; an internal injury, esp. to the brain, which may result in a behavioural disorder of organic origin' (*OED* 2a). The shift to the realm of the psychic, which can be traced through the work of John Erichsen, Jean-Martin Charcot, Sigmund Freud, Josef Breuer and, more recently, Dominick LaCapra, Cathy Caruth, Kirby Farrell, Ruth Leys and Ann Cvetkovich, among others, retains the language of the wound and injury but variously associates it with both behavioural responses to physical injury and, crucially for this article and work in the humanities, to 'emotional shock', the effects of which are still being felt. As Caruth summarizes, 'trauma is described as the response to an unexpected or overwhelming violent event or events that are not fully grasped as they occur, but return later in repeated flashbacks, nightmares, and other repetitive phenomena'.[2] She goes on to argue that this opens a paradox in the traumatic experience: 'that the most direct seeing of a violent event may occur as an absolute inability to know it; that immediacy, paradoxically, may take the form of belatedness'.[3] To deploy trauma in criticism, or to name as traumatic a sporting defeat, a collapse in financial markets, war or a natural disaster, points to the way in which trauma refuses to be contained by medical discourses, working its way into other areas of expression and enquiry. Thus trauma emerges, especially in late twentieth- and early twenty-first-century culture as a physical wound, a psychiatric condition and a trope in criticism and in culture more generally. In its various configurations, from the medical to the public to the critical, trauma provides a way of describing and structuring experience. As Farrell puts it: '[i]t would be hard to overestimate the plasticity and the elemental power of the concept. People use trauma as an enabling fiction, an explanatory tool for managing unquiet minds in an overwhelming

I am grateful for comments and advice I received on earlier versions of this article at Quorum, the Department of Drama at Queen Mary, University of London's research seminar and at 'Scaena: Shakespeare and his Contemporaries' at Anglia Ruskin University during 2008. My thanks also to Sarah Annes Brown, Margaret Healy, Mark Houlahan, Julie Scanlon, the Shakespeare Centre Library and Archive and the National Theatre Archive.

[1] See American Psychiatric Association, *Diagnostic and Statistical Manual of Mental Disorders: DSM-III*, 3rd edn (Washington, DC, 1980) and the most recent published definition of PTSD in: *Diagnostic and Statistical Manual of Mental Disorders: DSM-IV-TR*, 4th rev. edn (Washington, DC, 2000).
[2] Cathy Caruth, *Unclaimed Experience: Trauma, Narrative and History* (Baltimore and London, 1996), p. 91.
[3] Caruth, *Unclaimed Experience*, pp. 91–2.

world.'[4] In this work, criticism utilizes some of trauma's key clinical terminology and redeploys it as a way of explaining particular cultural products and their relationship to larger cultural formations and concerns.

I am interested, then, in the ways in which the figuration of trauma as the repeated return to a wound that is not fully accounted for, known or resolved, enables an analysis of relationships between a performance of a Shakespeare play – in this case Gregory Doran and Antony Sher's production of *Titus Andronicus* (1995) in South Africa – and various violent events and histories. While some of the key diagnostic features of trauma in its codification as PTSD appear to invite relatively straightforward structural comparison with particular forms of cultural production, such as the use of flashbacks or dream sequences in film, theatre and literature in which a subject returns to or repeats a traumatic event, my work does not seek to offer pretended clinical diagnoses of individuals (characters, directors, writers, performers) or particular performances projects through an application of PTSD symptoms, an activity that would be institutionally misplaced as well as being reductive. Rather, this article locates performances of Shakespeare as part of what might be described as a widespread turn to the traumatic that pervades contemporary culture, a phenomenon that Farrell marks as 'post-traumatic culture' whereby trauma is not simply an individual phenomenon but one where 'the entire culture is figuratively afflicted'.[5] Operating as part of 'trauma culture', performance can be read as offering a traumatic response to events, belatedly 'working through' that which is not yet fully known or accounted for, returning in manifold ways to what Caruth describes as the 'wound that cries out'.[6] Performance's belated 'working through' in response to various events and histories is both dependent on a traumatic event but also generative in relation to it: it participates in the articulation of the wound as much as it is made by it. Indeed, in Cvetkovich's model, trauma has the potential to become enabling, producing 'new practices and publics' and expanding 'the category of the therapeutic beyond the

confines of the narrowly medicalized or privatized encounter between clinical professional and client'.[7]

In my focus on the way in which performance might negotiate or respond to various traumatic wounds or events, I am not privileging either performance or criticism with fully knowing an event, or offering some kind of authentic experience of it, but rather as offering a *way* of knowing such an event: here a traumatic response can be termed, like the work of criticism and psychoanalysis, as a mode of interpretation. In using a model in which performance is designated as interpretative and generative rather than simply responsive to trauma, I also seek to avoid pathologizing the notion of 'working through' – freighted as it is with the language of psychoanalysis – as a treatment which, if successful, entails the 'end' of trauma and the 'cure' of the subject/culture, or one in which a repeated return to the event or 'acting out' stands as what LaCapra calls a 'melancholic feedback loop' in which the subject fails to resolve the trauma.[8] Instead, I want to consider 'working through' as an ongoing negotiation with various traumatic events, predicated on the understanding that there is no unmediated return to an originary moment of trauma or before trauma. In this work I am interested especially in how performance might offer an articulation of traumatic events either in the moment of performance or in the discourse that surrounds productions. Given the difficulties that attend the relationship between trauma and representation – conventionally figured as one of impossibility – I am concerned with the ethical implications of attempts to represent trauma in performance. In particular, I am interested in the ethics that surround what Leys, in relation to Walter Benn Michaels's analysis of the

---

4 Kirby Farrell, *Post-traumatic Culture: Injury and Interpretation in the Nineties* (Baltimore and London, 1998), p. x.

5 Farrell, *Post-traumatic Culture*, p. 2.

6 Cathy Caruth, *Unclaimed Experience*, p. 4.

7 Ann Cvetkovich, *An Archive of Feelings: Trauma, Sexuality and Lesbian Public Cultures* (Durham and London, 2003), p. 10.

8 Dominick LaCapra, *Writing History, Writing Trauma* (Baltimore, 2001), p. 21.

Holocaust, describes as the 'possibility of "remembering" someone else's fate'.[9] In this article I argue that, in 'working through', performances of Shakespeare memorialize and remember those events and histories. In this figuration, performance thus stands as a storehouse of trauma, archiving the event in the moment of performance and in its material and affective traces.

TITUS ANDRONICUS IN SOUTH AFRICA

Stimulated by a series of workshops run by the Studio, the National Theatre's developmental arm, in Johannesburg in the wake of South Africa's first democratic post-apartheid elections, Gregory Doran's production of *Titus Andronicus* with expatriate South African Antony Sher in the title role and a South African-based cast was a joint venture between the Studio and Johannesburg's Market Theatre. This collaboration is an example of the kind of artistic exchange made possible since 1991 when the United Nations lifted the cultural boycott on South Africa, sanctioned by its 1968 Resolution.[10] The production was developed through auditions in Johannesburg, two weeks of workshops in London and a rehearsal period in Johannesburg, before opening for an eight-week run at the Market Theatre in March 1995, with the first anniversary of the April 1994 democratic elections falling during the run. The play was subsequently performed at the West Yorkshire Playhouse's Courtyard Theatre in Leeds, the National's Cottesloe Theatre and at the Almagro festival in Spain during July 1995. Since its inception by Barney Simon and Mannie Manim in 1976, the Market Theatre has sought to present 'their audiences [with] a reflection of the world in which they lived', mainly through 'the development of indigenous work that reflects our aspirations and our lives'.[11] Given that Shakespeare has been used for conservative pedagogical and pro-apartheid political ends in South Africa as David Johnson and Martin Orkin have shown in their respective studies, as well as being co-opted for anti-apartheid work of the kind Orkin has considered, what, then, is at

stake in a performance of *Titus Andronicus* – a play which stages a series of violent acts and racial tensions – in post-apartheid South Africa in a theatre that promises 'a commitment to our community in a time in need of healing, understanding, sharing and reconciliation'?[12] In particular, how might a play that stages a resolution where power is purchased, to some extent through the incorporation and expulsion of those that are perceived as 'other', acts which are primarily localized on the bodies of a Moor and a woman, be performed in a culture in which 'black' and 'coloured' populations, have been systemically oppressed and in a theatre that is actively engaged in projects of reconciliation and healing? As will become apparent, this is a production that is certainly traced by the traumatic spectre of apartheid and its ongoing effects but it also encodes a range of other traumas that, collectively, raise questions about the possibility of representation and the ethical implications of rehearsal and performance. I am interested especially in the way in which a performance of *Titus Andronicus* was used as a precursor for exploring a series of violent events and histories, which, in turn, generated what might be described as archives of trauma.

Perhaps wary of forcing a relationship between the play's narrative and South Africa's racial politics, Doran has claimed that the production was 'certainly not presenting allegory'.[13] And indeed,

---

[9] Ruth Leys, *Trauma: A Genealogy* (Chicago and London, 2000), p. 285.

[10] See Resolution 2396 (XXIII) of the committee on the Policies of Apartheid of the Government of South Africa (A/7348, par. 12, p. 20), accessible via www.un.org/documents/ga/res/23/ares23.htm (accessed 25 Sept. 2008); and Resolution A/RES/46/79 of the committee on the Policies of Apartheid of the Government of South Africa (A/7348, par. 9, p. 33), accessible via www.un.org/Depts/dhl/res/resa46.htm (accessed 25 Sept. 2008).

[11] Programme, *Titus Andronicus*, Cottesloe, 1995, n.p.

[12] Programme. See David Johnson, *Shakespeare and South Africa* (Oxford, 1996) and Martin Orkin, *Shakespeare Against Apartheid* (Craighall, 1987).

[13] Gregory Doran, *Woza Shakespeare! 'Titus Andronicus' in South Africa* (London, 1997), p. 179. *Woza Shakespeare!* is divided into sections variously written by Sher and Doran. All subsequent references will be given in parentheses in the text.

the production did not offer a sustained allegorical reading in which the action of the play was deployed as a straightforward analogy between the narrative of Shakespeare's text and South Africa. Yet the production simultaneously instituted a South African frame of reference for engaging with the play, repeatedly turning to iconic South African images and sounds, many of which worked to make associations between aspects of the play and South Africa's history of racial conflict, especially as it was codified during apartheid. In addition to the use of South African accents, music and settings, such as the Zulu song used at the beginning of the production and the inclusion of red Johannesburg earth as part of Nadya Cohen's set design, a series of ethnic parallels was forged with respect to casting. Thus Doran conceived of the Andronici as Afrikaners: 'Titus's family are of old Roman stock, with a self-righteous belief in their own importance. Like the Afrikaner nation, they are God-fearing and pure-bred' (48). Sher worked to enact this concept through appearance and costume, noting his intention for 'the facial look of all the Andronici to be very old-style Afrikaner' (120). To this end he grew his beard, had it square cut and cropped his hair in a military crew cut. Consequently, reviewers read Titus as Afrikaner in both South Africa and the United Kingdom and, on several occasions, associations were made between Sher's Titus and Eugène Terre'Blanche, leader of the Afrikaner Weerstandsbeweging (Afrikaner Resistance Movement), which campaigns for an independent Boer state.[14] As a counterpoint to Sher's Afrikaner Titus, the images of Aaron, played by Sello Maake ka Ncube, who was, on occasion, manacled around the neck and hands, invited spectators to read his plight in the context of the oppression of black people in South Africa and more widely, reinforced by the speeches in which Aaron asserts his subjectivity and identifies the inequalities that attend being black. Doran makes his desire for these connections explicit in his assertion that South African audiences 'can feel the weight of oppression and subjugation on his [Aaron's] shoulders'.[15] The question of how to figure the Goths in relation to this black/Afrikaner dichotomy was

explained during a National Theatre Platform session. Thus the 'Afrikaner rigidity in the Romans' was contrasted with the Goths who, in a catch-all ethnic category, 'could be everything else including black', 'poor whites' or 'mixed race that could come from Cape Malay, from Indians'.[16] Here the specificity of 'other' South African identities was negated in favour of a generalized 'otherness', in much the same way that the production's representation of the Andronici, Aaron, the Nurse and the Boy, who were also played by black actors, did not create sufficient space to acknowledge the diversity of black and white cultures in South Africa.

Although the production did not offer a seamless analogy between the text and South Africa, the South African frame of reference offered by these images does, however, invite allegorical readings of the kind Doran claims to be resistant to: Titus is identified as Afrikaner, and, on occasions with an explicitly white-separatist Afrikaner, Aaron carries the weight of racial oppression in South Africa, the fall of Rome is linked to the fall of the Andronici-Afrikaners and this shadows the end of apartheid; somewhat disturbingly given the contemporary political situation of the play's production, this regime is reinstituted in modified form at the close of the play. The production at once sought to engage with the violence perpetrated in South Africa yet in the moment of performance this violence was refracted through the

---

[14] See, for example: Digby Ricci, 'Titus Topples into the "Relevant" Pit', review of *Titus Andronicus*, Market Theatre, *Weekly Mail & Guardian*, 31 March 1995; Mark Gevisser, 'What's Wrong with Relevance?', review of *Titus Andronicus*, Market Theatre, *Weekly Mail & Guardian*, 7 April 1995; Robert Greig, 'Schlock-horror, Elizabethan-style', review of *Titus Andronicus*, Market Theatre, [South Africa] *Sunday Times*, 2 April 1995; Michael Coveney, 'A Magical Mastery Tour', review of *Titus Andronicus*, Courtyard, *Observer*, 16 July 1995; Charles Spencer, review of *Titus Andronicus*, Courtyard, *Daily Telegraph*, 14 July 1995.

[15] Doran, interview with Robert Lloyd Parry, '*Titus Andronicus* in South Africa,' *Plays International*, Aug. 1995, pp. 10–11; p. 11.

[16] Platform, *Titus Andronicus*, National Theatre, 21 July 1995, National Theatre Archive, audio recording, ref. no. 1456.

action of Shakespeare's play of Goths and Romans. In this way the histories of violence in South Africa to which the performance turned were at once legible, aided by scenography, casting and the mission statement of the Market Theatre, among other factors, and placed under erasure by a play-text that deals with at least two additional temporalities, Ancient Rome and Elizabethan England, and the cultural authority of Shakespeare and the National Theatre. Images of South Africa, especially its history of racial segregation, were in effect spliced into Shakespeare's text, forcing equivalences between the text and South Africa, even as the analogies broke apart under the narrative requirements of the text and developments in post-apartheid South Africa. In this way the 'local' images to which the production had recourse operate as traumatic fragments. These fragments neatly identify the way in which the production might be said to offer a traumatic turn to South Africa, especially in relation to apartheid; it identified some of its key images, yet did not integrate them seamlessly into the narrative of Shakespeare's play. Instead the fragments pierced the Shakespearean narrative, turning the spectator repeatedly to traumatic aspects of South Africa's history, traumas that are reinforced in the fate of Aaron. Pertinent though these images are, it was, however, in the audition, workshop and rehearsal processes that the production's traumatic turns were most explicitly developed. I am, then, concerned to identify the various traumatic histories and events that were brought to bear during these preparation phases and the implications of this work for the moment of performance. In the course of this exploration I will draw extensively on *Woza Shakespeare! 'Titus Andronicus' in South Africa*, the text of which is based on diaries Doran and Sher kept during the production, marking both their professional and personal relationships. *Woza Shakespeare!* is, of course, a partial and selective document and one that works both to represent and occlude the voices of others. With this partiality in mind, I want to read this text as a document which, like the production it seeks to account for, offers a working through of a series of violent events and histories.

One of the most striking aspects of the audition, workshop and rehearsal processes as they are documented by Doran and Sher is the way in which various activities were structured in order to create an archive of trauma for members of the cast to draw upon in performance. These activities included autobiographical storytelling, watching films, listening to visiting speakers and individual research work. This kind of work is indebted to various method acting systems of training, originating from Constantin Stanislavski's work at the Moscow Art Theatre and popularized by Lee Strasberg at the New York Actors' Studio in the 1950s. These training methods emphasize an actor's use of their memory and the creation of sense impressions such that they will be able to recall these in performance and hence play the role 'truthfully'. As Peter Brook summarizes, the method actor is 'trained to reject cliché imitations of reality and to search for something more real in himself'.[17] An engagement with 'real' experience pervaded the preparation of *Titus Andronicus*; as Sher puts it in an interview: 'we were concerned with studying people with real examples of violence'.[18] The exercises used to focus this concern – many of which aimed to create an archive of traumatic memories resulting from real experiences to be capitalized on in the moment of performance – in turn raise questions about the ethical engagement with such material, especially in relation to the 'use' and representation of such experiences in performance. In this production the act of performance became about more than playing the role; it was simultaneously characterized as about honouring (and I use the word advisedly as will become clear below) the experiences that were shared and encountered in the audition, workshop and rehearsal periods.

The production's drive to utilize personal experiences of trauma was evident from the outset of the audition process. As Sher recalls, in order to cast Lavinia, Doran used an exercise where he asked actresses to place socks over their fists to represent Lavinia's amputated hands and 'without

---

[17] Peter Brook, *The Empty Space* (1968; London, 1990), p. 30.
[18] Doran, interview with Robert Lloyd Parry, p. 10.

using speech, to communicate the story of some traumatic event in her life' (50). In this work, it was Jennifer Woodburne who made her case most convincingly: '[h]er sock-fisted, dumb-tongued story – about an intruder breaking into her flat one night – is very upsetting, without a hint of charades to it' (50). In this exercise Woodburne was asked to draw on her own experience of a violent event and communicate it through performance. Here the task stages a communicative model of trauma and makes a claim for the efficacy of performance in carrying out the work of communication. That is, the exercise is predicated on the notion that performance has the capacity not only to represent a traumatic event, but that in so doing it is able to communicate or transmit something of the emotional affect of that event, registered in Sher's comment that the performance is 'very upsetting'. The use of performance as a mode of transmitting what Caruth would call 'simple knowledge' of a traumatic event is antithetical to an understanding of trauma in which the action of trauma hollows out the point of traumatic reference and resists literal representation.[19] However, Caruth's Freudian-inflected model shares with Doran's a similar belief in the communicative power of trauma or 'the historical and personal truths it transmits', where it is the responsibility of the spectating subject to listen to the 'wound that cries out'.[20] In Doran's model, the performance of trauma is credited with the capacity to transmit such personal truths, the success of which is registered at the level of content (Sher was able to understand easily the situation that Woodburne performed) and affect (Sher found the performance upsetting).

Work on the transmission of trauma also recurred in the workshop phase of the preparation process in London, but here the work of communication was also figured as commodity production. Early in this process, which comprised a series of activities and research rather than work on the playtext, an activity that was reserved for the rehearsal period in Johannesburg, Sher records that, as 'part of our work on violence, we've asked each member of the group to recount a personal experience of it' (73). Here the workshop space was mod-

elled as a kind of therapeutic space where members of the group were invited to talk through various experiences. Interestingly, these are acts that were repeated in therapeutic contexts in South Africa since a newspaper advertisement, contemporaneous with the production, advises that 'The Trauma Clinic offers one to one counselling to victims of violence and group debriefings', a 'service provided by the Centre for the Study of Violence and Reconciliation'.[21] Further, the documentation of the Truth and Reconciliation Commission records a series of individual testimonies of experiences of violence and oppression, from 1995 until the Commission closed early in 2002, identifying the way in which South Africans were invited to share publicly their experiences in the aftermath of apartheid.[22] While the workshop, the therapy session and the state-sanctioned site of testimony are not reducible to one another, they do share an interest in the enactment and elucidation of emotional states. In the workshop, this interest can be framed in terms of affective labour, or that which is designed to produce emotional affects in others and/or the self. Here the individual experiences of violent events, while still retaining their primary relationship to the teller, take on the status of commodities, available for consumption as material for performance. Subsequently, Sher records that one member of the group recounted the rape and murder of a family member 'in a calm, quiet voice, both far away from, and very near to, the edge of tremendous emotion' (73). In the course of this narrative Sher describes how another member of the narrator's family was given police photographs of the crime scene, depicting a bed with blood where the head and genitals would have been; the narrator explained that the family member kept the photos because '[t]hey were part of *us* ... my

---

[19] Caruth, *Unclaimed Experience*, p. 5.

[20] Caruth, 'Introduction', in *Trauma: Explorations in Memory*, ed. Caruth (Baltimore, 1995), pp. 3–12; p. 8.

[21] Trauma Clinic advertisement, *Star*, 8 May 1995.

[22] For details of the Truth and Reconciliation Commission, including transcripts of the testimonies, see: www.doj.gov.za/trc/trc_frameset.htm (accessed 28 Sept. 2008).

family . . . part of our history' (73, Sher's emphasis and ellipsis). Just as the photographs function as mementos, signs to be incorporated into the family's history, the individual experience of violence was offered as a memento to the cast, something for them to hold, return to and incorporate within their own performances. The narrative also offered the group specifically South African contexts for violence as it touched on the difficult topics of interracial violence and its relation to the operation of the law during apartheid and attempts to redress wrongful imprisonment in its aftermath. As Sher reports, the murdered woman was white; one of the men convicted of her death was black and was subsequently pardoned as part of the amnesty that followed Mandela's release. Sher notes that in his role as chair of the session it is his 'job now to draw comparisons, to fit this personal story into the scheme of our work – but it's difficult to speak' (73). Here he imagines a way in which the personal experience of violence will somehow be able to be deployed in relation to work on Shakespeare's play. However, he notes that the group sat in silence and that he found it difficult to speak, thinking of how he would respond to the event and photographic evidence if it pertained to a member of his own family.

In this episode, the individual experience of violence was reiterated and narrativized and thus made available as an emotional commodity in the workshop process. What emerges though is that the commodity produced through the labour of the workshop process threatened the process itself: Sher was unable to assimilate easily the experience into the work of the production and Doran finished the session early in response to further silence from the group. Here the traumatic narrative thus operates as a remainder, a surplus; it was both desired as part of the workshop process, doing the work of producing emotional affects that can be redeployed in performance, and simultaneously threatened this process. Here the narrative, not yet fully comprehended, forced participants, at least in Sher's account, to return to traumatic events – real and hypothetical – that he was unable to incorporate seamlessly into an understanding of

the play. Whereas this episode suggests that traumatic narratives resist a straightforward application to the play and the business of the workshops, the rehearsal process also models the opposite position, most clearly in relation to Maake ka Ncube's rehearsal of the moment in which Aaron encounters his child and considers Tamora's injunction to kill him, with the line 'is black so base a hue?' (4.2.71) Doran says that he encouraged Maake ka Ncube 'to honour that thought' (161), which denotes the moment in the play where Aaron begins to assert his subjectivity. He goes on to note that this instruction 'releases something. And suddenly we're blasted with his anger. A lifetime of the humiliations of apartheid, decades of his people's struggle, centuries of his race's oppression, howl up through Sello now as he delivers the line' (161). Here Doran envisages a rehearsal model where the lived experiences of the actor (in this case with respect to apartheid) are able to be welded, through the work of rehearsal, to the character. The resulting force of this archive of personal and cultural history provides the means by which to perform Aaron. In this work, however, the trauma of apartheid and a history of racial oppression was not simply deployed in the service of enabling Maake ka Ncube to play Aaron but, aided by casting, location and scenography, his performance returns the spectre of apartheid to the field of performance and criticism.

In addition to producing an archive or storehouse of traumatic personal memories for performance, even if these sometimes proved difficult to use in relation to the play, the experiences of others, in keeping with research-based exercises that often formed part of workshop and rehearsal processes, were also co-opted for this work. As part of this work, Sher recalls that they watched a documentary about the My Lai massacre, which offers testaments from both Vietnamese women and American Vietnam veterans. In his observation that the My Lai massacre is a 'useful model for the Roman-Goth war' (91), and that the experiences of the Vietnam veteran are a 'good example of how real life confounds the clichés about violence' (91), Sher highlights the way in which violent events were offered as a way of understanding aspects of *Titus*: here events and experiences were given utility value, available to be used and deployed as part of the workshop process. However, Sher goes on to observe that the South African cast 'are curiously unmoved by him [the veteran] and the film' (91). He accounts for this reaction by suggesting that having 'grown up with violence, they view it in a more cynical, less sentimental way than Greg and I', and that '[t]hey often find aspects of the violence *funny*' (91, Sher's emphasis). He comments further that perhaps the Vietnam War is 'just too far away from their own experience' to engage with (91). Here Sher locates the South African cast as having a culturally determined response to violence, and one which Sher believes works well in relation to the play: as Sher notes earlier in *Woza Shakespeare!*, '[t]he rhythms of Elizabethan and African society are strangely compatible: the violence and beauty and *humour* in both' (19, Sher's emphasis).

What emerges most clearly from the My-Lai massacre documentary episode is the way in which the attempted loading of the traumatic experiences of Vietnam onto that of contemporary South Africa and *Titus Andronicus* seemed to fail. That is, despite Sher's designation of the material as having a utility value for understanding the play, it left the cast apparently 'unmoved'. By contrast, Sher credits the specificity of local experiences with offering possibilities for the kind of traumatic 'turning to' that the production engages with. As Gys de Villiers, who played Saturninus, recorded in his newspaper diary, videos of pre-election violence in 1986 'affects us far more than the Vietnam video'.[23] Indeed, Sher records how the cast's reactions changed when they watched Michael Buerk's 1987 report on South Africa for the BBC, which included footage of violence, including a scene where a man is knifed to death by a group of people. For Sher, this footage once again provides a model for the action of the play: 'without this kind of research, actors wouldn't think of playing them [the play's several stabbings] as happens here' (93). Sher notes how the cast 'watch it in shocked silence – some weeping – these are images from their own nightmare. Like photos of a loved one

raped and murdered, this *belongs* to them' (93, Sher's emphasis). Here Sher credits the research work, which he claims shows the cast 'images of themselves' (91), with providing access to their own history, which, in turn, will feed directly into the practicalities of enacting *Titus*'s scenes of violence. As with the effects produced through the individual narratives of violence, the workshop was once again recoded as space where traumatic incidents are turned to and where the work of mourning can take place. The grief that Sher reports in relation to the experiences of watching acts of violence was, however, once again commodified and made available to be recycled in the act of playing *Titus*. The work of mourning thus functions to produce a practical and emotional archive for use in performance. For Sher, though, the moment of performance also entails a responsibility to the images they have watched and the stories the cast have shared: '[o]ur exploration of violence had been hard going, but worthwhile. When we come to reproduce it, we will be compelled, as Greg puts it, "to honour the real thing" . . . . The South Africans have a very intense, *personal* attitude to violence' (91, Sher's emphasis). Notwithstanding Sher's generalizations about the character of his (ex-)compatriots, he acknowledges a responsibility to the subjects whose stories have been commodified in the process of the workshop just as he reaffirms that one of the key drivers for the production is to institute a South African frame of reference for the violence.

In what follows I want to push Sher's sense of ethical responsibility to the experiences of others and the implications for exercising this responsibility in the act of performance further through a consideration of Jennifer Woodburne's preparation for the role of Lavinia, as it is recorded by Doran and Sher. Woodburne's commitment to engaging with traumatic events was evident throughout the audition, workshop and rehearsal process. In this work she drew on the research material provided by Doran and Sher, and her own research,

---

[23] Gys de Villiers, 'Not to Praise, but to Conquer', *Sunday Times Magazine*, 12 March 1995.

as the following sketch reveals. Thus Woodburne used the image of the man who was stabbed in Buerk's documentary as a point of comparison for the moment in the play when Tamora sanctions her sons' rape of Lavinia (125). She attended a talk Doran and Sher arranged to be given to the cast in London by Lindy Wootton from the North Westminster Victim Support Scheme, and drew on Wootton's experiences with rape victims as a context for her work on Lavinia. In addition, Woodburne also conducted her own medical research, using her mother's connections as a medical technologist at Groote Schuur Hospital to research Lavinia's hand and tongue amputations. On Woodburne's behalf, her mother questioned colleagues about the effects of Lavinia's injuries and Woodburne was also given access to medical text books which depict, as Sher records, images of severed hands and facial gunshot wounds, photocopies of which she brought to workshops (81). In the course of her research Woodburne also met a cancer patient with no tongue and a stream of saliva running from his mouth, and used this experience to explore what it would be like for Lavinia to have such injuries (144). Woodburne also spoke to a doctor about the difficulty of eating with Lavinia's injuries, employing this knowledge to explain the scene where Titus has to cajole Lavinia into eating (144). The results of Woodburne's research are revealed in the video of the production made by the South African Broadcasting Corporation in association with the Market and the National at the end of the production's run in South Africa, during which Woodburne is shown with streams of saliva running from her mouth.[24] Woodburne's use of research materials was also evident from her dressing mirror which Sher notes was covered with images that had been collected on the cast's notice board, including topical images of violence such as the ubiquitous image of a girl in Grozny, covered in white dust and splashes of blood, in close proximity to an exploded shell, and that of Ambrose Sibiya, a Zulu man who had his hand cut off with a *panga* (machete) (199).

Woodburne's development of her character thus rested, at least in part, on the research, appropriation and commodification of the experiences of others. Indeed, this drive toward commodification is registered sharply in her response to the image of the girl wounded by the shell in Grozny, an image Sher says Woodburne wonders if she 'could use . . . for Lavinia's make-up . . . The way her lips are outlined in red, her eyes too' (81). This drive is, however, also traced in Doran and Sher's narrative by Woodburne's sense of responsibility to her research subjects in which her performance is cast as a kind of testimony to these individuals. Thus, when the production was under threat of cancellation due to funding problems, Sher says that Woodburne 'was most worried about the people who'd helped her research Lavinia's injuries', and he remembers her saying: 'I felt such responsibility to them. If we didn't do the play, I would've sort of cheated them' (143). This sense of responsibility also recurs in Sher's record of Woodburne's response to her mirror of images. Sher recalls Woodburne giggling and saying 'I can hardly see myself', before going on to ask, 'without the smile . . . "How am I going to do justice to all these people?"' (199). In these comments Woodburne is represented as reading herself into the trauma of others, envisaging herself as a surrogate for their suffering. In identifying the way in which her own image has been partially occluded by the images of others, Sher depicts Woodburne as offering an image of herself as all but erased by the experiences of others. In Woodburne's subsequent comment, performance is designated as the mode by which she seeks to honour the experiences of the others with whom she has engaged. These kinds of sentiments are echoed by Sher who comments: 'I believe we are achieving what Greg urged . . . we're "honouring" the personal stories we heard, those films we watched, Jennifer's research' (156, Sher's ellipsis).

Woodburne's performance operates, then, as a kind of Kristevian 'transposition', refiguring both the experiences she has engaged with and her

---

[24] *Titus Andronicus*, South African Broadcasting Corporation, Market Theatre, 13 May 1995, Shakespeare Centre Library, videotape, accession no. 83390189.

own position as an acting subject whose performance is marked and changed by the experiences she has encountered. As Kristeva notes: transposition 'specifies that the passage from one signifying system to another demands a new articulation of the thetic – of enunciative and denotative positionality'.[25] Woodburne's intertextual or transpositional performance, which presses the experiences she has encountered into a new signifying system of the acting subject, also raises questions about the ethics of the process of transposition. That is, while Woodburne sought to do justice to the people whose experiences she has engaged with, her polysemic performance, which deployed cancer and other medical narratives as easily as documentaries, personal narratives, medical advice and the experiences of those working with victims of violence, does, however, run the risk of conflating, or forcing an equivalence, between various kinds of traumatic experiences, bringing them to bear in a performance context that has little relation to their original contexts, and thus risking the occlusion of the specificity of their narratives. This kind of conflation is not only evident in Woodburne's performance as the production collectively drew on South African contexts alongside images of Ayatollah Khomeini, Vietnam prisoners of war, acts of self-harm, transcripts of therapy sessions, newspaper clippings of state-sanctioned surgical hand amputations in Iraq, the Grozny girl and Ambrose Sibiya, as well as various dramatic and filmic references, such as *Tamburlaine*, *Henry V*, *Patton* and *La Strada*. In this series of references the production's concern with relationships between South Africa and Shakespeare's text were spliced with other cultures, events and (auto)biographical narratives. Again, the production invites a consideration of the ethical implications of the deployment of these images and narratives variously in rehearsal and in the moment of performance. That is, to what extent was the production able to realize its sense of responsibility towards its research subjects in performance, such that that responsibility might be communicated to others? Even though an utterance is, as Mikhail Bakhtin suggests, subject to centrifugal forces that posit its potential for multiple

meanings, the meaning(s) of an utterance are, however, also shaped and determined by centripetal forces, that shift according to the context of the utterance, which work to unify its meaning(s).[26] In the case of the performance, the various voices that Woodburne and the production sought to honour are, given the constraints of the mode of performance (a Shakespeare play) whose clearest external points of reference are South Africa, the theatrical institutions of the Market and the National, and the star duo of Sher and Doran, at least partially occluded, or sacrificed, in the moment of performance. Given Woodburne's sense of responsibility to her research subjects and the fact that *Woza Shakespeare!* offers Doran and Sher's subjective experiences of the production, it is then perhaps ironic that Woodburne's archive of trauma and her narrative of responsibility, alongside that of other members of the production, emerges perhaps most directly not in performance but in *Woza Shakespeare!*

Whereas *Woza Shakespeare!* provides ground for an analysis of the way in which the production sought to engage with Shakespeare's narrative in relation to a range of violent acts and events, an analysis of responses to the production identifies the way in which this 'trauma work' failed to reach a high capacity audience in Johannesburg. One of the crucial requirements for the successful operation of a transmission model of trauma that informed much of the workshop and rehearsal work – spectators – was largely absent in South Africa. In Johannesburg the production played to what Doran describes as 'poor houses' (222), in contrast to high-capacity performances in the United Kingdom. Sher seemed at once baffled by this response – 'how can the people of Johannesburg not be *interested* in our experiment with Shakespeare?' – but also at pains to account for this phenomenon, citing fears about security,

---

[25] Julia Kristeva, *Revolution in Poetic Language*, trans. Margaret Waller (1974; New York, 1984), p. 60.

[26] M. M. Bakhtin, *The Dialogic Imagination: Four Essays*, ed. Michael Holquist, trans. Caryl Emerson and Michael Holquist (Austin, 1981), p. 272.

transport links, mixed reviews and, most especially, the aftermath of the cultural boycott. Sher expresses this through several media, including *Woza Shakespeare!* (205–43), a letter to the Johannesburg *Star*, an interview in the *Evening Standard* and during the Platform session at the National.[27]

Sher's letter to the *Star* prompted a series of letters in response and the debate was played out over a week and a half in the paper's opinion pages, concluded by a second letter from Sher. Collectively, these letters suggest that the poor houses were the result of a number of factors, including the fears about security, particularly with respect to the central city location of the theatre, ticket prices, especially in relation to high levels of unemployment, inadequate transport links, performance times, the emigration of middle-class citizens who form the basis of audiences of theatres such as the Market, a resistance to Shakespeare (or to 'localized' Shakespeare) and fleeting visits by celebrity actors and directors, apathy, antipathy of the reviewers, the violent content of the play and the cultural boycott (and Sher's support of it).[28] These responses go some way toward identifying the material conditions, born of economics, geography, ethnicity, education and culture that resulted in low-capacity audiences. And yet another possibility remains born of the lived experiences of the trauma of apartheid: perhaps the performance of a violent Shakespeare play in a production that attempted to offer specifically South African contexts for violence in the wake of the first democratic elections and the lead up to the establishment of the Truth and Reconciliation Commission in July 1995 was too reductive, too inadequate, in the face of the ongoing legacy of apartheid, even as those same acts proved popular at a remove in the United Kingdom and in Spain. Here the wound cries out but the act of listening to this particular theatrical instantiation of trauma was resisted in marked contrast to the public 'performances' of the Truth and Reconciliation Commission.

Despite resistance to the production and the difficulties that attend making the various violent acts and personal histories of trauma legible in the moment of performance, Shakespeare's play and

the workshop and rehearsal activities that attend its production, were, as I have suggested, appealed to as ground for working through violent events and histories. In the repeated traumatic returns to acts of violence – personal, historical, contemporary, South African, global – performance comes to be conceived as a mode of mourning. This relationship between the play's action and mourning is articulated in Doran's director's note where he asserts that the play's acts of brutality 'rather than appearing gratuitous or extreme, seemed only too familiar, and our attention turned instead to how people deal with that violence, to the impact of grief, and man's capacity for survival'.[29] The work of performance was thus offered as a way of exploring violence and grief, both in terms of the narrative arc of the play but also, as I have suggested, at the level of the performer and the company, even as that work was not communicated to its largest potential audience in Johannesburg.

Alongside the exploration of grief and the designation of performance and its preparation as a mode of mourning, Doran also worked to offer the conclusion of the production as an act of reconciliation and healing. In his director's note Doran explains how in working through the play in a South African context, it 'took on new meaning for us, as a struggle to discover the nature of Justice, and, ultimately as an appeal for reconciliation and healing'.[30] In this vein, the play's concluding speeches, which focus on the punishment of Tamora and Aaron, were tempered by shifting Marcus's speech to the end of the play. The

---

27 Sher quoted in Clare Bayley, 'Lines of Least Resistance', *Independent*, 31 May 1995. See Antony Sher, 'SA Theatre is in Deep Trouble', *Star*, 26 April 1995; Platform, *Titus Andronicus*, National Theatre; and Michael Owen, 'Sher, Shaken to the Roots', *Evening Standard*, 30 July 1995.

28 See Editorial, 'Centre-stage Debate', *Star*, 4 May 1995; Israel Motlhabane, 'The Answer to Theatre Blues', *Star*, 4 May 1995; Ian Fraser, 'The Truth is, You Just Can't Eat Art', *Star*, 5 May 1995; Garalt MacLiam, 'There's No Business in Slow Business', *Star*, 8 May 1995; Joyce Ozynski, 'Signs Look Fine for Theatre', *Star*, 11 May 1995; and Sher, 'A Fond Farewell – For Now', *Star*, 12 May 1995.

29 Doran, Director's note, programme.

30 Doran, Director's note, programme.

last lines of the production, reprinted in the programme, thus became: 'O, let me teach you how to knit again / This scattered corn into one mutual sheaf, / These broken limbs again into one body' (5.3.69–71). Doran argues that:

These words hold such resonance in South Africa, where the new political orthodoxy is reconciliation. But in order for this unifying idea to be meaningful, justice must be done and be seen to be done.

We want Marcus's words to resonate with the audience, for them to hear the echo (179).

The production's claims were explicitly linked to the social world of Johannesburg and South Africa more widely on the opening night when Ben Ngubane, the Minister for Arts and Culture, addressed the audience at the end of the production. He pledged three million rand to the Market Theatre and Mark Gevisser reports Ngubane as saying: 'If there is one message to be got from this [the play] . . . it is that violence begets violence and that reconciliation is the only answer', a comment Gevisser reads as symptomatic of the new South Africa's capacity to 'squeeze reconciliation out of any stone – even one as dense and bleak as *Titus Andronicus*'.[31] Here reconciliation is presented as the dominant mode of engagement in relation to violence both in the play and in culture. While the production finished with a plea for reconciliation, resonating with the rhetoric that surrounds post-apartheid South Africa which was formalised in the order to establish the Truth and Reconciliation Commission, shortly after the end of the play's South African run, this plea was synchronized with one of the production's final images of Aaron chained around the neck and hands. While Doran does not claim a one-to-one correspondence between the end of the play and

contemporary South Africa, his desire for a resonance with respect to a call for justice and reconciliation is also traced by a history of racial oppression in South Africa. Shakespeare's play is employed as a kind of panacea to heal a fractured culture but as this analysis suggests, the wounds continue to seep and were far from contained by the narrative of the play and its performance.

The auditions, workshops, rehearsals, production and responses in relation to Doran and Sher's *Titus Andronicus* thus negotiate a complex set of relations between trauma and performance. In this work Shakespeare's text is used as a kind of aide-mémoire for engaging with a range of traumatic experiences, especially in relation to those wrought by apartheid, and the production simultaneously used those experiences as a means through which to engage with the play. What I have sought to show is that this is not a linear relation, whereby experience can be neatly mapped onto the action of the play and vice versa. Rather, the production and its documentation highlight the difficulties that attend traumatic representation, especially in relation to the way in which the production sutured Shakespeare's narrative to particular violent events and histories. Further, the 'turn to' apartheid and the other violent and painful events and histories, medical and otherwise, that the cast used as part of their preparation process, raises questions about the ethical appropriation of the experiences of others in performance, especially in relation to acts of responsibility and the possibility for making that sense of responsibility legible in performance. And in this difficult work the production thus stands as an archive that works to memorialize traumatic memories and experiences.

---

[31] Mark Gevisser, 'What's Wrong with Relevance?'.

'O, THESE ENCOUNTERERS': ON SHAKESPEARE'S MEETINGS AND PARTINGS

DAVID HILLMAN

Moments of meeting and parting, in Shakespeare as elsewhere, are powerfully charged. Each joining or separation is a unique event. The coming-together or parting of two characters is invariably a moment of great uncertainty at which there is the potential for something new (whether destructive or creative): however familiar the other may be, new possibilities unfold with each meeting; however short the interval between this meeting and the projected next one, new dangers subtend any separation. No-one can ever be sure that something unexpected will not take place in the interim; this might be the last time these two characters will meet on these precise terms (if at all).

Opening gambits and parting shots can tell us a great deal. One could, if one wished, read into the moment of first meeting the future development of the essential part of a relation; here we could make helpful use of Kenneth Burke's notion of the 'entelechial principle'– the thorough working-out of the implications intrinsic to any beginning.[1] And if one can read all such moments as instances of 'prophetic greeting' (*Macbeth*, 1.3.76),[2] one can also see in the form a parting takes a consummation of everything that has preceded it, reading backwards from the eventual ending or *telos* – what Burke called 'prophesying after the event'.[3] One might even think of the entire development of a relation as contained in the seeds present at its very beginning – as a long drawn-out processing of what has taken place in those first few moments – and of a parting as a recapitulation or re-enactment of all that has gone before.

From a psychoanalytic point of view, one could say that all partings are re-experiencings of an original separation from the maternal other, and that all comings-together are imbued with a fantasised potential for fusion with the originary maternal container. If meetings are always linked with the sense of an impulsion towards cohesion and unity – what Freud termed the life drive (eros) – partings are indelibly marked with a tinge of the death drive (thanatos), that which undoes connections and destroys things. These are transformational moments, when the possibility of radical change for the self opens up. Hence, such moments can be filled with both excitement and terror; a meeting (like a separation) can change a life, or end it. 'Thou met'st with things dying, I with things new-born' (*The Winter's Tale*, 3.3.113–14): at the extreme ends of the spectrum, the possibilities embodied in meeting and separation are imagined in Shakespeare as either death-dealing or

An early draft of this essay was presented at a seminar I convened at the International Shakespeare Conference in Stratford-upon-Avon, August 2008. I am grateful to the members of the seminar, and especially to Lars Engle, for their helpful comments. Thanks also to John Kerrigan and Adam Phillips for their responses to that draft.

[1] See Kenneth Burke, *Kenneth Burke on Shakespeare*, ed. Scott L. Newstok (West Lafayette, Indiana, 2007), p. 161. As Newstok points out, the notion of entelechy is Aristotelian in origin (p. 279 n.9).

[2] All quotations from Shakespeare are from *The Riverside Shakespeare*, ed. G. Blakemore Evans (Boston, 1974), except those from *Troilus and Cressida*, which are from David Bevington's edition (London, 1998).

[3] Burke, *Kenneth Burke on Shakespeare*, p. xxi.

copulative/procreative (and often as both). Meetings – like the clash of Capulets and Montagues at the opening of *Romeo and Juliet* – no less than partings, have the potential for instant violence (for what Romeo calls 'the appertaining rage / To such a greeting', 3.1.63–4); and, as is implicit in Juliet's 'Parting is such sweet sorrow, / That I shall say good night till it be morrow' (2.2.184–5), separation can have its own jouissance. The sorrow of parting is sweetened by the heightening of the very emotion that makes it sorrowful; and, perhaps, by the potential for a renewed coming-together (which would be impossible without any separation).

The example of Juliet's first encounter with Romeo underlines the immediacy with which the emotions I am pointing to can take place upon the meeting of two characters, as if the uncertainty pertaining to such moments can itself act as a catalyst for underlying dynamics to emerge. So, Imogen and her lost brothers 'at first meeting lov'd' (*Cymbeline*, 5.5.379) – the positive side of the potential of a first meeting to Posthumus's hilariously overwrought imagining of Iachimo's (supposed) coming-together with Imogen:

> Perchance he spoke not, but
> Like a full-acorn'd boar, a German one,
> Cried 'O!' and mounted; found no opposition
> But what he look'd for should oppose and she
> Should from encounter guard.
>
> (*Cymbeline*, 2.5.15–19)

Posthumus's bitter hysteria reveals the powerful (comic and tragic) potentialities underlying such moments, infused as they are with ignorance and uncertainty, and hence with the potential for extremes of scepticism. When *King John*'s Constance demands: 'let belief and life encounter so / As doth the fury of two desperate men, / Which in the very meeting fall, and die' (3.1.31–3), her odd metaphor brings together the immediate and mortal danger of first meetings with the problem of belief: it is because one never knows what will take place upon meeting and parting that these moments can be seen to be wrapped up in the dynamics of faith and doubt in Shakespeare. Upon first encountering an other (even a familiar other),

external signs come to the fore – signs of status, of social and personal identity, of good or bad will, and so on. Outward markers are scanned with particular urgency during the first moments of a coming-together, and it is this hyperattention to externality that marks these scenes of meeting and parting as powerfully subject to scepticism.[4] On occasion, Shakespeare plays with the jingle of 'leave' and 'believe': 'his curses and his blessings / Touch me alike; th'are breath I not believe in. / I knew him, and I know him; so I leave him' (*Henry VIII*, 2.2.52–4).[5]

The explosive potentialities of these transitional moments emerge quite clearly in the vocabulary of encountering and leaving. Words such as 'meet' (in Elizabethan English: to encounter, to do battle with, as well as to make love to) and 'go' (to leave, but also to die, and, again, to have sex, as in Lear's 'The wren goes to't, and the small gilded fly / Does lecher in my sight' – 4.6.112–3) periphrastically refer to both violent and sexual activity, as does Sir Toby's innuendo-filled insistence upon Sir Andrew's 'accosting' Maria: '"Accost" is front her, board her, woo her, assail her' (*Twelfth Night*, 1.3.56–7). These terms become at times outright euphemisms to describe acts of love or of aggression. Indeed, the term 'encounter' itself is used in Shakespeare to denote both sexual goings-on ('the loose encounters of lascivious men', *Two Gentlemen of Verona*, 2.7.41) and hostile battle ('Bold in the quarrel's right, rous'd to th' encounter', *King Lear*, 2.1.54); frequently it is used of both at once, as in Posthumus's 'what . . . she / Should from encounter guard' (quoted above), or when Don Pedro promises to 'take her hearing prisoner with the force / And strong encounter of my amorous tale' (*Much Ado*, 1.1.324–5), or in *Venus & Adonis*'s 'Now is she in the very lists of love, / Her champion mounted for the hot encounter' (595–6). It is precisely because of the explosiveness or dangerousness of these moments of getting-together

---

4 See David Hillman, *Shakespeare's Entrails: Belief, Scepticism and the Interior of the Body* (Basingstoke, 2007), pp. 23–32.

5 See also: 'I could neither believe nor misdoubt. Pray you, leave me' (*All's Well*, 1.3.124–6).

or departing that euphemisms are needed,[6] and that divinities are habitually invoked at meeting and parting in understated forms of prayer ('adieu', 'God be with you' – the origin of 'God buy ye' and hence of 'good bye' – Godspeed, 'God gi' god-den' (*Romeo & Juliet*, 1.2.57), 'God and Saint Steven give you godden' (*Titus*, 4.4.42–3) and so on). The various conventional niceties and rituals of politeness (what Theseus calls 'greet[ing] with premeditated welcomes' (*A Midsummer Night's Dream*, 5.1.94), and Goneril refers to disparagingly as 'compliment of leave-taking' (*King Lear*, 1.1.302)) help to structure and defuse such moments. As Hamlet puts it, 'th'appurtenance of welcome is fashion and ceremony' (*Hamlet*, 2.2.371–2). Conventional physical and rhetorical forms of meeting and parting code relations of hierarchy and social and emotional distance, the rhetoric of initial appeal or closure being highly formalised, indeed clichéd; so that a certain irony might be discerned in Juliet's bidding farewell to conventionality itself in the balcony scene: 'Fain would I dwell on form, fain, fain deny / What I have spoke, but farewell compliment!' (*Romeo and Juliet*, 2.2.88–9).

But the verbal utterances that accompany meetings and partings are in a sense supplementary, for the more primal, dangerous potentialities of encounters and partings are almost invariably deflected by non-verbal, physical acts (such as those Lavatch draws attention to: 'make a leg, put off's cap, kiss his hand', *All's Well*, 2.2.10) – acts that are, precisely, symbolic sublimations of aggression or sexuality: the bow, the curtsy, the handshake, the wave, the embrace, the doffing of the hat, the kiss:

'Now let me say "Good night", and so say you;
If you will say so, you shall have a kiss'.
'Good night', quoth she, and ere he says 'Adieu',
The honey fee of parting tend'red is;
    Her arms do lend his neck a sweet embrace;
    Incorporate then they seem, face grows to face.
                    (*Venus and Adonis*, 535–40)

Here the 'honey fee of parting' – the kiss – becomes an overt attempt by Adonis to ward off and escape from Venus's aggressive sexuality; in Venus's imagination of the encounter between Adonis and the boar, something like the opposite takes place, unveiling the violent drive underlying kisses: 'He thought to kiss him, and hath kill'd him so . . . Had I been tooth'd like him I must confess, / With kissing him I should have kill'd him first' (1110–18). It seems worth considering why kisses are, across many cultures, so commonly the way close friends, family members and lovers greet and part (which is part of the reason that Armado's 'I will kiss thy royal finger, and take leave' (*Love's Labour's Lost*, 5.2.882) isn't altogether appropriate). Kisses are both the way into and the way out of sexuality; they can act as both forerunners and aftertastes: the kiss, writes Robert Burton, is 'the prologue of burning lust'; 'to kiss and to be kissed . . . [is] a most forcible battery, as infectious, Xenophon thinks, as the poison of a spider';[7] kisses are what Adam Phillips calls 'a threat and a promise, the signature as cliché of the erotic'.[8] Kisses are dangerous, ambiguous gestures; they entail using the lips *instead of* teeth or labia (hence implying how close the aggressive and the erotic may be). 'In kissing, do you render or receive?' asks Cressida during her extended welcome to the Greek camp (*Troilus and Cressida*, 4.5.37). Her pointed question highlights both the ambiguous nature of one of the most common embodiments of greeting and leave-taking, and the difficulty in establishing the appropriate hierarchy at such moments.

The moment of meeting or parting involves first and foremost the establishment of a relation between bodies: 'Incorporate then they seem'. And the relation needs to be both tactile and tactful (or, sometimes, tactile and tactical: Lady Macbeth to her husband, on greeting Duncan: 'bear welcome

---

[6] We could even question whether the traditional dramaturgical usage of the Latin *'exit'/'exeunt'* is a kind of euphemism – cf. the common (and comical) use of Latin for sexual terms as a kind of obscurantism; and note too the very common resort to foreign words at moments of greeting and parting: *ciao, sayonara, auf Wiedersehen, au revoir*, etc.

[7] Robert Burton, *The Anatomy of Melancholy*, ed. Floyd Dell and Paul Jordan-Smith (New York, 1927), p. 701.

[8] Adam Phillips, *On Kissing, Tickling and Being Bored* (Cambridge, 1993), p. 100.

in your eye, / Your hand, your tongue, 1.5.64–5).
The need for tact starts early: 'If a stranger comes
into sight and looks the baby in the face too
quickly, the baby will break down in crying and
sobbing.'[9] Kisses, handshakes and embraces are all
essentially messages of peace, non-aggression pacts:
I kiss you – rather than biting or cannibalizing
or having sex with you; I shake your hand or
embrace you – rather than raise my hand against
you. Antony, parting from Octavius: 'Look, here
I have you [*embracing Caesar*]; thus I let you go,
And give you to the Gods' (*Antony and Cleopatra*,
3.2.63–4); the aggression here is barely concealed –
part of Antony surely wants to squeeze the life out
of Caesar, to 'give [him] to the Gods' by making
a human sacrifice out of him. They are necessary
rites of passage, whether of 'docking' or disengag-
ing, and it is worth noting (these various actions
are indeed so conventional that it is easy to forget
how culturally specific they are) that the actions
deployed in these minor ceremonies are the same
in both cases – the implication being that the threats
needing to be defused are similar at both ends of an
encounter. In addition, in order to function properly, they must be mutual. Both sides must find
the right distance, we could say, from the other
(what is appropriate at this moment? An embrace?
A handshake? A kiss? On the lips or on the cheek?);
getting it wrong can have dire consequences. There
are of course significant differences between these;
a fundamental distinction can be drawn between
salutations that involve touching (and hence being
touched) and those that do not; the former seem
to entail a greater sense of shared participation in
the moment. Timing too is important: how long to
hold the handshake or embrace, the precise *moment
juste* to lean forward for the kiss or to raise oneself
up from the bow or curtsy. These spatial and temporal calibrations can be decisive for a relationship,
and just as we must make these delicate judgements
constantly in life, these are of course decisions the
director and the actors, consciously or otherwise,
must make at numerous points in a production:
spatial and temporal corporeal arrangements are
crucial at entrance and exit, meeting and parting.
It is also worth noting that all greetings and leave-

takings seem to have an inherently theatrical quality, derived in part from the ritualized structure of
these moments, in part from the frequent sense of
having an audience at such junctures. We can perhaps think of these moments as blurring the line
between 'real life' and theatre; hence the actors'
curtsies or bows at the end of a performance combine the formal parting from the role and from the
audience.

Greetings and farewells are prime examples of
what the philosopher J. L. Austin calls 'explicit
performatives' – statements whose illocutionary
force is quite clear. Such 'deliberately pure performative phrases'[10] embody conventional rules of
meeting and parting, rules that help to smooth the
transitions involved in such moments. As Austin
points out, with expressions such as these (precisely because they are so formalised) 'there is a
special scope for insincerity'[11]: 'When someone
says "I welcome you" or "I bid you welcome",
we may say "I wonder if he really did welcome
him?" writes Austin (adding: 'though we could
not say "I wonder whether he really does bid him
welcome?"').[12] A welcome, in particular, is a kind
of promise, with all the potential for a gap between
avowal and full intention – hence, for example,
Timon's 'hollow welcomes' that need 'Ceremony
. . . To set a gloss' upon them (*Timon*, 1.2.15–16).
Though – unlike most performative utterances
(such as promises, apologies, etc.) – greetings and
leave-takings cannot exactly be revoked ('I take

[9] T. Berry Brazelton and Bertrand G. Cramer, *The Earliest Relationship* (Reading, MA, 1990), p. 119.
[10] See J. L. Austin's *How To Do Things With Words*, ed. J.O. Urmson and Marina Sbisà (Oxford, 1976), and 'Performative Utterances' in his *Philosophical Papers*, ed. J. O. Urmson and G. J. Warnock (Oxford, 1961), pp. 233–52, where Austin (very briefly) discusses the form 'I welcome you' (p. 239) and 'device[s] such as raising the hat, saying 'Salaam', or something of the kind' (pp. 245–6). Stanley Fish's important essay on *Coriolanus* argued that it is a 'speech-act play': 'How to do Things with Austin and Searle: Speech Act Theory and Literary Criticism', *MLN* 91 (1976), pp. 983–1025; as I will argue below, following Lars Engle's helpful suggestion, *Troilus and Cressida* can be thought of as similarly profoundly concerned with speech acts.
[11] Austin, *How To Do Things With Words*, p. 161.
[12] Austin, *How To Do Things With Words*, p. 79.

back my "hello"'? 'I unbid you farewell'?), they can remain unfulfilled or empty even when apparently reciprocated:

York. Whom have we here? Buckingham, to disturb me?
    The King hath sent him sure; I must dissemble.
Buckingham. York, if thou meanest well, I greet thee well.
York. Humphrey of Buckingham, I accept thy greeting.
          (*2 Henry VI*, 5.1.12–15)

And Shakespeare can joke about the potential for greetings to become mere formalities, as in Grumio's playfully rude 'Welcome, you; how now, you; what, you; fellow, you – and thus much for greeting' (*Shrew*, 4.1.111–12). The good wishes implied in welcomes and farewells are especially vulnerable to being purely formulaic (Aumerle to Richard: 'would the word "farewell" have length'ned hours / And added years to his short banishment, / He should have had a volume of farewells', *Richard II*, 1.4.16–18). John Kerrigan has recently described the way the witches' use of 'All hail' in *Macbeth* colours all the formulae of 'the ubiquitous practice of greeting' in the play: 'The ambiguity of welcome is underwritten by the slipperiness of the word [hail].'[13] The play pushes greetings and welcomes into realms of dangerous moral uncertainty, associating them repeatedly with dissimulation and betrayal, so that they could all be characterised as 'Such welcome and unwelcome things at once' (*Macbeth*, 4.3.138).[14] Indeed, something similar can be said of the curtailment or de-ritualization of partings in the play, from the Captain's description of Macbeth's brutal 'nev'r shook hands, nor bade farewell to him, / Till he unseam'd him from the nave to th' chops' (1.2.21–2) and Malcolm's relation of Cawdor's death ('Nothing in his life / Became him like the leaving it', 1.4.7–8), to Malcolm's 'let us not be dainty of leave-taking, / But shift away' (2.3.144–5) and Lady Macbeth's 'At once, good night. / Stand not upon the order of your going, / But go at once' (3.4.117–9). One could hazard that there is a kind of inevitability connecting *Macbeth*'s ambiguous welcomes and its arbitrary or truncated partings. The various

broken greetings and leave-takings can all be taken as preparing the way for Macbeth's view of life as a poor player who 'creeps in' and, once done with his strutting and fretting, simply 'is heard no more' (5.5.20–6): like an actor unable to pull off his entrances and exits, the characters in this play seem unable or unwilling to negotiate the delicate timing of transitions, including those embodied in greetings and valedictions.[15] There is no notion in Macbeth's soliloquy of a proper parting or exit which might give retrospective coherence to life.

But the ambiguity that emerges in *Macbeth* is in a sense inherent to all greetings and partings. 'All hail' interestingly balances out a deferential and an assertive position (as Kerrigan points out, 'the witches use "haile" not only as a greeting but as an imperative').[16] Something similar can be said of the odd use of the verb 'to bid' in relation to welcomes and farewells. The *OED* tells us that the verb merges two Old English verbs, *biddan* (to ask or entreat) and *bëodan* (to proclaim or command) – speech acts coming, respectively, from a position of relative weakness or power; Shakespeare often draws out these impulses (e.g., 'obedience bids I should not bid again', *Richard II*, 1.1.163). But to bid welcome or farewell doesn't quite take on either the strong sense of giving an order or injunction (as in forbidding, or as in Fortinbras's 'Go bid the soldiers shoot', *Hamlet*, 5.2.403), nor does it quite embrace the weaker sense of proffering, inviting, or making an offer (e.g. 'I bid for

---

[13] John Kerrigan, *Archipelagic English: Literature, History, and Politics 1603–1707* (Oxford, 2008), pp. 107, 105. A.R. Braunmuller, in his edition of *Macbeth* (Cambridge, 1997), points out that Shakespeare (in *3 Henry VI*, 5.7.33–4, *Richard II*, 4.1.169–71) associates the phrase 'all hail' with Judas's betrayal of Jesus: see his note to 1.3.46. Cf. also *Love's Labour's Lost*, 5.2.340: '"Fair" in "All hail" is foul, as I conceive'.

[14] See Kerrigan, *Archipelagic English*, p. 110: 'Titles at the end of *Macbeth* are significant chiefly in the vanity which they share with the elaborate welcomes which so often incorporate them.'

[15] Indeed, Macbeth ends his soliloquy with an implicit dismissal of the formalities of greeting: '*Enter a Messenger.* Thou com'st to use thy tongue; / Thy story quickly' (5.5.28–9).

[16] Kerrigan, *Archipelagic English*, p. 104.

you as I do buy', *Cymbeline*, 3.6.70): '*To bid wel-come, adieu, farewell, good-bye, good morning*,' says the *OED*, is 'now used without analysis, "bid" being little more than = "say, utter, express"'.[17] But the word's etymology nicely captures the tricky business of getting the power balance right at moments of meeting and parting.

Similarly, the expression 'to take (one's) leave' originally meant 'to obtain permission to depart' (*OED*, 'leave' *sb.*) and only later came to mean 'to bid farewell': there appears to have been a crossover between the substantive 'leave' (= permission) and the verb 'leave' (= depart); between, that is, *giving* leave and *taking* leave. Hence, one can both take someone's leave and take leave *of* someone. Again, we can discern an uncertainty or shimmering on the border between positions of deference and forcefulness, passivity and activity – one that Shakespeare often exploits (e.g., 'If thou get'st any leave of me, hang me; if thou tak'st leave, thou wert better be hang'd', *2 Henry IV*, 1.2.88–90; 'Ay, good leave have you; for you will have leave, / Till youth take leave and leave you', *3 Henry VI*, 3.2.34–5; 'Give me now leave to leave thee', *Twelfth Night*, 2.4.72). Giving and taking leave: the verbs seem to imply that something material is being conferred or withheld. And Shakespeare often has some fun with the link between actual debts and the emotional power of greetings and leave-takings: 'A man is never undone till he be hang'd, and never welcome to a place till some certain shot be paid and the hostess say "Welcome"' (*Two Gentlemen*, 2.5.4–7); 'fear no more tavern-bills, which are often the sadness of parting' (*Cymbeline*, 5.4.159); or, as we have seen, Adonis's 'honey fee of parting'. Indeed, the very etymology of the verb 'to leave' gives evidence of the difficulties the action of departing involves: it derives from the Old English *læfan*, to remain. By definition, any act of departing leaves behind a ghost of one's lost presence – a remainder, a leftover, a debt.

* * *

Shakespeare's plays written during the early 1600s, and especially *Hamlet*, *All's Well That Ends Well* and *Troilus and Cressida*, evince a particularly acute awareness of the ambiguities and ambivalences of the rhetoric of greeting and leave-taking. The remainder or debt left behind upon leave-taking is an explicit concern of *Hamlet*, a play that repeatedly draws links between parting and death. If funereal rituals can be described as the fullest form given to a ceremony of leave-taking, the difficulties of parting are given emphasis through the play's repeatedly truncated funerals. The undevoured 'funeral bak'd-meats' which 'Did coldly furnish forth the marriage tables' (1.2.180–1) are only the most salient image of unpaid funerary debts in the play; as numerous critics have pointed out, Polonius's 'hugger-mugger' (4.5.84) burial and Ophelia's 'maimed rites' (5.1.219) similarly figure the cutting short of these rituals of taking leave of the dead. It is indeed characteristic of the play, and especially its protagonist, to find partings peculiarly charged. Hamlet's resistance to endings may be taken to derive in part from the evocative farewell of the Ghost of his father ('Adieu, adieu, adieu! remember me', 1.5.91); and we might speculate that it is precisely his father's inability to *take* his leave upon his death ('Cut off . . . Unhous'led, disappointed, unanel'd', 1.5.76–7) that both brings him back as a Ghost and contributes to the triple emphasis on 'adieu'. Indeed, it is as if Hamlet makes the reiteration of farewells a crucial lesson he learns from the Ghost's parting words ('Now to my word: / It is "Adieu, adieu! remember me" / I have sworn't', 1.5.110–12). So, we witness his repeated injunctions to Ophelia ('Farewell . . . Get thee to a nunn'ry, farewell . . . To a nunn'ry, go, and quickly too. Farewell', 3.1.132–40); and his reiterated 'Good night . . . Once more good night . . . So again good night . . . Good night, mother' (3.4.159, 170, 177, 217) in the closet scene. One thinks here too of Hamlet's characteristically punning response to Polonius's 'My lord, I will take my leave of you': 'You cannot, sir, take from me anything that I will more willingly part withal – except my life, except my life, except my life' (2.2.213–17); the pun (my leave/my life) turns on and invokes a

---

[17] *OED*, bid, *v.* II. 9.

question about what precisely is 'taken' or taken away with a departure.

Perhaps here we can discern an asymmetry between greetings and partings. Where the repetition of a welcome usually betokens heartiness (Hamlet to the Players: 'You are welcome, masters, welcome all. I am glad to see thee well. Welcome, good friends', 2.2.421–2), the repetition of a parting can figure a kind of pathos, one which emerges clearly in *Hamlet* – but one which can come perilously close to bathos: 'And farewell friends; / Thus Thisbe ends; / Adieu, adieu, adieu' (*A Midsummer Night's Dream*, 5.1.345–7). It is *Timon*'s Apemantus, characteristically, who makes fun of the tendency to reiterate a parting in his response to one of the Athenian Lords' 'Fare thee well, fare thee well': 'Thou art a fool to bid me farewell twice . . . Shouldst have kept one to thyself, for I mean to give thee none' (*Timon*, 1.1.262–6). It is, conversely, the Sonnets' submissive lover who dares not 'chide the world-without-end hour' of absence 'When you have bid your servant once adieu' (*Sonnets*, 57.5–8). The repetition of farewells may imply many things: a kind of pleading or weakness, a ridiculous self-dramatization, a fobbing-off, an uncertainty about how things stand at the moment of parting. In *Hamlet*, they seem to betoken above all a reluctance to part, an ambivalence about what Michael Neill calls *Hamlet*'s 'twin fears of ending and no-end'.[18] But as the psychoanalyst Michael Balint has written, 'The profoundly tragic situation is that the more efficiently one clings, the less one is held by the object.'[19] *Hamlet*'s partings have been shown by William Kerrigan to be close to the heart of the play, its 'good nights' at once 'formal, intimate, poignant, comic, mad, unflappable, ordinary, sweet, and prayerful, a thing of childhood and a thing to be said at the end of a life.'[20] These 'good nights' may be very different from Juliet's repeated 'good nights' in the balcony scene ('Sweet, good night . . . Good night, good night! . . . dear love, adieu! . . . good night indeed . . . A thousand times good night! . . . Good night, good night!', 2.2.120, 123, 136, 142, 154, 184), but both work to usher their plays towards the tones of tragedy, gently evoking what Sidney called 'the sweet violence of

tragedy'.[21] The ending of *Hamlet*, though, seems to gesture towards a new relation to parting, one evoked not only in Horatio's final 'Good night, sweet prince' (5.2.359) but also in the calmness of Hamlet's question: 'what is't to leave betimes?' (5.2.223–4).

If the plots of Shakespeare's plays can be described through arcs of separation and joining – the tragedies tending to move from central moments of coming together (such as Othello's marriage to Desdemona and their joyful reunion in Cyprus) to final acts of separation (though of course for Othello and Desdemona the final separation of death is also a (first?) coupling), the comedies swivelling in the opposite direction – greetings and farewells can be taken as miniature encapsulations of these genres: 'In the instant of our encounter, after we had embrac'd, kiss'd, protested and, as it were, spoke the prologue of our comedy . . . ' (*Merry Wives*, 3.5.72–5). One could say, then, that the common characterisation of *All's Well That Ends Well* and *Troilus and Cressida* as generically and tonally 'problematic' has a good deal to do with the problematization of proper welcomes and farewells – the difficulties in getting the distance right at these charged moments. As Patricia Parker has pointed out, *All's Well* is 'a play that is literally filled with farewells . . . but also with iterations of *farewell* in its double sense of an ending or separation and a wish for the way to come'; *All's Well*'s plot 'proceeds through a series of displacements or farewells . . . as well as a putting off of conclusions that are premature or threaten to be too near'.[22] The mixed feelings inherent to 'fare*well*' are of course writ large in the equivocalities of the '*Well*s' of the play's title.

---

[18] Michael Neill, *Issues of Death: Morality and Identity in English Renaissance Tragedy* (Oxford, 1997), p. 217.

[19] Michael Balint, *Thrills and Regressions* (London, 1959), p. 79.

[20] William Kerrigan, *Hamlet's Perfection* (Baltimore, 1994), p. 62.

[21] Sir Philip Sidney, *The Defence of Poesy*, in Gavin Alexander, ed., *Sidney's 'The Defence of Poesy' and Selected Renaissance Literary Criticism* (London, 2004), p. 47.

[22] Patricia Parker, *Shakespeare from the Margins: Language, Culture, Context* (Chicago, 1996), pp. 186, 193.

Typical here is the King's pained attempt to part from his lords in 2.1 ('Farewell, young lords . . . And you, my lords, farewell . . . Farewell, young lords . . . I say farewell . . . Farewell', 2.1.1–23). It is the spectre of his impending death, presumably, that makes this leave-taking so fraught; the desire for (emotional or aesthetic) closure (of a stage in a relationship or of a scene) is – as Frank Kermode has shown in a more general context[23] – inextricable from the dread of endings. Hence, perhaps, the repeated deferrals of leave-takings in the play: it is the pressure to resist endings, to dilate farewells, which lends the play so much of its tonal uneasiness. Parolles's advice to Bertram to take a fuller farewell from his companions follows hard upon the King's extended leave-taking: 'Use a more spacious ceremony to the noble lords; you have restrained yourself within the list of too cold an adieu. Be more expressive to them . . . After them, and take a more dilated farewell' (All's Well, 2.1.50–7). Taking his cue, perhaps, from the King, Parolles counsels Bertram to be more expansive – though the 'dilated farewell' he recommends may be little more than a matter of the ceremonial decorum he thinks appropriate to the court. 'Spacious', even more than 'dilated', captures the issue of not just temporal but bodily calibration – of the difficulty of getting the physical distance right between parting characters – something which is brought out too by Bertram's lament to the other young lords: 'our parting is a tortur'd body' (2.1.36) – that is, presumably, overstretched, as on a rack. The play ends, however, with what feels like an abrupt curtailment (too cold an adieu), and – tellingly – with the King's conditional and unconvincing gesture towards a new beginning: 'All yet seems well, and if it end so meet, / The bitter past, more welcome is the sweet' (5.3.333–4).

One might put the problem worked out in All's Well this way: if proper greetings and partings can't be negotiated, how can anything (and in particular a love relation) get going, or end? And, concomitantly, how can comedy, or indeed tragedy, take place? Troilus and Cressida takes this a step further: here the very idea of joining and separating is negated by the profusion of go-betweens, messengers and panders inserting themselves at every turn, at one and the same time permanently linking characters *and* making it virtually impossible for them to come together.[24] The go-betweens fill the transitional space that would normally need to be crossed by greetings and valedictions; these brokers thus function as breakers of the necessary circuits of community. Indeed, if All's Well is a play of failed or 'tortur'd' partings, Troilus and Cressida adds to this a panoply of troubled or broken greetings. It is full of welcomes that are either too hot or too cold, as well as of farewells that are either unduly truncated or painfully – indeed sadistically – dilated. The play offers a catalogue of different kinds of greetings: we are given Aeneas's over-ceremonious mock non-recognition of Agamemnon ('How may / A stranger to those most imperial looks / Know them from eyes of other mortals? . . . I ask that I might waken reverence', 1.3.223–7); the simultaneously both premature and predetermined first kiss between Troilus and Cressida, before the exchange of any words between them ('Why do you not speak to her? . . . So, so; rub on, and kiss the mistress', 3.2.44–8); Paris's description of Diomedes's 'most despiteful'st gentle greeting' (4.1.34) to the Trojan princes; the over-hasty greeting of Aeneas and Troilus ('My lord, I scarce have leisure to salute you', 4.2.61); and the extravagantly discourteous 'welcomes' of Cressida and, in parallel, of Hector to the Greek camp in Act 4 scene 5. This scene epitomizes the issues around greeting in the play; here, the 'welcoming' of both these Trojan characters by the Greeks brings out the shakiness of all sociability in Troilus and Cressida, the way spitefulness shines through the apparently 'gentle' rhetoric; as Jane Adamson has written of this scene: 'When was a welcome so like a spit in the eye?'[25]

---

23 Frank Kermode, *The Sense of an Ending: Studies in the Theory of Fiction* (New York, 1979), esp. p. 7.

24 On go-betweens in the play as destroying community, see David Hillman, 'The Worst Case of Knowing the Other? Stanley Cavell and *Troilus and Cressida*', *Philosophy and Literature* 32 (2008), 74–86, esp. pp. 81–2.

25 Jane Adamson, *Troilus and Cressida: Harvester New Critical Introductions to Shakespeare* (Brighton, 1987), p. 122.

The barely latent malevolence underlying the courtesies of greeting is exposed in Agamemnon's salutation to Hector:

> Worthy of arms! As welcome as to one
> That would be rid of such an enemy –
> But that's no welcome. Understand more clear:
> What's past and what's to come is strewed with husks
> And formless ruin of oblivion;
> But in this extant moment, faith and troth,
> Strained purely from all hollow bias-drawing,
> Bids thee, with most divine integrity,
> From heart of very heart, great Hector, welcome.
>
> (4.5.164–72)

The general doth protest too much. For one thing, 'this extant moment' is a radically compromised notion in *Troilus and Cressida*; as Linda Charnes has argued, 'this play afflicts the characters with a historical "knowledge" that contaminates most, if not all, of their verbal intercourse'.[26] For another, neither 'faith and troth' nor 'divine integrity' are exactly hallmarks of Agamemnon, whom we have already witnessed (1.3.13–30) deploying the concept of something 'Strained purely from all hollow bias-drawing' for his own propagandist aims. Moreover, the framing of this welcome in relation to the imminent (but, in terms of the audience, already past and taken-for-granted) destruction of Troy undermines the conditions of fulfilment of Agamemnon's ostensibly 'more clear' understanding.[27] By the time the Greek leader arrives at 'From heart of very heart, great Hector, welcome', the greeting is deeply compromised – hence, perhaps, Menelaus's need to 'confirm [his] princely brother's greeting' (4.5.175) a moment later. Achilles's greeting of Hector shortly thereafter is even more openly belligerent:

> Now, Hector, I have fed mine eyes on thee;
> I have with exact view perused thee, Hector,
> And quoted joint by joint . . .
> Tell me, you heavens, in which part of his body
> Shall I destroy him? Whether there, or there, or there?
>
> (4.5.231–43)

Achilles' greeting is indistinguishable from an attack; he welcomes Hector to the Greek camp as one might welcome a joint of meat served to the table, or as a cannibal might greet his captured enemy.[28]

We have already witnessed this kind of erotic-aggressive blazoning (indeed, *sparagmos* would be a more appropriate term here) of the body at the moment of greeting with the welcoming of Cressida to the Greek camp. The barely sublimated sexuality of the Greek generals' reception-line in the passing round of Cressida is abundantly clear. The heightening of attention to the other's body that is so prevalent at moments of meeting – the reading of the body in order to greet the other appropriately – all too easily slips into raw, openly belligerent, sexualized 'quot[ing]':

> There's language in her eye, her cheek, her lip,
> Nay, her foot speaks; her wanton spirits look out
> At every joint and motive of her body.
> O, these encounterers, so glib of tongue,
> That give accosting [Q, F a coasting] welcome ere it
>   comes,
> And wide unclasp the tables of their thoughts
> To every tickling [Q: ticklish] reader! Set them down
> For sluttish spoils of opportunity
> And daughters of the game.   (4.5.56–64)

Sexuality has become so fused with all other forms of human relatedness in Ulysses's disparaging view that he assumes that there will be no ambiguity about the term 'encounterers', as if all women who come into any kind of contact with others are automatically 'of the game'. Whether the welcome he envisages is 'accosting' (i.e. aggressively advancing) or 'a coasting' one (i.e. indirect, sidling), the pun on the (physical as well as economic) costliness of all such welcomes remains in force; and indeed 'ere it comes' might be taken to bring out the latent sexuality of the 'welcome'. Later, Ulysses will say of Cressida that 'She will sing any man at first sight' – and Thersites clarifies the lewd innuendo

---

26 Linda Charnes, *Notorious Identity: Materializing the Subject in Shakespeare* (Cambridge, MA, 1993), p. 76. On the way the play's protagonists all struggle – in vain – to occupy the present moment, see Hillman, 'The Worst Case', pp. 79–80.
27 I am grateful to Lars Engle for helping me see this point.
28 On the play's cannibalism, see Hillman, *Shakespeare's Entrails*, pp. 69–79.

with his rejoinder, 'And any man may sing her, if he can take her clef' (5.2.10–13).

Through the course of the play, it is the ever-manipulative Ulysses who pays the most acute attention to the language of welcomes and farewells, who seems oddly attuned to the power of these moments. It is he who comes up with the plot (vis-à-vis Achilles) to 'either greet him not, / Or else disdainfully' (3.3.52–3); he who suggests the 'kissing-game' upon Cressida's arrival in the Greek camp ('NESTOR Our general doth salute you with a kiss. / ULYSSES Yet is the kindness but particular; / 'Twere better she were kissed in general', 4.5.20–2) – and then accuses her of giving 'a coasting welcome'; and he again who generalizes about and personifies greetings and partings:

> For Time is like a fashionable host
> That slightly shakes his parting guest by th'hand
> And, with his arms outstretched as he would fly,
> Grasps in the comer. Welcome ever smiles,
> And Farewell goes out sighing.   (3.3.166–70)

Throughout the play, though, 'envious and calumniating Time' (line 175) is hardly the most hospitable of hosts, and our brief glance at the various greetings in this play has already hinted at what lies behind Welcome's outstretched arms – how undifferentiated the smile is from 'mastic jaws' (1.3.73). With welcomes like these, who needs farewells? Both, in this play, are little more than pretexts or manipulations, revealing the sheer precariousness of the civility (and civilization) depicted. For just as *Troilus and Cressida* exposes the problematics of greetings, it also shows the difficulties of partings. These are epitomized by Cressida's vain attempts to leave the scene before going to bed with Troilus:

CRESSIDA For this time will I take my leave, my lord.
TROILUS Your leave, sweet Cressid?
PANDARUS Leave? An you take leave till tomorrow
     morning –
CRESSIDA Pray you, content you.   (3.2.135–9)

And again by the anti-climactic rhetoric of Troilus and Cressida's post-coital parting ('Are you aweary

of me?', 4.2.8). Indeed, the play even opens up the question of whether one can take leave of oneself (and hence, presumably, welcome oneself):

> I have a kind of self resides with you
> But an unkind self that itself will leave
> To be another's fool . . . I would be gone.
>   (3.2.143–6)

But of course, Cressida stays. When she does eventually 'leave / To be another's fool', her valedictory words to the spirit of Troilus are again equivocal: 'Troilus, farewell! One eye yet looks on thee, / But with my heart the other eye doth see' (5.2.113–4). In this scene Diomedes repeatedly bids farewell to Cressida: 'Good night . . . No, no, good night . . . and so good night . . . Foh, foh! Adieu . . . Why then, farewell . . . Farewell till then' (5.2.30–112). But these come across as little more than manipulative gestures – 'whetstone[s]' (5.2.79), to use Thersites's word, to sharpen Cressida's appetite. Every parting in the play is tinged with a sense of unfinished business (e.g. Hector's 'the issue is embracement: Ajax, farewell' (4.5.149) Ajax's 'Farewell – who shall answer?' (2.1.124); Cassandra's 'Farewell – yet soft!'(5.3.89)). Indeed the play as a whole is notorious for not being able to close properly, with a variety of false endings each opening out onto another speech or scene (e.g. Troilus's 'march away. / Hector is dead. There is no more to say. / Stay yet . . .', 5.11.21–3). Each ending, each valedictory speech act, has a sting in its tail. And, concomitantly, the play has from the start signalled the problematic status of welcomes with, and in, its aggressive Prologue, which informs us that the play 'Leaps o'er the vaunt and firstlings of those broils, / Beginning in the middle' (lines 27–8)[29] – in the process implicitly dispensing with introductory gestures.

It is no coincidence that *Troilus and Cressida* both problematizes the starting-points and end-points of all 'encounters' and is perhaps the Shakespearian play that most inextricably mingles sex and war.

---

[29] Note the implicit critique of the 'vaunt' – the beginning – in the word's hint of boasting.

For the play makes all meetings and partings at once disturbingly close to the overtly sexual *and* implicitly death-dealing. *Troilus and Cressida*'s juggling with valedictions and greetings removes it from the arenas of either tragedy or comedy by making these speech acts both deeply satirical and deadly serious. In the end, what the play problematizes is the possibility of the social community that enables welcomes and farewells to work at all.

A PLAY OF MODALS: GRAMMAR AND POTENTIAL ACTION IN EARLY SHAKESPEARE

LYNNE MAGNUSSON

'what men may do'
(William Shakespeare)

'Yes, we can.'
(Barack Obama)

GRAMMAR, HISTORY AND METHOD

The relation between grammar and early modern drama is overdue for renewed analysis. To illustrate my point, the particular grammatical form I wish to focus on in this article is the Early Modern English modal auxiliary verb and the extraordinary work it does in articulating potential action in the new drama of the late sixteenth century, especially as that work is evidenced in such early Shakespeare plays as *Titus Andronicus* and *Richard III*. The 'close encounters' will be with dramatic exchanges taking shape around 'a play of modals', dialogic interactions highlighting and making theatrical meaning out of what might seem inconsequential linguistic detail – modality and its expression in modal auxiliary verbs. A long-standing semantic category for what becomes grammaticalized in languages in various ways, definition of modality is vexed and contested: I understand it here as concerned with the speaker's assessment of, or an agent's orientation to, the possible truth of a proposition or the potentiality of a state of affairs.[1] By the 1590s, during a period of particularly rapid linguistic change in Early Modern English, a group of modal verbs including 'may', 'must', 'can', 'will', and 'shall' had become differentiated in syntactic form from the full lexical verbs they derived from in Old English, losing their non-finite forms, no longer taking non-verbal objects, and generally followed by infinitives without a *to*-link.[2] They were also undergoing semantic and pragmatic changes that resulted, as we shall see, in a system with a curiously double register of meanings for auxiliary verbs like 'must' and 'may'. Modern-day linguists brought this double register into focus when they distinguished between epistemic modality, concerned with gradations of knowledge or belief about the truth of propositions, and deontic modality, concerned with duty, obligation and permission.

---

[1] Classic studies are John Lyons, *Semantics*, vol. 2 (Cambridge, 1977), pp. 787–849; Michael R. Perkins, *Modal Expressions in English* (London, 1983); F. R. Palmer, *Mood and Modality* (Cambridge, 2001); Jennifer Coates, *The Semantics of the Modal Auxiliaries* (London and Canberra, 1983); Joan Bybee, Revere Perkins and William Pagliuca, eds., *The Evolution of Grammar: Tense, Aspect, and Modality in the Languages of the World* (Chicago and London, 1994), pp. 176–242. On historical approaches and Early Modern English modal auxiliaries, see Matti Rissanen, 'Syntax', *The Cambridge History of the English Language*, vol. 3: 1476–1776, ed. Roger Lass (Cambridge, 1999), pp. 187–331; Merja Kytö, *Variation and Diachrony, with Early American English in Focus* (Frankfurt am Main, 1991); Anthony R. Warner, *English Auxiliaries: Structure and History* (Cambridge, 1993), pp. 135–97; Elizabeth Closs Traugott, 'Historical Aspects of Modality', in William Frawley, ed., *The Expression of Modality*, (Berlin and New York, 2006), pp. 107–39. For a cognitive approach, see Günter Radden and René Dirven, *Cognitive English Grammar* (Amsterdam and Philadelphia, 2007), pp. 233–65. I am grateful to Paul Stevens, Carol Percy, David Schalkwyk, Alysia Kolentsis, Scott Newstok, Judith Weil and Sylvia Adamson for comments that helped shape this paper.

[2] Rissanen, 'Syntax', p. 231.

I will argue that these qualities made modals of interest to a dramatist like Shakespeare in a number of ways, ways interconnected with wordplay, plot construction and character psychology, and contributing overall to what one might loosely call a play's 'potential action'. First, they opened up complex possibilities for a special kind of polysemy and wordplay, given the multiple uses with puzzling overlaps that were developing for these linguistic forms. Second, as key syntactic expressions in English of possibility, necessity, and probability – a part of the terrain of modality that was debated by Aristotle, by medieval scholastic logicians, and by Reformation theologians as well as by present-day linguistic semanticists – the modal verbs had a significant role to play, I will argue, in the playwright's invention of possible worlds and crafting of dramatic plots. Third, as we shall see, these small words assumed an important role in constructing particular kinds of subjectivity and inter-subjectivity oriented to potential action, where they foregrounded a speaker's stance in relation to knowledge and belief, or served as pivots for one or more speakers' competing interpretations of ability, duty and obligation, or for conflicting assertions of will and desire. Furthermore, they became part of the furniture of politeness, whereby speakers actively register relative social positioning in their immediate speech contexts and implicitly acquiesce to (or subtly challenge) a provisionally accepted social and power structure.[3] As such, they can be sophisticated tools for the construction of character and social dialogue in drama. This article, then, explores Shakespeare's practices in 'close encounters' of a specialized linguistic kind, not as a linguist might, to seek evidence about the history of Early Modern English or to characterize the specialized forms of Shakespearian grammar, but as a rhetorician or critic might, to ask where the interaction of modality and the Early Modern English verbal system opened up special opportunities that could be exploited in dramatic art and what Shakespeare did with these in his early plays.

The most immediate purpose of this essay is methodological – and I need to explain this before proceeding to examples. I aim to contribute to the underdeveloped interdisciplinary conversation between literature and linguistics, a dialogue largely neglected while literature and history were relearning how to talk to each other. As Sylvia Adamson and Jonathan Hope have both suggested, the linguistic code itself, the changing material of Early Modern English, is part of 'the context of material and cultural circumstance'[4] that historicist critics need to take seriously. A few pioneering studies have already begun to open up the subject of modals in relation to early modern English drama and literary culture, and it is important to see what has been accomplished and what remains unconsidered. Hugh Craig's expansive article, 'Grammatical Modality in English Plays from the 1580s to the 1640s', brought the topic to life in relation to drama, using word counts to show increasing frequencies of certain modal verbs and offering speculative claims that these changes correlated to a 'deepening subjectivity' and 'enhanced sophistication' over this sixty-year period.[5] He also suggested that individual dramatists occasionally foregrounded modal verbs to highlight 'tussles of the will', an idea that Alysia Kolentsis develops to interpret the 'absolute shall' scene in *Coriolanus*.[6] Craig's quantitative approach prevented him, however,

---

3 For applied studies of modality, politeness and power relations, see Susan M. Fitzmaurice, 'Tentativeness and Insistence in the Expression of Politeness in Margaret Cavendish's *Sociable Letters*', *Language and Literature*, 9.1 (2000), 7–24; Lynne Magnusson, 'A Rhetoric of Requests: Genre and Linguistic Scripts in Elizabethan Women's Suitors' Letters', in James Daybell, ed., *Women and Politics in Early Modern England, 1450–1700* (Aldershot and Burlington, 2004), pp. 51–66.

4 Sylvia Adamson, 'The Code as Context: Language-change and (Mis)interpretation', in Kirsten Malmkjær and John Williams, eds., *Context in Language Learning and Language Understanding* (Cambridge, 1998), pp. 137–68, esp. p. 165; Jonathan Hope, 'Shakespeare's "Natiue English"', in David Scott Kastan, ed., *A Companion to Shakespeare* (Oxford and Malden, Mass., 1999), pp. 239–55.

5 *English Literary Renaissance*, 30 (2000), 32–54; p. 32.

6 Craig, 'Grammatical Modality', p. 45; Kolentsis, '"Mark you/His absolute shall?" Multitudinous Tongues and Contested Words in *Coriolanus*', in this volume, pp. 141–50, and 'Shakespeare's Telling Words: Grammar, Linguistic Encounters, and the Risks of Speech,' University of Toronto Doctoral Dissertation, 2008, esp. pp. 143–89.

from considering the complex semantics of the modals and their strange polysemy, a topic that Brian Cummings raised in his magisterial study, *The Literary Culture of the Reformation: Grammar and Grace*, where he showed how the Early Modern English modal verbs triggered debates in translating scriptural passages into English, as they repeatedly gave rise to indeterminacies that left open such key points of theology as whether God's foreknowledge or predetermination was being invoked.[7]

Cummings's book treats Reformation theologians equipped with scholarly vocabulary and categories from university logic and grammar for arguing about modality. Although Shakespeare would not have been so fully equipped, grammar-school boys of his time, who were drilled daily until they had fully memorized Lily's Latin 'Accidence', or the parts of speech and their inflexions, would have had a rudimentary and suggestive vocabulary for a part of this terrain. More than his later work, Shakespeare's earliest plays repeatedly refer to and even quote directly from the book that was to remain the standard Latin grammar textbook in England from the Reformation through the seventeenth century. Popularly known as 'Lily's Grammar', although it was a collaborative work repeatedly revised after William Lily's death in 1523, the version studied by Shakespeare would have comprised two parts: *A Shorte Introduction of Grammar*, in English, introduced the lower-form schoolboys to the parts of speech, and the *Brevissima Institutio*, in Latin, provided more advanced instruction in syntax.[8] When Jack Cade, in *The First Part of the Contention . . . of York and Lancaster*, accuses Lord Saye of corrupting 'the youth of the realm in erecting a grammar school', the speech alludes to the contents of the *Shorte Introduction* or 'Accidence' as Saye is further blamed for having 'men about thee that usually talk of a noun and a verb and such abominable words as no Christian ear can endure to hear' (4.7.31, 36–8). When Queen Margaret in *Richard III* calls Queen Elizabeth a '*sign* of dignity' and offers to '*Decline* all this' (4.4.90, 97, emphasis added), she uses the *Grammar's* terminology. And when Demetrius in *Titus Andronicus* reads Latin verse from a scroll delivered

with weapons from Titus, Chiron correctly identifies it as 'a verse in Horace' that he 'read . . . in the grammar long ago' (4.2.22–3) – specifically, in Lily's *Brevissima Institutio*.[9] If the history of grammar in use has importance, so too has the history of grammatical categories, and, as Ian Michael has established, in identifying 'moods' of verbs, 'the most significant addition in the renaissance period is the innovation, apparently by [Thomas] Linacre, of the category and term "potential"'.[10]

Early sixteenth-century users of Lily's Grammar learned of only five traditional moods or 'modes' differentiating speaker's attitudes – indicative ('sheweth a reason trewe or false'), imperative ('biddeth or commandeth'), optative ('wissheth or desireth'), conjunctive – or, as later termed, subjunctive ('hath euermore some Coniunction ioyned with him' and 'dependeth of an other verbe in the same sentence'), and infinitive ('hath neither numbre nor person').[11] By mid-century, editions of Lily's Grammar had incorporated Linacre's innovation, the suggestively named 'Potentiall Mode'. Linacre had defined it as signifying 'a thyng as mayyng or owyng to be doone', identifying its 'sygnes in englysshe' as '*may, might, wold* or *shuld*' and noting its 'lyke voyce' or form in Latin 'to the subiunctyve mode'.[12] This is an interesting point, since it suggests that the 'potential' mode may not

---

[7] (Oxford, 2002). On modals and Donne, see also Lynne Magnusson, 'Donne's Language: The Conditions of Communication', in Achsah Guibbory, ed., *The Cambridge Companion to John Donne* (Cambridge, 2006), pp. 183–200.

[8] John Colet and William Lily, *A Shorte Introduction of Grammar* (1567), introd. by Vincent J. Flynn (New York, 1945); for a brief account of the history and editions, see pp. iii–xii.

[9] T. W. Baldwin, *William Shakspere's 'Small Latine & Lesse Greeke'*, vol. 1 (Urbana, 1944), pp. 567–9, 578–9.

[10] *English Grammatical Categories and the Tradition to 1800* (Cambridge, 1970), p. 115. For a helpful literary application, see Margreta de Grazia, 'Lost Potential in Grammar and Nature: Sidney's *Astrophil and Stella*', *Studies in English Literature, 1500–1900*, 21 (1981), 21–35.

[11] Five modes appear in John Colet and William Lily, *Grammatices rudimentis* (1527); six, including the potential, appear in Lily, *A Shorte Introduction of Grammar* (1549) and (1567), from the latter of which I have taken the definitions (sig. B2v).

[12] *Progymnasmata Grammatices Vulgaria* [1512], sig. C3.

have been introduced by Linacre into Latin grammar due to a formal distinction in Latin but instead due to the emerging use in English of the modal auxiliary verbs, interpreted as 'signs'. Here is the drill John Brinsley presents in his 1612 *The Posing of the Accidence* to assist schoolboys in learning Lily's definitions by heart:

Q. How know you the Potentiall Moode?
A. It sheweth an abilitie, will, or duetie to doe any thing.
Q. What signes hath it?
A. May, can, might, would, should, ought or could: as, *Amem*, I may or can loue. (p. 16)

Thus, in instruction in the grammar of Latin (a language relying on inflections), a grammar of Early Modern English (a language relying more on word order and function words) is also taking shape that is on the whole overly dependent on the Latin tradition, but with explanations sometimes tacitly acknowledging differences, as is the case where the potential mode implicitly recognizes the special status of an English grouping we today call modal auxiliary verbs.

As a tool for dramatic analysis, the historical category of the 'potential mode' is a suggestive concept, encouraging us to see how the mental action of speakers may be linguistically realized as a significant aspect of dramatic events, but it is too limited a category to account for the 'play of modals' in Shakespeare. The foregrounding of 'may' and 'can' as its chief 'signs' neglects their close formal and semantic relation to 'must', 'will', and 'shall', grouped with them in modern grammars as key modal auxiliary verbs, and the idea of 'potential' fails to account for uses of modals to qualify logical propositions, the function that modern-day semanticists, following classical and medieval logicians, have classified as 'epistemic'. In this article, rather than insisting on one terminology or another, I will come at Shakespeare's engagement with the English modal auxiliary verbs by way of close encounters in *Titus Andronicus* and *Richard III*, since what I am claiming to unearth is a knowledge-in-practice, Shakespeare's creative collaboration or co-creation from the outset of his

career with the ever-evolving collective resources of the language.[13]

TITUS ANDRONICUS

A richly articulated moment of conflict between Titus Andronicus and his sons will serve as a preliminary example of a play of modals, illustrating related character effects, plot-building and word-play:

TITUS
Traitors, away, he rests not in this tomb . . . .
Here none but soldiers and Rome's servitors
Repose in fame, none basely slain in brawls.
Bury him where you *can*; he comes not here.

MARCUS
My lord, this is impiety in you.
My nephew Mutius' deeds do plead for him.
He *must* be buried with his brethren.

[QUINTUS and MARTIUS]
And *shall*, or him we *will* accompany.

TITUS
'And *shall*'? What villain was it spake that word?

[QUINTUS]
He that *would* vouch it in any place but here.

TITUS
What, *would* you bury him in my despite?

MARCUS
No, noble Titus, but entreat of thee
To pardon Mutius and to bury him.
(1.1.346–60, emphasis added)

In an obvious way, it is an encounter of wills that comes to a head in the foregrounding of and sparring with the modal auxiliary verbs, *can*, *must*, *shall*, *will*, *would* – the father's will against the sons' wills, with their uncle Marcus, as so often in the play, standing between, trying to mediate. In a more subtle way, the play of modals here is also an

---

13 Shakespeare may have also collaborated in *Titus Andronicus* with George Peele, often argued to have had the chief share in 1.1. The issue is complicated by speculation that Shakespeare, tidying a collaborator's work, added the Mutius material, discussed below: see Gary Taylor, *William Shakespeare: A Textual Companion* (Oxford, 1987), p. 115 and Stanley Wells, *Re-Editing Shakespeare for the Modern Reader* (Oxford, 1984), pp. 99–103.

encounter between reasoning and wilfulness, or between a world conceived as a necessary logical construct and a separate world of possibility opened up in the social negotiation or contest over power. Titus states his position on Mutius's entitlement to burial in the Andronici tomb as a logical syllogism, or more precisely its rhetorical cousin an enthymeme, setting out argument and conclusion: the tomb houses Rome's servants; Mutius was slain in a brawl, not in service of Rome; therefore, he does not qualify to be housed in the Andronici tomb. Indeed, Titus's determination – 'he rests not in this tomb' or 'he comes not here' – is not cast as a subjective modal expression, *his* view among other possible views. It is his brother and his sons who open up the play of modals. Casting his determination in the present indicative, Titus makes a categorical assertion, rather than using 'must' or 'may' to cast it in terms of 'potential' as a more or less strongly asserted possibility.

Titus is so taken aback by his sons' response not simply because they oppose (in the contested word 'shall') their wills to his will, but more disconcertingly because they interrupt his world view, a view in which the Rome he returns to is as an unchanging verity – with duty, piety, necessity all implacably bound up into one. To envision a state of affairs as possible is to envision uncertainty and competing worlds, and it seems the peculiar characteristic of Titus at the outset of this play to lack this basic kind of imagination of the co-presence of multiple possibilities. Elsewhere in this scene, Titus seems completely stunned as the world repeatedly changes course around him. As Aristotle said in the *Rhetoric*, 'what is improbable *does* happen',[14] and Titus is to find himself in a world he never imagined – after such unexpected reversals that even the adaptable Marcus inquires, 'How comes it that the subtle Queen of Goths / Is of a sudden thus advanced in Rome?' (389–90). But here it is his brother and his sons whose modal expressions alert him to what *could* or *would* be, shock him into wondering, 'What, *would* you bury him in my despite?' Thus, the interplay of the dialogue in this 'close encounter' with necessity and possibility illustrates one significant facet of modality that can

be tapped for dramatic effect both in relation to the construction of character and the construction of plot. For a playwright to create the illusion in dramatic characters of interiority, it is usual (contrary to this uncharacteristic example of Titus) to make them appear, in linguist Michael Perkins's description of fundamental human attitudes, to 'think and behave as though things might be, or might have been, other than they actually are, or were'.[15] Furthermore, as Aristotle in the *Poetics* summarizes the fundamentals of dramatic plot, 'the poet's function is to describe, not the thing that has happened, but a kind of thing that might happen, i.e. what is possible as being probable or necessary'.[16] A play then, at its outset, characteristically creates the sense of multiple possible worlds (or states of affairs) and, by its finale, creates the illusion of a necessary state of affairs. Modals can intensify or facilitate this basic work of drama. Titus is such a distinctive character precisely because his initial mindset is so entirely at odds with this basic expectation of dramatic form, its orientation to uncertain futures and open possibilities that relate closely to modal concepts.

The complex example I have been analysing also illustrates, in a way that can be epitomized by Marcus's 'must', a second significant feature of the developing modal system pertinent to the dramatist's art: that is, its peculiar polysemy that crosses over between what linguistic semanticists, following logicians, have called epistemic and deontic modality. Whether or not we have wrestled with these technical terms – and I am not suggesting that Shakespeare had labels for modal categories – in using present-day English we tacitly make such a distinction in the pragmatic inferences that allow us to hear the *must* in 'You *must* be crazy' as marking the speaker's estimated level of knowledge or belief and the *must* in 'You *must* stop this crazy behaviour' as compelling or imposing an obligation. Epistemic is more closely connected to speaker subjectivity as an expressed stance to knowledge claims about

---

[14] *The Basic Works of Aristotle*, ed. Richard McKeon (New York, 1941), p. 1431.

[15] Perkins, *Modal Expressions*, p. 6.

[16] *Basic Works*, p. 1463.

the world; deontic to the intersubjective dance of obligation and permission, the forces and counterforces that bind people especially as these are played out in verbal interaction and social relations. Marcus's 'He *must* be buried with his brethren' can be understood as epistemic, insofar as it concludes an implied enthymeme supplying an alternative to Titus's – that is, the 'must' pertains to the realm of knowledge and belief, signalling Marcus's high level of assurance (still falling short of Titus's certainty) about what he holds to be the case; or it can be understood as deontic – that is, pertaining to what binds, or to the realm of duty, obligation, permission, and prohibition, and, specifically, pressing an obligatory duty upon his interlocutor.[17] In the microcosmic drama represented by this 'play of modals', one can regard Marcus's equivocal 'must' as a kind of hinge between Titus's stance of categorical reasoning where action issues out of logical necessity and his sons' stance of demand with action conditioned by intersubjectively mandated obligation. This claim, it may be objected, makes heavy weather of one very small word, and yet, I would argue, the ambiguity or lack of distinction here is related to a non-trivial aspect of the larger play, for the character Titus, to the end of the play, seems to have a misplaced and beleaguered confidence that what binds people's actions is or should be coextensive with or issue out of reasoned certainties. For we have a reprise of Titus's syllogistic habit at the climactic moment of Act 5 scene 3. Inquiring of Saturninus 'Your reason' (5.3.39) for judging Virginius's slaying of his deflowered daughter to have been 'well done' (36), he makes what he proclaims to be 'A reason mighty, strong, effectual' (42) his compelling motive for slaying Lavinia. 'Die, die, Lavinia' (5.3.45): there can be few deaths in Renaissance drama that issue so pointedly out of a syllogism. Titus's tragedy resides partly in this misapprehension about how the Roman world makes sense. In playing out the language of the encounter and making Marcus's equivocal 'must' the hinge between Titus's and his sons' separate registers, it is almost as if Shakespeare happens, in practice, upon a puzzle that linguistic theorists have endlessly struggled to

analyse: how ambiguities inhere in the linguistic system of modal auxiliary verbs in English (both Early Modern and present-day) and what, if anything, connects the apparently divergent meanings – epistemic and deontic – of the same form.

It is, however, the sons' 'And shall' (1.1.355) that becomes the flashpoint of the dramatic encounter over Mutius's burial, and this illustrates how modals facilitate the fine calibration of relationships, for what it brings into the foreground and unsettles is how the power structure is normally held in place and reinforced partly by the selections that speakers make among these small social levers. Sons do not customarily select the commanding or edict-enforcing 'shall' in interchanges negotiating futures with respected fathers, and it is this violation that is signalled by Titus's reiteration, '"And shall"? What villain was it spake that word?' Taken together with the secondary meaning of the word 'villain' (as menial serf or low-born rustic), Titus's repetitive retort acts to put the son back into his subordinate place, and while Quintus does not give in, his choice of the hypothetical 'would' in 'He that *would* vouch it any place but here' beats a retreat on the politeness front, which Marcus then capitalizes upon ('No, noble Titus, but entreat of thee / To pardon Mutius'), trying to preserve relationships while achieving Titus's disfavoured outcome. Politeness is politics writ small, and modal choices are integral elements of its ideological apparatus.

In this first 'close encounter' with modals in a fragment of Shakespearian text testing out potential action, we have glimpsed their contribution to all three of the categories I first outlined – to plot construction, to subjectivity of character and relationship, and to (in this instance) a relatively subtle form of stylistic wordplay.

RICHARD III

Let us turn for a second example to an encounter in *Richard III* where the spotlight is very much placed

---

[17] Another reading of this ambiguity might emphasize objective versus subjective deontic modality, depending on whether the compelling force is interpreted as an ethical norm or speaker-related.

on the polysemy of a modal verb, and, significantly, on the auxiliary *may*, which displayed a different range of meanings in the 1590s than it does today:

QUEEN ELIZABETH
My lord, you do me shameful injury
Falsely to draw me in these vile suspects.

RICHARD GLOUCESTER
You *may* deny that you were not the mean
Of my Lord Hastings' late imprisonment.

RIVERS She *may*, my lord, for –

RICHARD GLOUCESTER
She *may*, Lord Rivers; why, who knows not so?
She *may* do more, sir, than denying that.
She *may* help you to many fair preferments,
And then deny her aiding hand therein,
And lay those honours on your high desert.
What *may* she not? She *may* – ay, marry, *may* she.

RIVERS What 'marry, *may* she'?

RICHARD GLOUCESTER
What marry, *may* she? Marry with a king:
A bachelor, and a handsome stripling, too.
Iwis your grandam had a worser match.
                              (1.3.88–102, emphasis added)

The interplay here among Edward IV's Queen Elizabeth, Richard Duke of Gloucester, and the Queen's brother Lord Rivers about the Queen's agency in the incarceration of Clarence and Hastings is opaque without some attention paid to the history of the English modal *may*, which had at least three senses in Shakespeare's day, even if many editors have passed it over in this example without explanatory comment.[18] In present-day English, the modal verb *may* in main clauses is limited to two main interpretations: the epistemic perhaps-*may*, indicating the speaker's qualified level of commitment to a proposition as possible, is the primary use; we are all familiar with the deontic permission-*may*, reporting on or granting permission, though this use is fading away. In the 1590s, both these meanings had become available, but they coexisted with an earlier sense: the dynamic or ability-*may*,[19] which was more obviously associated with the original Old English lexical verb, 'maighen', to have the physical ability or might. Thus, this third and prior sense, ability-*may* (generalized by

this period to encompass mental as well as physical ability, or even to register an enabling condition external to the agent), was basically interchangeable with 'can', which was to replace it altogether in this interpretation by about 1700: hence, Lily's treatment of them as synonymous in illustrating the 'Potentiall mode' as showing an ability: 'as Amem, *I may or can loue*'.[20]

When Richard, speaking directly to Queen Elizabeth, tells her 'You may deny that' you caused Hastings' imprisonment, it does not make sense to interpret it as permission-*may* (Richard giving her permission to deny) or as *ability-may* (reporting to her on her own ability). This must be the epistemic perhaps-*may*, Richard's speculation that perhaps she will deny harm-doing to Hastings (based on her prior denial of harm-doing to Clarence). Even then, it is an odd assertion to make, standing, as it does in the Oxford *Complete Works*, as a completed sentence, full stop. An actor's voice will need to interpret the sentence on the written page as a speaker's utterance, perhaps as headed towards an anticipated 'but' and cut off as the actor-Rivers collaborates by interrupting, talking over. One asks, then, what is going on when Richard cuts off River's retort against Richard's 'may':

RIVERS She *may*, my lord, for –
RICHARD GLOUCESTER
She *may*, Lord Rivers; why, who knows not so?

Richard seems to be teaching Rivers a logic lesson, as if to say, there's nothing to argue against in my saying 'She [perhaps] may', for 'she perhaps may' entails rather than contradicts 'she perhaps may not', and so offers no possible ground for objection. But Rivers must have heard, and begun to answer, to a different 'may' – it's permissible, or justifiable for her to deny it, he seems

---

[18] A notable exception is John Jowett, ed., *The Tragedy of King Richard III* (Oxford, 2000), p. 178.

[19] I borrow these shorthand forms for the three uses from Sylvia Adamson, 'Understanding Shakespeare's Grammar: Studies in Small Words', in S. Adamson *et al.*, eds., *Reading Shakespeare's Dramatic Language: A Guide* (London, 2001), pp. 210–36; p. 220.

[20] *A Shorte Introduction of Grammar* (1567), sig. B2v.

to have begun to argue. But, as Richard elaborates his mocking catalogue of what 'She may do', he seems almost seamlessly to shift from one sense of 'may' to a second and a third: from, first, perhaps-*may* – of course, it's self-evident that it's logically possible that she will do any of these things, to, second, ability-*may* – by the time he is asking 'What may she not?', it makes sense as 'What *can't* she do?', given that she's displayed her ability to get *you* preferments. But, as he mockingly multiplies uses of 'may' ('What may she not? She may – ay, marry, may she'), provoking and answering Rivers with the dizzying double punning on 'marry' and 'may', he is also asking: what is not permitted to her? Just who marries with a king is not a matter of intrinsic ability: it is a matter of social regulation and entitlement, and the Queen clearly hears in Richard's taunting the implication that a female of lowly social origin, the 'country servant-maid' that Elizabeth, a few lines later, says she would rather be 'Than a great queen' (1.3.107–8), is properly a creature bound and restricted by prohibitions, limited by what she 'may not' do and by the permission-granting of others, to whom she should or must yield obedience. Richard's mockery implies a fascinating construction of gender and class in terms of interpersonally regulated 'may nots'. He baits her, here and elsewhere, by projecting onto her a wrongfully appropriated sense of power and entitlement.

Thus, Shakespeare here again exploits the peculiar polysemy of the modal system, to create puns quite unlike the sharply focused lexical puns featuring words that are homophones, separate words with an accidental coincidence of sound. The modal punning works differently, drawing both its interest and its difficulty from the sliding between not entirely determinate meanings that are interconnected in complicated or puzzling ways and are demanding on the hearer's collaboration in meaning-making through pragmatic inferences. We are all missing something – readers, editors, players, auditors – if we just quietly gloss over these demands in happy ignorance of language changes. Furthermore, the play here with modals is not just about wordplay: as in *Titus Andronicus*, modal possibility and necessity are linked to the engine of the dramatic plot. While Richard himself is the character most actively engaged in plot-making, the stage villain recreated as playwright surrogate, not only does he impute a wrongful sense of entitlement to Queen Elizabeth, he also exploits modals to create a sense among the other characters that she is the engineer of the plot. In Act 1 scene 1, when Clarence acknowledges that his jailer is not to blame – 'We know thy charge, Brackenbury, and *will* obey' – Richard's 'must' cements his identification of the Queen's power with the force of necessity: 'We are the Queen's abjects, and *must* obey' (1.1.106–7, emphasis added). In Act 1 scene 3, the same scene in which Richard's 'mays' turn to mockery the unearned prerogative or power of Queen Elizabeth, Richard imparts a strange flavour to his 'musts', using them in 'citations' of his rivals' speeches, to imply that the Queen's entourage has mocked and wrongfully imputed responsibility to him: 'I *must* be held a rancorous enemy. / Cannot a plain man live and think no harm, / But thus his simple truth *must* be abused / With silken, sly, insinuating jacks?' (1.3.50–3, emphasis added). He represents himself as the passive object or 'abject' of their must-making, although in the two preceding scenes it is Richard who has turned himself into an engineer of plot necessity, the play's must-maker.

If, as we have seen, character interactions involving contests over modals have dramatic potential that Shakespeare exploits, so too do contesting modals in a character's self-talk. 'Cannot', the modal of disability, is introduced early on as a key term in Richard's lexicon: 'since I cannot prove a lover...I am determinèd to prove a villain' (1.1.28–30). What he 'cannot' prove is precisely what he does prove by wooing Lady Anne in Act 1 scene 2. He who has accused Queen Elizabeth of unlocking the social prohibitions of 'may not' to find her way to illegitimate power and agency finds a way around the 'cannot' barriers, or root impossibilities, of Anne's attachment to Richard's victim, 'Edward her lord, . . . A sweeter and a lovelier gentleman . . . The spacious world *cannot* again afford' (1.2.227–32, emphasis added) and of his own physical disability, 'Upon my life she finds, although

I *cannot*, / Myself to be a marv'lous proper man' (240–1, emphasis added). If 'must and will' sums up the sweep of necessity that catches up Richard's victims, the negotiation of impossibilities in contradictions like 'cannot and will' or even 'cannot and must' become his motto. It is well worth noting that Richard is not the only plot-maker in Shakespeare's early plays who allies 'cannot and must' in negotiating possible futures. At the outset of *Titus Andronicus*, Aaron, in direct contrast to Titus, is the character with most reason to see his world as optionless, for restricting his agency and control of events are a number of disabling conditions: he is identified as a 'blackamoor' (4.2.51sd), marked off by characters in the play as 'barbarous' (2.3.78) and as racially other; he is also a slave, enslaved, moreover, at the play's outset to the vanquished mistress of a conquered people. With Aaron thus motivated to embrace the modal of disability, Shakespeare builds in unexpected surprises to help make him an interesting character and make the plot seem both 'improbable' and 'necessary'. Consider the 'play of modals' when Aaron instructs Chiron and Demetrius on how to achieve their perverted goal of 'loving Lavinia':

> 'Tis policy and stratagem *must* do
> That you affect, and so *must* you resolve
> That what you *cannot* as you *would* achieve,
> You *must* perforce accomplish as you *may*.
>
> (2.1.105–8, emphasis added)

Compare the tune of Richard's soliloquy at the conclusion of Act 1 scene 1, where he catches up the opportunity of King Edward's anticipated death and negotiates his own special brand of agency. Richard's opening – 'He *cannot* live, I hope, and *must not* die' (1.1.145, emphasis added) – foregrounds, at least momentarily, a disorder of logic that is linked to conundrums that modal logicians have never ceased debating, concerned with, as Aristotle put it, 'the mutual relation of those affirmations and denials which assert or deny possibility or contingency, impossibility or necessity'.[21] In Thomas Wilson's words from *The Rule of Reason*, it brings together 'repugnant propositions',[22] although Richard quickly shows the way around

the apparent contradiction or impossibility by articulating his plan in terms of timing ('Till George be packed with post-haste up to heaven' (1.1.146)). As his reflection brushes King Edward (and, it would also seem, God) out of the controlling position so that 'the world' is left 'for [Richard] to bustle in' (1.1.152), he continues on with projections of what he 'will' do. These focus almost entirely on what his opening soliloquy announced 'I *cannot* prove' – that is, 'a lover' (1.1.28, emphasis added): his plan is to 'marry Warwick's youngest daughter' (1.1.153), overriding the disabling conditions of his 'deformity' and her hate. A self-conscious rhetorician, Richard catches himself up and alerts the audience to a key rhetorical figure deployed or transformed in his own speech: the figure that Patricia Parker has done so much to explain – that is, hysteron proteron, the preposterous,[23] or, as Richard varies its usual proverbial equivalent of the cart before the horse: 'But yet I run before my horse to market' (1.1.160). He points, at least in part, to a disordered temporal sequence as his speech unfolds his mental planning. But beyond this, I would argue, the 'disordered speech' of hysteron proteron shows itself in his 'preposterous' and inverted sequencing of modals. It is not only the general thrust of the 'cannot and must' logic. Even his final 'must-making' conclusion – 'then must I count my gains' (1.1.162) – while it ties his plan tidily into the playwright's imperative to make his contingent plot seem necessary – is arse-backwards as a representation of Richard's cognitive scheme: people do not customarily represent what they hope for and look forward to as a matter of obligation or necessity.

ORDERS OF MODALS

These last examples bring out an intriguing way that Shakespeare plays with modals to achieve

---

[21] 'On Interpretation', *Basic Works*, p. 54.

[22] *The Rule of Reason* (1553), ed. Richard S. Sprague (Northridge, California, 1972), p. 50.

[23] 'Hysteron proteron: or the Preposterous', in Sylvia Adamson, Gavin Alexander and Katrin Ettenhuber, eds., *Renaissance Figures of Speech* (Cambridge, 2007), pp. 133–45.

stylistic effects that are also integrally tied to sub-jectivity effects in his characters and to speech action as micro-plot-development. If Shakespeare is able to create something original in Aaron's or Richard's character by making felt their disordering of modals, this can register and be interpreted only if there are recognizable orders of modals. We rec-ognize orders of modals today when we rehearse or improvise motivational schemes, either in our own self-talk or in advice to others. I came across one such scheme when I visited Moreton-in-Marsh in the Cotswolds recently, carved as a motto over the door of Dormer House School: 'I am I can I ought I will', it read, offering a cognitive map for its students' decision-making and action plans and capturing therein in modals the school's ethos of instilling assertive self-confidence in its pupils. To some extent things have not changed since Shake-speare's day, in the *longue durée* meshing social rela-tions and modals, cognition and modals, for we find in the poetry and drama of the late sixteenth century a similar kind of path-making as characters map out their resolution-making processes in rela-tion to some doubtful future. One way, however, that these orders of modals have certainly changed is reflected in the Dormer School's omission of verbs like 'may' and 'must' associated with permis-sion, prohibition, or compulsion. (It may be pre-mature to isolate those linguistic changes in which a history of *mentalité* can be said to be inscribed, but the vanishing permission-granting *may* and its replacement by the increasingly non-authoritarian approval signalled with *can* are suggestive.) Con-sider some of the schemes built up out of Early Modern English modal verbs to lay open the men-tal processing of speakers, schemes which seem to be proliferating in lyrical poems and plays printed between 1590 and 1610:

Vertue awake, Beautie but beautie is,
I may, I must, I can, I will, I doo
Leaue folowing that, which it is gaine to misse
(Astrophil and Stella)

Oh no I dare not, oh I may not speake!
Yes, yes, *I dare, I can, I must, I will* (*Fidessa*)

OCTAVIA How now *Octauia*, whither wilt thou flye?
Shall these same hands attempt impietie?
I may, I can, I will, I ought, I must,
Reuenge this high disgrace . . . (*The Virtuous Octavia*)

MERRY Peace conscience, peace, thou art too
    scrupulous,
Gaine doth attended this resolution,
Hence dastard feare, *I must, I can, I will,*
Kill my best friend to get a bag of gold: . . .
                                        (*Two Lamentable Tragedies*)

TULL[Y] *I shall, I must, I will, I will indeede,*
Euen to the greatest I will answere it
                                (*Every Woman in her Humor*)[24]

This sort of modal play, as if ascending a scale or climbing a ladder of modals, becomes com-mon enough in this period to merit the status of a rhetorical figure. It has something of the flavour of *gradatio*, or climax, but it lacks the doubling back in word repetition.[25] Perhaps the reason it has no Greek or Latin name is that it arises out of auxiliary verbs, features in Early Modern English grammar that distinguish the language from inflection-based Latin. While these exaggerated staircase lines of modals are rare in Shakespeare, my point is that they illustrate a cultural context articulating intel-ligible orders of modals, recognizable ways to sort and arrange cognitive operations that are becom-ing grammaticalized in the Early Modern English modals. These patterns for mental organization made available by combining modals are complex,

[24] Sir Philip Sidney, *Astrophil and Stella* (1591), Sonnet 47, lines 9–11, quoted from *Poems*, ed. William A. Ringler (Oxford, 1962); Bartholomew Griffin, *Fidessa* (1596), Sonnet 55; Samuel Brandon, *The Virtuous Octavia* (1598), III. 55–60; *Two Lamentable Tragedies* (1601), attributed to Robert Yaring-ton, sig. B3v; Anon., *Every Woman in her Humor* (1609), sig. E3. For thoughtful comments on Sidney's Sonnet 47 in rela-tion, respectively, to modals and to the potential mood, see Kolentsis, 'Shakespeare's Telling Words', pp. 61–2 and De Grazia, 'Lost Potential', p. 23.

[25] Abraham Fraunce actually cites the example from Sidney's Sonnet 47 of *Astrophil and Stella* as an illustration of '*Apo-siopesis, Reticentia*, concealing', 'when the course of a speach begun is in such sort staid, that some part thereof not vttered' (*The Arcadian Rhetorike* [1588], sig. F7), but this effect need not be part of the complex mental action inscribed in these sequences.

without compulsory sequence; they are strongly oriented to pragmatic inferencing, contextual meaning-making that demands the hearer's contribution – a contribution that can effectually be helped out in the theatre by the actor's spoken interpretation. The critical importance of pragmatic inferencing shows in how dependent the sense of 'will' is on positioning in these modal ladders: compare, for example, the order in Octavia's 'I will, I ought, I must, / Reuenge' to Merry's 'I must, I can, I will, / Kill'. William Bullokar's *Bref grammar for English*, published in 1586, comments on the 'eq[u]iuocy in Wil, Wilt, and Would, som tym shewing wilingnes, some tym a commaundment, som tym a wishing mæntt by them' (p. 33). Thus, 'will' before 'must' is more likely to register the speaker's wishing or willingness, while 'will' after 'must' registers commandment or self-commandment, a determination-*will*. We are always being called upon to make these low-level inferences in Shakespeare's plays, as where, in *The Taming of the Shrew*, we interpret the first 'will' in Petruccio's 'And will you, nill you, I will marry you' as treating Kate's wishes or volition, whereas we interpret the 'will' in 'I must and will have Katherine for my wife' (2.1.265, 274) in Bullokar's sense of commandment. Often, Shakespeare's selections and combinations of modals demand more alert and active interpretation by hearers, with his complex 'plays of modals' contributing to the distinctive psychology of his characters. Looking forward to Shakespeare's middle and late plays, consider, for example, the hysteron proteron or inversion of the expected modal gamut 'can and will' in Angelo's 'Look what I *will* not, that I *cannot* do' (*Measure for Measure*, 2.2.53, emphasis added)[26] or the subtle catachresis of Caliban's 'I must eat my dinner', where the enslaved subject's quiet resistance is registered by how his modal counters his master's must-making, even if he is soon brought, in an aside, to concede, 'I must obey' (*The Tempest*, 1.2.332, 374). It is as if what I have been calling 'orders of modals' supply a cognitive mapping or psychological ground, tacit understandings of how the drives and counter-drives, internal and societal, expressed in modal verbs characteristically interact, and the ways in which Shakespeare's dramatic art plays unexpected variations upon them.

POTENTIAL

With modals, people and playwrights are able to stage conflicts or negotiations within and between selves over uncertain futures, calling up a complex array of competing drives. What is brought into play is not just warring passions but the fine-tuned and culturally inflected estimations of ability, obligation, volition and knowledge as they relate to future actions, conflicts and negotiations in which we can recognize the mind in motion: a psychology in the potential mood. They also suggest the close connection between subjectivity and intersubjectivity, for modal language equally provides material for the fine-tuned calibration of social relationships and collective action-making. Furthermore, beyond contributing to Aristotle's possible and necessary plot effects, the interplay of modals allows Shakespeare and other Renaissance dramatists to tap directly into how people actually do plot action, individually or collectively, in their cognitive processes and their interactions. In the 'play of modals' we can see how potential action, whether as the mental deliberations of one character or the social negotiation of pairs and groups, is built into the fabric of the drama.

The close encounters of this essay, highlighting Early Modern English modal auxiliary verbs in two of Shakespeare's early plays, are intended to serve as a prologue to the wider possibilities for reading modality and its cueing of potential action in the Shakespeare canon and in the plays of

---

26 The complex dialogic play of modals in *Measure for Measure* 2.2 and 2.4 is treated in sophisticated ways, using different vocabularies, in George T. Wright, 'Supposing a Measure for *Measure for Measure*', in *Hearing the Measures: Shakespearean and Other Inflections* (Madison, WI, 2001), pp. 73–95, esp. pp. 84–9 and in William Dodd, 'Destined Livery? Character and Person in Shakespeare', *Shakespeare Survey* 51 (1998), 147–58.

his contemporaries. Of course, while my practice here has been to isolate the modal verbs, it is important to recognize that small grammatical function words like *may, must, can, will, would,* or *shall* never do all the work in plays by themselves. Staying with verbs, it would be productive, for example, to situate a study of the modal auxiliaries and the 'potential mode' in *Richard III* in relation to the play's engagement with the 'optative mode' – which articulates speakers' wishes for actions and outcomes outside their own control. On a larger canvas, this study has suggested how modal analysis overlaps with approaches like those deriving from speech-act theory that understand dramatic utterance not simply as expression or communication but as an integral part of a play's action, as what David Schalkwyk has called 'transformative speech acts'.[27] Also productive to explore

would be overlaps with the recent work on early modern forensic rhetoric and on England's participatory legal culture, work that theorizes how the plays' constructions of 'likelihood' and 'intention' suggest character interiority.[28] Readings attentive to modality and to a conception of potential action will be most valuable where the methods I have been setting forth in this article are used to complement other approaches to the worlds of possibility that Shakespeare's plays open up.

---

[27] 'Poetry and Performance', in Patrick Cheney, ed., *The Cambridge Companion to Shakespeare's Poetry* (Cambridge, 2007), pp. 249–59; pp. 241–2.

[28] On forensic constructions of likelihood and intended action, see Lorna Hutson, *The Invention of Suspicion: Law and Mimesis in Shakespeare and Renaissance Drama* (Oxford, 2007); Luke Wilson, *Theaters of Intention: Drama and the Law in Early Modern England* (Stanford, 2000).

MERRY, MARRY, MARY: SHAKESPEARIAN WORDPLAY AND *TWELFTH NIGHT*

THOMAS RIST

'MARRY, THAT "MARRY" IS THE VERY THEME': COMEDY AND MARRY–AGE

Marriage and merriment form two points in a triangular configuration of meaning in Shakespearian comedy. The importance of the first term is well attested to in recent criticism. In Catherine Bate's phrase, Shakespearian comedies are about courtship 'if they are about anything': 'Men and women meet, match, marry and mate. This is the eternal story which Shakespeare's comedies retell again and again.'[1] Understood as 'wit', merriment's place within Shakespearian comedy is, if anything, still more critically established. Samuel Johnson famously (if too negatively) observed it in his *Preface to Shakespeare* (1765):

A quibble is to Shakespeare, what luminous vapours are to the traveller; he follows it at all adventures, it is sure to lead him out of his way, and sure to engulf him in the mire. It has some malignant power over his mind, and its fascinations are irresistible. Whatever be the dignity or profundity of his disquisition, whether he be enlarging knowledge or exalting affection, whether he be amusing attention with incidents, or enchaining it in suspense, let but a quibble spring up before him, and he leaves his work unfinished. A quibble is the golden apple for which he will always turn aside from his career, or stoop from his elevation. A quibble, poor and barren as it is, gave him such delight, that he was content to purchase it, by the sacrifice of reason, propriety and truth. A quibble was to him the fatal Cleopatra for which he lost the world, and was content to lose it.[2]

Johnson's ahistorical bias against Shakespearian wordplay is as notorious today as his recognition of Shakespeare's tendency to such play is recognized. Recent commentators, however, have not only removed the negative connotations of Shakespearian 'quibbles', but have argued for such wordplay's especial import:

Wordplay itself has frequently been reduced to the purely decorative 'quibble', treated with the same sense of dismissal as Johnson's of Shakespeare's 'fatal Cleopatra', an eighteenth-century prejudice that still lingers in powerful forms. But . . . comic wordplay and what Kenneth Muir called the 'uncomic pun' lead us to linkages operating not only within but between Shakespeare's plays, across the often arbitrary boundaries of genre. And . . . the terms of the wordplay make possible glimpses into the relation between the plays and their contemporary culture, in a period when English was not yet standardised into a fixed orthography, obscuring on the printed page the homophonic networks possible before such boundaries were solidified.[3]

With the more recent 'turn to religion' in early modern literary studies,[4] such 'historical semantics'

I am grateful to Stanley Wells and Derek Hughes for their helpful comments on earlier drafts of this article.

[1] See Catherine Bates, 'Love and Courtship', in *The Cambridge Companion to Shakespearean Comedy* (Cambridge, 2002), pp. 102–22; pp. 103 and 102.

[2] See Samuel Johnson, *The Yale Edition of the Works of Samuel Johnson: Volume VII: Johnson on Shakespeare*, ed. by Arthur Sherbo, 2 vols. (New Haven and London, 1968), I, p. 74.

[3] See Patricia Parker, *Shakespeare from the Margins: Language, Culture, Context* (Chicago, 1996), pp. 1–9, cited in Ewan Fernie et al., eds., *Reconceiving the Renaissance: A Critical Reader* (Oxford, 2005), p. 378.

[4] For introduction, see Ken Jackson and Arthur Marotti, 'The Turn to Religion in Early Modern Studies', *Criticism*, 66 (2004), 167–90.

bear not only on the 'historical study of race, gender and class', as Patricia Parker observed in 1996,[5] but also on that fourth and related 'determinate category of cultural identity', early modern religion.[6]

One homophonic play peculiarly Shakespearian is that between 'merry' and 'marry', which, as Fausto Cercignani observed in 1981, 'rests on partial antithesis rather than complete identity'[7] – as in the following example:

Hold then; go home, be merry, give consent to marry
Paris   (*Romeo and Juliet*, 4.1.90)[8]

In this instance, 'merry' and 'marry' juxtapose in the line to produce precisely that kind of pun Parker noted as operating 'between Shakespeare's plays' and 'across the arbitrary boundaries of genre'. For Shakespeare repeatedly returns to the merry-marry association, even stretching the wordplay so that 'marry' is only present by its denotative content. For example, 'And if you can be merry then, I'll say / A man may weep upon his wedding day' (*Henry VIII*, Prologue, 31–2) juxtaposes 'merry' and the denotation of marriage ('wedding day'). 'As merry as when our nuptial day was done' (*Coriolanus*, 1.6.31) similarly juxtaposes the word for, and state of being, 'merry' with the phrase and denotative content of 'nuptial day'. In a variation on this favoured Shakespearian play, 'Wives may be merry, and yet honest too' (*Merry Wives of Windsor*, 4.2.105), the state of wifehood juxtaposes with a state of merriment; 'Be merry, and employ your chiefest thoughts to courtship' (*Merchant of Venice*, 2.8.43) presents another development of the same idea.

Playing on two of the fundamental aspects of his comedy, however, Shakespeare's merry-marry association also answers to that other aspect of Shakespearian wordplay observed by Parker: one which 'make[s] possible glimpses into the relation between the plays and their contemporary culture'. For, homophonically, 'Marry' has a second meaning in the period: it denotes the Virgin Mary. Shakespeare's knowledge of the Virgin is not in doubt. In *Romeo and Juliet*, for example, she is invoked as an imprecation: 'Jesu Maria, what a deal of brine!' (*Romeo and Juliet*, 2.3.69).

However, 'Marry' (meaning, 'by the Virgin Mary', and described by the Norton editors as 'a mild oath'[9]) is extremely frequent in Shakespeare: by my count from Spevack's *Complete and Systematic Concordance to the Works of Shakespeare* (1970), it occurs in the Shakespearian corpus 238 times – far more frequently than "Zounds', an oath popularly associated with Shakespeare but occurring only 28 times, and far more frequently also than 'Christ', which, including its variants, only occurs 16 times.[10] Indeed, Shakespeare's invocation of 'Marry', denoting the Virgin, is also notably frequent by contrast with other dramatists of the period: Marlowe uses the term 9 times; Webster uses it 25 times; Dekker uses it 30 times (though three of these are from plays co-authored with Webster: *Northward Hoe* and *The Famous History of Thomas Wyatt*); Jonson uses the term 32 times; and 'Middleton' (including his collaborations) uses the term 117 times.[11] Shakespeare, in fact, uses the term more than these five contemporary authors did together. Thus, whether because this means of referring to the Virgin remained ingrained in popular speech, or because Shakespeare especially favoured it, as these statistics perhaps suggest, Shakespeare imprecated via the

5 Fernie, *Reconceiving the Renaissance*, pp. 378–9.
6 See Julia Reinhard Lupton, 'The Religious Turn (to Theory) in Shakespeare Studies', *English Language Notes*, 44 (2006), 145–9; pp. 145–6.
7 See Fausto Cercignani, *Shakespeare's Works and Elizabethan Pronunciation* (Oxford, 1981), p. 85. Notably, this Shakespearian linguist agrees with Parker that Shakespearian wordplay 'requires historical interpretation' since Shakespeare 'exploited different modes of pronunciation . . . for dramatic purposes' (Cercignani, pp. viii and ix).
8 Unless otherwise stated, line references for the diverse plays cited in this section are all taken from *A Complete and Systematic Concordance of the Works of Shakespeare*, by Marvin Spevack (Hildesheim, 1970).
9 See *The Norton Shakespeare: Based on the Oxford Edition*, ed. Stephen Greenblatt et al. (New York, 1997), p. 222, n. 8.
10 See Spevack, *A Complete and Systematic Concordance of the Works of Shakespeare* (1970).
11 These statistics derive from my tracking of the word 'Marry' in the works of the various authors via *Literature Online*. I have distinguished carefully, of course, between different uses of the word.

Virgin to an unusual extent. And in many cases 'imprecation', in the sense of a 'prayer, invocation, petition, entreaty',[12] seems appropriate to Shakespeare's sense and use of the term. Encouraging us to recognize a sacred sense for 'Marry' in less clear-cut examples too, the following Shakespearian instances of the term all overtly suggest prayer: 'Marry, Amen', occurring in both *Twelfth Night* and *Henry VIII*; 'Marry and Amen', in *1 Henry IV* and in *Romeo and Juliet*; 'Marry, God forbid' in *The Taming of the Shrew*, *Hamlet* and *Sir Thomas More*; 'Marry, God forfend' and 'Marry, God defend his Grace', in *2 Henry VI* and *Richard III* respectively.[13] 'Marry, here's grace and a codpiece' (*King Lear*, 3.2.40) presents a more ambivalent example of sacred usage, but the wit in such a line depends on its self-conscious juxtaposition of the sacred and the profane.

Marian imprecations can also be the subject of humour in the form of wordplay, sacred or otherwise: 'Hume must make merry with the Duchess' gold; / Marry, and shall' (*2 Henry VI*, 1.2.87–8) is one example linking 'Marry' to merriment itself. And the following, wholly self-conscious play of words merrily, but overtly, links marriage (the second in our triangular configuration of meanings) with Mary: 'Marry, that "Marry" is the very theme' (*Romeo and Juliet*, 1.3.63). Thus, there is clear evidence of Shakespeare being aware, and playing off, the homophonically similar terms 'merry', 'marry' and 'Marry', suggesting, since merriment and marriage are so important in Shakespearian comedy, that the place of 'Mary' in that comedy deserves an especial consideration. Moreover, since 'Middleton' too juxtaposes 'Marry', (denoting the Virgin) with marriage, we know Shakespeare's contemporaries were susceptible to such play.[14] A word, however, on why this theatrical perspective has not – to my knowledge – been considered before.

Part of the problem is the recentness of the 'turn to religion' in Shakespearian studies. The tendency towards distaste for the Shakespearian pun – exemplified in Johnson – would seem another likely reason, and the need to check individual Marian puns – not encouraged by that tendency – would also seem relevant. However, in English literary history, oaths deemed innocuous today have frequently been registered as problematic: 'damned!', for example, has a long history of being spelled 'D–d', as if to empty it of a theological sense too dangerous to spell out fully. In Shakespearian England, the anti-Catholic 'Acte to restraine Abuses of Players' (1606) forbade using the words 'God', 'Christ Jesus' or the 'Holy Ghost' on the public stage 'jestingly or profanely',[15] again illustrating how terms commonly imprecated today were taken seriously and – since outlawing these terms was an innovation – that contemporary sensitivities regarding the sacred were fluid.[16] Relevantly, therefore, Shakespeare's fleeting, frequent, and sometimes pointed allusions to 'Marry' reflect the Virgin's traditional importance in the culture, as scholars especially emphasize regarding role-models for women. As Lisa Jardine remarked in 1983, Marina Warner has 'ably shown' how 'absence of sexuality early became a defining virtue of Mary', who became the 'second Eve' and 'ultimate icon of female virtue' for the period, while more recently historians have emphasized Marian veneration as an especial site of early modern sensitivity.[17] Behind Shakespeare's frequent and direct allusions

---

12 See the *OED* definition 2.

13 For details, see Spevack's *Concordance*.

14 In the collaborations *No Help Like a Woman's* and *A Match at Midnight* we find the following plays on Marry (the Virgin) and marriage: 'Marry if a wedding dinner . . .' and 'Marriage, a cloying meate, marry . . .'. Information taken from *Literature Online*.

15 Clare notes that the Act resulted from an anti-Catholic development in Parliament. See Janet Clare, *'Art Made Tongue-Tied by Authority': Elizabethan and Jacobean Censorship* (Manchester, 1990), pp. 104–6.

16 For detailed discussion of such periodic changes in sensitivity, see especially the chapter 'Obscenity and Profanity: Sir Henry Herbert's Problems with the Players and Archbishop Laud, 1632–34', in Richard Dutton's *Licensing, Censorship and Authorship in Early Modern England* (Basingstoke, 2000), pp. 41–61.

17 See Lisa Jardine, *Women and Marriage in the Age of Shakespeare* (Hemel Hempstead, 1983), p. 77. For the relation of the cult of Mary to that of Elizabeth, see pp. 177–8. For Marina Warner's study, see *Alone of All Her Sex: The Myth and the Cult of the Virgin Mary* (London, 1990). For discussion of Mary's contested place in early modern England, see Christine Peters, *Patterns of Piety: Women, Gender and*

to 'Mary' in the form of imprecations, then, lay a culture infusing such allusions with a meaningfulness we should not overlook – especially in *Twelfth Night*. John Manningham saw the play on 2 February, which as the Oxford editors note, 'was Candlemas, the festival of the blessing of candles to celebrate the Purification of the Blessed Virgin Mary'.[18] In 1623, that High Anglican Charles I saw the play on the same day. The third early performance that is datable was Easter Monday 1618: it is indeed 'interesting that the earliest recorded performances should have been at a celebratory feast'.[19] For observers such as Manningham, Charles I or his entourage, the Marianism of the text, which I now bring out, must have stood out.

THE SECOND EVES:
TWELFTH NIGHT

Although the Virgin was married, scholarship has often portrayed Marianism as an expression of desires antithetical to those of physical love. In de Rougemont's classic study, as Shakespearians observe,[20] Marianism originated in a Christianity seeking to meet 'the same profound desire' as had grown up toward the poetically 'Idealized Woman', associated by de Rougemont with the Troubadours, but so as 'to counter' that erotic expression.[21] Such a juxtaposing model gains superficial corroboration from Shakespearian comedy, since it typically presents conversions of 'maids' (synonymous for virgins in the period) into married women, suggesting an antithetical relationship between the two states of life and one in which the former is, if not quite an evil, then at least an undesirable state, marriage being the end of comedy. At the opening of *Twelfth Night*, however, Olivia does *not* desire marriage, or indeed, since she keeps herself 'like a cloistress' (1.1.27), *any* form of male-female life, presenting an early complication. It is a complication that the play centrally develops, moreover, since although she eventually marries, she does not marry according to her desire: seeking to marry 'Cesario' (in whose person Viola is disguised) Olivia mistakenly marries Viola's brother,

Sebastian. Thus, the play outlines a narrative arriving at the generic norm of marriage without compromising Olivia's initial rejection of female-male desire. As we shall see later, moreover, hers is a marriage in which sexuality is in the background.

I have already suggested that the contemporary culture could easily have associated Olivia's early stance in the play with Marianism, but the text itself registers it in just such terms. As he 'catechizes' her in Act 1 scene 5, Feste seven times mocks the man-shunning Olivia as 'madonna' (1.5.38, 52, 55, 57, 61, 63, 65) – an image the Oxford editors Roger Warren and Stanley Wells note for its 'Catholic overtones – referring to the Virgin Mary'.[22] They are right to do so, despite acknowledging that the *OED*'s first examples of 'madonna' that 'unmistakably allude to the Virgin Mary are from 1644 and 1645':[23] the following anti-Catholic response to the Campion trial, for example, written by Meredith Hanmer (1543–1604) and published in England in 1581, shows the *OED* in need of updating:

They [Jesuits] make an Idol of the Pope, so that *Christian Franken* being a Jesuit; and seeing the worship that was done unto him, saieth: *I verily tooke him for Christ, or rather some greater thing.* I will pass over their Idolatry and superstition, in worshipping *La Madonna di Loreto* [*sic*], *our Lady of Larctum in Italy. Gregory de Valentia*, the Jesuit, is not ashamed to defend in three several tracts, that the adoration of the sacrament, the honouring of Saints, and the worshipping of Images and relics is no Idolatry: concluding most blasphemously in on[e] respect: *prayse be unto God, and to the most blessed virgin Mary,* joining the creature, as partaker of praise with the creator.[24]

Religion in Late Medieval and Reformation England, ed. by Anthony Fletcher *et al.* (New York, 2003), pp. 207–45.

[18] See *Twelfth Night*, ed. Roger Warren and Stanley Wells, The Oxford Shakespeare (Oxford, 1994), p. 4; all textual citations of *Twelfth Night* from here on are from this edition.

[19] Warren and Wells, eds., *Twelfth Night*, p. 4.

[20] See, for example, my citation from M. M. Mahood on wordplay in *Romeo and Juliet* below.

[21] See Denis de Rougemont, *Love in the Western World*, trans. by Montgomery Belgion (New York, 1966), p. 117.

[22] See Warren and Wells, eds., *Twelfth Night*, p. 105, note 38.

[23] Warren and Wells, eds., *Twelfth Night*, p. 105, note 38.

[24] Citation from Chapter 3, ' The Hypocrisy and Superstition of the Jesuits', in Meredith Hanmer's *The Jesuits' Banner* (London, 1581). Text taken from *Early English Books Online*

Here, in 1581, 'madonna' clearly stands for the Virgin in English, making Shakespeare's uses of the word connote Mary as the Oxford editors suggest; searching through *Early English Books Online* reveals 'madonna' denoting the Virgin in three further English texts describing Italy (where the usage was common) of 1582, 1586 and 1590.[25] It should be emphasized, however, that much more than the bare use of the term in Shakespeare's play suggests the Virgin. When, for example, Feste asks, 'Good madonna, why mourn'st thou?', Olivia replies, 'Good fool, for my brother's death' (1.5.61–2), the text suggesting in such moments an iconographic *pietà* in which Olivia plays Mary.[26]

Pointedly, therefore, Olivia's comic trajectory is from a position of noted *Marianism* to one of *marriage*, presenting her very plot (a word in Shakespeare regularly connoting both dramatic action and intrigue simultaneously[27]) as an enlarged play on words. It implies a punning understanding of the bodies performing feminine parts ('characters') that is brought out by Feste in allusion to Maria: 'as witty a piece of Eve's flesh as any in Illyria' (*Twelfth Night*, 1.5.25–6). Maria's staged body is here viewed as a piece of 'wit'. Linking Eve and 'Maria' according to the standard Marian typology, moreover, the wit is telling – and it has expansive, comic implication. Maria is a 'second Eve' in a sense wittily contrasting with Olivia: while Olivia reportedly desires a cloistered life, only arriving at marriage by accident, Maria actively curries the favour of Sir Toby Belch through the course of the play, eventually marrying him. Thus, while Olivia is a second Eve in the theological sense of the typology, Maria is 'second Eve' in a more literal and parodic sense: showing Eve's typological sexuality. And thus, in both cases, the play of feminine character is a play on words drawing on the Marian.

MARY AND MARRIAGE

Feste's designation of Olivia as a 'madonna' is not a neutral one. Bringing out simmering religious antagonisms, Warren and Wells note how

the Catholic term 'will antagonise the puritan Malvolio',[28] but, being used to mock Olivia too, the term is also the opposite of neutral in a second sense. That, moreover, bears crucially on the essential comic matter of marriage. Challenged to redeem himself in the eyes of his 'lady' (1.5.33) by making her laugh, Feste gets Olivia's permission 'to prove you a fool' (1.5.52–3), leading to the 'catechism' following:

FESTE Good madonna, why mourn'st thou?
OLIVIA Good fool, for my brother's death.
FESTE I think his soul is in hell, madonna.
OLIVIA I know his soul is in heaven, fool.
FESTE The more fool, madonna, to mourn your brother's soul being in heaven. Take away the fool, gentlemen.
OLIVIA What think you of this fool, Malvolio? Doth he not mend? (1.5.61–9)

Contemporary Protestants normally objected to emotional mournings for the dead, so Feste lightly reflects a Protestant critique of a Catholic devotional attitude even as he mocks a 'puritan'.[29] In regard to the genre, however, the moment is crucial. Olivia's final line implies her softening

---

(accessed 24.3.2008). I have modernized spellings and punctuation where appropriate.

[25] See Anthony Munday, *The English Romayne Lyfe* (London, 1582); also George Whetstone, *An Heptameron of Ciuill Discourses* (London, 1582); also Richard Jones, *The Booke of Honor and Armes* (London, 1590). Whetstone also refers to the 'Madonna de Loreto'; Jones refers to the papal founding of the 'Cavalieri di Madonna', translating this as the 'Knights of St Mary'. Munday's allusion is in a marginal note on a passage dealing with images of Mary; it speaks of 'A new Pilgrimage risen up in Rome, called Madonna de Môte'. Documents cited from *Early English Books Online*, accessed 24.3.2008.

[26] For another Shakespearian manipulation of the traditional *pietà*, see Katharine Goodland's 'Inverting the Pietà in Shakespeare's *King Lear*', in Regina Buccola and Lisa Hopkins, eds., *Marian Moments in Early Modern British Drama* (Aldershot, 2007), pp. 47–74; p. 48.

[27] See, for example, the opening speech of *Richard III*: 'Plots have I laid, inductions dangerous'.

[28] Warren and Wells, eds., *Twelfth Night*, p. 105, note 38.

[29] I explore the contemporary attitudes to mourning at length in *Revenge Tragedy and the Drama of Commemoration in Reforming England* (Burlington, VT, 2008); see also Goodland, pp. 49–56.

towards Feste, as well as, perhaps, her even joining of him in the guying of Malvolio. Both softening and guying, however, imply her new mood, and in what follows her attention turns to matters other than mourning, Olivia even coming to praise a light-hearted (rather than mournful) outlook with declamatory enthusiasm: 'To be generous, guiltless, and of free disposition', in her impassioned phrase, 'is to take those things for bird-bolts that you [Malvolio] deem cannon bullets' (1.5.86–8). Thus, Feste's subtle but persistent ironising of Olivia's 'madonna', his mockery of her devotional *pietà*, delivers her from sadness to a more comic mood, softening her up not only for himself but also for the young 'Cesario', whom the play will shortly place in her way. Thus, a pivotal moment in the comedy – the transition from sadness to a light-heartedness facilitating romance – turns emphatically on Olivia's Marianism and presents it as this romantic plot's primary anti-comic impulse.

ECHOES OF THE PIETÀ

Since the movement of romantic comedy is towards marriages and, normally, their celebration, Olivia's madonna posture does not overtly return, thus reinforcing assessments as to its anti-comic status and perhaps encouraging us to see the play as somewhat anti-Marian. However, any such anti-Marianism is deeply qualified by the play itself. Olivia does not return to her initial Marian posture, but the play builds variously on its associations, firstly by punctuating its comedy with a series of mournful outlooks. Linking love and death, Viola will welcome one such moment sung by Feste as 'a very echo to the seat / Where love is throned' (2.4.20–1).

In the first of the play's ironic reversals, it is largely the songs of Feste – Olivia's mocker – that maintain echoes of 'madonna'. His first song, which spells out a comic rationale in 'Journeys end in lovers meeting' (2.3.41), goes on to dwell on comic merriment with a *carpe diem* notable for its melancholy anticipation of death:

> What is love? 'Tis not hereafter,
> Present mirth hath present laughter.
>   What's to come is still unsure.
> In delay there lies no plenty,
> Then come kiss me, sweet and twenty,
>   Youth's a stuff will not endure.   (2.3.45–50)

Even as it encourages embracing the present, the song dwells on the death of youth and 'hereafter', presenting if not Olivia's madonna overtly, then its anti-comic echo. Such echoes amplify, moreover, as the play progresses. Here is the first verse of Feste's second song:

> Come away, come away, death,
>   And in sad cypress let me be laid.
> Fie away, fie away breath,
>   I am slain by a fair cruel maid.
> My shroud of white, stuck all with yew,
>   O prepare it.
> My part of death, no one so true
>   Did share it.   (2.4.50–7)

Like the second stanza of the song that will follow, this is a (romantic) dirge, the echoes of Olivia's Marian posture not fading, as one would expect of an echo, but growing stronger. Moreover, the song plausibly imagines romantic love, our subject of comedy, becoming subject to death, and prepares us for a revised understanding of comedy itself even as it 'prepare[s]' the body of its lover's corpse. 'O prepare it', indeed, invites the singer's audiences to help bury a lover, the play thus back-tracking on Feste's earlier mocks and their result: Olivia downplaying her *pietà* and talking up 'free disposition'. Feste, who is here singing for Orsino, will go on to criticise the Duke for indulging an emotional 'nothing' (2.4.77), but the criticism is both understanding and sympathetic: 'Now the melancholy god *protect* thee', he begins, 'for thy mind is a very opal' (2.4.72; 73–4; my emphasis), the last image presenting Orsino's melancholy as valuable as well as changeable. The close of the play will show Feste absorbed by melancholy, singing to himself, rather than to Orsino, of wind and rain and reiterating that 'the rain it raineth every day' (5.1.382, 386, 390, 394), as if nature wept. The stanzas of this final song graduating from boyhood, to manhood, to marriage before ending, indeed, with the throwaway about the 'great while ago the world begun' that is 'all's one', the conclusion to the song seems deliberately to evade the end to which such an 'ages of man' naturally leads, highlighting the poignancy of human death by seemingly seeking to avoid talking about it.[30]

Thus, Feste and the play conclude with the very strains they previously made anti-comic. Echoing Olivia's madonna rather than emerging from it directly, the strains are not reducible to Marianism entirely, their frame of reference being also wider than Marian in a more specific sense. It is relevant that Orsino describes his desires as 'like fell and cruel hounds' pursuing him (1.1.21), an image evoking a second point of reference for virginity and death: Diana. Though thus allusively present, however, Diana is far less significant to the action than Olivia's 'madonna': unlike the madonna, whom, we have seen, is named seven times, Diana is never named, her presence being thus literally only indirect; more importantly still, it is on the idea of the madonna, rather than on Diana, that, as we have seen, the action turns from anti-comic to comic, giving Mary a pivotal centrality in the action that is never accorded the goddess. However, Diana does help in a more general sense, pointing up the virginal focus of the play in which Mary is pre-eminent – a focus bearing importantly on the eventual, final marriages. It also bears on the person of Viola – Orsino's eventual partner and the most expressive of the play's female maids. I consider this second topic first.

VIOLA AND SEXUALITY

Suggesting a maiden un-deflowered even in her name, Viola is pursued through *Twelfth Night* by a series of sexualising descriptions. In Orsino's musical allusion to the 'small pipe' [which] / Is as the maiden's organ' (1.4.31–2), for example, the audience is invited to laugh at a highly intimate and (it seems) unintentionally precise description of Viola's privity – a word denoting the genitals in the Renaissance and aptly emphasising the inappropriateness of Viola's implicit exposure. In later reflecting on disguise as a 'pregnant enemy' (2.2.28), and on comic intrigue itself as a virgin's 'knot too hard to untie' (2.2.41), Viola will continue to be dogged by innuendo always sexualising her. A key feature of her soliloquy in Act Two, Scene Two from which these last phrases come, however, is that for Viola – unlike those chuckling in the audience – such sexuality is troubling: 'now alas the day' (2.2.38) is just one phrase from the speech implying distress. The source of this distress, however, is Viola's initial decision to disguise herself as a eunuch (1.2.53), a decision bearing on sexuality the occasion for which deserves attention:

VIOLA Who governs here?
CAPTAIN A noble duke, in nature, as in name.
VIOLA What is his name?
CAPTAIN Orsino.
VIOLA Orsino. I have heard my father name him.
    He was a bachelor then.
CAPTAIN And so is now, or was so very late,
    For but a month ago I went from hence,
    And then 'twas fresh in murmur – as you know,
    What great ones do the less will prattle of –
    That he did seek the love of fair Olivia.
VIOLA What's she?
CAPTAIN A virtuous maid, the daughter of a count
    That died some twelvemonth since, then leaving her
    In the protection of his son, her brother,
    Who shortly also died, for whose dear love,
    They say, she hath abjured the sight
    And company of men.
VIOLA   O that I served that Lady
    And might not be delivered to the world
    Till I had made mine own occasion mellow,
    What my estate is.
CAPTAIN   That were hard to compass,
    Because she will admit no kind of suit,
    No, not the Duke's.   (1.2.22–43)

These lines introduce the characters Viola will mainly contend with – Orsino and Olivia – as well

---

[30] For more general comment on Feste's evasiveness here, see Warren and Wells, eds., *Twelfth Night*, p. 73.

as the threads of the triangular love-plot eventually entangling her. Notably, however, despite showing interest in Orsino's marital status, Viola's initial preference is service to Olivia until her 'occasion mellow / What my estate is'. 'Estate,' here, is ambiguous, as, to some extent, is the phrase as a whole, but one of the term's connotations refers generally to Viola's nature,[31] making her withdrawal from the prospect of Orsino – despite the reassurance by the Captain that Olivia is not interested in him – a withdrawal based on her own sense of un-readiness. Thus, the scene moves first from interest in Orsino as a potential marriage prospect to hesitation and withdrawal from that prospect into the safer world of Olivia. When it transpires that this avenue is not open to her, Viola takes refuge in the eunuch-disguise at Orsino's court. In doing so, however, her reticence towards Orsino is specifically associated with a sexual ambivalence that plagues her, as I have suggested, until the resolution of Act 5. Notably, Viola is thus like Orsino in his image of Actaeon: hunted by a desire seemingly forbidden – in M. M. Mahood's words, 'according to Freud because *amour-passion* is inimical to the Race, according to de Rougemont because it is contrary to the Faith'.[32] De Rougemont's emphasis on religion being more suggestive for the analysis thus far, what kind of resolution for Viola is possible?

THE SPIRIT OF MARRIAGE

Three marriages ornament the close of *Twelfth Night*, but none of them clearly fulfil the violent 'desires' (1.1.21) expressed by Orsino or heard elsewhere in the play, as in Viola's imagined 'loyal cantons of contemned love', which are described to Olivia as sufficient to enforce an unwilling lover's 'pity' (1.5.259, 265). Sebastian's marriage to Olivia is effectively a mistake – albeit one he welcomes – and on Orsino's part, at least, the marriage to Viola is predicated on a friendship he develops with her male (*sic*) persona in the course of the play, his threat to 'kill' her just moments before proposing to her (5.1.115) – seemingly for having come

between him and Olivia – accentuating a marriage not knowingly based on desire. The most that can be said of Sir Toby and Maria's marriage is that they share a love of intrigue and rather mean comedy: his observation that 'She's a beagle true bred, and one that adores me' (2.4.167) shows on his part little either of desire or romance, while her invitation to Sir Andrew to 'bring your hand to th' buttery-bar, [i.e. her breasts] and let it drink' (1.3.66), for example, does not suggest a body bound to Sir Toby; the play only acknowledges their marriage by briefest report.

In *Twelfth Night*, then, marriage is not primarily an expression of desire; only Viola achieves a partner she initially seeks out, and her emotional path to that achievement is ambiguous. Marriage being thus largely distinguished from desire, what completes the comic road to marriage is something less easy to define; in Sebastian and Olivia's case, as we have noted, it is largely a chance encounter and mistaken identity that give rise to the marriage, though there are miraculous connotations to the action which contemporaries could have recognized as suggesting divine intervention.[33] The marriage itself, however, is given its own, particular character in Olivia's address to Sebastian:

---

[31] See *OED* estate, *n*.1.a.

[32] M. M. Mahood, 'Wordplay in *Romeo and Juliet*', in Lawrence Lerner, ed., *Shakespeare's Tragedies: An Anthology of Modern Criticism*, (London, 1963), pp. 17–32; p. 19. For de Rougemont's study, again see *Love in the Western World* (1956). For his treatment of the cult of the Virgin conflicting with erotic and courtly love, see especially pp. 117–18. De Rougemont's view that the cult of the Virgin was constructed by 'the Church and clergy' to combat eroticism is no longer tenable – scholars such as Dyan Elliott, whom I cite below, have shown that much of the Christian impetus towards chastity was popular and even came from women; however, de Rougemont's broader sense of religion constructing culture, and providing tension with the erotic, remains useful, providing – as Mahood recognized – a historicizing alternative to Freud.

[33] Edmund Spenser, for example, tells us that chance is (or can be) guided by God. See *The Faerie Queene*, Book 1, Canto XI, stanza 45, line 6: 'It chaunced (eternal God that chaunce did guide)'. Such providential outlook is common to Protestants and Catholics in the period.

> If you mean well,
> Now go with me, and with this holy man,
> Into the chantry by. There before him,
> And underneath that consecrated roof,
> Plight me the full assurance of your faith,
> That my most jealous and too doubtful soul
> May live at peace. (4.3.22–8)

Chantries, as the *OED* makes plain, are endowments 'for the maintenance of one or more priests to sing daily mass for the soul of the founders or others specified by them':[34] the church in which Sebastian and Olivia are to plight their troths is of the kind roundly condemned by Reformers as manifestations of the purgatorial and Catholic cult of the dead,[35] becoming here, however, a locus for the 'chants' for the dead that we have observed echoing through the play. Thus, the forum for guaranteeing marriage reconnects Olivia forcefully to the Catholicism of her initial, Marian *pietà* and remembrance of a dead brother, transforming the earlier suggestion that such remembrance and love are incompatible to imply the opposite: love (or at least the 'true' love of marriage) is now grounded in such remembrance.

The choice by Shakespeare of a 'chantry', rather than a church more neutral, for Sebastian and Olivia's troth-plighting is not the only notable feature of the passage. The very religious rationale for chantries resonates in Olivia's description of her love as like a 'doubtful soul' needing to 'live at peace', reinforcing the passage's wider association of marriage and remembrance of the dead and further distinguishing the true love of marriage – the end of comedy – from such romantic love as Olivia pursued after Feste's intervention in Act 1 scene 5.

The chantry as a basis for love and marriage initiates a broader spiritual discourse persisting to the end. Observing that '"Spirit" could mean "devil" in Elizabethan English', the Oxford editors comment on the 'suggestion of witchcraft' surrounding Viola's discovery of her brother, arguing that the latter 'securely banishes any hint of the supernatural or diabolical by celebrating the human and natural'[36] – in the following exchange:

> VIOLA If spirits can assume both form and suit
> You come to fright us.
> SEBASTIAN   A spirit I am indeed,
> But I am in that dimension grossly clad
> Which from the womb I did participate.
> (5.1.229–32)

I am not convinced that the suggestions of either spirituality or witchcraft are banished by Sebastian's lines. Tracing his origins back to the 'womb' asserts Sebastian's material humanity, but 'A spirit I am indeed' is a remarkably strong assertion of spiritual identity, being only qualified, rather than negated, by the lines that follow. The case gains the corroboration of 'context' when we consider the scene in *The Comedy of Errors* that Shakespeare is here reworking;[37] it begins with an abbess:

> ABBESS
> Most mighty Duke, behold a man much wronged
> *All gather to see them*
> ADRIANA
> I see two husbands, or mine eyes deceive me.
> DUKE
> One of these men is *genius* to the other:
> And so of these, which is the natural man,
> And which the spirit? Who deciphers them?
> DROMIO OF SYRACUSE
> I, sir, am Dromio, Command him away.
> DROMIO OF EPHESUS
> I, sir, am Dromio, Pray let me stay.
> ANTIPHOLUS OF SYRACUSE
> Egeon, art thou not? Or else his ghost.
> (5.1.332–9)[38]

---

34 See the *OED* chantry 3.

35 For sustained, recent discussion of that cult, see Peter Marshall, *Beliefs and the Dead in Reformation England* (Oxford, 2002); religious problems concerning purgatory are well known to Shakespearians from *Hamlet's* critical history.

36 Warren and Wells, eds., *Twelfth Night*, p. 65.

37 As Warren and Wells note (p. 66), the scene 'not only looks forward to the endings of the late plays, but back to that of *The Comedy of Errors*'.

38 Quotation from *William Shakespeare: The Complete Works*, edited by Stanley Wells, Gary Taylor, John Jowett, and William Montgomery (Oxford, 1986); the quotations from *Love's Labour's Lost* following are from this edition too.

The overlap between the two scenes implies that the idea of twins having a spiritual connection had an enduring interest for Shakespeare, rather than being something quickly cast off. Moreover, this passage from *The Comedy of Errors* reminds us that, for both Shakespeare and his age, 'spirit' could suggest 'ghost': a likely association for *Twelfth Night*, in view of its dead, its seemingly dead and its chantry, and one implying a continual rather than brief dramatic interest in the spiritual.

Most significantly, since marriage begins in a chantry, the spiritual discourse carries through to the marriage of Viola and Orsino. Orsino's final anticipation of the 'golden time' of marriage highlights the spiritual:

> When that is known, and golden time convents,
> A solemn combination shall be made
> Of our dear souls.   (5.1.372–4)

The emphasis is on a union of souls rather than of bodies, the poet who gave us the 'marriage of true minds' in Sonnet 116 again conceiving a marriage other than physical – an idea underlined if we also hear in Orsino's verb a noun recalling both Olivia's 'cloistered', and later 'chantried' life: 'convents'. Pointing, then, to a spiritual marriage where virginity might be preserved, the close answers to Viola's initially conflicted interest in Orsino, as, indeed, it answers to the conflict initially in Olivia. Today, perhaps, virgin marriage seems impossible, but in fact what Dyan Elliott has called simply the 'Spiritual Marriage' has a long history in Christianity which continued into early modern times.[39] Moreover, Orsino's proposed marriage of souls is only impossible by a broadly naturalistic standard that is not his concern. Referring to the 'Golden Age', his notion of a 'golden time' of marriage is as ideal and mythological as realistic. Being both of the past (as normally for the Golden Age) but also welcoming what is to come, it defies naturalism again, and the play conveniently closes – leaving us two pairs of four virgins[40] – so that no further clarification is possible.

'TIS MARIA'S HAND

This article has argued for a *Twelfth Night* substantially turning on Marian ideas of virginity familiar to Shakespeare and which the play's first audiences were well placed to observe. Since these ideas play so large a part in the comedy, and especially in its conception of romance, it is natural to wonder where else in Shakespeare such interest might be visible, romantic comedy being a Shakespearean staple. An immediate answer is in the much earlier *Love's Labour's Lost*, a play juxtaposing asceticism with love before ending with an evocation of feminine life that anticipates the early, 'cloistered' Olivia.[41] Having forced the king to a year's penance in 'some forlorn and naked hermitage / Remote from all the pleasures of the world' (5.2.787–8), the play's Princess says he can marry her if he stays the course:

> Then at the expiration of the year,
> Come challenge me, challenge me by these deserts,
> And by this virgin palm now kissing thine,
> I will be thine.   (5.2.796–9)

She then goes on to describe what she will do while waiting for him:

>   and till that instance, shut
> My woeful self up in a mourning house,
> Raining the tears of lamentation
> For the remembrance of my father's death.
>   (5.2.799–802)

The parallels with *Twelfth Night* are notable. Besides sharing tensions between romantic love and virginity with the later comedy, this passage depicting the Princess is remarkably like that of Olivia in Valentine's description:

---

[39] See Dyan Elliott, *Spiritual Marriage: Sexual Abstinence in Medieval Wedlock* (Princeton, 1993).

[40] Associating himself with Diana, Orsino implies his virginity; Sebastian calls himself a 'maid' (5.1.257).

[41] For juxtaposition of love and asceticism in *Love's Labour's Lost*, see my 'Topical Comedy: On the Unity of *Love's Labour's Lost*', in *The Ben Jonson Journal*, 7 (2000), 65–87.

The element itself till seven years' heat
Shall not behold her face at ample view,
But like a cloistress she will veilèd walk
And water once a day her chamber round
With eye-offending brine – all this to season
A brother's dead love, which she would keep fresh
And lasting in her sad remembrance.

(Twelfth Night, 1.1.25–31)

While the Princess seeks seclusion for one year, Olivia seeks it for seven; while the Princess mourns a father, Olivia mourns a brother, Shakespeare varying his imagery slightly; however, both women mourn family, shut themselves away from men and weep; moreover, both inhabit suggestively monastic houses, similarities between the two passages even applying to word choices: 'father' anticipates 'son', 'Raining' is like 'water', 'woeful' anticipates 'sad' and 'remembrance' is in both. Shakespeare was revisiting an idea when he initially depicted Olivia at home.

Yet he concluded the dilemmas of his two heroines with at least one significant difference: at the end of *Love's Labour's Lost*, virgin asceticism coexists with the seemingly contrary state of marriage only in the sense that they are parts of a sequence; in *Twelfth Night*, however, the contrary states become united, the final marriage of 'souls' allowing them to coexist. It is a development allowing us to see a final pun in the play, in which 'hands' given in marriage are like Marian handwriting. 'Give me thy hand', Orsino proposes to Viola (5.1.266), but less than a hundred lines later Olivia is deciphering the plot against Malvolio: 'Alas, Malvolio, this is not my writing / Though I confess much like the character, / But out of question 'tis Maria's hand' (5.1.336–8). Olivia and Maria twinning as first and second Eves, the puritan has ironically been mistaking the sinner for the saint; indeed, though Malvolio (quoting Maria's riddle) says 'M.O.A.I doth sway my life' (2.5.106), his life, sequentially, is 'swayed' one way by Maria and the other way by Olivia. What Olivia's words in Act 5 bring out, however, is an implied meta-theatre connecting narrative and marriage: the false narrative 'plot' in which Malvolio was to marry Olivia was written (in the form of a letter) by Maria, the first Eve, being set right by Olivia, the second Eve or Mary. 'Hands' of narrative combining with hands given in marriage, the end points up the play's status as romantic comedy self-consciously; that the comedy was of a *Mary*, however, playfully reminds us that its narrative was always 'Marian' too, to 'marry' and 'Mary' being thus one and the same by the close of *Twelfth Night*.

A SUBTLE POINT: SLEEVES, TENTS AND 'ARIACHNE'S BROKEN WOOF' (AGAIN)

HESTER LEES-JEFFRIES

To observe that *Troilus and Cressida* is a play full of puns is hardly news: nearly two centuries ago, William Hazlitt described the whole play as 'a kind of double entendre',[1] and at times it is a play which could well be summarized by that now passé bowdlerizing editorial shorthand, 'with a bawdy quibble'. As Patricia Parker comments in the opening paragraph of *Shakespeare from the Margins* (1996), 'Wordplay itself has frequently been reduced to the purely decorative "quibble" . . . [yet] both comic wordplay and what Kenneth Muir called the "uncomic pun" lead us to linkages operating not only within but between Shakespeare's plays.'[2] *Troilus and Cressida* provides rich material for such an approach: its puns are dense and both uncomic and revoltingly (or even painfully) funny, and its quibbles are frequently not at all 'quibbling', but rather substantive, far-reaching and unsettling, a crucial part of the play's thick verbal texture and unstable moral universe.[3] They cannot be dismissed. Here I offer a close reading of one passage from the play, which pays attention not simply to quibbles, puns and other forms of linguistic play, but also to the material context of the passage, in terms of both performance issues and early modern material culture.[4] We are getting better at attending to the material circumstances of performance, at considering what impact such awareness might have upon the more purely linguistically oriented close reading of texts, and, indeed, at breaking down the distinctions between 'text' and 'performance'. But the degree of slippage between the categories of the verbal, the visual and the material in *Troilus and*

Cressida can still take us by surprise by showing that there could be a pun on a thing, or a quibble that is in part material. Such fluidity and expansiveness of interpretation seem to have been second nature to Shakespeare and his audience.

The exploration of the play's interest in duplicity and doubleness, of which puns and wordplay are but one manifestation, has become a critical commonplace, and the *locus classicus* of that commonplace, as evinced by the titles of at least two influential essays on the play,[5] is Troilus's great

---

[1] *Characters of Shakespear's Plays*, *c.*1817, quoted in Jane Adamson, *Troilus and Cressida* (Brighton, 1987), p. 87.

[2] Patricia Parker, *Shakespeare from the Margins: Language, Culture, Context* (Chicago, 1996), p. 1. It is perhaps significant that Muir was not only the editor, but one of the great champions, of *Troilus and Cressida*.

[3] 'Pun' and 'quibble' are more or less interchangeable; 'quibble' is perhaps more trivial or less exact, and it is as such that I am using it here.

[4] In an essay in *Shakespeare Quarterly*, Linda LaBranche observes that in *Troilus and Cressida* 'Visual patterns . . . operate thematically by helping to establish the play world's milieu through characteristic behaviors, abiding tensions, and predominating values; and they operate dramatically by guiding audience expectation, by shifting sympathy, and by regulating tone. Visual images also, however, link diverse moments in the play by providing recurring figures, situations, or conflicts; and in this respect they belong to a larger category of dramatic devices – what Alan Dessen calls "linking analogues" – that Shakespeare employs to create a network of cross-references throughout the play.' 'Visual Patterns and Linking Analogues in *Troilus and Cressida*', *Shakespeare Quarterly*, 37 (1986), 440–50; p. 447. She does not discuss either 5.2 or the role of material objects within the play.

[5] J. Hillis Miller, 'Ariachne's Broken Woof', *The Georgia Review* 31 (1977), 44–60; Elizabeth Freund, '"Ariachne's broken

speech of anguished erotic, and existential, bewilderment in 5.2:

> This, she? No, this is Diomed's Cressida.
> If beauty have a soul, this is not she.
> If souls guide vows, if vows be sanctimonies,
> If sanctimony be the gods' delight,
> If there be rule in unity itself,
> This is not she. O, madness of discourse,
> That cause sets up with and against thyself!
> Bifold authority, where reason can revolt
> Without perdition, and loss assume all reason
> Without revolt! This is and is not Cressid.
> Within my soul there doth conduce a fight
> Of this strange nature, that a thing inseparate
> Divides more wider than the sky and earth,
> And yet the spacious breadth of this division
> Admits no orifex for a point as subtle
> As Ariachne's broken woof to enter.
> Instance, O instance, strong as Pluto's gates:
> Cressid is mine, tied with the bonds of heaven.
> Instance, O instance, strong as heaven itself:
> The bonds of heaven are slipped, dissolved and
>   loosed,
> And with another knot, five-finger-tied,
> The fractions of her faith, orts of her love,
> The fragments, scraps, the bits and greasy relics
> Of her o'er-eaten faith, are bound to Diomed
>
> (5.2.140–63)

Much beloved of critics as a suggestive point of entry into the play as a whole, the almost wilful obscurity and density of the speech has often led to its being savagely cut in performance, as it was in the recent production by Cheek by Jowl.[6] Yet it is in the physical circumstances of performance that this speech is most resonant; even without the benefit of footnotes, some aspects of it might (at least to a seventeenth-century audience) be clearer than it appears on the page. There is no doubt that this is a crucial moment in the play, not just for its characters and plot, but also for its staging (it is the superb culmination of a series of scenes of voyeurism and surveillance in the play), its language (here are three of the play's characteristic tropes of wounding, food and fabric, coupled with a mangled classical reference) and what might be called its tone: like the play and the scene itself, Troilus's speech oscillates dizzily from perspective to perspective, from the particular to the general, from the microscopic to the vast. It is this last aspect in particular that this essay explores, suggesting that the allusive density of Troilus's language is here underpinned and reinforced by the scene's material context, going beyond Hazlitt's 'double entendre', Parker's quibbles and Muir's 'uncomic puns' to what are, in effect, puns on things.

Two more conventional puns frame this scene, anticipating and echoing Troilus's dazed observation that 'This is and is not Cressid' and alerting the audience or reader not only to the vexed question of Cressida's identity, so contested in 5.2 itself, but to the ways in which both language and things can be as slippery as people. One is the well-known climax of the first movement of 4.6, the Greek camp scene in which Cressida is kissed 'in general', when Ulysses's devastating résumé, or rather assassination of Cressida is followed by a flourish as Hector enters with the Trojans and the Greeks respond 'The Trojan's trumpet' (4.6.65).[7] Describing this and other puns, François Laroque coins the phrase

---

woof": The Rhetoric of Citation in *Troilus and Cressida*', in Patricia Parker and Geoffrey Hartman, eds., *Shakespeare and the Question of Theory* (New York, 1985), pp. 19–36. As Barbara E. Bowen puts it, 'The phrase became a kind of motto for deconstruction, largely because of J. Hillis Miller's treatment of the passage as an exemplary moment for a deconstructionist poetics', *Gender in the Theater of War: Shakespeare's Troilus and Cressida* (New York, 1993), p. 156. See also Yves Peyré, 'Iris's "Rich Scarf" and "Ariachne's Broken Woof": Shakespeare's Mythology in the Twentieth Century', in Jonathan Bate, Jill L. Levenson and Dieter Mehl, eds., *Shakespeare and the Twentieth Century* (Newark, 1998), 280–93; his discussion of hair and labyrinths very much complements my discussion here.

6 The Cheek by Jowl production of *Troilus and Cressida*, directed by Declan Donnellan and designed by Nick Ormerod, played at the Barbican Theatre, London, in June 2008. 'Troilus' long lament is often shortened... Most consistently excised are 141–151' [i.e. 'O madness of discourse... Ariachne's broken woof to enter', 145–155 in the Oxford edition quoted above], William Shakespeare, *Troilus and Cressida* (Shakespeare in Production), ed. Frances A. Shirley (Cambridge, 2005), p. 208.

7 Heard as 'The Trojan strumpet'. The pun was first suggested by A. P. Rossiter in *Angel with Horns* (1961), although subsequent editors have sometimes expressed scepticism. It is unclear from both Q (Troyans) and F (Troians) whether this refers to 'the Trojan', that is Hector, or the Trojans in general.

'anamorphosis played with the ear', and his plastic turn of phrase is significant: it is not simply one word, one sound being pulled in two directions but one thing, one woman.[8] The second such pun comes in the midst of the confusion of the battle scenes in Act 5. Troilus and Diomedes meet, as Troilus has promised, in battle. Thersites offers a commentary on their encounter: 'Hold thy whore, Grecian! Now for thy whore, Trojan! Now the sleeve, now the sleeve!' (5.4.22–3), and a few lines later Diomedes instructs his anonymous servant 'take thou Troilus' horse. / Present the fair steed to my Lady Cressid' (5.5.1–2). When Diomedes and Troilus meet again, Troilus challenges Diomedes: 'O traitor Diomed! Turn thy false face, thou traitor, / And pay the life thou owest me for my horse' (5.6.6–7). The detail of Troilus's horse being won from him by his rival is taken directly from Caxton, but given the context, it is hard not to hear 'whore' as well. Was Cressid here?

J. Hillis Miller notes that *logos* is derived from *legein*, 'to gather, as wheat is gathered into sheaves, *or as bits of string are gathered into hanks*' (my emphasis), and argues that

Troilus's speech brilliantly works out the implications of the division of the mind into two when the simple narrative line of monologue becomes the doubled line of dialogue. When one logos becomes two, the circle an ellipse, all the gatherings or bindings of Western logocentrism are untied or cut.

The metaphor of the thread recurs in Miller's essay: he speaks of the 'other Cressid' as 'a knot made of bits of used string spliced piecemeal together' (building on 5.2.159–60), of the accusation that the play as a whole is 'an incoherent string of episodes' and of Troilus's speech itself as 'a rope of words . . . [which] no longer functions as the tightrope supporting a single line of thought'. The loss of authority and the rise of fragmentation and the 'non-system' is akin to

that *mise en abyme* present, for example, in the way a rope is made of braided or intertwined smaller cords, each of which in turn is made of smaller threads enwound, and so on down to the smallest filaments twisted to form the smallest thread,[9]

but he does not go on to make the connection from this lexis that he so clearly borrows from Troilus's speech back to the performed, material centre of 5.2.

This is an article about tents and sleeves, but it begins with a fine silken thread, for Elizabeth Freund's question, 'How subtle is "a point as subtle as Ariachne's broken woof"?',[10] is less rhetorical than she might have thought: this speech is held together by a web of textile references, some metaphorical, some half-heard, some materially present in the scene itself. Charles Nicholl's enjoyable new biography of Shakespeare, *The Lodger: Shakespeare on Silver Street*, which is about the playwright's relationship with a family of Huguenot tire-makers,[11] ably draws together many of the textile references in the plays which most likely date from the time of Shakespeare's residence on the corner of Silver Street and Monkwell (or Muggle) Street, in Cripplegate Ward, near what is now the Barbican.[12] The exact dates of his residence are uncertain, with Nicholl being unable to be more precise than *c.*1603–*c.*1605, the period of the

---

Bevington and Burrow (Penguin) give the former; Dawson (Cambridge) and Muir (Oxford) prefer the latter.

[8] Laroque goes on to make a useful comparison between *Troilus* and *Twelfth Night*: 'In the darker world of the problem plays, the double is no longer externalized as the twin in the comic game of errors but it is perceived as an instance of moral duplicity, of the "bifold authority" that leads Troilus to the door of madness.' François Laroque, 'Perspective in *Troilus and Cressida*', in John M. Mucciolo, ed., *Shakespeare's Universe: Renaissance Ideas and Conventions* (Aldershot, 1996), pp. 224–42, pp. 235, 238.

[9] Miller, 'Ariachne's Broken Woof', pp. 44, 54, 55–6.

[10] Freund, 'Ariachne's Broken Woof', pp. 19–20.

[11] That is, makers of women's head-dresses, a craft involving the making of frames of gold or silver wire, embroidery in silk and metal thread, beading, sequinning, ribbon and lace-work and other ornamentation, and also wig-making. Nicholl gives a full and illuminating account of tire-making and the Mountjoys' work in particular: Charles Nicholl, *The Lodger: Shakespeare on Silver Street* (London, 2008), pp. 139–71.

[12] Nicholl does not mention that, like their more famous sometime lodger, the Mountjoys are remembered in the name given to one of the blocks of flats in the Barbican Estate: Mountjoy House comprises 64 flats and penthouses, but it is dwarfed by the 44-storey Shakespeare Tower.

probable composition of *Othello*, *Measure for Measure*, *All's Well That Ends Well*, *Timon of Athens* and *King Lear*.[13] He notes almost in passing that '*Measure for Measure* and *All's Well* are two of that group traditionally called the "problem plays", or the "dark comedies" – also in this group is the earlier *Troilus and Cressida* (*c*.1602), which falls outside my defined time-period but belongs with it in mood.'[14] *Troilus and Cressida* contains a number of striking textile references, and while it would be facile on that basis alone to date it (or any other play, in default of other evidence) as a 'Silver Street' play, when the dates of both composition and residence remain uncertain, it does certainly strengthen the play's connection with *Othello*, with which it shares many concerns and a number of linguistic features.[15]

Nicholl does not pay much attention to the play, save when he draws from it an example to illustrate the conclusion of his discussion of the processes of tire-making, the materials and processes of production with which Shakespeare presumably became familiar while he lived with the Mountjoys:

[Shakespeare] is familiar with the scene whose outlines I have tried to construct: he observes and enquires, and what he sees and hears is stored away in that capacious and miraculously accessible memory, to be used in turn as raw material in the manufacturing of metaphors –

Thou immaterial skein of sleave-silk, thou green sarsenet[16] flap for a sore eye, thou tassel of a prodigal's purse ...   (*Troilus and Cressida*, 5.1.28–9)

Sleep that knits up the ravelled sleave of care ...
          (*Macbeth*, 2.2.35)

Be't when they weaved the sleided[17] silk
With fingers long, small, white as milk ...
          (*Pericles*, 15.21–2)

Breaking his oath and resolution like
A twist of rotten silk ...   (*Coriolanus*, 5.6.97–8)

... The earliest is Thersites' ingenious insult from *Troilus* ... It is redolent of the tire-shop. The author's eye has taken in not only the skein of sleave-silk, which is 'immaterial' both visually – light, flossy, frothy – and because it is irrelevant or unusable until separated into

spinnable filaments, but also the sarcenets and tassels which are part of the tiremaker's decorative arts ...[18]

As Nicholl goes on to point out, the better-known reference to sleave-silk is the one from *Macbeth*, often misunderstood as a reference to knitting, as if 'care' were an out-at-elbow jersey. But, nevertheless, Thersites's curious epithets hurled at Patroclus in 5.1, incongruously delicate, vivid in their specificity and (im)materiality, establish an important context for the scene that follows, and for Troilus's speech in particular. 'Ariachne's broken woof' is as subtle as a spider's web, certainly, but it is also, and more specifically, as fine as sleave, unravelled silk, the raw material that is twisted into threads for weaving or embroidery, or braided into tassels. Such materials would be found in a tire-maker's workshop for the manufacture of ribbons and *passementerie*, the braids, laces and other trimmings made to order for each

---

[13] Nicholl, *The Lodger*, p. 27. As is discussed below, *Othello* at least can be dated slightly earlier.

[14] Nicholl, *The Lodger*, p. 28.

[15] As Michael Neill notes at the conclusion of his discussion of the date of *Othello*, 'The one thing we can say with some certainty was that *Othello* was the next tragedy that Shakespeare wrote after *Hamlet*. In mood, if not perhaps in strict chronology, these two plays belong with the darker "Jacobean" Shakespeare; and the action of *Othello* centres on the relationship between two figures who are infected with a more extreme version of the misogyny and sexual nausea that taints the hero of the earlier tragedy – qualities that are equally conspicuous in two of the plays that have most in common with *Othello* stylistically and that are probably closest to it in time, *Troilus and Cressida* (1601–2) and *Measure for Measure* (1603–4). All things considered, then, a date of 1602–3 is as close as we are likely to get – at least in default of some hitherto unsuspected evidence for more precise dating': William Shakespeare, *Othello*, ed. Michael Neill (Oxford, 2006), pp. 403–4. The shared concern with textiles and tokens in *Troilus* and *Othello* certainly supports this dating.

[16] Sometimes spelled 'sarcenet'; a very fine, light silk. The cumulative effect of Thersites's insults is to label Patroclus a lightweight; the 'tassel of a prodigal's purse' is presumably insubstantial because it is ineffectual in keeping the purse closed, and also perhaps because constant use has made it fluffy. Like his immediate predecessor Osric, Patroclus is a 'water-fly'.

[17] Synonymous with 'sleaved'.

[18] Nicholl, *The Lodger*, p. 166.

commission.[19] 'Sleave' and 'sleave-silk' are, in fact, two slightly different things, although they are sometimes used interchangeably. 'Sleave' refers to the filaments themselves, in their 'ravelled' state; 'sleave-silk', in a skein (as Thersites refers to it) is silk that is able to be separated into such filaments. The ultimate etymology is from 'slive', to cleave, split, divide. There is the potential for slippage and doubleness here: sleave-silk is a thread that can be divided, and sleave the filaments into which it can be divided. Sleave-silk incorporates the possibility or fact of division as well as the parts into which it can be divided, a quality invoked elsewhere in Troilus's speech: as Troilus uses it, 'fractions' (line 161) refers both to the parts into which a thing can be divided (the more familiar modern sense, but used by Shakespeare possibly for the first time in this way) and the process of that division, the fact of breaking, which is the more usual early modern sense.[20] 'Fraction' is notably the technical term for the ritual breaking of the Host in the Eucharist; here Troilus's language veers towards sacrilege as he tries to convey the enormity of his experience.

There are at least four more conventional quibbles at work in this speech. Best known is 'Ariachne' herself, Shakespeare's notorious conflation of 'Ariadne' and 'Arachne', whose combination results in a kind of constructive interference. The hubristic woven cloth of the text (*texere*, to weave) here incorporates both the insubstantial filaments of the spider's web and the thread given by the soon-to-be-abandoned Ariadne to Theseus, to guide him through the labyrinth. (That thread was usually referred to as a 'clew' in the sixteenth-century, the term also being used for the silkworm's cocoon.)[21] 'Woof' is both a collective term for the horizontal threads in a piece of woven fabric (by the late seventeenth century it can refer metonymically to the fabric itself) and the word applied to a single such thread. 'Breadth' is the usual term for a width of cloth, but here it is used for the space where that material used to be; it also calls to mind the 'hair's breadth', than which the 'subtle point' is even more finely-spun. And 'A *Point*, is a thing *Mathematicall*, indiuisible . . . it neither hath length, breadth, nor thickenes.'[22]

These etymological quibbles, several notably concerned with the whole and the part, cumulatively make Ariachne's broken woof present both visibly and invisibly in this scene. The subtle point that is the sleave, the silken clew, the broken filament of the spider's web or the tapisser's loom is invisible, too finely spun (*subtilis*) to be seen, but it is presented homophonically by the (presumably silken) sleeve, Troilus's gift to Cressida at their parting, which is both repeatedly named and materially present in the scene. The broken thread is aurally present as a strand of sleave-silk, named for the possibility of its division into the finest filament that an embroiderer could manage and vividly invoked by Thersites in the preceding scene. As the meaning and value of the sleeve shift, are emptied out and redefined, so it participates in the oscillation from micro to macro that Troilus's speech describes: the sleeve is both the ultimate exterior, all surface, and the embroiderer's thread, the finest filament, the smallest possible thing, the whole and the part, and also the fact of their division. The word is heard as both, but cannot be both, and yet it is.

Like some of the more obscure matter of Troilus's speech, the sleeve often disappears in production[23] and critics, when they have addressed

---

[19] On the small silk industry in sixteenth- and seventeenth-century London, see Natalie Rothstein, 'Silk in the Early Modern Period, *c.*1500–1780', in David Jenkins, ed., *The Cambridge History of Western Textiles* (Cambridge, 2003), vol. 1, pp. 528–61.

[20] 'Division' can also be used in both these senses, for both the act of dividing and the parts into which something is divided.

[21] Thomas Moffett's 1599 poem *The silkewormes, and their flies* includes a neat Virgilian parody in its dedication to the Countess of Pembroke: 'I neither sing *Achilles* baneful ire, / Nor Man, nor Armes, nor Belly-brothers warres, / Nor *Britaine* broiles, nor cities drownd in fire, / Nor *Hectors* wounds, nor *Diomedes* skarres . . .' (unsigned leaf, ?A1r).

[22] *The elements of geometrie of the most auncient philosopher Euclide of Megara*, trans. Henry Billingsley (London, 1570), *1r, B1v. The first part of the definition is from the Preface by John Dee.

[23] The sleeve may well be an incomprehensible object in a production set in any period other than the early modern: 'The exchange has often been updated with the costumes . . . Guthrie had both present gloves. Sometimes Troilus hands her a ribbon or band and she may give a scarf'

it at all, have tended implicitly to follow Jan Kott in averring 'Never mind the medieval props. She could equally well have exchanged rings with Troilus. Details are not important.'[24] Yet details *are* important: the sleeve is Shakespeare's invention, and it is therefore worth probing further. Chaucer's lovers exchange rings, and Cressida gives Troilus a brooch, which she later gives to Diomedes.[25] In Marston's *Histrio-mastix*, not printed until 1610 but probably performed in late 1599 or early 1600, there is a (very) short play of Troylus and Cressida, the entirety of which is concerned with love-tokens: Cressida has given Troylus her 'garter blue' which he wears on his 'valiant elboe'; she also gives him her 'skreene'.[26] Clearly the exchange of tokens loomed large in the imagining of these characters. Editors suggest that Shakespeare took the sleeve from a detail later in Chaucer's poem, when Cressida gives Diomedes 'a pencel of hire sleve'.[27] It becomes the focus of attention in 5.2, not only verbally (it is mentioned three times by name) but physically, as it is given first by Cressida to Diomedes, snatched back by her, snatched again by him, with her trying and failing to get it back. It is subsequently mentioned once by Troilus in 5.3, and six times by Thersites in 5.4. Douglas C. Sprigg notices the prominence of the sleeve in 5.2, and persuasively describes the way in which it becomes the focus of the action, paying particular attention to its use as a means of both titillation and (attempted) control first by Cressida, then by Diomedes, 'a dance on tiptoe'. 'In a previous scene, the audience has witnessed the sleeve used to pledge an oath of chastity and fidelity. Now it watches the sleeve used as a promise of fornication and betrayal.'[28] Sprigg concludes that, in *Troilus and Cressida*, 'complex concepts and relationships are reified and made palpable by material objects and physical actions. The abstract is made visible.'[29] Yet his ideas can be taken much further. To employ an appropriately textile metaphor, objects and actions are also woven seamlessly into the linguistic texture of the play, played on and with as both words and things.

The sleeve has multiple associations and functions not only in these scenes, but in the play and in early modern culture. Perhaps most obviously (and as Sprigg discusses it), it is a token exchanged between lovers (it should not be forgotten that it is an exchange, with Cressida giving Troilus her glove), gift-exchange being a typical part of the courtship process and conventionally seen as leading almost inexorably to the eventual formation of a marriage contract.[30] (That this exchange takes place after both the parodic troth-plighting engineered by Pandarus in 3.2 and the consummation of the relationship between the lovers emphasizes the relationship's irregularity.) It becomes an ironic chivalric token when worn by Diomedes in his helm, part of the archaic and nostalgic discourse of chivalry and knightly honour associated with Hector in particular in the play. The wearing of sleeves as tokens in the context of court tournaments like the Accession Day Tilts was not unknown, but it

(Shirley, *Troilus and Cressida*, p. 187). In the 2008 Cheek by Jowl production, in modern dress, Troilus gave Cressida a large, shawl-like scarf of coarsely woven silk.

[24] From *Shakespeare Our Contemporary* (1964), quoted in Priscilla Martin, ed., *Shakespeare: Troilus and Cressida: A Casebook* (London, 1976), p. 148.

[25] 'They spake of sundry thynges...And pleyinge entrechaungeden hire rynges, / Of whiche I kan nought tellen no scripture; / But wel I woot, a broche, gold and asure, / In which a ruby set was lik an herte, / Criseyde him yaf, and stak it on his sherte' (III. 1366–72). Troilus's reaction to seeing the brooch on a 'cote-armure' that his brother Deiphebe has won from Diomede is described at V.1646–1701. Quotations are taken from *The Riverside Chaucer*, ed. Larry D. Benson (Oxford, 1988).

[26] This is presumably her 'fire-screen', a small, rigid fan, which is rather impractical given her subsequent instruction to him to 'Within thy helmet put the same, / Therewith to make thine enemies lame' (John Marston, *Histrio-mastix. Or The player whipt* (1610), C4r).

[27] *Troilus and Criseyde*, V.1043. 'Pencel' here could either mean a chivalric token, as Diomedes wears Troilus's sleeve, in his helm, or a small pennant or streamer made out of a sleeve. Chaucer probably means the former.

[28] Douglas C. Sprigg, 'Shakespeare's Visual Stagecraft: The Seduction of Cressida', in Philip C. McGuire, David A. Samuelson, eds., *Shakespeare: The Theatrical Dimension* (New York, 1979), pp. 149–63; pp. 158, 159.

[29] Sprigg, 'Shakespeare's Visual Stagecraft', p. 159.

[30] See David Cressy, *Birth, Marriage, and Death: Ritual, Religion, and the Life-Cycle in Tudor and Stuart England* (Oxford, 1997), chapters 10 and 11, especially pp. 263–6.

was unusual; gloves were more usual, as seen in the miniature portrait of George Clifford, Earl of Cumberland, fighting as Queen Elizabeth's champion in the persona of the Knight of Pendragon Castle, her glove in his hat.[31] When Troilus states baldly, as he swears vengeance on Diomedes, 'That sleeve is mine that he'll bear in his helm' (5.2.172), there is an ironic recollection of his earlier response to the news of Cressida's exchange for Antenor: 'How my achievements mock me' (4.2.72). An 'achievement' or hatchment is a heraldic record of honours won, a crest or badge, such as might be worn on a helmet, and Diomedes will wear the sleeve in such a manner to mock him on the battle-field.

But, perhaps more affectingly in the context of the play's action, the detachable sleeves that were the norm in the sixteenth and early seventeenth century belonged in pairs, and they were commonly referred to as such, 'a pair of sleeves', in inventories, invoices and other documents of the period.[32] A single sleeve is already useless except as a token or symbol, and in 5.2 its symbolic valency is contested and radically altered. As Carol Rutter puts it, 'These piecemeal tokens of absent bodies are loaded with the promise of metaphor, for hands pledge hearts, and chivalric arms defend female honour. But the tokens are likewise cruelly ironic, for they are, literally, emptied out of meaning. The sleeve comes without the arm, the glove without the hand.'[33]

Troilus's reference to the 'subtle point' adds further emphasis to the redundancy of the sleeve: a 'point' is, in early modern usage, not simply the end of a thread, or a very small thing, but a garment tie, such as would be used to tie a sleeve to a doublet. But this sleeve can no longer be joined to anything; it has no function or purpose. It is probably worth noting that both sleeve and glove have some sexual symbolism, the limp sleeve figuring at the same time Troilus's impotence, in both scene and plot, as well as Cressida's genitals, and the glove (which Cressida evokes in a momentary fantasy of masturbatory sensuality, 'Thy master now lies thinking on his bed / Of thee[34] and me, and sighs, and takes my glove / And gives memorial

dainty kisses to it', 5.2.82–4) much the same. The glove in particular is made sordid by association with the 'five-finger-tied' knot of Cressida and Diomedes's hands, Thersites's 'potato finger' (5.2.56) and the word 'tickle', first heard in the prologue and repeated many times thereafter, which is so characteristic of the play's grubby, digital diction.[35]

More pertinently, however, the sleeve also figures exteriority, the legible outward surface as opposed to the unknowable interior. The sleeve was where livery badges, denoting household allegiance and status, were fixed:[36] this is why Iago will 'wear [his] heart upon [his] sleeve / For daws to peck at', disclosing his identity as clearly as any badge. Yet it is the first part of his speech that is the more important context here, a statement of inwardness, concealment and secrecy:

> Others there are
> Who, trimmed in forms and visages of duty,
> Keep yet their hearts attending on themselves . . .
> And such a one do I profess myself . . .

---

[31] The large-scale miniature by Nicholas Hilliard, in the National Maritime Museum, Greenwich, probably dates from 1590, when the earl became the Queen's champion. In the 'Rainbow' portrait of Queen Elizabeth, painted in about 1603 by Marcus Gheeraerts the Younger (now at Hatfield House) the Queen has a jewelled glove pinned to her elaborate lace ruff.

[32] Janet Arnold, *Queen Elizabeth's Wardrobe Unlock'd: The Inventories of the Wardrobe of Robes prepared in July 1600 edited from Stowe MS 557 in the British Library, MS LR 2/121 in the Public Record Office, London, and MS V.b.72 in the Folger Shakespeare Library, Washington DC* (Leeds, 1988), pp. 149–53.

[33] Carol Rutter, *Enter the Body: Women and Representation on Shakespeare's Stage* (London, 2001), p. 112.

[34] I.e. the sleeve.

[35] Compare De Flores in Middleton and Rowley's *The Changeling*, on picking up one of Beatrice-Joanna's gloves: 'She had rather wear my pelt tann'd in a pair | Of dancing pumps, than I should thrust my fingers | Into her sockets here' (Thomas Middleton, *Five Plays*, ed. Bryan Loughrey and Neil Taylor (London, 1988), 1.1.228–30).

[36] When the dying Mercutio flings at Romeo the accusation that 'I was hurt under your arm' (3.1.103) the implication is both that he has been physically stabbed by Tybalt while being restrained in Romeo's arms, and that, in figurative terms, he has been wounded while fighting on Romeo's behalf, as one bound to him by ties of kinship and service.

For when my outward action doth demonstrate
The native act and figure of my heart
In compliment extern, 'tis not long after
But I will wear my heart upon my sleeve
For daws to peck at. I am not what I am.

(1.1.49–51, 55, 61–5)

The sleeve is the ultimate exterior, the polar opposite of inwardness. From 5.2 of *Troilus and Cressida*,
therefore, the sleeve can be linked in the greater
scheme of the play to the gorgeous Greek armour,
concealing a 'putrefied core' (5.9.1) in pursuit of
which Hector loses his life, and in the context of
the relationship between the lovers, to the way in
which Cressida in particular is presented in terms
of concealment and withholding, and her lack of
interiority. 'Yet hold I off', she avers in her only
soliloquy in the play: 'Then, though my heart's
contents firm love doth bear, | Nothing of that shall
from mine eyes appear' (1.2.282, 290–91).[37] Many
of the crucial moments in the love plot happen
off-stage: Cressida never gives a reason why she has
changed her mind and decided to yield to Troilus's
protestations (and she does not even appear in the
play between her speech at the end of 1.2 just
quoted and her meeting with Troilus in 3.2), and
the reasons for her transference of her affections
to Diomedes can be, and have been, interpreted
in many ways. Her protestation to Diomedes 'He
that takes [the sleeve] doth take my heart withal',
to which Diomedes abruptly replies 'I had your
heart before. This follows it' (5.2.87), anticipates
Shakespeare's subsequent coinage in *Othello* of the
proverbial 'to wear one's heart upon one's sleeve'.

Troilus and Cressida, and especially in 5.2, provides a way of getting from *Hamlet* to *Othello* in
terms of a consideration of the relationships
between words and things: the 'remembrances' that
Ophelia tries to return to Hamlet are usually represented as letters, but they are surely things as well,
which have been accompanied by

words of so sweet breath composed
As made the things more rich. Their perfume lost,
Take these again; for to the noble mind
Rich gifts wax poor when givers prove unkind.

(*Hamlet*, 3.1.100–3)

The handkerchief in *Othello* may be the most
famous love-token, perhaps the most famous material object, in the canon, but it is composed of
words, of story, as much as of linen and silk. In a
play as interested in questions of relative value as is
Troilus and Cressida, it is important that the tokens
exchanged between the lovers have no intrinsic or
functional value of themselves – that they are not
rings – but rather that their value is entirely contextual, verbally constructed, and therefore mutable
and open to constant redefinition. In 4.4 the actual
exchange of the sleeve and the glove is casual:

TROILUS   Wear this sleeve.
CRESSIDA   And you this glove. When shall I see you?

(4.5.69–70)

Far more time is spent, as is surely proper, over the
lovers' protestations of truth and fidelity, the voic-
ing of their doubts and fears. As with so much else
in the play, Troilus's question, 'What's aught but
as 'tis valued?' (2.2.51), and his subsequent debate
with Hector are pertinent; there is in Troilus's long
speech in this same scene a strong and substantive connection with his speech in 5.2. Troilus
tells his father and brothers, as they debate (or at
least rehearse: this is, after all, presumably a discussion that they have had before in the seven years
since the beginning of the war) the reasons for and
against the keeping of Helen,

We turn not back the silks upon the merchant
When we have soiled them; nor the remainder viands
We do not throw in unrespective sewer
Because we now are full...   (2.2.68–71)

In 5.2, the silks are not merely soiled but ripped
apart, reduced to shreds and tattered threads; only
the 'fractions', 'orts', 'fragments, scraps, the bits
and greasy relics' still remain.

There are in fact two strands of textile imagery
at work in the scene, both reinforced by material referents. 5.2 takes place in or in front of
Calchas's tent. There is no stage direction giving
the location, but it is a reasonable inference: in 5.1
Ulysses says to Troilus of Diomedes, 'Follow his

---

[37] It is unclear whether Alexander is still present to the end of
the scene. Bevington includes a Long Note on this.

torch, he goes to Calchas' tent' (5.1.82) and Thersites adds that Diomedes 'uses the traitor Calchas his tent' (93–4); in the brief exchange between Diomedes and Calchas at the beginning of 5.2, Calchas is apparently 'within'.[38] As R. A. Foakes points out, 'tents' or their cognates are referred to more than thirty times in *Troilus and Cressida*,[39] both as a synecdoche for the Greek camp (the Prologue announces the siege in terms of tents: 'now on Dardan plains / The fresh and yet unbruisèd Greeks do pitch / Their brave pavilions' (13–15), and Troilus's last big speech in the play addresses the Greeks themselves via 'You vile abominable tents / Thus proudly pitched upon our Phrygian plains' (5.11.23–4) and as specific locations for the action. As Foakes in particular has suggested, it is possible that the tents were staged in some way, as they may have been for the night-before-Bosworth scene in *Richard III* and possibly for its pre-Agincourt equivalent in *Henry V*, as well as in other plays; the surviving 'plot' for the second part of *Seven Deadly Sins*, for example, calls for a tent on the stage with Henry VI asleep in it.[40] At the very least, it seems likely that the inner stage (if its presence can be assumed) would have been used for the interior of Calchas's tent, from which Cressida enters and to which she retreats to fetch the sleeve; the entrance might have been represented with a canvas awning or curtain. In modern productions 'the Greek camp is often denoted by a cloth pulled across the stage to suggest a tent', and the scenes in Achilles's tent have similarly used extra curtains or hangings, or not bothered, suggesting the more intimate, private setting with furniture.[41] Nick Ormerod and Declan Donnellan's striking traverse staging for Cheek by Jowl located Troy at one end of the stage and the Greek camp at the other, with a simple canvas awning above the Greek 'end' serving as all the tents, whether Agamemnon's, Achilles's or Calchas's, with the action spilling out across most of the acting area.

As the sleeve figures the macro-context and the filament of sleeve-silk the micro, there is a similar play with word and thing concerning tents, for a 'tent' in Early Modern usage is not simply a canvas pavilion, but also a piece of medical para-

phernalia, the small roll of cloth inserted into a wound to clean it or, sometimes, to act as a drain. Tents therefore keep wounds open, or probe them, wounds such as the 'open ulcer of my heart' and the 'gash' to which Troilus initially compares his love for Cressida (1.1.53, 62), and the 'sore' and the 'wound' of Pandarus's bawdy song to Helen and Paris in 3.1 (111–22). Inevitably, this is a pun made by Thersites: in response to Patroclus's question 'Who keeps[42] the tent now?', Thersites replies 'The surgeon's box or the patient's wound' (5.1.10–11); like his reference to sleeve-silk twenty lines later, the quibble proleptically announces the context for the scene in Calchas's tent which follows.

A surgical tent might be linked further to the 'pledget', the usual word for a small bandage or pad

---

[38] As Bevington notes, Calchas seems to be staying with Menelaus (4.7.163), and Calchas's tent is therefore Menelaus's, one of the subtle ways in which the parallel between the play's two love-triangles is reinforced.

[39] R. A. Foakes, 'Stage Images in *Troilus and Cressida*', in Marvin and Ruth Thompson, eds., *Shakespeare and the Sense of Performance* (Newark, 1989), 150–61; p. 153.

[40] Discussed by Foakes, 'Stage Images', p. 153. Foakes concedes that 'some of the Greek tents could be imaginary, or painted cloth'; I think that he is over-literal in his suggestion that the many references to tents mean that there were a number of different tent 'locations' or even structures on the stage; it seems unlikely, by way of contrast, that the 'orchard' setting for 3.2 involved large numbers of trees. Some plays, especially in the private houses, may have made use of what David Bevington has called 'simultaneous staging', whereby different areas of the stage represented different locations, sometimes through the use of canvas 'houses' or booths. This seems to have been employed in some of Lyly's plays written for the first Blackfriars company in the 1580s, and I have suggested that its conventions may have influenced the presentation of the fountain in *Cynthia's Revels*, allowing it (in Bevington's words) 'to exert [its] felt presence when... not actively in use'. See my *England's Helicon: Fountains in Early Modern Literature and Culture* (Oxford, 2007), pp. 227–30. Even in these terms, however, surely one tent would do.

[41] Shirley, *Troilus and Cressida*, pp. 112, 140. All four of the productions of *Troilus and Cressida* that I have seen (RSC, dir. Sam Mendes, The Pit, 1992; RSC, dir. Ian Judge, Barbican Theatre, 1996; National Theatre, dir. Trevor Nunn, Olivier Theatre, 1999; Cheek by Jowl, dir. Declan Donnellan, Barbican Theatre, 2008) have been played more or less on a permanent set, relying on curtains, hangings and lighting effects for the changes of location.

[42] Either 'remains in' or 'looks after'.

of soft cloth used to cover a wound (and sometimes used interchangeably with 'tent'): when Cressida returns with the sleeve Thersites comments 'Now the pledge, now, now, now!' and Cressida herself describes it as a 'pretty, pretty pledge' (5.2.66, 81): this 'tent' does indeed probe Troilus's wound. But there is again a bawdy edge, particularly in light of the treatment of 'wounds' in Pandarus's song: the gift of the sleeve as a 'pledge' figures the transfer of sexual 'ownership' of Cressida from Troilus to Diomedes, and the invisible orifex is also Cressida's, described as she is by Thersites as 'secretly open' (5.2.25). Like Helen, Cressida is reduced to a 'placket', an opening in a piece of cloth.[43] Tents are both exteriors and interiors, spaces into which people and objects can go, and things which can themselves occupy space. A 'tent' is also the term for the frame on which embroidery or tapestry is stretched for working,[44] and as such it is implicit in the invocation of the 'broken woof'; 'to tent' is at once to embroider, to probe or search a wound (Hamlet announces that he will 'tent him to the quick' (2.2.599) when he is planning the play as a test of Claudius's guilt), and to tempt; the 'tent scene' in the Greek camp invokes all three of these senses.

A seventeenth-century audience might expect the tent to be hung with tapestries, or for its entrance to be evoked with a tapestry hanging: tapestries were usually taken on progress to provide both decoration and insulation for unfamiliar or makeshift accommodation, and aristocratic generals would be likely to have taken them on campaign also. Jill Levenson opens her discussion of Trojan tapestries by observing:

When Shakespeare wrote his great, unloved play about Priam's Troy (c. 1601–2), his audience knew the plot and characters primarily from two sources: literature and wall-hangings . . . Henry VIII possessed more than two thousand pieces, dozens of them depicting the Nine Worthies, Hector, the history of Helen and Paris, and the siege of Troy . . . some of these crown tapestries about the Trojan legend lasted until the reign of Charles I.[45]

Even ordinary Londoners would probably have seen Cheapside hung with tapestries and other cloths draped out of the windows, the customary and most basic form of street decoration for royal triumphs and mayoral processions in early modern London. In this context, textile objects within the play, as well as the play itself, have a particular currency: it resonates, therefore, in the play's savage epilogue, when Pandarus instructs his fellow bawds to record his cynical moralizing in their 'painted cloths'. A painted cloth is emphatically not a tapestry, although Katherine Duncan-Jones is probably too absolute in her reasoning, on the basis of Pandarus's line, that painted cloths were only 'a popular and cheap form of wall-covering in taverns and brothels', as if they were not to be found in more gentle homes as well.[46] But there is perhaps a significant gesture here back to *The Rape of Lucrece* (the story of Lucretia being, like that of the Trojan war, a favourite subject for wall hangings and paintings), where first Tarquin, like Pandarus, is contemptuous of the facile moralizing and poor quality of such hangings ('Who fears a sentence or an old man's saw / Shall by a painted cloth be kept in awe', 244–5): Pandarus is the old man offering both his 'saws' and his 'sores'.

Far better known is the lengthy ekphrasis later in *The Rape of Lucrece* of 'a piece / Of skilful painting made for Priam's Troy' (1366–7), showing the city's fall, through which Lucrece mediates her own suffering after the rape. As she describes it, the legendary figures depicted here are everything that their dramatic counterparts in the later play are not, and she focuses in particular on Hecuba, a character who is conspicuous by her absence in the Trojan play (and who had been so affectingly and effectively evoked in *Hamlet*). For most of the play's history, Cressida has not been seen as a

---

43 In Early Modern usage, 'placket' can refer both to a woman's apron or skirt and to the opening in it.

44 *OED* 'tent' *n.*[5]; slightly more familiar now is the 'tenter', as in 'tenterhooks', on which woollen cloth was stretched for finishing, in order that it dry evenly.

45 Jill L. Levenson, 'Shakespeare's *Troilus and Cressida* and the Monumental Tradition in Tapestries and Literature', *Renaissance Drama*, 7 (1976), 43–83; pp. 43, 47–8.

46 Katherine Duncan-Jones, ed., *Shakespeare's Poems* (London, 2007), p. 48.

victim of rape (although it now seems common-place to refer to 4.5, the kissing scene, as the 'gang rape scene');[47] she is the anti-Lucrece. Yet as Laurie Maguire points out in her discussion of Cressida's flippant remark to Pandarus in 1.2 that she will lie 'upon my back to defend my belly' (256), one of the play's many cruces,

No editor before 1998 has glossed this perplexing phrase. In a note exploring variant interpretations, the play's most recent editor, David Bevington, suggests that Cressida 'may regard sexuality itself as a defence'. Lorraine Helms is less tentative and more explicit. Cressida 'will accept concubinage to avoid rape'. In other words, 'surrender becomes her last line of defense'. Like most victims of abuse, Cressida protects herself by submitting.[48]

Unlike Lucrece (and except according to Dryden), Cressida does not commit suicide; unlike Lavinia, she is not murdered (or executed or euthanased). Instead she simply disappears: her final occlusion in the play comes in Troilus's abrupt dismissal of her letter as 'Words, words, mere words, no matter from the heart' (5.3.111). Oddly, this is a letter that the audience has not previously heard of or seen being written, and of which the content is never known; it exists, instead, only as a thing to be torn apart.[49] The shared matter and contexts of these texts are made resonant in *Troilus and Cressida*'s last few lines by Pandarus's emphatic reference to the painted cloth. Lucrece sews,[50] Lavinia sews, Philomel sews;[51] Cressida is fit matter only for a painted cloth, a 'dissembling luxurious drab'. Shakespeare was thinking of Lucretia again at around this time in *Twelfth Night*, when he made Olivia's seal a 'Lucrece', and had the riddling letter refer to 'silence like a Lucrece knife' (2.5.91, 104), and it is perhaps important that there were editions of *The Rape of Lucrece* in 1594, 1598, 1600 and 1607, of *Titus Andronicus* in 1594 and 1600 and that in sixteenth-century Lancashire at least, 'drab' referred not only to 'a dirty and untidy woman; a slut, a slattern' or 'a harlot, a prostitute, a strumpet' but also to a kind of coarse, heavy cloth.[52]

In the comic world of *Twelfth Night* the twins can become human puns, as they are constantly taken one for the other: 'One face, one voice, one habit and two persons, / A natural perspective, that is and is not' (5.1.213–4). Like Iago, Viola states 'I am not what I am' (3.1.139) – but in the bitter, relentlessly material world of *Troilus and Cressida* Cressida is, and is not without the possibility of a *deus ex machina* double and a happy ending.[53] As Juliet Dusinberre puts it, in her discussion of beauty and in particular the word 'fair' in the play, 'the word is no longer the signifier of the thing, but the evasion of its reality';[54] the word is also the complication and the contradiction of that reality, quite literally 'both/and'.[55] In J. Hillis Miller's terms, the logos

---

47 See Rutter, *Enter the Body*, pp. 115, 131, and Shirley, *Troilus and Cressida*, pp. 191–4 ('Since the 1980s the action has threatened to become a sanctioned gang rape, with Diomedes finally rescuing her', p. 194).

48 Laurie Maguire, 'Performing Anger: The Anatomy of Abuse(s) in *Troilus and Cressida*', *Renaissance Drama* NS 31 (2002), 153–83; pp. 161–2, quoting Bevington's Long Note on 1.3.251 and Lorraine Helms, 'Still Wars and Lechery: Shakespeare and the Last Trojan Woman', in Helen M. Cooper *et al.*, eds., *Arms and the Woman: War, Gender, and Literary Representation* (Chapel Hill, 1989), pp. 25–42; p. 38.

49 There is a contrast here with Chaucer's poem, in which the lovers' lengthy letters are quoted in their entirety. Lavinia and especially Lucrece are both presented as writers and shown in the act of writing.

50 On his way to her chamber, Tarquin 'spies / Lucretia's glove wherein her needle sticks' (316–7).

51 'Fair Philomel, why she but lost her tongue / And in a tedious sampler sewed her mind. / But, lovely niece, that mean is cut from thee. / A craftier Tereus, cousin, hast thou met, / And he hath cut those pretty fingers off / That could have better sewed than Philomel' (*Titus Andronicus*, 2.4.38–43); Lavinia's lute has 'silken strings' (46).

52 *OED* 'drab' n¹ 1, 2; n² A.

53 In the 2008 Cheek by Jowl production, a very quick change allowed Lucy Briggs-Owen to double Andromache in 5.3; Marianne Oldham doubled Helen and Cassandra in the same production. In some ways Cressida is Helen's double too: they share the same position in the play's homosocial economy of woman-as-trophy/spoil.

54 Juliet Dusinberre, '*Troilus and Cressida* and the Definition of Beauty', *Shakespeare Survey 36* (Cambridge, 1983), 85–95; p. 93.

55 See Janet Adelman's discussion of this moment in '"This Is and Is Not Cressid": The Characterization of Cressida', in Shirley Nelson *et al.*, eds., *The (M)other Tongue: Essays in Feminist Psychoanalytic Interpretation* (Ithaca, 1985), pp. 119–41; pp. 129–30.

splits once more into its constituent strands, as the contested sleeve homophonically frays and unravels into an emblem of division and fracture rather than union, fidelity and truth – but it remains a sleeve. The sleeve and the tent in 5.2 of *Troilus and Cressida* are much more than prop or setting,

but they are also far more active than mere quibbles or even staged, materialized metaphors: they are inseparable from and instrumental in their linguistic context, speaking objects, material puns, 'thing-play'. A subtle point, but one, I hope, worth making.

THE LOOK OF OTHELLO

MICHAEL NEILL

The heart of a man changeth his countenance.
> Thomas Wright, *The Passions of the Minde in Generall* (1604)

Othello deals with the savage heart.
> Queen Victoria in David Geary and Willie Davis, *Manawa Taua / Savage Hearts*

The 'rejection of color as a criterion for evaluating men' is highly paradoxical. It is based on a highly charged inside/outside distinction, a fall into constant reversals of black and white.
> Christopher L. Miller, *Blank Darkness*

'Pigmentation,' explains the Duke in Charles Marowitz's *An Othello*, 'is the outward face of the inner soul – for just as clouds are white as they appear to the naked eye, so are they white in the inner soul or substance, and just as milk is white in its outer appearance, so is milk white in its inner soul or substance, and so, in a sense are *all* things white, if they are indeed white, and if black, perforce the same applies.'[1] Marowitz's reworking of *Othello* was produced in 1972 as a direct response to the Civil Rights struggle in his native United States and to the emergence of Black Power separatism in the later phase of that upheaval. In a strategy of deliberate anachronism, Marowitz interrogates Shakespeare's *Othello* by juxtaposing modern idiomatic dialogue with passages lifted directly from the original text: thus, as the action unfolds, the Duke discards his antique eloquence to become a caricature of Southern white prejudice, suggesting a direct line of descent from Shakespeare's Venetians to twentieth-century segregationists. The Duke himself emerges as the intellec-tual descendant of Shakespeare's frequently quoted contemporary, George Best, for whom the 'black and loathsome' colour of 'all those Moors that are in Africa' was an indelible mark of reprobation, 'a spectacle of disobedience to all the world' visited upon them by God for the sin of their ancestor Ham.[2] In a crudely platonic reading of bodily signs that insists upon the symmetry of 'outward face' and 'inner soul', the Duke revisits one of the most conspicuous preoccupations of Shakespeare's play – its tormented probing of bodily surfaces. He uses 'face' metaphorically, of course; but the metaphor is one that, in the context of a disquisition on colour, inevitably tends to literalize itself, becoming a metonym for the body, as though the Duke were paraphrasing the defiant proclamation of Shakespeare's first Moor, the villain of *Titus Andronicus*: 'Aaron will have his soul black, like his face' (3.1.205).[3] In this article I want to explore the role of faces and bodies in *Othello* and to consider how the fierce scrutiny to which they

The first version of this essay was delivered as a plenary paper at the meeting of the Deutsche Shakespeare Gesellschaft at Weimar in 2007. I am grateful to the organisers, especially Professor Andreas Höfele and Dr Tobias Doering, for generously providing me with an opportunity to rethink some of my ideas about the play.

[1] Charles Marowitz, *An Othello* in *Open Space Plays* (Penguin, 1974), p. 284.
[2] George Best, in Richard Hakluyt, *The Principal Navigations, Voyages, Traffiques, and Discoveries of the English Nation*, ed. Walter Raleigh, 12 vols. (Glasgow, 1903–5), vii. 263–4.
[3] All Shakespeare plays other than *Othello* are cited from G. Blakemore Evans, ed., *The Riverside Shakespeare* (Boston, 1974). Emphases are my own.

are exposed may allow us – in spite of Marowitz's strategic gloss – to re-inspect the significance of colour in the play: to see it less as prefiguring the modern discourse of 'race' and more as a device for figuring forth the play's peculiar cognitive anxieties. For if *Hamlet* often seems to be about listening, and *Lear* about learning to see, *Othello* – though it remembers the horror of *Hamlet's* poison through the ear (2.1.288; 2.3.341) – is fixated, from the moment of Iago's urgent 'Look to your house, your daughter and your bags!' (1.1.80), upon looking. This fixation corresponds, of course, to the play's jealous preoccupation with the unreliability of appearances and the treacherous potential of the histrionic art. In *Othello*, as Peter Stallybrass remarked some years ago, 'it is the *body* which is insistently the object of interpretation ... Othello's demand for "ocular proof" is but one example of the obsessively staged desire to *see* – to trace the body's surfaces as if they were the visual proof of a finally staged signification.'[4] But at a deeper level, I want to suggest, the articulation of this well-known scopic obsession has the effect of agitating our sense of the deeply vexed relationship between the looker and the looked-upon. At the heart of the play's torment lies a fundamental cognitive uncertainty that seems inscribed in the very lexicon of observation, so that the word 'look', in both its nominal and verbal applications, can refer either to the subject's gaze or to the object's appearance. In early modern culture such uncertainty was no doubt exacerbated by the obsessive preoccupation with the unreliability of visual impressions that has been so richly documented by Stuart Clark;[5] but it answers only too uncomfortably to what we now know about the ways in which the brain processes and renders coherent the confused mass of information relayed to the visual cortex.

BODIES AND LIES

Silence is best, besides there is a *tact*...
Which keeps, when push'd by questions rather rough,
A lady always distant from the fact –
The charming creatures lie with such a grace,

There's nothing so becoming to the face.
They blush, and we believe them.

Byron, *Don Juan,* Canto 1,
stanzas 178–9 lines 1418–25

Lying, we are inclined to think, is one of the distinctive accomplishments of humanity – or rather of human culture: other animals, even if they possess the necessary degree of reflective consciousness, cannot properly lie, because they lack that pre-eminent instrument of deliberate falsehood – language. Our nearest relatives, the chimpanzees, we might concede, are able to practice rudimentary forms of deceit, since they have access to a primitive language of gesture. But the attitudes and intentions of most creatures – for members of their own species, and for others whom necessity has taught to read their repertory of expression – appear to be conveyed by involuntary signals, which may or may not serve to mislead, but which, unlike the devious contrivances of speech, are rarely, if ever, crafted to do so.

Because human faces and bodies retain much of this capacity for unconscious communication, we tend to believe – as the science of physiognomy once insisted[6] – that they too cannot lie: properly scanned they will allow us unmediated access to the mysterious inner being of others – something that language at best can only struggle to express, and that frequently enough it seeks to conceal by obfuscation, distortion or outright falsehood. The eyes, we like to say, are 'windows to the soul'; the movements of the facial muscles are understood to constitute an eloquent repertory of 'expression'.

---

4 Peter Stallybrass, 'Reading the Body: *The Revenger's Tragedy* and the Jacobean Theatre of Consumption,' *Renaissance Drama,* n.s. 18 (1987), 121–48; p. 121. For a recent reading of *Othello* that has some points of contact with my own, see Sibylle Baumbach, 'Othello and the Physiognomy of the Mind', in *Shakespeare and the Art of Physiognomy* (Penrith, 2008), pp. 145–61.

5 See Stuart Clark, *Vanities of the Eye: Vision in Early Modern European Culture* (Oxford, 2007); this was a period in which, as Clark wittily puts it, 'Europeans lost their optic nerve' (p. 2).

6 A convenient summary of the history of this pseudo-science is given in Baumbach, Chapter 2, 'A Brief Overview of Physiognomic Thought and Theory'.

Moreover, our habits of reading expression predispose us to the assumption that the lineaments and cast of a particular countenance, even in repose, will map the nature of the personality 'behind' them: the very word 'character' implies that our individual natures are in some way inscribed upon our persons, precisely as in Marlowe's *Tamburlaine* the heroic personality of Techelles is legible in his 'martial face' and the 'characters graven in [his] brows' (*1 Tamburlaine*, 1.2.169–70). Our sense of who we ourselves are is profoundly entangled with the image we see in the mirror – despite the fact that we may choose at times, like Hamlet, to privilege an inwardness that 'passes show'.[7] Even more decisively, the vagaries of our relationships with others, including the most intimate forms of love and friendship, are governed to an extraordinary degree by what we believe we recognize in their faces, as if we were all naive Platonists like Marowitz's Duke.

'I have always hated that woman', an elderly man is reported as having said about the wife of the former British Prime Minister, 'She's got such a horrible mouth.'[8] For this anonymous physiognomist, it was as if the shape of Cherie Blair's lips constituted an infallible index to her nature. In much the same fashion, George W. Bush famously claimed to have gazed into Vladimir Putin's eyes and seen his soul. In fact a great deal of what we believe we know about other people is a function of such intuitive conjecture. It is surely the case that, as they age, faces will to some extent bear the marks of 'character', in so far as that consists of a constellation of emotional habits that translate into habitual expressions. Even the requirements of speaking one's mother tongue appear to have subtle effects on one's facial muscles, so that faces may acquire a particularly 'English', 'French' or 'Italian' aspect that is only partly a function of genetically determined resemblances. But so ingrained are our habits of reading character that it is extremely difficult to separate what we genuinely learn to detect in the faces of others from less accountable forms of 'instinctive' attraction and repulsion – the reflexes with which even small children react to the mien

of strangers, including the largely unmarked faces of their own contemporaries.

As Darwin first recognized, the reasons for our unthinking assumptions about the ready legibility of the self and others lie in a biological history that has endowed the human face with a uniquely complex musculature that renders it among the most richly expressive surfaces in the animal kingdom. That development necessarily involved the symmetrical evolution of the human brain as a finely tuned instrument for decoding the voluntary and involuntary messages transmitted by facial expression: the movements of the face, Darwin wrote, 'reveal the thoughts and intentions of others more truly than do words, which may be falsified'.[9] It turns out, however, that the capacity to falsify the transmission of information is by no means confined to the sophistications of speech: higher animals are capable of managing bodily expression in order to practice forms of deliberate deceit,[10] and in the case of humans such

---

[7] In *The Wisdom of Solomon Paraphrased*, Thomas Middleton gives this notion a wittily moralizing twist: building on the idea of the mirror as an emblem of self-knowledge, he develops an elaborate conceit of the face in the mirror as the embodied figure of Wisdom herself:

> She is my glass, my type, my form, my map,
> The figure of my deed, shape of my thought,
> My life's character, fortune to my hap,
> Which understandeth all the heart hath wrought,
> What works I take in hand, she finisheth,
> And all my vicious thoughts diminisheth.
> My facts are written in her forehead's book,
> The volume of my thoughts, lines of my words.
> The sins I have she murders with a look . . .
> Chapter 9, lines 103–11

Cited from Gary Taylor and John Lavagnino, eds., *The Collected Works of Thomas Middleton* (Oxford, 2007), pp. 1941–2.

[8] Anonymous train passenger, reported by Melissa Brown in her review of Cherie Blair's autobiography, *The Guardian Review*, 24 May 2008, 8.

[9] Charles Darwin, *The Expression of Emotions in Man and Animals*, ed. Paul Ekman (London, 1998), p. 359. I am grateful to Roger Payne of the Ocean Alliance for his advice on matters of animal behaviour.

[10] See, for example, the arguments of Roger Fouts, *Next of Kin* (New York, 1997).

sleights of communication are even more common. Darwin himself recognized that humans had developed ways of concealing information with a repertory of false expressions that rendered the face a less than fully reliable index to attitude and emotion. Yet this aptitude for deception was itself compromised in turn, he thought, by the incomplete nature of voluntary control: 'When movements, associated through habit with certain states of mind, are partially repressed by the will, the strictly involuntary muscles, as well as those which are least under the separate control of the will, are liable still to act, and their action is often highly expressive.'[11] The work of Paul Ekman and others has shown that this propensity for involuntary revelation, while by no means universal, is extremely common. Such 'leakage' as Ekman calls it, appears in 'micro-expressions' that often contradict the 'macro-expressions' managed by the conscious will. Thus if, of the whole body, 'the face is equipped to lie the most, [it is also equipped] to leak the most.' Ekman's researches show, however, that untrained observers typically fail to recognize its unconscious signals; whilst even trained ones may be tempted into the opposite mistake of supposing that their absence is necessarily evidence of truthfulness.[12] To complicate matters further, identification of a concealed emotion offers no infallible clue as to its cause: so that even the most minute observers may easily fall into what Ekman revealingly calls 'Othello's error' – the conviction that an expression of fear, for example, is necessarily evidence of guilt.[13] The rich and usually spontaneous eloquence of facial expression turns out to be confused by the unavoidable possibility of misprision by the observer on the one hand, and by the capacity for deliberate deception on the part of the observed on the other. It is no wonder then that, as often as we assume the communicative transparency of faces, we are troubled by a sense of their opacity: indeed there is a whole somatic vocabulary – 'to face something out', 'to put a good face on something', 'to save face', 'on the face of things', 'two-faced' – that imagines the face as a kind of

mask, as though 'visage' and 'vizard' were one and the same.[14] This is precisely the assumption that Iago makes, when he boasts his possession of one of those deceptive 'visages of duty' that mask a heart attending on itself (Othello, 1.1.50–1);[15] and it is not for nothing that Renaissance drama's most famous alliance in fraud links two characters named Subtle and Face.

In the theatre, of course, visages are never more than histrionic vizards – albeit ones that audiences must scan for clues to an imagined inner life. Since Shakespeare was himself an actor, it is hardly surprising that his writing exhibits recurrent anxieties about the contradictory semiotics of the human countenance. Sometimes its aspect seems maddeningly opaque; at others it appears miraculously readable, its script a supremely legible index of character and intention. Thus the innocent Henry VI recognizes in the face of his doomed uncle, Gloucester, a 'map of honour, truth and loyalty' that exactly traces the inward character of history's 'Good Duke Humphrey' (2 Henry VI, 3.1.202–3); in The Winter's Tale, Polixenes, confronted by Leontes's angry 'countenance' is convinced that 'I saw his heart in's face', just as he is able to decipher in the lineaments of Camillo's 'chang'd complexions' information about his own immediate peril that the other is reluctant to divulge (1.2.368–70, 381–2, 447). In Coriolanus, Aufidius's servingmen

---

[11] Darwin, Expression of Emotions, p. 54.

[12] See Ekman, 'Darwin, Deception, and Facial Expression,' Annals of the New York Academy of Sciences, 1000 (2003), 205–21

[13] Ekman, 'Darwin', p. 218; in fact it is Iago who most conspicuously encourages this error when he proceeds to discover proof of Bianca's guilt in the fearful pallor of her face (see below, p. 117). Ekman also makes clear that the cruder repertory of signals which we somewhat misleadingly call 'body language' is equally unreliable since, although 'most people do not censor their body movements', the body is nevertheless easier to 'command' than the face (p. 210).

[14] Interestingly, both words have their root in the same Latin verb, videre (to see); but where one denotes something seen, the other (cognate with visor) describes that which covers and protects it.

[15] All references to Othello are cited from the Oxford edition, ed. Michael Neill (Oxford, 2006).

at first give the banished hero short shrift, claiming that the porter must have had '[no] eyes in his head' to 'give . . . entrance to such companions' (4.5.12–13), but, on discovering his true identity, claim to have recognized the signs of inner worth upon his countenance from the beginning – though they are hard put to describe them:

SECOND SERVINGMAN Nay, I knew by his face that there was something in him. He had, sir, a kind of face, methought – I cannot tell how to term it.

FIRST SERVINGMAN He had so, looking as it were – Would I were hang'd but I thought there was more in him than I could think.   (4.5.154–9)

By the same token, if the lineaments of the face constituted the scripture of the self, in its changing expressions one might discover a lucid register of motive and intention: thus Hamlet – much though he prides himself on his own ability to keep secret 'that within which passes show' – convinces Horatio that by 'rivet[ing their] eyes to [Claudius's] face' in the Mousetrap scene they will be able to penetrate the public masquerade of the King's 'seeming' and uncover the secret of his fratricidal history (*Hamlet*, 1.2.85; 3.2.84–7).

In early modern thinking, this belief that the face (and the body more generally) could serve as an infallible index to the nature and workings of the inner self amounted to something more than a mere folk-belief, since it was supported by theorists of physiognomy. Thus in his psycho-physiological treatise, *The Passions of the Minde in Generall* – a text almost exactly contemporary with *Othello* – Thomas Wright maintains that because 'The heart of a man changeth his countenance . . . .wise men often, thorowe the windowes of the face, behold the secrets of the heart'; citing Proverbs 27.19, he goes on to declare that 'as the face of those that looke into waters shine unto them, so the hearts of men are manifest unto the wise'.[16] Mastery of this art is especially important for men in authority, Wright argues, since 'superiors may learn [as Othello vainly seeks to do with Iago in the first part of the temptation scene] to coniecture the affections of their subiects mindes, by a silent speech pronounced in their very countenance'.[17] By the same token, no inferior should venture to 'fixe his eyes vpon his superiors countenance; and the reason is, because it were presumption for him to attempt the entrance of the privy passage into his superiors minde, as contrariwise it is lawful for the superior to attempt the knowledge of his inferior'.[18]

Women, those notoriously 'leaky vessels', were especially liable to lay open their privy passages,[19] rendering them, in Wright's estimate, conveniently subject to ocular penetration: their 'passions may be easily discovered; for as harlots by the light and wanton motions of their eyes and gesture may be quickly marked, so honest matrons, by their grave and chaste lookes, may be soon discerned . . . The Scriptures also teach vs, in the face of a harlot, to reade the impuritie of her heart . . . The fornication of a woman shall be knowen by the lifting vp of her eyes, and in her eye-bries.'[20] So,

---

[16] Thomas Wright, *The Passions of the Minde in Generall* (London, 1604), pp. 27–9. An earlier version, which Shakespeare may have known, called simply *The Passions of the Mind*, had been published in 1601. For further discussion of the evidential value attributed to faces and to '"colour" in its legal, rhetorical, theatrical, theological and physiognomical senses', see Subha Mukherji, *Law and Representation in Early Modern Drama* (Cambridge, 2006), Chapter 4, '"Painted Devils": Image-making and Evidence in *The White Devil*.

[17] Wright, *Passions of the Minde*, p. 29.

[18] Wright, *Passions of the Minde*, p. 29. The powerful, it might be argued, were to some degree protected from the kind of impertinent scrutiny that Wright deplores by the idea of a nobleman's 'countenance' (or 'port') as consisting in everything that publicly declared and exhibited his rank and prestige, including his retinue of servants and clients; though from another point of view this diffusion of identity through a kind of social 'face' might also render him more vulnerable.

[19] See Gail Paster, 'Leaky Vessels: The Incontinent Women of Jacobean City Comedy', Chapter 1 of *The Body Embarrassed: Drama and the Disciplines of Shame in Early Modern England* (Ithaca, NY, 1993), pp. 23–63.

[20] Wright, *Passions of the Minde*, p. 29. By contrast, in Wycherley's *The Country Wife* (1675), Dainty Fidget declares that 'women are least masked when they have the velvet vizard on' (5.4.111–12), whilst in Congreve's *The Double Dealer* (1693), a play much interested in physiognomy, Mellefont somewhat paradoxically declares that 'women may most properly be said to be unmasked when they wear visors; for that secures them from blushing, and being out of

in *Troilus and Cressida*, Ulysses claims to be able to read Cressida's face and body like an open book:

> There's language in her eye, her cheek, her lip,
> Nay, her foot speaks; her wanton spirits look out
> At every joint and motive of her body.
> O, these encounterers, so glib of tongue,
> That give a coasting welcome ere it comes,
> And wide unclasp the tables of their thoughts
> To every ticklish reader!
>
> (*Troilus and Cressida*, 4.5.55–61)

Similar assumptions about the legibility of the countenance and the eloquence of the body's 'silent speech' are widely dispersed in *Othello*: just as Iago urges Cassio to discover the signs of lascivious invitation in Desdemona's face – 'What an eye she has! Methinks it sounds a parley to provocation' (2.3.21–2) – and just as he schools Roderigo to discover in Desdemona's courtesy to Cassio 'an index...to the history of lust and foul thoughts' (2.1.249–50), so he persuades the 'encaved' Moor to scrutinize Cassio's countenance for proof of his secret guilt: 'mark the fleers, the gibes, and notable scorns / That dwell in every region of his face....I say, but mark his gesture', all the while knowing that Othello's 'unbookish jealousy must construe, / Poor Cassio's smiles, gestures, and light behaviours / Quite in the wrong' (4.1.78–83, 97–9). Desdemona, appealing for Cassio's reinstatement, prides herself on her own 'judgement in an honest face'(3.3.50); and her famous insistence that she 'saw Othello's visage in his mind' (1.3.250), though it ostensibly inverts the method of physiognomy, nevertheless contains the implicit assumption that she is able to look through his face to discover the 'quality...honour, and... valiant parts' to which her own soul is consecrated. Othello's matching conviction that his 'parts...and...perfect soul' can '*manifest* [him] rightly' (1.2.31–2), reflects a similar confidence in the visibility of his inward characteristics[21] – one that, ironically enough, seems warranted when, in the final scene, a terrified Desdemona recognizes in her husband's look the 'portents' (5.2.46) of her own imminent murder:

> And yet I fear you, for you're fatal then
> When your eyes roll so....
> Alas, why gnaw you so your nether lip?
> Some bloody passion shakes your very frame.
>
> (5.2.37–45)

In spite of the apparently ready legibility of the countenance, however, physiognomy, proves to be a difficult and worryingly inexact science. Even Thomas Wright cautions that its wisest practitioners must sometimes depend upon conjecture, since they can never

> exactly understand the heartes which bee inscrutable, and onely open vnto God, but...by coniectures they may aime well at them: for he which beholdeth his face in the water, doth not discerne it exactly, but rather a shadowe, than a face; even so he, that by externall phisiognomy and operations, will divine what lyeth hidden in the heart, may rather conceive an image of that affection that doth raigne in the minde, than a perfite and resolute knowledge.[22]

For Pierre Charron, exterior signs are an even less reliable guide: to know the truth of a man, he maintains

> We must look into his inward part, his privy chamber...beholding him with all visages, feeling his pulse, sounding him to the quick, entering into him with a candle and snuffer, searching and creeping into every hole, corner, turning, closet, and secret place. For this is

---

countenance, and next to being in the dark, or alone, they are most truly themselves in a visor mask' (3.1.284–8).

[21] Lear's dying words, as he gazes at the corpse of the daughter whose very name identifies her with the heart, imply that he has learned to read the truth of her inner being in her face – a truth that the audience are invited to witness, even as the enigmatic spectacle leaves them painfully excluded from it: 'Do you see this? Look on her! Look her lips, / Look there, look there!' (*King Lear*, 5.3.311–12).

[22] Wright, *Passions of the Minde*, p. 27. Wright's phrasing here resonates intriguingly with Horatio's and Gertrude's account of the hearers' response to the mad Ophelia in *Hamlet*: 'They *aim at it* / And botch the words up fit to their own thoughts, / Which as her winks and nods and gestures yield them, / Would make one think there might be thought...'Twere good she were spoken with, for she may strew / Dangerous *conjectures* in ill-breeding minds' (4.4.9–15).

the most subtle and hypocritical, covert and counterfeit of all the rest, and almost not to be known.[23]

In Shakespeare the reliability of the physiognomical interpretation on which his characters depend is frequently exposed to similar question. Thus in *The Rape of Lucrece,* when the protagonist calls to mind a set of Homeric portraits, she appeals in apparently straightforward terms to the revelatory power of an art that so perfectly renders character in facial expression:

> In great commanders, grace and majesty
> You might behold triumphing in their faces....
> In Ajax and Ulysses, O what art
> Of physiognomy might one behold!
> The face of either cipher'd either's heart;
> Their face their manners most expressly told:
> In Ajax' eyes blunt rage and rigor roll'd;
> > But the mild glance that sly Ulysses lent
> > Show'd deep regard and smiling government.
> > > (*Rape of Lucrece,* lines 1387–1400)

On closer inspection, however, Lucrece's tribute is mined by ambiguity, for we cannot be entirely sure whether the painting's '*art of physiognomy*' belongs to the cunning of the representation or to the guile of those it represents, nor whether 'cipher'd' means that each man's painted face exactly registers his character, or that the truth of his heart is actually rendered in some blankly enigmatic code; and if it is their 'manners' of which their faces speak, then what of the thoughts and emotions that manners so often conceal? Indeed the 'mild glance' of 'sly Ulysses' bears witness to a 'smiling government' (self-possession) that renders his 'deep regard' (consideration) ultimately opaque to the beholding eye, recalling Richard of Gloucester's delight in his own ability to 'smile, and murther whiles I smile', or Hamlet's bitter recognition that 'one may smile, and smile, and be a villain' (*3 Henry VI,* 3.2.182; *Hamlet,* 1.5.108). No wonder that in the suspicion-riven world of Claudius's Denmark even Laertes's grief for his murdered father is subject to doubt: 'was your father dear to you? / Or are you like the painting of a sorrow, / A face without a heart?' (4.7.107–9).

This notion of the face as a contrivance of art is one that takes a peculiar charge from its theatrical context: Hamlet may be angrily dismissive of the exaggeratedly histrionic expressions of malice with which the murderer opens the dumb-show ('leave thy damnable faces and begin'), but he finds the spectacle of the First Player's exhibition of grief for Hecuba – in which 'all the visage wann'd... his whole function suiting / With forms to his conceit' (2.2.554–7) – deeply perplexing; and his perplexity reflects back on the audience's own habit of naïvely submitting to the impression of inner feeling crafted by the actor's countenance. However, it is not so much the contrived opacity of the hypocritical deceiver – what Sonnet 127, anticipating *Othello* as much as *Macbeth* in its play on the lady's dark looks, calls 'Fairing the foul with art's false borrow'd face' – that appears most disturbing, but unknowability of a less grossly manipulative, if even more baffling kind. What is at issue in such cases is misconstrual that (as in Sonnet 137) may be as much the product of the willed blindness of love as of any deliberate deception, since it depends upon the falsehood of 'eyes, corrupt by over-partial looks... Whereto the judgement of [the] heart is tied'. In Sonnet 93, tormented by the uncertain relation between face and heart, the poet comes to see in the beloved's beauty the repository of a dangerously occluded truth. Here is a character that is precisely *not* charactered in the visage:

> So shall I live, supposing thou art true,
> Like a deceived husband, so love's face
> May still seem love to me, though alter'd new;
> Thy looks with me, thy heart in other place:
> For there can live no hatred in thine eye,
> Therefore in that I cannot know thy change.
> In many's looks the false heart's history
> Is writ in moods and frowns and wrinkles strange,
> But heaven in thy creation did decree
> That in thy face sweet love should ever dwell;
> Whate'er thy thoughts or thy heart's workings be,
> Thy looks should nothing thence but sweetness tell.
> > How like Eve's apple doth thy beauty grow,
> > If thy sweet virtue answer not thy show!

---

[23] Pierre Charron, *Of Wisedome,* trans. Samson Lennard, 2nd edn (London, 1630), pp. 6–7.

Not surprisingly, then, as often as Shakespeare's lookers are persuaded of the transparency of the human countenance, others find such confidence confounded by events. In comedy this can lead to the ludicrous mistakings produced by the treacherous collusion of eyesight and imagination in a play like *A Midsummer Night's Dream*. In tragedy its consequences can be fatal; thus in *Richard III*, Hastings ensures his own destruction by his guileless misreading of the king: 'there's never a man in Christendom / Can lesser hide his love or hate than he, / For by his face straight shall you know his heart' (3.4.51–3). Flattered by Buckingham's suggestion that it is he, more than anyone, who can claim to be 'inward' with Richard (3.4.8), Hastings makes himself deaf to the Duke's sardonic observation upon the opacity of visages – a warning that is itself a dazzling piece of rhetorical prestidigitation whose swirl of pronouns mockingly enacts the elusiveness of inner truth:

> We know each other's faces; for our hearts
> He knows no more of mine than I of yours,
> Or I of his, my lord, than you of mine
> *(Richard III, 3.4.10–12)*

If Richard's unknowability is that of a protean performer who can 'frame [his] face to all occasions' (*3 Henry VI*, 3.2.185), his prophetic nemesis, Queen Margaret, while equally inured against the involuntary 'blush' of shame, renders herself indecipherable through the inexpressive fixity of a 'face [that] is vizard-like, unchanging / Made impudent with use of evil deeds' (*3 Henry VI*, 1.4.116–8). Hers is the impenetrability for which Macbeth yearns under the scrutiny of 'the tender eye of pitiful day' (*Macbeth*, 3.2.47) – as if fearful that the tenderness of the imagined eye might fatally soften the object of its gaze.[24] If Lady Macbeth imagines dashing out the brains of her own baby, it is precisely because she needs to cauterise the 'tender' emotion produced by the look of it, 'smiling in my face' (1.7.54–8). *Macbeth* works a series of variations on the proverbial injunction 'to beguile the time with a fair face' (Dent T340.1), but complicates it with the knowledge that the defensive look of the false countenance enables the very shame-

lessness that it seeks to conceal. Concerned that her husband's face is too much an open 'book, where men / May read strange matters', Lady Macbeth famously urges him to undo that effeminate openness: 'look like th'innocent flower / But be the serpent under't' (1.5.61–6). Macbeth, in his turn, will exhort his Lady to 'mock the time with fairest show'; since 'False face must hide what the false heart doth know,' he urges her that they must 'make our faces vizards to our hearts, / Disguising what they are' (1.7.81–2, 3.2.34–5). But the brazen mask he envisages is one that is designed to baffle self-scrutiny as much as external inquisition: 'To know my deed, 'twere best not know myself' (2.2.70). No wonder that the saintly Duncan, brooding on the betrayal of Macbeth's namesake Cawdor, is made to lament the empty pretence of physiognomy, insisting that 'There's no art / To find the mind's construction in the face (1.4.12–13).[25] No wonder either that Lear, baffled by his elder daughters' falsehood, persuades himself that he will need to 'anatomize Regan [in order to] see what breeds about her heart' – a fantasy later mimed by Edgar as he tears open Goneril's letter to her treacherous brother: 'To know our enemies' minds, we rip their hearts' (*King Lear*, 3.6.76–7; 4.6.260).[26]

---

24 For a brilliant account of the treacherously ambiguous character of visual perception in *Macbeth*, see Clark, *Vanities of the Eye*, Chapter 7, 'Sights'. Clark observes how the play adds to 'hypocrisy in word and deed...a kind of hypocrisy of the eyes' (p. 255); his analysis does not, however, extend to a consideration of the equivocal character of the 'look' and the uncertainties of phyiognomical scrutiny.

25 Compare the complaint of Roxano in Middleton and Dekker's *The Bloody Banquet*: 'I have some skill in faces – and yet they never were more deceitful. A man can scarce know a bawd from a midwife by the face, an hypocritical puritan from a devout Christian, if you go by the face' (1.4.114–17), cited from Taylor and Lavagnino, *Thomas Middleton*, p. 648.

26 Cf. also Cloten's threat to the loyally discreet Pisanio: 'Close villain, / I'll have this secret from thy heart, or rip / Thy heart to find it' (*Cymbeline*, 3.5.85–7). In Congreve's *Double Dealer*, though Careless justifies his suspicion of Maskwell by appealing to 'physiognomy' (1.1.134), Lady Touchwood, for whom Maskwell's very smile 'speaks in ambiguity', complains that 'Ten thousand meanings lurk in each corner of [his] various face', and wishes she might use her dagger to

More than any other character in Shakespeare, it is Iago who prides himself on the artful opacity of his own countenance, and the inaccessibility of his thoughts and feelings to the scrutiny of others. Even as his soliloquies unmask him to the audience, allowing them to glimpse the corrosive emotions that 'gnaw my inwards', he relishes his ability to ensure that 'Knavery's plain face is never seen till used' (2.2.288, 303). Iago boasts to Roderigo of the penetrative power of his own gaze – of his ability to see through Cassio's 'counterfeit' eye to the 'salt and most hidden loose affection' it conceals (2.1.234–6), whilst he discovers in the speaking bodies of Desdemona and Cassio the 'index and obscure prologue' to an entire 'history of lust and foul thoughts', proofs of an 'incorporate conclusion' (249–54). Yet even as he interprets these supposedly deceitful appearances, Iago delights in teasing his slow-witted victim by proclaiming his own mastery of deceitful 'seeming', the treacherous 'flag and sign of love' with which he wins Othello's trust (1.1.155), the 'forms and visages of duty...shows of service' (60, 50–2) with which he means to advance his own 'peculiar end':

For when my outward action doth demonstrate
The native act and figure of my heart,... 'tis not long
    after
But I will wear my heart upon my sleeve
For daws to peck at: I am not what I am.   (61–5)

Beneath Iago's 'outward action', he contrives to suggest, there is only the '*act* and *figure*' of inwardness to be discovered – not the open heart itself, but another performance, another impenetrable face.[27]

In the temptation scene, the success of Iago's stratagem depends precisely on the histrionic skill with which he manipulates Othello's increasingly desperate sense that he is witness to eloquent facial signatures whose precise meaning nevertheless remains frustratingly illegible to him – 'dilations, working from the heart' that remain (in his famously paradoxical phrase) obstinately 'close' (closed, secret) to the observing eye:

Thou dost mean something....
And when I told thee he [Cassio] was of my counsel
In my whole course of wooing, thou criedst 'Indeed?'

And didst contract and purse thy brow together,
As if thou then hadst shut up in thy brain
Some horrible conceit. If thou dost love me,
Show me thy thought....
...By heaven, I'll know thy thoughts.

                              (3.3.111–19, 165)

'You cannot,' comes the svelte reply, 'if my heart were in your hand' (166): the immateriality of thought, Iago keeps reminding the Moor, renders it inaccessible to view: even were Othello to 'rip his heart' like Edgar, or to eviscerate him as Lear longs to do Regan, it would not serve to reveal the 'foul things' which his 'honesty' paradoxically requires that, for his general's own good, he must keep hidden (141, 157). Ironically, Iago's performance can be as convincing as it is because there is indeed 'some monster in [his] thought / Too hideous to be shown' (110–11). Of course it has nothing to do with any privy information deriving from his own ability to 'spy into abuses,' the 'scattering and unsure observance' of which, with wry self-deprecation, he boasts to Othello (3.3.151,155); as the audience knows, it is merely the issue of the monstrous parthenogenesis that he planned, in the fullness of time, to bring out of the darkness of his inner 'hell...to the world's light' (1.3.392–3). To that extent Othello reads Iago's face correctly, recognizing its deformed emotions, only to misattribute their meaning.

---

uncover the truth of his nature: 'Oh! That they were written in thy heart, / That I with this, might lay them open to my sight' (5.4.52–5). For further discussion of anatomical conceits in Shakespeare, see Patricia Parker's essays, '"Dilation" and "Delation" in *Othello*,' in Patricia Parker and Geoffrey Hartmann, eds., *Shakespeare and the Question of Theory* (New York, 1985), pp. 54–74; 'Fantasies of "Race" and "Gender": Africa, *Othello*, and Bringing to Light,' in Margo Hendricks and Patricia Parker, eds., *Women, 'Race', and Writing in the Early Modern Period* (London, 1994), pp. 84–100; and '*Othello* and *Hamlet*: Spying, Discovery, Secret Faults,' Chapter 7 of her *Shakespeare from the Margins: Language, Culture, Context* (Chicago, 1996); also Michael Neill, *Issues of Death: Mortality and Identity in English Renaissance Drama* (Oxford, 1997), Chapters 2–4.

27 The meanings of 'figure' include 'external form', 'appearance; posture', 'bodily shape', 'image, likeness', 'part enacted', and (in heraldry, as in French) 'face' (*OED n.* 1a, 1c, 4a, 9a, 11a, 10c).

It is important to understand, however, that the effectiveness of Iago's tactic does not depend simply on the obvious way in which his seeming reluctance to divulge what he pretends to know works to convince the Moor of his privileged insight: 'This honest creature . . . sees and knows . . . much more than he unfolds' (3.3.246–7). At least equally damaging is what Iago's emphasis on his own inscrutability implies about the unreadability of faces and bodies generally – and therefore about the opacity of Desdemona's person in particular. Thus, just as Othello determines to 'see before I'll doubt' (193) – reassuring himself that his wife's ability to see *him* as he really is ('she had eyes and chose me', 192) is somehow the guarantor of her own inner goodness – so Iago pounces on Othello's words to divert his general's gaze from his own body to Desdemona's: capitalizing on Brabantio's libellous insistence upon the impossibility of his daughter's 'fall[ing] in love with what she feared to look on' (1.3.99) and on his warning that 'daughters' minds' can never be judged by 'what you see' (1.1.169–70), he contrives to suggest that Desdemona's outward person too must be the secret repository of 'a will most rank, / Foul disproportions, thoughts unnatural' (3.3.236–7) – the same 'foul' and 'monstrous' truths that Othello once seemed to glimpse hidden in Iago himself:

> Look to your wife, observe her well with Cassio;
> Wear your eyes thus . . . look to't.
> I know our country disposition well:
> In Venice they do let God see the pranks
> They dare not show their husbands; their best
>   conscience
> Is not to leave't undone, but keep't unknown.
>   (200–7)

The result – according to the play's sinister logic of 'changing places'[28] – is not only that Othello's 'dangerous conceits' begin to 'poison' him like the 'poisonous mineral' of Iago's gnawing jealousy (2.1.287–8; 3.3. 328–31), but that his former determination to 'see' Iago's thoughts is transmuted into his notorious obsession with 'ocular proof' of Desdemona's secret infidelity: 'Make me to see't' (3.3.362, 366). Iago pursues his advantage by goad-

ing this would-be 'supervisor' with suggestions and refractions of a scene that (with wicked irony) he represents as being just as inaccessible as his own tantalisingly withheld thoughts – even as he conjures its enormities into imaginary view:

> Would you the supervisor grossly *gape* on?
> *Behold* her tupped? . . .
> It were a tedious difficulty, I think,
> To bring them to that *prospect*. Damn them, then,
> If ever mortal *eyes* do *see* them bolster
> More than their own . . .
> It is impossible you should *see* this,
> Were they as prime as goats, as hot as monkeys . . .
>   But yet I say
> If imputation and strong circumstances,
> Which lead directly to the door of truth,
> Will give you satisfaction, you might have it.
>   (397–410 (emphasis added))

The 'door of truth' of which Iago speaks is like the 'closet door of nature's secrets' which the anatomist John Banister offered to open to students of the body.[29] It ought to give access to the 'privy passage' of the self imagined in Wright's *Passions of the Mind*; but the best Iago can offer in place of such disclosure is the ambiguous spectacle of those 'imputations and strong circumstances' that (in a deliberately blurry metaphor) are said to 'lead directly' to the door without opening it – the disturbing sexual displacements of his own dream narrative (415–27).

'Yet we *see* nothing done,' Iago disingenuously confesses, only to offer a charade of ocular proof in his visually suggestive fiction of the handkerchief:

> Have you not sometimes *seen* a handkerchief
> Spotted with strawberries in your wife's hand? . . .
>   Such a handkerchief –
> I am sure it was your wife's – did I today
> *See* Cassio wipe his beard with.   (433–9)

The handkerchief notoriously becomes a metonym for Desdemona's body: it renders her 'a common thing', like the sexualized body of Emilia with

---

28 See Michael Neill, 'Changing Places in *Othello*,' in *Putting History to the Question: Power, Politics, and Society in English Renaissance Drama* (New York, 2000), pp. 207–36.
29 John Banister, *The Historie of Man* (London, 1578), B1v.

which earlier Iago assimilated it (3.3.305); and with its blood-red embroidery, 'conserved of maiden's hearts' (3.4.74), it appears (as if uncannily reversing Iago's refusal to wear his heart upon his sleeve) to exhibit the secret truth of Desdemona's passionate heart to Othello's inflamed imagination. Associated by its name with that instrument of silent expression, the hand – a limb that, according to early modern physiology, was linked directly to the heart by a 'master vein' running from the ring-finger – the handkerchief is passed from hand to hand, as women are imagined passing from man to man; and when Othello next confronts Desdemona he pounces immediately on her hand, as though by scrutinizing it he could penetrate the inward secrets that her face so treacherously conceals:[30]

Give me your hand. This hand is moist, my lady . . .
This argues fruitfulness and liberal heart:
Hot, hot and moist! This hand of yours requires
A sequester from liberty . . . 'Tis a good hand,
A frank one . . .
A liberal hand. The hearts of old gave hands,
But our new heraldry is hands, not hearts. (3.4.34–45)

From the hand Othello returns again to the handkerchief, tracing its mysterious 'wonder' to the magical arts of the Egyptian who gave it to his mother, and attributing to this sibyl the very power to uncover inner truth with which he now believes himself endowed by the spurious conjuring of Iago's handkerchief trick: 'She was a charmer and could almost read / The thoughts of people' (3.4.56–7). The loss of this magic token, he insists, would have exposed his mother to the judgement of 'my father's eye', just as Desdemona's 'precious eye' is now exposed to his own inquisitorial gaze (lines 54–65). 'Fetch't, let me see't,' he commands, as if to look at it might indeed allow him to share in the Egyptian charmer's mind-reading.

Goaded as he is by Iago's enigmatic reminders of the deceitfulness of appearance and the inaccessibility of the inner self – 'Men should be that they seem – / Or those that be not, would they might seem none' (3.3.130–1); 'Her honour is an essence that's not seen, / They have it very oft that have it not' (4.1.15–16) – Othello never

achieves proper confidence in his ability to read what Ulysses calls the 'language' of the countenance, settling instead (under Iago's tutelage) into an acceptance of his wife's handkerchief as a substitute both for that elusive 'essence' and for the body he believes has been stolen from him: 'he had my handkerchief . . . By heaven, that should be my handkerchief . . . By heaven I saw my handkerchief in's hand . . . I saw it in his hand' (4.1.21, 153; 5.2.64, 213). In the infamous 'brothel scene' he pulls Desdemona to him: 'Let me see your eyes – / Look in my face', he demands, as if he – whom Iago once described as having 'devoted and given up himself to the contemplation, mark, and denotement of her parts and graces' (2.3.304–5) – might now discover in her looks the 'mystery' of her corrupted sex (4.2.25–30), and thereby confirm for himself the falsehood that 'Heaven truly knows' (39). What he sees, however, provokes only a litany of tormented questions: 'Why, what art thou? . . . What committed? . . . What committed? . . . What committed? . . . Are not you a strumpet? . . . What, not a whore? . . . Is't possible?' (33, 72, 76, 80, 82, 86, 87). Wright's lexicon of whorish expressions ought to help him here, but it does not: it is as though Desdemona's visage remained, in spite of everything, a mere vizard – ironically rendered impenetrable to him by virtue of the very thing that should exhibit the truth of her being: the fairness of her skin. Maddened by her appearance, he strikes her in front of Lodovico, and then orders her 'Out of my sight' (4.1.238). Just as he has warned Iago, it is the look of her, 'her body and her beauty' that fatally serve to 'unprovide [his] mind' (4.1.198–9) because he can never again be sure that he knows what he sees. As with the watchers on the Cyprus waterfront, for whom the difference between 'the main and th'aerial blue' is blurred by the very intensity of their gazing, so Othello finds his frantic scrutiny of Desdemona

---

30 For a full account of the overdetermined symbolism of the hand in early modern culture and the complex links made between the hand and individual identity, see Neill, '"Amphitheaters in the Body": Playing with Hands on the Shakespearean Stage', in *Putting History to the Question*, pp. 167–203 (esp. p. 184, n. 44).

resulting only in the tormenting uncertainty of 'An indistinct regard' (2.1.40–1). The look of his own face, it turns out, is equally subject to misconstrual.

READING COLOUR

[B]ehind that physical portrait . . . there is a psychological portrait. And if we could only read that, it would tell us how intelligent that tribe is, how stupid, how cunning, how ambitious. How faithful, for heaven's sake . . . .Isn't it just possible that that combination of black hair and strong chin and clear complexion is much more than a haphazard confluence of physical accidents? That they constitute an ethnic code we can't yet decipher? . . . Are they saying to us – these physical features – if only we could hear them – are they whispering to us: crack our code and we will reveal to you how a man thinks, what his character traits are, his loyalties, his vices, his entire intellectual architecture . . . a rebel at heart maybe, maybe even a traitor.
Brian Friel, *The Home Place*

I am spoken to not in words, which come to me quaint and veiled, but in signs, in conformations of face and hands, in postures of shoulders and feet . . . Reading the brown folk I grope, as they grope reading me: for they too hear my words only dully, listening for those over-tones of the voice, those subtleties of the eyebrows that tell them my true meaning . . . Across valleys of space and time we strain ourselves to catch the pale smoke of each other's signals.
Magda, in J. M. Coetzee's *In the Heart of the Country*[31]

For Coetzee's Magda even the 'subtleties of the eyebrows' belong to a species of language that can be 'listen[ed] to', something that Hendrik and Klein-Anna, the 'brown-folk' of her narrative – servants from whom she is cut off by the 'language of hierarchy, of distance and perspective' that is her 'father tongue'[32] – must learn to decipher, since what she imagines as 'the true language of the heart' that might bridge the 'contraries' of master and slave is as unavailable to them as it is to her. If the face is indeed, as Othello's language in the brothel scene declares, a textualized surface, it is on 'this fair paper, this most goodly book' that the truths of the heart ought to be inscribed. But it is, of course, at precisely the point when Othello's gaze fixes upon the fairness of Desdemona's appearance that colour complicates the lexicon of facial expression. In European culture, the language of the face includes the propensity of the countenance to change colour in response to inward feelings: the inward truths of emotion reveal themselves in the pink blushes of embarrassment, shame, or guilt, the red flush of anger, the 'dark looks' attributed to suspicion and suppressed fury, the pallor of fear and cold rage, the supposed 'yellow' of cowardice, and even in the 'green-eyed' gaze of jealousy.

Black skin, however, appeared to confuse the seemingly natural eloquence of 'complexion' – a term that reassuringly linked temperament to appearance. In the early modern discourse of colour and ethnic difference, the anxiety attaching to blackness resulted from a seeming paradox: on the one hand theologically based conjecture, iden-tifying it as the mark of inherited sin, offered reas-suring confirmation of a correspondence between outward appearance and inward reality, face and self; on the other hand, by its failure to exhibit the familiar vocabulary of changing hues, black-ness threatened to confound the semiotics of the face altogether; and on Shakespeare's stage, with its habit of metatheatrical self-consciousness, this notion of blackness as concealment must have been reinforced by the knowledge that a black face was never more than 'blackface', a sooty vizard that placed the actor's 'inner' reality at a double remove from the audience's scrutiny – but that, far from being indelible, might be conjured away by the magic of the theatre, like the colour of Niger's daughters in Jonson's masques of *Blacknesse* and *Beautie*.[33]

---

31 Brian Friel, *The Home Place* (London, 2005), pp. 14–15, 33; J.M. Coetzee, *In the Heart of the Country* (Har-mondsworth, 1982), pp. 7–8.

32 Coetzee, *In the Heart of the Country*, p. 97.

33 For an essay that highlights the metatheatrical use of both blackface and female make-up on the early modern stage, see Sujata Iyengar, 'Blackface and Blushface', Chapter 5 of *Shades of Difference: Mythologies of Skin Color in Early Modern England* (Philadelphia, 2005). Cf. also Dympna Callaghan, '"Othello was a White Man"; Properties of Race on Shake-speare's Stage', in Terence Hawkes, ed., *Alternative Shake-speares 2* (London, 1996), pp. 192–215.

When Aaron, in the passage I quoted earlier, brags of his wish to have his soul black like his face, he draws on a habit of reading pigmentation that was deeply ingrained in early modern culture. As Karen Newman and others have shown,[34] attempts to understand the significance of phenotypical difference in this period, though by no means uniform, were conditioned by scriptural texts that seemed to identify whiteness with purity and blackness with sin. 'Can the black Moor change his skin?' the prophet Jeremiah had demanded, 'or the leopard his spots? *Then* may ye also do good that are accustomed to do evil' (Jeremiah 13:23). This is the text that underlies Gertrude's confession in *Hamlet* when she responds to her son's denunciatory tirade by discovering in her 'very soul . . . such *black* and grained *spots* / As will not leave their tinct' (*Hamlet*, 3.4.90–2); and it supplies the title-page motto for a pamphlet whose title resonates suggestively with the stigmatization of Othello by both Iago and Emilia: Thomas Adams's *The Blacke Devill* (1615).

Although Adams at one point (no doubt remembering Jeremiah) calls the subject of his diatribe 'this *Moore',* his 'black devil', is purely metaphoric – a figure for the open villainy of creatures in whom 'hyde and carcasse, hand and heart, shadow and substance, seeming and being, outward profession and inward intention, are [equally] *blacke,* foule, detestable'.[35] In the context of ethnicity, however, what the prophet had offered merely as a persuasive visual analogy, became an instrument for decoding the significance of bodies that might be seen as bearing the ineradicable marks of George Best's 'natural infection'.[36] It is Othello's 'sooty' skin that rhetorically justifies Brabantio's denunciation of his son-in-law as a 'foul thief', since 'foul' (an adjective that occurs no fewer than 19 times in the play) could mean 'dirty-coloured' or 'black', as well as 'ugly', 'filthy' and 'wicked': this, Brabantio insists, is a creature who could have overcome Desdemona's virginal reluctance to marry and her instinctive aversion to his appearance only through a mastery of the so-called 'black arts' – the foul 'charms' that he has allegedly practised upon her, and rendered her 'blind' to

what, he claims, she once 'feared to look on' (1.1.70; 1.2.62–79; 1.3.61–7).

From the point of view of Aaron, it is the very indelibility of blackness that constitutes its virtue: 'Coal-black', he boasts, with sardonic defiance, 'is better than another hue, / In that it scorns to bear another hue' (*Titus Andronicus*, 4.2.99–100); its refusal to change is the visible proof of a perverse integrity. Unlike those fraudulently 'white-lim'd walls [and] alehouse painted signs', Tamora's sons, his nature is as self-consistent as his colour is impermeable, since 'all the water in the ocean / Can never turn the swan's black legs [or his own black face] to white' (98, 101–2); whiteness, by contrast, is something dangerously fungible, a 'treacherous hue, that will betray with blushing / The close enacts and counsels of [the] heart' (117–18).[37]

Aaron here simply inverts the usual early modern assumption that their seeming inability to blush was a sign of the fundamental shamelessness of dark-skinned peoples, whilst (as Thomas Wright

---

[34] Karen Newman, '"And Wash the Ethiop White": Femininity and the Monstrous in *Othello*', in Jean E. Howard and Marion F. O'Connor, eds., *Shakespeare Reproduced: The Text in History and Ideology* (New York, 1987), pp. 143–62.

[35] Thomas Adams, *The Blacke Devill or the Apostate* (London, 1615), sig. B3v. Compare Beatrice-Joanna's response to Deflores in *The Changeling*, the 'ominous, ill-faced fellow' whom she considers suited to murder by his very appearance: 'Blood-guiltiness becomes a fouler visage, / And now I think on one' (2.1.53; 2.2.39–40); 'honest' Deflores, significantly, is Middleton and Rowley's reworking of Iago.

[36] See above, n. 2.

[37] A similarly defiant apology for blackness is offered by Zanthia, the villainous black Moor of Fletcher and Massinger's *Knight of Malta*, whose colour is denounced as 'hell's perfect character' (4.1.77), but who boasts that her 'black Cheeke [cannot] put on a feigned blush / To make me seeme more modest then I am. / This ground-worke will not beare adulterate red, / Nor artificiall white, to cozen love' (1.1.193–6). Cf. also the Moorish Zanche in Webster's *The White Devil* who, familiar with the proverbial impossibility of 'wash[ing] the Ethiop white (5.3.261–2), professes herself 'proud / Death cannot alter my complexion,/ For I shall ne'er look pale' (5.6.229–31). On darkness as a trope of mystery and impenetrability in the period, see Kim F. Hall, *Things of Darkness: Economies of Race and Gender in Early Modern England* (Ithaca, NY, 1995), pp. 46–9.

argued) the blushing of white skin revealed a 'natural inclination to virtue and honesty'.[38] Of course there is a vicious contradiction in Aaron's boasting, since though he claims an absolute consistency between his black appearance and his dark interior, he also insists that, by comparison with the 'treacherous colour' that so readily exposes the falsehoods of Chiron and Demetrius, his complexion triumphantly conceals the counsels of his heart, rendering him, in the last resort, dangerously illegible: rather as Hamlet's 'nighted colour' and 'customary suits of solemn black' cast their 'inky cloak' over the dangerous matter 'within that passes show' (*Hamlet*, 1.2.68–85) the Moor's blackness at once enables and (paradoxically) bespeaks a kind of concealment. So it is too with Adams's black devil, with his 'brasen face, which no foule deed, nor reproofe for it, can make to change colour. How can it be otherwise? For a *blacke Devil* can no more blush, then a blacke Dog.'[39]

But if blackness is shown to be two-faced, so, oddly enough, is whiteness: though it is customarily associated with goodness and truth, in the case of Bianca, whose natural fairness is encoded in her very name, her extreme pallor at the sight of the wounded Cassio, is seized upon by Iago as proof of her guilty fear:

> Look you pale, mistress?
> Do you perceive the gastness of her eye?...
> Behold her well, I pray you, look upon her:
> Do you see, gentlemen? Nay, guiltiness
> Will speak though tongues were out of use.
>
> (5.1.104–9)

Moreover, even the apparently shamefast language of the blush, that seeming guarantor of 'virtue and honesty', is not to be relied on, making whiteness a 'treacherous hue' in more than one sense. The blood that suffuses the blusher's cheek can, after all, bear witness to vicious guilt as much as to virtuous shame: thus Hamlet discovers in the 'looks' of Rosencrantz and Guildenstern 'a kind of confession... which [their] modesties have not craft enough to colour' (*Hamlet*, 2.2.279–80); while Brabantio can insist that his daughter's maiden innocence is demonstrated by 'a spirit so still

and tender that her motion / Blushed at herself' (*Othello*, 1.3.96–7). Similarly, in *Much Ado About Nothing*, Claudio interprets the 'thousand blushing apparitions' that suffuse Hero's 'angel whiteness' (4.1.159–61) as being either a deceitful 'sign and semblance' of maiden shame, or an involuntary confession of guilt:[40]

> Behold how like a maid she blushes here!
> O, what authority and show of truth
> Can cunning sin cover itself withal!
> Comes not that blood as modest evidence
> To witness simple virtue?...
> Her blush is guiltiness, not modesty. (4.1.34–42)

The word 'blush', it is worth remembering, meant a 'look' or 'glance' before it described a flushed cheek[41] – suggesting that this supposed revelation of inner truth might itself only be a product of the aggressive gaze.

A white face, from this perspective, comes to seem as tormentingly opaque as a black one; and the meaning of its 'look', Claudio's misprision suggests, is simply a function of the look that is cast upon it.[42] It is paradox of this sort, I suggest, that provides the basis for the more extensive and sophisticated treatment of colour anxiety in *Othello*, where the markers of what later came to be called 'racial' difference, serve as a crucial vehicle for the play's worrying at fundamental issues of

---

[38] See Sujata Iyengar, 'Heroic Blushing', Chapter 4 of *Shades of Difference*, p. 107.

[39] *Blacke Devill*, sig. L1.

[40] Similarly, in *The Revenger's Tragedy*, a play much concerned with vizards, masquing, and deceptive faces, the disguised Vindice longs for shameless 'Impudence... [to] turn my visage / And if I needs must glow let me blush inward / That this immodest season may not spy / That scholar in my cheeks, fool bashfulness' (1.3.5–12).

[41] *OED n.* 2 – cf. the still current 'at first blush'.

[42] In an astute analysis of this passage Iyengar observes how Hero's face is shown as equally opaque to her defender, the Friar: 'Claudio and the Friar create the symptoms they interpret and describe simultaneously. They can have no direct access to her thoughts and feelings; any claims based on an interpretation of her face are unavoidably misleading because it seems to offer a window to her heart but in fact can grant observers no such thing' (*Shades of Difference*, p. 126).

cognition. The default assumption in Shakespeare's Venice, we know, is that the colour of the face corresponds to the disposition of the heart. However, Desdemona's conviction that she 'saw Othello's visage in his mind' (1.3.250), and the Duke's reassurance to her father – 'If virtue no delighted beauty lack, / Your son-in-law is far more fair than black' (lines 287–8) – attempt to force a disjunction between inward and outward hue. In this they anticipate the celebration of 'Fayre NIGER' and 'his beautious race' in Jonson's *Masque of Blacknesse* (1605), 'Who, though but blacke in face, / Yet are they bright / And full of life and light' (99–104), or of the King of the Moors in Middleton's *Triumphs of Truth* (1613) who, though he appears 'As far from sanctity as my face from whiteness', boasts that 'However darkness sits upon my face, / Truth in my soul sets up the light of grace' (424–30). But Brabantio instinctively interprets the Moor's 'foul' colour as the unanswerable proof that he is 'damned' (1.2.62–3); and Iago, with his pious insistence that 'Men should be what they seem' (3.3.130), misses no opportunity to demonstrate that outward blackness is precisely the 'flag and sign' of an ineradicably evil 'nature': 'what delight' he asks Roderigo, can Desdemona possibly 'have to look on the devil?' (2.1.220–1).[43] Ironically in the play's final scene, even the good-natured Emilia will succumb to this construction of colour when she sets the angelic fairness of Desdemona against the tell-tale 'dirt' of her 'filthy bargain' – a murderer whose crime proves him 'the blacker devil' (5.2.155, 162, 131).

Part of Othello's tragedy is that, as an acculturated 'Moor of Venice', he so readily internalizes the Venetian reading of colour. It is surely significant that, confronted with Brabantio's charge that his 'witchcraft' has blinded Desdemona against the foulness of his looks, he seeks to deflect it by offering a 'round unvarnished tale' (addressed to the 'grave ears' of the senate) that presents their falling in love as a function not of looking but of speaking and hearing: 'It was my hint to speak . . . This to hear / Would Desdemona seriously incline . . . and with a greedy ear / Devour up my discourse . . . My story being done, / She gave me for my pains a

world of sighs . . . She wished she had not heard it . . . And bade me, if I had a friend that loved her, / I should but teach him how to tell my story / And that would woo her. Upon this hint I spake' (1.3.91, 125, 142–66). Brabantio's sarcastic 'I never yet did hear / That the bruised heart was pierced through the ear' (217–18), is as much a comment on the plausibility of Othello's narrative of wooing, as it is a dismissive response to the Duke's consolation; and when the Duke attempts further solace by reinforcing Desdemona's insistence on the fairness of the Moor's inward visage (287–8), he gives Brabantio a chance to return to the treachery of eyesight in a way that will come to resonate in Othello's consciousness with fatal effects: 'Look to her, Moor, if thou hast eyes to see: / She has deceived her father, may do thee' (290–1).

In the temptation scene, Iago will remind Othello of his father-in-law's jibe at precisely the point where the Moor seems about to persuade himself that, regardless of the ensign's insinuations, Desdemona's ability to love him in spite (or is it because?) of his appearance must be the guarantor of her truth:

> She did deceive her father, marrying you;
> And when she seemed to shake and fear your looks,
> She loved them most . . .
> She that so young could give out such a seeming
> To seel her father's eyes up, close as oak –
> He thought 'twas witchcraft! (3.3.209–14)

With terrifying swiftness Iago succeeds in twisting Othello's proof inside out, effortlessly turning the Moor's gaze back upon his own 'looks' in the process. The effect of this trick is to begin his

---

43 Compare the treatment of the lascivious Moor Zanthia/Abdella in Fletcher and Massinger's *Knight of Malta*, as a 'devils seed' (5.2.209) whose 'black shape' is said to be 'hels perfect character' 4.1.76–7, as if her demonic nature were inscribed upon her person, so that even 'hell fire cannot parch her blacker then she is' (5.2.176–7). That Othello was in the minds of these dramatists is suggested by the echo of Iago's 'you'll have your daughter covered with a Barbary horse' (1.1.210) in Norandine's closing dismissal of Zanthia as a 'Barbary mare' and of her lover Montferrat as a 'French stallion' (5.2.314).

victim's capitulation to Brabantio's reading of his appearance – starting with the self-lacerating speculation of 'Haply, for I am black' (266), and ending with the masochistic characterization of Desdemona's disgraced name as 'begrimed and black / As mine own face' (lines 389–90). At the fatal moment when the Moor calls up 'black Vengeance' against the 'fair devil' his wife, it is as if he has learned to recognize within the 'hollow hell' of his own 'bosom' (447–9, 478), the same 'foul [i.e. black] things' whose lurking presence Iago mockingly acknowledged hidden in the 'palace' of his own 'breast' (140–2).

The tortured logic that issues from Othello's sense of heightened visibility means that his colour – far from acting as protective camouflage, like Aaron's black face – seems to render him transparent. Where the shameless Iago, remains defiantly opaque to the end ('What you know, you know', 5.2.301), Othello even begins to imagine his skin as subject to the revelatory transformations of the blush. Merely to 'speak [Desdemona's] deeds,' he insists, would be enough to suffuse his face with shame – to 'make very forges of my cheeks / That would to cinders burn up modesty' (4.2.74–5). Yet of course the figure that he chooses is oddly self-contradictory, for the only effect of these hot blushes, it seems, is to return the Moor's face to its originary condition, to the blackness of cinders which the burning rays of the tropical sun were supposed to inflict on African skin: the shamefastness of the cheek transmutes into the fire of Hamitic shame. The Moor's colour, it appears, is like a fate that he cannot escape – something written as indelibly upon his face as 'hell's perfect character' is inscribed upon the black countenance of his kinswoman Zanthia in *The Knight of Malta*.[44]

Othello's famous self-inculpation at the point of death, when – after the vision of damnation in which he imagines fiends snatching his soul and whipping it from the 'heavenly sight' of Desdemona – he symbolically 'turns Turk', is like his final acknowledgement that the Duke's 'fair' Moor has indeed become Emilia's 'blacker devil'. It amounts to an act of apostasy uncannily like that of which Thomas Adams accuses his 'blacke Devil' – one

that suggests an unexpected symmetry between blackness and its typological opposite, the fairness of Iago's 'heavenly shows':

> Whilst this *blacke Devil* had a white face, & carried the countenance of religion, he . . . seem'd of that number for whom there was a continual remembrance in good mens intercessions . . . But when the white scarffe is plucked off this *Moores* face, and his *blacke* leprosie appeares . . . then is he singled out as an enemy to *Christ* . . . Whilst this *blacke Devil* mantled his tawny skin, and ulcerous hart with dissimulation of piety, there was outwardly some hopefull likelihood of his reformation . . . His *Hypocrisie* hath deceiued the world; his *Apostasy* hath deceived himselfe.[45]

Just as Othello comes to internalize the white reading of his own black face, so he has learned to see his wife's fair face as the guarantor of her goodness: 'Look where she comes –' he exclaims in the middle of the temptation scene, calling on her beauty as witness, 'If she be false, O then heaven mocks itself' (3.3.280). It is an extraordinary moment: since Othello has been rapt in soliloquy, his hortatory 'Look' can only be addressed to the audience, as if inviting them to confirm his reading of her fairness. But 'fair', as Macbeth's Witches in their triumphant celebration of doubleness will declare, can also be 'foul'. Just as the Duke seeks to console Brabantio with the reflection that Othello's colour is a mere vizard and that, seen from within, the General resembles one of those paradoxically named 'white Moors' who are 'far more fair than black', so Iago will persuade his victims that, by the same token, Desdemona's fair face is a mask for hidden 'foulness': 'There's none so foul and foolish thereunto' he tells Desdemona, playing on this confusion of opposites, 'But does foul pranks which fair and wise ones do' (2.1.140–1). 'Foul' is precisely the word that Othello will use to justify his wife's murder: 'O, she was foul!' (5.2.198) – blackening her in the same language that Emilia uses to endorse her husband's reading of the Moor's colour. In his sinister word-games with Desdemona upon their arrival

---

44 See above, n. 37.
45 *Blacke Devill*, sigs. K4v–L1.

in Cyprus, Iago is already thinking of the 'history of lust and foul thoughts', the secret 'pranks', 'foul disproportions, [and] thoughts unnatural' that he will convince first Roderigo and then Othello (2.1.250; 3.3.205, 237) are concealed by Desdemona's white skin. 'If she be black,' he says, juggling derisively with the play's physical and moral chiaroscuro, 'and thereto have a wit, / She'll find a white that shall her blackness fit' (2.1.132–3). In this dazzle of obscene word-play, Desdemona's 'wit' is nothing less than that source of dangerous 'knowledge' that lies between her legs – *Lear*'s 'forfended place'; and Cassio is the white/wight whose supposed 'fit[ness]' to 'fill it up' will successfully reveal her hidden black (3.3.250–1, 389) – thereby exposing her fairness as no different from the 'white-limed walls' of Aaron's fair-skinned hypocrites, or the 'whited sepulchres' of Matthew 23:27.

Iago's sleight of hand is given additional plausibility by a familiar strain of folk-allegory to which Othello's oxymoronic characterization of Desdemona as a 'fair devil' draws attention. 'The white devil,' proverb lore insisted, 'is worse than the black' (Tilley, D310), suggesting that whiteness is as likely to be a sign of false virtue and hypocrisy as of true purity. It was, of course, this same proverb that would supply the title not only for Webster's tragedy of courtly hypocrisy but for a second Thomas Adams pamphlet, *The White Devill, or, The Hypocrite Uncased* (1613).[46] For Adams the type of white devilry was Judas – 'A Devill he was, blacke within & full of rancour, but white without, and skinned over with Hypocrisie'[47] – a figure with a striking resemblance to Iago, in that he is not only the embodiment of false service, but a 'purser... [who] shuts himselfe into his pouch,' and who moves 'from covetousnes to hypocrisie, from hypocrisie to theft, from theft to treason, [and] from treason to murder'.[48] Given that Iago is so conspicuously made the covetous keeper of Roderigo's purse (1.1.2; 1.3.333–64; 4.2.186–200), it is perhaps not an entire coincidence that the Ensign's first betrayal of his General is made to echo Judas's treachery towards his master in Gethsemane;[49] and Iago does, of course, boast of

his shameless white devilry to the audience, as he schemes to 'turn [Desdemona's] virtue into pitch': 'When devils will the blackest sins put on, / They do suggest at first with heavenly shows, / As I do now' (2.3.336–45).

The sweetest pleasure of Iago's stratagem lies in blackening Desdemona by persuading Othello that the 'heavenly shows' of his own white devilry are to be found in the 'divine Desdemona' (2.1.73), the woman whose fair countenance Cassio (2.1.85–6), Othello (3.3.281, 5.2.142–3, 273, 277), Gratiano (5.2.206), and Emilia (5.2.131, 135) all identify with the goodness of 'heaven'.[50] The effect of Iago's insinuations is to transform Desdemona's body in the Moor's eyes into an incarnate lie – one whose 'unproviding' beauty conceals the bodily falsehood

---

46 Commenting on Webster's self-conscious play with the theatrical reality of cosmetic whiteness and artificial blackface, Iyengar concludes that the thrust of his play is to show that in face 'the white devil is *indistinguishable* from the black' (*Shades of Difference*, p. 139).

47 The uncasing of the white devil is enacted in Middleton's *A Game at Chess*, where the Black Knight Gondomar orders the upper garment removed from the White King's Counsellor Pawn: 'The whiteness upon him is but the leprosy / Of pure dissimulation. View him now: / His heart and his intents are of our colour' (3.1.261–3).

48 *The White Devill, or, The Hypocrite Uncased* (London, 1613), sigs. B1, F1.

49 Ernst Honigmann's Arden 3 commentary on Othello's 'Keep up your bright swords' (1.2.59) cites John 18.1–11, where Christ, betrayed by Judas (as Othello has been by Iago), is arrested by officers 'with lanterns and torches and weapons' (18.3; cf. s.d. at l.53.1) and orders Peter 'Put up thy sword into thy sheath' (18.11).

50 There is, of course, an interesting comparison to be made with the so-called Dark Lady sonnets, since they also deal with matters of love and false appearance. In them the enigma of the other is notoriously registered in a rhetoric of colour, playing on the familiar opposition between foul (meaning black as well as ugly) and fair (light-skinned as well as beautiful) in a manner that anticipates the recurrent oppositions of *Othello*; thus in Sonnet 139, for example, the poet blames himself for the 'over-partial looks' that serve to 'put fair truth upon so foul a face' since love compels the eyes to 'see not what they see'. Cf. also Dondolo in Middleton's *More Dissemblers Besides Women*, who boasts of his 'Gypsy-minded' deception: 'Though my face look of a Christian colour, if my belly were ripped up you shall find my heart as black as any patch about you' (4.2.46–9).

of her adulterous 'lying' with Cassio. In 4.1, as if echoing the clown's puns at the beginning of 3.2, Othello struggles to keep the promiscuously coupled meanings of 'lie' apart, but cannot do so; and his speech disintegrates into a fantasy of dismembered bodies that anticipates his resolve to 'chop [Desdemona] into messes' (4.1.193):

Lie with her? Lie on her? We say 'lie on her' when they belie her. Lie with her? 'Swounds that's fulsome! Handkerchief – confessions – handkerchief? . . . Pish! Noses, ears, and lips . . . O, devil!   4.1.33–40

This same fantasy of a body that 'lies' in a tormentingly double sense, will return to him in 5.2, when he is confronted by Desdemona's uncle, Gratiano, and seeks to persuade him of the deceptive truth of what shows fair, and what foul : 'O, she was foul! . . . there lies your niece . . . I know this act shows horrible and grim' (5.2.198–201).

Nowhere is Othello's baffled fixation upon the his wife's fair body more conspicuous than in the famous, and much illustrated, moment, at the beginning of the last scene, when, torch in hand, the black man parts the curtains of the nuptial bed to reveal Desdemona's sleeping form in all its immaculate whiteness: now is his chance to act out the fantasy of physical violation that would lay the proof of his 'cause' open to view. He has convinced himself that (as her name – 'Desdemon' (4.2.41; 5.2.25) – unluckily suggests) his wife is a 'fair devil' whose colour, like the theatrical make-up that whitens the boy-actor's face, is merely a 'well-painted' sign of 'hypocrisy against the devil', the false mask of one who is in reality, a 'black weed' (3.3.478; 4.1.249, 6; 4.2.67–8). Purging himself of his wife's image, one to which he attributes something of the dark magic of which he himself was accused by Brabantio ('Forth of my heart those *charms*, thine eyes, are blotted'), he imagines a revenge that will leave her bed emblazoned – like the handkerchief whose embroidery is sinisterly imbrued with 'maidens' hearts' (3.4.74) – with the marks of her hidden iniquity: 'Thy bed, lust-stained, shall with lust's blood be spotted' (5.1.36–7). But what he has not reckoned upon, ironically enough, is precisely the look of her.

Despite his resolve to 'chop her into messes' (4.1.193), Othello cannot bring himself to violate the flawless surface of his wife's body: 'I'll not shed her blood, / Nor scar that whiter skin of hers than snow, / And smooth as monumental alabaster' (5.2.3–5). To stain the 'lovely fair' (4.2.68) of Desdemona's white skin with blood would be to mark it with the red of shameful passion, thereby rendering visible her hidden foulness and advertising her private history as a 'public commoner': matching the red and white of the handkerchief in which he repeatedly 'sees' the evidence of her guilt, this sanguinary blush might, by seeming to 'write whore' upon the 'fair paper' of her flesh (4.2.71–3), appear to constitute the final 'ocular proof' he so desperately needs. But instead, the death he inflicts upon her leaves her body unmarked, a smooth, unblemished surface resembling the deathly beauty of 'monumental alabaster', or the virginal flawlessness of 'one entire and perfect chrysolite' (5.2.5, 143). Othello may accuse Desdemona of 'ston[ing] his heart' (5.2.65), but it is her body that the gorgon stare of his imagination turns to stone. To become stone, after all, would be to become all surface, to be incapable of that within which passes show, to be reduced to a condition in which there can no longer be any contradiction between outward and inward, face and heart, because the face in its unmoving and unmoved condition can speak only of itself, and its blank stare has only one thing (or nothing) to say.

Yet this act of erasure does not work quite as it should. When Othello, recognizing his terrible error, imagines himself at the day of judgement, he is drawn once more to the spectacle of Desdemona's inert whiteness: 'O ill-starred wench, / *Pale as thy smock*, when we shall meet at count, / This *look* of thine will hurl my soul from heaven, / And fiends will snatch at it' (5.2.272–4; emphasis added). 'Look' here refers as much to the deathly appearance of her body as to the look of reproach he imagines her giving him. This is the 'heavenly sight' that, in a revealing variation upon a familiar trope, has him in 'possession' – ironically, just as a demonic spirit might possess him. 'What delight,' Iago had demanded of

Roderigo, could Desdemona have 'to look on the devil?' (2.1.220–1): now it is as if the very pallor of her skin had the power, by its contrast with his own blackness, to reveal the devil in him. The terrible 'look' he imagines, of course, is nothing more than a function of how he now looks at her – itself determined by how he has learned to see himself. The looking-glass he makes of his wife cannot properly reflect who he himself is – 'he that *was* Othello' (282) – but it shows him, with a finality that even Iago could not have hoped for, how he *looks*. There is an ironic parallel here with the way in which Iago himself finds in the appearance of Cassio a glass for his own deformity ('He hath a daily beauty in his life / That makes me ugly', 5.1.19–20); but where Iago's reaction is to break the mirror that threatens, in his favourite phrase, to 'unfold' him, Othello's is to submit to the image in his Venetian glass. Nothing remains then, but for the Moor to kill the 'malicious . . . turbaned Turk' whom he now accepts as his own dark double, the 'outward face of [his] inner soul'. No wonder that Lodovico cannot himself bear to contemplate 'the tragic loading of [the] bed' that he sternly orders Iago to 'look on': 'The object,' he declares with a shudder, 'poisons sight – / Let it be hid' (363–4). *Othello*, he reminds us, is a play where looks can kill.

RED BUTTON SHAKESPEARE

ROB CONKIE

INTRODUCTION

This article is cued by Andrew Hartley's provocative discussion of the logical impossibility of performance criticism; he writes that

One's sense of what happened on stage is shaped by perspective, which may be about where in the house you were sitting (to one side, close enough to be spat upon by the cast, peering through opera glasses from The Gods) or it may be about where you happened to be looking at a given moment.[1]

It is also, akin to my previous writing on, and wrestling with, the indeterminacy of meanings generated by theatre production,[2] structured in order to facilitate these multiple perspectives. Thus, somewhat perversely perhaps, I have fixed upon the model of interactive sports coverage, whereby the viewer can, by virtue of the remote control red button, appreciate the spectacle from a number of alternative perspectives. On the football (soccer) pitch these include: regular viewing angle; bird's eye view; goal-to-goal; 'player-cam'; highlights reel; 'fanzone'.[3] For the purposes of this close reading[4] of (a section of) performance, *King Lear* (3.7, the blinding of Gloucester) at the reconstructed Globe in London (2008), the perspectives upon, or from, which I originally wanted to focus were: the yard – 'front and centre'; upper gallery; the Lord's rooms; production archives; focus on a specific player; groundlings – a focus on the audience; facial expressions; delivery of text – pauses, inflection, emphases. I have incorporated the majority of these perspectives: they, in turn,

are followed by alternative readings of the play and production as a whole which are informed by the various perspectives of the (closely read) blinding scene.

I have, albeit too neatly, aligned details of the production with the various viewing perspectives. Thus, watching the production as a 'groundling', front and centre, if such a designation has currency in a circular playhouse, I have focused on the actions and gestures of the actors. From the upper gallery, not quite The Gods as in theatres such as the Olivier (London) or the old Royal Shakespeare Theatre (Stratford-upon-Avon), I have concentrated on the overall blocking and movement of the scene. These descriptions are of the type John Russell Brown labels the 'factual details of staging at particular moments',[5] the former notes

---

[1] Andrew Hartley, 'The Schrödinger Effect: Reading and Misreading Performance', p. 233 in this volume. An earlier version was given as a seminar paper in 'Shakespearean Close Reading, Old and New' at the International Shakespeare Conference, Stratford-upon-Avon, 2008.

[2] Rob Conkie, 'Sudokothellophobia: Writing Hypertextually, Performatively', *Shakespeare Survey 60* (Cambridge, 2007), 154–69.

[3] Player-cam focuses exclusively on one player (for 15 minutes); Fanzone is a commentary on the game by an extremely zealous fan from either side.

[4] This article was shaped especially by its early contexts of reception: firstly, as a contribution to the 'Shakespearean Close Reading, Old and New' seminar at the 2008 ISC (see note 1, above); and secondly, as part of the Shakespeare in Performance network discussions on theatre reviewing; more of this later.

[5] John Russell Brown, 'Shakespeare's Secret Language', seminar paper, 'Shakespearean Close Reading, Old and New', p. 2.

attesting to the micro-details of the action and latter to the macro. This part of the article resembles an extended prompt-book. The left side view turned out to be a less than ideal vantage point, at least for the production as a whole. However, not being able to see very well did focus the aural narrative of the production, especially as I was directly beneath the thunder-making machine, so I have here recorded sound effects, vocal inflections, non-textual vocals and audience responses. From the right side view I ignored the action on stage and looked only and more closely at the audience, mainly in the yard, as they watched the scene. I have focused, in particular, on three teenagers leaning against the 'front' edge of the stage and have attempted to describe their body language, facial expressions and verbal responses. Susannah Clapp, reviewing the production for the *Observer*, provides an apposite summary of my intentions here:

The audience's ultra-audible reactions to all this – gulps and shudders and gasps and sniggers and bleats of encouragement, as if everything were being seen for the first time – are an amplifying layer to the action, an echo-chamber which demonstrates how quick-changing are the moods and incidents before you. If you recorded their reactions you'd hear the beat of the play. The Globe is Shakespeare's electro-cardiogram.[6]

The next part of the article attempts to give eyes and ears to these multiple perspectives via four parallel columns spread over two pages each. Column 1 reproduces the text of the scene, including the deletions.[7] Column 2 documents the actions, gestures and movements of the scene; column 3 is the aural or soundtrack recording of the scene; column 4 is the description of the audience. The notes in columns 2, 3 and 4 are recorded chronologically and in parallel with the moment that the text is spoken. Thus, the description of the text-in-production is 'thickened' by 'interactive' cross-references to its delivery, embodiment, staging, acoustic accompaniment and reception. In doing this, I am attempting to at least partially address Pascale Aebischer's reservations about writing about performance: she argues that

Performance is characterised by its ephemerality, spontaneity, productive interaction between spectators and actors, and the subjectivity of its reception . . . In writing about performance, a physical, three-dimensional medium is flattened into two dimensions, leading inevitably to distortions and misrepresentations.[8]

My intention, with the full acknowledgement that I may be multiplying these distortions and misrepresentations, is to provide perhaps two-and-a-half dimensions; to raise the flattening, and to grasp or glimpse the ephemeral, spontaneous and subjectively received interactivity.

The most recent publication about London's reconstructed Globe theatre, *Shakespeare's Globe: A Theatrical Experiment*, echoes both Aebischer's concerns above and my attempts to tackle them via the Red Button structure which follows below. The editors explain that 'Rather than flattening opposing positions, we have set up a structure that highlights differences in approach in order to propose a new kind of criticism that can incorporate a more complex understanding.'[9] Indeed, the structure of the first part of the book on the 'Original Practices' Project is organized in a very similar fashion to my parallel columns: Stage action; Stage appearance; Music and sound; Actor/audience interaction. Given that Christie Carson goes on to explain that 'the volume has been designed to mimic the theatrical process of creation in that it allows each contributor to speak to his or her area of expertise in order to provide an integrated debate',[10] and that I too am attempting to offer an integrated 'mimic[ry of] the theatrical process', this synchronicity is perhaps not overly surprising. And lastly on this theme, the Globe has sought, as

---

6 Susannah Clapp in *Theatre Record*, 28 (2008), p. 499.

7 The deletions are scored by a faded text; the production was based on the Folio text of the play; the quotations hereafter are from the New Penguin edition of the play, edited by George Hunter (1972) and introduced by Kiernan Ryan (2005).

8 Pascale Aebischer, *Shakespeare's Violated Bodies: Stage and Screen Performance* (Cambridge, 2004), p. 17.

9 Christie Carson and Farah Karim-Cooper, *Shakespeare's Globe: A Theatrical Experiment* (Cambridge, 2008), p. 6.

10 Carson, *Shakespeare's Globe*, p. 30.

many professional (Shakespearian) companies do, to archive its productions on video. Unlike most of them, the productions at the Globe have been recorded from three perspectives; the cameras are labelled 'face-on', 'lozenge' (which refers to a diamond shape; the camera is at 45 degrees from face-on) and 'side-on'. The intention has been to preserve some of the three-dimensionality which the theatre architecture orchestrates and which this article attempts faintly to replicate. Thus, I have illustrated columns 2, 3 and 4 with screen captures from this archival footage which almost precisely represent the same moment on stage[11] from the three various perspectives. The face-on images, which offer a clear view both of the groundlings and of the octagonal stage projection (more of that below), illustrate the column dealing with, appropriately enough, the front and gallery view of the production. The lozenge images, which are closer to the stage and show less of the audience, but also, importantly, the balcony spaces, illustrate the soundtrack column. Finally, the side-on images, which are also from considerably above the stage, illustrate the audience response column.[12] You have just finished reading the Introduction; what follows is the Interaction and then the Interpretation, the hermeneutic drive of which will be impelled by the various viewing perspectives.

---

[11] An asterisk marks the textual moment which is represented by the screen captures. The actors featured are: Peter Hamilton Dyer (Cornwall), Kellie Bright (Regan), Joseph Mydell (Gloucester), Kurt Egyiwan, Beru Tessema, Ben Bishop (Servants).

[12] Unfortunately every one of the side-on recordings was poorly focused but this does at least preserve the anonymity of those 'photographed' as well as figuring the verticality of the space. I am enormously indebted to Globe Librarian Jordan Landes and Archivist Victoria Northwood for their help with these materials.

ROB CONKIE

INTERACTION

3.7

Enter Cornwall, Regan, Gonerill, Edmund, and Servants

Through the centre doors

CORNWALL
Post speedily to my lord your husband; show him this
letter: the army of France is landed. Seek out the villain
Gloucester.

DSC, facing outward

Exeunt some of the Servants

REGAN
Hang him instantly.

GONERILL
Pluck out his eyes.

At the right pillar

Left pillar

CORNWALL
Leave him to my displeasure. Edmund, keep you our
sister company: the revenges we are bound to take upon
your traitorous father are not fit for your beholding.
Advise the duke, where you are going, to a most
festinate preparation: we are bound to the like. Our posts
shall be swift and intelligent betwixt us. Farewell, dear
sister: farewell, my lord of Gloucester.

Enter Oswald

How now! where's the king?

Centre door

OSWALD
My lord of Gloucester hath convey'd him hence:
Some five or six and thirty of his knights,
Hot questrists after him, met him at gate;
Who, with some other of the lord's dependants
Are gone with him towards Dover; where they boast
To have well-armèd friends.

Cornwall kisses Gonerill on the cheek.

CORNWALL
Get horses for your mistress.

Cornwall brings forward a chair, slowly and deliberately.

GONERILL
Farewell, sweet lord, and sister.

CORNWALL
Edmund, farewell.

Exeunt Gonerill, Edmund, and Oswald

Go seek the traitor Gloucester,
Pinion him like a thief, bring him before us.

Exeunt other Servants

Though well we may not pass upon his life
Without the form of justice, yet our power
Shall do a courtesy to our wrath, which men
May blame, but not control.* Who's there? the traitor?

Enter Gloucester, brought in by two or three

REGAN
Ingrateful fox! 'tis he.

He enjoys a long, sexual kiss with Regan, near right
pillar.* He continues looking at Regan, not at the
brought forth Gloucester.

Drums play

This is the last scene before the interval, almost 90 minutes into the production. Concentration is perhaps starting to wander. As Patrick Marmion wrote in the *Daily Mail*, 'with the interval held back for nearly two hours, the first half is particularly cruel on the £5 "groundlings" forced to stand in the open top arena' (*Theatre Record* 495).

Drums stop. Very fast text. Cornwall has a very deliberate speech pattern. He speeds up and slows down for effect. It is a controlled venom.

Indeed, a number of people are leaving before this scene, perhaps with sore feet or backs or perhaps delicate stomachs and aware of what is to come.

Cornwall responds 'ah'

trA-A-Aitor, long pause, Gloucester . . .

bring-him, pause, before-us . . . Then a LONG pause

Sounds of struggle from offstage, including Gloucester's muffled cries

The audience switch their focus from the kiss next to the right pillar to the centre doors, through which Gloucester is being brought.

CORNWALL
Bind fast his corky arms.

Turning to face Gloucester

GLOUCESTER
What mean your graces? Good my friends, consider
You are my guests: do me no foul play, friends.

Gloucester standing behind the chair (slightly USC; locus)

CORNWALL
Bind him, I say.

Servants bind him

REGAN
Hard, hard. O filthy traitor!

With a thick rope, his arms by his side

GLOUCESTER
Unmerciful lady as you are, I'm none.

Gloucester gestures his innocence with his hands (which should be pinioned).

CORNWALL
To this chair bind him. Villain, thou shalt find-

*Regan plucks his beard**

There are three servants behind Gloucester, Cornwall is to his left and Regan to his right.
Cornwall stretches his arms theatrically.

GLOUCESTER
By the kind gods, 'tis most ignobly done
To pluck me by the beard.

REGAN
So white, and such a traitor!

GLOUCESTER
Naughty lady,
These hairs, which thou dost ravish from my chin,
Will quicken, and accuse thee: I am your host:
With robbers' hands my hospitable favours
You should not ruffle thus. What will you do?

CORNWALL
Come, sir, what letters had you late from France?

REGAN
Be simple-answered, for we know the truth.

CORNWALL
And what confederacy have you with the traitors
Late footed in the kingdom?

Enter the lute player, above right.
Cornwall clicks his fingers to motion the Servants back.

REGAN
To whose hands have you sent the lunatic king? Speak.

GLOUCESTER
I have a letter guessingly set down,
Which came from one that's of a neutral heart,
And not from one opposed.

Cornwall clips the back of Gloucester's head.

CORNWALL
Cunning.

Cornwall and Regan semi-circle Gloucester.

REGAN
And false.

CORNWALL
Where hast thou sent the king?

GLOUCESTER
To Dover.

Gloucester cries 'oh' as he is pinioned

Gloucester emphasises 'UNmerciful lady'

'Come sir', almost as if to the musician; from above he plays a pleasant tune on his lute. After a considerable pause, Cornwall speaks to Gloucester, 'what letters . . . ?'

Regan stretches the vowel on 'simple' . . . trA–A–Aitors

Singing from above accompanies the lute.

I suspect many in the audience do not know what is coming next; their attention is wandering.

This text is done very swiftly.

Bang

    Bang

A young woman is startled by Regan's venom.

        Bang

REGAN
Wherefore to Dover? Wast thou not charged at peril–

CORNWALL
Wherefore to Dover? Let him first answer that.

GLOUCESTER
I am tied to the stake, and I must stand the course.

REGAN
Wherefore to Dover,* sir?

GLOUCESTER
Because I would not see thy cruel nails
Pluck out his poor old eyes; nor thy fierce sister
In his anointed flesh stick boarish fangs.
The sea, with such a storm as his bare head
In hell-black night endured, would have buoy'd up,
And quench'd the stellèd fires:
Yet, poor old heart, he holp the heavens to rain.
If wolves had at thy gate howl'd that stern time,
Thou shouldst have said 'Good porter, turn the key,'
All cruels else subscribed: but I shall see
The wingèd vengeance overtake such children.

CORNWALL
See't shalt thou never. Fellows, hold the chair.
Upon these eyes of thine I'll set my foot.

GLOUCESTER
He that will think to live till he be old,
Give me some help! O cruel! O you gods!

REGAN
One side will mock another; the other too.

CORNWALL
If you see vengeance,–

First Servant
Hold your hand, my lord:
I have served you ever since I was a child;
But better service have I never done you
Than now to bid you hold.

REGAN
How now, you dog!

First Servant
If you did wear a beard upon your chin,
I'd shake it on this quarrel. What do you mean?

CORNWALL
My villain!

They draw and fight

First Servant
Nay, then, come on, and take the chance of anger.

REGAN
Give me thy sword. A peasant stand up thus!

Takes a sword, and runs at him behind

Cornwall, moving from the left pillar to USC takes off his dark jacket to reveal a crisp white shirt.

[Cornwall gets Gloucester's eye from the upstage ledge of the right pillar]

Again, Cornwall looks at Regan, not Gloucester, as he says this.

Cornwall puts his finger 'in' Gloucester's eye, pulls it out, complete with lengthy eyestalks, and throws it backstage.

Regan daubs herself with Gloucester's blood so that she has red eye-shadow.

The servant steps in between Cornwall and Gloucester.

Cornwall takes a sword from the other servant but is slashed across the belly.

Regan takes a dagger from the unwitting other servant, and stabs 1st servant from behind.

Note the lute ↓ player.

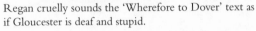

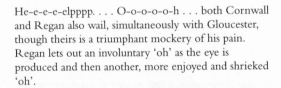

Regan cruelly sounds the 'Wherefore to Dover' text as if Gloucester is deaf and stupid.

Gloucester's reply separates each word of the first two lines, giving special emphasis to his defiance.

Regan gives a surprised laugh.

He-e-e-e-elpppp. . . . O-o-o-o-o-h . . . both Cornwall and Regan also wail, simultaneously with Gloucester, though theirs is a triumphant mockery of his pain. Regan lets out an involuntary 'oh' as the eye is produced and then another, more enjoyed and shrieked 'oh'.

The audience are a mixture of laughter and 'eurrgh' sounds; mostly laughter, for a good few seconds. This gives way to tittering.

Backing away from the front of the stage and not leaning on it.

Open-mouthed, and moving up and down, as if to protect themselves but still be able to see.

Shrink and turn away; again, hands over mouth and then wringing of hands.

First Servant
O, I am slain! My lord, you have one eye left
To see some mischief on him. O!

Dies

CORNWALL
Lest it see more, prevent it. Out, vile jelly!*
Where is thy lustre now?

GLOUCESTER
All dark and comfortless. Where's my son Edmund?
Edmund, enkindle all the sparks of nature,
To quit this horrid act.

REGAN
Out, treacherous villain!
Thou call'st on him that hates thee: it was he
That made the overture of thy treasons to us;
Who is too good to pity thee.

GLOUCESTER
O my follies! then Edgar was abused.
Kind gods, forgive me that, and prosper him!

REGAN
Go thrust him out at gates, and let him smell
His way to Dover.

Exit one with Gloucester

How is't, my lord? how look you?

CORNWALL
I have received a hurt: follow me, lady.
Turn out that eyeless villain; throw this slave
Upon the dunghill. Regan, I bleed apace:
Untimely comes this hurt: give me your arm.

Exit Cornwall, led by Regan

Second Servant
I'll never care what wickedness I do,
If this man come to good.

Third Servant
                    If she live long,
And in the end meet the old course of death,
Women will all turn monsters.

Second Servant
Let's follow the old earl, and get the Bedlam
To lead him where he would: his roguish madness
Allows itself to any thing.

Third Servant
Go thou: I'll fetch some flax and whites of eggs
To apply to his bleeding face. Now, heaven help him!

*Exeunt severally**

Cornwall holds Regan by the thigh as she takes out
Gloucester's other eye. Note the young woman ↑
unable to watch. . . . Regan puts her hands over, and
perhaps inside, Gloucester's eyes.

Regan points 'downstage' towards the front.

This exit is postponed, or takes a very long time,
because Gloucester and his aide are the last figures off
the stage.

Cornwall and Regan share another long kiss.

Cornwall's shirt and Regan's face are covered in blood.
Gloucester is helped, his hand outstretched, downstage
and over the extra thrust, down its steps and through
the audience, who part to allow him through. A sword
and the chair are left on stage.

Again, all three of them scream as the other eye is taken out. 'O-o-o-u-u-u-t-t-t' – Gloucester, 'No, no' – 'v-i-i-i-i-l-e j-e-e-ll-y.'

A father shields his daughter who, right next to the octagon, turns away from the scene.

'Where / is / thy / lu-u-u-stre / now?' Again, there is laughter, not as much as before, and 'eurggh' sounds from the audience.

Backing away from the stage again, pointing at the blinded Gloucester.

Regan is panting, sort of post-orgasmic sighing.

'h-A-A-A-t-es thee.'

Looking at one another grinning.

On the kiss the audience cannot help but laugh.

The song and lute continue

There is murmuring in the audience

Applause

Starting to discuss what happened.

INTERPRETATION

It might be worth briefly explaining my choice of the blinding scene as exemplary of what K. A. Ewert has described as 'a production's inflected moments where we most intensely feel meaning being made'[13] – my metonymic engine driving the play and production as a whole. I should confess that I have arrived at these comments somewhat *ex post facto*, and that my selection of the blinding scene as central and illuminating of the whole was largely intuitive or arbitrary. Nevertheless, J. I. M. Stewart's focus on this scene explores, irrespective, or perhaps even because, of its physical barbarity, the 'disinterested aesthetic concern'[14] which creates a structural, thematic and expressive completeness. Jay Halio, in a brief note, also focuses upon the structural underpinning and importance of the scene, though the structure he appeals to is mythopoetic, the scene's 'profound underlying motivation'.[15] These observations are further underlined by the history of the play in performance, where, in many productions, including the one under discussion here, the blinding of Gloucester immediately precedes, and builds up to, the interval, a fact sometimes explained by the desire to prevent audience members coming back late after the break in order to avoid the violence.

Watching the production from the 'front and centre' of the yard focused a particular kind of response. Indeed, the front and centre of the yard was itself focused by an extra thrust, an outcrop of staging made of a short jetty and an octagonal platform which projected another twenty feet into the yard, and from which steps descended into the yard and facilitated entrances and exits through the groundlings (as well as this, an additional façade was inserted on the 'upstage' wall with sliding doors which removed about four feet of the stage depth). One problem of this imposed architecture, at least from my overall, if not front and centre, perspective, was that it reduced the wooden O into a D or perhaps an arc. Thus, as significant amounts of the action occurred on the projected octagon, in the midst of the spectators, as it were, the staging seemed to treat the pillars as a proscenium arch and

to leave most of the stage area closest to the exits largely ignored. This meant that the yard areas to the 'side and back' were mostly unpopulated, even when the production was sold out, and that upper gallery seats to the back and side represented very poor viewing value. I will return to the benefits this afforded me for the aural reading of the play, but, by contrast, front and centre, at £5, if you could stand for the pre-interval 100 minutes, represented excellent value.

The discomfort produced by such a long time standing perhaps encouraged the groundlings to empathize with the pain Gloucester was about to go through: and this is the key to my yard interpretation. Here, front and centre, and so often directly appealed to, this position foregrounded the notion of empathy, sympathy and identification with the dispossessed or those suffering within the play. Like Miranda's viewing of the tempest, the groundlings could proclaim of both the blinding and this play's own storm scene, as well as other moments, 'O, I have suffered / With those that I saw suffer!' (*The Tempest*, 1.2.5–6). Thus, the key lines of the production, in terms of this reading or perspective, were Lear's heartfelt

> Poor naked wretches, wheresoe'er you are,
> That bide the pelting of this pitiless storm,
> How shall your houseless heads and unfed sides,
> Your looped and windowed raggedness, defend you
> From seasons such as these? O, I have ta'en
> Too little care of this.   (3.4.28–33)

This speech was delivered from the octagonal platform and predominantly and directly to the yard audience. The rest of the theatre was still and silent and David Calder's Lear was able to conversationally and empathetically discourse with those just a few feet from him, in stark contrast to the noise

---

[13] K. A. Ewert, 'Close Enough Readings? Or, Trying to Ascribe the Actor's Part in Analyzing Performance Texts', seminar paper, 'Shakespearean Close Reading, Old and New', p. 1.

[14] J. I. M. Stewart, 'The Blinding of Gloster', *The Review of English Studies*, 21 (1945), 266–70.

[15] Jay Halio, 'Gloucester's Blinding', *Shakespeare Quarterly*, 43 (1992), 223.

of the storm and his almost-doomed attempts to shout above it. Unfortunately, each time I saw the production the weather was perfectly clement and thus any of the unique kinds of new Globe frisson which develop from atmospheric serendipities were absent.[16]

Though such bad weather was absent (during my visits), the 'poor naked wretches' were palpably present. At times they were amongst the yard audience with strange sound devices stressing the atavistic nature[17] of the play (I cannot seem to keep the aural reading discrete from this one), and they were sometimes also on stage, in particular during the hovel scene (3.6). Benedict Nightingale observed that 'You won't see many Lears . . . discover such sympathy for the world's "poor naked wretches", here a swarm of vermicular men.'[18] They came up through the trap with a loud crash and then gathered 'upstage' on pillows as Lear madly arraigned his elder daughters. That these accusations were offered also to the audience forced an incongruity with the words; as Lear shouted and pointed outwardly it made no sense when the Fool joked and also pointed to the audience, 'I took you for a joint-stool' (Q sc. 13.47), when several such stools were on the stage itself. Also up from the trap, and mostly naked and wretched, was Poor Tom and he too did many of his 'set pieces' from the added stage projection. Lear identified with Poor Tom: as part of the younger man's antic disposition was to wave to imagined creatures in the yard and lower gallery, the older man's genuine lunacy followed suit and mirrored his mad-fellow; he watched him wave and then he, too, waved, comically straining to see at whom he waved. The identification was most poignant after twice (again comically) wondering whether Poor Tom had bequeathed his lands and all to his daughters, Lear understood their common situation and slowly embraced him. Here, the two men were identified as distressfully dispossessed; the groundlings, and the audience as a whole, were invited to sympathize with them and they did on several occasions via an audible 'aaaah' response.

Gloucester, of course, was about to be included in this fraternity of distress and dispossession and the audience was similarly invited to sympathize with him. Ironically enough, Joseph Mydell's Gloucester was presented as so sympathetic that many of the reviewers found it difficult to identify with him. Nightingale thought him 'a Gloucester so mild that you half-expect him to help out at his own eye extraction'[19] and Nicolas de Jongh reckoned somewhat heartlessly that 'Joseph Mydell's Gloucester suffers minimally'.[20] Perhaps the actor had read these reviews because later in the run he seemed to have acquired something of an edge, particularly in this scene. Though he looked back and forth at his interrogators as they spat their questions at him, he stared straight ahead into the audience on that moment when perhaps he moved from being, as Julie Carpenter observed, 'ineffectual',[21] to defiant and determined: 'I am tied to th' stake, and I must stand the course' (3.7.52). It was almost as if he was drawing strength from the yard for what he knew was inevitably coming, a baiting, whipping or worse. And then when his eyes were ripped out the audience responded very vocally (see below). As a final moment before the interval of powerful connection, Gloucester staggered with the help of a servant from the chair to the octagonal platform. Arm outstretched and trying to find his newly-blinded way, his first steps toward Dover were down into the yard and through the shocked, amused, entertained and included audience.

From above, the change, in relation to watching the scene and the play from the centre of the yard, was not of inclusion to exclusion but of participant to observer. Thus, whereas the 'poor naked wretches' text exemplified the groundling perspective, from this upper gallery point of view the most

---

[16] Victoria Northwood alerted me to the remarkable weather for the production on 1 May; the rain began on Lear's 'I shall go mad', the line prior to Cornwall's 'Let us withdraw; 'twill be a storm' (2.4.281–82), it gathered momentum by the time Cornwall advised 'Come out o'the storm' (2.4.304) and was torrential until Poor Tom was discovered in his hovel.

[17] Stewart, 'Blinding Gloster', p. 265.

[18] Benedict Nightingale, *Theatre Record* 28, p. 495.

[19] Nightingale, *Theatre Record* 28, p. 495.

[20] Nicolas de Jongh, *Theatre Record* 28, p. 497.

[21] Julie Carpenter, *Theatre Record* 28, p. 496.

resonant part of the play (for me) was Gloucester's Kottian despair, 'As flies to wanton boys are we to th' gods; / They kill us for their sport' (4.1.37–8). And whilst the production might have cast those on the ground as wretches, this architectural perspective cast the viewers, for their most expensive tickets, as gods watching the action unfold, present but removed. This experience, of witnessing the cruelty at a remove, of watching the movements unfold with far less direct contact or acknowledgement from the actors, reinforced a detached and voyeuristic relation to the mercilessness on display and made an explicit connection (again, for me) to the horrific images of torture from Abu Ghraib. It would have been possible, of course, to read the scene in the light of those recent abuses without the advantage of the upper gallery perspective but it served to focus several interesting parallels. Firstly, the notion of experiencing the violence at a mediated remove: in the upper gallery this was as a detached god looking down, akin to the *film noir* overhead camera; in the case of the Abu Ghraib images their availability was not within touching distance, as for a groundling, but by photographs accessed through the Internet. Thus, in both cases was a theatricalized violence moved from a private to a public sphere and, even more disturbingly, a significant aspect of that theatricality was of a masochistic sexuality.

This aberrant sexuality was introduced to the scene by Cornwall. Preparing to torture Gloucester, Cornwall took off his jacket, a gesture half world wrestling and half pornographic film. The kiss he shared with Regan as he rationalized their 'wrath' was prolonged and sexual and it was clear that his ensuing violence was a means of proving and igniting his virility and that it would take the form of a sex game. This fantasy was reinforced by his continuing to stare lustfully at his wife as he declared (to Gloucester) that 'Upon these eyes of thine I'll set my foot' (3.7.66). If, as Jay Halio, after the psychoanalysts, observes, the blinding represents a 'symbolic castration of Gloucester',[22] in this production it also served, albeit briefly, considering Cornwall's imminent death, as an erotic stimulus, a savage Viagra. Regan was very quick

to catch on, such that she confirmed what Aebischer has revealed to be almost a theatrical cliché in the middle daughter's portrayal, that of 'ferocious sexuality'.[23] At first – and I am prematurely sampling the aural record of the production again here – Regan's non-verbal response to the removal of Gloucester's first eye was of shock and thrilled surprise but the sound almost immediately developed into a kind of pre-orgasmic moan. From the blood of this first eye she perversely daubed herself with eye-shadow but further indulgences were to follow. Spurred on by the thrill of dispatching the servant, Regan joined Cornwall so that she extracted the second eye herself. She raised her knee and Cornwall gripped her thigh as they both screamed in echoed pleasure at Gloucester's excruciating pain. This time, with the blood on her hands from her own act of violence, she covered her face with it, luxuriating in the bloodlust. When she taunted her victim with, 'Thou call'st on him that hates thee' (3.7.86), she fingered his eyeless sockets and offered a brutal enactment of the castration trope. This godless sexuality, with its all-too-contemporary (if also Jacobean) confluence of violence and eroticism, was on view to the gods who were either powerless or simply too disinterested, akin to the majority of western liberal response to Abu Ghraib, to intervene.

I have had some difficulty in deferring the soundtrack reading of the scene and play, so integral has it been to the other perspectives, but here I privilege that particular perspective or, perhaps more accurately, hearing. The sounds I am focusing upon include delivery of text, non-verbal sounds, sound effects, music and audience responses; this last series of sounds also blurs my interpretative categories. As mentioned earlier I was alerted to this reading because of my attempt to watch the play from the 'back' and 'left side' of the stage. Not able to see much of the action, which was obscured by the stage left pillar when relatively static and on the octagonal platform, and being beneath the thunder and wind machine, I focused

---

[22] Halio, 'Gloucester's Blinding', p. 222.
[23] Aebischer, *Shakespeare's Violated Bodies*, p. 180.

instead on what I could hear; I suppose, to paraphrase the most illustrative text from the rest of the play, from here I was seeing the play 'feelingly'. Or, to push this slightly further, this was a Gloucester-like blind-spot which enabled an other-sensory perspective.

Ironically, the blinding scene itself was perhaps best apprehended from this vantage point; whilst much of the play was obscured from here, the unwatchable was clearly on view, located at the locus. Perhaps the director Dominic Dromgoole had intuitively hit upon Bruce R. Smith's contention that 'An actor may occupy the position of greatest *visual* presence at the geometric center of the playhouse, but he commands the greatest *acoustical* power near the geometric center of the space beneath the canopy.'[24] I have already mentioned the various screams and moans from the stage and I will later return to the various groans and laughter in the audience, but the most striking element of the soundtrack in this scene was of the accompanying lute and song: interestingly, the former sound was diegetic, that is, contained within the world of the play, whereas the latter sound was non-diegetic, working in the same way as a film score. As Cornwall prepared to extract the information he required from Gloucester he gestured to a musician above, perhaps a paid employee of Gloucester's own castle if this is not making of the play too realistic a world, and clicked his fingers to cue a song. The lute player duly obliged with a gentle tune and continued to play throughout the torture scene and until the interval. The singer joined in later but given that she repeated her musical motif at various moments in the production I have described this music as non-diegetic. The website from which I obtained these definitions notes that 'A play with diegetic and non-diegetic conventions can be used to create ambiguity (horror), or to surprise the audience (comedy)'[25] and both of these effects were certainly created in this scene. The instruction and intrusion of the lute, I would argue, even more forcefully than associations to Abu Ghraib, connected this scene to Quentin Tarantino's controversial debut film *Reservoir Dogs*.

The obvious connection here is between the torture – in particular, the severing of the police officer's ear in the film and the extraction of Gloucester's eyes in the play – and also in the way extreme and aestheticized violence uncomfortably juxtaposes with comedy. Stevie Simkin has written similar comparative analyses and observes that 'Early modern tragedies, like graphically violent horror movies, often walk a fine line between seriousness and camp, between shock and laughter.'[26] He goes on to provide examples from *The Duchess of Malfi*, *'Tis Pity She's a Whore*, *The Atheist's Tragedy* and especially *The Revenger's Tragedy*. He also notes, appositely for this discussion, that 'At the other end of the spectrum, the blinding of Gloucester in Act 3, Scene 7 of *King Lear* (1604) provokes nothing but shock and horror, unless performed ineptly, or with parodic intentions'.[27] These ideas were, and were not, borne out by the new Globe's staging of the blinding of Gloucester; shock and horror were probably present, although the measuring of such responses might prove difficult, but there was also considerable laughter and the scene was performed neither ineptly nor with parodic intentions. The laughter was an effect, I think, of the appeal to the *Reservoir Dogs* culture, where not just Gloucester, but many of the audience themselves, were stuck in the middle with Cornwall and, Miss Blonde, Regan.

The repeated similarities of the two torture scenes beg the question of whether it is more Tarantino, as famous for his creative plagiarism as Shakespeare, who has influenced the new Globe staging of Gloucester's blinding, or whether he has ripped the scene off, in a demonstration of cycles of violence, from his Jacobean forebear. In any case, the following parallels and juxtapositions may be observed:

---

[24] Bruce R. Smith, *The Acoustic World of Early Modern England: Attending to the O-Factor* (Chicago, 1999), p. 214.

[25] http://filmsound.org/terminology/diegetic.htm, accessed June 2, 2008.

[26] Stevie Simkin, *Early Modern Tragedy and the Cinema of Violence* (Basingstoke, 2006), p. 192.

[27] Simkin, *Early Modern Tragedy*, p. 193.

1. the victims are both 'tied to a chair'[28] (KL > RD)
2. the torturers both theatrically remove their jackets as if 'getting down to business' (RD > KL)
3. the victims both cue their own torture (KL > RD)
   a. Gloucester's protestations that he 'would not see thy [Regan's] cruel nails / Pluck out his [Lear's] poor old eyes' and that he 'shall see / The wingèd vengeance overtake such children [Gonerill and Regan]' (3.7.54–5, 63–4) prompts his punishment: 'See't shalt thou never' (3.7.65)
   b. Marvin, the police officer, probably wishes he hadn't defiantly proclaimed, 'you can torture me all you want'
4. the victims are tortured to playful musical accompaniment (RD > KL)
   a. Gloucester's lute player
   b. K-Billy's Supersounds of the Seventies plays Stealer's Wheel tune 'Stuck in the Middle with You'
5. the victims have their faces horrendously disfigured, eyes and ear (KL > RD)
6. the victims wounds are mocked (RD < > KL)
   a. Regan fingers Gloucester's eye-sockets as she reveals Edmund's treachery
   b. Blonde speaks into Marvin's severed ear
7. both torturers are interrupted (and eventually killed) by an appalled spectator
8. the appalled spectators who intervene are both killed by accomplices of the torturers

One moment where the two scenes diverge is the actual viewing of the disfiguring violence: the audience at the Globe can decide for themselves whether to look away; in the film, this decision is made (directorially) for the audience.

There is one detail of this scene, especially well-viewed from the 'left back' position, that I have yet to discuss, and it is akin to the perverse, 'black comedy' described above. The Globe's props department, perhaps striving for anatomical authenticity, provided eyes (both of which were hidden on the 'upstage' side of a pillar ledge) with lengthy and blood-dripping eyestalks. In my view, it was

these grotesque, tentacle-like sinews that prompted the audience's prolonged laughter and groaning after each gouging, and so exaggeratedly gruesome were they that I cannot believe that they were not intended to produce a mixture, in what was a constantly funny production, of comedy and horror. Perhaps the ambivalent presentation and reception might be theorized along Bakhtinian lines where the dislocation is produced because the comical grotesque of corporeal materiality properly associated within the 'lower bodily stratum' was here relocated to the eyes, more typically figured as windows to the soul. Stewart cites, in order to contest it, Robert Bridges's argument that Shakespeare's frequent depiction, and, regrettably, seeming celebration, of all kinds of debasement, was more a reflection of the audience than the author; he describes, after Bridges, 'the depraving effect of the playhouse public upon Shakespeare's art'.[29] In this production such depravity was staged in order to provoke and appeal to a playhouse public whose appetite for spectacular violence, both shocking but also comical, was fed not by bear-baiting, whipping and hanging but by parallel representations – maiming, dismemberment and decapitation, in cinemas and at home on DVD.

In moving towards a conclusion, I want to reflect on some critical writings about Gloucester's blinding, especially as they relate to audience reception, and also as they were either consolidated or challenged by the experience of being in, and watching closely, an audience watching that act at the new Globe. Edward Pechter's argument that 'In the main our range of response is limited to mental action – sympathy, antipathy, perhaps judgment; and no other play of Shakespeare's . . . involves an audience so directly

---

[28] The quotations which refer to the scene from *Reservoir Dogs* are taken from Simkin's description, which highlights parallels with *The Revenger's Tragedy*; see *Early Modern Tragedy*, pp. 194–96. Simon Brown made some helpful observations on these parallels.

[29] Stewart, 'Blinding Gloster', p. 264.

and deeply with its characters'[30] sounds like a Hazlitt-like commitment to the play on the page, but he attributes these responses to spectators, not readers. He omits, lacking the advantage of an open-air theatre space, performative responses such as laughter, gasps, groans and chatter or physical movement such as turning away, shifting position or leaving the theatre altogether. However, Stewart, also lacking an approximate reconstruction of Shakespeare's theatre, supposes that 'the physical conditions of the Elizabethan public playhouse . . . evoked far stronger suggestions of participation on the part of the spectators than a modern theatre allows'.[31] He also wonders of the 'ruder part of the audience', those in the yard, whether they would respond to the blinding of Gloucester 'with malevolent glee'.[32] Though the 'ruder part' of the new Globe audience laughed at the blinding I detected not a hint of malevolence. In that three of my closely read subjects were teenagers I might colloquially (and perhaps patronisingly) relate their response as, 'Oh my God, I can't believe they did that; that was so gross.' A measure of this absence of malice was the silence that invariably greeted Regan's callous order, and the best joke of the scene, to 'Go thrust him out at gates and let him smell / His way to Dover' (3.7.92–3). Indira Ghose has written that this line is 'saturated with a savage sense of humour that the play incessantly replays',[33] but not once in the productions, either live or recorded, which I witnessed, did this line receive even a titter of response. Stewart's surmise about the 'ruder part' of the audience was confirmed to some degree, however, given that the spectators in the upper gallery did not, as far as I could tell, respond with the horrified laughter in the way that their less financially able, and usually somewhat younger, co-audiences had. Thus, not only has the new Globe focused further dimensions of audience response, it has also, especially by virtue of the methodology deployed here, revealed the way audience response can be differentiated according to the specific place of reception.

Pascale Aebischer has provided the most recent and concentrated analysis of this scene in the theatre:

It is one thing to know that Gloucester is blinded, but quite another to listen to and, especially, to *watch* the mutilation, to use our own eyes to watch the removal of somebody else's eyes in a space (the theatre) that is so contained that the audience, if it does not intervene, is made to feel complicit in the violence perpetrated.[34]

Aebischer to some extent overstates her argument when she writes 'that today theatregoers still find the scene literally unwatchable'[35] and I feel there are aspects of this complicity debate that require further teasing out. Simkin has similar reservations about Quentin Tarantino's explication of comedy and complicity in the ear-severing scene:

'I kinda defy anybody to watch Michael Madsen do that dance and not kind of enjoy it', he remarks on the DVD commentary, claiming that the comic lead into the torture implicates the audience: 'You are a co-conspirator.' However, Tarantino makes no attempt to analyse any further what this might mean in terms of audience response, or the audience's *awareness* of its response. Perhaps this lacuna, conscious or not, is simply a recognition that the scene does not have the power to do any such thing.[36]

I will return to these ideas shortly. There were occasional gestures in the new Globe audience that attested to the scene being 'literally unwatchable', hands in front of faces, turning away and such, but for the most part people looked on, even if between their fingers, with a mixture of shock and fun. I certainly, as a committed researcher, watched closely and much enjoyed the spectacle, even though I decided years ago, after watching David Fincher's brilliant film *Se7en*, that I would

---

[30] Edward Pechter, 'On the Blinding of Gloucester', *English Literary History*, 45 (Summer 1978), 181–200; p. 183.

[31] Stewart, 'Blinding Gloster', p. 269.

[32] Stewart, 'Blinding Gloster', p. 268.

[33] Indira Ghose, *Shakespeare and Laughter: A Cultural History* (Manchester, 2008), p. 198. Ghose lists a number of theories of laughter that pertain to the reaction to Gloucester's torture: 'a strategy of self-defence that enables us to face sources of fear or pain', p. 7; 'a hydraulic safety-valve for the unconscious', p. 9; 'Laughter at horror simultaneously invokes and domesticates precisely those aspects of the world that induce terror in us', p. 200.

[34] Aebischer, *Shakespeare's Violated Bodies*, p. 159.

[35] Aebischer, *Shakespeare's Violated Bodies*, p. 159.

[36] Simkin, *Early Modern Tragedy*, p. 197.

not subject myself to such films, the most recent and joyless incarnation of which has been the torture porn made famous by the *Saw* franchise. I watched, enjoyed, but in no way felt complicit in the stage violence that I witnessed. I must concede that I probably erred in watching the blinding scene from the upper gallery on my third visit to the production: by this time I was fully aware of what would unfold – de-sensitized, as it were – and thus the potential of the scene to implicate me in its terror was somewhat dissipated. If I had first watched the production from above I might have been appalled not only by the grotesque actions played upon the stage, but also by the barbaric and heartless responses of the £5 'stinkards'.

Perhaps part of the reason for me rejecting the notion of being complicit in the yard (and yet suspecting that I may have felt otherwise in the upper gallery) is explained by Aebischer's use of the word 'contained'; the implication, as I read this, is that the confinement of the theatre space exerts a kind of moral stifling of the ethically compromised spectator. The new Globe, again along Bakhtinian lines, might be thought of as an open and excessive rather than classical and closed space, and one that resists containment in the way that a darkened proscenium auditorium perhaps does not (at least as easily). Accordingly, the upper gallery space might be figured as in between the yard and a darkened auditorium in its capacity to contain (incidentally, sitting in the Gods at the Globe you are protected from the rain but neither can you see much of the sky). Thus, in the least contained yard space the visceral impact of the violence is shared by the collective, visible and unruly audience and made comic.[37] What Simkin describes as 'the audience's *awareness* of its response' is multiplied by the audience members' awareness of each other, although it might be worth also problematizing the post-modern ironic response as exemplified by, for example, Ricky Gervais's politically incorrect humour. Finally, though, perhaps Aebischer is right about complicity if the laughter and groaning exhibited by the yard audience could be

said to represent an intervention. Aware of their own response and unable to silently acquiesce to the horrors they see depicted, even as they know they are fictional, but also reflective of real events they have witnessed through hyper-real representations, the audience resist their implication in the events through groans, giggles, laughter, shielding their eyes or turning their backs.

It is not surprising, I suppose, that my analyses should highlight such contemporary readings of the historically staged text given that my interpretative structure has been inspired by recent developments in viewing technology. Perhaps Dominic Dromgoole's background in directing new writing also emphasizes the contemporary within the historical in his new Globe productions. Though I would probably have identified the specific intertexts without this structure it has certainly focused, in particular, my commentary on identification / sympathy and on complicity / intervention. The metonymic task of reading the play and production as a whole via the closely read part – of using Gloucester's extracted eyes as interactive and interpretative red buttons – has proven beyond the limits of this single article, but I can imagine future 'fan-zone' work where the four or more perspectives are contributed by different viewers watching a production at the same time. At a recent meeting of performance-focused Shakespearians in Stratford-upon-Avon, come together to consider the purpose and future of theatre reviews, six separate reflections upon this *King Lear* production, including the first draft of this article, were discussed. The most striking observation of all, offered by someone who did not see the production, was that the six papers might have described six different productions. I have here attempted to articulate variance, to provide two and a half dimensions, but I forecast and invite more concertedly collaborative, indeed *Rashomon*-like, tellings of theatrical stories.

---

37 This is akin – as my students have informed me – to the de-eroticization of pornography when viewed publicly, which usually becomes comic.

'MARK YOU / HIS ABSOLUTE SHALL?': MULTITUDINOUS TONGUES AND CONTESTED WORDS IN *CORIOLANUS*

ALYSIA KOLENTSIS

FIRST CITIZEN Before we proceed any further, hear
me speak.
ALL Speak, speak.
FIRST CITIZEN You are all resolved rather to die
than to famish?
ALL Resolved, resolved.
FIRST CITIZEN First, you know Caius Martius is
chief enemy to the people.
ALL We know't, we know't.
FIRST CITIZEN Let us kill him, and we'll have corn
at our own price. Is't a verdict?
ALL No more talking on't. Let it be done. Away,
away! (1.1.1–12)

The first moments of *Coriolanus* capture the clamour and defiance of 'a company of mutinous Citizens' and provide a fitting initiation into a dramatic environment that is saturated with competing forms of language. With this demonstration, a collision of voices that will be maintained and exploited over the course of the play is powerfully introduced. On one hand, the dominant noise belongs to the starving and querulous mob, whose chanted words seem unhinged from their typical interactive and communicative functions. The doubled words, all clipped vowels and hard consonants, acquire an incantatory quality more in line with extra-linguistic sounds than with units of dialogue. Yet even in the midst of this collective howl, a counter-force emerges. Out of the din rises the enlivening voice of the First Citizen, clarifying and directing the sound of the multitude. The result is a confluence of verbal styles; the mob's chanting is offset by a discrete, articulate voice, so that two systems of language – the excited babble of a group,

and the exhortative voice of an orator – collide. The pattern of competing voices that is established here is repeated throughout the play and, indeed, the various implications of 'voice' provide a potent subtext. The mob's racket provides a visceral signal of the warring voices that will populate the play, and the words of the individual citizens that emerge from the rabble reinforce the point. There is an early, marked emphasis on the conflict between command and resistance, especially in regard to permitted speech. Almost immediately, the citizens direct one another about what might be said about Caius Martius:

FIFTH CITIZEN Nay, but speak not maliciously ...
SECOND CITIZEN What he cannot help in his
nature you account a vice in him. You must in no
way say he is covetous.
FIRST CITIZEN If I must not, I need not be barren
of accusations. He hath faults, with surplus, to tire
in repetition. (1.1.33, 39–44)

As this first scene establishes, what is spoken and what is not said are of paramount importance, subject to the dictates of the commanding *must*. The point is cemented soon afterward as the tribunes

An excerpt of this material was presented at the Shakespeare Association of America annual meeting in 2008; I am grateful to seminar members for advice and insight. I would like to extend particular thanks to Lynne Magnusson, who provided thoughtful commentary on early drafts. My conversations with her have helped to clarify and refine my perspective on this material. Thanks also to Ian Lancashire, Jeremy Lopez, Carol Percy and Paul Werstine for their helpful comments on an earlier version of this article.

isolate what they deem the most telling aspect of Caius Martius's behaviour:

BRUTUS   Marked you his lip and eyes?
SICINIUS   Nay, but his taunts.

(1.1.255)

In the world of *Coriolanus*, words are held up as shared – and disputed – capital, and we are taught to pay attention to them above all else. The misanthropy so easily associated with Coriolanus is endemic to all of the play's characters; the climate of war extends to battles over language, where questions of who is permitted to speak, and which words are sanctioned, predominate. The first scene demonstrates the range and impact of different 'voices' that are variously discrete, collective, commanding and resistant. And what is highlighted about the nature of language is its communal – and hence contested – status. Instructions governing its appropriate use are rampant, its content cannot be agreed upon, and it is understood to be at once vital and maddeningly ineffectual: the prevailing compulsion to 'speak, speak' is countered by the suspicion that all of this talk only gets in the way of any real action. The First Citizen's protest of 'why stay we prating here?' (1.1.46) seems the natural response to a milieu in which so many voices – the 'multitudinous tongue' so loathed by Coriolanus (3.1.159) – are forced to coexist. The confused and desirous cry to 'speak' resonates through all of the action that unfolds over the next five acts. In fact, the details of verbal sparring and negotiation – the linchpins of dialogue around which linguistic exchange is structured – are in *Coriolanus* put on display. This article suggests that the minute details of encounters between speakers, including easily overlooked words such as verbs of volition and obligation, hold important information about power and compliance in the play. These words project a speaker's attitudes and desires into the realm of social discourse; at the same time, they tell us something about control, particularly over a contested future. For this discussion, I will focus on the most prominent example, the 'absolute shall' scene in which Coriolanus rails against the tribunes' impudent use of a powerful

word from which they are presumably debarred. The scene suggests how small words are at stake in *Coriolanus*: held up for scrutiny, surrounded by proprietary anxiety, and fought for, they are 'words with victims' that enact the struggle for social control.

My analysis here is grounded in the word *shall*, part of the category of modal verbs (others include *may*, *can*, *will* and their variants) that act as markers of necessity, possibility, volition and obligation, among other things. Speakers use modals to express things like permission and prediction, but these verbs also indicate a speaker's stance toward the conditions of his or her speech – in other words, they encode speakers' attitudes toward what they are saying and toward the audience that they are addressing. Therefore modal verbs, which 'pragmatically convey strong speaker-centred meanings',[1] represent one of the few ways that the self is grammaticalized, a means by which a speaker's self-positioning is integrated into the very structure of the language. Because it 'refers to the range of different ways in which speakers can temper or qualify their messages'[2] modality exposes how a speaker thinks, indicating his stance toward his own words and to the context in which he utters them. *Shall*, the commanding modal marker of obligation, has particularly strong associations with power and antagonism: it linguistically inscribes power relations, traces speaker expectations, and illuminates and insists on specific rules of social interaction. Such a word carries particular resonance in the conflict-focused milieu of drama, and especially in a play such as *Coriolanus*, which showcases tensions among civic duty, familial authority and responsibility, and personal ambition: '*Shall* expresses aspects of obligation and desire, and therefore showcases the boundary between the demands of a speaker's

---

[1] Susan Fitzmaurice, 'Tentativeness and Insistence in the Expression of Politeness in Margaret Cavendish's *Sociable Letters*', *Language and Literature*, 9 (2000), 7–24; p. 17.

[2] Suzanne Eggins and Diana Slade, *Analysing Casual Conversation* (London, 1997), p. 98.

public world and the wishes of his private one.'[3] So when Volumnia churlishly insists that the reluctant Virgilia go visiting with her – 'She shall, she shall' (1.3.75) – her modals of obligation inscribe not only her preferred version of the future, but also her social rank as Coriolanus's mother and Virgilia's elder, and the concomitant conviction that her wishes take precedence. Because they are a projection of speaker attitudes and desires into the realm of social discourse, modal verbs such as *shall* are socially charged words that act as a (frequently contested) site of contact between the self and the world. These words create an intersubjective space in which the various wants and expectations of speakers compete and clash, and so must be carefully negotiated.

In addition to encoding a stance specific to each speaker, modals tell us something about control, particularly over fraught future time. Rissanen notes that all modal verbs inscribe an attitude about human control vis-à-vis the future: 'they indicate either some kind of human control over events ('permission', 'obligation,' 'volition'), or human judgement of what is or is not likely to happen ('possibility', 'necessity,' 'prediction').'[4] Therefore, speakers' modal expressions convey their perceptions about what is required, expected or possible in the future. In the formal lexicon of modal theory – rooted in notions of actual and possible worlds – modal verbs such as *shall* represent a speaker's conscious attempt to transform a 'situation representation' (that is, a possible outcome in the future) into a 'world representation' (an actual, verifiable future outcome).[5] The effect of *shall* is that 'the situation representation turns out to be a true description of a world situation because the world situation is brought about by an agent.'[6] In other words, the defining feature of *shall* usage is the belief that one's own actions can bring about a future outcome: it is not merely hoped for, but actively sought. As a word that designates a speaker's capacity to bring about some future action, *shall* is held up in certain encounters as a prize to be claimed. In these heated contests, the 'victor' who lays claim to *shall* sees his or her intention for the future fulfilled.

Another important feature of the modals is their grammatical slipperiness. Pseudo-verbs with unique properties, they were in a state of transition during the early modern period, and so had potential for a 'wider range of meanings' in Shakespeare's English.[7] This semantic fluidity is important to my discussion because the early modern *shall*s of *Coriolanus* have a stronger association of obligation – retaining something of the old English *sceal* ('liable for debt') – and subtly different implications, than those of present-day English. As these origins suggest, *shall* is a forceful word which harnesses a specialized semantic legacy, one characterized by disparate power and required action. Therefore, while there are limited ways to articulate future action in the linguistic code of Early Modern English – with *will* and *shall* being staple components – these options are not identical. In using a modal expression such as *shall*, thereby suggesting or insisting that one is obliged to do something, speakers demand control over both their addressees and the future action dictated by *shall*. What is particularly interesting in terms of *Coriolanus* is that its spotlight on sanctioned language extends to the use of modals, as a play with an unusually high percentage of these words. In a quantitative study of grammatical modality in early modern English drama, Hugh Craig notes the elevated proportion of modal verbs in the tragedies, and observes that 'the highest count of all is in [Shakespeare's] last tragedy, *Coriolanus*'.[8] Craig suggests that the proliferation of modals can be traced to the play's preoccupation with 'tussles of will' and 'the applying and resisting of social leverage', the intersubjective

3 Joan L. Bybee, Revere Perkins and William Pagliuca, *The Evolution of Grammar* (Chicago, 1994), p. 262.

4 Matti Rissanen, 'Syntax', in *The Cambridge History of the English Language*, 6 vols. (Cambridge, 1999), vol. 3, p. 231.

5 See discussions in Alex Klinge, 'The English Modal Auxiliaries: From Lexical Semantics to Utterance Interpretation', *Linguistics*, 29 (1993), 315–57; pp. 325–53, and Michael Perkins, *Modal Expressions in English* (London, 1983), p. 14.

6 Klinge, 'English Modal Auxiliaries,' p. 350.

7 Rissanen, 'Syntax', p. 210.

8 Hugh Craig, 'Grammatical Modality in English Plays from the 1580s to the 1640s', *English Literary Renaissance*, 30 (2000), 32–54; p. 45.

jousting that the modals tend to enact: 'the diffi-cult relations between the individual will and the world, the tragic misfit between the two, are the special territory of *Coriolanus*, and the modals play a considerable part in articulating this struggle.'[9] The curious abundance of these words in the play, and their capacity to offer insight into a speaker's subjective perspective as well as interactive rela-tionships, make them a compelling object of study. Furthermore, an appraisal of the modal choices at work in the play – with a particular focus on the dialogue's contested *shall*s, weighted with the sense of obligation as well as the contested potential to control future outcomes – offers a commentary on the nuances of modals in use. This discussion aims to show that a reconsidered language-based approach to *Coriolanus*, grounded in close readings of the play's striking linguistic collisions between characters, exposes how modal expressions such as *shall* can sharpen our understanding of coer-cion and compliance in the play, and can unveil the transformative moment when the future is determined.

Language is consistently 'at stake' in *Coriolanus*, most apparently in the play's concern with the intricacies of pragmatic language use, its engage-ments with public forms of language and with ver-bal negotiation. Language is placed in the spot-light, both at the large-scale level of competing language systems and registers, and on the smaller scale of grammatical play and manipulation. Cori-olanus himself is a key figure in a language-based analysis of the play as an active participant in and manipulator of its broad linguistic networks. He purports to stand alone and declares his mistrust of words, fashioning himself as a soldier whose skill on the battlefield does not extend to the world of communication: 'When blows have made me stay I fled from words' (2.2.72). At the same time, however, he establishes himself as an astute reader of the systems of linguistic circulation in the play, and the skill that he consistently demonstrates in a wide array of speech situations suggests that he is neither as reticent nor as inscrutable as has some-times been suggested. Indeed, Coriolanus is one of Shakespeare's most verbose figures, speaking 'one

quarter of the play's 3,200 lines, a part larger than any in the tragedies except for Hamlet, Iago, and Othello'.[10] While he – the war-bred man who is 'ill-schooled / In bolted language' (3.1.323–4) – tends not to engage in the self-revealing rhetoric of some of Shakespeare's more renowned solilo-quists, the details of his interactive dialogue are worth examining. Commonplace words such as *shall* encode clues about a speaker's self-positioning, and they confirm that there are many means of tracing linguistic subjectivity in drama. Alan Sin-field asserts that these revealing aspects of dia-logue include 'self-reference and self-questioning (including soliloquy), indecision, lying', and he isolates the representation of a character making a decision as the 'nucleus of intersubjective drama'.[11] Decisions, projections, questions: such processes are enacted in the ordinary function words of the language. Moreover, Coriolanus is depicted as an astute critic of communication who pays vigilant attention to the nuances of dialogue, railing against any perceived violation. Words deemed by him to be bold or defiant – 'shall' (3.1.92), 'traitor' (3.3.69), 'boy' (5.6.105) – are subject to his pub-lic scorn and scrutiny. These censorious lessons serve to tell us something important about Cori-olanus: he knows how social language works, and is sensitive to the power contained in single words. Furthermore, he is eager to inform his listeners of his attunement to these details; his status as arbiter of communication is evidently very important to him. It is this kind of pragmatic language-in-use that is held up in this play, and that augments the potency of the linguistic collisions that are of par-ticular interest to me here.

Act 3 begins with the tense anticipation of conflict, opening on a Roman street with the entourage of proud patricians set to encounter the scheming tribunes.[12] There is a certain accent

---

[9] Craig, 'Grammatical modality,' pp. 45–47.

[10] Russ McDonald, *Shakespeare's Late Style* (Cambridge, 2006), p. 52.

[11] Alan Sinfield, *Faultlines: Cultural Materialism and the Politics of Dissident Reading* (Oxford, 1992), p. 59.

[12] Shakespeare's depiction of this encounter is markedly dif-ferent from North's account in *Plutarch's Lives of the Nobel*

placed on acts of social speech, both in the under-current of impending confrontation – the suspense of observing the colliding factions who are bound to argue – and in the patterns of the dialogue itself. The scene begins with a question posed by Coriolanus – 'Tullus Aufidius then had made new head?' (3.1.1) – and continues as an interrogation-style dialogue featuring Coriolanus as the sole questioner. He attempts to pry details about Aufidius from Lartius, and displays a particular interest in what Aufidius has *said*: 'Saw you Aufidius?... Spoke he of me? LARTIUS: He did, my lord. CORIOLANUS: How? What?' (3.1.8, 12). The types of questions posed by Coriolanus, used to elicit information, are classified in the lexicon of discourse analysis as '*wh*-interrogatives'. They are typical of speakers wishing to take 'an initiatory role' since they serve the various authoritative functions of interrogation, challenging prior talk, and achieving commands.[13] The pattern unveiled by these questions is that of a firmly established, rule-bound speech community. Coriolanus is its leader, organizing the parameters of the interaction, constraining the responses of others, and demanding and receiving information in a manner reminiscent of breathless gossip. The exchange sets up Coriolanus not simply as an active participant, but as the primary controller of a linguistic exchange that highlights the significance of words themselves, the 'how' and 'what' of speech.

Given this dictatorial display, it is unsurprising that Coriolanus attempts to extend his position as regulator of discourse even when he encounters the antagonistic tribunes. To Sicinius's impertinent imperative – 'Pass no further' – he retorts in disgusted surprise with further questions: 'Ha, what is that?... What makes this change?' (3.1.27–9). The situation escalates as the tribunes refuse to 'give way,' and even Coriolanus's supporters beg him to speak '[n]ot in this heat, sir, now... No more words, we beseech you' (3.1.67, 79). The apex comes after Coriolanus again offers evidence that '[h]is heart's his mouth' (3.1.257) by indignantly claiming that all of his words – whether spoken in 'choler' or 'patience' – are indicative not of passing whims but of enduring convictions.

Sicinius responds by threatening to subdue that 'mind' which communicates its unfiltered thoughts without pause; in so doing, he effectively vows to terminate Coriolanus's power of speech:

SICINIUS   It is a mind
  That shall remain a poison where it is,
  Not poison any further.
CORIOLANUS   'Shall remain'?
  Hear you this Triton of the minnows? Mark you
  His absolute 'shall'?
COMINIUS   'Twas from the canon.
CORIOLANUS   'Shall'?
  O good but most unwise patricians, why,
  You grave but reckless senators, have you thus
  Given Hydra here to choose an officer
  That, with his peremptory 'shall', being but
  The horn and noise o'th' monster's, wants not spirit
  To say he'll turn your current in a ditch
  And make your channel his? If he have power,
  Then vail your impotence; if none, awake
  Your dangerous lenity. If you are learned,
  Be not as common fools; if you are not,
  Let them have cushions by you. You are plebeians,
  If they be senators; and they are no less
  When, both your voices blended, the great'st taste
  Most palates theirs. They choose their magistrate,
  And such a one as he, who puts his 'shall',
  His popular 'shall', against a graver bench
  Than ever frowned in Greece. By Jove himself,
  It makes the consuls base, and my soul aches
  To know, when two authorities are up,
  Neither supreme, how soon confusion
  May enter 'twixt the gap of both and take
  The one by th'other.   (3.1.89–115)

Coriolanus's extended retort is the product of a speaker familiar and comfortable with powerful words, and who is able to shape them to serve his interests. Skilfully constructed, withering and defiant, the speech in every aspect shows Coriolanus's bids for linguistic mastery. Coriolanus's invec-

---

Grecians and Romans. As Lee Bliss remarks, Shakespeare's version positions the tribunes as calculating agitators, so that when they meet Coriolanus's party in the street, they have 'already instigated the decision to refuse Coriolanus the consulship, thus creating an ironic, un-Plutarchan, context for the patricians' confident entry procession', 'Introduction', *Coriolanus*, (Cambridge, 2000), p. 180.

13 Eggins and Slade, *Analysing Casual Conversation*, p. 87.

tive virtually parses the future-altering, hierarchy-determining modal verb, and it offers an interesting commentary on social language systems in the play. He first condemns Sicinius for his presumptive authority in using *shall*, suggesting that he – a delegate of the mere 'minnows' in the social pond – is in fact impotent to execute it. His interrogation of the authority behind this word invokes the familiar critical terrain of J. L. Austin and Stanley Fish; in speech act terms, Coriolanus objects that Sicinius's *shall* cannot perform as a *shall* because he does not have the requisite influence to speak it.[14] He further takes offence at Sicinius's use of *shall* in such a public denunciatory fashion, demanding that fellow listeners 'mark' his temerity. With this speech, one of the driving concerns of *Coriolanus* – who is permitted to say what to whom – is laid bare.

Coriolanus is not merely affronted, however; there are signs of fear beneath his fury. The *shall*s in his speech are successively modified by three striking adjectives: 'absolute', 'peremptory' and 'popular.' Interestingly, his first target is Sicinius's 'absolute' *shall*; the initial sting, it seems, lies less in the insolence of Sicinius's utterance than in its unequivocal force. His outrage seems natural given that it is typically Coriolanus who is aligned with the absolute – Volumnia's rebuke that he is 'too absolute' (3.2.40) resonates throughout the play – and his reaction suggests a puerile propriety toward this territory. Yet his objection also gives voice to fears about the very scenario that is being enacted before us: Coriolanus the vocal leader is here stopped short by a usurper seeking the position of privilege in a speech event. As Coriolanus knows, there can be only one determiner of the 'absolute'; the word's very definition precludes plurality. Sicinius appropriates the very word that denotes the linguistic sovereign, the commanding *shall* that singles him out as one who 'speak[s] o'th' people as if you were a god / To punish' (3.1.85–6). By robbing him of this word, Sicinius assumes the sovereign position and ensures that Coriolanus take his place as the 'man of ... infirmity' that the people believe him to be (3.1.86). The fear of being subjected to the destructive control of

others is further evident in Coriolanus's assessment of 'peremptory shall'. The etymological roots of 'peremptory' lie in the Latin *perimere*, meaning 'to thoroughly destroy,' and this meaning has in a legal sense been transmuted to 'put a decisive end to'. In one sense, Coriolanus's use of this modifier intensifies his argument for the preposterousness of Sicinius's position: it is absurd that Sicinius's self-appointed authority, nothing but the 'horn and noise o'th' monster', should carry any type of delimiting power. But the flip side of this semblance of absurdity is that it veers, terrifyingly, into the realm of reality. In this way, the absolute and peremptory *shall*s here deployed by Sicinius provide a grammatical prelude to the pivotal moment when Coriolanus is forced to stave off his own banishment with the counter-declaration to Rome and its inhabitants, 'I banish you' (3.3.127). What at first appears to be the railing of a petulant bully against losing his privilege to speak is in fact also a cry for self-preservation. Despite his aggressive claims for the invalid authority of the tribune, Coriolanus recognizes that this 'Triton of the minnows' represents an increasingly absolute threat, for the word that Sicinius wields with such insouciance has the power to put an end to, to destroy, and (as Coriolanus will soon discover) to send elsewhere. This scene acts as a pivot point – an unravelling begins, as Coriolanus begins to be victimized by the very modes of language that he once used against others. The reversal that has taken place in the language inscribes the potent dictates of those who rule and those who are ruled.

---

[14] See J. L. Austin's foundational work, *How To Do Things With Words* (Cambridge, 1962), and Stanley Fish's 'How to Do Things with Austin and Searle: Speech Act Theory and Literary Criticism', *Modern Language Notes*, 91.5 (1976), 983–1025. According to Austin's logic, Sicinius's *shall* violates the felicity conditions of a successful speech act. Austin's theory suggests that 'the particular persons and circumstances in a given case must be appropriate for the invocation of the particular procedure invoked' (15); otherwise, the speech act fails and is classified as a 'misapplication' (18). Coriolanus attempts to show that Sicinius does not constitute an 'appropriate' speaker, a position that lies at the heart of their tussle over *shall*.

In light of this dawning threat, the ending of Coriolanus's diatribe is particularly interesting. He closes with an appeal to social order, noting that when competing authorities collide, the result is confusion: 'when two authorities are up, / Neither supreme, how soon confusion/ May enter 'twixt the gap of both and take / The one by th' other' (3.1.112–14). Coriolanus here offers perhaps the best testament against claims that he strives to stand apart from linguistic communities, for he asserts that language – and specifically ordered, governed language – is necessary to determine where one stands in the world. It is when agitators begin speaking out of turn – 'And such a one as he, who puts his 'shall', / His popular 'shall', against a graver bench' (3.1.108–9) – that chaos ensues. Particularly noteworthy is that Coriolanus subtly conflates the social and personal implications of such bids for linguistic control. He first couches his disapproval in an argument for the retention of social distinction, so that senators and patricians may be prevented from being reduced to 'common fools'. For this reason, the 'popular shall' – quite literally, the *shall* of the people – is an oxymoron to Coriolanus; it is not only threatening but untenable, for the language of the people cannot reduplicate that of the patricians. The result of such laxity, according to Coriolanus, is a dangerous linguistic miscegenation, wherein 'when, both your voices blended, the great'st taste / Most palates theirs' (3.1.106–7); in other words, the resulting mingled voice will always favour the people. However, this general ideology is necessarily bound up with an awareness of what is at stake for Coriolanus personally, so that collective concerns, such as fear of tainted language, bleed into fears about individual self-protection. The speech begins with the tone of an outraged but still distanced orator; the subject is the derided 'he', the audience the collective 'you', and Coriolanus's own 'I' perspective is withheld.

Yet this impersonal mask begins to crack as the speech continues; after a frustrated appeal to 'Jove himself' (3.1.110), Coriolanus refers for the first time to his own pained state: 'My soul aches' (3.1.111). Further, as Cominius and Menenius attempt to halt his increasingly inflammatory rant

and shunt him away – 'Well, on to th' market place' (3.1.115) – the more of himself Coriolanus injects into his comments. When Menenius urges, 'Well, well, no more of that' (3.1.118), Coriolanus (ever in the guise of linguistic controller), proceeds undeterred: 'Though there the people had more absolute power – / I say they nourished disobedience' (3.1.119–20); he follows up with the equally assertive intention that 'I'll give my reasons, / More worthier than their voices' (3.1.122–3). The increasing frequency of personal pronouns suggests a burgeoning awareness of the implications of the citizens' seditious behaviour not only for the community at large, but for Coriolanus himself. More subtly, however, this self-reference represents a strategy for asserting control over the exchange. By positioning himself as a real force, an 'I' that cannot be disregarded, Coriolanus accelerates the conflict and renders it explicitly personal: the situation is transformed to him versus them, and he pits himself against precisely what they strive to expropriate (the 'absolute power' of their 'voices'). What began as a pundit's speech on the Roman political process has revealed itself as a vicious personal battle, and Coriolanus's defensive stance is a means of protecting his most valued attribute: his understanding of his own place in the world. Identity is shaped by the very conditions on which Coriolanus comments: who may speak, and from what context and perspective. If it is true that 'Coriolanus fears not being himself more than anything',[15] then this fear is rooted in the act of speaking. As William F. Hanks explains, it is inherently connected to one's stance in the world: 'To speak is inevitably to situate one's self in the world, to take up a position, to engage with others in a process of production and exchange, to occupy a social space.'[16] Furthermore, as William Dodd notes, personal identity 'is defined by the commitments and identifications which provide the frame or horizon within which I can try to determine

---

[15] Alexander Leggatt, *Shakespeare's Political Drama* (London, 1988), p. 194.

[16] William F. Hanks, 'Notes on Semantics in Linguistic Practice', in *Bourdieu: Critical Perspectives* (Chicago, 1993), p. 139.

from case to case what is good, or valuable, or what ought to be done, or what I endorse or oppose. In other words, it is the horizon in which I am capable of taking a stand.'[17] And it is largely through grammatical modality, a substantial contact site between 'I' and 'world', that such a stand – the very fabric by which identity is created – is established. Coriolanus envisions himself one way, but is not permitted to realize this vision; the stand that he wants to take is not available to him. He reacts against the attempt to shake him from the stance through which he identifies himself, and is distressed because such an attack means relinquishing the self that is familiar to him, being forced to play 'a part / That [he] shall blush in acting' (2.2.145).

Moreover, not only is Coriolanus forced to relinquish his customary modes of self-positioning, he must also succumb to a new version of the future, renegotiated by others. Evidence for this reframed future is apparent as Coriolanus's rant is brought to an end, not by the pleas of his cohort, but rather by the pithy and brutal directive of the tribunes:

BRUTUS   He's said enough.
SICINIUS   He's spoken like a traitor and shall answer
            As traitors do.

(3.1.164–6)

With these words, the tribunes lay down thundering proof of the power that Coriolanus fears that they hold. Brutus's terminating words are definitively peremptory, putting a decisive end to the possibility of speech, while Sicinius's vow that he 'shall answer' acts as the trump card. This *shall*, hardly as impotent as Coriolanus had initially tried to categorize it, is confirmation that they have won, for it represents the 'absolute shall' that has now categorically changed hands from one set of rule-makers to another. Recall that the first verbal conflict in the scene occurs when the tribunes demand that Coriolanus and his party 'stop', even as the senators insist 'Tribunes, give way. He *shall* to th' market-place' (3.1.33). Sicinius's *shall* at the end of the scene confirms how the dispute over Coriolanus's immediate future is ultimately resolved, for it is the tribunes' version of the future that will be

carried out: Coriolanus shall not go to the market place; he shall be punished as a traitor. The decisive force of *shall* has been cemented: 'someone or something outside the subject decides what the subject is obliged or permitted to be'.[18] Herein lies the ignominy for Coriolanus; it is not merely that he has been defeated so publicly in a verbal sparring-match, but that he has lost authority over all parties, including himself. The outcome of the 'absolute shall' scene shows that the victim-making capacity of *shall* has effectively claimed Coriolanus. Indeed, it is only after Brutus and Sicinius utter these final condemning words that Coriolanus finally addresses his prosecutors, in the taunting, defensive language appropriate to the angry prisoner that he has become: 'Thou wretch, despite o'erwhelm thee!'; 'Hence, old goat!' (3.1.166, 179). The progression that we have witnessed over the course of this scene – a trajectory beginning with Coriolanus's incredulous protests and ending with his forced position of passive defensiveness – grants us at least partial access to his inner world, and the ways that he perceives himself. Dodd observes that it is during moments of verbal conflict, in which social power switches hands and identity is reappraised, that questions of selfhood are addressed:

Some of the clearest traces of this confrontation are, I believe, to be found at those junctures where Shakespeare allows his 'given' characters to place their selves at risk by embracing (or willfully shying away from) the openness of dialogue as they negotiate rights and obligations that were formerly part and parcel of their social standing. Our sense of their personhood, our impression that at such moments they are 'unified subjects meaningfully acting in the world,' surely owed much to the way that transactional dialogue offers characters a *point d'appui* from which they can objectify, at one and the same time, their old, static, 'given' selves and their new, dynamic, negotiated selves.[19]

---

[17] William Dodd, 'Destined Livery? Character and Person in Shakespeare', *Shakespeare Survey 51* (Cambridge, 1998), 147–58, p. 151.

[18] Lars Hermeren, *On Modality in English: A Study of the Semantics of the Modals* (Lund, 1978), pp. 95–6.

[19] Dodd, 'Destined Livery?', p. 158.

The details of Coriolanus's speech unveil the machinations behind his self-appraisal and self-positioning; they permit us to observe his fear, rebellion and intimidation. At the end of the 'absolute shall' scene, we are witnessing the fallout of a self renegotiated.

The change in speech tendencies is not restricted to Coriolanus; also noteworthy is the new momentum that the word *shall* acquires for those who have been pitted against Coriolanus up to this point. In the aftermath of the 'absolute shall' conflict, the tribunes and the citizens begin to use the word with abandon, offering support for Craig's claim that *Coriolanus* makes more use of modal verbs than any other play of Shakespeare. *Shall* has been held up by Coriolanus as a powerful word that designates control, a word worth sparring over so that its winner may wield it like a prize. Having publicly won the right to claim 'absolute shall', the tribunes treat the word as a taboo profanity that they repeat with relish. It carries the intoxicating weight of something formerly inaccessible, but newly discovered to be within their grasp.

MENENIUS You worthy tribunes –
SICINIUS He shall be thrown down the Tarpeian rock
  With rigorous hands. He hath resisted law,
  And therefore law shall scorn him further trial
  Than the severity of the public power
  Which he so sets at naught.
FIRST CITIZEN He shall well know
  The noble tribunes are the people's mouths,
  And we their hands.
ALL PLEBEIANS He shall, sure on't.
                                              (3.1.265–72)

Sicinius seems to take particular delight in interrupting Menenius's feeble plea with his new injunction. The references to 'scorn' and 'the people's mouths' uphold the focus on the power and legitimacy of speech, and underscore the fact that the tribunes have won a decisive victory in this contested realm. Even the rhythm of the lines emphasizes the word; the repeated 'law' holds semantic properties that recall *shall*, and the lines 'He shall well know' and 'He shall, sure on it' carry alliterative force. In subsequent scenes, the new currency bestowed on *shall* ensures that the

word imparts a weightier blow when it is used against Coriolanus. Indeed, it becomes a byword of sorts in Sicinius's proceedings against him; in his plotting with Brutus, Sicinius isolates *shall* as a literal call to arms: 'Assemble presently the people hither, / And when they hear me say "It shall be so / I'th' right and strength o'th' commons", be it either / For death, for fine, or banishment, then let them, / If I say "Fine", cry "Fine!", if "Death", cry "Death!"' (3.3.12–16). True to his word, in his hortatory address to the citizens, Sicinius transforms this modal phrase into a rallying cry: 'I'th' people's name / I say it shall be so' (3.3.108–9); 'There's no more to be said, but he is banished / As enemy to the people and his country. / It shall be so' (3.3.121–3). The plebeians' response to the jingoism is fervent, even ecstatic: 'It shall be so, it shall be so! Let him away! / He's banished, and it shall be so!' (3.3.110–11). The desperate mob of the play's opening scene has come a long way; newly capable of backing their words with achieved power, they are in a sense answering their earlier call to 'speak, speak'.[20]

The confrontation between Coriolanus and the tribunes exemplifies Coriolanus's preferred method of expressing convictions about himself and the state of his world: not through the self-reflective musings of soliloquy, but rather during the skirmishes in which he seems so at home. It has been suggested that his reluctance to question himself renders him inaccessible: 'Unlike the protagonists of most of the other major tragedies, he never asks "Who am I?" or "What have I become?"'... when not absorbed with his sword and its work, he is usually seen waging verbal battle against not only the common people, both as citizens and soldiers, and the tribunes, but against senators and patricians as well.'[21] Yet the details

---

20 Further evidence for the reversal is that it is now Coriolanus who resorts to this plaintiff position. Facing his prosecutors, he says 'First, hear me speak' (3.3.38), and his interrogative *shall* (which appeals to the authority of the addressee rather than the speaker) confirms the transfer of power: 'Shall I be charged no further than this present? / Must all determine here?' (3.3.40–1).

21 Bliss, 'Introduction', pp. 40–1.

of Coriolanus's verbal performance offer a revealing linguistic profile, for it is through these linguistic collisions that he makes himself known to us. As Dodd notes, dialogue provides a valuable store of information by showcasing the speaker in the process of self-positioning and negotiation: 'interactional dialogue can become a site for the production of self as agency – self as aware of and responding to transpersonal "discourses", as opposed to being simply voiced or subjugated by them.'[22] Given this lens, some of Coriolanus's most prominent and affecting lines might be read slightly differently. Consider his famous declaration as he is confronted with the pleading presence of his wife and mother: 'I'll never / Be such a gosling to obey instinct, but stand / As if a man were author of himself / And knew no other kin' (5.3.34–7). This *cri de coeur*, often cited as an appeal to autonomy and detachment, may alternatively be read as a testament to linguistic mastery. Coriolanus's desire to be 'author of himself' – as the one who originates, who causes an action or event to come into being – perhaps speaks less to a desire for severed intimacy than to a wish for control over uncertain future events. It is, in a sense, a wish to return to his acknowledged role as 'god to punish' rather than man of infirmity, capable of falling prey to instinct. Coriolanus is well aware that language is built on mutual exchange, and his consistent goal in linguistic encounters is mastery; he relishes these reciprocal situations when they allow him to affirm his dominance. This is why the 'absolute shall' scene represents such a resounding defeat. By calling prominent attention to the impinging *shall*s of the tribunes, Coriolanus discloses his deep fear of being outstripped as the regulator of discourse. And as the repercussions of the 'absolute shall' scene show, the very words to which Coriolanus feels exclusively entitled are ultimately turned against him. This transformative encounter in dialogue represents the moment in which Coriolanus's future is forcefully re-determined. The parameters of Coriolanus's battle to speak his place in the world, and the details of the loss of this fight, are thus inscribed in the minute details of linguistic exchange, the telling and contested words that all of the 'voices' in this play strive to claim as their own.

---

[22] Dodd, 'Destined Livery?', p. 156.

CHAGALL'S *TEMPEST*: AN AUTOBIOGRAPHICAL READING

HANNA SCOLNICOV

Marc Chagall's black-and-white lithographs illustrating *The Tempest*,[1] executed by the artist in 1975 at the age of eighty-eight, offer a very personal, autobiographical reading of the plot and characters of the play. Chagall's single attempt to illustrate a Shakespeare play[2] is almost unknown among art historians and Shakespeare scholars alike and barely mentioned in the many books written on the painter.[3] Except for the Bibliothèque Nationale, the book is also surprisingly missing from the online catalogues of the great libraries that I searched.

The publication details, which attest to the authenticity of the work, appear in the front and end matter. The volume was published in Monte Carlo, by Editions André Sauret, under the supervision of Charles Sorlier. The hand-set text, in the new font Romain du Roi engraved by Philippe Grandjean, was printed by the Imprimerie Nationale of France, while the original lithographs by Marc Chagall were printed on the presses of Fernand Mourlot in Paris.

Alongside the English text of the play, the book contains fifty original lithographs by Marc Chagall, of which thirty-one are full-page *hors-texte* illustrations and nineteen serve as headers or footers to the printed text, some of them half-page size. The total run was of two hundred and fifty numbered copies, plus twenty copies for contributors (numbered I to XX), printed on Vélin d'Arches paper, small folio size, 243 pages, loose sheets vellumboxed, and signed by the artist.

The copy I had access to is number 156. I came across it two years ago, when the lithographs were about to be put on display at Tel-Aviv University Gallery and I was asked to write the catalogue article for the exhibition.[4] To my great surprise, I could find no bibliography on this volume and the Chagall scholars I approached reacted in disbelief over the very existence of such a work. But there it was, donated many years ago to the Gallery, published by Chagall's well-known publisher, and signed. I found myself conducting primary research on that work, identifying the scenes and characters depicted and analysing them in relation to the text of the play, and even attempting to establish the

---

[1] William Shakespeare, *The Tempest*, illustrated by Marc Chagall (Monte Carlo. Éditions André Sauret, 1975), 243 pp.

[2] One exception may be the bridal picture of his first wife Bella and himself with an animal's head, and an angel in flight above, perhaps the indefatigable Puck, titled *Midsummer Night's Dream*, 1939, Museum of Grenoble, reproduced in *Homage to Marc Chagall*, ed. San Lazzaro (New York, 1969), p. 32. But, it should be noted that the animal head seems to be that of a goat, not an ass. The goat, which is often represented by Chagall, I take to stand for Chagall himself, and the hybrid nature of the figure is common in many of his paintings.

[3] Brief references to this book are found in Monica Bohm-Duchen, *Chagall* (London, 1998), p. 325: 'As he grew older and more frail, Chagall's work in the graphic medium began gradually to take precedence over his work in other media. In 1972–5 he produced illustrations for *The Odyssey*, and in 1975 for *The Tempest*'; and also in *Chagall e la Bibbia*, ed. Giovanni Battista Martini and Alberto Ronchetti (Milan, 2004), p. 174.

[4] Hanna Scolnicov, 'Chagall's lithographs for Shakespeare's *Tempest*', in *Marc Chagall: Illustrations for the Story of the Exodus and Shakespeare's Tempest*, exhibition catalogue (Tel Aviv, Genia Schreiber University Art Gallery, 2007).

correct placement of full-page illustrations that had become misplaced.

Producing Shakespeare's text with original lithographs, in a collectors' edition, indicates that this is a book meant to be leafed through and enjoyed for its visual images. It is obviously inconvenient to read from such a large, loose-leaf volume, but the size of the book allows for impressive images, and is also reminiscent of the size of the First Folio. This edition takes us back to the text as book, as material object, meant to be enjoyed in the privacy of one's home. Here then is another tome to match the books in Prospero's library in Milan (1.2.110), and especially those volumes with which Gonzalo furnished the barque, along with the provisions needed for survival (1.2.160–168), and which Caliban sees as the source of Prospero's power, without which 'he's but a sot' (3.2.85).[5]

Unlike large canvases relating to Shakespeare's plays, the illustrations of *The Tempest* were intended to stand side by side with the printed text and add a visual dimension. Illustration does not presume to be an autonomous art or a translation of the verbal into the pictorial medium but remains dependent on the text. Illustrations are meant to supplement the written word and enhance its meaning, but, like the written work, they too are meant to be 'read' along with the words.

On the title-page, Chagall lays his claim to a kind of co-authorship with the playwright, thus indicating the relationship between the verbal and visual texts. 'Shakespeare' appears above the larger lettering of 'The Tempest', and 'Marc Chagall' – and not 'Illustrations by Marc Chagall' – appears below, in the same font size. Here then is the art of two very different geniuses, working in different media and in different cultures and periods, yoked together.

The frontispiece (Illustration 16) depicts a relatively large image of Shakespeare at the top, Prospero down front right, Ariel, in the shape of an angel, to the left, and the ship rocking on the waves in the centre. From outside the freely sketched oval that encloses the world of the play emanate the bold rays of 'Jove's lightning' (1.2.201) that strike

16. Frontispiece: Shakespeare, Prospero, Ariel.

the ship. The proportionate size of the figures would seem to indicate the hierarchy of powers responsible for the tempest: playwright, powerful magician and messenger spirit.

Although they appear alongside the text, the illustrations do not necessarily illustrate a particular segment of text or a particular event in the play. Instead, they often illustrate the characters and indicate the relationships between them as well as the themes: the force of the supernatural storm, the power of music and the redemptive power of love and romance. In other words, the pictures convey the spiritual dimension of the events, their noumenal rather than phenomenal dimension. Not so much what the eye sees, but what the mind conceives. One can say that Chagall illustrates not the overt plot, but Prospero's spiritual journey.

---

[5] All quotations from *The Tempest*, ed. David Lindley (Cambridge, 2002).

17. Storm at sea.

The sea-storm (p. 21) (Illustration 17), a bravura scene in the theatre, becomes in Chagall's rendering an image of human disaster, as the distraught passengers try to save themselves by jumping overboard. Taking his cue from Ariel's report to Prospero, Chagall portrays here the 'fever of the mad' and the 'tricks of desperation', the 'quit[ting] of the vessel' and the plunging into 'the foaming brine', and Ferdinand crying out as he leaped, 'Hell is empty, and all the devils are here' (1.2. 209–15). This cannot be shown in the theatre, but is provided as an explanation of the mechanism behind the opening shipwreck scene. Chagall presents the storm, with hindsight, as the manifestation of Prospero's magical powers, represented by Ariel controlling the storm from above (p. 65).

Like Shakespeare, Chagall treats the storm as a literalization of the general upheaval in the world that must occur if the social wrongs committed in the past are to be healed. Chagall's own predicament as creative artist and Jew, caught up in the political turmoils of the Revolution in Russia and the Second World War in France, nourishes his understanding of Prospero's deposition and exile from Milan.

Chagall's lithographs follow the modern trend in setting store by the original and individual artistic interpretation. Instead of using classical models, Chagall created his visual images for Shakespeare's characters by identifying them with his own personal world. The ambiguity of dramatic time and place in *The Tempest* made it relatively easy for Chagall to relate the events and characters of the play to his own personal biography and private mythography. Paradoxically, by interpreting the play in his subjective and autobiographical manner, Chagall managed to universalize the aristocratic Renaissance plot and turn it into a metaphor for the tempestuous journey of life and the final coming to terms with it, and finding peace and reconciliation.

Chagall seems to ignore the Jacobean context of the play and does not strive for 'authenticity' or verisimilitude in dress or landscape. Unlike the more familiar eighteenth- and nineteenth-century paintings that treat the play as an edifying neo-classical drama, Chagall transposes the events into a minor, folkloric key. Chagall's illustrations are rooted in both Russian and Hassidic popular narrative art. He provides a free and imaginative interpretation that is not indebted to any pictorial or theatrical tradition of illustrating Shakespeare. The only artistic tradition, if one can call it that, to which he was committed was his own unique visual language, developed over so many years, and his only iconographic reference (or source) is self-reference to his own mythography.

His use of an English, rather than French, text is puzzling, since, despite the time spent in the US during the later War years, Chagall could not have read the play in the original. The very question of the language in which he read the play (Yiddish? Russian? French? – these are the options) is currently unanswerable and further problematizes the relationship of his visual rendering to the

153

18. Ariel imprisoned in the pine tree.

verbal text.[6] Be this as it may, the emotional and ideational understanding of the play exhibited by the pictures suggests an intimate acquaintance with it.

As illustrations, the meaning of Chagall's lithographs is dependent on their correspondence to the play. But while the verbal text is a reading text and, potentially, a theatrical script, the illustrations are intended solely for the reader. It is therefore perhaps not surprising to discover that, despite Chagall's lifelong engagement with the theatre, his illustrations for *The Tempest* relate exclusively to the play, without either recording a production or anticipating one.

Chagall illustrates events taking place in the dramatic present, as well as past, expository events from 'the dark backward and abysm of time' (1.2.50). He represents purely narrative passages, such as Prospero's life in his palace, when still the Duke of Milan (p. 27), his sea-voyage of twelve years ago with the infant Miranda, or Ariel's confinement in the cloven pine tree (p. 71)

(Illustration 18). Likewise, the foul witch Sycorax, who never makes an appearance in the play, is pictured by Chagall, chiding the grown-up Caliban (p. 49).

The lack of differentiation between what is told and what is shown is especially striking in view of Chagall's close ties with the theatre, for which he had often created sets and costumes.[7] Indeed, the illustrations for *The Tempest* often seem to disregard the theatrical aspects of the performance, treating the play as a purely literary work, irrespective of what is to be shown on the stage.

Curiously, some of the more 'theatrical' events of the play are neglected by Chagall. For example, there is no illustration of the discovery of Ferdinand and Miranda 'playing at chess' (s.d. following 5.1.171), the wedding masque or the hatching of the aristocratic conspiracy. Likewise, the comic conspiracy too is omitted, except for one minor half-page illustration (perhaps showing Stephano, Trinculo and Caliban inebriated – but it is not a clearly recognizable moment in the play).

In two of the lithographs, the one showing the setting and the other the removal of the banquet, Chagall illustrates the stage directions, without paying any attention to the characters appearing in the scene and to the dialogue. Furthermore, the setting of the banquet (p. 165) offers no particular

---

6 I interviewed Prof. Benjamin Harshav (28.5.08), who has written extensively on Chagall and Yiddish culture, and he was of the opinion that Chagall could have read the play in Yiddish translation, or perhaps in Russian, or might have had the play read to him in French by his first wife Bella. He may also have watched a Yiddish or Russian performance. However, any of these would have taken place many years earlier. 'Chagall knew no English, spoke Russian to Bella and French to Virginia, and read Yiddish newspapers' (Benjamin Harshav, *Marc Chagall and the Lost Jewish World: The Nature of Chagall's Art and Iconography* (New York, 2006), p. 28).

7 See, e.g., *Marc Chagall: An Exhibition of Paintings, Prints, Book Illustrations and Theatre Designs, 1908–1947, at the Tate Gallery, February 1948* (London, 1948); Dennis Milhau, 'Chagall and the Theater', in *Homage to Marc Chagall*, ed. San Lazzaro (New York, 1969), pp. 101–8; *Marc Chagall and the Jewish Theater*, exhibition catalogue (New York, Guggenheim Museum, 1992); Ruth Apter-Gabriel, ed., *Chagall: Dreams and Drama*, exhibition catalogue (Jerusalem, Israel Museum, 1993); Beate Reifenscheid, *Chagall und die Bühne* (Bielefeld, 1996).

19. The vanishing banquet.

interpretation for the 'strange shapes' mentioned in the stage directions (s.d. following 3.3.19) and described by Gonzalo as 'of monstrous shape' (3.3.31), picturing them simply as waiters carrying in platters. It is only the amazement of the audience watching this feat from the bottom left corner, and the awkward slant of the tables, that hint at the strangeness of the feast. In the removal of the banquet (p. 171) (Illustration 19), Ariel appears not 'like a harpy' (s.d. following 3.3.51), but in the figure of an avenging angel, presiding, sword in hand, over the vanishing of the banquet.

Most of Chagall's work is, in one way or another, autobiographical. He is interested in himself as the creative artist, in himself as the embodiment of the dispossessed, exiled Jew, and he is interested in the drama of his nuclear family. These three themes appear again and again in his paintings and can also be seen as leitmotifs in his illustrations for *The Tempest*. Chagall interprets the figure of the magician as himself, the ageing artist, bidding farewell to his art; he identifies the exiled Duke's predica-

ment with his own double exile, first from Russia, then from Europe; finally, he views the relationship between Prospero and Miranda in terms of his own relationship as a widower left with his only daughter Ida. Clearly, Chagall read the play as a metaphor for his own life story.

In *The Tempest* lithographs, Chagall creates a pictorial world that reflects his own autobiography. The pictures carry a sense of naïve authenticity that suits the primitiveness of the New World image created by Shakespeare. From Chagall's point of view, the play becomes a fairy-tale with highly realistic implications, a generalized story that provides the structure of many particular life-stories, but especially the life-story of the artist himself.

Taken together, the lithographs define a fictional world that is both circumscribed and coherent. In this world, Prospero is the only real character. The illustrations draw our attention to this idiosyncratic feature of *The Tempest*. Unusually for Shakespeare, this is a one-character play, the play about Prospero's fantasy of settling his account with his enemies, and the entire trajectory of this plot is unrealistic. Finally reconciled with his former enemies, he promises to tell them 'the story of my life' (5.1.302). At the beginning of the play, he has already recounted to Miranda the story up to that point, and the rest of the play ties together all the remaining loose ends. The elements of both biography and fantasy in the play were clearly picked up by Chagall.

Like the play itself, Chagall's lithographs can be seen as meta-art, as art about the artist and his art, about his sources of inspiration and his attitude to his own creative power. Throughout his life, Chagall was interested in the self-reflexive aspect of art, picturing himself holding his palette and paintbrushes. Such a self-portrait of the artist is naturally missing in the *Tempest* lithographs, since Chagall is committed to illustrating the events and characters of the play. Here, the autobiographical elements can only enter through his personal interpretation of the play and there is no explicit self-portrait. Chagall's autobiographical reading of the play needs to be seen within the double context of his artistic output and the complex story of his life.

20. *Towards the Other light.*

21. Prospero, Ariel, Ferdinand, Miranda.

Chagall produced his very last work, titled *Towards the Other Light* (1985), (Illustration 20),[8] the day before he passed away at the age of ninety-eight, i.e. a decade after the completion of his work on the lithographs for *The Tempest*. In this work, he depicts himself seated in front of his easel, palette in hand, with the familiar pair of lovers on the painted canvas presenting him with a bouquet. Not only is there an angel hovering above and touching his head, blessing him and perhaps waiting to take him away, but the painter himself is now ready for flight, with a pair of wings on his back. Here, as in many earlier pictures, Chagall duplicates himself as both the painter and the object of painting, in the act of producing a self-portrait of himself as a young man with his wife.

The idea of the self-portrait is not coextensive with the idea of autobiography, since the self-portrait in itself lacks a narrative dimension. The narrative element enters the picture through the juxtaposition of the old artist with his younger self, whom he is portraying, together with independent, outside knowledge of Chagall's life and art. In the lithographs that accompany *The Tempest*, the narrative element is pre-given by the play, but Chagall's autobiographical reading turns this narrative into a symbolic representation of his own life.

The four figures in Chagall's moving last picture can easily be related to his conception of the four main characters of *The Tempest*, namely, Prospero, Ariel, Ferdinand and Miranda (p. 193) (Illustration 21). Of these, the three human characters enact the archetypal drama of patriarchy, the passage of the unmarried maid from her father's control to her husband's possession. The conflict between father and future husband is crystallized in another print (p. 77), showing the powerful mage casting the spell on Ferdinand, who holds out his sword, while the distressed Miranda stands close by, torn between obedience to her father and love for Ferdinand, and the detached Ariel looks on from above.

---

[8] In Bohm-Duchen, *Chagall*, fig. 228.

Chagall represents the romance of Ferdinand and Miranda in the likeness of his familiar pair of lovers (p. 141), i.e. himself as a young man hugging his first wife Bella, and interprets Prospero as the ageing artist. This can be understood as another simultaneous projection of Chagall, assuming the double role of young lover and old father, of both Ferdinand and Prospero. Add to this Prospero's total control of Miranda, and the three central characters become collapsed into a unified autobiographical representation of patriarchal control. Chagall's visual interpretation of Miranda is ambiguous, as both beloved and daughter, referring both to Bella and Ida.

Ariel completes the quartet of characters, adding a spiritual and inspirational dimension to the drama of the nuclear family. The figure of the winged Ariel is reminiscent of the angels that hover over many of Chagall's paintings. The winged angel is a figure that haunts Chagall's imagination. In his youthful 'Apparition',[9] he turns away from his easel towards the angel, asking for help and guidance. In Chagall's very last picture, the angel is still there. Due to his Hebrew name, Ariel is more than a mythical figure of artistic inspiration. Ariel – literally, the lion of God – or, in his variant names, Erel or Uriel, is one of the archangels, an important figure in post-Biblical angelology, an angel of air and fire, of retribution and of artistic inspiration. Leaning on a long tradition of Talmudic and Kabalistic angels, Chagall interprets Ariel as his own private source of artistic inspiration and power, and also his own attendant angel. Ariel becomes tinged with a holiness that is indebted to folklore no less than to religion. Illustrating the play afforded Chagall the opportunity to examine his relationship with his guardian angel, who, he felt, had accompanied him wherever he went. In Chagall's autobiographical reading of the play, Ariel becomes identified with Chagall's own angelic daemon. The idea of seeing Ariel as a guardian spirit is not alien to the tradition of reading the play, as for example in Shelley's poem 'With a guitar, to Jane'.[10]

Illustrating *The Tempest* at the age of eightyeight, Chagall could easily see himself as a demiurge who had created a dream-world with the help of his attendant spirits but was now facing the impending dissolution of all the beauty he had produced. Like the ageing theatrical magician, he too was ready to take leave of his art, his creative powers and the creatures he had created. For him too, the revels were about to end, the actors were all spirits, his world was about to melt into thin air and his life to be rounded with a sleep (4.1.148–58). Prospero's final vision of life itself as an insubstantial pageant about to fade breaks down the boundaries between the spiritual and concrete worlds, as practised by Chagall throughout his career. Shakespeare and Chagall, two totally disparate artists, working in different media and belonging to very different cultures, are thus discovered to share a common artistic and existential vision.

The moment of the loss of his artistic powers is depicted by Chagall as a moment of leave-taking. He shows Ariel flying upward (p. 197) over the billowing sea, the boat on the horizon, with Prospero lifting his hands towards him in a gesture that expresses release, farewell and blessing at one and the same time. In this lithograph, Chagall expresses the emotional content of Prospero's Epilogue: the overthrowing of his charms, the sad, though successful, coming to an end of his project, the loss of 'spirits to enforce' and 'art to enchant', and the desire for release and reconciliation. Ariel can be seen again, his weightless figure treading the waves, fulfilling his master's last mission (p. 211). The departing spirit is so important to Chagall that he adds a very personal scene to the play, depicting the pair of lovers, held by Ariel, flying above the boat (p. 217) (Illustration 22). This paean to love refers back to Chagall's repeated depictions of himself flying with Bella in his arms, as in, for example, *Over the Town*.[11]

---

9 *The Apparition* (blue and white: 1917–18), reproduced in Ruth Apter-Gabriel, *Dreams and Drama*, fig. 31; (colour: 1924–25/c.1937), reproduced in Susan Compton, *Marc Chagall: My Life – My Dream, Berlin and Paris, 1922–1940* (Munich, 1990), fig. 24.

10 *Shelley: Selected Poetry and Prose*, ed. Carlos Baker (New York, 1951), p. 428.

11 *Over the Town* (1914–18), reproduced in Apter-Gabriel, *Dreams and Drama*, fig. 14.

22. Ariel flying with Ferdinand and Miranda.

23. The island full of music.

Having received Prospero's promise of 'calm seas, auspicious gales' (5.1.312), the ship finally sets off on its journey back home, its sails filled with wind, and two hands blessing its journey, depicted by Chagall in a moving little vignette (p. 234). Prospero's Epilogue to the play is preceded by his full-page figure, towering over the tiny lovers, the flying Ariel and the temporary sojourners on the island crowded into one corner (p. 237). Prospero's posture expresses a new humility and acceptance. The play was his life story and, like Shakespeare, who gave Prospero the last word, Chagall too gives him pride of place in the final lithograph.

Prospero's magic appears to be, to a large extent, the magic power of music. Ariel succeeds in foiling the conspiracies hatched on the island and saving the evil-doers from themselves by singing and playing on the pipe and tabor. Shakespeare's island is full of music, as are also Chagall's paintings, with their repeated depiction of the iconic figures of the Jewish fiddler and of other musicians

(p. 187) (Illustration 23). The spirits that echo Ariel's songs are presented by Chagall as little winged creatures playing various wind and string instruments and hovering above the human figures on the enchanted island.

Chagall realized the potential hybridity contained in Shakespeare's characterization of Ariel and Caliban and depicted them as liminal and hybrid creatures. Liminality and hybridity are of the very essence of the mythological world. Chagall's well-known interest in drawing hybrid creatures, part animal and part human, mermaids and cocks with human faces,[12] amplifies Shakespeare's own fantasy of mythical creatures in this play. Ariel and Caliban appear as basically human figures, but Ariel is provided with wings and Caliban is presented, even before he hides under

---

[12] E.g., *The Bay of Angels*, 1962, lithograph, 57 x 78 cm, and *The Blue Nymph*, no date, lithograph, 59 x 50.5 cm, reproduced in Fernand Mourlot, *Chagall Lithographe: 1957–1962*, vol. 2 (Monte Carlo, 1963).

24. Caliban conjoined to a fish.

the gabardine, trailing a fish-tail behind his back (p. 119). Another hybrid creature, a cross-looking harpy, half-bird, half-woman, watches him from above. Later on, Caliban is shown conjoined to a huge fish, its head appearing behind his shoulder and its tail trailing at the back of his legs (p. 127) (illustration 24). In this fantasy world, another fish flips its way through the bushes and yet another dives in from above. A few years earlier, Chagall had made some lithographs of the biblical prophet Jonah. In one of them, *Jonah against a Blue Background* (1972),[13] he depicted Jonah as a similar hybrid of man and fish, in the sea, with a far-off boat.

On the face of it, the depiction of the supernatural beings, Ariel, Caliban and the tiny musical spirits that inhabit Chagall's island, would seem to point to the illustrations as belonging to the surrealist movement in art and Chagall is known to have befriended some of the leading surrealist artists in Paris. Chagall was interested in the world that is

hidden from the eye – the magical world below the surface. Shakespeare's unrealistic and irrational romance would invite a surrealist interpretation. The surrealist strain in Chagall's art[14] could easily accommodate the fantasy elements of the play and the breaking down of the demarcation between the visible and the invisible, the real world and its spiritual content.

Chagall's world of the imagination is indeed sometimes taken to be a manifestation of Surrealism. But his view of art differs from that of the surrealists on two main points.[15] Firstly, the surrealists, as the modernists in general, aimed at eliminating the artist from the work of art, presenting it, as it were, objectively. By contrast, Chagall was clearly and consistently interested in presenting himself as the artist responsible for his work. Secondly, the surrealists attempted to tap the unconscious directly, representing it in all its incoherence, bypassing the conscious artist, who imposes order and meaning on his work. They advocated automatism and the objective representation of dream worlds. Chagall's figures may have issued from his own subjective world of images, but they were consciously developed into a private mythology and iconography. Taken together, Chagall's works provide an image of his own person, his private history, his ideas, beliefs and emotions. Furthermore, the very fact that these lithographs are illustrations of Shakespeare's text negates their being classified as surrealist, showing that these cannot be incoherent dream-images or automatic drawings issuing directly from the unconscious.

In these illustrations, as in other works, Chagall uses elements from Surrealism, without himself being a surrealist, as well as elements from

---

[13] *Jonah against a Blue Background*, 1972, 42 × 57 cm, reproduced in Charles Sorlier, *Chagall Lithographe: 1969–1973*, vol. 4 (Monte Carlo, 1974), fig. 661.

[14] 'Chagall detests realistic art in all its forms . . . he transforms and transfigures [natural forms].' See Raissa Maritain, 'On Chagall's Surrealism' (1958), in Jacob Baal Teshuva, ed., *Chagall: A Retrospective* (Paris, 1995), p. 145.

[15] Cf. Jean-Michel Foray, 'Un rendez-vous manqué', *Chagall Surréaliste?*, exhibition catalogue (Nice, Musée National Message Biblique Marc Chagall, 2001), pp. 8–16.

25. Ariel flying over the sea.

Futurism. One of the most moving pictures in *The Tempest* series shows Ariel posed over the sea in a wonderful diagonal line, playing the violin, Chagall's own favourite instrument (p. 105) (Illustration 25). Ariel's diagonal flight repeats the pronounced diagonal movement in a number of Chagall's early works. So, for example, in *The Traveller* (1917),[16] in *en avant, en avant* (1918), a study for the first anniversary of the Revolution,[17] and *Costume Design for Mikhoels* (1920).[18] The diagonal movement in these pictures, their élan, is a hallmark of artistic and political Futurism.[19] The forward and upward thrust expresses the Futurist liberation from the past, from the dogmas of the well-made and well-balanced picture, but also, at the same time, the dynamics of revolution, the march forward, *en avant, en avant*. Although he is not stretching his legs, but only soaring diagonally and playing his violin, Ariel shares with these Futurist images their poetic power.

The revolutionary fervour of Chagall's early days in Russia, expressed in his study for the first anniversary of the Revolution, may also enfold a personal pun. According to a well-known anecdote, recounted by Chagall in his memoirs, written in 1922, the great revolutionary poet Mayakovsky had written a dedication to him in one of his books: 'God grant that everyone may *chagalle* like Chagall.'[20] Mayakovsky was punning on the Russian word 'chagalle', meaning 'march forward'.[21] This intertwined linguistic and visual pun underlines Chagall's personalized sub-text in everything he paints, his striving to march forward and liberate himself from the dogmatic thinking of the contemporary artistic establishment. Another possible verbal/visual pun around Chagall's name plays upon the Russian word for a song-bird, the goldfinch, *chegol*.[22] This could explain the abundance of birds in many of the illustrations to the play, as in many other of his works. For example, in the lithograph depicting the musical spirits, two of them bearing Chagall's own features, there appear two birds, the one clapping cymbals, the other with a violin. So, in addition to Chagall's customary self-representation as the lover, one could say that he appears another four times within this single picture.

[16] Apter-Gabriel, *Dreams and Drama*, fig. 8.

[17] Étude pour le premier anniversaire de la Révolution: *en avant, en avant*, (1918), crayon and gouache on framed parchment paper, 23.4 × 33.7 cm. Musée National d'Art Moderne, Centre Pompidou, Paris. Reproduced in *Chagall Surréaliste?*, p. 43.

[18] Apter-Gabriel, *Dreams and Drama*, fig. 9.

[19] See Benjamin Harshav, in *Marc Chagall and the Jewish Theater*, exhibition catalogue (New York, Guggenheim Museum, 1993), p. 17a.

[20] *Ma vie*, traduction de Bella Chagall (Paris, 1957), p. 220. See also, Ruth Apter-Gabriel, 'Chagall in Russia', in Apter-Gabriel, *Dreams and Drama*, p. 15.

[21] The poem 'The March of Time' appears in Vladimir Mayakovsky, *The Bathhouse* (1930), *The Complete Plays of Vladimir Mayakovsky*, tr. Guy Daniels (New York, 1971), pp. 256–9. The typographical setting of the lines is in itself in a repeated diagonal form, not uncommon in Mayakovsky's poetry.

[22] I am indebted to Dr Elena Tartakovsky for helping me with the Russian.

CHAGALL'S *TEMPEST*: AN AUTOBIOGRAPHICAL READING

Of all his plays, *The Tempest* is the only one in which Shakespeare identifies, almost explicitly, with his protagonist as creator. It is perhaps for this reason that Chagall found the play congenial to his own view of art as necessarily including the artist within his work. Chagall found the way to make Shakespeare's play a vehicle for his own self-expression and, in the process, revealed the crucial importance of angelology in the Judaeo-Christian tradition to the relationship of Prospero with Ariel.

Chagall's solipsistic view of the world, in which he is both creator and protagonist, both artist and subject-matter, highlights Shakespeare's own identification with Prospero in their shared tragic perception of their art and life fading, like 'this insubstantial pageant', into thin air. Chagall managed to tighten the underlying structure of the play and interpret it as a play about the spiritual life of the artist and his struggle with the recalcitrant materials of his art and the tempest of his life.

READING ILLUSTRATED EDITIONS: METHODOLOGY AND THE LIMITS OF INTERPRETATION

STUART SILLARS

That Shakespeare's plays were published in his life-time to a degree almost unparalleled in the works of other dramatists may or may not reflect their construction, at least in part, for reading rather than performance; doubtless this debate will long continue. But one implication of the publication statistics, as revealed and analysed by Lukas Erne,[1] is irrefutable: there was a large and continuing market for these volumes, implying an eagerness to consume the plays through reading. The recent work of Andrew Murphy[2] has made clear the continuing force and extent of this eagerness and its satisfaction through publication, doing much to adjust the focus of literary history to encompass popular as well as scholarly editions. By definition, the former have had wider circularity. In the 1770s, John Bell claimed sales of 3,000 copies simply for the first number of his serial Shakespeare,[3] shortly after Samuel Johnson's two editions of 1765 had sold about half that number.[4] Nearly a century later, Charles Knight boasted sales of 700,000 for the various serial forms of his complete edition, extending the figure to one million when a later printing, selling for two shillings, was included.[5] Both the Bell and the Knight are, of course, illustrated editions, forming part of the tradition beginning with Rowe – whose editions with pictorial frontispieces appeared when the Folios were the only other editions, and were neither easily nor cheaply available for most readers. The tradition continues through the second editions of Pope and Theobald, through those of Hanmer and Bell, to the Victorian serial printings, first those of Charles Knight and 'Barry Cornwall', to its climax and

conclusion in the volumes of Howard Staunton, the Cowden Clarkes and John Dicks. Given this profusion, it seems hard to argue against the proposition that the illustrated edition was increasingly the initial encounter with the plays for many, if not most, readers from the beginning of the eighteenth century to the close of the nineteenth.

So much for the currency of the illustrated edition: what of its value within the complex exchange system of performance, reading, and the limitations of critical study? I'd like here to begin to explore some of the problems of critically addressing the illustrated edition, conscious that the address is inevitably a dual one. It is concerned both with attempting to recover something of the variety of reading experiences that these editions offered their diversity of original readers; and also with exploring, defining and delimiting appropriate critical devices to be adopted by readers today. The two are, of course, inevitably intertwined, and any insights into earlier readings will emerge only through the lens of later practices. But, following the not inconsiderable precedent of

---

[1] *Shakespeare as Literary Dramatist* (Cambridge, 2003).

[2] See *Shakespeare in Print: A History and Chronology of Shakespeare Publishing* (Cambridge, 2003) and *Shakespeare for the People: Working-Class Readers, 1800–1900* (Cambridge, 2008).

[3] The claim is recorded, though without citation, by Stanley Morison in *John Bell, 1745–1831: Bookseller, Printer, Publisher, Typefounder, Journalist, &c.* (Cambridge, 1930).

[4] The figure is taken from William St Clair, *The Reading Nation in the Romantic Period* (Cambridge, 2004).

[5] Knight gives these figures in *The Bookseller*, 1 July 1868, p. 41. For further discussions of this claim, see Andrew Murphy, *Shakespeare for the People* (Cambridge, 2008), p. 83.

Erwin Panofsky, the task can be approached in the hope that the later stance will represent an act of *Gewalt* or creative violence in its readings.

A key aspect of the process is identifying the range of critical disciplines involved in the mingled endeavours of recovery and reframing. Clearly, what is involved is far more than an act, say, of textual close reading or performance history – whatever those terms may be taken to mean – although both have their functions in the process. Another will involve engagement with art historical issues of medium, style and tradition, most particularly in terms of what might be conveyed through systems of reference known to contemporary artists and their audiences. While individual performances may not be an immediate source of reference, there may well be elements of allusion to stage business, the organisation of the stage, or larger conventions of action or presentation. At a more complex level, there is the difference in medium between dynamic representation on stage and the static medium of print, which will involve the reader in further acts of negotiative interpretation. And all of this must be carried on with an awareness that it is the illustrated edition, and not merely the illustration, that is the object of concern, intertwined with the effort to recover models of the reading experience that it offers.

One way of addressing these issues is to look at some early images. Here, for purposes of comparison, are François Boitard's design for Rowe's *The Winter's Tale* in 1709,[6] and Hubert Gravelot's for *All's Well that Ends Well* in the second edition of Theobald in 1740.[7] Boitard's image (Illustration 26) has clear implications of theatre in the curtain, forestage and what might well be a painted drop, with perhaps the shadow of a curtain before it, at the rear. But since the play was not performed between 1700 and 1709, when Boitard was in England, these elements must reflect a generalised theatricality, not record a performance, even one heard of from an intermediary. The design derives equally from a tradition of painting, the curtained throne at the right appearing in many earlier ceremonial images that reflect state visits or encounters between captives and victors.

But there are subtle forces at work in the use of these allusions. The sculptures in the niches to the rear play against the figure enthroned to the right, exploiting the ambiguity of the moment in which Hermione apparently moves from sculpted likeness to human figure, while the poses of the two female figures closest the throne, the nearer of which is surely Paulina, suggest intense concentration surrounds the latter's command, 'Music, awake her, strike!' (5.3.98).[8] The presentation of Leontes, hand open in amazement, echoes this mood. His placement at some distance from the figure, and on a physically lower plane, suggests, to an audience trained to recognize symbols of rank and worth, that the returned Hermione is of far higher moral stature than he, reinforcing the longer truth of the play's movement. To be fully effective, the engraving depends on the reader's skill in decoding this breadth of reference and teasing manipulation of form. Allusion to theatre merges with larger negotiation of artistic style and construction of meaning, and the whole is validated by the reader's awareness and analytical skill.

Contrast this with Gravelot's treatment of *All's Well That Ends Well* (Illustration 27). This engraving makes its effect through a far more immediate stylistic vocabulary, presenting a more representational encounter in a recognisable street. Again, it cannot record a performance, the play receiving its first post-Restoration staging by Henry Gifford in 1741, the year after the engraving was published. While the setting might be feasible in the contemporary European theatre, the deep recession that it implies is unlikely on the English stage.

---

[6] *The works of Mr. William Shakespear; in six volumes. Adorn'd with Cuts. Revis'd and Corrected, with an Account of the Life and Writings of the Author. By N. Rowe, Esq.* London: Jacob Tonson, 1709.

[7] *The Works of Shakespeare: in eight volumes . . . With notes, explanatory, and critical: by Mr. Theobald. The second edition,* 12 vols., London : H. Lintott, C. Hitch, J. and R. Tonson, C. Corbet, R. and B. Wellington, J. Brindley, and E. New, 1740.

[8] Line references to the plays throughout are to the most recent editions of *The New Cambridge Shakespeare.* Where quotations are made from earlier editions discussed in the text, the line numbers refer to the equivalent passages in the New Cambridge edition.

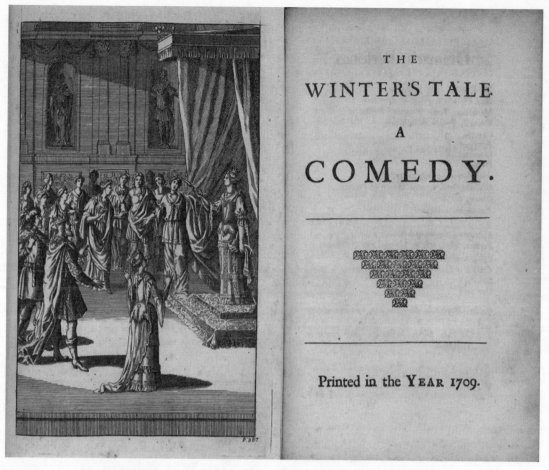

26. François Boitard, engraved by Elisha Kirkall: frontispiece to *The Winter's Tale* (Rowe, 1709).

More important, perhaps, is the carefully developed chiaroscuro, surely impossible in any theatre of the period, that ensures that Helena and the widow are in deep shadow before Bertram, Rossillon and a passable suggestion of the stage direction's 'whole army'. The gestures, too, are less reminiscent of the elaborate codes developed by le Brun and others for stage and canvas, instead reflecting the careful anatomical drawing that Gravelot developed during his stay in London. The use of attributes is carefully controlled to those that are instantly recognisable: the colours of the army are self-explanatory, and the staff carried by Helena conveys the meaning of a traveller without

demanding its decoding as a pilgrim's staff. The fall of the draperies has a Rococo elegance that subtly shifts the image towards the immediately fashionable, suggesting that the onlooker has simply turned a corner and encountered the scene. In short, the stress is far more on a moment of action, presented with a vocabulary and technique that is wholly print-based, than on the larger conceptual thrust achieved in the composition and allusiveness of the Boitard. As a result, the scene invites the reader to respond emotionally rather than intellectually, experiencing a momentary encounter rather than speculating on an implied, though unspecified, consequence. The task presented is

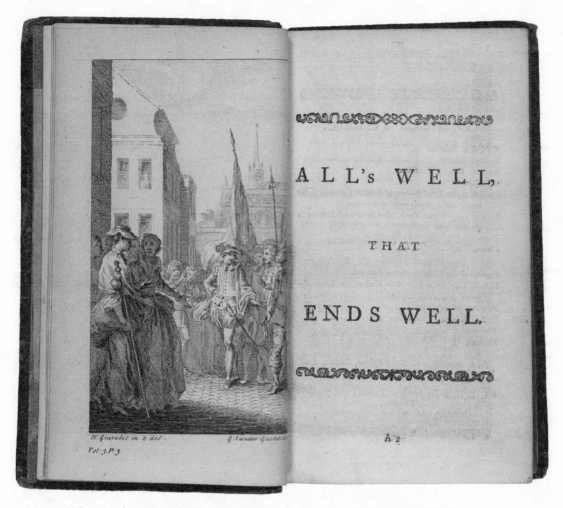

27. Hubert Gravelot, engraved by Gerard Vander Gucht: frontispiece to *All's Well that Ends Well* (Theobald, 1740).

one of emotional contemplation, not conceptual decryption.

This discussion suggests many of the approaches necessary to absorb the effect of these two representative images, and also raises questions that underlie the task. Perhaps the most fundamental need is the sorting-out of the system of relations that each image has with contemporary theatre, artistic style and reading practice. Another dimension – another axis with which the above relationships intersect – is the selection of moment for illustration, with its consequent implications

about the play itself and the way it is presented to the reader. These axes of interpretive practice raise another question: to what kinds of reader are the images addressed, and how should we, in turn, define the experience they offer? It's impossible, of course, to define all kinds of their original readers, but certain principles can I think be established. One is the implicit consequence of style and the construction of idea within the images themselves. As E. H. Gombrich demonstrated in *Art and Illusion*, and Erwin Panofsky explored in almost all of his art historical writing, structures of representation and the methods by which the onlooker decodes and assimilates them are matters of convention and consensus that change with systems of belief, philosophy and society. The present-day critic's act of reading must, then, to some degree, attempt to recover systems of meaning and reading before moving to explore the effect of an image on the reading experience offered for the play that it presents.

Not all contemporary readers, of course, will be skilled in these techniques of reading images. But many will have assimilated them without conscious effort: as far as I know, no educational establishment provides tutorials in MTV iconography for the channel's primary audience. When we turn to the issue of relating the image to the play, the effect upon the reader is infinitely various, but we can and must distinguish between two major groups; those who have read the play before, and those who come to it afresh. Elsewhere, I have called these the qualified reader and the new reader – the former term used to denote limitation, as much as preparation, by previous experience, not the successful negotiation of a contemporary examination.[9] For the new reader, both images will be generally suggestive of concerns or event; for the qualified, they will reinforce or challenge earlier ideas of the play. Any present-day stance towards these images, and the others of which they are representative, should at least show an awareness of this duality, as well as of the skills of image assimilation available for each period or generation.

The question of reader response brings with it an issue fundamental to the working of a frontispiece. By its placing, the frontispiece acts to define, in a variety of degrees and emphases, a key concept or key moment within the play before the verbal text is provided, in consequence suggesting the trajectory of action or an essential of argument or idea that will inevitably colour the reading experience to come. It is worth pausing for a moment here to recall that the word frontispiece comes originally from architecture, where it refers to the main frontage of a building, designed to reveal its purpose and character. Later, it was employed to describe what is now known as the title-page, which often provided a visual, emblematic synopsis of the contents of the book – the series of diagnostic portraits clustering around the title in Burton's *Anatomy of Melancholy*, for example, or the complex iconography of the Folio of Ben Jonson's *Works*. The purely typographic frontispieces that appeared in many of Shakespeare's quartos at first sight have no relation to this tradition; but, in making reference to key episodes of the play's action, they direct the reader in constructing the play's trajectory in a way much like that of many pictorial frontispieces. From these earlier forms, the power of the frontispiece over the reader becomes clear: it will have a major influence on the experience that follows. In the case of Shakespeare's plays, this will most likely mean establishing the moment presented as a point of climax in event or idea, stressing the nature of a character or relationship or, less frequently, revealing a particular issue as a major point of focus.

Seen within this larger frame, the frontispiece is revealed as a significant determinant in the reader's experience of the play. For the new reader it will offer one or more suggestions about what is to follow, opening various possibilities of action and idea to be confirmed, rejected or redefined through interaction with the pages that follow. For the qualified reader, it will reinforce or challenge an established interpretation of the play, much as seeing a new production will redefine an earlier experience. For both kinds, this will modify the reading experience: and identifying precisely how this act of visual privileging functions, in itself and as part of the longer sequence of reading, must surely be a key component of any subsequent critical analysis. This, of course, raises a further question: do the images reflect prevalent stances or generate them? This suggests that a grasp of other interpretations, performed or written, should be at least a part of the analytic process of reading these editions today. And this takes us back to the earlier question concerning the relations between images and

---

9 For a fuller discussion of these terms and their implications, see *The Illustrated Shakespeare, 1709–1875* (Cambridge, 2008), pp. 22–3.

performance practice, revealing the innate connections between all of the questions posed by the interpretation of illustrated editions, and the techniques that they demand of the scholar.

The reading experience offered by the contribution of an illustrative frontispiece is a very specific one, but some of its elements are shared with the placing of images elsewhere in a printed edition of a play. A special caution must be applied to eighteenth-century editions with pictorial frontispieces, which brings with it further implications about how the visual and verbal texts these combine were read then, and should be approached now. Both of John Bell's Shakespeares, the 'Acting' edition of 1774[10] and the 'Literary' of 1788,[11] were first issued in serial form, for binding by their purchasers. Various forms of each of these editions contained engravings showing scenes in naturalistic settings, or individual actors in character. Many surviving copies include both sets of images, bound in different locations within the volumes according to the owner's preference. Importantly, some move the engravings originally presented as frontispieces, the naturalistic scenes, into the body of the play, binding them opposite the lines they illustrate. Others locate the actors' portraits in this position. The two forms respectively present an imagined, non-theatrical visualization of event, and a stylised account of an individual performance which will in some cases function as a recollection of one witnessed by the reader-purchaser-binder. To an extent, then, one privileges the play as a performative entity, the other as something constructed imaginatively through reading. But another physical form – in my experience the most common of those surviving – binds both images at the opening of each play, as a new kind of double frontispiece.[12]

The result is the production of a quite new visual experience for the reader. Overall, this formal variation suggests that, just as each copy of the First Folio must be seen as an individual bibliographic statement, so bound copies of early illustrated editions must be seen as existing in a number of separate forms, reflecting the preferences of their readers in a very literal construction of the plays. It is one that is quite radical for the time, since separate plates were usually inserted as right-hand, or recto, images, to avoid 'offset', the imprinting of one image against the surface of the other. Their opposed placing is clearly the result of a conscious decision by reader or binder to make both simultaneously visible. This may be evidence of a specific dimension of reading, extending the practice of shared reading aloud to the discussion of the engravings and the readings they present. In a culture where conversation is highly regarded as a mark of cultural discernment, this seems not at all unlikely, although there is no tangible evidence to record such events taking place.

Whatever the theory and practice that produced this layout, such presentation of images effectively constitutes a self-contained conceptual summation of the play in a single page-opening, often generating critical readings of no little significance. Illustration 28 shows such a combination from a copy of the 1788 *Henry V* in the Folger Shakespeare Library,[13] pairing an image of Sarah Siddons as Princess Katherine with one showing Pistol's capture of a French soldier. Each may be read separately, the former as one of many presentations of the leading woman actor of her generation, invariably seen in a profile to reveal elegant,

10 *Bell's Edition of Shakespeare's Plays, as they are now performed at the Theatres Royal in London, regulated from the prompt books in each house. With notes critical and illustrative by the authors of the 'Dramatic Censor'*, 5 vols. with 4-volume 'continuance', London : Printed for John Bell, and C. Etherington at York, 1774. The publication history of the edition is complex and its dates uncertain. For a full discussion, see Kalman A. Burnim and Philip H. Highfill Jr., *John Bell, Patron of British Theatrical Portraiture: A Catalog of the Theatrical Portraits in his Editions of Bell's Shakespeare and Bell's British Theatre* (Carbondale and Edwardsville, IL, 1998), pp. 10–13.

11 *Bell's Edition: Dramatic writings of Will Shakespeare, With the Notes of all the various Commentators; printed complete from the best editions of Sam. Johnson and Geo. Steevens*, 20 vols. [1785–88], London: Printed for, and under the direction of, John Bell, 1788.

12 I have discussed the two editions, and the reading experiences they offer, at greater length in 'Seeing, Studying, Performing: *Bell's Edition of Shakespeare* and Performative Reading', *Performance Research*, 10:3, 'On Shakespeare', edited by Peter Holland and William Sherman (September 2005), pp.18–27.

13 Folger call number PR 2752 1788a copy 2 Sh.Col. vol. 12.

28. Edward Burney, engraved by J. Thornthwaite: 'Mrs. Siddons in Princess Katherine,' bound facing P. J. De Loutherbourg, engraved by Hall: frontispiece to *King Henry V* (Bell, 1788).

sweeping gestures, and appealing as much to a cult of celebrity as to an interest in the character represented. The engraving of Pistol presents independently a scene that might be read both as an instance of nationalist triumphalism, or a darkly comic undermining of such values through the equation with Pistol's character. The omission of this scene in production by Kemble, Macready and, later, Charles Kean, implies more than the independence of the illustration from stage practice, showing also the discomfort that the events produced in performers and audiences.

Taken together, the two offer a different range of interpretations. At a simple narrative level, the two aspects of the play, defined through widely separated social gradations, may be the dominant impression. Other readers might extend this to see a sharp, and ironic, contrast between the refined grace of Siddons as Katherine and the clumsy vigour of Pistol. But the juxtaposition invites a more suggestive reading. The resemblance between the figures of Katherine and the French soldier, both presented in profile, in postures suggesting different degrees of supplication, draws a visual parallel between the play's two engagements, bringing them together as variants of a single trope of conquest – and one that, in both cases, is linked with financial expediency. This acts as a counter to the more insistently heroic reading of the kind that would be expected from a presentation of the play at the end of the eighteenth century, opening up a series of questions about contemporary political, as well as performative and critical, approaches to the histories.

The counter-argument to this reading, of course, is that it results from an interaction caused by the binding process that is not necessarily the consequence of a critical or interpretive decision by binder or purchaser. But no matter: the convergence is presented to the reader every time she or he opens the physical book, the visual pairing insistent even if at a subconscious level of perception. For the new reader, all kinds of links will be possible between the two images, which will in some measure define key elements of the action, much as the image on the cover of a magazine privileges the article it illustrates. For the qualified reader, the references, and the link, may contradict or reinforce earlier assumptions – in parallel, perhaps, to the responses of a theatregoer seeing a new production of a play seen many times before. But in all these circumstances the encounter with the images affects the reader's perception at a level that makes an early critical insinuation about the play's structure and ideas. And the dual visualization in itself makes a very strong conceptual point about the dual identities of the plays themselves, as both entities realized in performance and texts available in print.

The nature of the reading experience assumes a somewhat different identity for engravings placed within the body of the play. The edition of Bellamy and Robarts issued serially between 1788 and 1791 was the first to include two plates, each placed opposite a page of dialogue.[14] This material doubling makes possible the visual linking of events in the play that are individually of considerable, though not necessarily connected, interpretive force, affecting the reader's construction of the trajectory and ideas of the play. The effects of this are immediately apparent in *Antony and Cleopatra*, where the two engravings show Antony's attempted suicide and Cleopatra's death, a pairing that immediately reveals the play's dual tragedic

progress. A rare sheet of instructions to the printer, bound in error with one of the Folger's Bellamy and Robarts editions, reveals that information was provided on where to place the prints. Again, however, editions exist in different forms, although whether through error or personal preference it is impossible to say. My own copy places both images on right-hand pages (see illustrations 29 and 30).[15] Each event is given equal status, and the engagement with the death of Antony must, to a reader encountering the text for the first time in progressing through the volume, have seemed at first sight to suggest a more usual tragedic progression; but this would surely have been displaced when the death of Cleopatra is revealed, in both word and image, as something of far greater consequence. The visual pairing thus becomes an important interpretive statement on a larger scale than the momentary, drawing attention to the play's extension of tragedic structure.

But this may not always be the case, especially when the different forms in which the edition survive is considered. In my copy the image faces a page of text that begins with Cleopatra's final words:

> As sweet as balm, as soft as air, as gentle –
> O Antony!–Nay, I will take thee too: —
>   [*Applying another asp to her arm.*
> What, should I stay, — [*Dies.*   (5.2.305–7)

The page continues with the entry of the Guard, the death of Charmian, the entry of Dolabella and, finally, that of Caesar. That all of these take place opposite the engraving effectively maintains the presence of the dead Cleopatra during these subsequent events, intensifying both them and the death itself, which becomes a mute presence analogous with that on stage, where the body remains during the subsequent exchanges. One of the more complex tasks for the reader of a play is to remain aware of the presence of non-speaking characters: the visual statement makes this powerfully apparent,

---

[14] *The Plays of William Shakespeare, complete in eight volumes* [1788–91], London: Printed for Bellamy and Robarts, 1791.
[15] Folger call number PR 2752 1791a1 c.1 Sh.Col. vol. 5.

29. Edward Burney, engraved by Goldar: first illustration to *Antony and Cleopatra* (Bellamy and Robarts, 1791).

reinforcing the pathos of the death itself through its continuing force on the action.

Here, the currency of the play is driven forward; but a copy in the Folger collection incites a quite different response by the image being placed on a left-hand page (Illustration 31). It faces Cleopatra's speech beginning 'Give me my robe; put on my crown; I have / Immortal longings in me' (5.2.274–5). The engraving shows events from a little later, with Charmian lying dead beside Cleopatra and Dolabella leaning over her shoulder, and this makes clear the events that will follow from Cleopatra's speech on the facing page. In a sense this advances the action by showing what will shortly follow the speech on the page, but its larger effect is to slow, if not suspend, the reader's progress through the play. Making the outcome inevitable, it adds to the pathos of the final speech, creating an emotional and narrative caesura or meditative suspension. Fundamental to this is the physical placement of the engraving, which forces the eye back and thus inevitably breaks the usual left–right reading movement. Image and word thus combine to produce a specific response to this climactic moment,

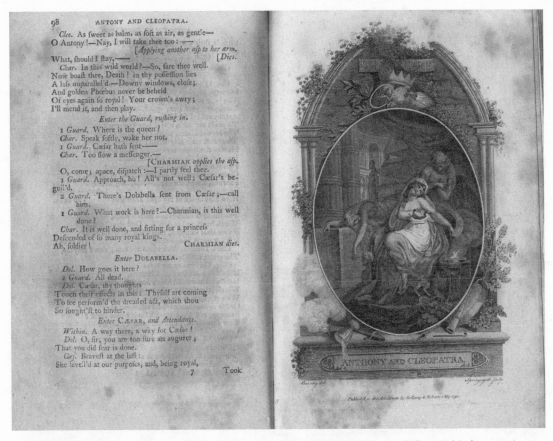

30. Edward Burney, engraved by Springsguth: second illustration to *Antony and Cleopatra* (Bellamy and Robarts, 1791).

the halt increasing its intensity in a manner that depends on the interaction of the two elements.

This stress on emotional engagement is matched by the general tenor of the image, which reflects contemporary *sensibilité* in selecting moments of emotional engagement rather than those of rapid action, or a larger visualization of language or idea across the breadth of the play. The placing recommended by the binding instructions produces an experience parallel to that of a stage performance; the earlier location offers something closer to the technique more frequent in a novel, holding back a moment of climax for maximal effect. Neither is necessarily preferable: they simply work in different ways. To the range of other aesthetic categories that must be considered when exploring the read-

ings offered by the illustrated edition, then, must be added two more: the history of emotional presentation in visual texts, and the engagement between the illustrated drama and the illustrated novel, a major form since the 1740s when Hubert Gravelot provided engravings for Fielding and Richardson. Whether or not the decision to bind the images in these two different ways rested on such considerations is impossible to answer, and in a sense irrelevant: the form of the text is what remains, and the effect on the reader is consequential upon this material circumstance, not on the motivation behind it. There is one more element worthy of note in this edition. Both the versions discussed here take place in a volume with an allegorical frontispiece, 'Shakespeare holding up the mirror to

31. Alternative binding for second illustration to *Antony and Cleopatra* (Bellamy and Robarts, 1791).

dignified guilt' (Illustration 32) and are thus placed beneath its emotional and conceptual shadow. For the present-day reader this poses a further challenge, in accepting a mindset that can accept both the emotional involvement of the death scene and the narrative statement of a moral criticism of the works of Shakespeare that the frontispiece presents.

These variations in physical form, and the consequent diversity of readings they produce, reveal the need to see eighteenth-century editions as individual acts of construction, or perhaps even as acts of adaptation to parallel those of production. When read, they are events that have their own perfor-

mative actuality, both when absorbed by individual readers of different levels of experience, and when rendered in the collective, shared reading often undertaken within small groups and the discussion which must, we assume, have flowed from it, in pursuit of the new pastime of conversation. They need to be seen very much in this light. Just as the adaptations and burlesques of the eighteenth-century stage are now seen as negotiations between a notional authentic text and a series of ideological, theatric, aesthetic and social currents, so the individual illustrated editions should be placed within these larger frames, and valued as individual

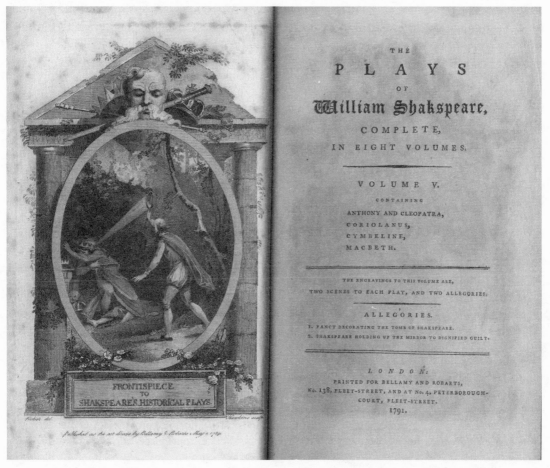

32. Richter engraved by Hankins: 'Shakespeare holding up the mirror to dignified guilt'. Frontispiece to Volume 5, Bellamy and Robarts, 1791.

presentations of the plays. All these elements must form part of any present-day attempt to explore, and clarify, the nature of these editions and the reading experiences they originally generated.

Changes in the physical processes of book production in the first third of the nineteenth century, in particular due to the use of mechanical case-binding, render irrelevant some, though by no means all, of the practices discussed above, but they also introduced new elements just as important. Charles Knight's *Pictorial Shakspere*, published serially between 1838 and 1842,[16] reveals a wholly new method of play reading that does much to displace

the reductive representation of the gulf between scholarly and popular editions of the plays – a distinction always fraught with dangerous implications for the later critic. Knight's approach is largely concerned with a clearly stated, though never fully argued, assumption of the importance of historical accuracy – that is, the presentation of the plays

---

[16] *The Pictorial Edition of the Works of Shakspere. Edited by Charles Knight*, 56 parts, London: Charles Knight and Co., 56 monthly parts, 1838–43. Issued as 7 volumes, with an additional supplementary volume containing the life of Shakespeare. Subsequent versions included 'The National Edition', 3 vols., London: Routledge, 1858.

in a manner authoritatively showing the period in which their action occurs – and which rested on genuine and extensive historical research.

This mindset is implicit within the structure of the plays. Knight breaks the plays by introducing sections of 'Illustrations' at the end of each act, which contain both illustrations in the earlier sense of the word – exemplary and clarifying footnotes – and visual depictions of specific places, costumes, customs or other elements mentioned in the play. The play is thus punctuated by visual and verbal annotations that contribute to a particular order of scholarly reading – one that focuses on fashionable antiquarianism rather than the *apparatus criticus* of scholarly editions of an earlier or later period. The result is to fracture reader involvement, acting against the assumption that, since the plays have pictures, they are read in the same way as the illustrated serial novels which are their immediate contemporaries, and denying the kind of involvement offered by the Bellamy and Robarts example discussed earlier. Further, as the sections headed 'illustrations' contain visual material to extend the commentary on the plays, so the use of illustrations moves towards a similarly explanatory function: the images are there to offer clarification of referential elements such as setting, costume or accoutrement, and far less to offer interpretive comment or emotional amplification.

Alongside his edition of Shakespeare, Knight produced a breathtaking array of educative publications – it is as if he is the publishing embodiment of the Victorian work ethic.[17] Two of the most widely disseminated were his *Penny Magazine*,[18] which appeared between 1832 and 1846, and his history of London, published from 1841 to 1846. That the plays are being approached from a material, antiquarian basis essentially the same as the stance adopted in these publications is shown by the use of woodblocks shared between the two kinds of publication. Thus, an image of the Bloody Tower occurs in both *London* and *Richard III*, and one of the Holbein Gate both in the former and in *Henry VIII*.

This use may perhaps be explained as a specific kind of textual annotation, but the same sharing

of material occurs in places within the text itself, with, for example, the same woodblock used to show the banquet scene in *Henry VIII* and to support the discussion of Westminster Hall in *London*. But Knight's edition is not wholly concerned with visualising material circumstance. The illustrated title-pages – frontispieces in the older sense of the word – are generally what Knight referred to as 'Imaginative embellishment' to balance the 'realities' that were the basis of the plays,[19] and presenting the reader with a complex of intellectual and imaginative involvement of a level even greater than that of the frontispiece and textual engravings of the Bellamy and Robarts *Antony and Cleopatra*. The intellectual gymnastics demanded for the comprehension of these ranges perhaps reach their climax with *Pericles*,[20] where the treatment of Gower suggests that original readers were capable of supple shifts of approach while turning the volume's pages. The simple, materialist approach is taken in the presentation of the same wood engraving of Gower's tomb as headpiece to the 'Notice on the Authenticity of *Pericles*' (Illustration 33) that is used in the discussion of St Mary Overies in the appropriate volume of *London* (Illustration 34). That this occurs at the end of the play adds further to the complexities established at its outset. The frontispiece-title shows Gower in the

---

17 The full range of his activities has recently been described by Valerie Gray in *Charles Knight: Educator, Publisher, Writer* (Aldershot, 2006). Knight's own account of his activities, which should perhaps be approached with a little caution, is given in his autobiography, *Passages of a Working Life during Half a Century: With a Prelude of Early Reminiscences*, 2 vols., London : Bradbury & Evans, 1864.

18 The title-page of the first number reads as follows, revealing the extent of its production and distribution: *The Penny Magazine of the Society for the Diffusion of Useful Knowledge.* London: Charles Knight and Co., 22 Ludgate St, New York, William Jackson, 102 Broadway, Boston. J. H. Francis; Philadelphia, Orrin Rogers; Baltimore, W. N. Harrison; Washington, DC, James Burchenal.

19 'Advertisement' to *Comedies*, vol. 1.

20 This appeared in the seventh volume of the collected edition. Headed 'Doubtful Plays', it also included *Titus Andronicus* and *The Two Noble Kinsmen*, as well as fourteen other plays at one time suggested as part of the canon, remarkable at a time when the majority of scholarly editions rejected these.

[Gower's Monument.]

NOTICE

ON

THE AUTHENTICITY OF PERICLES.

THE *external* testimony that Shakspere was the author of Pericles would appear to rest upon stronger evidence, as far as regards the fact of publication, than that which assigns to him the authorship of Titus Andronicus. That play was not published as his work till after his death: Pericles was published with Shakspere's name as the author during his lifetime. But this evidence is not decisive. In 1600 was printed 'The first part of the true and honourable history of the Life of Sir John Oldcastle, &c. Written by William Shakespeare;' and we should be entitled to receive that representation of the writer of 'Sir John Oldcastle' as good evidence of the authorship, were we not in possession of a fact which entirely outweighs the bookseller's insertion of a popular name in his title-page. In the manuscript diary of Philip Henslowe, preserved at Dulwich College, is the following entry :—" The 16th of October, 99. Received by me Thomas Downton of Philip Henslowe, to pay Mr. Monday, Mr. Drayton, Mr. Wilson, and Hathaway, for The first part of the Lyfe of Sir

111

33. Headpiece to 'Notice on the Authenticity of *Pericles*' (Charles Knight, 1838–43).

of that day, the chorister as bishop, and his companions as prebends, walked in procession to the church, preceded by the dean and canons. As he went he was feasted by the people, and bestowed in return his blessing, which was highly coveted.

We arrive now at one of the most interesting events in the history of St. Mary Overies—its restoration about the close of the fourteenth century, when the poet *Gower* contributed the principal funds. This church was doubtless endeared to him by a peculiar tie: he was married here, in 1397, to Alice Groundolf, by the celebrated William of Wickham, who then held the see of Winchester; and here their ashes repose. A small monument marked the site of her resting-place, according to Leland, which has long disappeared; his is doubtless destined to last as long as the beautiful edifice which enshrines it.

[Gower's Monument.]

This monument, now in the south transept, was originally in a part of the north aisle of the nave, called St. John's Chapel, where it was placed in accordance with the poet's directions as expressed in his will. He writes, " I leave my soul to God my Creator ; and my body to be buried in the church of the Canons of the blessed Mary de Overes, *in a place expressly provided for it.*"

The gratitude of the canons to their generous benefactor was marked by their long continuing to perform a yearly obiit to his memory, and by hanging up a tablet beside the monument with the inscription " that whosoever prayeth for the soul of John Gower, he shall, so oft as he so doth, have a M and a D days of pardon." Of the sumptuous beauty of this monument our engraving furnishes the best description ; we confine ourselves, therefore, to a notice of the inscriptions, and of such other portions as are not there distinguishable. Each of the three

34. J. W. Archer, engraved by J. Jackson: Illustration to St Mary Overies, *London*, volume I (Charles Knight, 1844).

35. J. Jackson: Title-page, *Pericles* (Charles Knight).

foreground, and behind him what seems to be a representation of the play's conclusion, suggesting his function as narrator (Illustration 35). The Persons Represented page which follows (Illustration 36) presents Gower above the list of characters with, beneath, a storm-tossed ship. The visual suggestion in both complements the character's liminal function, as presenter-chronicler held between action and audience. The placing above the character list serves to present this distance in a manner peculiar to the medium of the play in print, separating the reader even from the distanced involvement that Gower has on stage. Yet opposite this image there is a comparatively naturalistic engraving of the play's opening, with Pericles received by Antiochus and his daughter in a formal, classical setting appropriate to the play's notional setting of Antioch. Knight's authenticity is asserted at the end of Act 1, where the port of Tyre is shown

as a small tailpiece in the style of a contemporary topographical engraving. The reader is thus presented with a printed version of the distanced narrator, visually introducing characters to balance his theatrical function of introducing events; the events themselves; and an image of the geographical setting – a compound that suggests considerable sophistication in the assimilative and ordering skills demanded of the reader. At one level – in the storm and the image of Antioch – there is novelistic involvement; at another – in the presence of Gower – there is performative narration; and at yet another there is an antiquarian visualisation of the play's setting. To this must be added the quotations from Gower's *Confessio Amantis* that are presented as the 'Illustrations' after each act, and the engraving of the monument to Gower that prefaces the concluding 'Notice'. All this suggests a skilled control of readerly engagement that has no difficulty in code-switching between an academic awareness of source and allusion, a subtle grasp of the difference between the stage and print functions of Gower, and a novelistic immersion in character and event. And, of course, the sophistication is not only the reader's, but also the text's, in the transmediation of the play's complicated structures into the form of a printed edition, which is itself presented at the intersection of scholarly and popular states.

This response should not, however, be taken to typify the processes followed by readers of popular Victorian editions of the plays. While Knight's volumes, and those of the other Victorian editors, lack the degree of variation in individual binding and location of engravings found in those of Bell, Bellamy and Robarts and others from the preceding century, they still exist in enough different material forms to instil caution in the critic attempting to recover their effect on the reader. Some later editions of Knight's plays, those issued in bound volumes after the original serial issue, and some of those issued in the USA, place the 'Illustration' sections together at the end of each play, and thus offer a more continuous trajectory of the plays, perhaps engendering a more immediate imaginative engagement in the reader. The

36. J. W. Whimper: Persons Represented, and J. Jackson: headpiece to Act 1 scene 1, *Pericles* (Charles Knight).

most forceful example of variation in progressive versions of Victorian editions is shown in Howard Staunton's Shakespeare, which contained several hundred wood-engravings after designs by Sir John Gilbert. Published in serial parts in the 1860s and in three volumes immediately thereafter, it went through a large number of subsequent printings in many different physical forms.[21] But only in the *Library Shakespeare* of 1873–5[22] did it achieve its most complete integration between word and image, a relation made possible by the use of the original woodblocks within a much larger page and two-column setting of the play. The increased space makes possible the use of subtly paired images that anticipate action, draw out parallels, move the reader onward to new action, or control and define the reading experience in other ways. Thus, for

example, an image of Bolingbroke before Richard II appears opposite an image of the gardener being overheard by the Queen and her ladies, the symbolic link tightened by the gardener's gesture (Illustration 37). The serial issues, and the three-volume edition, place the images on different pages, and the continuity and resonance are much diminished. So, too, is the contrast of the play's modalities, the performative iconography of ritual statecraft in Richard, the symbolic realism of the gardener laid

[21] *The Plays of Shakespeare. Edited by Howard Staunton; the illustrations by John Gilbert; engraved by the Brothers Dalziel*, London: G. Routledge & Co., 1856–60.

[22] *The Library Shakespeare Illustrated by Sir John Gilbert, George Cruikshank and R. Dudley*, 3 vols., London: William Mackenzie, 1873–5.

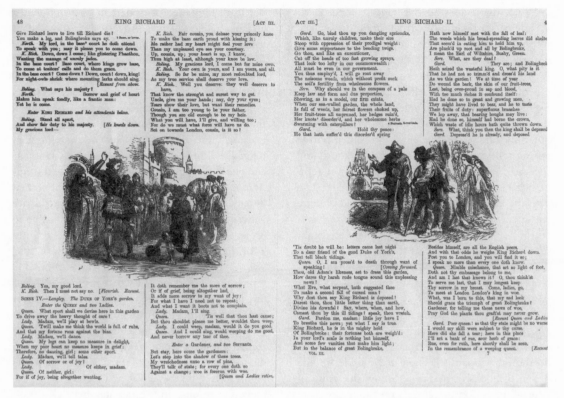

37. John Gilbert, engraved by the Dalziel brothers: page-opening from *Richard II* Act 3 scene 3 (The Library Shakespeare, 1873–5).

bare in visual conflict by the opposition of the two images.

At the time of this edition, the nature of the reading experience is made complex by its apparent similarity to that offered by the illustrated novel, which by this time has moved from the emotional and conceptual identity suggested in the Bellamy and Robarts edition discussed earlier towards something of larger currency and greater complexity. But, just as it is too easy either to dismiss or to venerate Boitard's designs for Rowe as records of contemporary performance, it is misleading to see Gilbert's edition as the consummation of the visual novelization of the plays. As in the earlier medial relation, there is some value; again, as in the earlier relation, it is not what it seems. The diversity of the illustrations in their viewpoint and location has taken over the function of the omniscient narrator –

literally, in a sense, because all-seeing; but not all-depicting, since withholding of visual information is an important tool in the continuously illustrated edition's equipment. It offers a control of progression, involvement and distance that parallels that of a narratorial presence, but the result is a performative reading of a rather different kind, since the detailed textual operations of dialogue and event are primarily – and, in most cases, initially – set by the play-text itself. Negotiation with the theatre, then, has been displaced by negotiation with the novel – but not only the novel, but with the multiple forms of illustrated journalism that proliferated from the founding of the *Illustrated London News* in 1841, many of which employed the same artist-engravers who worked on illustrated Shakespeares. These intersections demand another relational awareness in any sustained critical address.

What, then, does all this suggest for a critical approach to editions with illustrations, and the interpretations that may be deduced from them, for contemporary readers and for later scholars? One is that a range of disciplines needs to be brought together in any initial effort at understanding. Essential is a grasp of the larger aesthetic frames of the period of their production. The theatre is one, but only one: important also are contemporary artistic styles and methods of representation, and specific methods of reading associated with systems of belief or the organization of knowledge. The physical processes of book production and binding are also essential, as the earlier examples of the variety of bound forms have shown. There are other suggestive areas. Perceptual psychologists point out the importance in the Western tradition of elements on the right rather than the left: academics who lecture about images will generally stand on the side that is the audience's left of the images they are discussing, to give greater impact to image than performer – although, strangely, politicians often do the exact opposite. Those responsible for the design of books or magazines know the value of a 'tease' image on the cover, and the importance that this has in prioritizing the reader's reaction.

Discussion of these physical elements must also take into account the consequences of any valid reading of the printed text, so that we are in a sense moving into the territory of reader response criticism, modified by the physicality of the textual object. In reply to this I would also propose a new heresy, that of the material accident. This would work in parallel to the intentional fallacy, and propose that, whether or not the structure offered to the reader is the product of an accident of binding, it is still a powerful determinant on the reading that is derived. It is not enough to say that this is just the result of a binding error – what a world is in a 'just' . . .

There are many other physical elements that demand close study, something that the discussion of illustrated editions shares with the examination of other editions of Shakespeare, consideration that draws the practice closer to the larger discipline of book history. Subscription lists convey important details of the range of readers in terms of gender and place of residence. Advertising copy can be valuable in suggesting the nature of the intended readers, in some cases offering goods of a price that suggest a readership quite other than the devoted artisans that are habitually, and perhaps misleadingly, seen as a key constituent of the readership of the early serial novel. And, most striking perhaps, because most often overlooked in contemporary references, the names and locations of stationers and booksellers given on the title-pages of the editions need full citation, to reveal the extent of their distribution, instead of the uniform and reductive pattern of style sheets designed with reference to present-day, rather than much earlier, publications. That, for example, Bell's 'Acting' edition of 1774 was sold by a stationer in York as well as in London reveals the importance of what was then seen as a provincial interest in the plays, and suggests interesting possibilities for further discussion of the relation between performance and reading. All these factors will have had a powerful effect in defining the nature of the readers of initial editions, impacting in turn upon the nature and complexity of the process of reading and consequent debate.

There are also larger implications about the detail of critical practice. Since the reading of these volumes involves a variety of relations between text and image, the whole critical vocabulary needs, if not overhaul, then careful examination. That word 'text' is as troublesome as ever; but there has to be a term for the words themselves, in distinction from the images, during analysis and discussion. 'Play-text' is appealing, but ultimately invalid, as it suggests a basis for performance. 'Letterpress' is too specific, and too mechanical. Perhaps the best solution is the simplest – 'words'. This has the advantage of releasing 'text' for a reference to the whole book – or, to use the fashionable curatorial term, the 'object'. The fragmentation of literary studies has tended towards a separation of the multiple identities of textuality, isolating visual, literary, social, bibliographical and other textualities. My approach would be quite the reverse, merging these and other aspects, resting on the etymology of the word (from *texere*, to weave), to use 'text' about the whole fabric of the individual illustrated edition, the material broadcloth from which the reading experience is sewn. In the creative confusion that it generates, this is a metaphor of, if not quite a parallel to, the earlier experience in its relation to the construction of the play in the mind of the reader. Construction – or, perhaps, production: it is, after all, an act which, I have been arguing, is one that is equivalent to that of performance, and one in which the reader has a more active involvement in decoding, interpreting and bringing together the currency of the play through the unified fabric of word and image.

If we are fully to address the nature and identity of the the experience of reading the illustrated edition, throughout its history, and so validate a very considerable channel through which the plays became known, we need to address areas of this kind, and so explore the nature of response that they generate. Such a practice might, in consequence, reveal itself as a parallel to the history of performance and performance criticism. In drawing attention to this area of Shakespeare reception it will do much to explore earlier constructions and experiences: and, with luck, it might even be regarded as controversial.

CLOSE ENCOUNTERS WITH ANNE BRONTË'S SHAKESPEARE

PAUL EDMONDSON

In considering the Shakespeare that Anne Brontë knew, three kinds of close textual encounters emerge. First, the Shakespearian text the Brontë family might have read, and the context in which they read it; second, Anne Brontë's actual copy of Shakespeare's plays and how she might have read them; and third the kinds of Shakespeare allusions which are traceable in her two novels, *Agnes Grey* and *The Tenant of Wildfell Hall*. These close encounters with a reader and her writing will further our understanding of Shakespeare's importance in relation to Anne Brontë's creativity as well as to her life.

Shakespeare's impact on the work of the Brontë sisters is considerable. In Charlotte's novel, *Shirley*, there is a chapter entitled '*Coriolanus*'. Shakespeare is there appropriated as an emotional and political nexus for the relationship between Caroline Helstone and Robert Moore. Shakespeare is appropriated, to a lesser extent, in *Jane Eyre* and *The Professor*.[1] In Emily's *Wuthering Heights*, Shakespeare's influence is much more submerged, just one of the imaginative and influential threads that Emily weaves together.[2]

Although it includes the *Life of Sir Walter Scott*, the Lord Wharton Bible and Milton's *Paradise Lost*, no edition of Shakespeare is listed in the inventory of 'Books belonging to or inscribed by members of the Bronte family and held in the Brontë Parsonage Museum'. This should not be too surprising. The inventory is small and the most commonly read books tend not to survive. The Brontës' knowledge of Shakespeare can be safely assumed.

Lynne Reid Banks imagines the reading environment of the Brontës in her 1986 biographical novel, *Dark Quartet: The Story of the Brontës*:

When he [the Reverend Patrick] saw Branwell in a reverie over some book, written in a more permissive age, Patrick wondered if he was wise in allowing his children access to any volume in his library or that at Ponden Hall, which they frequently visited to borrow books. At first he had felt that they were safe from the grosser allusions in Shakespeare, for instance, by virtue of an inability of their essentially innocent minds to understand. Now he was no longer sure.[3]

Even the Brontës have begun looking for sex in Shakespeare. Perhaps the Rev. Patrick might have made sure that his children were kept safe from Shakespeare's sexier passages by acquiring the relatively recent four-volume edition of twenty plays in *The Family Shakespeare* (1807), edited by Henrietta Bowdler (1754–1830), which cut all the so-called 'grosser allusions'. Or, he might have

This article would not have been possible without the kind assistance of: Karin Brown (The Shakespeare Institute Library), Ann Dinsdale (The Brontë Parsonage Library), Chris Hay (Birmingham Central Library), Andrew Murphy (University of St Andrews), Coreen Turner (The Brontë Society), Betsy Walsh (Folger Shakespeare Library), and Georgianna Ziegler (Folger Shakespeare Library).

[1] Adrian Poole discusses Charlotte Brontë's appropriation of Shakespeare in *Jane Eyre, Shirley*, and *The Professor* in *Shakespeare and the Victorians* (London, 2004), pp. 102–10.

[2] I examine Shakespeare's influence on Charlotte and Emily Brontë in 'Shakespeare and the Brontës', *Brontë Studies*, 29.3 (2004), pp. 185–98.

[3] Lynne Reid Banks, *Dark Quartet: The Story of the Brontës* (London, 1976; repr. Harmondsworth, 1986), p. 66.

steered his children towards the ten-volume, completely Bowdlerized edition of 1818 (the year Emily was born) finished by Henrietta's twin brother, Thomas.

A translation of August Wilhelm Schlegel's *Lectures on Dramatic Art and Literature* was published in 1815; William Hazlitt's *Characters of Shakespeare's Plays* appeared in 1817 and his theatrical criticism, *A View of the English Stage*, appeared in 1818. It is likely that the Brontë family relished these classics among Shakespearian criticism. Their favourite novelist, Sir Walter Scott, was himself profoundly influenced by Shakespeare. They might have read with interest, too, Anna Jameson's *Characterisations of Women, Moral, Poetical and Historical* of 1832. Later this became known as *Shakespeare's Women*, a character study of the leading roles. The kind of cultural climate in which the Brontës read Shakespeare is alluded to in Jane Austen's *Mansfield Park*:

Shakespeare one gets acquainted with without knowing how. It is part of an Englishman's constitution. His thoughts and beauties are so spread abroad that one touches them every where, one is intimate with him by instinct. . . .

'No doubt one is familiar with Shakespeare in a degree,' [replies Edmund Bertram], 'from one's earliest years. His celebrated passages are quoted by every body; they are in half the books we open, and we all talk Shakespeare, use his similes, and describe with his descriptions.'[4]

The Brontës were probably aware of Edmund Kean's (1787–1833) flashes of lightning across the London stage, sharing what Adrian Poole calls the Victorian yearning for his 'physical intensity, excitement, and force'.[5] They might have read with interest the reviews of William Charles Macready's (1793–1873) Shakespearian productions at the Theatre Royal, Covent Garden. John Forster vibrantly reviewed Macready's productions of *King Lear* and *Coriolanus* in February and March 1838 for *The Examiner*. Charlotte herself saw William Charles Macready as Macbeth and Othello and writes to her friend Margaret Wooler on 14 February 1850:

I astounded a dinner-party by honestly saying I did not like him . . . The fact is the stage-system altogether is hollow nonsense . . . they comprehend nothing about tragedy or Shakespeare and it is a failure. I said so – and by so saying produced a blank silence – a mute consternation.[6]

Charlotte knew the Shakespeare she preferred. On 4 July 1834, she supplies her friend Ellen Nussey with a recommended reading list:

If you like poetry let it be first rate, Milton, Shakespeare, [James] Thomson, Goldsmith, Pope (if you will, but I don't admire him), Scott, Byron, [Thomas] Cam[p]bell, Wordsworth and Southey. Now Ellen don't be startled at the names of Shakespeare, and Byron. Both these were great Men and their works are like themselves, You will know how to chuse the good and avoid the evil, the finest passages are always the purest, the bad invariably revolting you will never wish to read them twice, Omit the Comedies of Shakespeare and the Don Juan, perhaps the Cain of Byron though the latter is a magnificent Poem and read the rest fearlessly, that must indeed be a depraved mind which can gather evil from Henry the 8th from Richard 3d from Macbeth and Hamlet and Julius Caesar.[7]

Here Charlotte recommends Shakespeare as a writer among other writers, but he emerges as the one whom she is most keen to impress upon Ellen. There is an implied criticism of the bowdlerized edition lurking at the back of 'you will know how to chuse the good and avoid the evil'. Charlotte's advice to 'omit the comedies' does not necessarily mean that she herself did not like them, only that they are not part of her selective reading list. Perhaps she thought that in themselves the comedies would not lead to the intellectual improvement that Ellen was apparently seeking. Charlotte also makes explicit mention of *Henry VIII*, the play so admired by Henry Crawford in *Mansfield Park,* with all his associations of Shakespeare being part of an English constitution. Charlotte's recommendations

---

[4] Jane Austen, *Mansfield Park*, ed. Tony Tanner (Harmondsworth, 1966; repr. 1985), p. 335.
[5] *Shakespeare and the Victorians* (London, 2004), p. 7.
[6] *The Letters of Charlotte Brontë*, ed. Margaret Smith, 3 vols. (Oxford, 2000), vol. 2, p. 344.
[7] *The Letters of Charlotte Brontë* (Oxford, 1995), vol. 1, p. 130.

to Ellen Nussey might reflect the overriding taste of the sisters: the histories, the tragedies and Shakespeare's Roman plays are at the top of the list. But Anne Brontë's actual copy of Shakespeare survives, bearing witness to its owner's particularly inflected reading habits, preferences, and influences. How?

The Rev. Patrick Brontë died on 7 June 1861, having outlived his last surviving child, Charlotte, by six years. Surprisingly, the trustees of Haworth church decided not to elect the Rev. Arthur Bell Nicholls, Charlotte's widower, as the new incumbent. He returned to Banagher in Ireland with two dogs called Plato and Cato, books, manuscripts, Charlotte's writing desk, sewing and paint boxes, and some paintings (he folded Branwell's famous portrait of his sisters now in the National Portrait Gallery). The local auctioneer, Cragg, sold the rest of the Parsonage's contents on 1 and 2 October 1861 (485 lots raising a total of £115 13s 11d). The Rev. Nicholls's Brontë mementoes, which he had spread through his second marital home, were sold by his widow after his death in 1906. Although it was possible to trace many of the auctioned pieces and reinstall them in the Parsonage Museum, no edition of Shakespeare was retrieved.

So we arrive at Folger PR2752 1843h Sh. Col.: Anne Brontë's copy of Shakespeare, which was apparently taken back to Ireland with the Rev. Nicholls in 1861. Henry Folger purchased it from a bookshop in Iowa in July 1910, together with a signed copy of W. C. Bennett's *The Triumph of Salamis* (presented to Charlotte). The same purchase also included a prayerbook presented to the Rev. Patrick Brontë in 1827 and Charlotte's copy of J. B. H. de Saint Pierre's *Paul et Virginie* (1823).

The Shakespeare is *The Dramatic Works, with numerous illustrations on steel and wood* published by I. J. Chidley, 123 Aldersgate, London 1843, not in any way a distinguished or important edition. It is lightly illustrated, with an image at the beginning of each play. Its volumes are tiny: 5.5 cm by 8.7 cm (2.2 by 3.42 inches), and they are 2.6 cm (just over an inch) thick. Volume three of the five-volume edition is missing. The Folger Shakespeare Library's Head of Reference, Georgianna Ziegler,

is quite right: this is exactly the kind of edition you can imagine Anne Brontë reading.

The ordering of the plays suggests it is probably a reprint of Samuel Johnson and George Steevens's fourth edition of Shakespeare, 'revised and augmented', and first published in 1793. The last volume has a flower pressed between its pages, as the catalogue has it, 'by the owner of the book': Anne Brontë herself, or perhaps Charlotte in memory of Anne?

The volumes are not annotated. Anne's signature and date appear at the front of volumes two and four. These appear to be in the same hand. Volume five includes the undated inscription 'Mr Brunty', 'Mr Bramby', or 'Mr Branty', with the definite inscription 'Thorp Green' underneath. This is in a different hand to the writing in volumes two and four. The librarian of the Brontë Parsonage's collection suggests that these inscriptions are almost certainly the bookseller's way of identifying the volumes (the Brontë Parsonage owns several similar examples).

The opening endpapers of volume one carry the most information. This signature is written in a different ink to volumes two and four and is thought to be authentic: 'Anne Brontë, / Thorp Green, / May 8th 1844/1844'. Although the ink seems to have smudged for her, it is possible that the repeated '1844' was made by another hand (see illustration 38).

Anne was the governess for the Rev. Edmund Robinson of Thorp Green Hall, Little Ouseburn, about twelve miles from York, for five long years. She went there in May 1840. Her brother Branwell joined her in his post as personal tutor from 1843. Brother and sister remained in Robinson's employment until July 1845, when Branwell was dismissed. Anne's signature is the hand of a twenty-four-year-old woman in what seems to have been her own intimate, portable, and indeed travelling copy of Shakespeare's works.

These volumes of Shakespeare that Anne had with her during her time at Thorp Green represent her desert-island reading. The imaginative and dramatic flights that Shakespeare encouraged helped to counterbalance her time away from home.

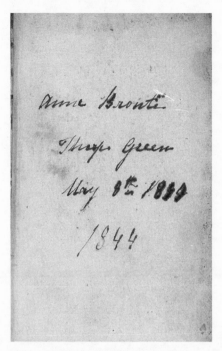

38. Anne Brontë's signature at the front of volume 1 of her miniature copy of Shakespeare, reproduced actual size: 5.5 × 8.7 cm.

Perhaps she was given the books while at Thorp Green, either by a member of the family, who considered her to be a great reader, or even by Branwell when he started work. His arrival there in 1843 coincides with the edition's first appearance in print.

On Anne Brontë's reading in general, Josephine McDonagh comments that:

it is often held that Anne's reading was more confined than her sisters, her tastes more sober and pious. Allusions and citations in *The Tenant* suggest otherwise. Her reading seems to have been every bit as eclectic as her sisters'. The novel refers to an extraordinary range of writings: the Bible, liturgical texts, hymns and sacred poetry, as well as works by Milton, Pope, Scott, Thomas Moore, Cowper, and Burns, the satirist Peter Pindar and the anti-Jacobin Frere. There is frequent quotation from Shakespeare, and allusions to Jacobean dramas, restoration comedies, and the stage melodramas that Anne may have seen in Scarborough . . . conduct literature, medical advice books, and temperance tracts are also invoked.[8]

Anne signed other books while at Thorp Green including her song book (signed June 1843), *Rabenhorst's Pocket Dictionary of the German and English Languages* (dated 14 September 1843), and *Lessons in German Literature* (dated 7 March 1844). There is, too, the Rev. John Valpy's Latin text book (dated November 1843), no doubt the one referred to in chapter seven of *Agnes Grey*; Valpy himself adapted *King John* and *The Merchant of Venice* for the stage in the early nineteenth century. Within just over a year of Anne writing her name in her copy of Shakespeare, in her 'birthday note' of 31 July 1845, she mentions that she 'has begun the third volume of *Passages in the Life of an Individual*', an early draft of what would later become *Agnes Grey* (submitted in April 1846 and appearing towards the end of 1847).

A close encounter with Anne's copy of Shakespeare represents a unique insight into how a member of the Brontë family read. *Agnes Grey*, a thinly veiled, fictional autobiography, helps to support this view. The Robinson family at Thorp Green had four daughters (the eldest was fourteen, the youngest died aged two and a half in March 1841) and one son (aged nine). Anne's life looking after them must have made almost continuous demands on her time. She was one of the Rev. Robinson's live-in servants and there would have been precious little opportunity to read, let alone write. But Shakespeare might have been perceived as being made up of manageable portions of text: verses, lines, speeches, scenes, and acts. Suddenly breaking off from a play might, for Anne, have been more tolerable than breaking off from a novel. Reading Shakespeare might have given her the kind of flexibility she would have needed as a reader at a time when she had to be available to the children's and the family's every need. But in tracing Anne Brontë's implied presence through these volumes, we are tracing an invisible reader.

It is reasonable to suppose that Anne herself was the only person ever properly to read these

---

8 Anne Brontë, *The Tenant of Wildfell Hall*, ed. Herbert Rosengarten, with an introduction and additional notes by Josephine McDonagh (Oxford, 2008), p. xxxi.

volumes of Shakespeare. This is not the kind of edition in which to look up a reference. Charlotte probably saved Anne's copy, an intimate reminder of her late sister's close encounters with Shakespeare whilst away from home. There is evidence throughout each of the four surviving volumes of a reader having turned down the top corner of the page where she has broken off, as Giacomo in *Cymbeline* remarks: 'Here the leaf's turned down' (2.2.45). This page turning is consistent, approximately 3.8 cm (one and a half inches) from the outer page. It is done neatly and respectfully. The corners have long been folded back into place, but the creases remain. The reader seems to have broken off regularly, and there seem to be three types of break. One: at a natural break in the text, for example between Act 3 scene 3 and Act 3 scene 4 of *Hamlet*, suggesting that she was treating the ends of scenes rather like the ends of chapters. Two: during a scene, suggesting a sudden interruption. The third kind of break is less easy to define and might signal the marking of a particular passage, the corner being turned down as a possible aide-mémoire.

Here are two richly suggestive examples of this third kind of break. The first is biographical and comes in volume one during *Much Ado About Nothing*, and could point to Leonato's 'I cannot bid you bid my daughter live' (5.1.271) at the top of the page. Did these words of a distressed father prompt Anne to reflect on her own father's grief on the deaths of her older sisters Maria and Elizabeth? The second example is where Shakespeare meets Anne's own biography and fiction. It comes from *Coriolanus*, which her sister Charlotte particularly prized (see illustration 39). Volumnia praises her young grandson for having chased a butterfly and torn it to shreds. In Chapter 2 of *Agnes Grey* the heroine has a spirited exchange with the young Tom Bloomfield. On discovering that he sets traps for birds, Agnes asks him why:

'Papa says they do harm.'

'And what do you do with them, when you catch them?'

39. *Coriolanus* in volume 4 of Anne Brontë's copy of Shakespeare, showing some evidence of page-turning at the top of p. 13.

'Different things. Sometimes I give them to the cat; sometimes I cut them in pieces with my penknife; but the next I mean to roast alive.'

'And why do you mean to do such a horrible thing?'

'For two reasons; first, to see how long it will live – and then, to see what it will taste like.'

'But don't you know it is extremely wicked to do such things? Remember, the birds can feel as well as you, and think, how would you like it yourself?'

'Oh, that's nothing! I'm not a bird, and I can't feel what I do to them.'

'But you will have to feel it, Tom – you have heard where the wicked people go to when they die; and if you don't leave off torturing innocent birds, remember, you will have to go there, and suffer just what you made them suffer.'

'Oh, pooh! Papa knows how I treat them, and he never blames me for it; he says it's just what *he* used to do when he was a boy.'[9]

---

[9] Anne Brontë, *Agnes Grey*, ed. Robert Inglesfield and Hilda Marsden (Oxford, 1991; repr. 1998), p. 18.

As Volumnia, Valeria and Volumnia's daughter-in-law Virgilia reflect:

> VOLUMNIA One on's father's moods.
> VALERIA Indeed, la, 'tis a noble child.
> VIRGILIA A crack, madam.
>
> (*Coriolanus*, 1.3.68–70)

Anne might well have wanted to mark the passage about tearing a butterfly as an example of bad behaviour, perhaps one even to share with her young charges, if not to write home about. Or perhaps it reminded her of the behaviour of the children Joshua and Mary Ingham of Blake Hall, the first family for whom she was governess (from April to Christmas 1839). Writing in the new year to her friend, Ellen Nussey, Charlotte referred to the Inghams as an

unruly, violent family of Modern children such for instance as those at Blake Hall – Anne is not to return – Mrs Ingham is a placid mild woman – but as for the children it was one struggle of life-wearing exertion to keep them in anything like decent order.[10]

None of Anne's other books suggest that she was in the habit of turning down pages. But this does not mean that she did not do so here. *Agnes Grey* contains several episodes of disrupted reading of the kind represented by Anne's copy of Shakespeare. The supreme moment of the solace of reading destroyed in a Brontë novel comes at the beginning of her sister Charlotte's *Jane Eyre*: 'shrined in double retirement' in a window-seat with *Bewick's Book of British Birds*, Jane is cruelly interrupted by John Reed (whose surname suggests something with which to beat children, as well as the pastime he is preventing Jane from enjoying).[11] Reading, and the solitariness it brings, were much to be prized. 'Reading is my favourite occupation when I have leisure for it, and books to read,' admits Agnes to Mr Weston the curate.[12] For a governess, reading takes place in stolen moments: 'on a bright day in the last week of February, I was walking in the park, enjoying the threefold luxury of solitude, a book, and pleasant weather,' recalls Agnes.[13] She

also recalls her studies being interrupted by Miss Rosalie Murray:

On the afternoon of the fourth, as we were walking beside the park palings in the memorable field, each furnished with a book (for I always took care to provide myself with something to be doing when she did not require me to talk), she [Rosalie] suddenly interrupted my studies [with an exclamation].[14]

Agnes mentions the practice of walking around whilst reading again: 'Being too much unhinged for any steady occupation, I wandered about with a book in my hand for several hours – more thinking than reading, for I had many things to think about.'[15] It is not too much of an imaginative leap to suggest that Anne used occasionally to walk around with her small volumes of Shakespeare, perhaps saying some of the speeches out loud, rather as she and her siblings used to do whilst 'making out', walking around the dining room table in the parsonage, that is, talking to each other of their imaginary worlds, characters, and writings.

The evidence of the page-turning suggests that, at least from this edition, Anne read *Much Ado About Nothing*, *A Midsummer Night's Dream* (folded down at the beginning of Act 1 scene 2, which may suggest she got no further with it, at least at Thorp Green, though this comedy seems to have been a favourite of the Brontës), *The Winter's Tale* (folded down at the first appearance of Autolycus, a natural break in the play), *Henry VIII*, *Timon of Athens*, *Coriolanus* and *Pericles*. By far the most page-turnings occur during *King Lear*, *Romeo and Juliet*, *Hamlet* and *Othello*, suggesting that either she encountered interruptions more regularly when reading these plays, or that she returned to them

---

10 24 January, 1840, *The Letters of Charlotte Brontë* (Oxford, 1995), vol. 1, p. 210.
11 Charlotte Brontë, *Jane Eyre*, ed. Q. D. Leavis (Harmondsworth, 1966; repr. 1985), p. 39.
12 *Agnes Grey*, p. 130.
13 *Agnes Grey*, p. 86.
14 *Agnes Grey*, p. 118.
15 *Agnes Grey*, p. 150.

more often (indicative of her possibly favouring, like her sisters, Shakespeare's tragedies more than his comedies).

But many more plays than these are alluded to during the course of her two novels. Three kinds of literary connections with Shakespeare can reasonably be made: the acknowledged, unambiguous verbal allusion; an *unacknowledged,* unambiguous verbal allusion; and an allusion (possibly submerged) made possible by its narrative situation, mood, or thematic context. Among these variations, Anne Brontë uses sequences of allusions to establish the overarching mood of a particular episode.

During the course of *Agnes Grey* (1846/7) and *The Tenant of Wildfell Hall* (1848), Anne alludes to about twenty-five Shakespeare plays: about two-thirds of the canon, more, apparently, than her two sisters put together. Curiously, of those she does not refer to, four are included in volume three of her edition (*Henry IV Parts One and Two, Henry V,* and *Henry VI Part One*), the volume which is missing. On the possible evidence of page-turning, she does seem to have read three for which I have not identified an allusion. Perhaps these were less well known to her: *Pericles, Timon of Athens* and *Henry VIII.* Plays to which she alludes in both of her novels include: *Much Ado About Nothing, The Two Gentlemen of Verona, As You Like It, Love's Labour's Lost, Hamlet* and *Othello.* In *The Tenant of Wildfell Hall* she develops an allusion to a single play more carefully than in *Agnes Grey*, producing a greater effect of self-conscious artistry and Shakespearian texture.

What follows are a few select examples. The allusions seem compelling because of their immediate context and phrasing. In some instances it could be the mention of a single word which, because it is used in a similar context to its Shakespearian counterpart, might be classed as an allusion and brings to mind a Shakespearian moment, a backdrop to Anne's own creative voice.

A good example of this kind is a previously unnoticed, possible allusion to *All's Well That Ends Well* in *Agnes Grey*. In Chapter 17, entitled 'Con-

fessions', Agnes absorbs herself in the notion that even though everything is being done to keep her away from Mr Weston, she can still think of him. She writes:

And yet . . . how dreary to turn my eyes from the contemplation of that bright object, and force them to dwell on the dull, grey desolate prospect around, the joyless, hopeless, solitary path that lay before me. It was wrong to be so joyless, so desponding; I should have made God my friend, and to do His will the pleasure and the business of my life; but Faith was weak, and Passion was too strong.[16]

In *All's Well That End's Well*, Helen confesses in soliloquy:

> My imagination
> Carries no favour in't but Bertram's.
> I am undone. There is no living, none,
> If Bertram be away. 'Twere all one
> That I should love a bright particular star
> And think to wed it, he is so above me.
> . . .
> But now he's gone, and my idolatrous fancy
> Must sanctify his relics.   (1.1.81–6; 96–7)

Both Agnes and Helen share a feeling of dejection, and turn to a religious consolation to answer their troubles. But it is that word '*bright*', a 'bright object' for Agnes, and, more memorably, 'a bright particular star' for Helen that connects Anne Brontë's imagination with Shakespeare's. In both instances, the woman is in love with a man who she is afraid does not return her affection. In Helen's case this will mean pursuing him across Europe with only a token reconciliation at the end, 'all yet seems well'. Agnes will be rewarded, but not until she has spent months of worry away from Mr Weston in the fashionable watering place (probably Scarborough), working in her mother's school. Like her namesake in *A Midsummer Night's Dream*, Helen lavishes her affection on a man who treats her badly. Perhaps it was *All's Well That Ends Well* that encouraged Anne to name her heroine Helen in *The Tenant of Wildfell Hall*, who in Chapter 38 looks

---

[16] *Agnes Grey*, pp. 147–8.

out onto the evening sky and takes comfort in 'one bright star... shining through.'[17]

Agnes awakes at the beginning of Chapter 7 after a tempestuous day, like a character in *The Tempest*:

feeling like one whirled away by enchantment, and suddenly dropped from the clouds into a remote and unknown land, widely and completely isolated from all he had ever seen or known before... with a world of waters between himself and all that knew him.[18]

Her charming sympathy and companionship with Matilda's dog, Snap, whom she has carefully nursed 'from infancy to adolescence' (p. 112), as well as her coming between the animal and danger a few pages later, is evocative of the servant Lance for his dog Crab in *The Two Gentlemen of Verona*. The only Shakespeare allusion glossed in modern editions is a rare moment of humour. The narrator says, 'As I cannot, like Dogberry, find it in my heart to bestow *all* my tediousness upon the reader' – much to the reader's relief.[19]

A Shakespearian comic heroine, Rosalind, frames *The Tenant of Wildfell Hall*. The end of Anne's own preface sounds a little like Rosalind's epilogue to *As You Like It*. She considers whether or not it matters that a man or woman wrote the book, and whether men and women will enjoy it differently:

in my own mind, I am satisfied that if the book is a good one, it is so whatever the sex of the author may be. All novels are or should be written for both men and women to read, and I am at a loss to conceive how a man should permit himself to write anything that would be really disgraceful to a woman, or why a woman should be censured for writing anything that would be proper and becoming for a man.[20]

Anne Brontë is keen to maintain her disguise as Acton Bell, firmly tantalizing her public and remaining just behind the mask in the same way as the boy playing Rosalind.

Eighteen direct Shakespearian allusions are noted in modern editions of *The Tenant of Wildfell Hall*.[21] These refer directly to: *As You Like It*,[22] *Hamlet*,[23] *Henry VI Part Two*,[24] *King Lear*,[25] *Macbeth*,[26] *Measure for Measure*,[27] *The Merchant of Venice*,[28] *A Midsummer Night's Dream*,[29] *Much Ado*

---

[17] Anne Brontë, *The Tenant of Wildfell Hall*, ed. G. D. Hargreaves (Harmondsworth, 1979; repr. 1985), p. 346.

[18] *Agnes Grey*, pp. 57–8.

[19] *Agnes Grey*, p. 59.

[20] *The Tenant of Wildfell Hall* (Harmondsworth, 1979; repr. 1985), p. 31.

[21] The editions collated are: *The Tenant of Wildfell Hall*, ed. Herbert Rosengarten, with an introduction by Margaret Smith (Oxford, 1993); *The Tenant of Wildfell Hall*, ed. Herbert Rosengarten, with an introduction and additional notes by Josephine McDonagh (Oxford, 2008); *The Tenant of Wildfell Hall*, ed. Stevie Davies (Harmondsworth, 1996).

[22] Chapter 14: 'chewing the cud of bitter fancies' alluding to *As You Like It*, 4.3.102: 'Chewing the food of sweet and bitter fancy'. Rosengarten and Smith, pp. 108 and 475.

[23] Chapter 39: 'set the table on a roar', alluding to *Hamlet*, 5.1.186–7 Rosengarten and Smith, pp. 335 and 482; also Chapter 20: 'to the top of his bent', *Hamlet*, 3.2.372: 'They fool me to the top of my bent'. Rosengarten and McDonagh, pp. 149 and 428.

[24] Chapter 32: 'melts away and makes no sign?', alluding to *Henry VI Part Two*, 3.3.29: 'He dies and makes no sign.' Rosengarten and Smith, pp. 278 and 482.

[25] Chapter 30: 'play the fool or madman', alluding to *King Lear* 3.4.73: 'turn us all to fools and madmen'. Rosengarten and Smith, pp. 246 and 481.

[26] Chapter 14: 'exertions not loud but deep', alluding to *Macbeth*, 5.3.29: 'Curses, not loud but deep'. Rosengarten and Smith, pp. 111 and 475. Also chapter 22: 'like the ghost in *Macbeth*', p. 181; also chapter 33: 'with their false, fair faces', alluding to 1.7.81–2, 'Away, and mock the time with fairest show. / False face must hide what the false heart doth know', pp. 284 and 482. Also Chapter 32: 'loose upon him, like a cloak', alluding to 5.2.20–2: 'Now does he feel his title / Hang loose about him, like a giant's robe / Upon a dwarfish thief.' Rosengarten and McDonagh, pp. 241 and 434.

[27] Chapter 17, 'if I hate the sins I love the sinner', alluding to *Measure for Measure* 2.2.37: 'Condemn the fault, and not the actor of it?' Davies, pp. 150 and 506.

[28] Chapter 9: 'my still unquiet soul' alluding to *The Merchant of Venice*, 3.2.303–4: 'For never shall you lie by Portia's side / With an unquiet soul.' Rosengarten and Smith, pp. 77 and 474.

[29] Chapter 16: 'grow, live, and die in single blessedness', alluding to *A Midsummer Night's Dream*, 1.1.78. Rosengarten and Smith, pp. 132 and 476. The allusion recurs on pp. 186 and p. 420. Also chapter 31: 'through flood and fire', alluding to 2.1.5, pp. 261 and 481.

About Nothing,[30] *Othello,*[31] and *Twelfth Night, or What You Will.*[32]

Here are two more which are as yet unglossed in modern editions. Helen Huntingdon's words to Mr Hargrave towards the end of volume two, 'I only ask your *silence* on one particular point . . . to absent yourself again, for a while,'[33] recalls the dying Hamlet's command of Horatio:

> Absent thee from felicity a while,
> And in this harsh world draw thy breath in pain,
> To tell my story. . . .
> The rest is silence.   (5.2.299–301; 310)

There could be no more potent an allusion than this to convey Helen's desperation and conclude a volume.

An allusion to *Othello* makes it the best Shakespearian example with which to illustrate a steady and encroaching marital infidelity. While walking in the park Helen sees and hears her husband make an affectionate exchange with the unfortunately named Lady Lowborough. This is reminiscent of Iago's attempt to convince Othello that Desdemona is playing false with Cassio and the scene he stages between Cassio and Bianca, who exchange Desdemona's fateful handkerchief. When Helen challenges her husband with her observations he responds enigmatically, 'I *shall* catch it now!', a little like Othello's 'Perdition catch my soul / But I do love thee', just seconds before Iago will irrevocably catch him (3.3.91–2). *Othello* is one of the plays which contain the highest instances of page-turning in Anne's Brontë's Shakespeare.

Anne Brontë's close encounters with Shakespeare's text are manifest not only through the allusions in her novels but are traceable through the physical state of her copy of Shakespeare. Per-

haps even more than her sisters, Anne herself takes central place when it comes to using, re-working, re-fashioning and re-appropriating Shakespeare. If *Agnes Grey's* autobiographical complexion is true, then Anne Brontë's reading was often interrupted while she was working as a governess at Thorp Green. But interruptions during Shakespeare did not matter too much. She could turn down the corner of her page and look up. After all, he was part of her Englishwoman's constitution.

And what about that missing third volume? Anne might well have lent this to brother Branwell during their time together at Thorp Green. It contained the plays about the wild Prince of Wales and his subsequent reformation. Branwell might have left it behind him in his hurry to get away, after his alleged liaison with Mrs Robinson, the vicar's wife. It is my view that between 1843 and 1845 Anne Brontë found in her miniature copy of Shakespeare a consolation devoutly to be wished and at the same time (re)discovered there a guiding muse for her two subsequent novels. Of the twenty-three Brontë-related citations currently listed in the World Shakespeare Bibliography online none relate explicitly to Anne. It is hoped that this article redresses that balance.

---

[30] Chapter 26: 'everything handsome about him', alluding to *Much Ado About Nothing*, 4.2.83: 'one that hath two gowns and everything handsome about him'. Rosengarten and Smith, pp. 219 and 480.

[31] Chapter 39: 'what wife? I have no wife', alluding to *Othello*, 5.2.106. Rosengarten and Smith, pp. 340 and 483.

[32] Chapter 27 quotes *Twelfth Night*, 2.4.31–4. Rosengarten and Smith, p. 225. Also chapter 30: 'play the fool or the madman', alluding to *Twelfth Night*, 1.5.126: 'a fool and a madman', pp. 246 and 481.

[33] *The Tenant of Wildfell Hall* (Harmondsworth, 1979; repr. 1985), p. 343.

SHAKESPEARE AND THE MAGIC LANTERN

JUDITH BUCHANAN

In 1841/2, a magic lanternist calling himself 'Timothy Toddle' wrote down, for his own reference, the running order for his slides. Alongside each numbered and titled slide, he scripted an accompanying commentary. Toddle, it seems, wanted to ensure both the correct sequencing of his material and the fluency of his public patter. His show opened, as was customary, with an introductory 'Welcome' slide and closed with one reading 'Good Night' and another 'God Save the Queen'. Between these end points, the show consisted of approximately 180 other slides, ranging significantly in theme and tone. The surviving running order reveals that in the midst of slide sequences such as 'A very clever trick of clowns', 'Miss Lucy swinging from a Walnut tree', 'Punch and Judy', 'Mr Pickwick running after his hat' and 'Lord Byron – a poet of the first rate talent but of the most seductive & dangerous principles', Toddle also dropped in slides illustrating two dramatic moments from *Macbeth*, each accompanied by a summarized narration of the relevant section of the drama and some select Shakespearian quotation.[1]

Subsequently, Toddle's script passed to another lantern-lecturer who, in c.1870, made some modifications and additions to it in a discernibly different hand.[2] This later lanternist's additions included two further Shakespearean sequences, from *Hamlet* and *Richard III* respectively. As had been the case for the original *Macbeth* section, both additional Shakespearian sequences were accompanied by some scripted narration and gobbets of appropriate quotation.

The Toddle document is, as far as I am aware, unique in the insight it offers into the flavour of a nineteenth-century magic lantern show in its totality.[3] It tells of the variety of types of slide that could be included in a single show, the extent and tenor of the commentary that might accompany them and, through its passage down the century and subsequent modification, the adaptability of such shows according to the preferences of the lanternist, the prevailing cultural climate and the current availability and modishness of particular slides. Later in this article, in the context of a discussion of other uses

---

[1] This surviving hand-written lantern reading consists of six sheets of paper folded and sewn into a booklet of 24 pages. Topical news items mentioned in the script (the recent birth of the Prince of Wales and the imminent opening of the Thames Tunnel) help to date it to 1841 or early 1842. The surviving manuscript, complete with later additions, is now held by the Magic Lantern Society of Great Britain (MLS). A helpful transcription of it is reproduced in Dennis Crompton, David Henry and Stephen Herbert, eds., *Magic Images: The Art of Hand-Painted and Photographic Lantern Slides* (London, 1990), pp. 47–53.

[2] This later lanternist also had the revised manuscript booklet bound (or rebound), presumably to ensure its continued usefulness as a blueprint for entertaining lantern shows. Given the surviving evidence about known lanternists, it seems reasonable to assume that Toddle's successor was also male. I take the c.1870 date of the later handwritten modifications from Crompton, Henry and Herbert. The slides themselves from the Toddle collection have not, as far as we know, survived.

[3] Many slide readings produced by slide manufacturers to accompany the sale of particular themed sequences (typically of ten to fourteen slides each) survive. However, the scope of Toddle's script surpasses these, designed as it was to incorporate such mini-stories within a script for the entire show.

of Shakespeare within the institutional life of the magic lantern, I discuss the particular, and evolving, contribution of Shakespeare to the scripted lantern entertainment originally designed by Toddle. Two fundamental pieces of evidence provided by this manuscript of relevance to the current enquiry are, however, worth noting at this introductory stage: first, Shakespeare's presence within magic lantern shows at all, as one in an eclectic mix of narrative and non-narrative subjects; and second, the augmentation of the Shakespearian aspects of the show later in the century as a greater range of such slide sequences became available and their popularity increasingly assured.

* * *

The nineteenth century witnessed a diverse range of engagements with Shakespeare, both earnest and satiric. Many of these forms of Shakespearian cultural expression have been well documented and discussed.[4] This is not, however, the case for Shakespeare in the magic lantern. On the few occasions when nineteenth-century Shakespearian lantern sequences have been discussed, they have tended to be cited (including by me) principally to compromise the claim that 1899 (when Herbert Beerbohm Tree made his pioneering film of *King John*) constituted a definitive beginning for the history of 'screened Shakespeare'.[5] In this article, I treat Shakespeare and the magic lantern as a subject in its own right rather than as an introductory tool for retrospectively redefining the history of Shakespeare in another medium. To clarify the import and profile of Shakespeare's presence in the magic lantern, I begin with an account of the culture and operations of the lantern *per se*. I then turn to the particular, and ranging, uses to which the lantern put Shakespeare as one element within its considerable and influential repertoire of entertainment and edification.

THE LANTERN: MECHANISMS, USES, PROFILE

A technological curiosity in the latter half of the seventeenth century, through the eighteenth and nineteenth centuries the magic (or optical) lantern then became a well-established, and increasingly influential, part of European education and socially diverse entertainment. By the 1890s, it had accrued a rich technological, artistic and sociological history on both sides of the Atlantic.[6] Lanterns formed part of ghostly exhibitions, church meetings, travelling shows, variety divertissements and special lectures.[7] For those who could afford such things, the lantern also formed an increasingly regular part of domestic entertainments.[8] For present purposes, however, it is public lantern shows, and the

---

[4] See, for example, the exploration of the Victorian predilection for puncturing the cultural sanctity of Shakespeare through burlesques, comic songs, cartoon sketches and skittish poems in Richard W. Schoch, *Not Shakespeare: Bardolatry and Burlesque in the Nineteenth Century* (Cambridge, 2002).

[5] Discussions of Shakespeare lantern exhibitions as context for the story of Shakespeare on screen include John Collick, *Shakespeare, Cinema and Society* (Manchester, 1989), pp. 12–32 and Judith Buchanan, *Shakespeare on Silent Film: An Excellent Dumb Discourse* (Cambridge, 2009), pp. 25–42. The current article subsumes and develops that section.

[6] An estimated 75,000–150,000 lantern shows of varying styles were on offer in America each year in the latter half of the nineteenth century. See Terry Borton, *Cinema before Film: Victorian Magic Lantern Shows and America's First Great Screen Artist, Joseph Boggs Beale* (forthcoming). Pre-publication excerpts posted at: www.magiclanternshows.com/filmhistory.htm, hereafter Borton online. For a history of American lantern shows, see also Charles Joseph Pecor, *The Magician and the American Stage* (Washington, DC, 1977) and Xenophon Theodore Barber, 'Evenings of Wonders: A History of the Magic Lantern Show in America', unpublished PhD dissertation, New York University (1993).

[7] For an iconographic history of lantern shows and audiences, see David Robinson, ed., *The Lantern Image* (London, 1993).

[8] For Samuel Pepys's 19 August 1666 account of a lantern show in his home, see Robert Latham and William Matthews, eds., *The Diary of Samuel Pepys*, vol. 7 '1666' (London, 1972), p. 254; for Charles Dickens's plans to host a lantern exhibition at home for his son's birthday party, see letter of 31 December, 1842, reproduced in M. House, G. Storey, K. Tillotson *et al.*, eds., *The British Academy Pilgrim Edition of the Letters of Charles Dickens*, vols. 1–12 (Oxford, 1965–2002), vol. 3 (1974), p. 416. For advice to amateur lanternists on subjects suitable for a 'parlour entertainment' for 'the domestic circle', see Anon, 'The Magic Lantern: Its Construction, Illumination, Optics & Uses', *The Optical Magic Lantern Journal and Photographic Enlarger*, vol.1 no.1 (15 June, 1889), pp. 2–4 (3).

varied audiences that attended these, that will be of interest.

The lantern worked by projecting onto a wall or screen images drawn, painted or eventually printed onto glass slides. These slides were inserted in turn into a slot in the side of a box (lantern) illuminated from behind first by a candle and then, as the technology developed, by a paraffin flame, a carbon arc, a gas discharge lamp and, in time, an electric bulb. The projection could be in vivid colour and the projected image sharp and clear. The use of more than one lantern trained on the same point on the screen, or a lantern that contained multiple slide-loading points (a diunial or triunial) enabled images to replace each other in rapid succession, creating the impression of movement. As early as 1713, Jonathan Swift had reported of a lantern show that 'I went afterwards to see a famous *moving* picture, and I never saw anything so pretty'[9] (my emphasis) and, by the mid-nineteenth century, the lantern's range of possible effects simulating movement was striking. It was, for example, possible to create the popular 'dissolving views' by bringing up the light on one slide while simultaneously taking it down on another, the transition from one version of a scene to another (a winter landscape transmuting 'magically' into a summer one, a dormant volcano into an erupting one, a dancing beauty into a dancing skeleton and so on) being timed to best effect by the accomplished expertise of the lanternist himself. Some slides ('slip' or 'slipping' slides) also included adjustable mechanical sections that could be moved or removed mid-projection and/or a pulley system that enabled a section of the slide to circulate repeatedly. In this way, for example, a fountain could be seen spouting water continuously, a sleeping man could accidentally swallow a rat each time he opened his mouth to snore, a rosebud could open into bloom and return to bud, or bathing beauties could be seen alternately dipping into and emerging from the water.[10] By the deft manipulation of the effects levers, pulleys or turning handles on the slides and by the changing of the slides themselves, therefore, the sudden or gradual animation of a person or transformation of a scene could be implemented by the lanternist.[11]

A lantern presentation would typically incorporate both a musical accompaniment (most frequently from a piano), and a vocal commentary provided by a live lecturer. The commentary was sometimes offered by the lanternist himself from his slide-loading position behind the lantern, sometimes by a separate lecturer at the front of the hall. In some cases, it would have been scripted ahead of time; in others it was extemporized. And sometimes (as may have been the case for Toddle), a prepared script would have allowed a confident lecturer then to extemporize at will from a scripted prompt. Writing in 1889, Henry Cooper argued that the chief determinant of a successful lantern exhibition was the quality of the commentary:

The lecture must be the backbone of the entertainment. The slides may be as good as possible. The lenses of the best construction, but if the description of the pictures be faulty, they will avail nothing to satisfy modern taste.[12]

Styles of commentary varied from the flippantly jocular to the designedly edifying and educative. Nevertheless, there was general agreement that the level of preparation of the spoken accompaniment, and the degree of fluency and interest with which it was delivered, was a key influence in making or marring a show:

---

9 Swift, *The Journal to Stella*, ed. George A. Aitken (London, 1901), Letter 62 (March 1713), p. 530. Quoted in Laurent Mannoni, *The Great Art of Light and Shadow: Archaeology of the Cinema* (Exeter, 2000), p. 121.

10 A single, exquisitely painted, English 'wreck and rescue' slide from *c*.1840, for example, showed a small rowing boat moving across a troubled sea from a foundering vessel to the shore, while the waves moved up and down threateningly around it. This effects slide combined lateral movement (of the boat) with vertical movement (of the waves) – a bravura example of the lanternist's art. I am grateful to Richard Manwaring Baines for showing me this delightful effects slide from his collection.

11 For a mid-nineteenth-century description of the various ways in which movement on the screen could be generated in lantern shows, see Benjamin Pike Jr., *Catalogue of Optical Goods* (1848), quoted in George Kleine, 'Progress in Optical Projection in the Last Fifty Years', *Film Index* (28 May, 1910), p. 10.

12 *The Optical Magic Lantern Journal and Photographic Enlarger*, vol. 1 no. 1 (15 June, 1889), p. 8.

let the slides of some interesting story be passed through the lantern in succession without a word of context, what is the result? – Weariness and yawning. Here is the secret, then – the story behind.[13]

A lantern show working at its best, of course, allowed the linguistic elements to work in sympathetic collaboration with visually pleasing slides to create a bright and engaging composite presentation.

The stock-in-trade lantern sequences in need of enlivening commentary tended to fit the following broad types: phantasmagoria, morality tales warning against the dangers of drink, Bible stories, travel narratives/geography lessons/missionary reports (lantern tours of the Holy Land were a favourite), tales for children (*Cinderella, Dick Whittington, Little Red Riding Hood, Aesop's Fables* and *Alice's Adventures in Wonderland* were all popular), adventure stories (notably *Robinson Crusoe, Robin Hood* and *Don Quixote),* sentimental melodramas (tales of penury, bereavement, personal sacrifice and cold weather), comic sketches (with titles such as 'Lady on kicking donkey', 'Punch with growing nose', 'Monkey riding cat'), grand historical subjects (Wellington's battles, the death of Nelson, kings and queens of England), and pictorial accompaniment to well-known stories, poems and songs (in addition to the ever popular Defoe, authors such as Bunyan, Milton, Swift, Dickens, Longfellow, Coleridge and Tennyson were also regularly plundered as a source for slide sequences).[14]

SHAKESPEARIAN EXCERPTS IN THE MAGIC LANTERN

Though not central to this stock repertoire, Shakespeare nevertheless made many appearances in the Magic Lantern and, reciprocally, enlisted the lantern in more traditional theatrical Shakespearian productions on occasion too. As early as 1821, for example, Edmund Kean included lantern slides in his stage *King Lear* at Drury Lane to augment the visual effects of the production.[15] Moreover, the memorializing of celebrated theatrical perfor-

mances was sometimes aided by projecting images of famous stage actors in Shakespearean roles as part of touring, culturally edifying or more tonally varied lantern lectures. Slides of paintings such as 'Mrs. Siddons in the Character of Queen Catherine', 'Mr. Kean in the Character of Richard the 3rd' or 'Ellen Terry, as Lady Macbeth' helped to promote and sustain the celebrity of Shakespearian players by bringing their image to larger and more diverse audiences than could have attended the performance of place-specific and time-bounded theatre productions.[16] And while theatrical culture was being given a wider profile in this way, in a mutually beneficial exchange of cultural authority, the lantern was thereby acquiring kudos as a vehicle both for celebrating, and reflecting upon, artistic greatness. Such culturally respectable fare might even have helped provide the compensation for, or wholesome distraction from, some of the more frivolous, or slightly saucy, slides that sometimes appeared on lantern programmes.

In the various collaborations between the lantern and Shakespeare, however, the lines of appropriation were usually more unilaterally drawn as the lantern adopted and adapted Shakespearian material for its own satirical, visually diverting or educational purposes. A single Shakespearian image was even occasionally used as an economical point of collective recognition to illustrate a lantern lecture about something else entirely: Lady Macbeth in night-gown bearing dagger and drugged posset could, for example, contribute to phantasmagoria horror shows as a signifier of

---

[13] Amy Johnson, 'Is the Lantern Played Out? No', *The Optical Magic Lantern Journal and Photographic Enlarger*, vol. 5 no. 67 (1 December, 1894), pp. 208–9 (209).

[14] In a further article entitled 'Is the Lantern Played Out? – No', Albert Tranter specifically extolled the virtues of the lantern 'as an aid in illustrating imaginative poetry', citing examples from Coleridge and Shelley: *The Optical Magic Lantern Journal and Photographic Enlarger*, vol. 7 no. 80 (January, 1896), p. 10.

[15] See Terence Rees, *Theatre Lighting in the Age of Gas* (London, 1978), pp. 81–3.

[16] Crompton, Henry and Herbert, *Magic Images*, p. 53. The Ellen Terry slide is from the author's private collection.

night-time terror or metaphysical torment; Lear and Poor Tom could emblematize 'delusional insanity' and 'feigned insanity' respectively as part of a lantern lecture on mental illness.[17]

The approach of Toddle and his successor, however, was less brazenly utilitarian than this. Rather than raiding a Shakespeare play for a tropic character to serve as passing illustration for something else, they allowed a series of Shakespearian dramatic moments a life of their own. In line with the comparable treatment accorded *The Pickwick Papers*, for example, they worked on the assumption that their audience had some prior knowledge of the source text.[18] Reference to one or two celebrated dramatic moments from a play could, therefore, through the evocative use of a few slide images, be assumed sufficient to conjure the broader drama. Moreover, the accompanying commentary could attach the dramatic excerpt − if in slightly perfunctory manner − to the language and narrative context of its Shakespearian origins.

In the following extract from the Toddle manuscript (with spelling, lineation, punctuation and introductory titles retained), the sections from either side of the Shakespearian sequences are also quoted, to showcase not only the quantity and character of the scripted commentary but also the local specifics of the exhibition context:

36. Elegant Flower call'd the Turks Cap −
See how nicely they fit a Turks Hd.
The Turks are proud of their Caps & are looking
    Round for Admiration.

*37 Artificial Ice at the Colosseum Regents Park

*37a Scene from Hamlet −
Whither will thou lead me
Speak Ill go no further
Mark me − I will −
I am thy fathers Spirit − Now
Hamlet hear 'tis given out
that sleeping in mind orchard
A Serpent stung me, but know
thou noble youth the Serpent that
did sting thy fathers life now
wears his Crown.

King Richard
The King enacts more wonders
than a Man − His horse is
slain − but all on foot he fights
seeking for Richmond in the
throat of Death

The Death of Richard
God & your Arms be praised
victorious friends the Day is
ours the Tyrant Dog is dead

38. The Combat between McDuff & Mackbeth.
Mackbeth had surprised McDuffs
Castle during his absence &
had barbarously murdered his
wife and Children − Macduff
exclaims
Gentle Heaven − front to front
bring thou this fiend of Scotland
& myself − within my swords
length let him, and if he
scape then Heaven forgive him too

At length they meet in Battle. McDuff
cries out Then yield ye Coward
& live to be the Show & Gaze of time

I will not yield & so lay on
McDuff − and death to him
who first cries hold enough

38A Paul Pry − I hope I don't
intrude − Ive just lookd
in to see whats going forward
and hope to have a slice of Cake
bye & bye

---

17 The hand-coloured slide of 'Lady Macbeth' is reproduced in Mervyn Heard, *Phantasmagoria: The Secret Life of the Magic Lantern* (Hastings, 2006), p. 290. The line-drawn slides of Lear and Poor Tom, drawn by 'A.J.C.', are held in the Archive of the Bethlem Royal Hospital, Box A07/1, inventory nos. LSC-090 and LSC-091 respectively.

18 On the prevalence of 'Shakespearean phrases, aphorisms, ideas, and language' within the nineteenth-century imagination, see Lawrence W. Levine, *Highbrow/Lowbrow: The Emergence of Cultural Hierarchy in America* (Cambridge, MA, 1988), pp. 31, 37−8. On how well Shakespeare was known and how frequently quoted in nineteenth-century America, see also pp. 27−8.

38B Hodge giving his dog a bone
Well then jump & you shall
have it.

38C The Escape of Mary Queen of Scotts for
Lochleven Castle[19]

Even where, as here, there were minor inaccuracies in a quoted script, accompanying the projection with a few choice Shakespearian quotations had the advantage of licensing the lantern lecturer to display both his erudition (real or assumed) and, in the interests of the entertainment, his declamatory power (hammed or otherwise). The tenor of Toddle's commentary across the manuscript as a whole suggests he was well versed in extracting maximum comic potential and dramatic excitement from his slides. The choice of Shakespearian sections certainly makes provision for an accompanying oratorical flair. The appearance of the ghost on the battlements (37a), for example, allowed for the heightened drama of some ghostly vocals in the commentary ('I am thy fathers [sic] Spirit . . . '). The script for the two scenes from *Macbeth* (the attack on Macduff's castle and the slaying of Macbeth) called both for a steeliness in delivery ('bring thou this fiend of Scotland . . . ') and for a resolute exchange, ideally to be conducted between differently modulated voices ('Then yield ye Coward . . . ', 'I will not yield . . . '). Although constituting only a fraction of the play, these two *Macbeth* scenes, as exhibited in the lantern, constituted their own contained mini-drama of action and consequence, the slaying of Macbeth coming as a focused act of revenge for the earlier slaughter of Macduff's family. Despite their brevity, therefore, these two scenes are allowed some narrative autonomy, implicitly standing as synecdochic reference to the play as a whole.

The scenes labelled 'King Richard' and 'The Death of Richard', showing the horseless Richard fighting on and dying, again provided the opportunity for some exclamatory drama in the commentary ('the Day is / ours the Tyrant Dog is dead'). It is, perhaps, notable that the script omits the line we might think almost required in this context – 'A horse! a horse! my kingdom for a horse!' (a line with a significantly popular profile, then as now).[20] While, however, its omission from the script may indeed mean that this line was never uttered as part of the show, it is also possible that the lanternist simply did not feel the need to script it in order to be able to produce it when the occasion demanded. Since the lanternist's booklet constituted, in effect, an aide-mémoire rather than necessarily a fully prescriptive script, it would have allowed for embellishment of exactly this sort. Indeed, it was fundamental to the identity of a lantern show that there was always the possibility of a joyous opportunism (or hapless meandering) in the way it progressed, depending on the flippant or learned digressions the individual lecturer chose to insert, the improvisatory flourish or dragging ponderousness with which he did so, and the receptivity or otherwise of the audience at any given show.

Since the Shakespeare slides from the Toddle lantern show have not survived, we cannot know precisely what they might have looked like.[21] Nevertheless, we can be fairly confident about their twofold function as inclusions on the programme: they both added dramatic excitement to the lineup and lent at least the semblance of cultural elevation to proceedings. However, sandwiching the culturally elevating material between a visual gag about the Turk's Cap (36) and a slipping slide showing a dog jumping for a bone (38B) would, presumably, also have ensured that the balance of the show as a whole did not in the process become too burdened by educational weight.[22]

---

19 The slide sequences numbered 37 and 37a (marked *) were amongst those interpolated by the subsequent lanternist. Crompton, Henry and Herbert, *Magic Images*, p. 51.

20 On the history of the pantomimic celebrity of this line, see Julie Hankey, *Richard III: Plays in Performance* (London and Totowa, NJ, 1981), p. 15.

21 The precedent provided by other surviving slides suggests these would have been sparely executed, line-drawn illustrations, hand-coloured prior to sale. Their primary purpose was to evoke the dramatic moment and clarify plot details pertinent to that moment.

22 It was, of course, a pattern of tonal variety on an exhibition programme that the moving picture industry would in due course emulate.

Brief excerpts from *Macbeth*, *Hamlet* and *Richard III* were not the only Shakespearian gobbets to be absorbed into a divertingly unfocused rag-bag of lantern offerings of this kind. From 1850 onwards, for example, several different English versions of slide-sets illustrating Jacques's 'Seven Ages of Man' speech from *As You Like It* became available for inclusion in variety lantern shows. These slide-sets were each structured as seven-slide sequences, with a scripted reading from *As You Like It* produced by the slide producer to be read alongside the projection and the possibility of accompanying light animation effects to enliven some of the ages.[23] Such sequences provided a contained brush with Shakespeare while combining the considerable virtues of reassuring familiarity, a ready-made internal structure (from first to last age) and, significantly in the context of the broader show, winning brevity.

ABRIDGED SHAKESPEARE IN THE MAGIC LANTERN

In the latter half of the nineteenth century, however, the engagements of slide-manufacturers with Shakespeare became more narratively ambitious as they turned their attention to representing whole Shakespearian plots in compressed form. Each lanternized sequence adapted from a single Shakespeare play was composed of between eight and fourteen plot-evocative slide images. Typically, these were sequenced so that one charged dramatic moment ceded to the next without any plot-retarding, or tension-easing digressions into inconsequential business along the way. The chosen slide images served as the graphic hooks upon which the narration of the story could then be hung. Wherever possible, slide artists seem to have chosen their individual images to resonate with the pictorial version of the play that already had a profile in the public imagination. This existing profile drew upon well-known Shakespearian paintings, engravings, edition illustrations and memorable tableaux from theatre productions that iconized select moments from the plays. Even within the constraints of the eight to fourteen slide format, it would, for

example, have been unthinkable to produce a lanternized *Romeo and Juliet* that omitted an image of Romeo scaling Juliet's balcony, an *Othello* without the visual sensationalism of the murder of Desdemona, or a *Hamlet* that ignored the indulgent popular romantic imagery of Ophelia in the brook (a dramatic moment whose rich graphic life derived entirely from its extra-theatrical expressions). In referencing the broadly conventionalized visual identity of 'peak moments' from the plays, slide artists were also reaffirming the summarized version of each play this came to represent.[24] Late nineteenth-century lantern Shakespeare, therefore, both drew upon and contributed to an analogue, abbreviated visualized and narrativized version of the best-known plays – a version of manageable proportions in which the plays could circulate easily and intelligibly in consensually recognizable form.

In the nineteenth century, encountering Shakespeare in a partially allusive or vigorously abridged form was not an experience particular to the magic lantern. In fact, only a minority of people would have encountered a Shakespeare play principally either through reading an unexpurgated version or attending a full, worded production. In the mid-late nineteenth century, this was Shakespeare for the purists and the cultural elite only. Others certainly met Shakespeare, but their sites

---

23 Multiple versions of a *Seven Ages of Man* 7-slide sequence were issued, each with a published one-page version of the speech from *As You Like It* 2.7, to be read in conjunction with the exhibition of the slides. The MLS's Slide Readings Library holds three lantern scripts for *The Seven Ages of Man*: Millikin and Lawley of London's pre-1872 script (serial no. 91903); York and Sons of London's pre-1887 script (serial no. 90802); and Alfred Pumphrey of Birmingham's post-1875 script (serial no. 91677). It has not as yet proved possible to date these slide readings precisely. However, the active trading years of the issuing company in each case narrows the window of possibility.

24 The 'peak moment' approach to literary adaptation, according to which only the most dramatic moments are selected for representation in another medium, is discussed in Tom Gunning, 'The Intertextuality of Early Cinema: A Prologue to *Fantômas*', in Robert Stam and Alessandra Raengo, eds., *A Companion to Literature and Film* (Oxford, 2004), pp. 127–143 (128).

of encounter were less rarefied: in popular songs, through the Lambs' simplified *Tales from Shakespeare* or in the more rough-and-tumble variety theatres and vaudeville houses on both sides of the Atlantic where Shakespeare had long been offered in truncated, simplified and often skittish versions.[25] Lanternized Shakespeare therefore joined a range of other pictorialized, dramatized, distilled and otherwise reduced retellings of Shakespeare in finding a form in which the plays could connect quickly with a popular audience.

The most popular of Shakespearean subjects for lantern treatment in the final quarter of the nineteenth century seems to have been *Romeo and Juliet*.[26] Theobald and Company of London, for example, produced a twelve-slide hand-painted sequence depicting a compressed version of the play with an accompanying scripted reading.[27] Another twelve-slide chromo-litho *Romeo and Juliet* slide sequence, 'splendidly coloured', is advertised by the culturally aspirational manufacturer, Robert H. Clark, in the January 1896 issue of the *Optical Magic Lantern Journal and Photographic Enlarger* as one in a list of slide sets for sale for four shillings each (a price suggestive of a premium product).[28] Three richly drawn *Romeo and Juliet* slides from a sequence produced by Newton and Company of London are in my own collection, and further versions survive in other collections, though the manufacturers in those cases have proved more difficult to trace.

Macbeth was also considered both sufficiently dramatic and sufficiently well known to be amenable to compressing for lantern treatment. In one skittish English lantern version from *c*.1880 entitled, as its opening slide colourfully announces, 'Ye Fearful Tragedie of Macbeth' (Illustration 40), an effects slide shows the three hand-drawn, hand-painted witches seen in profile and pointing in a chirpy parody of Fuseli's well-known painting. A superimposition lever enables these to appear as if from nowhere at the will of the lanternist. In a later slide from the sequence, a duelling Macduff cuts off Macbeth's head by means of a further mechanical effects lever. The appeal of this sequence could always then be comically enhanced by moving the

lever forwards and backwards in quick succession causing Macbeth's head to be alternately severed from and returned to his neck.[29]

BRIGGS'S 'SHAKESPEARE ILLUSTRATED' LANTERN SLIDE SERIES

It was, however, an American family firm of slide manufacturers and slide painters, Casper W. Briggs and Company of Philadelphia, that showed the most applied commercial interest in telling Shakespearian tales through the lantern. Briggs released two separate series of Shakespearian painted slide sequences, the first in the early 1890s, the second in 1908. The earlier of these went under the series title 'Shakespeare Illustrated'. The plays lanternized for this series included *Romeo and Juliet*,

---

[25] See Schoch, *Not Shakespeare* and Levine, *Highbrow/Lowbrow*, pp. 18–23. The popularity of the Lambs' *Tales from Shakespeare* (1807) gave their accessible version of Shakespearian 'stories' an important place in the education of many Victorians.

[26] The surviving slides, slide readings and other documentary records of manufacturers' slide catalogues point to the unrivalled popularity of *Romeo and Juliet* in this respect. However, the vagaries of what survives and what does not of this body of material should properly temper any absolute claim about relative production rates.

[27] The MLS's Slide Readings Library holds a script for the Theobald 12-slide *Romeo and Juliet* lantern sequence (serial no. 90478). On Theobald and Company's role in introducing chromolithography to English slide-production for their 'sets of twelve slides, the subjects including topographical scenes, nursery tales, and episodes from the Scriptures', see Stephen Herbert, *A History of Pre-Cinema*, vol. 3 (London, 2000), p. 90.

[28] Whole-page advertisement, *The Optical Magic Lantern Journal and Photographic Enlarger*, vol. 7, no. 80 (January, 1896), p. vii. Other available subjects advertised in the same issue that help to identify Clark's cultural placement in the market include: 'The Pilgrim's Progress', 'Red Riding Hood', 'Pictures from the Old Testament', 'Cinderella', 'The Slaves of Drink', 'Marley's Ghost', 'Punch and Judy', 'Pictures from the New Testament', 'Discovery of America by Columbus' and 'Scenes from Pickwick, &c'.

[29] I am grateful to the eminent lanternist and lantern historian Mervyn Heard for providing details about, and generously giving me access to, some of his remarkable nineteenth-century Shakespearian slides.

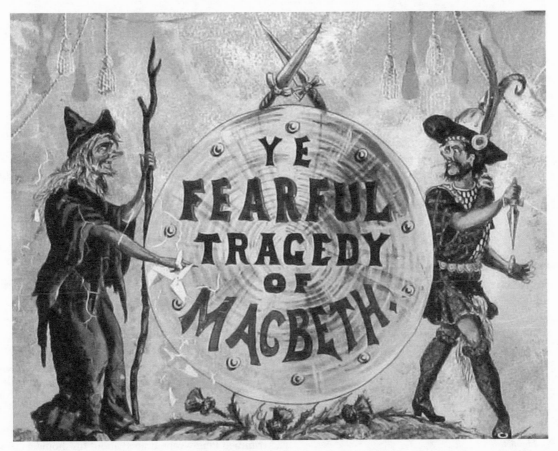

40. The introductory slide to a satirical lantern version of *Macbeth c.*1880?

A Midsummer Night's Dream, The Taming of the Shrew, The Merchant of Venice, As You Like It, Timon of Athens, The Merry Wives of Windsor, Twelfth Night, Hamlet, Othello, King Lear, Macbeth, Cymbeline, The Winter's Tale and *The Tempest.*[30] Each was represented by a set of (eight to fourteen) slides that, when projected in sequence with suitable narration and musical accompaniment, succinctly pictorialized the plot. The artist for Briggs's later 1908 Shakespearean series was one of America's most prolific and prominent lantern artists, Joseph Boggs Beale (1841–1926), employed by Briggs in the years after 1900. Titles from this second series included *The Merry Wives of Windsor, Hamlet, Romeo and Juliet* and *Othello.*[31] The slides from both series were mass-produced line-drawn images, collodion

30 The 1890s dating of the 'Shakespeare Illustrated' series is not definitive, but the mahogany of the wooden frame surrounds, the weight of the glass, the collodion used to coat the slides and the dates of the reproductions of the paintings from the *Art Journal* on which they draw, help identify the decade.

31 I am grateful to Terry Borton, the distinguished lanternist and lantern historian of the American Magic Lantern Theater, for kindly showing me his Joseph Boggs Beale Shakespearian slides of *Romeo and Juliet, Hamlet* and *The Merry Wives of Windsor* in Baltimore, NJ. Each sequence is a beautifully coloured, crisply worked plot compression celebrating the iconic 'moments' of each play while omitting sub-plots and suppressing complexities that might detract from the energetic forward trajectory of the pictorialized account. Beale and Briggs together made it their project 'to make great literature, history, and religion available on [the lantern] screen' for the benefit of a wide audience. See Borton online.

on glass, which were then hand-coloured for those customers who could afford the premium edition. Appropriate lines from Shakespeare have been hand-written onto the slide frame of some of the surviving slides. It is not clear whether this was done by Briggs before the point of sale, or by a particular lanternist who subsequently owned them, to help prompt his memory during the exhibition of his slides. Though plenty of published lecture scripts were marketed alongside dramatic slide sequences in this period to guide the lanternist in preparing the show, I have found no surviving trace of any such readings to accompany these particular sequences.

A remarkable collection of surviving Briggs Shakespearian slides is held in George Eastman House (Rochester, NY). By way of sample illustration of these, here I discuss the *Hamlet* sequence from the 1890s series and the *Romeo and Juliet* sequences from both the 1890s and the 1908 series.[32] After a brief descriptive introduction to the sequence as a whole in each case, I concentrate principally, for present purposes, on the striking effect of the single slide included in the run that is an artistic anomaly in the context of the rest of the sequence.

i) *Hamlet*
Ten slides survive specifically from Briggs's *Hamlet* sequence from the 'Shakespeare Illustrated' series. However, there is also another surviving slide entitled 'Shakespeare Reading Hamlet to his Family' which comes from a contemporary Briggs series released in parallel called 'English History: 1486–1603'. This slide would have formed an appealingly neat introduction (and/or conclusion) to the *Hamlet* sequence for any lanternist who owned both Briggs sequences. It shows a recognizably 'Droeshoutian' Shakespeare sitting at home in doublet and ruff recounting the story of *Hamlet* to his rapt and attentive family. The action of the *Hamlet* sequence itself is simply and clearly illustrated through a well-chosen series of exemplary, plot-packed cameo moments from the play: 'Hamlet – Ghost Scene', 'Hamlet's Soliloquy', 'Hamlet's advice to the players', 'Hamlet surprising the king

at prayer', 'Hamlet's interview with his mother', 'Ophelia scattering flowers', 'Ophelia', 'Hamlet – a Church Yard', 'Duel between Hamlet and Laertes', 'Hamlet kills the king'.[33] In addition to these extant slides, there may also have been a couple more that have not survived: perhaps one of the play-within-the-play and/or one of Hamlet's body being borne aloft as a suitable closing image for the story. Whatever the missing slides depicted, sufficient numbers survive to demonstrate clearly the manner in which the story was compressed for lantern projection – a distillation of a succession of iconic moments, each one densely packed with economically encoded narrative information. A description of the single slide 'Hamlet's interview with his mother' (Illustration 41) can serve as sample illustration of how much plot could be inventively condensed into one 'action image'.

In this one slide, Hamlet, in doublet, sword and cloak, though bare-headed, stands in the middle of his mother's room beneath the two gilt-framed portraits of King Hamlet and King Claudius respectively, which hang, square-on to our gaze, on the wall above the door. Hamlet points towards an arched alcove at the back right corner of the room where the translucent ghost of his father stands. The ghost is in armour with an ermine-trimmed kingly robe draped about his shoulders – the same robe that appears in both portraits and that Claudius himself wore in the previous slide. Despite being set back, the ghost seems larger than Hamlet – a colossus of a man (take him for all in all). His ghost, in Hamlet's vision and ours, is perspective-defyingly imposing, even from afar. Gertrude sits before Hamlet in right of frame, her hands clasped together and raised towards him

---

[32] It has occasionally been necessary to make an inferential discrimination to place a particular slide as part of the 1890s or the 1908 sequence. Such discriminations are not fail-safe but have been based on style of illustration, character of slide mount and placement of image within a run.

[33] These titles are taken from the (unprojected) edge of the slide. They were probably inserted by the manufacturer prior to sale, and would also have been used to advertise the sequence in the company's catalogue of commercially available slides.

41. Slide from the 'Hamlet' sequence of Briggs's 'Shakespeare Illustrated' series. Collodion on glass, 3.25 × 4 in. Title on slide: 'Act III, Scene 4 – Hamlet's interview with his mother'.

pleading, presumably, for his sanity and her life. She ignores his imperiously gestured suggestion that she should look upon the ghost. At Hamlet's feet in the left of the image lies Polonius's body, which has evidently recently fallen through the arras that hangs there.

In sum, therefore, this slide presents an economically organized pictorial account of the entire closet scene telescoped into one encapsulating moment, the narrative implications of which the lanternist-narrator could then embellish at will. For this slide, as for most in the sequence, aesthetics are clearly subservient to plot, and the aesthetics, though not crude, certainly lack nuance. Even the details of perspective, for example, can be compromised if this allows for greater narrative communicativeness.[34]

---

[34] Unlike some other slides of a similar date, Briggs did not make use of an appearing/disappearing lever-operated

42. Briggs's 'Shakespeare Illustrated' *Hamlet*. Title on slide: 'Act IV, Scene 5 – Ophelia scattering flowers'.

Distinguished clearly from this dominant story-telling mode, however, is the slide entitled 'Ophelia' (Illustration 43). Rather than having been specifically drawn by one of Briggs's slide artists for inclusion in this set, it is, by contrast, a reproduction of English painter Arthur Hughes's 1852 painting *Ophelia* – copied onto glass directly from a photographic plate taken of the *Art Journal's* printed lithograph.[35] Unsurprisingly, given its provenance, the image differs decisively in style and treatment from all others included in the sequence. It is

'effect' for their ghost. For a disappearing Shakespearian ghost, see the effects slide from an unidentified version of *Hamlet* reproduced in Crompton, Henry and Herbert, *Magic Images*, p. 51.

[35] I am grateful to the distinguished lantern historian Stephen Herbert for discussing this process with me. He tells me there may have been a copyright arrangement made between Briggs and the *Art Journal* for reproduction rights. Equally, however, Briggs may simply have taken copies of the images from the *Art Journal* without paying. There was precedent for both approaches. I have found no surviving evidence to suggest one way or the other in this case.

43. Briggs's 'Shakespeare Illustrated' *Hamlet*. Title on slide: 'Ophelia – Hughes'. From Arthur Hughes's 1852 painting *Ophelia*. This slide shows an Ophelia markedly different in style, presentation and associations from the Ophelia who appears elsewhere in the sequence.

conspicuously spare on narrative detail but rich in unexpected associations, technical acumen and significant whimsical charm. The Ophelia it presents is one who, unlike her more prosaic counterpart in the preceding slide (Illustration 42), for example, is appealingly suggestive of multiple other presences. Elaine Showalter has described the painting as showing:

a tiny waiflike creature – a sort of Tinker Bell Ophelia – in a filmy white gown, perched on a tree trunk by the stream. The overall effect is softened, sexless, and hazy, although the straw in her hair resembles a crown of thorns.

Showalter sees Hughes's Ophelia as a 'juxtaposition of childlike femininity and Christian martyrdom'.[36] There is certainly a spiritual quality to the painting. Ophelia's face is serene, abstracted, even Madonna-like, and her waiflike fragility is emphasized by her delicately outstretched arm and by the isolation of her figure in a landscape so much bigger than herself. The straw in her hair is incidentally evocative of a crown of thorns, but also, perhaps, of a halo. She is victim and saint, child and sprite, Ophelia and Madonna, and a complex anomaly as included in this pictorial sequence.

In the context of the projected show as a whole, the effect of this anomalous insertion must have been striking. Hughes's pre-Raphaelite Ophelia

[36] Elaine Showalter, *The Female Malady: Women, Madness, and English Culture, 1830–1980* (London, 1987), pp. 84–5.

inevitably differs markedly from the more pared down, naïve style of the same character's other appearances in the slide run. It is true that Ophelia's trailing, extended right arm in the 'Ophelia scattering flowers' slide might perhaps be seen as an anticipatory mimicking of the yet more delicately extended right arm of Hughes's Ophelia, so constituting a suggestive bridge into the succeeding slide. In practice, however, that single echoed gesture across slides serves, if anything, simply to draw attention to the markedly different character of the two images as a whole, and of the two versions of Ophelia on offer within them. The daring disruption of stylistic consistency across slides robs the sequence of a sense of artistic unity, and even of character stability. In doing so, however, it confirms the iconic status of the character whose role in the narrative transcends any single manifestation, or even style of presentation. Ophelia, that is, can look like this or she can look like that. She can inhabit this or that sort of landscape. She can be eroticized, infantilized or idealized. Throughout all such variations in interpretive emphasis, however, the mythic dimensions of the story she occupies enable her to remain incontrovertibly 'Ophelia', possessed of a range of accumulated dramatic and artistic meanings. The progress of the story can, therefore, accommodate the stylistic adjustments without dislocating.

Briggs and Company made a habit of appropriating existing works of art for their slide narratives, often embedding them, as here, in broader, line-drawn sequences as an unprepared-for visual treat to be happened upon unexpectedly in the midst of more ordinary artistic fare. The Hughes painterly insert is, therefore, just one of several artistic surprises to have been culled from the pages of the *Art Journal* and implanted in one of the 'Shakespeare Illustrated' sequences. The inclusion of a known work of art in such sequences may, of course, have served as a gratifying nod to the artistic cognoscenti who, having recognized its provenance, might murmur modestly to their neighbour of their familiarity with it.[37] The copying of works of art (woodcuts, engravings, half-tones and coloured prints) for lantern exhibition was, at any rate, a standard part of the repertoire for the major slide manufacturers. By the 1890s, the *Optical Magic Lantern Journal and Photographic Enlarger* was even issuing advice to the private collector about how best to do this. Published reproductions of works of art, the journal enthused, offer the lanternist 'an inexhaustible store from which to draw if due care is taken in the selection'. The journal did take the precaution of issuing the self-indemnifying caveat that '[i]n the first place, it is just as well to be on the safe side and not make copies of copyright pictures'[38] – advice that was by no means, however, always followed in practice. I do not know, for example, whether Briggs and Company requested copyright permission for their reproduction of paintings from the *Art Journal*. It would not, however, be entirely surprising if they did not.

ii) *Romeo and Juliet*

All fourteen of the slides from Briggs's 1908 *Romeo and Juliet* lantern sequence have survived, all drawn by slide artist Joseph Boggs Beale. Beale's lantern scenes have little interest in psychological depth or emotional intensity, but they do tell the story both clearly and prettily. They appear in the following sequence: 'The quarrel in the street', 'Romeo and others in mask', 'Juliet at the balcony', 'Romeo and Juliet at the Friar's', 'Romeo's duel with Tybalt', 'Romeo and Juliet at window', 'Juliet beseeching her father', 'Juliet drinking the sleeping draught', 'Capulet and family weeping over Juliet', 'Romeo and the Apothecary', 'Duel between Paris and Romeo', 'Romeo drinking the poison', 'Death of Juliet', 'Reconciliation of Capulets and Montagues'.

---

[37] As such, it would have fulfilled a similar function to the *tableaux vivants* on the nineteenth-century stage, which made recognizable artistic allusions for the gratification of those whose range of cultural reference allowed them to identify the visual quotation.

[38] Duncan Moore, 'Copying Printed Matter for the Lantern', *The Optical Magic Lantern Journal and Photographic Enlarger*, vol. 5, no. 67 (1 December, 1894), pp. 215–7 (216, 217). For coloured prints, the use of orthochromatic plates with a screen was recommended.

44. Briggs's 1908 *Romeo and Juliet*. 'Juliet at the balcony'. Collodion on glass with applied colour. 3.25 × 4 in.

In the third slide in the sequence, 'Juliet at the balcony' (Illustration 44), Juliet stands between twisted Grecian columns in the foreground, her poised upright stance, semi-coiled hair and the drapes in her white dress aligning her tonally with the classical and heroic status of the columns that frame her. Although her arms are outstretched before her as she apostrophizes the Romeo she believes absent, everything about her suggests a woman fully under control. Romeo is visible at a significant remove down the garden, too distant for any facial expression to be clearly discerned. His arms too are raised, but without that potentially charged gesture communicating passionate investment. In contrast to Romeo's remoteness and Juliet's careful restraint, however, a luscious drape hangs unchecked over the edge of the balcony in the foreground of the image. The slide painter – typically separate from the slide artist – has painted this drape a suggestive deep pink, distinguishing it

45. Briggs's 1908 *Romeo and Juliet*. Friar Laurence's Cell. Collodion on glass. 3.25 × 4 in.

clearly from the night-time pale blues, pale greens and silvers of the rest of the image. Given Juliet's classical poise and Romeo's distance, the deeply coloured, haphazardly draped cloth invitingly suggests the potential for a passionate intensity that might otherwise be thought beyond the emotional range of these central figures. It is, in fact, a balcony scene of careful spatial choreography but of only symbolically displaced passion.

Given the self-possession of this scene and the fact that the whole sequence emerges from the

designing vision of a single artist, it is perhaps no surprise that later images from the same sequence are comparably restrained.

At Friar Laurence's cell, for example, the young lovers embrace decorously, her head leaning on his shoulder and his head inclined gently towards hers as his arm gently encircles, and his hand rests gently upon, her shoulder (Illustration 45). The accompanying quotation, hand-written onto the lower frame of this slide, remembers the Friar's rather breathless words: 'FRIAR: "Come, come with me, and we will make short work, for by your leaves, you shall not stay alone till holy church incorporate two in one."' Though the lovers are fully attentive to one another in Beale's pictorialized imagining of it, nevertheless the embrace we *see* is considerably more chaste in character than might be supposed from the Friar's evident impatience to see them married.

Across the entire slide sequence, in fact, Romeo and Juliet are presented as conventionally fetching figures, conducting a conventionally fetching Victorian love affair – if one with a (decorously enacted) tragic end. Despite the energy of the Shakespearian lines suggested as suitable accompanying quotation by the inscriptions on the frame, and despite the significant drama of the Shakespearian moment referenced in each case, the images themselves consistently temper the heightened feelings that drive the play. For all their narrative clarity and pretty arrangements of characters and scenery, these images are, in fact, emotionally tepid.

Another slightly anodyne visual rehearsal of *Romeo and Juliet* is on offer in a late nineteenth-century slide sequence from English slide manufacturers Theobald and Company. In the Theobald balcony scene, Romeo is dandified in blue hose, burgundy doublet, Victorian moustache and feathered cap as he is suspended rather stiffly on a ladder approaching Juliet's parapet, while Juliet herself is scarcely present as a character at all – just visible, if slightly hazily, in the orangeate glow from the casement window. It is a scene which would clearly have served its purpose to facilitate a lively accompanying narration or recitation. However, while colour has been used with vibrant intensity on the slide, in other artistic respects it is conspicuously bland.

Whereas emotion seems absent from the Theobald balcony scene and is only emblematically suggested in the Joseph Boggs Beale one, it is, by contrast, potently and centrally present in the balcony scene slide from Briggs's earlier *Romeo and Juliet* sequence (from the 1890s 'Shakespeare Illustrated' series). As Arthur Hughes's painting of Ophelia was invited to disrupt the pretty artistry,

and stylistic consistency, of the otherwise unchallenging *Hamlet* sequence, so here an imported artistic insert injects some heightened emotional cadence into the story of *Romeo and Juliet*. The image 'Romeo At Balcony' (Illustration 46) is borrowed from the celebrated Viennese artist Hans Makart's remarkable 1860s painting *Romeo and Juliet*.[39] Unlike in the Theobald and the Beale balcony slides discussed above, this balcony scene depicts Romeo's reluctant departure after his night with Juliet rather than his first, less sexually expressive approach. But the Makart image is also stylistically clearly distinguished from the other two *Romeo and Juliet* balcony slides. Such is the strikingly realistic artistry in the portrayal of the two central figures, that – though painted by Makart – the image initially deceives the eye into believing it a photographic slide employing life models (a common device in the lanternizing of morality tales and of Dickens, for example). A fully engaged, and utterly believable Juliet leans over the edge of the balcony in order to embrace her departing lover. She steadies herself on the adjacent pillar with her left hand in order to use her right to keep her hold on his precariously balanced figure. He, meanwhile, appears to hang from her grasp, precariously kneeling on the rung of a rope ladder thrown over the side of the balcony parapet. His head is thrown sensuously and uncompromisingly back that he might gaze on Juliet. His physical dependence upon her seems total, and he apparently gives himself to it, and to the moment, without qualification. The light – presumably from the rising sun – falls transcendently upon both of their faces, locked together as they are in an exchange of desirous gazes.

In the degree of the passion so transparently on display and in its arresting reversal of gender roles, it is a striking image. This Romeo is no swashbuckling antecedent to Errol Flynn scaling the walls to hop manfully into Olivia de Havilland's castle

---

[39] At the time of writing, a photographic image of the Makart painting is available to view online at, for example: www.photographersdirect.com/buyers/stockphoto.asp?imageid=657464

46. Title on slide frame: 'Romeo At Balcony – Makart'. Series Title: 'Shakespeare Illustrated'. Collodion on glass. 3.25 × 4 in.

bedroom in Warner Brothers' *Adventures of Robin Hood* (Michael Curtiz, 1938), nor of any of the later agile filmic Romeos adept at displaying their effortless manhood on ivy-clad walls. Rather, this Romeo's arched back, thrown back head, ballet-ically languid legs and evident need of physical assistance patently feminize him. Correspondingly, though her own feminine grace is not thereby compromised, Juliet's physical poise and solicitous care for the physical welfare of her lover seem to cast her in the role of protector. As projected to lantern audiences of the late nineteenth century, it must have seemed a decisive rejection of the prettier and more decorous Shakespearian images of insipid balcony encounters being peddled else-where. In its unapologetic concentration on two young lovers whose bodies are visibly finding it tormenting to be torn from each other, the image is bodily, sensual and daring. As inserted into the midst of a run of plot-clarifying, line-drawn *Romeo and Juliet* lantern slides from which it is sharply distinguished in tone, detail and emotional force, the inclusion of this Makart painting constitutes an arresting injection of passionate animation.

* * *

Across the nineteenth and into the twentieth century, Shakespeare was used in magic lantern shows for a range of purposes: as a plunderable source for illustrations for lectures on other subjects; in excerpted form as part of divertingly mixed lantern shows; and in abridged form as whole Shakespeare plots were compressed into the requisite eight to fourteen slide format for pictorialized retelling. The lantern medium offered slide artists and painters the opportunity to produce bright, beautiful and occasionally partially animated 'action-images' from the plays, and these decorative artistic dalliances with Shakespeare in turn gave the lantern-showmen the pretext, and illustration, for a scripted recitation from, or extemporised retelling of, a Shakespearian play to an assembled audience. In peddling simplified, abridged and illustrated Shakespeare in this way, the lantern collaborated with a series of other media in consolidating an implicitly agreed truncated form in which Shakespeare could circulate intelligibly and accessibly.

The diverse range of other cultural forms upon which the lantern drew in its responses to Shakespeare, however, made of it a territory where approaches otherwise considered at odds might encounter one another in striking proximity. In mimicking the forms of satirical sketches, burlettas and cartoons, for example, and in embedding Shakespearian excerpts within a variety programme of self-consciously skittish lantern sequences, the lantern was implicitly puncturing the perceived dignity of its source. However, by inviting reflection on the projected image of Mrs Siddons as Queen Catherine or of Mr Kean as Richard III, in absorbing paintings by Hughes or Makart into its Shakespearian sequences and in accompanying its Shakespearian images with charged poetic quotation, the lantern could also participate in sustaining and promoting the cultural elevation of the material that it was elsewhere satirizing.

The dual tug of the reverential and the parodic in lantern approaches to Shakespeare serves well to remind us of one of the crucial conditions of lantern exhibition – namely, that no show had a fixed tonal character but was rather made, and remade, on each occasion by a lanternist's deft management of the technology (both the hardware of the lens and lamp and the software of individual slides and slide sequences), and by his rhetorical dexterity in mediating engagingly between the slides and the audience. Thus it was, for example, that material that might play earnestly in one show could potentially play satirically in the next, depending on the manner in which the slides were shown and the inflection given to the commentary by the lanternist (working in tune with the mood of the audience). A lanternized *Macbeth* for one audience, for example, could end with the gasp-worthy effects slide by which Macbeth's head was severed from his neck, while for another that same slide could gleefully return the severed head to its neck for anarchic or comic effect; the account of Hamlet's ghost could be presented as chilling to one audience but entertainingly hyperbolic to another; Romeo and Juliet's balcony encounter could be made to inspire a sigh or a giggle. It was not only, therefore, in the particularity of its cultural references that the lantern found itself caught between approaches. It was, in itself, a medium always in the balance, always dependent upon the particularities of the lanternist's use of his slides and of his accompanying performance to determine its tonal character.

In its weaving together of the exhibition of Shakespearian fine artistry with the retelling of Shakespeare narratives and the sampling of live Shakespearian language, the lantern's engagements with Shakespeare were unique. In time, however, this delicately poised, interestingly mutable medium that combined the dexterous use of technology with the unpredictable glories (and/or disappointments) of an individual performance would, as discussed elsewhere, be replaced by a different version of screened Shakespeare. The new medium of cinema would forego the pretty but frequently slightly saccharine Victorian and Edwardian artistry of painted slides in favour of the weight and interest of real, and often famous, Shakespearian actors enacting grand passion and dramatic moment. Even in its processes of institutional displacement, however, early cinema looked to the lantern as a model for emulation in various respects – and the lantern's established popularity as a vehicle for Shakespeare confirmed its worth in this respect. In 1908, for example, an article in the *Moving Picture World* reported that Shakespearian lantern shows were attracting audiences of 'thousands'.[40] This report specifically threw down the gauntlet to the film industry in the hope of inspiring it to attract yet greater crowds for filmed Shakespeare than had been possible for lanternized Shakespeare.

Part of the moving picture industry's response to that challenge involved appropriating some of the lantern's successful exhibition conventions. The lantern's legacy is, for example, particularly conspicuous in the presence of the moving picture lecturers who provided live commentary on Shakespearian (and other) moving pictures in some exhibition venues in the years between 1908 and 1914.[41] During that period, there was a lively and ongoing debate in the film trade press not only about the rhetorical competence or otherwise of the available speakers on the moving picture lecture circuit but, more fundamentally, about whether an accompanying commentary was needed at all in a medium such as the cinematograph. This was a debate that had never been pertinent in relation to lantern shows whose projected visuals, however beautifully painted, had never been expected to carry the burden of stand-alone meaning. Cuing an audience to gaze in particular ways at targeted aspects of the projected images was explicitly part

of the lanternist's brief as he mediated between image and audience. It was against precisely this intimate co-dependence and mutual accommodation between words and images that the film industry, by contrast, chafed. There, in time, the interposing presence of the lecturer became considered a cumbersome impediment to the medium's visual autonomy – a symbolic admission that the images themselves lacked sufficient clarity or eloquence to be able to communicate without linguistic supplementation.

By 1914, that debate was resolved and the style of film production had moved on so as to render the figure of the moving picture lecturer redundant – an antiquated reminder of a style of production and a mode of exhibition no longer *au courant*. At that point, the moving picture lecturer joined the host of lantern showmen who had preceded him – the dull and the charismatic alike – in being largely consigned to the historical record. But whereas the moving picture lecturer proved an expendable element of a medium that then had the gall to thrive without him, Timothy Toddle and his fellow lanternists had always been fully integral to what a lantern show was, a crucial part of that excitingly unpredictable triangulation of meaning-making between two-dimensional image, live commentary and audience that played its institutional part in the dissemination, promotion and sympathetic satirizing of Shakespeare for approximately a hundred years.

---

[40] W. Stephen Bush, 'Shakespeare in Moving Pictures', *Moving Picture World*, vol. 3, no. 23 (5 December 1908), pp. 446–7 (447).

[41] On the uses of lecturers in Shakespeare moving pictures of the early cinema period, see Buchanan, *Shakespeare on Silent Film*, pp. 10–13.

SHAKESPEARE AND THE COCONUTS: CLOSE ENCOUNTERS IN POST-APARTHEID SOUTH AFRICA

NATASHA DISTILLER

South African literary history is full of the effects of writers having had close encounters with the Shakespeare text. The results have been literary and personal, with writers displaying, and often-times clearly experiencing, a profound emotional connection to, especially, the plays. Since the days of the mission schools in colonial Southern Africa, Shakespeare has been a signifier of education, civility and erudition, as well as a vehicle for the expression of strong feelings. Encounters with the Shakespeare text have shaped hopes, allowed for public self-fashioning, and have influenced more intimate subjectivities as writers and scholars of a particular class stratification were educated in English Literature.[1] Something has changed, though, in terms of what a close encounter with Shakespeare enables. If Shakespeare used to be part of a marker of class and social mobility located in the terms of a discourse of progress and modernity, knowledge of Shakespeare now comprises a much more publicly ambivalent display. Shakespeare once had a particular currency, acquired personally but activated publicly, which he appears to be losing. This article will attempt to account for the change, suggesting that it reveals the gap between theory and lived experience. Close encounters with Shakespeare viewed through a post-colonial lens illustrate that culture is hybrid. Nevertheless, in the face of ongoing socio-economic power differentials which operate along raced and classed axes, the logic of a binary structure of identity continues to inform an experience of Shakespeare in South Africa long after our own cultural artifacts reveal that binary models are an artificial and inadequate

way to understand how people live, including how they live with Shakespeare.

Perhaps the most well-known example of a South African whose close personal encounter with Shakespeare profoundly influenced his work is Solomon Plaatje.[2] Plaatje, the author of the first novel in English by a black South African and the first translator of Shakespeare's plays into a Southern African language, was also the first secretary of the organization that became the African National Congress, now in government in post-apartheid South Africa. Plaatje's diverse writings, which are concerned with linguistic, land and political rights in the context of turn-of-the-twentieth-century South Africa, invoke Shakespeare's plays thematically and through direct quotation.[3] David Johnson[4] has suggested that one way to read Plaatje's love of Shakespeare is to understand him as having been duped by the false promise of British liberalism, such that his admiration for Shakespeare becomes a sign of his co-optation by a system that

My thanks to the attendees of the University of Cape Town's English Department research seminar series, summer 2008, whose useful comments helped to sharpen the argument of this article.

[1] Natasha Distiller, *South Africa, Shakespeare, and Post-Colonial Culture* (Lampeter, 2005); David Johnson, *Shakespeare and South Africa* (Oxford, 1996).

[2] See Tim Couzens and Brian Willan, 'Solomon T. Plaatje, 1876–1932: An Introduction', *English in Africa*, 3:2 (1976), pp. 1–99; and Tim Couzens, 'A Moment in the Past: William Tsikinya-Chaka', *Shakespeare in Southern Africa*, 2 (1988), 60–6.

[3] See Distiller, *South Africa*, pp. 109–22.

[4] Johnson, *Shakespeare*, p. 96.

was never going to deliver the socio-political equality it held forth as a possibility. According to this interpretation of Plaatje's Shakespearian writings, Africans can only lose by loving Shakespeare and the white culture 'he' supposedly stands for. They lose not only politically but at the level of identity too. We might say Johnson suggests Plaatje can be accused of being a coconut.

The term 'coconut' is one of several edible designations, including 'bounty' (from the American Bounty chocolate bar), 'topdeck' (a South African chocolate bar), 'apple', 'banana', and, of course, 'oreo' (from the American Oreo cookie), used to designate someone who, due to their behaviour, identifications, or because they have been raised by whites,[5] is 'black' on the 'outside' and 'white' on the 'inside'.[6] These terms are in operation in the UK, USA, South Africa, New Zealand and China, amongst other places. The focus on 'acting' or 'feeling' 'white' in a range of communities across the globe points to the ongoing prevalence of white privilege as a structuring principle of our neo-colonial world.[7] The different terms also speak to the imbrication of racial profiling with personal identity, in that ethnicity is yoked to skin colour, which in turn is presumed to designate a fixed identity. 'Coconut' specifically, although used in South Africa to denote black people (most often with a particular kind of education which includes fluency in English and a media profile, as in 'coconut intellectuals'), has provenance elsewhere as a term for people considered 'brown', not 'black': Asians, Indians, Latinos, Filipinos.[8] In all places, used by those who are claiming access to an authentic blackness of whatever shade, the term has derogatory implications of inauthenticity, artificiality and, sometimes, shameful or shameless aspiration. In South Africa, the appellation 'coconut' is currently in extensive circulation, and is closely tied to class mobility as indicated specifically through speaking a specific kind of 'white' English.[9]

Of course, this conceptualization of personal identity is crude in its essentializing of blackness and whiteness, and untenably reliant on notions of cultural authenticity. Assertions of cultural purity and their concomitant legitimations, invocations of tradition are nostalgic and political, if powerful, fictions. Without endorsing these implications of the trope of the coconut, I would like to explore the workings of the notion of the coconut specifically in relation to how Shakespeare might be experienced in post-apartheid South Africa. Recent local responses to the idea of Shakespeare, and of what a deeply personal familiarity with Shakespeare might mean, draw on the trope, so that a close encounter with Shakespeare is still reliant on a particular display of English literariness understood to exist in a binary relation to a putative Africanness. This despite our own literary archive, steeped in activism, which suggests that Shakespeare has been far more profound for the South Africans who have closely encountered 'him'. More than this, I want to follow through on coconut logic: is there a kind of artificiality, an inauthenticity, a hollowness at the core of such a display, which is activated because of the ongoing valency of a pernicious but, in real terms, ongoing binary? This discussion ultimately asks what the place of Shakespeare is in post-apartheid South African public culture. What does a close encounter with the Shakespeare text signify today?

[5] Minelle Mahtani, 'Mixed Metaphors: Positioning "Mixed Race" Identity', in Jo-Anne Lee and John Lutz, eds., *Situating 'Race' and Racisms in Space, Time, and Theory: Critical Essays for Activists and Scholars* (Montreal & Kingston, London, Ithaca, 2005), pp. 77–93; p. 90 n. 1.

[6] 'Apples' is a term used by Native Americans, and 'bananas' by Chinese about Chinese Singaporeans; see Tracy L. Mack, 'What Can You Learn from a Rainbow?', *Interracial Voice*, www.webcom.com/~intvoice/tracy.html.

[7] 'Rotten coconut' denotes someone who is brown on the outside and black on the inside, as in Indians who perform a hip-hop identity; see Nitasha Sharma, 'Rotten Coconuts and Other Strange Fruits', *Samar*, 14: Fall/Winter (2001), www.samarmagazine.org/archive/article.php?id=62. Sharma comments that while the fruit metaphors for acting white 'are perfectly healthy . . . this reference stigmatized those seen as "trying to be black" as "rotten" and "downwardly" assimilating'.

[8] Sarfraz Manzoor, *The Guardian*, 'The Coconut Conundrum', (Monday, 30 July 2007), www.sarfrazmanzoor.co.uk

[9] Catherine McKinney, '"If I Speak English Does it Make Me Less Black Anyway?" "Race" and English in South African Desegregated Schools', *English Academy Review*, 24:2 (2007), pp. 6–24.

I suggest ultimately that precisely the kind of problematic binary thinking which animates the trope of the coconut might now infuse the public representation of the experience of a close encounter with Shakespeare's texts. Although this binary logic is theoretically suspect and an inaccurate model for how identification occurs at the level of the everyday, it is being reinscribed in post-apartheid South Africa because it does in fact accurately reflect an experience of the world; it bespeaks the ongoing hierarchies of social and economic power. And Shakespeare belongs firmly to the privileged half of the binary, despite his regional history as a literary, political and, indeed, personal resource for discourses of resistance. Daily post-apartheid experience is trumping literary colonial history.

A more concrete way of posing this coconut question is to ask can Shakespeare, who has reached Africans through a particular historical process, ever be free of his colonial masters despite the existence of a rich African Shakespearian tradition, in the context of current relations of social and economic power in the country and in the world? If, as the range of South African texts discussed below suggest, the answer may be no, then the notion of the coconut might be useful in the expression of an authentic (I use the word advisedly) anxiety. This anxiety is encapsulated by the idea of the subject trying to be something he is not, and in the related reasons why someone would try to alter herself.

In Kopano Matlwa's debut novel, *Coconut*,[10] one of the protagonists has a Shakespeare-quoting uncle. This novel details the hopes and aspirations, and the costs, of two young women's searches for identities in South Africa in 2007. One, Ofilwe, belongs to the generation whose parents have acquired upper-middle-class status, and the other, Fikile, aspires to this status. The novel makes it clear that both young women have internalized aspects of whiteness, in different ways, and to different effects. They are, in their own ways, coconuts. Ofilwe feels alienated from her parents' culture and language, and Fikile loathes where she finds herself located culturally. Fikile's uncle is another kind of coconut.

Uncle is constantly quoting or paraphrasing Shakespeare as the ultimate expression of his distress.

'Oh, I am fortune's fool!' Uncle would begin, whimpering.
'Yes, Uncle,' I would sigh. No, Uncle, I would think. Not again, not now, please. I had homework to do . . .
'I have lost all my mirth, the earth seems sterile.'
'Yes, Uncle,' I would say again, for that was all that was expected from me . . . during these laments when Uncle would spew out pieces of Shakespeare as if he thought them up himself while lost in the abyss of his sorry existence . . . [11]
'I am dying, Fikile, dying . . . When beggars die, there are no comets seen,' he would sob . . .
'Yes, Uncle.'
'I am a godly man, Fikile.'
'Yes, Uncle.'
'I am an honest man, Fikile.'
'Yes, Uncle.'
'A righteous man, Fikile.'
'Yes, Uncle.'
'That it should come to this!'
'Yes, Uncle.'
'I struggle each day to keep a free and open nature.'
'Yes, Uncle.'
'The world is grown so bad that wrens make prey where eagles dare not perch.'
At this point, of course, I had long stopped listening . . .
He was speaking to himself . . . [12]

The reasons for Uncle's distress are imbricated in their Shakespearian expression. Uncle's knowledge of Shakespeare is a signifier of his proficiency in English, and thus a trace marker or remnant of the privileged education he had access to as a child, when he was taken into the household of the white family that employed his mother as a domestic worker. Very specifically, though, for Fikile, herself unashamedly aspirant to white economic and social privilege, Uncle's Shakespeare is an empty signifier. It comprises an arguably poignant but ultimately empty display of Englishness and white erudition.

---

[10] Kopano Matlwa, *Coconut* (Johannesburg, 2007).
[11] Matlwa, *Coconut*, p. 99.
[12] Matlwa, *Coconut*, pp. 100–1.

His ongoing monologue of quotes serves as a marker of his failure to achieve the promise of advancement implicit in the acquisition of a certain kind of education.

Uncle's distress is about his work situation, where he is being cynically used as 'window dressing' in the post-apartheid government's Black Economic Empowerment policy. It is Shakespeare who enabled this situation, marking Uncle as a black man with specific, although practically useless, talents:

'They use me, Fikile . . . I sit in my chair at the security desk and read my books . . . I love my books . . . My Hamlet, my kings – Richard and Lear – my Julius Caesar, my Antony and Cleopatra, my beautiful but yet so tragic Romeo and Juliet . . . Ah, but some rise by sin and some by virtue fall . . .

Oh Fikile, when Mr Dix approached me at my humble security desk and inquired about the books I read, I was only honoured to share with him the might, the mastery and supremacy that lay within those pages . . .

But he is mad that trusts in the tameness of a wolf, a horse's health, a boy's love or a whore's oath. I was a fool . . . I should have known those heavy white men in their dry-cleaned suits were not interested in my sonnets but in my black skin.[13]

Uncle's English, and specifically 'his' Shakespeare, indicate his ability to perform a proficiency that does not in fact result in anything. Mr Dix occasionally lends him a suit and takes him along to business meetings where he is introduced as a senior member of the business, forbidden from participating in the discussion, and whisked out of the room under the pretence of an urgent call as soon as possible. Uncle will never be a successful businessman, even as his English, exemplified by his Shakespeare, enables him to pretend that he is. It is his Shakespeare's performance value, together with Uncle's desperation – that is, the fact precisely that he is not what he seems, that he is poor – that makes him useful to his bosses (Fikile is narrating here):

'I am a man more sinned against than sinning.' Sniff-sniff. Bullshit. Absolute bullshit! Uncle knew very well that from that first day when Mr Dix asked him to read him passages from his books and asked him to recite the poetry, Uncle lauded over everyone; he was being inter-

viewed, assessed and evaluated for the position of black fake senior partner/CEO/co-founder/financial director or whatever position it was that spoke of transformation at Lentso Communications . . .

Uncle was just another hungry black man, hungry for a piece of the pie like the rest of us . . . Uncle is a liar and a fake . . . He's pathetic as a security guard and probably would have been fired by now if they hadn't found out that he spoke English so well.[14]

Uncle's English is a marker of education and the necessary element for attainment of what Fikile calls 'the soft life', which 'everyone . . . yearned for',[15] even as his propensity for displaying this education by quoting Shakespeare emphasizes his lack of attainment of financial success. Uncle is the failed version of the earlier, mission-schooled, upwardly mobile young man who, through the promise of Western education, would further the 'progress' of himself and, as a leader, his people, towards modernity. This figure, an important one in the history of writing in English in the region as well as in the development of a political leadership and a colonial petty bourgeoisie, is specifically gendered, a point made by Fikile when she mentions that his sister, as talented as he, was not thought worthy of education by the white family.

Fikile has no respect for what Uncle's Shakespeare signifies. Like one of Johnson's versions of Plaatje, Fikile depicts her uncle as a 'Yes-man'.[16] For her, his empty displays confirm that he is 'Such a twerp . . . Such a sorry, pathetic, little twerp . . . I loathed this man.'[17] The reason she hates him so much is that when he is particularly inconsolable – when he is most steeped in his lachrymose Shakespeare and has 'that sorry look' when he comes home from work – he sexually abuses her, which she experiences as 'comforting' him.[18] 'I hated that Uncle was such a sorry and pathetic and weak man and hated even more that I was the only one who

---

13 Matlwa, *Coconut*, pp. 101–3.
14 Matlwa, *Coconut*, pp. 108–9.
15 Matlwa, *Coconut*, pp. 108–9.
16 Matlwa, *Coconut*, p. 123.
17 Matlwa, *Coconut*, pp. 103, 104.
18 Matlwa, *Coconut*, pp. 111–12.

was able to comfort him.'[19] His sexual abuse of Fikile is a sign of his loss of manhood, and his close encounter with Shakespeare facilitates the expression of his failure and emasculation.

Uncle is a poor 'investment'[20] for the white family who educated him, and for his community. It is crucial to note, however, that Fikile is not rejecting the aspiration to whiteness she sees him as having squandered.

Uncle could have had it all and he screwed it up. The Kinsleys did so much for Uncle even though they didn't have to. I mean, he was only their domestic worker's son and yet they treated him like he was one of their own . . . If only they had known that all the money they were investing in tuition, school uniforms, piano lessons and expensive encyclopedias would one day go to waste. If only they had invested that money in me instead of Uncle . . . I knew that if I had been given half the chance Uncle had been given I would never have turned out to be a disappointment . . . I knew that if I was given the chance to meet the Kinsleys, then all my problems would be solved, for they would surely ask me to move into their home right then and there and change my name to something cute like Sarah Kinsley.[21]

As she dresses herself for work in the morning, putting in her green contact lenses and applying her skin lightening cream, Fikile observes,

[P]erhaps it is for the better that the conditions in this dump never improve. They can serve as a constant reminder to me of what I do not want to be: black, dirty and poor. This bucket [where she washes] can be a daily motivator for me to keep working towards where I will someday be: white, rich and happy.[22]

She is grooming herself towards this end, and, crucially, this involves educating herself in English.

I am now more confident in everything I do and am no longer uncertain of my capabilities. Nothing intimidates me. I have even started speaking in the English language even when I do not need to. I am no longer concerned with what I sound like because I have come to believe that I sound like any other English-speaking person. I use words like 'facetious' and 'filial' in everyday speech and speak English boldly . . . Not like Uncle, who spews out fragments of Shakespeare that make little sense to him or anyone else, but with insight and understanding.[23]

It is not Uncle's aspiration that disgusts Fikile. It is his failed aspiration, and Shakespeare is the signifier of this failure. Shakespeare is the display of a veneer of Englishness; by virtue of its incomprehensibility it is in fact evidence of what it is trying to conceal, a hollowness and lack of substance. This is in opposition to Fikile's 'insight[ful]' use of English. Her comment, that she now feels confident of sounding 'like any other English-speaking person', speaks to a long social history of accent in South Africa, and to the types of English spoken by most South Africans, now recognized as its own regional variant with the publication of the Oxford University Press *Dictionary of South African English* in 2002. This legitimation is lost on Fikile, though, who is striving to differentiate herself from most South Africans and enter a caste whose markers of belonging include various aspects of what Fikile identifies as whiteness: money, designer labels, western culture (symbolized by Avril Lavigne on the cover of her latest *Girlfriend* magazine), happiness, cleanliness, dignity and, of course, English spoken in a specific way, all the time (not just as a lingua franca or when talking to monolingual white South Africans). Fikile knows that 'the accent matters',[24] as do her real-life counterparts.[25]

Fikile's private fantasy of selfhood, her self-fashioning, embodies the centrality of Englishness to her aspirations:

My name is Fiks Twala. I have a second name, Fikile, which I never use because many find it too difficult to pronounce . . . I grew up in white environments for the most part of my life, from primary school right up to high school. Many people think I am foreign, from the UK or somewhere there. I think it is because my accent is so perfect and my manner so refined. Yes, I have always been different. I never could relate to other black South Africans . . . It's never been an issue for me

---

[19] Matlwa, *Coconut*, p. 114.
[20] Matlwa, *Coconut*, p. 125.
[21] Matlwa, *Coconut*, pp. 124, 125.
[22] Matlwa, *Coconut*, p. 118.
[23] Matlwa, *Coconut*, p. 137.
[24] Matlwa, *Coconut*, p. 154.
[25] See McKinney, 'If I Speak English'.

though. I guess you do not miss something you have never known . . .

I lived in England for a while, Mummy and Daddy still lecture there. I couldn't stand the weather, absolutely dreadful, so I moved back here . . . It's harder here though, you have to do everything for yourself. You can't trust anybody, not with all the crime and corruption. But ja, it's home, what can I say?[26]

Her motto is 'Fake it till you make it.'[27]

The kitchen staff at the restaurant she works at, all of whom would be working-class black people like Fikile herself, respond to her by shaking their heads and saying 'Shame' (an expression of pity in South African English). She responds, 'Stupid people . . . why are they feeling sorry for me?'.[28]

Even as Fikile cannot see what she is betraying, Matlwa is clear that 'authentic' working-class Africanness is poor compensation for hundreds of years of oppression and concomitant deprivation, even as she is aware of the complexities of the identity and class positions that have resulted. Fikile's co-worker, Ayanda, is a child of the post-apartheid privilege meted out to the small black middle class. He is working at the restaurant to try to reconnect with the authenticity he feels his privileged upbringing has cost him. Ayanda has a run-in with a racist white patron who wants a cheese sandwich without the cheese. Their interaction results in Ayanda's outburst, which Fikile calls 'talking all sorts of revolution shit':[29]

'They feel nothing. They see nothing, absolutely nothing wrong with the great paradox in this country. Ten per cent of them still living in ninety per cent of the land, ninety per cent of us still living on ten per cent of the land . . . Any fool . . . can see that there is a gross contradiction in this country.' What was Ayanda talking about? He lived in some loft his parents had bought him in Morningside [a previously whites-only upper-middle-class suburb] . . .

'How many of them do you hear saying that they want to leave the country? . . . "Oh the crime! Oh the poverty!" . . . So why don't they leave? Why the hell did they come here in the first place? . . . If they want to leave, I say the sooner the better.'

I knew he didn't mean that. He didn't mean any of it. Ayanda had tons of white friends . . . Ayanda had gone

to a white school, lived in white neighbourhoods all his life. He had the life that everybody dreamed of. The ass was just talking out of his arse. And we all knew it. I did, the kitchen staff did, and he did. So after that, he got back to work.[30]

The acquisition of the social and economic capital experienced by Fikile as whiteness has real, life-altering power. While English is crucial to this process, and Fikile works hard to fake her English identity until she can properly acquire it, Shakespeare bears a different relation to it. While Shakespeare stands for proficiency in English, he signifies, specifically, useless knowledge and a particular kind of display. Unlike English, Shakespeare is flashy but ultimately empty of real content and so empty of real power.

Has Shakespeare's display value become the defining element of 'his' post-apartheid South African incarnation? Has he become the marker, not just of the coconut, but, in the context of democratic and neo-liberal South Africa, the failed coconut? *Coconut*'s analysis of white privilege, accessible by those blacks who can perform the relevant, meaningful markers of Englishness, is pertinent and incisive. Shakespeare, as the exemplar of English, stands for access to this privilege. But Uncle's mobilization of the quotes to express his 'sorry state', the state in which he abuses a child, stands also for his failed attempt, his partial and ultimately unsuccessful access. Fikile does not reject the aspirations encoded in uncle's Shakespeare. Indeed, she is passionately committed to achieving them. What she does not buy is that Shakespeare is a viable pathway to this social mobility and, more vitally, a relevant marker of the psychic authenticity she feels precedes her right to this mobility.

Fikile is a canny young woman who has understood how privilege operates in post-apartheid South Africa and is single-minded in her desire

---

[26] Matlwa, *Coconut*, p. 146.
[27] Matlwa, *Coconut*, p. 147.
[28] Matlwa, *Coconut*, p. 146.
[29] Matlwa, *Coconut*, p. 152.
[30] Matlwa, *Coconut*, p. 153.

to better her social standing. By embracing white Englishness she has ensured that she will always be aspiring to something she can never quite be, a version of Ngugi wa Thiong'o's colonized African mind.[31] Crucially, Matlwa's novel explored these issues when South Africa was under the leadership of a president who is famous for quoting Shakespeare most specifically, as well as other canonized English writers, in his political speeches. In recent South African public discourse Thabo Mbeki's Shakespeare appears as a signifier of his self-fashioning and concomitant alienation from his constituency, standing for his positioning in an either/or formulation where a leader is either in a personal relationship with Shakespeare and all he represents or in touch with 'the' African people. Sometimes Shakespeare is mentioned along with other canonical writers, but Shakespeare is always present in this discussion. Like Uncle's Shakespeare, Mbeki's Shakespeare becomes emblematic of a fatal character flaw.

Writing at the time of the ANC presidential succession saga, in December 2007, author Rian Malan assessed Mbeki's career. Commenting on his image in South Africa as being more concerned with his global commitments than with what was happening in the country he was supposed to be leading, Malan writes tellingly of the display value of Mbeki's literate speeches:

At times, he seemed to be living a fantasy in which he starred as a great statesman, descending from the sky in the presidential jet and marching down a red carpet into a forest of microphones to deliver a speech laced with quotes from Yeats and Shakespeare, leaving the western world shaken to its racist core by the sight of an African more suave and civilised than it could ever hope to be.[32]

Relevant to Matlwa's depiction of an unimpressed Fikile, he adds, 'I say western advisedly, because it remains unclear whether Africans are impressed by this sort of intellectual flash. The audience whose approval Mbeki most deeply craved was white and western.'[33] Indeed, political journalist Xolela Mangcu, who places himself in the same intellectual tradition as Mbeki, comments, '[W]e have a president who at every opportunity is always more

interested in how clever he is than in empathizing with the rest of the population.'[34] Mbeki lost the party's presidential position to Jacob Zuma, who has been cast as a populist, and whose victory was a clear indication from the ANC membership that they were fed up with Mbeki's management style. Commenting on Zuma's first policy speech as ANC president, journalist Fiona Forde described Zuma's style and content:

Zuma... made his way to the podium with unmistakable authority... [H]e spoke with clarity and in a deliberate tone. His choice of words was simple, yet meaningful. There was not a word of Shakespeare this year... Instead, he delivered a straightforward statement and used his voice and not verbosity to give emphasis at every punch line.[35]

By inference, Mbeki's Shakespeare is obscure, elitist and obfuscating. It symbolizes the reason why he lost popular support, and organizational power. The charge of elitism, so encapsulated in Mbeki's penchant for Shakespeare, implicitly links him to 'the West' and all its putative interests – big business, 'white' culture – in a binary formulation where Zuma's plain speaking marks him as a man of 'the people'.[36] Reporting on the 2007 ANC national conference held at the University of the Limpopo in Polokwane at which Mbeki lost the presidency to Zuma, Kevin Bloom and Phillip de Wet took a moment to reminisce about Mbeki's image. They emphasize his English (both his

---

31 Ngugi wa Thiong'o, *Decolonizing the Mind: The Politics of Language in African Literature* (London and Nairobi, 1986).

32 Rian Malan, 'Requiem for a Lonely Man', *Sunday Independent* (16 December 2007), p. 9. Malan concludes: '[I]f it weren't for Aids, crime, unemployment, collapsing hospitals, crippled bureaucracies, Zimbabwe and the arms deal, we'd have to cast him as a great president.'

33 Malan, 'Requiem'.

34 Xolela Mangcu, *To the Brink: The State of Democracy in South Africa* Scottsville, 2008), p. 152.

35 Fiona Forde, 'No More Whispering in the Corridors, says Zuma', *Sunday Independent* (13 January 2008), p. 3.

36 If Mbeki is a coconut, Zuma is a chameleon, and his apparent demagoguery is belied by his ability to speak plainly to every interest group; Mbeki may be cast in the public mind as protecting the interests of the economic elite, but Zuma has not given any indication that he will threaten these interests.

education and acculturation, and his use of language), which sums up his contrast to Zuma and his class interests:

'But he's so well spoken!' That was a favourite phrase at the dinner tables of white South Africa, circa midsummer 1997 . . . Only ten short years ago, many of those who today equate Zuma with the impending apocalypse were heaping praise on the sophisticate who would inherit the country from Nelson Mandela. Mbeki, it was widely quoted, held a masters degree in economics from a British university [Sussex], the suits he wore were from Saville Row, there were even photographs of him in his younger days smoking a good English pipe. Such sentiments were further entrenched when, after Mbeki took power, he liberally salted his official speeches with references to Pliny the Elder, William Shakespeare and William Butler Yeats. Here was a man . . . with whom foreign investors and Caucasians everywhere could identify.[37]

Similarly, in Allister Sparks's assessment, Zuma

is essentially a man of the people, with a charm and warmth that endears him to the crowds. He would not be the philosopher president. You would not hear him quoting Yeats or Shakespeare or delivering speeches of literary grandeur, but he has his ear to the ground and he knows what's going on. As the Afrikaners used to say of their political equivalents, Hy weet waar die volk se hart klop [he knows where the people's heart beats]. He is clever, but not too clever . . . [38]

Read together with Matlwa's devastating assessment of African men who quote Shakespeare, Mbeki appears to be in danger of being called a failed coconut himself. However, as Isabel Hofmeyer has pointed out, the use of Shakespeare in political speeches by the post-apartheid political leadership continues a genre that was developed in the colonial mission schools.[39] The display value of the Shakespeare text in such a context is more than window dressing; it enters into a rhetorical tradition that makes use of the social power accrued to Englishness, for its own ends. This tradition, as Hofmeyer notes, is under-appreciated. Instead, Mbeki's Shakespeare is touted in the public realm as an indicator of his sense of himself as educated

and erudite, as anglicized, implicitly a sign of his failure to connect with his constituency.

Journalistic impatience with Mbeki's Shakespeare, which peaked during post-Polokwane reports, was in evidence before the 2007 conference, again as shorthand for all that was wrong with Mbeki's leadership. Political correspondent Vukani Mde began his 2006 assessment of Mbeki's State of the Nation address of that year by rejecting first the poet and then the president who needs him:

I've never liked Shakespeare. He is of very limited use to the modern writer. He wrote too much on too many subjects, and on many occasions made himself guilty of the twin infractions for which no writer can be forgiven: repetition and contradiction. In fact his oeuvre suffers from the same literary and philosophical pitfalls that litter the Bible. They are both impossible to quote without fear of contradiction, or worse, ridicule. But while I've always tolerated the Bible as a joint effort between people with different agendas, I make no such allowances for a lone Englishman from Stratford-upon-Avon who should have known better. I just don't do

---

[37] Kevin Bloom and Phillip de Wet, 'Fear & Loathing in Polokwane: The Big Stuff', *Maverick*, www.maverick.co.za/ViewStory.asp?StoryID=183105. And Anthony Sampson's 2001 glowing assessment of Mbeki, which focuses on his 'Englishness', concludes: 'His intellectual detachment allows him to see his country in a wider context, and his love of Shakespeare is part of his understanding that Africa's problems are part of the broader problems of the human condition. With this perspective he will not be easily lured, like so many African leaders, in the direction of dictatorship' ('President Select', *The Observer* [Sunday, 10 June 2001], www.guardian.co.uk/world/2001/jun/10/nelsonmandela.southafrica). The intervening years suggest Sampson had too much faith, both in Mbeki and in Shakespeare's influence. After the AIDS debacle (very publicly informed by Mbeki's surfing), and in the face of what Mbeki's Shakespeare has come to mean, Sampson's listing of the president's interests as 'Poetry, the internet' can only draw ironic sniggers from South Africans. Given the overall tone of the article, I am sure this was not Sampson's intention.

[38] Allister Sparks, 'Implications of a Zuma Presidency', *Homecoming Revolution* (28 November 2007), www.homecomingrevolution.co.za/hcrblog/?p=320.

[39] Isabel Hofmeyer, 'Reading Debating/Debating Reading: The Case of the Lovedale Literary Society, or Why Mandela Quotes Shakespeare', in Karin Barber, ed. *Africa's Hidden Histories: Everyday Literacy and Making the Self* (Bloomington and Indianapolis, 2006), pp. 258–77; p. 271.

Shakespeare. You can imagine my dismay then, when I realised President Thabo Mbeki meant to base his state of the nation literary effort on these two unreliable sources. I've just never understood our president's devotion to the man's writing. He runs to him at the slightest provocation, in increasingly silly attempts to lend poetic gravitas to the prosaic work of government. But poetry as a mode of communicating the ordinary unfortunately delivers ever-diminishing returns... I just fell asleep in the end... It was torture most foul.[40]

In an ironic repeat of a familiar colonial conflation which saw Shakespeare's texts as the secular equivalent of the Bible, and equally as important for the civilization of the natives,[41] Mde here addresses Shakespeare and the Bible as twin sources of an irrelevant, imposed, overrated culture. The symbolic power of this culture, disavowed as it may be by Mde, nevertheless resonates through this critique in his inability to resist the temptation to use Shakespeare himself. It is not just Shakespeare's pithy epithetic quality, as in the final sentence quoted above, that is available to this journalist writing in English. He concludes his article by turning Shakespeare against Mbeki, and benefits from both the poetry and the emblematic truth-value of the texts:

When historians chronicle [Mbeki's] so-called Age of Hope, they may praise faintly for the stunning successes, but will damn him for the devastating failures. Shakespeare said: 'The evil that men do lives after them, but the good is oft interred with their bodies.' So it shall be with Mbeki. Macbeth's lament [quoted by Mbeki in his speech] ends thus: 'Life is but a walking shadow. A poor player, that struts and frets his hour upon the stage and then is heard no more. 'Tis a tale told by an idiot, full of sound and fury, signifying nothing.' Like a mid-term state of the nation speech.[42]

Mde deploys the very authority he deplores, in order to perform the same rhetorical flourishes for which he damns Mbeki. Shakespeare clearly still has both symbolic and poetic clout. Mde is relying upon this clout to invest his statement, 'I just don't do Shakespeare' with provocation. At the same time, he does 'do' Shakespeare, in order to undo Mbeki's presentation, and implicitly, Mbeki's

self-presentation. The attack is as personal as it is political.

It is instructive that another text in the public realm at the time of the succession battle for presidency of the ANC when Mbeki's reign was being assessed, this time a political cartoon,[43] also invokes his well-known Shakespearian proclivities in order to turn them against him in a critique that aims at more than his political presence (Illustration 47).

The reference in the second frame of the bottom line to Zuma's 'comeback' 'explains' his ability to survive rape and corruption charges to become president of the ANC. Eve's reprimand, 'Didn't we tell you to stay away from beetroot?', references the health minister Manto Tshabalala-Msimang's ('Lady Manto') notorious comments about how to treat HIV, in the context of Mbeki's ongoing tacit support for AIDS denialism. Mbeki first accessed denialist positions on the Internet.

Mbeki's Shakespearian quote, 'I conjure you...', is met with Mother Anderson's 'Tell him to speak English'. Thus the cartoonists' comment, not only on Shakespeare's incomprehensibility, but on Mbeki's leadership style, from his hifalutin' speeches to his sometimes incomprehensible take on key issues like HIV or Zimbabwe. In order to fully appreciate the humour, a reader has to be familiar with Mbeki's reputation as depicted by Malan. Crucially, the reader does not have to be familiar with *Macbeth*, only with the most famous elements of the play in common circulation. *Macbeth* is the play most likely to be recognized by post-apartheid South Africans, since it is the most popular set work, not least because it is short and, according to teachers who have to present it to schoolchildren, full of action (not wordiness).[44]

---

40 Vukani Mde, 'Mbeki Struts and Frets His Hour Upon the Stage', *Business Day* (22 February 2006), www.businessday.co.za/articles/specialreports.aspx?ID=BD4A150829.

41 See Ngugi, *Decolonizing the Mind*.

42 Mde, 'Mbeki Struts'.

43 'Madam & Eve', by Stephen Francis and Rico, *Mail and Guardian* (30 November – 6 December 2007), p. 33. Permission to use the cartoon is gratefully acknowledged.

44 Distiller, *South Africa*, p. 231.

47. 'Madam & Eve', by Stephen Francis and Rico, *Mail and Guardian* (30 November–6 December 2007), p. 33.

This cartoon generates some of its humour by playing on Mbeki's characteristic love of Shakespeare, and using *Macbeth* to comment on a struggle for power that dominated the nation's public discourse for weeks, cleverly linking the play's concerns with legitimate leadership, political and personal betrayal, and murderous political machinations to similar issues in the ANC presidential succession saga (sans the literal murder, but very much in keeping with the tone of the events). But it also generates humour at a much more private cost to Mbeki, a man whose public persona is steeped in his performance of familiarity with the civilization Shakespeare represents, as we have seen. One of the cartoon's subtexts is the president's murderous stance on HIV; it ends, after all, with Mother Anderson's nightmare culminating in a vision of the health minister responsible for implementing Mbeki's denialism and perpetuating a refusal to embrace Western science. Mbeki is accused of practising precisely the kind of superstitious, 'heathen' behaviour commonly associated with stereotypes of the tribal African. It is instructive, then, to note that of all Shakespeare's plays, *Macbeth* is the one now most commonly proclaimed to have 'relevance' to Africans because of its tribal Scottish context and because, precisely, of the witches[45] (in colonial times the play most 'relevant' to the African elite was *Julius Caesar*). The *Madam & Eve* cartoon thus at once draws on Mbeki's erudition, and disciplines him for it, in the face of his behaviour around HIV, in which he assumes an anti-Western binary positioning when it suits his emotional and/or policy needs even as his deployment of Shakespeare is read as an acknowledgement of a respect for Western cultural norms.

What this analysis demonstrates once again is the prevalence of old binaries which by now should have no place in the new South Africa, one of which is Europe/Africa, which corresponds to associations with science/traditional medicine.

Mbeki's quoting of Shakespeare is revealed to be a veneer, beneath which his 'true' African self is revealed in his irresponsible, anti-democratic behaviour, his high-handed, ignorant and deadly approach to the HIV crisis.

Thus, despite actual literatures which provide content to a truly Africanized Shakespeare and which bespeak a syncretic South African identification process which is a more accurate reflection of how we are made than our history's various attempts to cordon off cultures from each other,[46] the associations with public deployments of a close encounter with the Shakespeare text suggest that Shakespeare does not have substantially more than display value in the current South African public arena. What is on display when Shakespeare is displayed is an affiliation with a positioning of privilege and concomitant socio-economic power, but no meaningful content, if not actively negative content. Thus Shakespeare is by now first and foremost the indicator of where cultural and economic power lie, which, because of ongoing relations of power that have not altered with the advent of democracy, tend to be constructed in a binary relation to a putative Africanness. Because of 'his' public image, Shakespeare easily becomes the ultimate tinsel in the window dressing, a more important literary, political and psychological history in the region notwithstanding. Is there room for a close encounter with Shakespeare in post-apartheid South Africa which can be represented in any but the most personal terms? Has Shakespeare grown not just old but white, here? Is he the fluff on the coconut?

---

[45] See Natasha Distiller, '"The Zulu Macbeth": The Value of an "African Shakespeare"', *Shakespeare Survey 57* (Cambridge, 2004), pp. 159–68; p. 162.

[46] See Sarah Nuttall and Cheryl-Ann Michael, eds., *Senses of Culture: South African Culture Studies*, (Oxford and New York, 2000); Distiller, *South Africa*; and Mangcu, *To The Brink*, p. 9.

THE SCHRÖDINGER EFFECT: READING AND MISREADING PERFORMANCE

ANDREW JAMES HARTLEY

The fixture of her eye has motion in't,
As we are mock'd with art.

(*The Winter's Tale*, 5.3.67–8)

It is, perhaps, to be expected that professional academic Shakespearians often make for cynical and jaded theatre audiences. They have, after all, seen it all before, if only in their heads. But alongside the bored response to what is familiar there is often something closer to indignation, a frustrated outrage – oft overheard in the intermission bar – about the extent to which the production is 'wrong'. Recent RSC offerings are a case in point. I thoroughly enjoyed the 2008 *Hamlet* (dir. Doran) and loathed the *Shrew* in the same season (dir. Morrison), but found some of my academic colleagues defended their likes and dislikes about the shows – in admittedly informal and spontaneous conversation – solely in terms of how they read the plays as text. Some objected to portions cut from the *Hamlet* script, others to the invasive nature of theatrical visuals (why isn't Hamlet wearing *shoes*?). I hated the *Shrew* production, it was alleged, because I misrecognized the play's unrelenting misogyny. Yes, this production was less romantic, less fun, than many others, but it got the play *right*. Now, I would argue that I hated that production not because of its conceptual approach, but because I found it tedious and unfunny despite the fact that it was trying hard – excruciatingly hard, in fact – to be the opposite. What I faulted the production for was a crassness of approach (as was the case with Morrison's *Macbeth* the previous year) coupled with woeful execution, and while I might be persuaded that this is in some way *interesting* I can't be persuaded that such failings are eradicated by the production's derivation from a particular reading of the play. Theatre has to be assessed as theatre, not as textual criticism or commentary, and while this in no way reduces critical response to an assessment of performative competence it does have implications for the kinds of intellectual exchange which are fittingly rooted in performance.

In what follows I would like to explore that critical response through the consideration of three elements of the scholarly approach to being an audience. First, I will explore the way that theatre demands the jettisoning of the very knowledge about a play we have worked so hard to achieve, via a metaphor from quantum mechanics. Second, I will reflect upon the literary academic's difficulties with the visual dimension of theatre and what I am calling 'necessary interpolation'. Finally, I will consider the way that we try to apply close-reading techniques to theatrical production in order – sometimes problematically – to render the medium more susceptible to the literary and argumentative skills upon which we rely in our consideration of other kinds of text.

I. THE QUANTUM MECHANICS OF THE SCHOLAR IN THE THEATRE

At the end of Act 3 scene 2 of *The Winter's Tale*, Hermione, beleaguered queen of Sicilia, dies – or 'dies' – off stage, and whether or not you choose to use the quotation marks says a lot about the way you think about the dramatic text and the story. One reading of the text says that Paulina has kept Hermione alive through the past sixteen years and that news of her death was greatly exaggerated. Paulina has visited the removed house which now houses the statue 'privately twice or thrice a day, ever since the death of Hermione' (5.2.104–5), and Hermione later confesses that she has preserved herself to see her 'issue' – Perdita – alive again (5.3.127–8).

An alternate reading takes Hermione's death as real, making her revival at the end a supernatural act. This latter reading refuses to pick up the hints from the second gentleman (perhaps taking them as evidence of magical practice), the demi-jokes about the remarkable realism of the statue in the final scene, and reads Hermione's remark about preserving herself in metaphysical terms. In other words, all of the textual evidence for her survival throughout the play can be read slightly obliquely as marks of wonder rather than cynicism. This reading also utilizes the convention that Shakespeare almost never misleads his audience/readership, so that we should take the announcement of Hermione's death at face value. Nothing in the first three quarters of the play subverts that idea and Antigonus's dream-vision of Hermione's ghost seems to reinforce it (3.3.38–45). The statue scene itself is particularly open to a magical reading; Hermione behaves like a statue for some 80 lines and – if we assume the 'awakening' begins at Paulina's 'music awake her, strike' – it takes her some six or seven lines to come fully to life. Even without extensive pauses, the transition seems to take time and is not simply a shrugging off of the statue ruse. The setting, Paulina's careful orchestration of the situation, her incorporation of music and reference to arts which some may consider unholy, all suggest a ritualized event with supernatural underpinnings drawing on elements of the play elsewhere which go beyond the real.[1] But such textual evidence requires an imaginative reader who can supply the atmosphere of the moment and ignore the evidence of a simpler and more rational version of events. In any case, the reader can choose or can opt to keep both contradictory possibilities in mind at once.

Students often want to know which it is: did she die, only to be magically revived, or has she been hiding out for over a decade and a half? Most of us have our preferences for how we like to think about the issue and both readings have their attendant problems which are too familiar to be rehearsed here. Importantly, of course, many of us read the play allowing for both possibilities, and we may not commit to one or the other at all, experiencing the play in the synchronic manner of someone who knows its whole even as one reads a particular line, finding meaning in the very contradiction.[2] That synchronic awareness allows all possibilities to coexist in the infinite hypothetical which is imaginative reading.

When the play is experienced in the diachronic manner of broadly naturalistic theatre, however, the issue becomes one of evidence to which the audience is exposed in a moment by moment

---

[1] The Delphos oracle's prophetic knowledge is the clearest element of a supernatural dimension though there are numerous plot elements including the bear and the falcon which led Florizel to Perdita that might be considered providential.

[2] James Siemon argues persuasively that the dramatic power of the statue scene trumps the minor expository details underscoring a more realist reading, but insists that the apparent contradictions between the two are fruitful and consistent with a patterning of ambiguity and ambivalence throughout the play. He reads the moment symbolically, seeing Hermione representing a mythic rebirth, the apparent contradictions 'give the fullest dramatic value to the possibilities for loss and for gain which the action of the play provides'. ' "But It Appears She Lives": Iteration in *The Winter's Tale*', *PMLA*, 89 (1974), pp. 10–16; p. 15. John Joughin makes a different but related case in arguing that the affirmation of one possibility wholly at the exclusion of the other produces 'an over-reductive schematic and distortedly unified account of particular events': 'Art, Truth, and Judgement in *The Winter's Tale*', in Hugh Grady, ed., *Shakespeare and Modernity* (London, 2000), p. 69. While this insistence may lend itself better to a readerly response to the play I take his point that the restored Hermione is pointedly not as she once was, representing a persistent past which cannot simply be sloughed off. Again, in theatrical terms the issue is not about which choice the production makes or if it opts to keep both readings in play, but about the power of the production to itself insist on its own semantic logic.

sequence, beginning with the announcement of the queen's death off-stage. Where it goes from there depends upon choices made or effects produced by the production, either tipping a wink to the audience (perhaps through stage action or one of those loathsome programme plot summaries) in ways perhaps playing for comedy or for a darker, more deliberately vengeful Hermione, or it may go so far (as in a recent Washington, DC production) to make Hermione's being stone no more a kind of magical – and traumatic – rebirth. A production might leave the issue ambiguously unresolved or it might make a single choice (though the audience may not all recognize that choice), and in a production which permitted a deviation from conventional realist narrative it may actively float both possibilities. The point is that until the truth is definitively revealed (the way the statue-Hermione comes down, for instance), no member of the audience can say for sure whether Hermione is alive or dead at the top of *this* production's statue scene, regardless of how well they know the play.

When a production makes a definitive choice, it closes off all other alternatives in ways which are not true of reading, teaching or thinking about the play as an abstraction in the mind which is (in Harry Berger Jr.'s terms) a kind of imaginary audition. Theatre makes effects which cause that hypothetical to be limited, and while it can leave some things open-ended, it must also commit: each line (generally) will be delivered only one way, by an actor whose stance, demeanour, costume, etc. all close off other options. The rehearsal process is a closing down of possibilities, a reduction of the infinite to a single choice or moment, each one followed by another experienced by the audience diachronically, and further reducing the infinite to the unique.[3]

In Schrödinger's infamous 'thought experiment', a cat sits in a box with a poisonous agent whose release depends upon the 50 per cent possibility that a radioactive isotope will decay, thereby killing the cat. According to quantum mechanics, a subatomic particle can exist in a combination of possible states and, according to the Copenhagen Interpretation, this combinatory variable only settles into a definite state upon observation. This is known as 'collapse' or 'measurement'. Schrödinger's hypothetical experiment challenged such a position by using what he saw as the palpable absurdity of what happens when the Copenhagen interpretation is applied to systems large enough to be seen with the naked eye, and not just to atomic or subatomic systems. What the critique amounts to is the idea that the cat in the box must exist simultaneously in both live and dead states until the box is opened and its future (or lack of one) is determined.[4] Each subatomic chance event determines a new universe: in one the cat lives, and goes on to have a causal relationship with the world around it; in another it dies and can affect its world only through absence. Until the moment of observation, there is only possibility (multiple cats in multiple states). Those hypotheticals crystallize into unalterable reality when observed.

Quantum mechanics aside, this is a pretty good way of thinking about theatre, where choices which come into being in the performance exist in an infinite number of hypothetical states until that moment of observation by the audience. This is not true on the page because of the way truth remains both indeterminate (Hermione can be alive and dead in my mind because there is nothing physical to confirm either) and shaped by the reader (I *want* her to be alive, so she is). The reading mind permits what Schrödinger calls a quantum superposition, our Hermione-cat existing simultaneously in both dead and alive states because the reader is a part of the thought experiment and there is no external observer. On stage, by contrast, where there are external observers (the audience), Hermione is

---

[3] It is undeniable that even a single choice can have multiple effects as far as the audience is concerned, but this does not alter the fact that the production's decision prohibits other options, if only for that single performance and regardless of how it is read by a disparate audience. An actor can opt to say a given line standing or sitting, but not both.

[4] Erwin Schrödinger, 'Die gegenwärtige Situation in der Quantenmechanik', *Naturwissenschaften* (November 1935). A translation by John D. Trimmer titled 'The Present Situation in Quantum Mechanics' is in J. A. Wheeler and W. H. Zurek, eds., *Quantum Theory and Measurement* (New Jersey, 1983).

what she appears to be at the moment it – whatever it is – happens, and not before. If it hasn't already been made clear, the form of her past is revealed by the way she comes down from being the statue, and no other information, belief or prior sense of the text is relevant. Only in the observed action does the universe coalesce into firm reality and meaning.

I am using Hermione as a conveniently Schrödinger-esque instance, but the idea might equally be applied to every single choice a performer or production makes, each theatrical *moment*, down to the delivery of each word, the stance, the gesture, the tone, etc. In the theatre, nothing is till it happens, and when it happens all other possibilities are banished to a parallel dimension – the production this one might have been but isn't. Theatre is thus creative in an absolute sense because it makes the story in the enacting of it, each choice mapping a path that negates all others and traces a unique and wholly novel identity. In the infinite range of hypothetical *Winter's Tales*, this one is born distinct and fresh in the air of the observed performative moment.

That moment may be found anywhere in a production. It may inhere in a particular textual crux which invites choices, such as Lear's 'Look on her, look, her lips. / Look there, look there' (5.3.286–7) where the actor's decisions have significant implications for the production as a whole. If he is focused on her lips, is he seeing what he thinks is movement, breath, life? If so is this a joyous moment that redeems the sorrows he has felt, or does it mean he dies deluded or – worse – wilfully blind to reality? Or perhaps the line is delivered in the grief or shock of *not* seeing movement/life; is that a moment of realization for the king alone, or is he instructing those around him (*Look: this is what all the fighting has led to* or *Look at the arbitrary and grinding nature of the universe*)? In 1993 Robert Stephens gave the last phrases of the line ('Look there, look there') while looking off-stage into a light the audience could see: his redemption. There are, of course, countless other valid choices which inform the semantic weight of the moment, none of which inhere in the words on the page.

Lear's death is a moment of particular resonance, but my point here is that it enacts the Schrödinger's cat logic of *all* theatrical moments which come into existence in front of the audience and which cannot be anticipated or disputed based solely on prior assumptions and textual knowledge. They are the nature of theatre, the effects of which cannot be built, as is sometimes argued, from a textual 'blueprint'.[5] An audience member who thinks that this Beatrice is too tall when she enters,[6] that this Hamlet is too sour, or the lighting too dark on this *Dream*'s too abstract set, is not experiencing the theatrical moment as a new phenomenon in the present, but archiving it before it has come fully into being, comparing it to other productions, weighing the extent to which it fulfils expectations derived from alien elements such as the way that audience member teaches the play. I recognize that critical contextualizing of this kind is unavoidable, that all audiences bring prejudices and assumptions about the play into the theatre, but that does not justify using such critical context as the basis of judgement about what a production 'gets right'.[7]

---

5 Though subtle and thoughtful in its analysis, June Schlueter and James P. Lusardi's *Reading Shakespeare in Performance* (Madison, Teaneck, 1991) rests, they say, on this assumption (p. 17).

6 Few elements of a production are as potent as casting and indicate the Schrödinger's cat effect more dramatically: an infinite hypothetical reduced to the single choice observed by the audience, a choice which coalesces into the basic reality of the show, obliterating all alternatives, many of which paraded through the audition room.

7 A deeply problematic phrase tossed around all too often by critics of all stripes which affirms only the authority of their assumptions as indefensibly as its theatrical equivalent invoked when something on stage does or doesn't 'work'. In *Reading Shakespeare on Stage* (Newark, NJ, 1995) Herbert R. Coursen has many intelligent and resonant things to say about reading Shakespeare on stage but there are times when he allows a prior sense of the play derived from what he believes the text does to determine his responses to moments in productions or to the entirety of the productions themselves. He condemns, for instance, the opening of an *Antony and Cleopatra* production which he otherwise thought very strong, because Philo and Demetrius entered and closed the door before beginning the opening speech. This was 'weak stagecraft' because it 'robbed us of a coming in in the middle of a conversation' as prescribed by 'Shakespeare's adaptation of the *in media res*

I keep using the word 'choices' to describe what a production does but the truth is that much of what we might consider 'choice' on stage is really a good deal less conscious, less deliberate and more the consequence of previous 'choices' which were themselves as much about evolution – even evolutionary accident – as deliberation. Part of the problem with the term 'choice' in describing what actors do, of course, is that it plays along with that old fiction that motivation is all, that meaning is created only by conscious decision by performers who control the audience's interpretive range. The quantum mechanical reading which I am calling the Schrödinger effect is useful because it throws its emphasis instead onto the audience (the observers) making a discovery, and by 'making' I mean both *finding* it and *producing* it. Actors and directors may *intend*, but this like other intentions (authorial and critical) is subject to the peculiar physics of the performative moment. As critics have to shelve their prior assumptions (Hermione is or is not dead before the statue scene), so practitioners have to abandon the illusion that what they mean to do determines what is seen to happen.

I have seen Leontes's jealous monologue ('Inch thick, knee deep . . . ') played by an actor who wanted to exploit the insidious communion with the audience ('now, while I speak this') by coming downstage and using direct audience address. He tried to project the character's neuroses into the house, finding 'comfort' in the notion that most of the other men in the theatre were in similar predicaments, even if they had not drunk and seen the spider. For some of those in the audience, the moment 'worked' perfectly, but others thought it meant he wasn't that upset by his wife's supposed infidelity. Some went so far as to assume that the jealousy was a trumped-up Vice-like excuse for assassinating Polixenes for political reasons they assumed they had missed. Some, reading the moment less in terms of character than in an apparent failure of acting, found the assumed intimacy jarring, a breaking of the fourth wall which disrupted their engagement with the story. Whatever we think of such a response, the actor's choice was overwritten by the audience response, clarifying the last element of my quantum mechanical analogy: different observers find different things in the same evidence. The person sitting next to you in the house may swear blind the cat was dead when you clearly saw it get up and walk around. You could ask the actor playing the cat but, in the end, you both know what you saw.[8]

Plenty of scholars would be quick to admit that they know little about how theatre is made. Few would admit that they don't know how to watch it. Some of this problem comes from seeing themselves as 'expert witnesses' in the trial of the production, people whose knowledge of Shakespeare makes them particularly good arbiters of the production's achievements. The problem is that they often aren't. Shakespearians can make lousy audience members, not simply because they are invariably jaded and sceptical, but because they are not representative of the target audience: the general public.[9] How many times have we heard otherwise smart academics railing at a production which did not enact their reading of a play, a scene, a character,

---

tradition' (p. 72). In attacking David Hare's *King Lear*, he says that only those moments played naturalistically as being about relationships 'worked' and that the stagey distance elsewhere amounted to 'a radical misreading of Shakespeare' (p. 76). I can't speak to the quality of the *Lear* production, but the attack is clearly about a disagreement concerning the subject matter of the play and the performative style: Coursen reads the play as being essentially about relationships and assumes it must therefore be played in a particular way. This, like the dismissal of the decision to begin *Antony and Cleopatra* with a pointedly private discussion, seems to me overly restrictive as a model for performative creation.

8 Some of these anxieties about controlling the way audiences read performances hinge, as W. B. Worthen has made clear, on issues of authority, though he is less interested in how an awareness of the problem might inform what practitioners actually set out to do.

9 Of course, many Shakespeare productions are not truly aimed at the general public, but I am speaking here particularly of regional productions who do not see themselves performing for Stanley Wells, Michael Billington and the RSC archive.

a moment?[10] Scholars have to learn to leave their preconceptions – even those they have worked hard to build through years of research and teaching – at the theatre door. This does not mean they have to suspend judgment, just that their judgement has to be grounded in something integral to *this* production's making of the play.

2. NECESSARY INTERPOLATION

All elements of the production enact a version of the Schrödinger effect, not simply those hinging on possibilities or cruces of which the text is aware, and this seems a particular source of anxiety for literary critics. By virtue of its genre, performance introduces signifying elements which interweave with the text without being determined by it. A glance, for instance, is rarely scripted. Neither is an actor's intonation or dialect, their style of movement or their deportment. The text rarely specifies aspects of a character's appearance as it is manifested on stage, but while some of these may be comparatively neutral – a particular hair or eye colour, say – others – her race, form of sexual appeal or manifest physical disability – are inevitably loaded with significance. Some are so intangible that we can term them only in the most ephemeral terms: 'stage presence' for instance or 'energy' (in the sense of aura or vibe). All of these come into being before our eyes regardless of our expectations and in ways closing off universes of alternate realities.

We go, it is sometimes said, to hear a play, rather than to watch it, and while this seems to hold on to an early modern notion of performance (with the largely bare stage untouched by designers) it denies the truth of theatre as a material entity with a visual dimension. The technologies of production and the emphases of our culture have shifted focus ever more towards the visual so that a set designer like Karl Eigsti[11] has been known to remark that if the set does not change every twenty minutes – even if it's just by someone throwing a jacket over the back of a couch – the audience's eye goes to sleep. There may be good reason to dismiss such stuff as clutter, but the impulse to do so among Shakespearians

often speaks to the notion that all elements of the visual not clearly demanded by the text are distractions from the words (*why isn't Hamlet wearing shoes?*). The shorthand for this is 'interpolation,' an intrinsically pejorative term which suggests (however tolerantly) that something has been added in ways rendering the resulting production impure. Often, of course, it means words, lines actually uttered on stage which have been imported from another play, fashioned by the director or some previous actor-manager, but it can also mean wordless scenes (like Henry Irving's Shylock returning to his empty house after dinner with Bassanio). At its broadest, interpolation is anything which shows the hand of the company somehow aggressively thrusting itself into the play.

But the idea that something can be inserted (usually problematically) between the page and the stage, is – needless to say – a binary which doesn't adequately map the process by which a dramatic text becomes a stage play. As readers we only notice costume details in Shakespeare's plays when they are particularly striking (like Hamlet's inky cloak and customary suit of solemn black) but we forget that costumes of some kind are always tacitly implied and must be chosen, usually out of nothing but the text's intimations of class, occupation and character, themselves subject to the larger conceptual frame of the production. The text may require a cup from which Gertrude must drink, for instance, but the nature of that cup, its aesthetic dimension, the way it attracts or deflects focus, its iconic associations (a golden chalice, crystal wine glass or Styrofoam disposable?) might only be inferred from the play script itself in the most indirect, provisional and subjective ways. In real terms, it isn't there, and the other cups which (matching or not) may populate that final scene

---

10 Such arguments are ultimately ghosted by an assumption – one we all know to be false – that the production is supposed to be a definitive embodiment of the play.

11 Karl Eigsti is a Broadway designer who has worked with Michael Kahn, Ed Sherrin, Robert Kalfin, Julianne Boyd, Tom Moore and others. A portfolio of his work is available at: www.karleigsti.com/clients/eigstik/nav/splash.shtml

are even less there in the text since their function is less explicit. Still less there are the other elements of the scene that have no reference point in the text: the candelabras, chairs and other furnishings which are invisible on the page but which necessarily affect the shape of the scene (particularly a scene involving stage combat) and its impression on the audience. At some level, therefore, all that is not scripted is interpolation, but to tag such theatrical effects with that pejorative is to misrecognize the medium as a mere transmitter for the text. Gertrude's undescribed costume and the cup from which she drinks her death are 'necessary interpolations', decisions made by the company for which there are no textual clues.

A further problem for largely literary academics is in the difficulty of translating the visual into meaning. Unlike music or art criticism, literary analysis uses the same medium as the art object under discussion, an affinity which facilitates an especially rich intercourse between the two. In the theatre, however, the verbal is surrounded – overshadowed, even sometimes occluded – by other semiotic apparatuses and phenomena such as sound, set, lighting and costume, all of which tend to float away from our usual critical vocabulary. We know how to parse Hamlet's major soliloquies but we are less fluent at naming the colour of the light which falls upon him as he performs them or the textures of his clothes. More to the point, we don't know what such things *mean* in the usual sense. We can approximate their *feel* – a nebulous term which feels itself at odds with the tough business of rigorous argument – and we can tell that they are a part of how that theatrical moment made meaning, but we are often at a loss to nail down what the meaning of those clothes or that light is. We turn into critical novices, looking for crude symbolism (red means blood, right? white is pure, maybe something vaguely Christian?) and, when we can't make it work, dismissing it all as irrelevant and annoying: another interpolation foisted upon us by the design-happy director and her team.

We know that colour need not be read this way, of course, that it may have thematic weight, may even be symbolic, but is as likely to be part of

another concern entirely, being a component of concerns as diverse as stage pictures, focal emphasis or character-driven realism. The problem is that when we watch Shakespeare – as opposed to when we watch theatre (or film or television) in which we have no textual investment – we start rooting around for meaning of an expressly verbal type. Designers don't generally think in those terms even when their inspiration *is* textual. They may find key elements of the set in image patterns appearing in the play, but their transmogrification into a visual form resonates in quite different terms, terms which the general audience member is intended to grasp subconsciously or viscerally. So Yukio Horio's set for Ninagawa's 1998 *Romeo and Juliet* substituted Italian streets for a series of grid-like frames creating three black corridors.[12] As well as suggesting differences in the Capulet and Montague cultures, these lines 'enabled us to focus on the speed of the young people', so that the speed of Romeo's simian ascent to Juliet's balcony emphasized the opposite of vertigo: a dramatic and theatrical self-confidence.[13]

Lighting designers, for instance, often seek prompts in the script, but such details – when Lorenzo and Jessica discuss the moonlight in the final act of *The Merchant of Venice*, for instance – supply a context for designers which is open to interpretation in terms of both how it should feel and how that feeling should be executed. For designer Linda Essig[14] the verse itself suggests that the moonlight in the scene should be approached 'in an infinite number of ways, the language freeing the designer to stray from the reality of moonlight (a cool, high-contrast, dimness) to express the poeticism of the language through color, angle

---

[12] Yukio Horio was the production designer for Takashi Miike's 2005, kabuki-inspired *Demon Pond*, and has worked with directors such as Kazuya Yamada, Paul Miller, Nishizawa and Ninagawa.

[13] Tony Davis, *Stage Design* (Crans-Près-Céligny, Switzerland: Rotovision, 2001), p. 118.

[14] Linda Essig has designed lighting for theatres throughout the US and is the author of *Lighting and the Design Idea* (2005) and *The Speed of Light: Dialogues on Lighting Design and Technological Change* (2002).

and texture'.[15] Elsewhere she makes it clear that such interpretive choices are also made according to issues of location, period, mood and character, as well as practical concerns such as actor visibility, and the way coloured light plays on certain costume fabrics or painted surfaces. Such concerns take us well outside of the text. Essig's remarks on a non-literal approach to a Shakespearian moon tellingly echoes lines by the seminal theatre writer Robert Edmond Jones whose discussion of designing a set on which Juliet can denounce swearing on the inconstant moon concludes: 'it is not the knowledge of the atmospheric conditions prevailing in Northern Italy which counts, but the response to the lyric, soaring quality of Shakespeare's verse'.[16] For Jones, a set is not a picture whose construction is something akin to interior decorating, but 'something conveyed, . . . a feeling, an evocation'.

It is a presence, a mood, a warm wind fanning the drama to flame. It echoes, it enhances, it animates. It is an expectancy, a foreboding, a tension. It says nothing, but it gives everything.[17]

The fecund metaphor of such a description, so alien to the language of contemporary literary discourse, reminds us of the artistry which is the aim of design work and which is so difficult to translate into the linear terms of critical semantics. When Ming Cho Lee[18] says that he prefers to 'let the design emerge from the life of the play'[19] or when Ralph Koltai[20] says that 'the play isn't about a door, it is about someone coming on stage'[21] they are thinking of the 'play' as something at least en route to becoming a production with a clear visual dimension which supports the human action on stage but which cannot be inferred from the script alone. Peter Hall says that he finds the origin of a production's design in any number of production elements which are only part of the play text in the most indirect and subjective terms:

Sometimes it is an object; sometimes it is a texture or a colour. Often it is a material. The whole of our RSC Wars of the Roses cycle in the Sixties revolved around steel – its texture and brightness and capacity to rust. This came from looking at the swords and weapons in War-

wick Castle's armoury. Steel gave us a dangerous metal world – a place of power politics and sudden coups – and a metal floor on which the tramp of Fascist feet sounded as the cycle proceeded to the tyranny of *Richard III*.[22]

Swords clearly have their place in these plays, but the expansion of the steel to form the fabric of the cycle's world is a constructive leap of a fundamentally different order from that of current literary criticism. While none of this is surprising, it should serve to remind us that designers are not playing to us, and that their response to the text is one mediated by aesthetic and other concerns which are neither single nor self-evident on the page, and are shaped by other interpretive choices involving the director, performers and the other designers. The result is an attempt to build a world in which a particular version of the play can live on stage for an audience which will respond emotionally, even viscerally, though the design element necessarily builds that version even as it responds to it.

I am emphasizing the visual by reference to what might be called 'tech or design heavy' productions, but the difference between these and more 'bare bones' or lab theatre productions is one of degree, not kind. While a black box show may rely more clearly on the bodies and voices of the actors, this does not reground the core of the production in the words of the play as is sometimes assumed, the visual continuing to shape audience experience through the semantic and aesthetic arrangement and interaction of those bodies. Even when

---

[15] Essig, *Lighting and the Design Idea*, p. 74.

[16] *The Dramatic Imagination* (New York, NY, 1941), p. 27.

[17] Jones, *Dramatic Imagination*, p. 26.

[18] Ming Cho is a Tony award winning Broadway designer whose productions of Shakespeare include a *Macbeth* at the Shakespeare Theatre, Washington, DC, in 1995.

[19] Davis, *Stage Design*, p. 38.

[20] Hungarian born designer Ralph Koltai may be the greatest innovator of current British theatrical design. In addition to work at the Royal National Theatre, he has worked on over 30 RSC productions and is an Associate Designer for the company.

[21] Davis, *Stage Design*, p. 26.

[22] John Goodwin, ed., *British Theatre Design: The Modern Age* (London, 1989), p. 13.

light, costume and set have minimal impact on the production, the staging remains dependent on basic theatrical contingencies such as the nature of the space, the arrangement of the stage, the kinds of interest created by levels (shaped either by structures or bodily stance), and the style of actor movement. Productions on bare stages without large-scale design elements necessarily foreground smaller visual components from actor coloration and body type to physical gesture and energy, all of which become semiotic elements in the production which are not determined by the play as text and are all, at some level, interpolations.

Part of the reason that Shakespearians are understandably unsettled by the visual, by the centrality of interpolation and the larger issue of the Schrödinger effect is that they imply a theatre which implicitly rejects the scholar's deep knowledge of the play's nature, range and meaning in textual terms, forcing them to treat the production as something new, external – even alien – to their prior experience and expertise as literary scholars.

3. READING PERFORMANCE

One of the ways that literary critics have responded to the unique properties of production has been to think of the production itself – the *whole* production (necessary interpolations and all) as a constructive rather than simply interpretive art object – as a species of text to be read. The close-reading methods derived from New Criticism and its more theoretically savvy successors can be applied to the examination of a performance on stage, the 'reader' substituting for the literary signifiers of text (diction, allusion, poetic structure and effects etc.) those of the stage (delivery, costume, light, gesture and so forth). In so doing, a performance is valorized – or so the argument goes – rendered worthy of serious discussion, documented for posterity and productively analysed.

Clearly there is much about this which is desirable. On the one hand, many of us – particularly those involved in the consideration of performance history – would love to have the kinds of accounts of performance which range far beyond

the reach of the average newspaper review and give us detailed readings of key moments, so that we know exactly how a particular Hamlet – say – delivered his opening line. In addition to simply nailing down the specifics which are usually lost in sweeping statements about actor competence and character orientation, such studies would open the door to the development of competing readings based on the same performed product, similar to the ways we build different readings of the same printed play. Such readings would generate whole new avenues of discourse, just as cultural studies has discovered that almost anything (films, paintings, ketchup bottles) can be read for significance. Better yet, good close-readings will make such discussion available to participants who didn't actually see the production but can now weigh in on what it meant . . .

And there's the rub, or part of it. The moment we open up discussion of a performance to people who haven't seen it, something is clearly *off*, and it indicates a problem with the logical paralleling of close-reading text and close-reading performance. When we close-read text, especially in the New Critical model, we study what is extant, self-contained and public, with the intention of generating something persuasive which will build on that distinctly public quality through transparency and rigour. The text is presumed to be available to both the critic and subsequent readers of that critic's work, and is generally visible in that work in the form of quotation. In other words, the close-reading textual critic is responsible only for analyzing what is extant, and his or her argument will collapse if it asserts things which are evidently incorrect, which demonstrate a tin ear for tone, for instance, which fail to identify a classical allusion, or which are otherwise premised on misreadings.

All of this is possible in the close-reading of film because the film, like the poem or play, exists outside the critical work devoted to it, but it is not true of performance on stage, and for two reasons. First, while it is comparatively easy to identify different extant versions of a play text or film, and respond to any notable differences from other versions in one's critical response, performance on stage is fundamentally protean, each performance within a production varying – sometimes subtly, sometimes drastically – according to the particular contingencies of theatre. People miss cues, light and sound effects don't work properly, doors stick, props malfunction. But it isn't simply about failure to deliver some quasi-ideal production which makes theatre unstable. Actors act differently from night to night, sometimes deliberately, sometimes in response to what other actors do or what the audience does (or doesn't do). Audiences don't have to be disruptive or counterintuitive in their responses ('failing' as audiences) to affect the particular energy of a performance, and this informs what happens on stage as the cast adjust to the mood of the house. A production of Goldoni's *The Servant of Two Masters* at Georgia Shakespeare recently, despite a professional cast and well-oiled stage crew, varied as much as ten minutes in running time from night to night simply because of the audience dynamic. The length of the show indicates substantial – if less easily measurable – difference from one show to the next and raises serious concerns about the 'text' of the show to be close-read. While I don't want to throw out the baby with the bathwater and claim that no meaningful continuity can be claimed between performances, it seems essential that the close-reading of a production must consciously address the single *performance* under consideration, or must compare multiple versions of the same moment in a run before it can begin to make any statement about the production as a whole.

The second problem with close-reading performance is less easy to navigate. I said above that fundamental to the close-reading of text is the continued existence and visibility of the text itself, so that the critic's reading can be held up against the words of the original 'text', usually bolstering its arguments through quotation which brings the primary text into the secondary reading. This is not possible in the case of theatre, which cannot be 'quoted' in an academic paper.[23]

In order to 'read' the performance in a way compelling for the critic's readers, the critic must first describe what happened on stage, thereby building what will then be analysed. Patricia Tatspaugh, for instance offers this wonderfully personal and specific reading of a moment from Michael Boyd's RST 2004 *Hamlet*:

Hicks's Ghost, the most terrifying I have ever seen, entered ever so slowly from the stalls onto the ramp, his long sword dragging behind him. His face and chest were chalk white; in one ear blood had congealed while from the other blood streamed down his bare chest. Hicks, dressed in a tattered skirt, bent his slender, muscular frame and contorted his mouth to resemble the expression in Edvard Munch's 'The Scream.' Holding the sword above his head, the Ghost commanded Hamlet to avenge his murder. (As the Player King, Hicks repeated the gesture when, imitating Pyrrhus, he raised an imaginary sword, which 'seem'd i' th' air to stick'.) Hicks's recollection of old Hamlet's murder was as chilling as his appearance. He stressed initial consonants and introduced details faster and louder until he reached the word 'revenge,' which he elongated. Gradually lowering the sword, he pointed it at the prince on 'Now wears his crown', dropped the weapon into a trap, enjoined Hamlet to 'Remember me', and fell headlong into the trap after it.[24]

This is a beautifully evocative passage with lots of specific detail and an admirable foregrounding of the author ('the most terrifying *I* have ever seen'). For a moment we can almost hear and see the ghost and feel the fear it inspires. What makes the

---

[23] It is true that in a multi media format such studies might insert video footage of the performance in question, but this is rare, partly because use of such video usually violates the Equity regulations of theatre companies which stipulates a different pay scale for actors who appear on screen (SAG rates or their equivalent). Such video may also violate the limited copyright terms of directors and designers whose work was intended only to be seen in the theatre. This is why most theatres which do have a video archive have strict regulations about where such video can be seen and how it can be used. As I argue below, moreover, video record, even if permissible, is not an adequate means of quoting stage performance, since it changes the genre of that performance, altering its visual and audio dimension, limiting the viewer's focus and otherwise not so much mediating the performance as transforming it.

[24] Patricia Tatspaugh 'Shakespeare Onstage in England, 2004–2005', *Shakespeare Quarterly*, 56 (2005), 450–1.

description successful as writing makes it something of a self-fulfilling prophesy as performance criticism, however, the trick of the effect being borne by the language which evokes the feeling. The prose is regular and resonant as it describes the ghost's slow entrance, the details undergirding the horrific effect: the chalk white face, congealed blood evoking the manner of his death, and that loaded reference to 'The Scream'. We get specifics of vocal articulation and emphasis, and a dramatic sense of conclusion as the spectre falls 'headlong' into the trap. It's a vivid, almost novelistic description, and is designed to convey the author's impression of the performance, though it is done so well that the reader has no room to question whether he or she would have focused on the same details, or whether others in the house found the ghost as scary as did the author.

My point is not that there is anything wrong with such evocative description – and there may be no real alternative – but that we need to be alert to the reader's response being at a certain remove from the original performative moment. Instead of having access to the primary text, as in conventional textual close-reading, the subsequent reader is dependent on the critic for a sense of what the text *was*, as well as what it *meant*. What happens, then, is that in the close-reading of performance, the text which is read is not actually the performance at all, but an intermediary text which is constructed by the critic in the essay for that purpose.

Apart from lending itself to a potentially disingenuous telling of what happened on stage in order to make one's reading more coherent or forceful, this *constructive* approach to the detailing of the intermediary text raises concerns about the reader's subjective engagement with what happened on stage. The core principle behind New Critical close-reading is that the critic can build an objective response through consideration of a text's component elements, a text which has ontological status. One's perspective, interest or background could – in principle (and in ways generally considered theoretically suspect these days) – be elided, replaced by a clear-sighted and rigorous considera-

tion of what was definitively *there*. Others may disagree, but their arguments would have to be equally objective and specific in their response, leading – again, in principle – to a quasi-scientific exactness in subsequent debate. Theatre, on the other hand, is a necessarily subjective business.

Lois Potter, another observant and shrewd reader of the theatre, responding to Gregory Doran's 2006 *Antony and Cleopatra* says:

In the heavily cut scene on Pompey's galley, Antony's attempt to explain how the Egyptian farmers work in harmony with the Nile was concurrent with, and finally totally swamped by, Lepidus's simultaneous questions about the pyramids and the crocodile. Antony finally gave up on his explanation with the same amused resignation that he had *obviously* learned through years with Cleopatra.[25]

And later in the same piece:

Enobarbus's famous barge speech seemed less like a monologue than usual, because his two listeners were so much part of it in their contrasting reactions: Agrippa, the ex-soldier, sat down on 'O, rare for Antony!' (2.2.205) and let himself be carried along by the story, while Maecenas, the prim civil servant, remained standing, *obviously* disturbed by its foreign policy implications.[26]

However right they feel, the 'obviouslys' elide both the author's subjective position and the extent to which event and response are being conflated so that the supposedly subsequent reading becomes compelling and, well, *obvious* to a point which makes it impossible to imagine reading the moment in another way. Again, this is not a critique of the writer (who does foreground her own subjective position expressly at other moments in the piece[27]) but a reminder of a particular pitfall of

---

25 Lois Potter 'Assisted Suicides: *Antony and Cleopatra* and *Coriolanus* in 2006–7', *Shakespeare Quarterly*, 58 (2007), p. 517 (my emphasis).

26 Potter, 'Assisted Suicides', p. 518 (my emphasis).

27 For instance: 'The fact that the scene got laughter and then won back the audience's sympathy was a source of wonder to many commentators. They differed as to the point at which Patrick Stewart laughed himself (I was told that it came after Diomedes' "Now, my lord" but on both the occasions when I saw him it was on "Too late, good Diomed" [4.4.118, 127]);

performance criticism: the impulse to totalize audience response.[28]

This pitfall is most evident when the article writer or reviewer uses specialist or personal knowledge to shape a sense of a staged moment. Speaking of Lindsay Posner's 2001 *Twelfth Night*, Russell Jackson remarks,

Olivia's household was represented permanently by the furnishing of the alcove on the right of the forestage: black furniture, including a piano, a grandfather clock, a small table, some austere chairs, and a row of ancestral photographs. There were also two telltale Beardsley drawings that slyly indicated her suppressed longings.[29]

Later, he adds:

Mark Hadfield's Fool had acquired an anthology of mannerisms and gags from several sources, including Harold Lloyd, Buster Keaton, and Little Tich – a famously agile and strikingly diminutive music-hall performer, whose yard-long shoes were alluded to but not quite imitated in Feste's oversized footwear.[30]

I don't dispute that the Beardsley drawing might indicate Olivia's suppressed longings or that Feste's footwear evoke Little Tich, but I am bound to ask: for whom? Both references draw on the particular echoes of cultural artifacts (and he assumes similar resonances for paintings by Klimt and Matisse in the same piece) which we can't assume the entire audience felt or knew. Jackson is not making that claim, of course, but the information shapes our sense of the production in ways which give it a specific shape based on his response which is, in turn, shaped by his frame of reference.

These moments frankly put those interpretive strategies and assumptions where the reader can see them, but reviewers and performance critics more commonly leave such assumptions unsaid: 'the sub-plot was equally hilarious and frightening,' for instance, or 'spectators headed for the intermission sympathizing with Viola's quandary'.[31] Ultimately, of course, the problem may be less about the writers of such criticism – who are, of necessity, constrained to write what they see in the way they see and interpret it – so much as it is with how we

read such accounts and recognize their inherently mediated quality.

One's sense of what happened on stage is shaped by perspective, which may be about where in the house you were sitting (to one side, close enough to be spat upon by the cast, peering through opera glasses from the gods) or it may be about where you happened to be looking at a given moment. Theatre does not control the gaze of the audience as film does, so what one was aware of cannot be considered a record of what everyone in the house was aware of. The descriptive 'text' of the production thus presented to be read by the critic in his study, is thus already a subjective response with special emphasis in which certain facts of the production have been ignored or devalued while others have been given weight. The 'text' to be read is thus already a reading, dependent on but different from the 'primary' text (the performance) and the criticism which follows is thus either tertiary (a reading of a reading of a text – a reader responding to a single audience member's response to a performance), or is an expansion of the secondary reading (the audience response) presented, inaccurately, as readings two and three collapsed into a response to the performance. In either case, what is lost to the critic's readers is a sense of the 'primary' text – the performance – in any unmediated way. If the performance itself is lost to subsequent readers, then what is the critic reading?

I suspect that it varied from one performance to another.' (p. 519)

28 It might be pointed out that Potter's very depth of experience separates her from other audience members. Her consideration of Enobarbus's speech is implicitly comparative ('less like a monologue than usual') and the reaction which then shapes her readers' response is itself shaped by material from outside the production. This is neither undesirable nor possible to avoid, but it does behove the reader to be aware that the depiction of the theatrical event is doubly mediated.

29 Russell Jackson, 'Shakespeare at Stratford-upon-Avon: The RSC's 2001–2002 Season', *Shakespeare Quarterly*, 53 (2002), 543.

30 Jackson, 'Shakespeare at Stratford-upon-Avon', p. 545.

31 Michael Shurgot, '*Twelfe Night, Or What You Will*, at the Seattle Repertory Theatre, September 13-October 20, 2007', *Shakespeare Bulletin*, 26 (2008), 178.

We might put this question another way: what is the close-reading of performance *for*? What is it supposed to achieve and – given its unavoidably subjective nature – who does it represent? The last question is the easiest to answer. Close-reading of performance represents the individual critic, and as such cannot claim any broader or more objective perspective. More challenging, however, is the question of purpose and achievement. For the sake of argument, let us assume that a given critic has extraordinary powers of observation and recall (I will later consider how such things might be simulated, to my mind, problematically), that she is able to recount in minute detail every element of Hamlet's 'nunnery' speech to Ophelia. She sets out to write an essay on the moment, acknowledging her subjective position as a single audience member and giving a detailed account of the performances she attended, perhaps even detailing nuanced differences between them. She then scrutinizes what she remembers and builds a brilliant reading of Hamlet's state of mind as inflected by the production's particular model of, say, patriarchy. This may be fascinating and insightful, but I find myself struggling to understand what exactly that reading speaks to. Because the issue of subjectivity does not simply alter what the critic perceived, it also dictates the value of the reading. If the production is lost to the subsequent reader of the critic's work, and cannot be revisited – except perhaps in memory if the reader also saw the production – then is not the *meaning* of the event as elucidated in the close-reading as subjectively defined as the perception of it? Is the close-reader not steadily further and further removed from the experience of anyone else in the theatre who experienced the production in the diachronic manner in which audiences generally do? And doesn't this render the reading a creative act which speaks less and less to the production itself?

Most audience members don't have anything like the perfect recall and comprehensive observational skills I mentioned above, and this further problematizes the situation as critics use other means to simulate them. We may have recourse to video archive, for instance, a technology which

nicely documents a production – or rather a single (usually) performance of a production – but which renders it as a quite different kind of event. And though the act of rewatching a single moment over and over again may allow us to write about it with a great sense of detail, it necessarily refashions the theatrical original as something quite different from what the audience experienced. An alternate strategy is to attend a production repeatedly, and some critics claim to do this ten, fifteen or twenty times in order to get a firm grasp on the production. But what is it that is being grasped here, when one behaves in so perverse a fashion, when one constructs a mode of watching so thoroughly alien to the rest of the audience?[32]

I am loath to suggest that the value of close-reading has to be tied to what a production may or not be *intended* to do, since that opens a different can of worms entirely, but it must surely be acknowledged that close-reading performance is – on some level – at odds with the experiential nature of theatre. This is a different objection from the one our students raise when they object to our 'over-reading' text, because text is there to be read. It persists, inviting speculation, connection, interrogation. Theatre, on the other hand, is ephemeral, and that ephemeral nature is a basic component of its semiotic method. To somehow freeze a performative moment in time in order to 'read it' is, I would argue, to deliberately and forcefully misread its essential nature. It changes what the 'text' being read is, and alters the mode of 'reading' itself, rendering a product which is generically at odds with what it purports to read. However brilliant the reading, the method used to produce it cannot be equated with audience response, since audiences do not – cannot – make their reaction to

---

[32] I have similar concerns about writing about productions from the inside, that is with privileged information derived from watching – or being somehow involved in – rehearsals. Considering how a production came into being and evolved can, of course, be of tremendous interest and value, but such knowledge is too often used to bolster a reading of the publically performed event in which the *intent* of the actors or director seems to overwrite what actually happened on stage and what audiences perceived.

a moment on stage conditional upon this kind of microscopic scrutiny. To suggest that this method produces more or better insights than those the original audience has is not simply to move the goalposts, it is to change the ball to a puck.

I am not arguing here for an end to the serious discussion of performed events, and I am delighted by performance work which embraces what I have referred to above as the Schrödinger effect and the production's necessary interpolation. What I am concerned about is the kind of close-reading which relies upon – for instance – video archive or repeat viewing, to create the (illusory) sense of a static text which can then be read in isolation, replaying the moment and sifting for meaning, like some barmy prospector panning for gold. If the meaning needs to be read in this way in order to be coherent, in what sense was it truly there for the people who experienced the production first hand? And if it wasn't apparent to the production's actual audience, what value is there in building that meaning for subsequent readers? Certainly there may be stimulating intellectual work to be done with such things, but let us not mistake them for readings of performances.

The appeal of close-reading in performance studies is partly the way it turns theatre back into text, stabilizing it, making it static and allowing us fundamentally (deep down in the very marrow of our bones, the sinews of our hearts and the neurons of our brains) *literary* critics to do what we know we're good at. At the same time (and according to the same deep-seated reptilian logic), close-reading respectabilizes what we have come to love – theatre – seeming to make it worthy of the kind of attention some of our colleagues are loath to grant to something so visceral and messy, tenuous and finite. But to treat performance as text's ugly step-child forces the construction of an aberration, something that was once alive but which has been cut up, flattened out and stitched together till it resembles a book. However understandable such an impulse may be, it must be resisted if we are to recognize the expressly theatrical meanings which theatre creates, regardless of how familiar we might be with the play itself. We must be prepared for our prior sense of a play to be trumped by what we experience in the theatre; we must learn to read that experience provisionally and in terms which suit the performative medium, and we must – like Leontes gazing upon the speechless statue of his 'dead' wife – awake our faith in production as more than the sum of its words.

BEHIND THE SCENES

ROBERT SHAUGHNESSY

The Royal Shakespeare Theatre is currently undergoing a radical transformation. Described in company publicity as 'one of the world's most iconic theatrical sites', the theatre closed in 2007 for refurbishment, to reopen in 2010 as, it is hoped, 'the best theatre for Shakespeare in the world'. The 1930s cinema-style auditorium reviled by generations of its users has been demolished, to be replaced by what is described by the Royal Shakespeare Company's Artistic Director Michael Boyd as 'a theatre which celebrates interaction . . . a bold, thrust-stage, one-room auditorium – a modern take on the theatres of Shakespeare's day'.[1] One of the distinctive elements of this latest attempt to reshape the conditions of Shakespearean performance is indicated by Boyd's description of the company's temporary replacement and prototype for the new theatre, the Courtyard, as 'a meeting place between audience and actors . . . where we can make some kind of fragile consensus together'.[2] Summoning an egalitarian and inclusive ethos long associated with thrust stages, as well as current discourses of conflict resolution, the remark suggests that getting physically closer to Shakespeare in Stratford confers benefits beyond the theatrical: the Courtyard stage, and its permanent successor, are envisaged as not only neo-Elizabethan performance spaces but also as forums for creative dialogue, collective problem-solving and democratic participation. This is not new, in that the open stage has been subject to such a quasi-political inflection throughout the entire history of theatrical modernism; what is relatively unusual about Boyd's concern for consensus-building is that it

emerges from a specific, and indeed acutely sensitive, local context. The extensive changes to the RST, carried out by leading architectural company Bennetts Associates, have been implemented subject to a degree of consultation that is unparalleled in the RSC's history. Having inherited from his predecessor, Adrian Noble, a reconstruction scheme (the flagship of the notorious Project Fleet) that was bitterly contested within the company and strongly opposed by Stratford townspeople, Boyd steered it towards general acceptability, in part by fostering the active involvement of local communities as stakeholders in the redevelopment process.[3] One such participatory initiative was the 'Theatre Memories' project, devised in partnership with four local schools, during which consultation about the redevelopment of the theatre was directly linked to the 'citizenship' component of the National Curriculum. Groups of pupils ranged in age between eight and fourteen were invited to collaborate in discussions about the proposed changes, acting as intermediaries between the RSC and the town by canvassing opinion on the streets

---

My thanks to Bridget Escolme, Darryll Grantley, Barbara Hodgdon, Peter Holland and Patrice Pavis for valuable behind-the-scenes help with this article.

[1] 'Transforming our Theatres', www.rsc.orguk/transformation, accessed 13 June 2008.
[2] David Ward, 'A Worthy Scaffold', *Guardian*, 21 June 2006.
[3] For an account of the controversies that surrounded Project Fleet, and of the philosophy of management that underpinned it, see Peter Holland, 'Shakespeare's Two Bodies', in Barbara Hodgdon and W. B. Worthen, eds., *A Companion to Shakespeare and Performance* (Oxford, 2005), pp. 36–56.

of Stratford, and visiting the Royal Shakespeare Theatre to inspect its facilities and to evaluate the advantages and disadvantages of the existing and projected configurations. Their findings overwhelmingly endorsed the RSC's plans, confirming the company's case that not only the stage but most of its surrounding infrastructure were in urgent need of modernization.[4] The consultative process involved taking the pupils on a backstage tour of the theatre and, although what the children made of this is nowhere documented, we can safely assume that their experience of the confinement and squalor of what the RSC's website frankly describes as the 'cramped' conditions behind the scenes reinforced their support for the reconstruction scheme. The website reinforces the point with a forlorn gallery of images illustrating the 'need for change' with shots of dressing rooms bleak as prison cells, and of narrow corridors choked with scenery and technical equipment. The reconstruction is envisaged not only as a matter of creating a safer and more conducive working environment for artists and stage crew; the reconfiguration and modernization of the spaces behind and around the stage extends and expands the work involved in the opening-up of the performance space itself. More than a refurbishment, it is a significant rethinking of what backstage space is and means, what and whom it is for, and to what uses it should be put. Demonstrably the product of a consensus, informed by the guiding principles of increased accessibility and community involvement, backstage at the new theatre will operate as part of a complex of public spaces and transit routes, to include a foyer linking the Swan and the RST, a public square, and a dedicated education studio. As Simon Erridge, director at Bennetts Associates, stated in an address to a Stratford-upon-Avon audience who had more interest than most in tracking the changes, the priority with regard to the rebuild of the theatre was 'how to make it more open to relate it to the site and to the town'.[5]

The visit by Stratford's school pupils was probably the first time in the history of theatre tourism that a group has been invited backstage in a theatre in order to connive at its demolition; and as such their tour provides a unique variation upon a practice that has in recent years become well established in the theatre industry. Prior to its closure last year, backstage tours of the RST had been offered for some years; currently tours are available at the Courtyard Theatre. In the United Kingdom, tours are run by numerous regional theatres, including, for example, the West Yorkshire Playhouse, the Birmingham Rep and the Theatre Royal, Brighton; in London, tours are or have been available at the Royal Court, the Royal Opera House, the London Palladium, Shakespeare's Globe and the National Theatre, amongst others. Generally, the tours attempt to strike a balance between information and entertainment, whilst often also contributing to their host organization's education and community outreach briefs. Their primary constituency is those who already have a fairly specialist taste for theatregoing, although some attempt to appeal to a broader tourist market. Up until the end of September 2008, the most notorious of these was offered by the Theatre Royal, Drury Lane, where one could pay £9 to take part in an hour-long event called *Through the Stage Door*, described as London's first 'Interactive Theatre Tour', in which three actors impersonated figures from the theatre's history, including Garrick, Grimaldi, Sheridan and Nell Gwynn, while taking participants on a journey from foyer to auditorium to subterranean prop storage area. Attempting to sugar the pill of theatre history with a sizeable dollop of showbiz mythology and saucy seaside-postcard-style innuendo, this tour inevitably emphasized those aspects of Drury Lane that might appeal to the star-struck and the prurient; as Gilli Bush-Bailey remarks, the story that the tour told of Nell Gwynn, 'like the theatre's underground tunnels, with all their Freudian

---

4 Gillian King, *Transforming Our Theatres: Citizen Project Report* (Royal Shakespeare Company, 2006); and, as director, *Theatre Memories* (Royal Shakespeare Company DVD, 2006).

5 Simon Erridge, 'A New Theatre for Shakespeare in Stratford: The Transformation of the RSC', address delivered to the 33rd International Shakespeare Conference at The Shakespeare Institute, University of Birmingham, 3–8 August 2008 (4 August).

associations, is a subterranean journey of sexually charged imagination'.[6]

The fairly crude tactics of eroticization employed here blatantly addressed backstage's historic appeal as a space of desire as well as of intrigue. As a subject of pictorial representation and as a romanticized fictional locale, backstage has been an area of interest for artists, playwrights, novelists and film-makers: the canon of work ranges from Hogarth's *Strolling Actresses in a Barn* (1738) to Richard Eyre's backstage movie *Stage Beauty* (2004).[7] Until recently, however, backstage has not been a subject for scholarly investigation; as Gay McAuley observes, what she terms 'practitioner space' is 'significantly the least documented, least analyzed, least theorized area of theatre space'.[8] Seen in a longer historical perspective, backstage areas have traditionally been fashioned by the theatre's hierarchies and divisions of labour, as well as by the exercise of managerial and proprietorial rights, while the management of the traffic between spectator and practitioner spaces is a key aspect both of the evolution of playhouse design and of the shifting social, cultural and sexual politics of the actor-audience relationship. The transgressive nature of backstage access (most obviously, to actresses' dressing rooms) has also been linked to its explicitly sexual character, as manifested, for example, both in the habits of male playgoers from the Restoration period through to the late nineteenth century and in repeated efforts to regulate, reform and ultimately curtail them. It was, it appears, precisely the arrival of women on the English stage in the 1660s that transformed backstage into a charged, spatially specific site of erotic interest: in pre-Interregnum theatre, playgoers' personal liaisons with the players seem to have taken the form of activities outside of and away from the playhouses (Jonson has Tucca in *Poetaster* invite the player Histrio to 'ha' good cheer tomorrow night at supper' (3.4.278–79)). The ease with which Restoration theatregoers could pass behind the scenes is documented by Samuel Pepys, who records an instance in 1667 when on a visit to the King's Playhouse he was invited 'up into the Tireing-rooms and to the women's Shift' to

observe Nell Gwynn dressing; after a pleasant idyll in the Scene Room, he eventually goes, almost as an afterthought, '[b]y and by into the pit and there saw the play; which is pretty good'.[9] This kind of behaviour (and worse) was the sort which, some three-quarters of century later, David Garrick's reforms at the Theatre Royal, Drury Lane, were determined to root out. His playbills announced that as 'the admittance of persons behind the scenes has occasioned a general complaint on account of the frequent interruptions to the performances, it is hoped gentlemen will not be offended that no money will be taken for the future'.[10] The evening of the opening performance in 1747 that famously began with Garrick and Samuel Johnson's prologue announcing the new contract between those 'that live to please' and the 'drama's patrons' ended with an epilogue, given with pointed irony to Margaret Woffington, which offered a mock lament for the new manager's curtailment of the audiences' backstage visiting rights, as a consequence of which 'Each Actress a lock'd up Nun must be / And priestly Managers must keep the Key.'

---

6 Gilli Bush-Bailey, *Treading the Bawds: Actresses and Playwrights on the Late-Stuart Stage* (Manchester, 2006), p. 5.

7 Notable Shakespeare-themed contributions to the cinematic genre include *To Be or Not to Be* (USA, 1942), *A Double Life* (USA, 1947), *Kiss Me Kate* (USA, 1953), *The Dresser* (UK, 1983), *In the Bleak Midwinter* (UK, 1996) and *Shakespeare in Love* (UK, 1998).

8 Gay McAuley, *Space in Performance: Making Meaning in the Theatre* (Ann Arbor, 2000), p. 26. Backstage space is also the subject of a brief discussion in Marvin Carlson, *Places of Performance: The Semiotics of Theatre Architecture* (Ithaca, NY, 1989); and Andrew Filmer offers an ethnography of performer behaviour offstage in 'Minding the Gap: The Performer in the Wings', *New Theatre Quarterly*, 24 (2008), 158–69. Case studies of backstage tours of non-theatrical settings, considered as a tourist activity, are offered by Nick Couldry, 'The View from Inside the "Simulacrum": Visitors' Tales from the Set of *Coronation Street*', *Leisure Studies*, 17 (1998), 94–107; and Sean Gammon and Victoria Fear, 'Stadia Tours and the Power of Backstage', *Journal of Sport Tourism*, 10 (2005), 243–52.

9 *The Diary of Samuel Pepys*, vol. 8, ed. Henry B. Wheatley (London, 1928), p. 127.

10 Reprinted in *The London Stage 1660–1800, Part 4: 1747–1776*, ed. George Winchester Stone, Jr. (Carbondale, IL, 1962), p. 7.

The comic register employed by the epilogue contains a mock-Shakespearian element: the prologue invokes Shakespearian authority in order to eradicate disorder onstage and to reverse the decline in dramatic manners and morals that began in the seventeenth century; the epilogue inverts and flouts that authority, concluding with a parodic reworking of Othello's 'Farewell the tranquil mind...' (3.3.350–62), bidding 'Farewel Coquettry, and all Green-room Joys / Ear-thrilling Whispers, *Deard's* deluding toys', and calling for its audience's aid, 'or else – our *Occupation's* gone'.[11] As a performer whose performance of sexuality was instrumental to both her onstage and celebrity personae, Woffington was the epitome of the culture of behind the scenes intrigue that both drew spectators to the playhouses and was a key component of its scandalous reputation; and her announcement of Garrick's reforms is an elaborate tease: playing upon the double entendre of a gentleman's rights of entry, the epilogue maps the eroticized anatomy of the theatre building onto the speaking body of one of its leading actresses (and one, moreover, renowned for her cross-dressing). This was titillating enough, but contemporary comment further suggests that behind the scenes was viewed as a space not just of heterosexual promiscuity and prostitution but also, because its boundaries were dangerously insecure, of sexual deviance and gender ambiguity. For the playhouse beau, access *backstage* was a continuation of his activities *onstage*; as Kristina Straub argues, his conspicuous exhibitionism (whether sitting on, moving around, or entering and exiting the performance space) unsettled the gendered distinctions between spectator and spectacle, but also rendered him, like the actors, a notoriously libidinous subject of the audience's, and the moralist's, gaze.[12] Thus James Ralph, reporting on the behaviour of theatre audiences in the 1720s, writes of 'the *Hermaphrodites* of the Theatre; being neither Auditors nor Actors perfectly, and imperfectly both', that is, 'those Gentlemen who pass their Evenings behind the Scenes, and who are so busy in neglecting the *Entertainment*, that they obstruct the view of the AUDIENCE': here, in Garrick's playbills, and elsewhere, the ready conflation of backstage

and onstage behaviour (tellingly figured in terms of indeterminate gender identity) suggests that, at least in some instances, behind the scenes is not necessarily the same thing as behind the scenery.[13] The capacity for inversion and reversal that is inherent in backstage space is also at play in a particularly salacious episode in the anonymously authored, scandal-mongering *Memoirs of the Celebrated Mrs Woffington* (1760), which recounts its eponymous heroine's adventures with a certain 'Mr L – ', who, we are told, '*knew* her behind the Scenes' while she was costumed in her signature breeches part of Sir Harry Wildair (thus enabling him to '*know* an Actress, when *acting the Man*'); given the author's predilection for innuendo, it is perhaps not too much of a stretch to read the combination of cross-dressing and backstage sex as code for sodomy.[14]

Nonetheless, even Garrick could not put a stop to the practice of audience interlopers cajoling or bribing their passage behind the scenes that easily, and backstage retained its place as what Tracy C. Davies calls a 'powerfully erogenous' zone within the metropolitan geography of sex throughout the eighteenth and nineteenth centuries (and perhaps beyond); and although, as Davies notes, 'most West End managers vehemently claimed to prohibit unauthorized access backstage, implying that despite popular belief to the contrary influential spectators could not approach actresses in their dressing rooms', in practice 'managers may have compliantly facilitated it'.[15] If the late Victorian

---

[11] 'Prologue Spoken by Mr. Garrick', and 'Epilogue Spoken by Mrs. Woffington', in *Prologue and Epilogue Spoken at the Theatre in Drury-Lane, 1747* (London, 1747), pp. 3–4.

[12] Kristina Straub, *Sexual Suspects: Eighteenth-Century Players and Sexual Ideology* (Princeton, NJ, 1992), pp. 7–8.

[13] James Ralph, *The Touch-stone: or, historical, critical, political, philosophical, and theological essays on the reigning diversions of the town* (London, 1728), p. 145.

[14] *Memoirs of the Celebrated Mrs Woffington* (London, 1760), p. 33. For a fuller account of the erotic dynamics of Woffington's stage and celebrity personae, see Nicola Shaughnessy and Robert Shaughnessy, eds., *Lives of Shakespearian Actors I: Volume 3: Margaret Woffington* (London, 2008).

[15] Tracy C. Davis, *Actresses as Working Women: Their Social Identity in Victorian Culture* (London, 1991), p. 150.

theatre's assiduous efforts to eradicate such goings-on by effecting a more decisive demarcation of the physical as well as social boundaries between audience and performer spaces were an index of reputability and seriousness, they were also entirely in keeping with the period's attempted transformation of backstage performer space into a realm of cloistered sequestration and individual preparation rather than of assignation, entertainment and casual socializing, and into a fit place for the kinds of representational work whose mechanisms of construction are carefully concealed. The post-Stanislavskian actor tends to be strongly protective of backstage, and often resistant to incursions from non-professionals; as Simon Callow puts it, this is the world of 'the romance of work, the juju of craft – and all secret. Our kingdom.'[16] For the performer intent on sustaining the 'unbroken line' of a characterization for the duration of a performance, backstage should offer a secure environment conducive to the maintenance of focus and concentration. Antony Sher seems to evoke this ideal when he indicates that the challenge of playing Shylock is that 'he is offstage for much of the performance and most of his emotional changes take place in the dressing room'.[17] As Jonathan Holmes has demonstrated, whether Shakespeare's text affords the resources to fashion such a continuous character trajectory is debatable;[18] moreover, backstage space is rarely as amenable to actors' physical and psychological needs as many would like, and although the battery-farm conditions of the dressing rooms at the RST represent an extreme case, performers' positioning within structures that since the late nineteenth century have necessarily prioritized the accommodation of machinery rather than bodies has largely been secondary and subordinate.

If the allure of theatre's backstage areas as sightseeing attractions resides in the secrets that they harbour, the promise of the theatre tour is that going behind the scenes affords privileged access to the 'reality' of the organization that its public façade disguises or conceals. As part of a wider cultural spectrum, backstage theatre tours belong to a tradition of workplace-centred tourism whose roots can be traced as far back as the late nineteenth century, but which has recently flourished and expanded in the context of the post-industrialized economies of twenty-first century Europe and the United States, where, Chris Rojek remarks, the increasing flexibility of work patterns and of leisure time means that 'the workplace where we can observe others at work, increases its attraction value as a leisure and tourist destination'.[19] In the United Kingdom behind the scenes tours are available in factories (the Mini factory in Oxford, the Wedgewood Centre in Stoke-on-Trent, Dartington Crystal in Devon), breweries (Shepherd Neame in Faversham, Fuller's in Chiswick) and farms (Abbey Home Farm in Gloucestershire). Tours that advertise a look 'behind the scenes' are also offered by various stately homes, university colleges, public institutions, heritage sites, sports stadiums and theme parks. Diverse as these venues are, the claims that are made on behalf of their tours are often remarkably similar: at Witley Court in Worcestershire, one is promised 'an exciting opportunity to explore parts of the Court seldom open to visitors'; at Durrell Wildlife Conservation Trust '[a]t least one opportunity to visit an area that is normally out of bounds to the public'; and at Chatsworth House 'an opportunity to explore those sections of the house that are not normally on show'; the Wimbledon Tour Experience 'gives you VIP access to restricted areas where even tournament ticket holders are forbidden to enter'. Most comprehensively of all, the Behind the Scenes Tour of Oxford's Christ Church College invites us to 'Visit the hidden Christ Church. With access to private gardens, this allows a unique access into the College's history, its architecture, student life, scenes associated with the world of Lewis Carroll and of course,

---

16 Simon Callow, *Being an Actor* (Harmondsworth, 1984), p. 182.

17 Interview with Michael Goldfarb, *Guardian*, 16 April 1987, quoted in Jonathan Holmes, *Merely Players? Actors' Accounts of Performing Shakespeare* (London, 2004), p. 40.

18 Holmes, *Merely Players?*, pp. 15–61.

19 Chris Rojek, *Ways of Escape: Modern Transformations in Leisure and Travel* (Basingstoke, 1993), p. 152.

the Harry Potter films.'[20] Here we may sample a particularly potent blend of site history, biography and fantasy which has significant parallels with the backstage activities that are planned for the new RST, as indicated by Simon Erridge: in addition to the standard building tour, visitors will also take a 'secret' backstreets route from the theatre to New Place and Shakespeare's Birthplace, thereby experiencing the opportunity to integrate the story of Stratford-upon-Avon's theatre into the larger compendium of biographical and mythical narratives, organized around the municipality's historic properties, from which, as Barbara Hodgdon has pointed out, it has traditionally been isolated.[21]

As the recurrence of certain key terms ('unique', 'exclusive', 'opportunity', 'normally' and 'not normally') indicates, the common theme of the behind the scenes or backstage tour is that it something out of the ordinary, that its participants, temporarily constituted as an elite, are being afforded rare and special privileges and a chance to make acquaintanceship with secrets (or, and the quasi-erotic terminology is not coincidental, with forbidden or secret parts), that it is a tourist experience that is something more than that, that it is tourism on different terms, or even that it is not, really, a tourist experience at all. Trading upon the impression that what is on offer is somehow unique and special, such tours lend themselves to ready classification within the influential model of tourist experience originated by the sociologist Dean MacCannell, in his classic 1976 study, *The Tourist*. Contending that '[t]ouristic consciousness is motivated by its desire for authentic experiences', he points to the example of how

tourists commonly take guided tours of social establishments because they provide easy access to areas of the establishment ordinarily closed to outsiders . . . the inner operations of these important places are shown and explained in the course of tour . . . on tour, outsiders are allowed further *in* than regular patrons.[22]

Operating within a more general conceptualization of 'touristic space' as 'a *stage set, a tourist setting*, or simply *set*',[23] 'behind the scenes' experiences appear to renegotiate the divisions between

the public and private areas of an institution or organization. The problem, of course, is that the promise of access to the authentic workings can be disingenuous, misleading or simply false: it is 'always possible that what is taken to be entry into a back region is really entry into a front region that has been set up in advance for touristic visitation'.[24] Proposing the term 'staged authenticity', MacCannell suggests that 'there is a staged quality to the proceedings that lends them an aura of superficiality, albeit a superficiality not always perceived as such by the tourist, who is usually forgiving about these matters'.[25]

Applied schematically, the concept of staged authenticity rehearses a clear and possibly simplistic dichotomy between truth and falsehood, as well as invoking a scenario of manipulation and deceit, and subsequent commentators have questioned MacCannell's emphasis upon the tourist's desire for authenticity; in particular, Maxine Feifer has suggested that the more typical experience in postmodern culture is that of the 'post-tourist'; a figure

---

[20] See 'Witley Court', www.english-heritage.org.uk; 'Behind the Scenes Tour', www.durrell.org/Visit-Durrell-In-Jersey/Guided-Tours; 'Behind the Scenes Days in 2008', www.chatsworth.org/events/bts_tours.htm; 'Wimbledon Tour Experience', www.londonpass.com/attWimbledonTour-Experience.asp; '"Behind the Scenes" Tours', www.chch.ox.ac.uk; all accessed 5 November 2008.

[21] Barbara Hodgdon, *The Shakespeare Trade: Performances and Appropriations* (Philadelphia, 1998), pp. 191–240. On the Stratford Shakespeare tourist trade, see also Graham Holderness, 'Bardolatry: Or, the Cultural Materialist's Guide to Stratford-upon-Avon', in Graham Holderness, ed., *The Shakespeare Myth* (Manchester, 1988), pp. 2–15; and Nicola J. Watson, 'Shakespeare on the Tourist Trail' in Robert Shaughnessy, ed., *The Cambridge Companion to Shakespeare and Popular Culture* (Cambridge, 2007), pp. 199–26. For discussions of Shakespearean tourism more generally, and of the Bankside Globe in particular, see Dennis Kennedy, 'Shakespeare and Cultural Tourism', *Theatre Journal*, 50 (1998), 175–88; and Susan Bennett, 'Shakespeare on Vacation', in Hodgdon and Worthen, *Companion to Shakespeare and Performance*, pp. 494–508.

[22] Dean MacCannell, *The Tourist: A New Theory of the Leisure Class* (London and Basingstoke, 1976), pp. 101, 98.

[23] MacCannell, *The Tourist*, p. 100.

[24] MacCannell, *The Tourist*, p. 101.

[25] MacCannell, *The Tourist*, p. 98.

whom John Urry characterizes as finding 'pleasure in the multiplicity of tourist games' and who knows 'that there is *no* authentic tourist experience, that there are merely a series of games or texts that can be played'; thus post-tourists 'almost delight in the inauthenticity of the tourist experience'.[26] Mac-Cannell himself acknowledges that the success of the system partly rests upon the tourist's willingness to entertain the fiction (or, in our terms, to willingly suspend disbelief). Moreover, his modelling allows some scope for play between the categories: rather than defining the relations of frontstage to backstage in terms of a simple binary, MacCannell describes tourist settings in terms of a 'continuum starting from the front and ending at the back', within which it is '*theoretically* possible to distinguish six stages': at the front lies the cultural façade in its simplest form, and at the back the region which, being out of bounds, 'motivates touristic consciousness'; between these we can encounter 'a front region that is totally organized to look like a back region' (stage three), 'a back region that is open to outsiders' (stage four) or 'a back region that may be cleaned up or altered a bit because tourists are permitted an occasional glimpse in' (stage five).[27] We notice that this appears to correspond to the proscenium model, invoking the spatial divisions and stylistic hierarchies of perspective staging, with the most 'inauthentic' and superficial actions performed front cloth, and the deepest truths of heart's desire located at the vanishing point upstage. To return to the thesis that underpins MacCannell's analysis, the touristic quest for 'authenticity' is symptomatic of a more fundamental alienation; '[s]ightseeing,' he contends, 'is a way of attempting to overcome the discontinuity of modernity, of incorporating its fragments into unified experience'.[28] Viewed in this light, the frontstage-backstage model does rather more than organize and stratify the relationship between visitor and alien cultures; it is a representation of the general cultural and ideological apparatus which positions the rootless and disaffected subject of modernity. Here MacCannell's thinking, perhaps unexpectedly, converges with a strand within theatre and performance studies over the

past two decades (itself akin to psychoanalytically inflected theories of the cinematic gaze), which has accounted for the persistence of the picture frame in very similar terms: as David Wiles (who has drawn a highly suggestive analogy between the classic picture-frame stage and Freud's mapping of the mind, whereby the forestage corresponds to the preconscious, the stage to the ego and backstage to the subconscious) suggests, the 'perspective stage . . . has proved to be one of the most powerful tools of western culture for manufacturing dreams'.[29]

The behind-the-scenes theatre tour, then, sits somewhere towards the back of the sociology of tourism's conceptual stage, at the higher end of the continuum, at stages four and five, though across the range of tours currently available we can discern a complex interplay between a variety of authenticities, staged and otherwise. As I shall indicate below, the tour of Shakespeare's Globe presents particularly complex challenges, in that, as a conjectural simulacrum of an early modern playhouse whose interior is as essential to its integrity and its claim to historic authenticity as its exterior, it is in a sense *all* frontstage. But even the apparently more straightforward theatre tours entertain a degree of negotiation of the idea of the authentic, and, in particular, a certain sensitivity surrounding the extent of the public's rights of access in practice. For health and safety reasons, as well as more obviously practical ones, backstage tours can only take place when performances do not; thus as an opportunity to view a working environment the theatre backstage tour fundamentally differs, for example, from the

---

[26] Maxine Feifer, *Going Places: The Ways of the Tourist from Imperial Rome to the Present Day* (London, 1985); John Urry, *The Tourist Gaze: Leisure and Travel in Contemporary Societies* (London, 1990), p. 11.

[27] MacCannell, *The Tourist*, pp. 101–2.

[28] MacCannell, *The Tourist*, p. 13.

[29] David Wiles, *A Short History of Western Performance Space* (Cambridge, 2003), p. 207. MacCannell's terminology of frontstage and backstage, it is important to note, derives less from a study of vernacular theatre architecture than from the influential performance-based paradigm of social interaction and region behaviour advanced by Erving Goffman in *The Presentation of Self in Everyday Life* (New York, 1959).

tour of the BMW Mini factory in Oxford, where participants witness actual, live assembly-line construction, or that of the Shepherd Neame Brewery in Faversham, during which 'your guide will take you through the heart of the brewery, enabling you to see how beer is made from barley to bottle and from hop to hand-pump!';[30] the best that the tour can usually offer is a glimpse of theatre in preparation, rather than theatre fully at work. The tour publicity for the Royal Opera House is admirably frank about this: whilst it entices with the possibility that a tour '*may* include opportunities to see the Royal Ballet in class, or the magnificent backstage technology in operation', it makes no promises, and indeed strongly cautions that, as a 'working theatre', 'plans may change at short notice' and hence tours 'vary according to what is available on the day and a visit to the auditorium is not guaranteed'.[31] We see here some quite delicate footwork around the issue of the degree and scope of access to the authentic backstage that the tour can reasonably claim to offer, which in itself reveals a deep structural irony: the closer we try to get to actual performance at work, the more likely it is that we will find ourselves excluded from it.

To turn now to a case study: the National Theatre has been operating backstage tours of its South Bank complex since the building opened in 1976, with the intent, from the outset, of not only rendering accessible, but also publicly legitimizing, an institution and a work of uncompromisingly modernist architecture which has been both celebrated and bitterly criticized. Presenting itself as a multi-tiered public forum whose terraces and foyers, bars and cafés are as much performance spaces as the auditoria they surround, the National strives to offer itself not just as a theatre building but as a metropolitan amenity, cultural centre and social rendezvous point, a composite concrete stage upon which, whether or not they are assembled in the interests of theatre, the citizens of Britain have the opportunity to meet face to face. In this context, the National's backstage tour is more than a visitor experience designed to lure in the curious; it is, in an important sense, a contribution to the institution's civic mission.

This is reflected in the price of the tour, which at £6 (with concessions available) compares pretty favourably with other London theatre tours and even more favourably with, for example, the leading sports stadium tours, the cheapest of which start at the same price for a discounted child's ticket. The tours are scheduled to run up to six times a day during weekdays and twice on Saturdays; although not originally conceived as a revenue stream for the organization, they are now fully integrated into its ticketing economy.[32] According to the National's web publicity, they continue to attract more than 20,000 participants a year. On the day I attend, it is with a group of around a dozen, gathered for the tour prior to the evening performance of Ayub Khan-Din's British-Asian comedy *Rafta Rafta* in the Lyttelton auditorium.[33] We begin at the frontstage location of the information desk in the main lobby, following the preliminaries ('Do feel free to ask questions; no photography, please') the transition to the outer reaches of backstage is effected when our guide flicks aside the rope barrier that cordons off the entrance to the Lyttelton. Properly speaking, we are not yet backstage, but it is hard not to feel a shudder of privilege as we take our seats in a frontstage zone that, because it is not yet open to the general public, is for now a backstage one, as we overhear radio-miked coded instructions relayed between the stage crew and the lighting box. Facing the Lyttelton's proscenium frame, we are told of how it can be expanded or contracted to crop the pictures it presents, and of how the stage can be inclined; and our guide's spoken commentary on the complexities of the theatre's hydraulics is not merely illustrated but graphically embodied in a fluent sequence of hand movements, capturing the workings of the most advanced scenic

---

[30] 'Brewery Tours', www.shepherd-neame.co.uk/tour/, accessed 10 June 2008.

[31] 'Backstage Tours', http://esales.roh.org.uk/tickets/tour/, accessed 10 June 2008.

[32] I am indebted here to the help and advice generously offered by the National Theatre's Nicola Thorold and Alison Rae, who took time to answer my questions and shared their own research on the theatre's backstage touring activities.

[33] This was on 23 October 2007.

technologies through the traditional arts of the solo storytelling performer. Anthropomorphically rendering the theatre machine as articulate body, this is the first of a series of performative micro-events which will encourage us not just to understand the National but, perhaps, to begin to love it. We pass through a door to the left of the stage and find ourselves at the beginning of the 'real' backstage, whose difference is immediately registered in terms of the drop in the quality of the environmental finish: drab and peeling paintwork, worn linoleum rather than carpet, and functional fluorescent working light, all of which, of course, enhance the impression of authenticity rather than diminish it. Onto the Lyttelton stage for a peek up into the flies, and a look at the set for *Rafta Rafta*; from a distance we admire the naturalistic detailing that extends even to the choice of a particular brand of tea-bags in the kitchen, before being taken behind the cyclorama where lies the gunmetal grey set for tomorrow's performance of Pinter's *The Hothouse* – which, in the absence of the human performing bodies it requires to animate it, has even more of an uncanny, *Marie Celeste* air about it, and just for a moment I imagine ours as a party of strange revenants, silent and unseen witnesses at scenes, slices of the real, that have been frozen in time. The impression evaporates as we enter the workshop behind the stage, an industrial-scale space filled with the aromas of hot metal, aerosol paint and sawdust, and the sounds of power tools, drilling and hammering, a working environment that is the domain of carpenters and painters who, accomplished practitioners of the Stanislavskian art of public solitude, proceed with the performance of their work duties as if we were invisible. Simultaneously a place of heavy manual labour and delicate artistry, the workshop confronts us with radical disparities of scale, between the displays of exquisitely intricate set models and large wooden flats stacked against the walls and suspended from skylights. As we move onwards to the prop storage rooms, we negotiate passageways dressed, to us it appears randomly, with fragments of scenery: a single door in a frame bearing the Magritte-like scribbled legend 'rehearsal door', classical columns, chairs; and everywhere chalked warnings, injunctions and instructions – do not remove, please replace. Whatever we make of it, this seemingly chaotic repository has an order and a logic which we must respect if not understand; indeed, the authenticity of the scene lies precisely in its refusal to organize itself legibly for our benefit.

It is when we reach the props store that the impressions that have been generated by the tour thus far begin to gather together in a more focused and – literally – material form. Standing on the Lyttelton stage and gazing into the flies, we heard that the central principle (and the achievement) of the National Theatre is its effectiveness and efficiency as a mechanism for keeping in rotation a repertory that in any season can consist of around twenty full productions as well as numerous supplementary activities, drawn from the entire range of classic and contemporary British, European and world theatre, operating across three auditoria, six, sometimes seven, days of the week, fifty-two weeks of the year; uniquely within the theatre industry in Britain, moreover, *everything* that contributes to production is generated, or recycled, in-house. As a model of self-sufficiency and resource management this is exemplary; what we also notice is that, at least in the first instance, one of the effects of this emphasis on the manufacture and movement of props and scenery is that it invites us to visualize the National's dramatic repertoire as a finely balanced ecology of rotating commodities. The tour can hardly be criticized for this, for it is what it can best show us and it is largely what we came to see; but to regard the operations of the institution only in this light is to leave unexamined the larger questions about its role and purpose, in particular those pertaining to its status as the theatre which, however complexly, plays a powerful part in the articulation of a national culture. Though it would be an oversimplification to describe the National as a state of the art machine geared towards the production of the art of the state, the National is, obviously, implicated in the manufacture of ideas and sensibilities as well as things.

For participants in the backstage tour, though, this is not really what we want to hear about. If the journey so far has taken us from the point of reception (the auditorium) through the place of inception and production (the workshop), and from realization to possibility, it now presents us with the opportunity to sample the National's material output at closer range. Gathered before the doors to the prop storage area (to which access is prohibited), we contemplate a kind of *Wunderkammer* display of items from past productions as we are told of the secrets of their fabrication: decanters and glasses of booze, breakable bottles, a retractable dagger, a latex tortoise (from Stoppard's *Jumpers*), a pie with a pastry topping fashioned in the form of two poodles (from the 2005 stage version of *Theatre of Blood*), and, of course, a Yorick skull. Exhibiting implements of intoxication and violence that have been contrived to function entirely without risk, the prop display inhabits the realms of the simulacra, as described by Jean Baudrillard, whereby 'substituting the signs of the real for the real' ensures 'the operation of deterring every real process via its operational double, a programmatic, metastable, perfectly descriptive machine that offers all the signs of the real and short-circuits all its vicissitudes'.[34] Although we venture backstage in pursuit of authenticity, these artifacts appeal to the post-tourist in us not because they are real (that would be disgusting or, worse, merely boring), but because theirs is the hyperreality of the ardently fake; their interest lies partly in the ingenuity with which they have been constructed (a review in the listings magazine *Time Out* enthusiastically notes that the props collection ranges from 'silicone broccoli florets' to 'giant chunks of polystyrene rubble'[35]), and partly in the aura that derives from their having been actually used on the National's stages. The display also focuses an image of theatre work as dominated by the paraphernalia of realism. If the emphasis upon the corporeal grotesque momentarily recalls the inanimate theatre of the macabre that we expect of the rival tourist experience advertised by the London Dungeon, it also marks the point on the tour where the theatrical body is most graphically figured, yet not present. It is also, not coincidentally, the most interactive section of the tour: thus far we have been enjoined to keep to the path, not to touch, to keep out, and definitely not to photograph, but our guide now encourages us not only to closely inspect the props, but also to handle and to play with them, surrogating ourselves as the performers in whose footsteps we tread. Interactivity does not end here: props and costumes are available for hire 'at reasonable rates' to performers, film-makers, events organizers and others across the amateur and professional spectrums (the RSC operates a similar system). Theatre may be the most transient and ephemeral of arts; yet the National's and the RSC's productions enjoy an afterlife in which, dissolved into their constituents, dispersed and fragmented, they are used and re-used in contexts their makers could never have anticipated: reportedly, the most popular items for hire are 'the seagull from *The Seagull* and the barber's chair from *Sweeney Todd*' and 'the restraining chair and chamber pot from *The Madness of George III*'.[36] Thus the National's props become national property.

The National's backstage tour does not, however, include a visit to the costume store, in part because the physical layout of the building is in this instance at odds with narrative concision: to go there would entail a lengthy and awkward detour. Nor does it include the actors' dressing rooms, the rehearsal rooms, or indeed any of the places where performers might be glimpsed at work, rest or play; anyone taking the tour in the hope of bumping into Simon Russell Beale in a corridor is likely to be disappointed.[37] What follows is the Cottesloe, the

---

34 Jean Baudrillard, *Simulacra and Simulation*, trans. Sheila Faria Glaser (Ann Arbor, 1994), p. 2.

35 Lisa Mullen, 'Backstage at the National Theatre', *Time Out*, 5 January 2007.

36 'Props Hire Store', www.nationaltheatre.org.uk/20629/costume-amp-props-hire/props-hire-store.html, accessed 22 July 2008.

37 As this article was nearing completion, however, the National Theatre launched a virtual tour of the building which does allow a glimpse of these areas and of actors in rehearsal, hosted by Simon Russell Beale himself; see 'Online Tour', www.nationaltheatre.org.uk/40631/online-tour/online-tour.html, accessed 5 November 2008.

metal outer casing of the symbolic heart of the plant, the Olivier stage's drum revolve, and, on the last leg, an excursus into the foyer and an elevator trip to the topmost circle of the Olivier auditorium. Perched vertiginously in a spot which is as far from any of the National's stages as it is possible within eyesight and earshot to get, we hear of the mechanisms housed within the Olivier's fly tower, and fancy wanders up and out, alighting upon the dominant features of the exterior façade that, as key components of what its architect Denys Lasdun called the building's 'self-advertising' capacity, spectacularly announce the National's ministry by functioning as massive projection screens and monuments to visionary theatre history, which at night, as one of its chroniclers has written, are 'dramatically lit to resemble the mythic scene sketches of Edward Gordon Craig'.[38] Meanwhile, inside and far below, we spot some actors: members of the cast of tonight's show, limbering up on the Olivier stage. From up here they look tiny, distant, and beyond reach.

This tour is almost at an end. The guide reveals that there is another reason for bringing us here, to the highest interior point in the complex. Shepherded out of the Olivier, we find ourselves on a high balcony which commands a spectacular overview of the place we began our journey, the place Lasdun thought of as the 'fourth auditorium': the sweeping foyer, bar and restaurant, and front of house space, buzzing with early evening theatregoers and others, some drinking, some idly studying the art displays, some paying varying degrees of inattention to the ambient noodlings of a jazz trio. It is, without question, an uplifting sight, charged with the power and pleasure of looking down, and palpable evidence that within its civic leisure industry remit, the building works; here we may survey the National's imagined community glimpsed, momentarily, as a totality.[39] If one of the effects of the tour has been to unsettle the divisions between inside and outside, to render performance space as public space and vice versa, to advertise and celebrate its machinery of production rather than attempt to conceal it, and, ultimately, to reveal the continuity between the arena, auditorium, land-

scape and city that Lasdun found in the Hellenistic model, then this finale is brilliantly judged.

Also, by returning us to frontstage space and inviting us to review it from another angle, the tour's narrative is afforded a satisfying, full-circle sense of closure. By foregrounding the imperatives of access, inclusion, participation and public use, the tour reiterates the National's long-established cultural mission whilst contributing to the growing portfolio of educational, performance and performance-related practices that the institution harbours within and around its premises. Stepping back for a moment, it also finally provides us with a vantage point from which to look forward to its prospects both as an organization and as a public building, within the immediate context of the National Theatre's approaching half-centenary in 2013, and in the wider context of future arts policy and provision in the United Kingdom. A sense of the likely shape of the latter can be gleaned from the publication, in January 2008, of *Supporting Excellence in the Arts*, Sir Brian McMaster's recommendations to the UK Government's Department of Culture, Media and Sport regarding the future of arts funding. Based on the conviction that 'excellent culture goes to the root of living and is therefore relevant to every single one of us', McMaster's report explicitly seeks to encourage 'excellence, risk-taking and innovation' whilst advocating the development of 'a light touch and non-bureaucratic method to judge the quality of the arts in the future'. Most relevant to the current discussion, however, is that one of the report's core concerns is how 'artistic excellence can encourage wider and deeper engagement with the arts by audiences'.[40] It is abundantly clear

---

[38] Simon Callow, *The National: The Theatre and its Work, 1953–1997* (London, 1997), p. 74.

[39] For a discussion of the erotics of overhead surveillance, see Michel de Certeau, 'Walking in the City', in *The Practice of Everyday Life*, trans. Steven Rendall (Berkeley, 1984), pp. 91–110. It is worth recording here that the rebuilt Royal Shakespeare Theatre complex incorporates an observation tower, from which the town of Stratford can be surveyed.

[40] Sir Brian McMaster, *Supporting Excellence in the Arts* (London, 2008), p. 6.

that the vast majority of backstage, frontstage and sidestage activities that take place in and around the National, the Royal Shakespeare Theatre, Shakespeare's Globe, and similar organizations are driven by the desire to engage actual and potential audiences with aspects of those companies' core activities; what is less certain is the degree and the quality of follow-through from one to the other, and whether they stimulate genuine passion and understanding or, to use McMaster's description of routine art, 'supply audiences with a superficial experience that provides immediate satisfaction but no lasting impact'.[41] Nonetheless, as we have seen, the opening up and opening out of both the theatre organizations and the buildings that house them has become one of the most visible manifestations of their commitment to widening participation and access. For the National's current artistic and executive directors, Nicholas Hytner and Nick Starr (who has emphasized that the National should be concerned with the 'authenticity' of the experience it offers), a transformation of backstage space is central to the execution of this brief. Announcing that it is his intention to redevelop the coach park behind the South Bank complex as an educational centre, Hytner has declared that he wants to 'make the National more porous' by 'knock[ing] through those bricks walls at the back, so people are able to look into our workshops'. As both a response to the public curiosity about backstage and a potential negation of its mystique, this is a bold plan, if not quite on a par with the current reconstruction of the Royal Shakespeare Theatre, but Hytner goes further: 'I'd even float something that would horrify most of my colleagues: that rehearsals should be visible and accessible.'[42]

Here, the principle of open backstage access is tested to the limit, touching upon the traditionally most secretive realm of theatre-making of all. This is very much in the spirit of McMaster's conviction that the 'best person to communicate about their art is the artist' and that artists should therefore 'be strongly encouraged to engage with their audiences';[43] yet it is not without its difficulties. One is that the commitment to extending access to all areas may, in the end, be at odds with what

we have seen is the fundamental appeal of backstage, which is that it is a place that fosters the impression (however illusory this may be) that it is available to the general public only through special dispensation; to open up the theatre runs the risk of rendering its workings merely routine. Whether an observed rehearsal is viewable as an authentically backstage activity is also debatable, given that the presence of outsiders in rehearsal can often inhibit performers (or, conversely, encourage exhibitionism), and shift the work away from the experimental and the exploratory and towards performance, or frontstage, mode. More contentious, though, is the issue of whether such access should be encouraged or allowed at all, and whether, just because the public is, as Hytner puts it, 'fascinated by how the performing arts are put together', this legitimates intrusion into an arena that the majority of modern practitioners still prefer to keep private, whose sanctity, according to Peter Brook, underwrites 'the essential bond of trust which is the basis for the actor and director's capacity to work together'.[44] Actors in rehearsal on the stage of Shakespeare's Globe may not (or may affect not to) mind the scrutiny of a constant stream of touring onlookers; elsewhere, the security of rehearsal space can be one of the most important factors in the encouragement of the 'risk-taking and innovation' through which 'excellence' is sought. At the same time, we need to recognize that the history of backstage itself suggests that the division

41 McMaster, *Supporting Excellence*, p. 18.
42 Quoted in Michael Billington, 'This Will Horrify my Colleagues', *Guardian*, 17 January 2008.
43 McMaster, *Supporting Excellence*, p. 17.
44 Peter Brook, *There Are No Secrets: Thoughts on Acting and Theatre* (London, 1993), p. 99. Qualifying the promise of his title, Brook accounts for his consistent refusal to permit observers at rehearsals by invoking the experience of allowing 'a very serious author to observe the process', who, despite being enjoined to 'publish nothing abut what he witnessed' went on to produce a book 'full of inaccurate impressions' which Brook clearly regarded as an act of betrayal. The reference, I assume, is to David Selbourne's highly critical *The Making of 'A Midsummer Night's Dream': An Eye-Witness Account of Peter Brook's Production from First Rehearsal to First Night* (London, 1982).

between private rehearsal and public performance is itself relative and contingent, the product of a frontally oriented theatre architecture and of the specific technologies of acting that have evolved within it, as well as of a more pervasive cultural binary between public and private that we may well also wish to interrogate.

Throughout this article I have focused primarily on the backstage desires of audiences and visitors while also indicating that these, like their quest for truth and authenticity, can never be fully satisfied.

I end by shifting the emphasis to the needs and preferences of the backstage performer, not just because the performer's rights to privacy ought to be respected, but because it is in the acknowledgement of legitimate boundaries that the desire for the authentic can be put in proper perspective. In the theatre, especially backstage, there are still mysteries to be preserved and secrets to be kept. Sometimes it may be in all our interests that there are walls that remain opaque, curtains that are kept closed and doors that stay firmly shut.

INNER MONOLOGUES: REALIST ACTING AND/AS SHAKESPEARIAN PERFORMANCE TEXT

ROBERTA BARKER

In Declan Donnellan's 2008 production of *Troilus and Cressida* for Cheek by Jowl, Helen of Troy (Marianne Oldham) initially featured as the Face that Launched a Thousand Copies of *Hello!* Magazine. Decked in a chic white evening gown, she delivered the play's Prologue while stalking with feline satisfaction among the soldiers who would die for her (illustration 48). Later, she and Paris primped and posed for a series of glamour photos, looking for all the world like a Shakespearian Brad Pitt and Angelina Jolie. When Pandarus began his song, 'Love, love, nothing but love', Helen proved her star power by joining her voice with his, offering, one critic asserted, 'the best singing of the night'.[1] At this point, however, something surprising happened. The song's lascivious words seemed increasingly to disturb her; her voice began to tremble, her eyes filled with tears, and by the end of the song she had to pause to compose herself. Soon the mask cracked altogether and she broke weeping from the stage. The audience had witnessed Helen's transformation from a plastic icon into a psychologically complex 'character' in the realist tradition.[2]

Depending on one's perspective, such an approach to Helen may appear either self-evident or thoroughly wrong-headed. Some version of realist acting informs most mainstream American and British productions of Shakespeare and his contemporaries. Its shaping force guarantees that many actors and directors will explore the inner objectives and past histories that drive their characters' words and actions, creating complex emotional subtexts to flow beneath the complex Shakespearian text. Moreover, many audience members will judge the resulting performances as much or even more in terms of the richness, plausibility and clarity of their implied emotional narratives as in terms of any relationship to the literary play-text. Yet this process has come under increasing fire from scholars, who have branded it ahistorical, apolitical and insufficiently conscious of its own tortuous relationship to the perceived authority of the Shakespearian text.

My article's modest aim is not to refute these important and well-taken critiques of realism, but rather to balance them by arguing for a closer analysis of the *processes* involved in creating

I should like to thank Cary Mazer, whose insights have informed every stage of this article's development.

[1] Philip Fisher, Review of *Troilus and Cressida*, dir. Declan Donnellan, *The British Theatre Guide*, accessed 20 July 2008, www.britishtheatreguide.info/reviews/CBJtroilus-rev.htm.

[2] Here and in the argument that follows, I use the terms 'realist' and 'realism' to describe a range of theories and practices of acting that are based to some extent on the 'System' of Konstantin Stanislavski. These approaches to acting have been given a number of other titles. In *Talking to the Audience: Shakespeare, Performance, Self* (Abingdon, 2005), p. 14, Bridget Escolme favours 'naturalism'. In his unpublished essay 'Two Cheers for Emotional Realism, or, Learning to Love Fallacious Characterology', p. 3, Cary Mazer prefers the more specific term 'emotional realism'. In her *Complete Stanislavsky Toolkit* (London, 2007), p. 17, Stanislavskian actor-teacher Bella Merlin uses 'psychological realism'. I have chosen 'realism' simply because this appears to have been the term Stanislavski favoured when describing the goals of his own work. See Samuel L. Leiter, *From Stanislavsky to Barrault: Representative Directors of the European Stage* (New York, 1991), p. 31.

48. Marianne Oldham as Helen of Troy in *Troilus and Cressida*, directed by Declan Donnellan (Cheek by Jowl, 2008).

and watching realist performance within its cultural context. I want particularly to consider the Stanislavskian notions of subtext and of the inner monologue as they helped to shape key scenes from Donnellan's *Troilus and Cressida* and from Trevor Nunn's production of *The Merchant of Venice* (Royal National Theatre, 1999). These scenes exemplify realist acting's tacit construction of the literary playtext not only as blueprint or source, but also as excess and as lack. Renewed engagement with the inner monologue as a primary performance text, neither governed by nor subsuming the spoken words of the script, may help us better to understand the productive tensions that shape much contemporary Shakespearian representation.

Cary Mazer defines realism as 'the mode of acting that arose (hand in hand with character criticism and with new forms of dramatic writing that increasingly pyschologized a play's

dramatis personae) in the nineteenth century [and] that was codified as the 'System' by Konstantin Stanislavsky'.[3] This 'mode of acting' was produced by a very specific historical view of human subjectivity, of its relationship to society, and of the process an actor must undertake to represent these effectively. Grounded in an age of scientific positivism and emerging contemporaneously with the rise of psychoanalysis, realism sought to replace what it perceived as the generalizations and stock typing of previous forms of stage characterization with a highly particularized and carefully observed mimesis of 'real' human behaviour.[4] Throughout his long and varied career, Stanislavski experimented with a range of techniques by which the actor could be trained effectively to achieve just such a convincing imitation of life.[5] Many of these techniques came together to form his 'System', a conception of the actor's process described in his written works and developed practically at the Moscow Art Theatre. In the System, character appears 'as a function of the motivational needs and drives of the individual agents of the drama in the encounter with the obstacles represented by

---

[3] Mazer, 'Two Cheers for Emotional Realism', p. 3.

[4] For one of the definitive statements of this position, see Emile Zola, *Le Naturalisme au Théâtre* (1881), ed. Chantal Meyer-Plantureux (Brussels, 2000).

[5] Stanislavski's career as an actor, director, and teacher spanned more than fifty years, over which time his theory and practice constantly evolved. From an early strong commitment to minute scenographic naturalism as the source of the actor's creativity he moved to an exploration of the psychological processes by which the actor could stimulate emotion and the physical processes by which the body and voice could be freed to convey it. At the end of his life he was still elaborating his 'Method of Physical Action', in which the actor focuses upon the score of his character's gestures in order to trigger emotional reactions in himself and his audience (see Merlin, *Complete Stanislavsky Toolkit*, pp. 185–96). In his new translation of Stanislavski's *An Actor's Work: A Student's Diary* (London, 2008), p. xvi, Jean Benedetti remarks upon 'the accidents of history' and of publication that caused most Western directors and actors to see the System as 'purely psychological' and to ignore its physical and textual emphases. The aspects of the System I focus upon in this paper are those that, thanks in part to these 'accidents', most dominate contemporary Stanislavskian acting training and practice in the English-speaking world.

social and material reality'.[6] The dramatic character possesses a deep psychology grounded in her past and present interactions with the 'given circumstances' of her environment.[7] She is constantly growing and changing as she seeks to reshape that environment by pursuing a sequence of goals and desires which result in highly specific actions and reactions.[8] Although these 'objectives' or 'tasks' are constantly in flux, the performer's actions remain logically and consistently rooted in her character's central goal, the 'super-objective' or 'supertask'.[9] The realist actor must search within herself to find the thoughts, will and emotions that allow her to identify with her character,[10] to chart moment-by-moment her character's evolving wants and needs, and to follow her on her 'journey' through the play.

Although this construction of character as psychologically complex, goal-driven and internally consistent grounds realist acting, it has become almost taboo in Shakespeare Studies and Performance Studies, especially in the wake of Cultural Materialism and the New Historicism. Much of the most influential scholarship of recent decades has focused attention upon early modern constructions of subjectivity as relational rather than individualistic, unstable rather than coherent and unitary.[11] For the early modern period, writes Stephen Orgel, 'character' meant 'both a written account of a person, and the letters – characters – in which the account [was] written'; dramatic characters, he reminds us, 'are not people, they are elements of a linguistic structure, lines in a drama, and more basically, words on a page'.[12] The scholarly critique of character has had a direct impact upon our understanding of performance practice on the early modern stage. John Russell Brown devotes a number of pages in his recent *Shakespeare and the Theatrical Event* to reminding readers that 'Elizabethans did not speak of the individual characters in a play, as we do' and that for Shakespeare's original audiences 'the player's physical enactment of imaginary emotion provided the dominating effect in performance, not the illusion of a certain kind of person, still less of a "character" in our present-day usage'.[13] Examining performance through a wider lens, Joseph Roach's *The*

Player's Passion similarly stresses the huge historical gap between the psycho-physiological theories of acting promulgated by Stanislavski and his disciples and the more rhetorical model of 'personation' that obtained in the early modern period.[14]

For performance theorists informed by poststructuralism, meanwhile, realist characterization emerges as problematic less because it is anachronistic than because it is fundamentally conservative, working merely to confirm the complacent individualism of today's dominant Western culture. Colin Counsell speaks for many such critics when he complains that 'Stanislavskian actors . . . [work] on the assumption that characters are coherent, unitary identities, whereas in real social life we all adopt a multiplicity of discursive and behavioral personae'.[15] Counsell reads individual identity in post-structural terms as constantly shifting, shaped

---

[6] Robert Gordon, *The Purpose of Playing: Modern Acting Theories in Perspective* (Ann Arbor, 2006), p. 53.

[7] Stanislavski, *An Actor's Work*, p. 52.

[8] Stanislavski's first English translator, Elizabeth Hapgood, translated the term by which Stanislavski denoted these goals or desires as 'objectives': see Konstantin Stanislavski, *An Actor Prepares*, ed. and trans. Elizabeth Hapgood (New York, 1936), p. 112. Stanislavski's latest translator, Jean Benedetti, renders it instead as 'tasks' (*An Actor's Work*, p. 142). As the former version is the more widely familiar to actors but the latter, perhaps, the more faithful to Stanislavski's Russian, I have used both terms as alternatives where necessary.

[9] See *An Actor Prepares*, pp. 248ff, for 'super-objective', and *An Actor's Work*, pp. 307ff, for 'supertask'.

[10] Stanislavski, *An Actor's Work*, p. 276.

[11] Well-known examples of such work include Stephen Greenblatt, *Renaissance Self-Fashioning* (Chicago, 1980); Francis Barker, *The Tremulous Private Body* (London, 1984); Jonathan Dollimore, *Radical Tragedy: Religion, Ideology and Power in the Drama of Shakespeare and his Contemporaries* (London, 1984); Catherine Belsey, *The Subject of Tragedy: Identity and Difference in Renaissance Drama* (London, 1985); and Alan Sinfield, *Faultlines: Cultural Materialism and the Politics of Dissident Reading* (Oxford, 1992), among many others.

[12] Stephen Orgel, 'What is a Character?', reprinted in *The Authentic Shakespeare* (London and New York, 2002), p. 8.

[13] John Russell Brown, *Shakespeare and the Theatrical Event* (Basingstoke, 2002), pp. 84, 86.

[14] See Joseph Roach, *The Player's Passion: Studies in the Science of Acting* (London, 1985).

[15] Colin Counsell, *Signs of Performance: An Introduction to 20th-Century Theatre* (New York, 1996), pp. 31–2.

by rhetorical constructions and ideological appa-
ratuses in which human subjects participate but
which they cannot fully control. In place of
this unstable subjectivity, realism offers a deceitful
'image of the illusory coherent self'.[16] Ric Knowles
concurs, complaining of 'the astonishingly linear,
prescriptive, and logocentric approach to dramatic
character and human subjectivity' that dominates
realist acting.[17]

In Shakespearian performance, this process
is compounded by the presence of the many-
splendoured author, The Inventor of the Human,
whose written text supposedly encodes his characters' magnificent three-dimensional wholeness.
W. B. Worthen has argued powerfully that the
Shakespearian realist actor's fixation on character
is inextricably linked to an obsession with the
playwright's authority. Actors seek coherent,
psychologized characters in the plays because
their realist training encourages them to do
so; they then ascribe the results to Shakespeare's
superhuman and transhistorical insight into human
nature. In this way, writes Worthen, 'Shakespeare
grounds characterization by effacing its rhetorical
agency, its rhetorical complicity in specifically
contemporary modes of ideological production'.[18]
Bridget Escolme expands upon the implications
of this situation:

In the name of making the plays accessible to modern audiences, the conventions of stage naturalism can
close down possible meanings for those audiences, while
implying that a particular version of what it is to
be human – the consistent, self-contained character –
should be recognised as universal, through the work of
Shakespeare, most 'universal' of playwrights.[19]

Like Counsell, Escolme objects to the hegemony of
a realist conception of character which sees human
beings as driven by inalienably individual needs,
values and experiences and encourages spectators
to identify with the coherent and universalized
psychologies they see onstage. Little room is left
for a sense of subjectivity as 'unstable and worked
for', or for a more uneasy and critical encounter
between early modern character and contemporary spectator.[20]

Such critiques notwithstanding, some version of
Stanislavskian realism continues to reign on most
mainstream contemporary English-speaking stages.
In 1997, Worthen showed how profoundly actors'
descriptions of their own craft 'are informed by
notions of a coherent and internalized characterization fully consistent with Stanislavskian mimesis'.[21]
A look at the most recent volumes of Cambridge
University Press's Players of Shakespeare, published
in 2003 and 2007, shows that this is still the case.[22]
Like the slim publications in Faber and Faber's
Actors of Shakespeare series, they show actors constructing three-dimensional characters shaped by
the given circumstances of their past and present
'lives'. In Saskia Reeves's Actors on Shakespeare volume on Much Ado About Nothing, for example, the
actress comments on the process by which she created Beatrice in Declan Donnellan's production for
Cheek by Jowl. She describes 'improvis[ing] many
times around the idea of Beatrice being adopted
into Leonato's household as a young orphan, growing up as if she were Hero's sister but always knowing Leonato wasn't her father'.[23] Surveying such
evidence, Worthen admits that

Despite decades of impugning Stanislavski and the techniques he developed or inspired, several Stanislavskian
principles – continuous characterization, . . . the need to
develop an inner life for the role, a consistent through-
line of action – suffuse thinking about acting today, and

---

[16] Counsell, Signs of Performance, p. 32.
[17] Richard Paul Knowles, 'Frankie Goes to Hollywood
    (North); or The Trials of the Oppositional Director', Cana-
    dian Theatre Review, 76 (Fall 1993), p. 6.
[18] W. B. Worthen, Shakespeare and the Authority of Performance
    (Cambridge, 1996), p.146.
[19] Escolme, Talking to the Audience, p. 152.
[20] Escolme, Talking to the Audience, p. 150.
[21] Worthen, Shakespeare and the Authority of Performance, p. 127.
[22] Robert Smallwood, ed., Players of Shakespeare 5 (Cambridge,
    2003); Robert Smallwood, ed., Players of Shakespeare 6: Essays
    in the Performance of Shakespeare's History Plays (Cambridge,
    2007). In a related volume, Performing Shakespeare's Tragedies
    Today: An Actor's Perspective, ed. Michael Dobson (Cam-
    bridge, 2006), Samuel West is exceptional among his peers
    in approaching the role of Hamlet in an explicitly anti-realist
    fashion.
[23] Saskia Reeves, Actors on Shakespeare: Much Ado About
    Nothing (Faber and Faber, 2003), p. 31.

particularly suffuse actors' descriptions of their work. This is hardly surprising. . . . Stanislavski is involved in the production of the bourgeois subject at the heart of modern realism: an individual, delimited, organic, non-commodified, spontaneous psyche. And, Stanislavski or no, it would be difficult to expect actors any more than the rest of us to stand outside this dominant mode of ideological transmission.[24]

As Andrew Hartley shows in his *Shakespearean Dramaturg*, any scholar who wishes to participate in genuine dialogue with a wide range of contemporary theatre practitioners must engage with the language of realist acting.[25]

But realism's continued occupation of the theatrical mainstream is not the only force that invites us, as students of Shakespearian performance, to consider it afresh. Another motivation may be glimpsed in Worthen's suggestion that the 'friction between texts and enactment in contemporary performance might help us to find the pulse of Shakespearean performativity'.[26] *Friction* is precisely the factor critics of realism generally diagnose as absent from its representations. 'System-atic acting', writes Counsell, is 'characterised by a smoothness, an absence of discord and disjuncture'; it 'eradicate[s] all signs of the stage's meaning-making process' and constructs the meanings *it* produces as 'non-constructed, as neutral, "natural", and non-partisan' realizations of the truths inscribed in the dramatic play-text[27] Yet Stanislavski's own writing sketches a rather more complicated relationship between the actor, the play-text and the audience than Counsell allows. In this first section of *An Actor's Work*, his alter ego Tortsov asks his students,

When a real actor embarks on Hamlet's soliloquy 'To be or not to be' does he merely deliver the author's ideas, which are not his own, as mere words, and merely carry out the moves the director has given him? No, he gives much, much more, and invests the words with something of his own, his personal representation of life, his heart, his living feelings, his will . . . He speaks not as the non-existing person, Hamlet, but in his own right, in the Given Circumstances . . . And he doesn't say the words just so other people can hear the lines and understand

them. It is essential that the audience should feel his inner relationship to what is being spoken.[28]

Stanislavski envisages an actor clearly distinguishable from the authority of the text he performs. His vision of his part should be at least as understandable to spectators as its lines. In effect, the spectator encounters two objects for interpretation: the spoken play-text and a parallel performance text constituted by the actor's 'inner relationship to what he is saying'. If the two can be separated, then the potential for 'friction' between them might help spectators to reconsider the possibilities and contingencies of both.

In order to test this hypothesis, I wish now to turn to one, pivotal aspect of the realist acting process: the exploration of subtext and of the 'inner monologue'. The very textuality of these Stanislavskian terms conveys the sense of a shadow play beyond the written/spoken one: a play constructed by the actor's mind, voice, body and interactions with her partners. In the first English rendering of Stanislavski's works, Elizabeth Hapgood translates the master as declaring firmly that '[i]t is the subtext that makes us say the words we do in the play': the character's unspoken thoughts drive her words, rather than vice versa.[29] In the second part of *An Actor's Work*, the teacher Tortsov declares that

The meaning of a work of art lies in its *Subtext*. Without it words are ineffectual onstage. When we create a performance the words are the author's and the subtext is ours. If it were otherwise, the audience wouldn't make

---

[24] Worthen, *Shakespeare and the Authority of Performance*, p. 212.

[25] Andrew James Hartley, *The Shakespearean Dramaturg: A Theoretical and Practical Guide* (New York, 2005), p. 65. The work of Carol Rutter offers a particularly fine example of such dialogue between a scholar and realist acting methodology; see, for instance, her reading of Zoe Wanamaker's Emilia in *Enter the Body: Women and Representation on Shakespeare's Stage* (London, 2001), pp. 142–77.

[26] W. B. Worthen, *Shakespeare and the Force of Modern Performance* (Cambridge, 2003), p.78.

[27] Counsell, *Signs of Performance*, pp. 32, 45.

[28] Stanislavski, *An Actor's Work*, pp. 279–80.

[29] Constantin Stanislavski, *Building a Character*, trans. Elizabeth Reynolds Hapgood (New York, 1949), p. 108. No directly corresponding passage appears at this point in Jean Benedetti's translation of Stanislavski.

an effort to come to the theatre to see the actor. They'd stay at home and read the play instead... Only there [in the theatre] can you feel the real, living heart of the play, the subtext that has been created by the actor and is re-experienced in every show.[30]

Once again, the actor's work is clearly separable from the author's. This time, the former is explicitly prioritized. In order effectively to convey her role, the actor must construct an 'inner monologue' that reflects the continuous sequence of images and ideas tumbling through her character's mind both as she speaks and when she falls silent. 'When this inner monologue – inaudible to an audience, but observable on the actor's face, in his behaviour, and his form of expression – has become part of the actor's conscious,' declares Stanislavski, 'then the role is ready'.[31] The literary play-text serves as a kind of cipher to be unravelled as the actor scans her character's words and actions for vital hints of her hidden thoughts and emotions.

Theatre artists often describe Shakespearian dialogue as fully self-sufficient, able to give the actor all the information she needs without recourse to the notion of subtext. In *A Shakespearean Actor Prepares*, actor Michael York describes Stanislavski's theory as largely inapplicable to Shakespeare, in whose writing 'text and subtext (if any) are one. The Shakespeare actor is recommended to *act the text*... The character has no thoughts except those expressed in the words.'[32] In a *Players of Shakespeare* essay on her performance as Hermione, actress Alexandra Gilbreath, too, insists that 'Shakespearean characters... say what they think on the line and in the moment, without subtext. The language *is* the subtext.'[33] At the same time, however, she tells us that Hermione's line, 'Take the boy to you: he so troubles me, / 'Tis past enduring' is not 'a serious request, just a momentary desire to be left in peace.'[34] Another actor might see these lines as deadly serious, fed by Hermione's stifled panic over her husband's strange behaviour. Gilbreath's interpretation is not self-evident; she is reading subtext after all.

Similarly, in his influential guide to *Playing Shakespeare* John Barton asserts that 'the nature

of the language tells us about the nature of the character, or maybe we should say the language *is* the character'.[35] He stresses the decisive and guiding force of the author's words even in cases of irony, where, he says, 'what Shakespeare does is to write down one word or group of words..., but he wants us to find two meanings to it'.[36] A few pages later, however, he admits that 'in a way irony can't be written down' and that we can never be 'absolutely sure' that Shakespeare intends a given character to speak ironically rather than seriously.[37] 'Talking about irony', Barton confesses, 'has led us inexorably to talking about interpretation'.[38] When interiority is at stake, Shakespeare's words are never fully transparent; each actor must diagnose and make clear the character intentions that lie behind them.

In its recognition of this aspect of an actor's work, the very notion of the inner monologue tacitly depends on a construction of the literary play-text as both excess and lack. The linguistically rich Shakespearian text exemplifies this conundrum. After all, if an actor is to convey to the audience the psychological necessity for an early modern play-text's elaborate imagery, he may need to formulate a very elaborate subtext. Antony Sher gives a highly detailed example of this process when, in the midst of a meditation on playing *The Winter's Tale*, he responds to Leontes's single line, 'Inch-thick, knee-deep, o'er head and ears a forked one' by concluding that the King's

subconscious is bubbling up into his wide-awake brain. And there's a peculiar arousal to it.... He's expressing disgust, yet – like a tabloid journalist – with juices

---

[30] Stanislavski, *An Actor's Work*, p. 403.

[31] In N. M. Gorchakov, *Stanislavsky Directs*, trans. Miriam Goldina (1952; Westport, 1973), p. 266.

[32] Michael York with Adrian Brine, *A Shakespearean Actor Prepares* (Lyme, 2000), p. 315.

[33] Alexandra Gilbreath, 'Hermione in *The Winter's Tale*', in Smallwood, ed., *Players of Shakespeare* 5, p. 81.

[34] Gilbreath, 'Hermione in *The Winter's Tale*', p. 80.

[35] John Barton, *Playing Shakespeare* (London, 1982), p. 59.

[36] Barton, *Playing Shakespeare*, p. 121.

[37] Barton, *Playing Shakespeare*, p. 131.

[38] Barton, *Playing Shakespeare*, p. 133.

flowing. The normal functions of self-censorship, of self-control, are leaving him. The world is becoming dream-like, or nightmarish, exactly as it does when you have a fever... Even if I can't explain him, I know this isn't about 'evil' behaviour; this is about someone in trouble, in pain.[39]

Paradoxically, this notion of the play-text as an excess demanding explanation contains its own opposite: the notion of the play-text as a lack that must be supplied. It gives the realist actor so many words, but not necessarily all the words he wants. Thus, Sher backs up his vision of a suffering Leontes by pointing out 'how Shakespeare sprinkles the text with references to illness', but then admits that these references leave him with a new question: '*what* disease, though?'[40] The play-text offers no answer; Sher must complete it by asking 'many experts in mental disorder... to put Leontes on the couch'.[41] Out of the responses to his quest to reconcile spoken word and inner life are born the vocal and physical details of his performance.

In his exploration of the actor's process, *The Actor and the Target*, Declan Donnellan riffs on Stanislavski in order explicitly to characterize the actor's experience of the play-text in terms of a tension between spoken words and interior emotion:

Feelings and words live in different dimensions, like polar bears and whales. Speech, like any other reaction, always ends in failure. Words can start to do wonderful things only when we realize they can hardly do anything at all... [A]lthough she may fear the immense size of the text, Irina [the actor] must remember that Juliet's [the character's] problem is the precise opposite. Where Irina fears her emotion is too small to support the text, Juliet will feel her emotion is too huge to be constrained within the tiny confines of words.[42]

The actor Irina 'fears' the inadequacy of her own feelings and skills to compass the grandeur of *Romeo and Juliet*'s celebrated and elaborate rhetoric; the text appears to her as excess. In fact, however, the text is lack; 'the tiny confines of words' are inadequate to convey the great bounty of Juliet's inner experience, for 'the word is always smaller than the

feeling'.[43] The actor must 'see what is at stake for the character' and must use the text, not as an end in itself, but as a tool in the character's struggle to respond to and transform the people and objects around her in a scene (her 'targets', in Donnellan's parlance).[44] 'The more the text can be broken down into reactions to different targets the more Irina will feel free', asserts Donnellan.[45] Only by discovering the stream of her character's responses to the stimuli she encounters will the actor be liberated into true expression. The subtext, which Stanislavski described as an 'underground spring',[46] *must* flow more widely and deeply than the text that serves as its source.

Donnellan's *Troilus and Cressida* offers an example of this process. Marianne Oldham's portrayal of Helen's shift from gay abandon to desolation may or may not have been inspired by certain words in the play-text; after all, Shakespeare's queen speaks of her 'melancholy' and reminds Pandarus that 'to make a sweet lady sad is a sour offense'.[47] But Oldham's actions – her flirtatious body language crumbling into a desperate effort to hide her tears, her photogenic smile battling the trembling of her lips – spoke far more loudly than her words, progressively revealing the great beauty's apparent confidence and self-satisfaction as mere window-dressing masking her guilt and grief over her deadly role as *casus belli*. Coloured by her feelings, the sexual double entendres in Pandarus's song – 'These lovers cry, / O ho, they die!' – took

---

39 Antony Sher, 'Leontes in *The Winter's Tale*, and Macbeth', in Smallwood, ed., *Players of Shakespeare 5*, p. 94. Escolme, *Talking to the Audience*, pp. 1–2, uses Sher's Leontes as a quintessential example of a Shakespearian performance in the Stanislavskian tradition.

40 Sher, 'Leontes and Macbeth', p. 94.

41 Sher, 'Leontes and Macbeth', p. 95.

42 Declan Donnellan, *The Actor and the Target* (London, 2002), p. 183.

43 Donnellan, *The Actor and the Target*, p. 184.

44 Donnellan, *The Actor and the Target*, p. 184.

45 Donnellan, *The Actor and the Target*, p. 187.

46 Stanislavski, *An Actor's Work*, p. 402.

47 William Shakespeare, *Troilus and Cressida*, ed. G. Blakemore Evans (Boston, 1974), 3.1.69, 72–3. All subsequent references to Shakespeare will be to this edition.

on dark nuances and served only to compound her depression.[48] Her inner monologue determined the possible meanings not only of the words she uttered, but of those others directed to her.

At least, this was *my* understanding of Oldham's performance. The complex negotiation between Shakespearian play-text and Stanislavskian acting demands the participation, not only of the actor and director, but also of the spectator who encounters the performance as part of a full theatrical event. Just as the actor began the realist process of characterization by decoding the literary play-text, so each individual spectator of realist acting must decode a huge range of signs – not only characters' words, but also the tones and rhythms of their speech, their physical gestures, their relationships to the stage space, their costumes, and so on – in an effort to understand the behaviours and relationships represented. Although the realist actor generally aims to convey her version of her character's inner 'journey' with the greatest possible clarity, each audience member will read it as fits his own spatial and ideological position, perceptions and biases. Like the actor herself, he is faced with both excess (why is the actor doing and saying *all that?*) and lack (*what* does it really mean?). The answers he finds may conflate the words the actor speaks with the inner life her performance implies ('Ah, Helen is anxious about the outcome of the war – no wonder she says, "This love will undo us all"'[49]). Alternatively, they may register some degree of tension between text and subtext, as when one of my companions at Donnellan's *Troilus* turned to me and asked, 'But was that really what the words *meant?*'

Academics are often justly accused of assigning to the Shakespearian words with which they are so familiar too great a priority in performance, where, as John Russell Brown reminds us, 'the manner of speaking them, the situation in which they are spoken, and the speaker's commitment to them...tend to dominate the effect'.[50] Yet the case of my companion suggests that even a listener hearing *Troilus and Cressida* for the first time might sense some contradiction between Helen's anguished interior monologue, so painstakingly

mapped by the actress, and her words, many of which *sounded* light-hearted. After all, profound angst is not necessarily the first emotion that springs to mind when one hears such a line as Helen's 'in love, i'faith, to the very tip of the nose' (3.1.127). I do not mention this sense of conflict between verbal text and acted subtext in order to raise the red herring of 'faithfulness' to the Shakespearian script; I am interested neither to criticize Oldham's acting for betraying Shakespeare's sacred intentions nor to praise it for triumphantly asserting the primacy of performance over literature. Rather, I want to suggest that the moment when a spectator catches herself thinking 'Wait – is that really what the words *mean?*' may be the instant that most strongly situates a production within its own historical moment.

In an interview about his *Troilus*, Donnellan acknowledged that contemporary wars in the Middle East were 'absolutely' among the leading inspirations for the production.[51] 'One of the things that the play is about is about self-deception', he continued, opining that as *Troilus and Cressida* unfolds 'people lose their self-deceptions' rather as those who believed that wars in Afghanistan and Iraq 'would be over by Christmas' have been forced to abandon *their* illusions.[52] In this context, a Helen whose beauty and joie de vivre were media-manufactured simulacra and whose own efforts at self-deception crumbled into distress was very much called for. The friction between public and private, textual and subtextual Helens reflected the production's effort not simply to criticize contemporary wars as morally bankrupt, but also to stress the human cost they wreak even upon those most responsible for them. Far from kowtowing to the authority of the Shakespearian play-text, Donnellan and Oldham negotiated openly with it to convey the ideas they felt psychologically and politically pertinent to a contemporary audience.

---

48 See *Troilus and Cressida*, 3.1.121.
49 See *Troilus and Cressida* 3.1.110–11.
50 Brown, *Shakespeare and the Theatrical Event* p. 1.
51 Declan Donnellan, 'Interview with Dominic Cavendish', 7 March 2008, www.cheekbyjowl.com/productions/troilusandcressida/podcast.html, accessed 20 July 2008.
52 Donnellan, 'Interview'.

A very similar use of inner monologues to negotiate with, complicate, and even combat the possible implications of a spoken play-text characterized
Trevor Nunn's critically acclaimed production of
The Merchant of Venice, which opened in 1999 on
the Cottesloe stage at the Royal National Theatre.
During a National Theatre platform discussion of
the production, Nunn admitted that he had long
been leery of approaching the play because of the
charges of anti-semitism and racism commonly laid
against it. He chose to stage it at the Cottesloe
because he believed that such small-scale environments 'give you the possibility of exploring plays
in great psychological detail and in great subtextual as well as textual detail'.[53] Such an approach,
he thought, would facilitate a re-examination of
the play's stageworthiness. David Bamber, who
played Antonio, also spoke of 'investigating the
play in . . . what we'd describe as a sort of naturalistic way, which means . . . ditching the givens,
ditching the generalizations'.[54] Nunn and his actors
conformed to the patterns described by Worthen,
citing Shakespeare as the ultimate source of all their
discoveries. The director praised the Bard as 'our
first great naturalistic dramatist' and Bamber maintained that the psychological details of the production *must* have derived from Shakespeare, since
'[t]he greatest living playwright in the world can't
have missed anything out. It's not like being in
an episode of *The Bill*'.[55] Yet a close analysis of
the inner monologues implied by one of the production's most celebrated scenes, Shylock's farewell
to his daughter Jessica, tells a rather different
story.[56]

In Nunn's staging, this scene's dominant set piece
was a table upon which a silver-framed photograph
sat flanked by candlesticks. On the archival video
of the production held by the Theatre Museum,
London, this photograph visibly depicts a smiling woman. Such detail would, of course, not
have been clear to most theatrical spectators even
in the intimate Cottesloe. Still, the shrine-like
surroundings of the photograph and the loving
reverence with which it was treated by Shylock
(Henry Goodman) and Jessica (Gabrielle Jourdan)
suggested that it depicted an absent loved one.

Any spectator familiar with Shakespeare's play-
text and hence with Shylock's reference to his
late wife Leah (3.1.121), would have been likely
to make the connection immediately. The scene
circled around this photograph as around a ful-
crum. Jourdan's Jessica entered hurriedly, responding to her father's repeated calls (2.5.4, 6) with
nervous eagerness to please. In a passage inter-
polated into an earlier scene (2.3), Nunn's audience had already seen Shylock berating Jessica in
Yiddish for a failure in housekeeping, provoking her description of his house as 'hell' (2.3.2).
Now, as he pressed his keys into her hand and
addressed her as 'my girl' (2.5.15), they once again
broke into a language associated with their shared
Jewish heritage. Ignoring Launcelot Gobbo, who
hovered on the fringes of the scene, Goodman's
Shylock led his daughter to the photograph of
her mother and began to sing 'Eshet Chayil' ('A
Woman of Valour'), a Hebrew hymn in praise of
an ideal wife and mother often sung or recited
at the celebration of Shabbat. His eyes filling
with tears, Shylock nodded in approval as Jessica – her own voice tremulous with emotion –
joined him. Even an audience member utterly
unfamiliar with the hymn or its contents might
have inferred that this was a familiar ritual which
bound father and daughter in their love and grief
for the departed Leah.

The tone of the scene changed radically, however, when Launcelot mentioned the possibility of a 'masque' (2.5.23). Already pacing the
room, troubled and 'right loath to go' (2.5.16),

---

[53] 'NT25: 1999 (*The Merchant of Venice*)', Platform Interview
with Trevor Nunn, Henry Goodman, Gabrielle Jourdan,
and David Bamber, 18 September 2001, Cottesloe Theatre,
Royal National Theatre (Audio Recording, Royal National
Theatre Archives).

[54] 'NT 25: 1999 (*The Merchant of Venice*)'.

[55] 'NT 25: 1999 (*The Merchant of Venice*)'.

[56] The analysis that follows is based upon two live viewings of
Nunn's production, one at the Cottesloe Theatre in September 1999 and one at the Olivier Theatre in March 2000, as
well as upon viewings of the archival videos of the production held by the Royal National Theatre Archives (filmed in
the Cottesloe with one camera) and the Theatre Museum
Archives (filmed in the Olivier with three cameras).

Goodman's Shylock whipped round in consternation on 'What, are there masques?' (2.5.28),
emphasizing the word 'masques' as if it were one
he feared as well as despised. Increasingly agitated,
he rounded on Jessica:

> Hear you me, Jessica;
> Lock up my doors, and when you hear the drum
> And the vile squealing of the wry-neck'd fife,
> Clamber not you up to the casements then,
> Nor thrust your head into the public street
> To gaze on Christian fools with varnish'd faces;
> But stop my house's ears, I mean my casements[.]
> (2.5.28–34)

Where Shylock and Jessica had earlier clasped
hands, intimate cohabitants of Shylock's 'sober
house' (2.5.36) and of the stage space, Jourdan's
Jessica now cowered away from her father. Her
flinching demeanor was justified at the climax of
the speech, 'stop my house's ears', when Shylock –
apparently quite spontaneously and without warning – struck her full across the face.

Reeling from the blow, she looked back at him
with shock, pain and reproach, to which he in turn
responded with immediately obvious remorse. He
delivered 'I mean my casements' with a placatory
gesture, as if recognizing a sudden lapse that had
horrified him as much as it had her. Apart from
a sudden return to suspicious threat when Shylock questioned Jessica about Launcelot's aside –
'What says that fool of Hagar's offspring, ha?'
(2.5.44) – Goodman played the rest of the scene
on an almost pleading note; he was even willing
to praise the much-despised Launcelot if it would
help him to re-establish some sense of reciprocal exchange with his daughter. As he departed,
reminding her of 'a proverb never stale in thrifty
mind' (2.5.55), he appeared to have succeeded, for
she joined in and capped his rhyme on 'fast bind,
fast find' (2.5.54). But the unity between them
proved illusory. He had scarcely left her before, her
tears bursting forth, she addressed his back with
vehement anger: 'Farewell, and if my fortunes be
not cross'd, / I have a father, you a daughter, lost'
(2.5.56–7).

As a spectator of this scene in action, first at the
Cottesloe and again in its revival at the Olivier, I
decoded two key inner narratives. The first concerned the psychological struggle between father
and child. The actors' intonations and physical
actions worked to show how thoroughly the two
were bound by their shared emotional history and
how emotionally painful their parting would be.
Shylock clasped his daughter's hand and touched
her face as he lead her toward her dead mother's
photograph; his inner monologue appeared to
link beloved daughter to much-missed wife. Tears
sprang to Jessica's eyes as she sang with him: signs
of her attachment to her parents and perhaps of
her guilt at her impending abandonment of her
father. The slap Shylock gave Jessica on hearing
Gobbo's mention of 'masques' demonstrated the
darker side of their relationship. Shylock's inability to control his temper and his anxiety for his
only remaining family remember resulted in abuse
which alienated the very child he so longed to
keep with him. He realized his terrible error and
tried to placate her with renewed gentleness, but
her apparent acceptance of rapprochement merely
concealed the burning anger that would drive her
decisively into Lorenzo's arms ('Farewell!').

The second key factor informing Shylock's and
Jessica's inner narratives in this scene was their consciousness of shared Jewish identity. This inner consciousness was most explicitly conveyed when the
two joined in singing 'Eshet Chayil'. Their performance of Jewish tradition seemed particularly
significant given the period setting of Nunn's production, which took place in a Europe on the brink
of the Holocaust. In Stanislavski's 'System', choices
about subtext are inseparable from decisions about
the 'given circumstances', and this key 'given circumstance' certainly affected spectators' potential
understandings of Shylock's inner monologue as
he quarrelled with his daughter. His slap to Jessica
expressed not only fatherly possessiveness, but also
pent-up anxiety about their precarious position as
Jews in a society whose apparent tolerance of them
could easily collapse during carnival masquerade.
The constant threat of abuse from *outside* the family
created abuse *inside* it. The aspects of the characters'

behaviour that might seem most disturbing to contemporary spectators – Shylock's stifling treatment of his daughter and Jessica's apparent willingness to abandon her father and religion – were not only explained psychologically but explained twice over.

In such moments, Nunn followed his illustrious predecessors from Henry Irving to Jonathan Miller by transforming *The Merchant of Venice* into a 'modern' statement about the prejudices and divisions that fracture social and familial relationships.[57] Did the production's Stanislavskian emphasis on the inner lives of its characters work to obscure this act of appropriation by assigning credit to the universality of Shakespeare's characters, as realism's critics tend to suggest? On the contrary, I would argue, choices such as the very obvious interpolation of 'Eshet Chayil' alerted spectators to the fact that they were watching a re-vision of the Shakespearian text. For some reviewers, such insertions appeared as unnecessary, even offensive, trespasses against the integrity of Shakespeare's vision. Alastair Macaulay, for instance, complained of the 'over-embellishment' involved in having Shylock speak 'additional lines of German [sic] at home' and lead 'Jessica in Yiddish [sic] duets'.[58] For the artists behind the production, however, such interpolations were amply justified by the need to clarify subtext. In an interview with Rivka Jakobson, Goodman confessed that 'there is no Hebrew in the play' but declared that he himself had brought the hymn into rehearsal and Nunn had chosen to put it into the show because

I thought this guy is . . . he does not have to be, but if you assume he is . . . an Orthodox Jew looking after his daughter. The mother is not there and therefore he has to perform the mother's functions. He has to keep the Sabbath table, he has to light the candles, and he would know all that.[59]

Goodman's sense of Shylock's interiority constructs the play-text as lack rather than as transhistorical plenitude. If the audience is fully to understand Shylock's heart, it *must* hear 'Eshet Chayil' and must see the widower, with tears in his eyes, stroke the face of the daughter who reminds him

of the dead Leah. By implication, this inner monologue and its outward manifestations critique the very Shakespearean play-text on which they rely as insufficiently aware of the deep Jewish culture they represent.

In another interview, Goodman acknowledged the necessity for such implied critique at the turn of the twenty-first century, remarking that 'now any production of the play brings with it the inevitable sensibilities of audience and actors in a post-Holocaust world'.[60] The actors' implied inner monologues were, in fact, far more concerned with solving the perceived 'dilemma of a post-Holocaust production'[61] by relating Shylock's and Jessica's actions to the psychological pressures of cultural marginalization and persecution than with conveying universalized human truths or affirming the Bard's authority. Unsurprisingly, then, Nunn's *Merchant* closed with a crumpled Jessica keening 'Eshet Chayil'. Her inner monologue of grief for her father and for her own loss of identity trumped the cheerful Shakespearian ending as subtext supplemented and justified the text's perceived limitations.

Still, here as at the performance of *Troilus* I witnessed, subtext did not necessarily succeed in remaking the text in its own image – at least, not for all spectators. In an article syndicated in a number of Jewish publications, scholar and activist Racelle Weiman responded to the television film

---

[57] For readings of this aspect of *The Merchant*'s performance history, see particularly James C. Bulman, *Shakespeare in Performance: 'The Merchant of Venice'* (Manchester, 1990) and John Gross, *Shylock: A Legend and its Legacy* (New York, 1992).

[58] Alastair Macaulay, 'Shakespeare Squeezed into a Forced Attitude', Review of *The Merchant of Venice* dir. Trevor Nunn (Cottesloe Theatre), *Financial Times*, 22 June 1999.

[59] Rivka Jacobson, 'On Jewishness, Shylock and Tevya: Rivka Jacobson talks to Henry Goodman', *British Theatre Guide*, accessed July 20 2008 www.britishtheatreguide.info/otherresources/interviews/HenryGoodman2.htm.

[60] Judi Herman, 'What's to be done with Shylock?' *Daily Telegraph*, 11 August 1999.

[61] This phrase is used as a section heading in Peter Reynolds's workpack on *The Merchant of Venice* (Royal National Theatre, 1999), created by the RNT for students who attended the production while studying the play.

based upon Nunn's stage production by arguing that although a director like Nunn 'can remove lines, he can shuffle them around, assign them to different characters, he can even add text, as long as it is not English . . . the bottom line is that the text remains the text'.[62] The spoken word resists the gestural score; Shylock still 'dreams of moneybags', even if he squeezes his daughter's hand tenderly as he mentions it. For Weiman, Nunn's and Goodman's insistence on Shylock's three-dimensional interiority merely created a mixture of offensive generalizations and untenable contradictions; his uncontrollable bursts of anger condemned him as a bad man who deserved what he got, and '[h]is strong identification as a religious man ma[de] his courtroom scene . . . even more outrageous'.[63] Like Goodman, Weiman recognized friction between play-text and theatrical praxis, but unlike him she accounted the play-text the winner in their combat.

The negotiation that took place between spoken text and embodied subtext in Nunn's *Merchant* had much in common with that in Donnellan's *Troilus*. In both, actors used realist processes to construct inner monologues by which they squared their characters with the demands they perceived in their own time and place. In both, the inner monologue tacitly superseded the verbal script as the dominant performance text. In both, the play-text's structures lodged in the minds of at least some members of the audience in a manner that countered the psychological narratives constructed by actors. Contradiction and struggle, rather than

smoothly coherent unitary identities, were the result.

Such tension between two performance texts, one born of editorial and print tradition and the other of theatrical praxis, is to be found everywhere on our stages. If we as scholars choose to emphasize either the text *or* the performance process as solely constitutive of theatrical meanings, we will undervalue the productive and instructive tensions produced when they clash with one another. If we treat realist acting as an easy scapegoat for the ills of mainstream Shakespearian theatre, we risk not only distancing ourselves from today's practitioners but also ignoring the true complexity of realism's negotiations with pre-realist drama. A more thorough exploration of the theatrical rhetoric by which actors construct and audiences read inner monologues can help to show us *where* a particular production places a Shakespearian narrative in relation to our time, *how* realist acting struggles to make the play-text 'work' for contemporary audiences, *why* such gyrations are accounted necessary – and perhaps also *why*, at some times and for some spectators, they fail in their missions. As historians of our own theatre, it behoves us to take subtext as seriously as spoken text and to look further into moments where they contradict as well as confirm one another. It behoves us, in short, to 'mind the gap'.

---

[62] Racelle R. Weiman, 'A Source of Continued Pain and Disappointment', *Jewish Federation Dayton*, 11 October 2001.
[63] Weiman, 'A Source'.

MORE JAPANIZED, CASUAL AND TRANSGENDER SHAKESPEARES

SHOICHIRO KAWAI

Tokyo is alive with Shakespeare productions. In 2007, for instance, there were fifty-two, excluding foreign productions, roughly one new Japanese production a week. This immense popularity of Shakespeare began in the early 1970s. Until the 1960s, Shakespeare's plays could be seen only two to seven times a year.[1] The Royal Shakespeare Company's first visit to Japan in 1970 with Terry Hands's *The Merry Wives of Windsor* and Trevor Nunn's *The Winter's Tale* (with Judi Dench as Hermione/Perdita) was presumably a powerful impetus. The term 'Shakespeare boom' first appeared in newspapers in late 1971, when they announced the line-up of Shakespeare productions for the following year: the highly regarded theatre company Bungaku-za held a 'Shakespeare Festival', producing three plays, and the Royal Shakespeare Company visited Japan for the second time with three Shakespeare productions directed by John Barton. There were many more Shakespeare productions in that year: twenty-one in total, an amazingly large number, although rather few by twenty-first century standards.

But 1972 seemed to have been an exception, for in 1973 the number of Shakespeare productions decreased to ten; nevertheless, a sense of momentum was gradually recovered when Yukio Ninagawa directed his first Shakespeare production, *Romeo and Juliet*, in 1974,[2] and in 1975 Norio Deguchi's Shakespeare Company started producing all the thirty-seven plays of Shakespeare, costumed in jeans and T-shirts, completing the cycle in six years. The 'boom' continued in the 1980s, and the construction of the Tokyo Globe in 1988 spurred

it on. By the time that the World Shakespeare Congress was held in Tokyo in 1991, the yearly output of Shakespeare productions amounted to well over forty, culminating in fifty-two productions (including foreign ones) in 1993. This was the first major peak and the number then declined a little in the late 1990s; the Tokyo Globe then closed down in 2002 because of deteriorating management, after it lost its position as a central venue for Shakespeare productions. In the twenty-first century, Shakespeare productions have become so frequent, diverse and eclectic that the Tokyo Globe seems to have lost its power to attract large audiences for visiting foreign Shakespeare productions.

In the last decade of the twentieth century, there was apparently a change in the way audiences appreciated Shakespeare's plays. The Japanese, familiarized with Shakespeare, seemed no longer to care for 'authenticity' in Shakespeare productions. English productions of Shakespeare still continued to be performed in Japan but it did not matter whether Shakespeare was performed in English, German, Russian or Japanese: audiences enjoyed the Berliner Ensemble's German *Richard II* and Peter Stein's Russian *Hamlet*, both of which came

---

[1] For figures on the number of Shakespeare productions in Japan until 1994, see Ryuta Minami, 'Chronological Table of Shakespeare Productions in Japan 1866–1994', in Takashi Sasayama, J. R. Mulryne and Margaret Shewring, eds., *Shakespeare and the Japanese Stage* (Cambridge, 1998), pp. 255–331. Data after 1994 is based on my own research.

[2] For Yukio Ninagawa's Shakespeare productions, see my chapter in John Russell Brown, ed., *The Routledge Companion to Directors' Shakespeare* (London, 2008).

to Japan in 2002. Appropriations of Shakespeare became a norm and people began to seek their own Shakespeares. This trend continues at the beginning of the twenty-first century.

Not surprisingly, theatre people in their thirties, who were brought up during the early 'Shakespeare boom', founded their own 'Shakespeare companies' in the 1990s. In 1990, Kaoru Edo founded the Tokyo Shakespeare Company to produce her own adaptations of Shakespeare as well as the plays of her award-winning novelist husband, Hikaru Okuizumi, such as *The Trial of Macbeth*. In 1993, Kazumi Shimodate founded his Shakespeare Company based in Tohoku in order to transform Shakespeare through the use of a northern dialect. In 1995, Canon Planning launched the 'Shakespeare for Children' series for family audiences every summer. One of the members, Takayuki Ayanogi, founded the Academic Shakespeare Company in 1996 in order to perform Shakespeare's plays twice a year, in addition to his participation in every production of the 'Shakespeare for Children' series until 2006. Another member, Kotaro Yoshida, formed the theatre company AUN with Yoshihiro Kurita and has been producing Shakespeare twice a year since 2000, while Kurita, after leaving AUN, began 'Ryutopia Noh-stage Shakespeare' in 2004, and has been producing Shakespeare every year since then.

The older generation has been similarly enthusiastic. In 1993, at the age of sixty, the celebrated actor Mikijiro Hira announced his decision to perform in the complete Shakespeare canon; he has steadily increased the number of the plays he has performed in. Starting in 1998, Yukio Ninagawa's 'Sai-no-kuni Shakespeare' series has produced Shakespeare twice a year at the Sai-no-kuni Theatre in Saitama prefecture; his twenty-first production (*The Winter's Tale*) is already planned for January 2009. Norio Deguchi also continues to work with his much rejuvenated Shakespeare Company, and Eizo Endo's Itabashi Theatre Centre has actively produced Shakespeare's plays every year since 1980. Some theatre companies that had begun by performing other plays have recently begun to perform Shakespeare's plays annually. Some exam-

ples of such companies are Types, which has been performing Shakespeare's plays since 2002, En, since 2005, and Studio Life, since 2006.

The fact that there are so many Shakespeare companies and Shakespeare series confirms the variety of ways in which Shakespeare is appreciated. Earlier, people used to try to learn something from Shakespeare but they now seem to want simply to be entertained by his plays. The Reduced Shakespeare Company's *The Complete Works of William Shakespeare (abridged)*, popular on the West End stage, was translated into Japanese and first performed by Japanese actors in 2002. It ran for a hundred performances in 2008. Some of Shakespeare's plays have also been adapted into rock musicals[3] and TV dramas.[4] There was even a professional wrestling match entitled *King Lear* in August 2008. According to a flyer, the champion 'Great King Lear' would try to defend his championship against two teams – the 'Regan WX' and 'Cornwall Kobayashi' team and the 'Goneril Taniguchi', 'Albany Benkei' and 'Oswald Imai' team – while 'Cordelia Ito' would fight a death match against 'Edgar Kasai'. The dramatization of the match involved actors and a violinist; however, it was basically a real wrestling match.[5] There is no telling how Shakespeare will be adapted next.

CHOOSE YOUR OWN SHAKESPEARE

The current age is one of 'my own Shakespeare', in which the theatregoer can pick from a long list of productions. If you have favourite actors, this will help you to choose your own series or company. Among others, the Shakespeare for Children series may be a typical new form for Shake-

---

[3] Two instances from 2006, Theatre Company Shinkansen's rock musical *Metal Macbeth* and Takarazuka Company's 'Rock Opera: *Rome at Dawn*', based on *Julius Caesar*, are discussed by Yukari Yoshihara in her 'Popular Shakespeare in Japan', *Shakespeare Survey 60* (Cambridge, 2007), pp. 130–40.

[4] Nippon Television Network Corporation broadcast 'Shakespeare Drama Special', two modernized drama programmes based on *King Lear* and *Romeo and Juliet*, on 6 and 7 April 2007.

[5] The match was produced in Yokohama by Big Japan Prowrestling.

speare in the twenty-first century, where people have begun to enjoy Shakespeare in a more casual manner. Although the series claims to be aimed at children, its high theatricality in the style of Theatre de Complicite has been highly acclaimed and has received many awards. The director Seisuke Yamasaki's method is simple, stylish and impressive. For stage settings, they use only the small wooden desks and chairs that can be found in old elementary schools. These desks and chairs are quickly rearranged on the stage in order to create a long table, a step, a throne, a hill, a gate or whatever is needed. To emphasize the magic of theatre, only eight or nine actors perform all the characters through quick changes.

At the beginning of every production, the actors appear on stage together as a chorus, all clad in black gowns and hoods, clapping their hands in rhythm and moving in a formation as if they are flowing along the stage. When some of them take off their gowns and hoods to reveal the costumes they are wearing underneath, they become characters in a new scene. Yamasaki is also a talented ventriloquist and he manipulates a *bunraku*-sized 'Shakespeare puppet' with a prominent head (Illustration 49). The puppet is a type of mascot for the series that never fails to appear on the stage in every production, commenting on the play for the audience and joining the actors by acting as a character. Each play is adapted to ensure that it falls within 'the two hours' traffic of [the] stage'. From the first production, the series was staged at the Tokyo Globe for eight consecutive summers until the theatre was closed in 2002. The Tokyo Globe was reopened in 2004 with Shoji Kokami's production of *Romeo and Juliet* in my own new translation and the Shakespeare for Children series returned to the Tokyo Globe in 2006 and 2007. However, the new Globe has been lacklustre in its support for Shakespeare productions under a new managing company more interested in young pop stars.

In 2008, for their fourteenth production of the series, Yamasaki's company performed *Cymbeline*. In this production, a hooded group dressed in black moves around the stage, clapping their hands as usual, some taking off their hoods and gowns in

49. Shakespeare Puppet as Jupiter, in *Cymbeline*, directed by Seisuke Yamasaki, 2008.

order to reveal a princess and her lover Posthumus, then the King, the Queen and her son. When a scene is completed, the characters are again assimilated into the group. The enjoyment involved in the transformation of characters is a particular feature of their work, as the production is heavily dependent on doubling: the Queen changes into Arviragus, who decapitates Cloten, and then Cloten is reborn as Guiderius. Thus, there is a good reason for the Queen and Cloten not to be present in the final scene. The denouement is not only happy but comical, as Iachimo, after confessing what he has done, dashes out and returns as Belarius in order to confess his past offence.

The use of the Shakespeare puppet in this production is also effective. It plays Jupiter, a character who can fly, and in 1.6 it appears as Cornelius's master, sitting cozily on the front of Cornelius's

50. Seisuke Yamasaki as Cornelius, Maki Izawa as Queen, in *Cymbeline*, 1.6, directed by Seisuke Yamasaki, 2008.

bike (Illustration 50). The puppet converses with Yamasaki-as-Cornelius and reveals to the audience that the drug that Cornelius has just handed over to the Queen is not a poison but a sleeping potion that makes the drinker look as if he or she is dead. Considering the fact that a sleeping potion with such a curious effect belongs to the realm of fantasy, in the same way that Jupiter's appearance does, the puppet suitably performs the function of diminishing the awkwardness of these fantastical devices.

Yamasaki's simple but dramatic staging may be comparable to Paul Stebbings's with his International Theatre Company London, which has been visiting Japan since 1992 and has performed Shakespeare's plays every year since 2001. Stebbings's company consists of only six or seven actors and uses no stage settings, thereby stimulating our imagination by evoking Elizabethan touring companies that performed with a limited cast. The per-

formances by Paul Stebbings's company are rhythmical, making good use of musical instruments and vocal sounds. The techniques of both companies may also be compared to those employed in Yasunari Takahashi's *The Braggart Samurai* (1991), a Kyogen adaptation of *The Merry Wives of Windsor*, staged by six Kyogen performers. This adaptation involves a fascinating scene where Falstaff is carried in a non-existent basket by two servants. Mansaku Nomura as Falstaff, supposedly seated in the basket, synchronizes his movements with the two carriers so that it looks as if he is really being carried.[6]

'Kyogenizing' Shakespeare is a good way of furthering our understanding of his plays, for Shakespeare is arguably more akin to Kyogen than

---

6 For *The Braggart Samurai*, see Yasunari Takahashi, 'Kyogenising Shakespeare/Shakespeareanising Kyogen' and its script in *Shakespeare and the Japanese Stage*, pp. 214–40.

to modern Western theatre. There are striking similarities in structure between the Noh stage and Shakespeare's stage at the Globe: two pillars on an empty space with no curtains, no backcloths and no stage set. In Takahashi's second Kyogen adaptation, *The Kyogen of Errors* (2001), based on *The Comedy of Errors*, there is a scene in which Mansai Nomura, the Kyogen performer playing two roles equivalent to Dromios of Ephesus and of Syracuse, has to be present both inside and outside the gate at the same time. Again, there is no real gate. Other Kyogen performers, all clad in black, somewhat similar to Yamasaki's chorus, stand in a line with their hands on one another's shoulders to indicate a gate, and Mansai, stepping before them, speaks to his other self, who is inside the gate. When a drum beats, the gate impersonators put down their hands and the gate disappears; at the same time, Mansai steps back through them and speaks as the servant inside the gate. When the drum-beat is repeated, the gate reappears and Mansai steps forward and speaks as the servant outside.

When *The Kyogen of Errors* was performed at the London Globe in 2001 I was commissioned to provide English surtitles. Watching a Shakespearian play first 'japanized' and then adapting it back into English was intriguing. Because there are many Japanese elements in such an adaptation, one cannot simply return to Shakespeare's original language. For example, in the final scene, Egeon and the Abbess's dialogue about their lost son is rendered in Noh chant or *utai*. This formality must be expressed in some way or other, and the following excerpt from the surtitles may indicate how this Japanized Shakespeare was rendered back into English:

> *Egeon.* Am I awake? Or in a dream?
> With joy I want to scream.
> Tempests are kind after all
> For such fortune did befall.
> But tell me if the other boy
> Is alive and well to our joy.
> *Abbess.* To Awaji Island our child
> Was taken by pirates wild.
> Alone to this abbey I came,
> And an unhappy nun I became.

51. Mansai Nomura as Richard III, Kayoko Shiraishi as Margaret, in *A Country Stealer*, an adaptation of *Richard III*, directed by Mansai Nomura, 2007.

The Japanese *utai* sounds graver and more serene than this doggerel and it contrasts with the hustle and bustle of the play. The success of this adaptation seemed to lie in its acceleration of the confusions and accentuation of the final reunion.

Another attempt at Kyogenizing Shakespeare is my own adaptation of *Richard III, Kuni-Nusubito or The Country Stealer* (2007), in which Mansai played Akusaburo (Richard), a character who intensely covets the throne (Illustration 51). Unlike the previous two Kyogen adaptations, this one was a collaborative effort, involving Kyogen, modern drama, mime and traditional Japanese music. When Akusaburo, having seduced Lady Anne, speaks the Japanese equivalent of 'Shine out, fair sun, till I have bought a glass, / That I may see my shadow as I pass', a mime artist slides down to Akusaburo's feet and imitates his actions, pretending to be his shadow on the ground. This representation of the shadowy nature of his character later stands up and becomes an observer, sometimes lending a helping hand to Akusaburo's wicked thoughts.

Although the setting, names, and costumes are rendered Japanese, the plot remains true to the original: it is a Japanese version of *Richard III* performed on a Noh stage. The conspiratorial team of Richard, Buckingham and Catesby are played by Kyogen performers in their unique acting style, and their victims are performed by modern actors; thus, one may clearly perceive how the normal world is thwarted by the wickedness humorously represented by Kyogen performers. In fact, Richard's often facetious direct address to the audience is very similar to that frequently employed in Kyogen. Further, it was not difficult to Kyogenize Richard's drama of winning the throne through treachery, for Kyogen is full of characters who hit upon some expedient to satisfy their desires. One has to add, however, that their crimes are always petty ones, no more than, for instance, stealthily drinking their master's *sake* without permission. Moreover, there is always complicity between the errant Kyogen character and the audience, although the character bears all the blame when the play ends with the routine of the offender running away, shouting '*Yurusaremase*' (Forgive me), and the offended running after him, repeating '*Yarumaizo*' (I will not).

Such complicity with the audience is explicitly established in this adaptation. For example, when the Lord Mayor is persuaded by Buckingham that they have to entreat Akusaburo to be their king, the Lord Mayor steps down in front of the Noh stage and speaks directly to the audience as his citizens, asking them to cry 'God save Akusaburo, our royal King!' Akusaburo instantly asks Hisahide (Buckingham), 'And did they so?', but Hisahide glares at the audience and says, 'No, so God help me. They spake not a word' (3.7.23–4), always getting a laugh.

Later, when Akusaburo appears with an array of bonzes (Buddhist monks) chanting a sutra, the Mayor appeals to him, saying 'your citizens entreat

you', and the audience knows that he is referring to them. When Hisahide pretends to be infuriated and gives up his entreaty, he walks among the audience asking them to leave: 'Come, citizens. 'Swounds! I'll entreat no more' (209). He speaks to several 'citizens' in the auditorium and, when he confirms that they will not move, he turns to Akusaburo with a histrionic look of surprise: 'Look, they will not budge an inch! Can you ignore their fervent wish?' Then, Akusaburo yields, confirming that he has been compelled by 'you' (pointing to the audience).

Comedy turns into tragedy, however, when Richard abandons Buckingham and decides to murder the young princes in the tower. Such brutality can never be staged in the mode of Kyogen, for all the characters in Kyogen are humane, whatever their human weaknesses. Moreover, there is no true villain in Kyogen. At this point, therefore, Mansai shifts his acting style to that of modern theatre in order to impersonate an archvillain. In conceiving our adaptation, we decided that the play is not simply a delineation of the nature of evil. Considering the fact that it is Shakespeare's first play in which the protagonist soliloquizes about himself, we decided that we should focus on how his 'conscience' overpowers him when he becomes conscious of his subjective self. The word 'conscience', repeatedly used in the play, carries its now obsolete meaning as 'consciousness' or 'inmost thoughts'(see *OED* 2.a and 3, quoting *Cymbeline* and *Timon*). Richard has to fall because he is confronted with his consciousness or his inner self. For this reason, the technique for depicting the 'existence' of the dead became important. Although Richard rationally thinks that the dead do not exist, they do exist in his mind to oppress him. Mansai decided that in this play, death should be signified when a Noh mask, carried by the shadow, is placed upon a character's face. In Akusaburo's dream before the final battle, the ghosts appear with Noh masks on. Because of the masks, they become more than the resurrected dead: they are agonizing psyches directly encroaching upon Akusaburo's spirit. In this way, we were freed from modern realism that laughs away occult phenomena. In the world of Noh, the return of the dead to the world of the living is a familiar motif and one may even argue that Noh masks themselves represent inscrutable psychic entities filled with deep-seated grudges.

The female parts – Anne, Queen Elizabeth, Margaret and the Duchess of York – were all played by Kayoko Shiraishi in order to emphasize the unison of their rancour and curses. There is a scene where Shiraishi transformed herself and became the four characters one after another, delivering their curses as she changed costumes (designed by Junko Koshino). Shiraishi, who has a long experience of playing Shakespearian characters, is a remarkable actress who has the strength to handle the formality of Noh and Kyogen. In a sense, she transcended the characters, so that her curses reverberated in harmony with those of the dead.

Akusaburo himself wore the mask of *Buaku*, or the wicked man, in the latter half of the play, and when he was killed in the battle, his body evaporated, leaving the mask on the stage. This suggests that any person who puts on the mask may turn into another Akusaburo. At the beginning of this play, a modern woman (Shiraishi) with a parasol, apparently on a holiday, visited this old Noh stage, where she found the *Buaku* mask. In the final scene, we returned to that first scene and again saw her holding the mask in her hand and reciting Basho's famous *haiku* about warriors fighting, dying and leaving a vestige behind. She then put down the mask and left the stage, without knowing that those psychic entities were still there on the stage, though the audience was allowed a glimpse of them. Shakespeare's plays are similar to the Noh stage, a vestige of an old culture, filled with passionate thoughts, and one has only to pick up a mask lying there to revitalize its hidden power.

The idea of performing Shakespeare on the Noh stage is not new, for Yukio Ninagawa used it in *The Tempest: A Rehearsal on a Noh Stage on Sado Island*, premiered in 1987 and revived in 2000. In this production, Prospero (Mikijiro Hira), acting like a theatre director, was imagined to be Zeami, the fifteenth-century Noh master, who, like Prospero, was once exiled to an island. As the subtitle

suggests, the structure of the production revolved around a rehearsal of *The Tempest*. Before the play began, the audience saw actors preparing themselves and even saw Ninagawa onstage giving notes to Hira. During the performance, the actors always remained onstage, watching one another perform. It worked brilliantly as a framework to underscore the metatheatrical structure of the play. Admittedly, in this production a small replica of a Noh stage on the main stage was not effectively used other than as a symbol.

The real Noh stage has been employed for Shakespeare productions by Yoshihiro Kurita in his Ryutopia Noh-stage Shakespeare series since 2004. Kurita's company enjoyed a triumphant success in April 2006 when they participated in the Craiova International Shakespeare Festival held in Romania with several critics agreeing that the most impressive production in the festival was their *Winter's Tale* (first performed in 2005 in Tokyo and Niigata and revived in 2008 in both cities and elsewhere). Praising the play's 'brilliant synthesis of Noh and Shakespeare', one British critic wrote in the *Financial Times*:

The formalized movement of Noh, its deliberation to the point of almost imperceptible slowness (such as Misaki Machiya's Perdita left rotating on stage throughout the interval), blended with what sounded like a more naturalistic delivery of the text. This does not solve all problems, but it was a work of luminous beauty both conceptually and as a piece of drama.[7]

We have to think twice, however, before we refer to 'the formalized movement of Noh' in this production, since it involved no Noh performers. No degree of imitated formality and slowness can turn a modern actor into a Noh performer. Kurita is honest in calling the series 'Noh-stage Shakespeare' because it is performed on a Noh stage; thus, he never pretends to aim for a synthesis of Noh and Shakespeare. Michael Hattaway rightly calls the production 'Noh-inspired', and one may indeed praise the production, as he puts it, in that

---

7 Ian Shuttleworth, 'The Bard Reinterpreted', *Financial Times*, 3 May 2006.

52. Ukon Ichikawa as Macbeth, Emiya Ichikawa (male) as Lady Macbeth, in *Macbeth 07*, Ryutopia Noh Theatre Shakespeare Series, directed by Yoshihiro Kurita, produced by Ryutopia, 2007.

'the control of [the actors'] movements and precision of the *mise en scène* made for an evening of sheer beauty and rarified pathos'.[8] Indeed, Kurita's Noh-stage Shakespeare is always precise and beautiful, and we might identify it as a synthesis of the Noh space and Shakespeare.

Kurita's strength lies in his profound knowledge of traditional Japanese dancing (*Nihon Buyo*) and Kabuki, which he has spent many years learning and which enables him to make beautiful use of traditional Japanese space. In this sense, his most successful production may have been *Macbeth* (2006, 2007) which featured two famous Kabuki actors. Ukon Ichikawa as Macbeth spoke and moved somewhat in Kabuki fashion, making Macbeth histrionic, while Emiya Ichikawa, the Kabuki *onnagata* or female impersonator, played Lady Macbeth more realistically (Illustration 52). The three witches were played by young women in red

kimonos with movements that suggested mechanical dolls. The presence of these girls who moved slowly in kimonos is actually a trademark of this series, and they certainly offered a tense and beautiful formality. Their doll-like movements helped the audience understand that they were manipulated by Hecate, whose role was performed by a celebrated expert of Japanese dancing. As always, Kurita's precise *mise-en-scène* made the drama suitable for performance on a Noh stage. Kurita also made full use of the bridgeway (*hashigakari*) on the stage, which is supposed to be a bridge between this world and the other. The two worlds may be the play world and the real world or this world and

---

8 Quoted from Michael Hattaway, 'The Craiova Shakespeare Festival of 2006 (25 April–3 May 2006)', on the website 'Shakespeare in Europe' (http://pages.unibas.ch/shine/CraiovaReport.htm), accessed on 29 July 2008.

the netherworld. Therefore, in the 2007 revival of this production, Lady Macbeth stood at the farther end of the bridgeway, waiting for Macbeth to join her, and Macbeth, having been killed, stood up and walked slowly on the bridgeway, moving towards her, indicating the departure of his soul. It was an intriguing moment with Kabuki theatricality becoming part of the Noh stage.

Kurita is a very experienced director of Shakespeare. Actor-director Kotaro Yoshida, co-founder with Kurita of the AUN theatre company, is now an essential part of the cast for Ninagawa's Sai-no-kuni Shakespeare Series and I shall turn to his work, as the standard-bearer for current Shakespeare productions. Born in 1959, Kotaro Yoshida has twenty-seven years of experience performing Shakespearian characters. As of October 2008, he has performed in more than twenty-three different plays of Shakespeare and participated in more than fifty-five Shakespeare productions. That twenty-seven of these productions, around half the total, have been performed in the first eight years of this century may be another indicator of how the demand for Shakespeare productions has increased in the new century.

Early in his career, Yoshida belonged to Deguchi's Shakespeare Company, and he has been awarded theatre prizes for his performances as Shylock in 1988 and as Hamlet in 2001 (a prize also in part for his role as Richard II under Yamasaki's direction in the Shakespeare for Children series). In a few years, he will have been a part of sixty different Shakespeare productions. This will be an extraordinary achievement, considering the fact that he is still only in his late forties and has already performed at the Royal National Theatre, at the Barbican and in large theatres in Japan. Moreover, he is a very good director at AUN and his interpretations of plays are insightful and persuasive.

He is particularly good at playing authoritative, powerful or violent characters: in *All's Well* (2006), he played a domineering King and made the last scene very problematic, as it ought to be; in *Richard III* (2008), he played a bloodthirsty Richard, butchering his victims with a baseball bat, reminiscent of Robert De Niro as Al Capone in the film *The Untouchables* (1987). His performance of the title role in *Titus Andronicus*, directed by Yukio Ninagawa and first performed in 2004, was so well received at Stratford-upon-Avon in 2007 that there is no need to repeat the details here. Since then, he has appeared in almost all the performances of the Sai-no-kuni Shakespeare series by Ninagawa (*As You Like It*, *The Comedy of Errors*, *Coriolanus*, *Othello*, *Lear* and *Much Ado*). His next title role was Othello in 2007. His was a masculine, violent Othello, contrasted with You Aoi's girlish and timid Desdemona. The stage set for the production was simple: staircases on both sides of the stage leading offstage and a long corridor suspended high above in the air. Because the corridor was almost at the level of the ceiling, when Othello watches Desdemona from there and misunderstands her, the distance between them renders his mistake an excusable one. Yo Takahashi played an insane Iago, who seems to be spurred by some obsession to destroy Othello (illustration 53). Yoshida's portrayal of Othello's fury was magnificent and, because he was so destructive, the question of Iago's motive was less problematic. His was a tragedy of vehement passions, turning from deep love to uncontrollable rage. Further, the audience was so overwhelmed by the radical change in Othello's passions that anything else seemed inconsequential.

TRANSGENDERED SHAKESPEARES

One can easily imagine how Shakespeare's young heroines were played by boys in the Elizabethan period. However, many find it more difficult to accept that boys performed the roles of older women in Shakespeare's plays. Presumably, one reason why there are so few mothers in Shakespeare's plays is that the Elizabethan players lacked any equivalent of the Japanese tradition of female impersonators (especially in Kabuki) and male impersonators in Takarazuka. In Japan, given these traditions, there is nothing awkward about transgender casting. Accordingly, in 2003, when Jonathan Kent directed a Japanese production of *Hamlet* with an all-male cast and the Kyogen performer Mansai Nomura in the title role, the

53. Kotaro Yoshida as Othello, Yo Takahashi as Iago, in *Othello*, 4. 1, directed by Yukio Ninagawa, Sai-no-kuni Shakespeare Series No. 18, 2007.

54. Issei Takahashi (male) as Beatrice, Keisuke Koide as Benedick, *Much Ado about Nothing*, directed by Yukio Ninagawa, Sai-no-kuni Shakespeare Series No. 20, 2008.

audience thoroughly enjoyed Eisuke Sasai's performance as Gertrude. Although Sasai is not a Kabuki actor, his performance in female impersonation was impeccable. So was the performance of Shinobu Nakamura, the Kabuki female impersonator who played Ophelia. Had they not known better, some members of the audience might have believed that the roles were being played by women.

The same is of course true of the performance of *Ninagawa Twelfth Night* in 2005 (revived in 2007), which was performed by an all-male cast because it was a Kabuki version. Kikunosuke Onoe's marvellous transformations from Viola to Sebastian and back again was sheer Kabuki magic. No Japanese would find the fact that all the female parts were played by men to be strange. Rather, this is considered to be a mode of expression: in Kabuki,

women's roles are played by men in the same way that men's roles are played by women in Takarazuka.

In this sense, it was natural that some director would have wished to see Hamlet played by a dashing Takarazuka male impersonator. Thus, Rei Asami and Mira Anju, both ex-Takarazuka star actresses, played the title role in Giles Block's *Hamlet* in 1995 and in Yoshihiro Kurita's musical version of *Hamlet* in 2002 (revived in 2004 and 2007) respectively.[9] What is interesting about Kurita's *Hamlet* is that not only Hamlet but also

---

9 Since Sarah Bernhardt, many women have played the role of Hamlet abroad; some of these productions were also performed in Japan, such as Andrzej Wajda's *Hamlet* at the Tokyo Globe in 1990, in which Teresa Krzyżanowska played Hamlet.

55. A young man (Dai Iwasaki) posing as Hermia, from a handbill for *A Midsummer Night's Dream,* produced by Studio Life, 2008.

Horatio was played by a woman while Gertrude and Ophelia were played by men who were just as talented as Kabuki female impersonators. Jun Uemoto, who played Ophelia, is known for his female roles; for instance, he had played a charming Olivia in *Twelfth Night* in the Shakespeare for Children series.[10]

Things began to change in 2004, when Kurita produced *King Lear* with an all-female cast as part of his Ryutopia Noh-stage Shakespeare, with a company that did not include any professional male impersonators. Many observers felt that the famous Kayoko Shiraishi was exceptional as Lear, for she was no conventional 'actress'. With her strong low voice, she played a tempestuous Lear.

The significance of this all-female *King Lear* might not have been noticed if it were not for Ninagawa's all-male production of *As You Like It* in 2004 (revived in 2007), with Hiroki Narimiya and Yuki Tsukikawa, both male, acting as Rosalind and Celia. Because Narimiya, the young star,

is not at all a female impersonator, the audience was constantly reminded of the fact that a boy is playing a girl. Further, we were not allowed to believe in the world in which Rosalind lived as a girl; instead, we saw Narimiya trying hard to play Rosalind, who, in turn, tried hard to play Ganymede. The difference between the sexes is strengthened in this production, contrary to the spirit of traditional transgender casting. The same is true of Ninagawa's all-male productions of *Love's Labour's Lost* (2007) and *Much Ado About Nothing* (2008), in both of which young handsome boys were transformed into dazzlingly charming heroines (Illustration 54). Many young female spectators swarmed to the theatre for these productions to see their favourite handsome pop stars playing

[10] In 2007, Kurita became more interested in refining his *Hamlet* as a musical play and decided to cast a woman as Ophelia and a man as Horatio; nevertheless, the transgender Hamlet and Gertrude remained the same.

a woman, and performances were always sold out. Naturally, one may expect criticism of Ninagawa's commercialism; however, the fact is that he is satisfying the needs both of the theatre management and of the drama. Being made acutely aware of the gap between the actor's and the character's gender is a significant theatrical experience, rethinking the terms of performance in Shakespeare's theatre.

As for the charm of transgender casting, one might recall Adrian Lester's impressive performance as Rosalind in Cheek by Jowl's all-male production of *As You Like It* (1991). Lester changed his voice in the epilogue and instantly reverted back to his own gender, astonishing the audiences by suddenly reminding them that he was not Rosalind. Mark Rylance may have intended a similar purpose in his performance of Cleopatra, Olivia and other female characters, although only young boys can be sexually ambiguous and enticing to this extent. Ninagawa must be aware of this as he employs attractive young boys, just like the producer of the new company Studio Life, a male version of Takarazuka. It is a company of handsome young boys, which suddenly decided to perform musical versions of Shakespeare. The atmosphere of the production can be clearly identified by observing the boy in a skirt on the flyer of their production of *A Midsummer Night's Dream* in 2008, a revival of the 2006 production (Illustration 55). There is naughty sensuality here, of a kind which would have provoked attacks from Puritans in Elizabethan times. Oddly, Japan's relaxed enjoyment of Shakespeare seems to redirect us back towards Elizabethan controversies.

TRANSLATION FUTURES: SHAKESPEARIANS AND THE FOREIGN TEXT

TON HOENSELAARS

At the 1994 meeting of the International Shakespeare Conference in Stratford, Inga-Stina Ewbank delivered an impressive plenary devoted to 'Shakespeare and Translation as Cultural Exchange'.[1] In this path-finding address, Ewbank observed that despite the cultural turn in Shakespeare studies, research into Shakespeare in translation was still mainly the pursuit of non-English-natives. Drawing on the work of Dirk Delabastita and Lieven D'hulst, Ewbank noted that – at least as perceived from the English omphalos – the study of translations was really 'an interesting and harmless occupation for researchers abroad'.[2] There was, she argued, still little 'reciprocity' between Translation Studies on the one hand and English and American Shakespeare Studies on the other. During the early 1990s, seminars on translation had indeed become an inalienable part of Shakespeare conferences, in Stratford and elsewhere, but the attendance rate by native speakers of English, she argued, remained negligible.[3]

Since 'Exchange' was the conference theme in 1994, Inga-Stina Ewbank sought to free Shakespearian translation from its Cinderella status and achieve a new, more fully integrated form of exchange around the topic. In an attempt to bring both non-native and native speakers of English together around their world author, Ewbank first countered the still widely held assumption that translation merely involved a potential element of corruption. Translation should not be seen as 'a somewhat embarrassing form of inverse colonialism' either.[4] In an attempt to change this prevailing hegemonic perception, Ewbank invited the con-ference to recognize first of all that, '[t]ranslation is never a purely philological activity but a collusive re-creation in which cultural differences cling to grammar and syntax and history mediates the effect even of single words'.[5] By shifting the emphasis from translation as a purely 'philological' activity to one that negotiates 'cultural' difference, Ewbank managed to make the term *translation* include a rather broad variety of activities. This could be the staging of Shakespeare by directors and actors. Alternatively, Shakespeare's plays – staged or screened – could be seen to translate actors into stars. Also the act of interpretation practised by academic critics was to be recognized as a form of translation. In the final analysis, any form of transmigration within the Shakespearian text itself, or involving the transmission of that text, was to be recognized as an open-ended form of translation, part of a process of cultural dynamics and exchange

I am grateful to Nina Geerdink (Free University, Amsterdam) for useful advice about the work of Jan Vos, to Paul Franssen (Utrecht University) for his comments and suggestions at various stages and to Dirk Delabastita (University of Namur) who has been my very distinguished guide through those areas of Translation Studies where Shakespeare rules supreme.
1 Inga-Stina Ewbank, 'Shakespeare and Translation as Cultural Exchange', *Shakespeare Survey 48* (Cambridge, 1995), pp. 1–12; p. 1.
2 Ewbank, 'Shakespeare and Translation', p. 1. Her reference point was *European Shakespeares: Translating Shakespeare in the Romantic Age*, ed. Dirk Delabastita and Lieven D'hulst (Amsterdam and Philadelphia, 1993), p. 19.
3 Ewbank, 'Shakespeare and Translation', p. 1.
4 Ewbank, 'Shakespeare and Translation', p. 2.
5 Ewbank, 'Shakespeare and Translation', p. 6.

between England and the European continent and beyond, in ever different media, in ever new, also non-European contexts.

It is difficult to do justice to the erudition and panache with which Inga Stina-Ewbank argued her case. It is easier to see, however, that since her 1994 address, the theme of 'translation' in Shakespeare studies has come a long way. Arden's *Shakespeare and Language* series, for example, commissioned an entire collection devoted to 'Shakespeare and the Language of Translation', thus producing the first book by a major English publisher devoted solely to the topic.[6] Quite recently, translation also became one of the 'Alternative Shakespeares', as Diana Henderson included Rui Carvalho Homem's fine essay on memory, ideology and translation (involving the troubled Portuguese politics of the mid-twentieth century) in the new volume in that famous Routledge series.[7]

The concept of 'translation' is ubiquitous in Shakespeare studies now and it has proved a source of inspiration for a range of remarkable and influential analyses, like Michael Neill's postcolonial 'Shakespeare and the Tropes of Translation', as well as Patricia Parker's *Shakespeare from the Margins* with its dazzling analysis of 'Translation, Adultery and Mechanical Reproduction in *The Merry Wives of Windsor*' and 'Translating, Conveying, Representing and Seconding in the Histories and *Hamlet*'.[8] And there is much else. Studies such as these have been responsible for effectively 'translating' the field of Shakespeare studies in recent years. But what does 'translation' stand for here? After all, much of this work is conducted at one remove from traditional Translation Studies. Neill's approach to the issue of 'translation', as he openly puts it, is 'only incidentally concerned with "translation" in its narrowly linguistic application'.[9]

There are, however, notable exceptions to this trend. Timothy Billings, for example, has worked extensively on Shakespeare's Asian connections, deftly fusing linguistic and cultural concerns.[10] And Liz Oakley-Brown has impressively studied the various Ovidian translations that feed into Shakespeare and English literature and also traced their afterlives.[11] Her research manages to weld

an in-depth knowledge of Latin and Early Modern English to a reconstruction of the cultural, reformatory processes conveyed by the available translations. Surely, the odd purist in the Ovidian field may have his doubts about the way in which Oakley-Brown reads the socio-cultural significance of Lavinia's communication via Ovid in *Titus Andronicus*, but the *real* as well as *rare* challenge that Oakley-Brown poses to Shakespearians is that of achieving a sustained emphasis on matters linguistic as they reveal their cultural significance.[12]

---

[6] *Shakespeare and the Language of Translation*, ed. Ton Hoenselaars and with a foreword by Inga-Stina Ewbank (London, 2004).

[7] Rui Carvalho Homem, 'Memory, Ideology, Translation: *King Lear* Behind Bars and Before History', in *Alternative Shakespeares 3*, ed. Diana Henderson (London and New York, 2008), pp. 204–20. The growing interest in 'cultural translation' in Shakespeare studies is part of a broader tendency in mainstream Translation Studies, where we may witness a comparable marginalization of the verbal component. See Kate Sturge, 'Cultural Translation', in *Routledge Encyclopedia of Translation Studies*, 2nd edn, ed. Mona Baker and Gabriela Saldanha (London and New York, 2009), pp. 67–70.

[8] Michael Neill, 'The World Beyond: Shakespeare and the Tropes of Translation', in his *Putting History to the Question: Power, Politics and Society in English Renaissance Drama* (New York, 2000), pp. 399–417; and Patricia Parker, *Shakespeare from the Margins: Language, Culture, Context* (Chicago, 1996), pp. 116–48 and 149–84 respectively.

[9] Neill, 'The World Beyond', p. 400.

[10] Timothy Billings, 'Caterwauling Cataians: The Genealogy of a Gloss', *Shakespeare Quarterly* 54 (Spring 2003), 1–28; and 'Masculine in Case: Grammar Lessons and Gender Identity in *Hic Mulier* and *The Merry Wives of Windsor*', in *Class, Boundary and Social Discourse in the Renaissance*, ed. Alexander C. Y. Huang, I-Chun Wang and Mary Theis (Taiwan, 2007), pp. 87–106.

[11] Liz Oakley-Brown, 'Translating the Subject: Ovid's *Metamorphoses* in England 1560–67', in *Translation and Nation: Towards A Cultural Politics of Englishness*, ed. Roger Ellis and Liz Oakley-Brown (Clevedon, 2001), pp. 48–84; '*Titus Andronicus* and the Cultural Politics of Translation in Early Modern England', *Renaissance Studies* 19 (2005), 325–47; and *Ovid and the Cultural Politics of Translation in Early Modern England* (Aldershot, 2006).

[12] A. B. Taylor's review of Liz Oakley-Brown, *Ovid and the Cultural Politics of Translation in Early Modern England*, in *Notes and Queries* (September 2007), 332–3.

Ewbank's invitation to see 'translation' as a cultural process has led to a legitimate broadening of interest, with great benefits, but the change has come at a price. The cultural turn that has affected Shakespeare and translation has led to a 'widened scope' but it has also, as Péter Dávidházi argues, 'resulted in a loss of focus', with the original core business involving the interaction of foreign languages moved firmly into the background.[13] To put it in W. B. Yeats's terms, flying in ever widening gyres, the translation falcon would seem to be losing the falconer.

When Dennis Kennedy introduced the attractive phenomenon of 'Shakespeare without his language', he sought to alert us to the creative practice of Shakespeare translated onto the continental European stages and, later, beyond, onto the Asian stages, not in his *own* language but rendered in *another* tongue.[14] However, the phrase 'Shakespeare without his language' now seems taken ever less to mean 'Shakespeare rendered in a language other than his own early modern English' and more and more 'Shakespeare translated in broadly cultural and intersemiotic terms, without too much attention to the purely linguistic otherness of a foreign tongue'. 'Shakespeare without *his* language' has come to be interpreted as 'Shakespeare without his *language*'.

In our appreciation of Shakespeare as a world author, the cultural turn has, among other things, led to the obfuscation of the national-linguistic distinctions that were originally razed as part of the historical process that produced international Shakespeare and, as we get matters into focus, we notice – perhaps to our surprise – that the study of this national, linguistic translation of Shakespeare is *still* mainly 'an interesting and harmless occupation for researchers abroad', more or less the way it was in 1994.[15] Yet, if we are really prepared to see Shakespeare as a world author, rather than as an English writer, can we afford to ignore the linguistic perspective on that world? Can we really afford to study his world status today, as well as the genesis of that position and neglect his historical progress through the various vernaculars of the world? Can we afford this in a world where English has, since

the Renaissance, replaced Latin and French as the *lingua franca*?

It seems to me that we cannot and I feel strengthened in this view by David Damrosch. In his challenging comparative study *What is World Literature?*, Damrosch proposes a number of flexible and realistic criteria to define 'world literature'.[16] World literature, he believes, ought to be understood as a double 'elliptical refraction of national literatures' – with the original, national traces of a work increasingly diffused and refracted as the work travels to cultures farther from home, while, at the same time, defining more clearly the work's position in its source culture.[17]

In his definition, Damrosch creates ample space for the role of language. World literature is writing that gains or loses in translation, by which he means that literature's complexity, unlike a tax return that has to be unambiguous both in terms of questions and answers, continually generates creative new readings and applications.[18] Finally, world literature, Damrosch argues, is 'not a set canon of texts but a mode of reading, a detached [= an individual] engagement with a world beyond our own'.[19]

Damrosch is not blind to the way in which our current urge for cultural contextualization may interfere with a more cosmopolitan perception of literature: 'The more one needs to know, say, about the courts of Queen Elizabeth and King James I

---

[13] Péter Dávidházi's review of *Shakespeare and the Language of Translation*, ed. Ton Hoenselaars, in *Translation and Literature*, 15 (2006), 122–9; p. 128.

[14] Dennis Kennedy, ed., *Foreign Shakespeare: Contemporary Performance* (Cambridge, 1993), pp. 1–18.

[15] At the same time, of course, it is interesting to note that Shakespeare's international success is also on a number of occasions due precisely to a range of competing regionalisms and nationalisms that seek to cordon off their own politico-cultural borders. Here the 'world' author becomes the 'local' author. See Dirk Delabastita, 'Anthologies, Translations and European Identities' in *Shakespeare and European Politics*, ed. Dirk Delabastita, Jozef de Vos and Paul Franssen (Newark, 2008), pp. 343–68.

[16] David Damrosch, *What is World Literature?* (Princeton and London, 2003).

[17] Damrosch, *What is World Literature?*, p. 283.

[18] Damrosch, *What is World Literature?*, p. 289.

[19] Damrosch, *What is World Literature?*, p. 297.

in order to understand Shakespeare, the less time one has available to learn much about the cultural underpinnings of French drama or Greek tragedy.'[20] Moving beyond this perhaps rather obvious Eurocentric focus to the postcolonial world at large, Damrosch adds: 'The more committed today's Shakespeareans become to understanding literature within its cultural context, the less likely they are to feel comfortable in comparing Shakespeare and Kalidasa.'[21]

Damrosch recognizes the problems posed by the issue of 'translation' in its narrowly linguistic application. With our recognition of literature's complexity and the way in which '[t]he balance of credit and loss remains a distinguishing mark of national versus world literature', it follows, as Damrosch puts it, 'that the study of world literature should embrace translation far more actively than it has usually done to date' and that '[t]he fullest response to the problem would . . . include learning more languages'.[22]

This is a lot to ask and Damrosch is not unaware of the fact. Therefore, in the concluding chapter to his book, appositely entitled 'World Enough and Time', he agrees that if we wish to study the dual refraction of Shakespeare and other literatures and wish to have at least a working knowledge of the other languages where Shakespeare travelled, one cannot help wondering 'who can really know enough to do it well?'.[23] The question here is really a rhetorical question and the answer is really as implicit as it is in the first exchange between Portia and Nerissa in *The Merchant of Venice*. In the second scene of the play, Portia tells Nerissa what she thinks of 'Falconbridge, the young baron of England'.[24] 'He is,' she says, 'a proper man's picture, but alas, who can converse with a dumb show?' (1.2.69–70). The description of Falconbridge has often been read as a confirmation of the early modern stereotype of the monolingual Englishman. A close look at the passage, however, reveals that the truth is more complex. Portia may confess that she says nothing to this man who 'hath neither Latin, French, nor Italian' (1.2.66–67), but she also admits that the problem is not Falconbridge's only. It is mutual: 'for he understands not me, nor I him' (1.2.65–66). In fact, Portia's command of the English language is the problem. As the Lady of Belmont, rather peevishly perhaps, puts it: Nerissa 'will come into the court and swear that I have a poor pennyworth in the English' (1.2.68).

When Damrosch asks, 'who can really know enough to do it well?' we may safely answer 'no-one, really'. Some may have no foreign languages at all, while others have only 'a poor pennyworth'.[25] This is also why Damrosch emphasizes the importance of collaborative work: 'While individual scholarship and teaching will always remain important, those who work on world literature are increasingly going to find that a significant share of their work is best done in collaboration with other people.'[26]

Any Shakespearian working on encounters of a multilingual nature is likely to agree and heed this call to unite. In fact, it echoes translator-cum-scholar Angel Luis Pujante's appeal, made during the late 1990s, in an attempt to rally scholars for research into the complex European identity of Shakespeare, his work and his afterlives:

[T]he history of Shakespeare in Europe is also part of the history of European culture. Despite obvious differences, the various European countries share much more than they sometimes believe or are led to believe; if culturally they have a great deal in common, the work to do on Shakespeare in Europe will have to be done in common.[27]

---

[20] Damrosch, *What is World Literature?*, p. 285.

[21] Damrosch, *What is World Literature?*, pp. 289–90. Kalidasa, the fifth-century Sanskrit poet and playwright has also been called the 'Sanskrit Shakespeare'.

[22] Damrosch, *What is World Literature?*, pp. 289–90.

[23] Damrosch, *What is World Literature?*, p. 284.

[24] *The Merchant of Venice* in *The Complete Works*, ed. Stanley Wells and Gary Taylor (Oxford, 2nd edn, 2005), 1.2.63–64.

[25] This instance of 'the pot calling the kettle black' neatly foils the more serious and complex treatment of Shylock by the Venetians.

[26] Damrosch, *What is World Literature?*, p. 286.

[27] Quoted from *Four Hundred Years of Shakespeare in Europe*, ed. Angel Luis Pujante and Ton Hoenselaars (Newark, 2003), pp. 17–18.

Pujante's rallying cry did not fall on deaf ears and the ideal expressed here has since been realized in the shape of the European Shakespeare Research Association, founded in Iasi (Romania) in November 2007.[28] However, an organization of this kind is not the sole requirement for a sensible dialogue across linguistic borders. There must also be a readiness to recognize the Babylonian curse and the will to problematize it. I was convinced of this during a recent correspondence with Douglas Bruster about various queries regarding his current work (with Eric Rasmussen) on the Arden edition of *Mankind* and *Everyman*. For his work on the original language of the Dutch source play for *Everyman*, Bruster of course had at his disposal the marvellous website – part of the symbolically named TEAMS project – with the English translation of the Dutch *Everyman* play.[29] As befits the specialist in Damrosch's perception, however, Bruster would not be satisfied with the available translation. Anyone familiar with the *boskos boskos* sequence involving Paroles in *All's Well That Ends Well* will know what caution is always required when relying on the translation of others. And to those not familiar with the scene, 9/11 and the Iraqi crisis should have sufficiently revealed what may happen when even a venerable institution like the FBI relies on English too much and ignores or mishandles 'translation'. By juxtaposing Bruster and the FBI in this way, I am not suggesting that the international Shakespeare research community is a more reliable institution than the Federal Bureau of Investigation, but I do think that linguistic curiosity is a rare virtue and could serve as a model for every man and for every woman.

This ambition would be more or less in line with what the US Government has been seeking to achieve since 9/11, after it had become clear that training speakers of Arabic, Urdu, Farsi and Chinese, among a host of other languages, was crucial to national security. It would also seem in line with the Modern Language Association of America's attempt – using David Damrosch as a point of reference – to respond to 'the nation's language deficit' (as it has been called) with a more humanistic, cosmopolitan vision.[30] Finally, on a perhaps more mundane level, it would seem to be in line with the objectives of Barack Obama, who, during an election campaign appearance at Powder Springs, Georgia, on 8 July 2008, sought to combat US xenophobia and persistent monolinguism with the following argument:

I don't understand when people are going around worrying about we need to have English only . . . Now, I agree that immigrants should learn English. I agree with that. But, but, understand this: instead of worrying about whether immigrants can learn English – they'll learn English – you need to make sure your child can speak Spanish. You should be thinking about how can your child become bilingual? We should have every child speaking more than one language. You know, it's embarrassing, it's embarrassing when Europeans come over here, they all speak English, they speak French, they speak German. And then we go over to Europe and all we can say is 'Merci beaucoup'. Right?[31]

If we manage to adjust our joint attitude along the lines sketched above and if we are prepared jointly to approach early modern literature with (its own) multilingual awareness, we may, as Shakespearians, envisage a creative and close encounter with old and new foreign texts, with translations of Shakespeare.

This encounter may take various forms. One of these is by returning to the vast number of near-contemporary, seventeenth-century texts that involve Shakespearian materials in translation. The texts that I shall consider in some detail here are in Dutch and not all of them are new to Shakespeare scholars. My first reason for looking at texts in my mother tongue in particular is that, just as Portia had to acknowledge a 'poor penny-worth in the English', I have to confess that my Sanskrit is

28 The website at www.um.es/shakespeare/esra/ records the history of the organization, its current structure and its research plans for the near future.
29 For *Everyman and Its Dutch Original, Elckerlijc*, ed. Clifford Davidson, Martin W. Walsh and Ton J. Broos, see the website of the Consortium for the Teaching of the Middle Ages (TEAMS) at www.lib.rochester.edu/camelot/teams/daevintro.htm.
30 Domna C. Stanton, 'On Rooted Cosmopolitanism', *PMLA*, 121 (2006), 626–40.
31 Personal transcription, CNN, 8 July 2008.

rather rusty. Despite our ideals and the recognition of their relevance, we remain limited in our linguistic means.

There is, however, another reason for turning to these Dutch translations. It is a truth universally acknowledged that translations age. In a comparable way our interpretations as academics who study these translations age. After all, the conditions under which we research and write are in a continual flux. Hence, the vast amount of work that nineteenth- and early twentieth-century philologists devoted to the seventeenth-century translations and adaptations of Shakespeare into Dutch – however brilliant in most cases – should not be accepted as conclusive. Yet, this is what seems to be happening most of the time. Given the difficulty of access to the materials in question – in practical terms and in terms of language, of course, both to the foreigner and to the twenty-first-century scholar – we have a tendency time and again to draw on the dusty work of forebears and only rarely to venture out into the field of these translations for a fresh look.

We may profitably go back to several of these translations, in an attempt to find out more about the interaction between the early modern author and the translator, the interaction, that is, during the years preceding that unprecedented rise of the continental European Shakespeare in countless languages and dialects and, preceding the author's journey beyond that continent, into world literature, assisted by generations of translators. Interesting as a starting point for such an investigation might be (i) the 1621 translation into Dutch of the first 810 lines of Shakespeare's *Venus and Adonis* and (ii) the better-known 1641 translation-cum-adaptation of *Titus Andronicus*, namely Jan Vos's *Aran and Titus*.

The 1621 translation of *Venus and Adonis* – published in The Hague – has long escaped scholarly attention. This may, in part, be due to the fact that studies of Shakespeare's afterlife tend to focus on the plays and the Sonnets and only rarely if ever on the narrative poems (which tend, rather, to attract readings of the way in which Ovidian and other materials metamorphosed into the Shakespearian

text itself).[32] But the main reason for this translation's neglect, certainly, is that the text refers to Shakespeare only obliquely. The title-page of the translation that appeared in The Hague in 1621 reads: 'The fiery story of the goddess Venus's love for the youth Adonis, as described by the learned Ovidius Naso in the tenth book of his *Metamorphoses* [lit. re-shapings, re-creations] . . . [now] put, until the first departure of Adonis, into rhyming Dutch verse by a member of a chamber of rhetoric. And now completed by I. W. vander Niss.'[33] Only a closer look at the *preface* to the translation – available in copies at the Royal Library in the Hague, the University of Amsterdam Library and the British Library – puts us on the Shakespearian trail. Here we read about the text as

having first been put into English by an English Poet and recently by an amateur [meaning: admirer, aficionado] into Low Dutch rhyme, until the first departure of Adonis.
[*wesende door een Enghels Poeet, eerst in Engels ende onlanghs door een beminder op Nederduytschen Rijm ghestelt, tot het eerste scheyden van Adonis.*][34]

The close correspondence between the Dutch version of *Venus and Adonis* and the Shakespearian text that we know, reveals that the 'English Poet' here can only be our Shakespeare.[35] Given the fact that all copies of *Venus and Adonis* until 1621 have

---

[32] For a discussion of translation in connection with Shakespeare's own sources (a topic that seems to enjoy a particular interest from anglophone scholars), see the work of Liz-Oakley Brown (see n.11) and Jonathan Bate, *Shakespeare and Ovid* (Oxford, 1993). Attention to the narrative poems on the continental side of the English Channel is rare too. An exception, therefore, is Christa Jansohn and Dieter Mehl, '*Venus and Adonis* und *The Rape of Lucrece* in der Übersetzung von Heinrich Christoph Albrecht', in *Shakespeare im 18. Jahrhundert*, ed. Roger Paulin (Göttingen, 2007), pp. 49–62.

[33] J. C. Arens, 'Shakespeare's *Venus and Adonis* (1–810): A Dutch Translation Printed in 1621', *Neophilologus*, 52 (1968), 421–30; p. 422. Translation is my own.

[34] Arens, 'Shakespeare's *Venus and Adonis*', p. 429, n.6.

[35] We can even determine that as a copy of *Venus and Adonis* the translator must have used Q9 (1602 [1608?]) or a later editon of the poem, where 'she murders with a kiss' (line 54) was changed to 'she smothers with a kiss' (Arens, p. 429 n.8).

'William Shakespeare' signing the Dedication to the Earl of Southampton with his full name, this narrative poem should have been least likely among Shakespeare texts to create any confusion on the score of its original authorship.[36] But the argument does not end here. Shakespeare is really presented not as the author of *Venus and Adonis*, but as the 'translator' of Ovid and I am using the term in its narrowly linguistic sense. What we see here is that (i) Shakespeare's poem is not recognized as 'the first heir of [his] invention', as Shakespeare himself describes it in the dedication to *Venus and Adonis*, and (ii) mentioned as an appreciated translator of Ovid, Shakespeare is metamorphosed not, like Adonis, into an anemone but into pure anonymity. The substitution here seems to have been inspired not by the fact that Shakespeare's narrative was so close to Ovid's as to be mistaken for an Englished version of the original, but rather by the profitable fame of the Roman poet and Shakespeare's lack of it.

My second text is the Dutch version of *Titus Andronicus* by Jan Vos, known as *Aran and Titus*. Looking at the Dutch play and the interaction between the early modern author and the translator, there is much that strikes the eye, even though, again, the name of Shakespeare is not mentioned. Much is uncertain about Jan Vos's *Aran and Titus*, which is both verbally and structurally indebted to the German translation of the tragedy that appeared in 1619.[37] What is certain, however, is that *Aran and Titus* also contains elements that do not occur in the German version of the play, but seem to be uniquely Shakespearian. Among other things, like Shakespeare's original but unlike the German version, the Jan Vos play includes the Ovidian sequence in Act 4, although Shakespeare's contrapuntal use of English and Latin has been replaced by a dialogue that is entirely in Dutch. Also, when Titus Andronicus reads from the *Metamorphoses* at the request of Lavinia (here named Rosalyne), the Dutch play follows Shakespeare's original in providing eight lines from Ovid's tale of Philomela, in Dutch.[38]

It is intriguing, certainly in the case of this free translation of a play containing so much that is unmistakably Shakespearian, that even in the Dutch context, the authorship (or translatorship) of *Aran and Titus* (originally: *Aran en Titus*), or parts of it, was never entirely unchallenged. Adriaen van den Bergh, the theatre aficionado who was acquainted with the strolling players and who translated Thomas Kyd's *The Spanish Tragedy* into Dutch in 1621,[39] claimed to have written a *Titus* play and parts of his *Titus* play, based on Shakespeare, may have entered *Aran and Titus*. The main reason for raising this issue within the present context is that Jan Vos, the author credited with *Aran and Titus*, was notoriously monolingual. He knew only one language, namely Dutch. Jan Vos's epitaph, written by J. V. Peterson, spoke of him as one,

Who, knowing no language other than Dutch, achieved more
Than many who, arrogantly displaying their foreign language learning,
Seem like strangers in their mother tongue.
[*Die, kennende geen taal dan Neêrduitsch, meer bedreef*
Dan veele, die verwaand met taalgeleerdheid prijken,
En vreemdelingen in hun Moederspraak gelijken.][40]

The curious fact of Jan Vos's monolingualism also explains why it was the prominent Dutch classicist,

---

[36] For information about the transmission of the English text, I rely on *Shakespeare's Poems*, ed. Katherine Duncan-Jones and H. R. Woudhuysen, The Arden Shakespeare (London, 2007).

[37] A survey of the interconnection between the different versions may be found in W. Braekman, 'The Relationship of Shakespeare's *Titus Andronicus* to the German Play of 1620 and to Jan Vos's *Aran en Titus*', *Studia Germanica Gandensia* 9 (1967), 9–117 and 10 (1968), 9–65. A review of the situation is provided in *Titus Andronicus*, ed. Jonathan Bate, The Arden Shakespeare (London, 1995), pp. 48–9.

[38] Jan Vos, *Toneelwerken: 'Aran en Titus', 'Oene', 'Medea'*, ed. W. J. C. Buitendijk (Assen and Amsterdam, 1975), lines 1714–22. The Dutch verse corresponds with *Metamorphoses*, Book VI, lines 519–26.

[39] The most detailed discussion of Adriaen van den Bergh remains Theo Verlaan, 'Adriaen van den Bergh: Het leven van een rederijker in de eerste helft van de zeventiende eeuw; zijn betrekkingen met het zwerftoneel, en met *Jeronimo*, een *Spanish Tragedy* van die naam', unpublished MA Thesis, Groningen University, 3 vols. (Groningen, 1983).

[40] Jan Vos, *Alle de gedichten van den vermaarden Poëet Jan Vos, Tweede deel.* (Amsterdam, 1671), sig. B2v. The text is also available at: www.dbnl.org/.

Caspar van Baerle, who translated, from the Latin, a number of lines from Seneca's *Thyestes* that found their way into the text of *Aran and Titus*. Van Baerle may also have translated the lines from Ovid in Act 4 – whose mediator has not been identified – but we cannot be certain.

Finally, the monolinguism of Jan Vos would seem to explain his extreme pride when in 1658 – presumbly through the mediation of Caspar van Baerle – *Aran and Titus* was translated into Latin:

On [the shores of] the [Amsterdam] River IJ my Titus
    spoke Dutch, his first language:
Now [the students at the grammar school at the town
    of] Tiel teach him Latin, for the ear of foreign
    nations.
In this way he becomes a citizen with the Spanish,
    British and Walloons [=French].
He who wants his fame spread wide, requires Latin
    interpreters.

[*Myn Titus sprak aan 't Y Neêrduits, zijn eerste taal:*
Nu leert hem Tiel Latijn, voor 't oor der vreemde volken.
Zoo wordt hy burger by de Spanjaart, Brit en Waal.
Wie veer vermaart wil zijn vereist Latijnsche tolken.][41]

The monolinguism of Jan Vos – who (to echo Ben Jonson) must have possessed very much less than Shakespeare's 'small Latin and less Greek' – tends to multiply the number of authors and translators involved in one or more versions of *Aran and Titus*, yet the name of Shakespeare remains conspicuously absent. Unmentioned, too, is Shakespeare where it concerns the remaining pages of Vos's complete works, which contain some twenty-five sonnets composed on the English or Shakespearian model, like the following, which served to accompany Gabriel Metsu's 1661 painting entitled *Woman in Childbed*, now in the Metropolitan Museum of Art, New York:

Written to acompany the painting of a woman in childbed, in
    the hall of Alderman Jan Jakobsen Hinloopen, painted by
    Gabriel Metsu.
What miracle does Metsu announce to our view?
It is living flesh and blood; yes silver, wool and silk.
Art, to our eyes, has a special power.
Nature, which generates all, dies of mere envy

Now that she sees how dead paint can be made to
    create things as full of life as this.
The female visitor to the childbed, who politely enters
    the bedroom
With her face and mouth seems to convey respect.
No shadows are used here to convey natural
    roundness. No.
Who wants to paint well must choose the noblest
    object.
A beautiful painting has gigantic power.
Anyone who seeks power by means of shadow will
    lose all his power.
For a long time visiting women in childbed was a
    female affair:
Now art invites the man too to visit this woman.
The arts bind more than the strongest bonds.

[*Op de schildery van een Kraamvrouw, in de zaal van den*
    E. Heer Scheepen Jan Jakobsen Hinloopen, door
    G. Moetsu geschildert
Wat wonder komt Moetsu aan ons gezicht vertoogen?
't Is leevendt vlees en bloedt; ja zilver, wol en zydt.
De kunst heeft op het oog een ongemeen vermoogen.
D'alteelende Natuur besterft van enkle spijt,
Nu zy uit doode verf zoo leevendigh ziet scheppen.
De vandster, die beleeft ter kraamzaal in komt treên,
Schijnt haar gezicht en mondt eerbiedelijk te reppen.
Hier zijn geen schaaduwen om 't werk te ronden:
    neen.
Wie wel wil schildren moet het allereelst verkiezen.
Een schoone schildery heeft overgroote kracht.
Wie kracht door schaaduw zoekt zal al zijn kracht
    verliezen.
Dus lang was 't vanden voor het vrouwelijk geslacht:
Nu noodt de kunst de mans om deeze vrouw te
    vanden.
De kunsten trekken meer dan d'allersterkste banden.][42]

Little or no work has been done on the Shakespearean sonnets of Jan Vos. Instead, Dutch scholars investigating the reception of the sonnet in the Netherlands have tended to focus on the work of the canonical poet and playwright Joost van den Vondel rather than Jan Vos. However, their predominant emphasis on the formal features of the sonnet – unchallenged by notions of an

---

41 Jan Vos, *Alle de gedichten van den Poëet Jan Vos* (Amsterdam, 1662), p. 467. The text is also available at www.dbnl.org/.
42 Jan Vos, *Alle de gedichten van den Poëet Jan Vos*, p. 654.

intertextual or a reader-oriented nature – has led to some trenchant observations about the so-called English sonnet that are worth keeping in mind, particularly with regard to the apparent ease with which the familiar form consisting of three quatrains (each with their own rhyme words) followed by a rhyming couplet so easily managed to generate poems of four, five or six quatrains (each with their own rhyme words) followed by a rhyming couplet.[43] The ideal of cohesion associated with the former model contrasts sharply with the Lego-like expansion drive of the latter and there are many such longer poems in the complete works of Jan Vos as well. Was the fourteen-liner a shorter version of the poems with four, five, or six quatrains, or the other way around? Extended research is needed to establish whether Jan Vos – the 'clever Fox', as his tombstone read[44] – was not only the literary mid-wife of *Titus Andronicus*, but also also one of the begetters of the Shakespearian sonnet in Dutch.

Considering some of the earliest Dutch translations and adaptations of Shakespeare's work, we begin to see that even though, already at an early date, Dutch readers and writers sufficiently appreciated the merits of *Venus and Adonis*, *Titus Andronicus* and the Sonnets to appropriate them, the players in the literary field and the rules by which they played, were not conducive to conveying Shakespeare's 'name' or 'fame' to countries beyond the Channel. At the same time, we witness a tendency against this. We see how the various movements in the Dutch literary field also produce (i) strong authorship claims, (ii) strong claims of translatorship (as in the case of Adriaen van den Bergh), as well as (iii) a clear recognition of the craft of translation (as in I. W. vander Niss's recognition of Shakespeare's qualities) and (iv) a firm conviction that translation was indeed to be the road to an international readership (as on the part of the proudly monolingual Jan Vos).

Further research into the texts I have mentioned as well as the many other early modern English materials in the early modern Netherlands should help create a more reliable assessment of the interplay between authorship and translatorship, original text and translation: it would certainly

include a discussion of Shakespearian materials like G. A. Bredero's romance play *Griane*, first acted in Amsterdam in 1612. In Act 4, a Time chorus ('De Tydt') describes how in the course of the years young Palmerin, child of the maligned daughter of the Emperor of Constantinople, is abandoned in the wilderness. The Time chorus recounts how Palmerin is found by a shepherd and how, ignorant of his royal origins, the prince grows up, to leave the woods in which he has always lived. Averse to life as a farmer and spurred on by his noble blood, the Chorus tells the audience, Palmerin eventually manifests his princely character, reunites his parents and clears them of the accusation of adultery. Bredero's *Griane* inevitably recalls *The Winter's Tale* (1611), also on the verbal level, and a renewed investigation into the echoes between these texts should shed new light on Anglo-Dutch relations and also enhance our appreciation of the spread and development of the romance genre during the early seventeenth century.[45] The 1654 translation-cum-adaptation into Dutch of *The Taming of the Shrew* – Abraham Sybant's *De Dolle Bruyloft* or *The Mad Wedding* – has received some attention in recent years, but a full reassessment of the complex gender issues that these plays share and their position in the Erasmian marriage counselling tradition is still due.[46]

---

43 See the following articles in *Tijdschrift voor Nederlandse Taal-en Letterkunde*: S. J. C. Budding, 'Vondel en het Shakespeare-sonnet', 13 (1894), 179–84 and 306–12; L. Strengholt, 'Sonnetten en pseudosonnetten bij Vondel', 86 (1970), 194–212; and C. F. P. Stutterheim, 'Sonnetten en pseudosonnetten bij Vondel en anderen', 94 (1978), 71–106. For a tentative reassessment, see *Klinkend boeket: Studies over Renaissance-sonnetten voor Marijke Spies*, ed. Henk Duits, Arie-Jan Gelderblom, Mieke B. Smits-Veldt (Utrecht, 1994). See also Jan Vos, ed. Buitendijk, pp. 19 and 24.

44 The tombstone describes the poet as 'de schrandre Vos, een gauw vernunft' ('the clever Vos [= Fox], a quick wit' (*Alle de Werken*, II, sig. B2v).

45 G. A. Bredero, *Griane*, ed. Fokke Veenstra (Culemborg, 1973), pp. 83–4 and lines 1750–1804. Veenstra does not discuss the Shakespearian connection, first established by C. H. den Hertog in 'De bronnen van Breeroos romantische spelen', *De Gids*, 4 (1885), pp. 500–46.

46 For a discussion of the options see Ton Hoenselaars and Jan Frans van Dijkhuizen, 'Abraham Sybant Tames *The Taming*

We should, however, also look beyond the work of Shakespeare, who was neither the only nor the most popular London playwright in the Low Countries during the first half of the seventeenth century. It is time to reassess the different versions of *The Spanish Tragedy* produced in the Low Countries between 1615 and 1638 (some of which could help clarify current English editions of the play), the 1617 translation of Thomas Middleton's *Revenger's Tragedy* by Theodore Rodenburgh (with a moralizing Induction and a considerable stage history in Amsterdam), as well as the Dutch rendering of Marlowe's *The Jew of Malta* (Leiden, 1645), John Mason's *The Turk* (Amsterdam, 1652) and even William Prynne's *Histriomastix* (Leiden, 1639).[47] These texts, approached as translations (defined in narrowly linguistic terms) but also as ambassadors between two prominent early modern cultures on either side of the Channel, form a formidable corpus. Here lie the traces of a veritable *sea change*, fully deserving our sense of wonder and academic commitment.

In the face of such a wealth of material in terms of texts and so much research in the offing, one may well wish to repeat Damrosch's question: 'Who can really know enough to do it well?' In terms of Shakespeare studies, the Babylonian curse has not been lifted and probably never will be lifted. For this reason, all sorts of collaboration will be required to access world texts and to assess or reassess them, although personal contacts rather than institutional bonds may be of greater value than we tend to assume. The important thing to stress in this context is that we should never give in to the tendency – noted by Damrosch in connection with the cultural turn in historical Shakespeare studies, mentioned earlier – 'to

downplay the importance of what [we do not] know'.[48]

In his early eighties, the venerable Johann Wolfgang von Goethe told his secretary Johann Eckermann: 'I do not like to read my *Faust* any more in German.' Instead, the multilingual German poet, reading 'translations as readily as originals', preferred to read *Faust* in a new French translation. Even though it was mostly in prose, it made the old man experience his own masterpiece again as 'fresh, new and spirited'.[49] It seems to me that Goethe's practice might feature as a model for us Shakespearians to follow. After years and years of reading Shakespeare's texts in Early Modern English, we might devote our time to reading him – or trying to read him – in Dutch, Swahili and Chinese, or in Klingon, the 'original' language from which Shakespeare, as Chancellor Gorkon in *Star Trek* would have us believe, was later translated into Early Modern English.[50] As with Goethe, so too Shakespeare, when read in ever new translations, may turn out 'fresh, new and spirited'.

---

of the Shrew for the Amsterdam Stage (1654)', *Ilha do desterro: A Journal of English Language, Literatures in English and Cultural Studies* (Brazil), 36 (1999), 53–70.

47 Cornelis W. Schoneveld, *Intertraffic of the Mind: Studies in Seventeenth-Century Anglo-Dutch Translation with a Checklist of Books Translated from English into Dutch, 1600–1700* (Leiden, 1983). See also Ton Hoenselaars, 'The Seventeenth-Century Reception of English Renaissance Drama in Europe', *SEDERI*, 10 (1999), 69–87; and, with Wouter Abrahamse, 'Theodore Rodenburgh and English Studies', in *The North Sea and Culture (1550–1800)*, ed. Juliette Roding and Lex Heerma van Voss (Hilversum, 1996), pp. 324–39.

48 Damrosch, *What is World Literature?*, p. 285.

49 Damrosch, *What is World Literature?*, p. 7.

50 Douglas Lanier, *Shakespeare and Modern Popular Culture* (Oxford, 2002), pp. 9–10.

AFTER TRANSLATION

YONG LI LAN

First and foremost, the problematic of translation is the allocation of the foreign.

Sakai Naoki[1]

I. BODY, SPEECH, TRANSLATION

Asian Shakespeare productions typically create an 'intercultural' action by introducing a gap between the verbal and embodied dimensions of the performance. As distinct from the older, looser notion of adaptation, intercultural performance strategies reflexively emphasize and capitalize upon the differences between the disparate cultural systems of theatre forms. In these stage encounters between cultures, Asian theatres have played a central role, and the classical forms in particular offer striking opportunities for juxtaposing their formalized conventions of music, singing, gesture, dance, costume and make-up, as well as their cultural and aesthetic foundations, against Western theatre conventions. By comparison with many theatre forms in Asian cultures, Shakespeare presents an exorbitantly word-heavy theatrical idiom. When the RSC *King Lear* played in Singapore recently with Ian McKellen in the title role, I was conscious of hearing the language as a startling, ringing dimension of a foreign culture, quite unlike how it sounds to me in London or Stratford-upon-Avon, simply because I was watching the performance within a community to whom it would not just be an archaic form of English but a culturally alien mode of performance. A comment overheard in the audience: 'Hey, I thought we coming to watch Gandalf – what is this

Shakespeare? We'd better go eat supper in the interval.' At the same time, a popular local television and film actor later said that McKellen's performance had been a revelation to him of how much the actor's voice could do. Reciprocally, Western reception of Asian performances has focused on their physical expressivity, beauty and spectacle, since these aspects necessarily captivate attention over speech in a language one doesn't follow. The review of the 2006 Craiova Shakespeare Festival at the online 'Theatre Record – The Chronicle of the British Stage' begins by quoting Stanley Wells: 'Before you put something of your own in [Shakespeare's] place,' he warned, 'make sure that you have something worthwhile to say.' While the review observes that the Japanese production of *The Winter's Tale* by the Ryutopia Noh Theatre Shakespeare Series 'delightfully exemplified the Wells problem', in what sense it did so remains highly ambiguous: '[the director] Kurita offered a style triumph very much his own, with his beautifully disciplined actors moving throughout with a rare grace. Almost all of Shakespeare's comedy had been ruthlessly excised, with no sign of Autolycus, or the young shepherd and his girlfriends; in its place was a coherent world of mythic, Japanese intensity.'[2] Perhaps the problem of having something worth saying in place of Shakespeare is not a question of what to say, but of how to

---

[1] Sakai Naoki, 'Translation', *Theory, Culture and Society*, 23.2–3 (2006), 73.

[2] See www.theatrerecord.org/Archives/2006/archive08–2006. html#top, accessed 29 December 2008.

speak – or translate – embodied effects of this kind without resorting to stereotypical displacements onto a foreign, mythic intensity.

For Asian theatre practitioners to choose Shakespeare now, and for their productions to return with Shakespeare to the West, something more of their own is expected, by both producers and audiences, than Shakespeare's play in translation. The most obvious difference that Asian practice can make to Shakespeare is to recast the action with a more powerful visual dimension and sensory impact. The greater weight given to embodiment in performance traditions provides not only the resources of traditional forms such as formalized acting and musical conventions, but alternative theatrical values, such as the presentational over the representational, that shape newer approaches. The altered equilibrium between speech and embodiment that arises from performing Shakespeare in interaction with these traditions and values necessarily foregrounds the Asian body over the verbal action translated or adapted from, or just notionally identified with, Shakespeare's play. Where a contemporary or international, rather than classical, performance idiom is used in such an intercultural strategy, it is nevertheless the aesthetic choices of stage presentation and acting style that define and dramatize local terms of engagement with the play and the original author Shakespeare, and that attract attention and critique, over the script – perhaps even more so where those choices are adapted from western performance styles.[3] This heightened corporeality is as much a matter of spectatorial positionality in reception as it is of theatre forms in production: to audiences habituated to logocentric western drama, the foreign appearance, sounds and 'world' of a different theatre form present a greater difference to Shakespeare than his words in a different language, idiom or social context, especially where that form has a highly developed vocabulary of costume, movement and music. Thus intercultural Asian Shakespeare inevitably recreates the familiar Orientalist polarization of body/mind as an East/West dyad. To bring the contrastive theatrical modes of Shakespeare and Asian performance into conjunction is to employ an old,

broad channel of cultural trade and expectation along which such productions circulate and whose terms they renegotiate and reanimate. What has been overlooked in this binary opposition of verbal to physical action, and literary versus theatrical values, is the third node of intercultural performance: that of translation.

Translation is commonly thought of as extraneous to the performance proper: a process of textual transfer completed prior to the performance and/or a facilitating aid for foreign audiences during its progress. It is worth noting, though, that the relatively recent technology of screened surtitles that concurrently translate the onstage dialogue has played a key role in the mobility of intercultural productions across linguistic boundaries.[4] Without this provision for following the words being spoken or sung, a spectator lacks access to the characters' minds and must remain an 'outsider' to the action,

---

3 For instance, Shen Lin contextualizes Lin Zhao Hua's adoption of European avant-garde methods in his production of *Richard III* (Beijing, 2001) within current trends in China where Shakespeare performance carries the symbolic value of English as the medium of the global market economy ('What Use Shakespeare? China and Globalization', in Dennis Kennedy and Yong Li Lan, eds., *Shakespeare in Asia: Contemporary Performance*, forthcoming).

4 The term 'surtitles' originated in the 1980s with the practice of presenting translations of the verbal content of European stage operas. See Peter Low, 'Surtitles for Opera: A Specialised Translating Task', *Babel*, 48:2 (2002), 97–110; Yvonne Griesel, 'Surtitles and Translation: Towards an Integrative View of Theater Translation', in Heidrun Gerzymisch-Arbogast and Sandra Nauert, eds., *Challenges of Multidimensional Translation*: Proceedings of the Marie Curie Euroconferences MuTra – Saarbrücken 2–6 May 2005, http://www.euroconferences.info/proceedings/2005_Proceedings/2005_Griesel_Yvonne.pdf, accessed 10 December 2008. In Asian contexts of performance, surtitling has also supported forms within their own language communities – for instance, it has replaced the scripts that used to be distributed during the performance to enable Beijing opera audiences to follow the lyrics, since the singing is not tonally matched to the words – or across different Chinese languages within a local community, where the Mandarin script allows other Chinese language groups to follow regional opera in Singapore; see Chua Soo Pong, 'Translation and Chinese Opera: The Singapore Experience', in Jennifer Lindsay, ed., *Between Tongues: Translation and/or/in Performance in Asia* (Singapore, 2006), p. 173.

precisely at the level of their physical presentation. At the same time, to treat the practice of translation during the performance (surtitling) as a kind of bridging convenience or concession for foreign audiences, a para-text to the primary theatrical presentation, is implicitly to conceive of intercultural performance as a monolingual event, one whose normative situation is 'inside' its 'own' linguistic and cultural community, 'out' of which it is translated. This representation of translation, as a process of 'source' to 'target' languages and situations, assumes that languages and cultures are discrete, enclosed spaces, according to which equivalences can be drawn between Asian treatments of Shakespeare and the English original, and on account of which productions designed for international circulation are regarded with suspicion as lacking an authentic cultural identity.

On the contrary, of course, bilinguality or frequently multilinguality is inherent in any reference to Shakespeare's text in an Asian language production (as well as in English-language Asian productions), where the co-presence of at least two (and usually more) languages and cultural systems is structural to the effect of that reference. Here one may adapt the distinction Sakai Naoki makes between a heterolingual address as opposed to a homolingual one. Sakai argues for the need to avoid assuming that in a situation where the speaker and listener share the same language, they are both presumably embraced within the unitary community of a single language – 'for such a group can only be posited imaginarily and *in representation*' (author's italics). In contrast, heterolingual address recognizes a 'non-aggregate' community, in which the 'mingling and cohabitation of plural language heritage in the audience' predicate varying degrees of communication, including the zero degree.[5] Considering, first, that audiences of many traditional Asian forms attend performances without expecting to follow some or even all of the words, second, that internal translation is also common and produces pleasure in the performance of translation, for instance in the Balinese dance drama *arja*, where each line sung in high Balinese by an epic character is repeated in contemporary Balinese by

a servant or clown,[6] and third, the cosmopolitan constitution of audiences in the urban Asian centres where intercultural and multilingual theatre practices are growing in number and diversity, then the cultural environment for performing Shakespeare in Asia at once accommodates, and suggests ways to exploit, the discontinuities between languages, and between language and embodiment.

My concern in this article is to restore the balance between the embodied and the verbal modes of performance in the reception of Asian Shakespeare, partly because the role of verbal language has been readily overshadowed by attention to the corporeal, but also in order to explore the changed status of Shakespeare's dominant, signature mode of verbal action in intercultural performance. In exploring the performativity of translation, I aim to illuminate the intersections between three fields: Shakespeare, intercultural theatre and translation studies. I consider several instances of Asian Shakespeare performance in which the spoken or sung dimension of the action, the translation of the verbal text in surtitles, and the corporeal, physical performance, do not merge into a cohesive whole, but sustain a separation and incongruence between each other. I propose that it is in the tension between them that the intercultural relation to Shakespeare and, conversely, Shakespeare's value for intercultural performance, are constituted. These productions all take place 'after translation' in the historical sense of coming after, and reacting against, well-established practices within their own countries for both translating Shakespeare's text and reproducing it in adapted Western realist theatrical conventions.[7] In contrast to the clearly delineated horizon of interpretation

---

[5] Sakai Naoki, *Translation and Subjectivity: On Japan and Cultural Nationalism* (Minneapolis, 1997), pp. 4–6.

[6] The term 'internal translation' was coined by Mary Zurbuchen, 'Internal Translation in Balinese Poetry', in A. L. Becker, ed., *Writing on the Tongue* (Ann Arbor, 1989), pp. 215–79. See also Ward Keeler, 'Balinese and Javanese Performing Arts', in Lindsay, *Between Tongues*, pp. 204–23.

[7] *Shingeki* in Japan, and *hua ju* in China. In colonial Singapore, conventional English Shakespeare was a staple production of expatriate theatre groups. In all three countries productions of Shakespeare's plays in these forms are still regularly mounted.

and audience competence expected in these earlier genres, intercultural practices, by virtue of bringing together elements from several disparate performance genres as well as Shakespeare, are extremely unpredictable and variable in reception, because they invoke and often challenge the spectator's sense of cultural belonging, ownership and history, as well as the aesthetic values invested in specific components. These unconscious investments perhaps only surface and acquire definition when provoked by such incongruence, and in this way enter into the intercultural event. Thus Asian Shakespeare performance can posit no ideal spectator, and instead requires a critic to recognize and treat her own culturally subjective position with greater self-reflexivity than has often been the case.

2. PARADOXES OF FAITHFUL TRANSLATION

I began to notice the performativity of translated surtitles during Ninagawa Yukio's 2003 production of *Pericles* at the National Theatre in London, when I realised that the English surtitles were screening Shakespeare's text, not a counter-translation of Matsuoka Kazuko's modern Japanese translation into its modern English equivalent. This practice created a curious paradox of faithfulness to Shakespeare. In the normative hierarchy of reception, surtitles are a second-order text that supplements the primacy of live, direct speech on stage, particularly if the surtitles are translating the spoken language. They thus remind the spectator (who reads them) that she is apprehending the action at one remove. But in this production, the precedence that the speaking human being ordinarily takes over a translated version of his or her speech was reversible, since the surtitles framed that speech as a live translation of a prior script – which at one level, of course, was exactly what was happening.[8]

The striking effect of a reversible two-way translation being enacted in Ninagawa's practice of closely following and surtitling Shakespeare's text is significant in several ways. First, the presence

of Shakespeare's original text acts as a guarantee of the performance's authenticity in terms of its fidelity to his play. A useful analogy here is the policy of the Royal Opera House Covent Garden in London of treating the opera libretto, not the specific stage performance, as the source text for the translated surtitles. This separates the progress of the surtitles from that of the stage production, and marks the 'neutrality' of the surtitles as a parallel text uncommitted to a specific production's interpretation, unimplicated in its contingency and ephemerality.[9] Similarly, the non-translation of the surtitles in Ninagawa's practice reassures audiences of the unchanging, uncontested stability of Shakespeare's text, and recreates the original order of its translation into Japanese.

Yet once this guarantee is in place, the surtitles are often superfluous, because the density of Shakespeare's language combined with the speed of the Japanese stage delivery make it impossible to watch and read simultaneously without missing something. And a spectator unused to reading Shakespeare may find herself little the wiser for the surtitles. On the other hand, without either following the spoken Japanese or reading Shakespeare's English, Ninagawa's stage images and stage business layer the basic plot situation with a great deal to watch and engage in. His sets frequently consist of multiple levels between which the actors move, so that single scenes and speeches are punctuated by a sense of transition to a different stage of the action, literally and figuratively. The

---

[8] Ninagawa's practice of surtitling based on the original text is not singular in theatre translation. Yvonne Griesel points out that 'the reference level contains existing canonical dramas or drama translations and plays a key role in T[heatre] T[ranslation]. My findings have clearly shown that a German original text performed in French translation, which reappears in its source language in the surtitles enjoys the highest authority. It is treated as a so-called sacred text, and the translator does not dare to make serious interventions in the textual structure, so as not to change the style and language of the original' ('Surtitles and Translation', p. 10).

[9] The two approaches to surtitling opera, focusing either on the libretto or the stage production, are discussed by Riitta Virkkunen, 'The Source Text of Opera Surtitles', *Meta*, 49 (2004), 89–97.

theatrical spectacle of the motifs and devices he employs, like the breathtaking cherry tree version of Birnam Wood, transfigure moments of inner drama, like Macbeth's later solitary speeches, with a potent visual force and suggestiveness. Throughout, the combination of choral and instrumental music, and of traditional Japanese with Western aural accompaniment, interweave contrastive emotive cues. All these interwoven or layered elements assert a vivid presence distinct from both the spoken level of the action and Shakespeare's English in the surtitles. The presence of Shakespeare's text, to which the dialogue is tied, but not its embodiments or its settings, demarcates the separation between speech and its presentational context. The surtitles thus *create* the untranslatable, which remains beyond the bounds of language in the way another cultural aesthetic can imagine, visualize and vocalize the 'same' play.

In Ninagawa's productions that have toured abroad, such as *Ninagawa Macbeth* (1985), *Tempest* (1988), *Pericles* and *Titus Andronicus* (2006),[10] the untranslatable is most often couched as the marvellous and fantastic, through the emphasis of his presentational style on exceeding the bounds of realism, and its surprises of scale and dynamic movement. The incongruence between Shakespeare's speech and elements of fantasy in the stage presentation challenge the kinds of meaning that are based on character realism and interpretation; that is, on the written text simultaneously present in the surtitles. The acting bridges Shakespeare's text and the stage presentation, and ranges from stylized to naturalistic, but often leans toward the former with formalized movements and melodramatic expression. In short, the surtitles pit the cultural authority of Shakespeare's text against a cultural environment of splendour, fantasy and suggestiveness that Ninagawa's style adds to and expands alongside the text. As many have noted, this powerful visual style depends less upon Japanese theatre traditions than a virtuoso synthesis of elements drawn from disparate sources.[11] Thus the wider implications of his practice are not for a meeting of Shakespeare and Japanese theatre, but of the conjunction of the verbal code – Shakespeare

performing through the surtitles as the 'original' language – and the growing ascendancy of the image, that is at once marked as Japanese and as a composite part of the shift in globalized, cross-cultural communications.

In the Ryutopia Noh Theatre Shakespeare Series' production of *Hamlet* in 2007, on the other hand, the sustained tension between Shakespeare's text in translation and its embodiment in different cultural systems served the opposite need for restriction in the presentation. This performance began with a shaven-headed figure in dark clothes (Hamlet) sitting cross-legged down-stage centre on the six-metre square *noh* stage, at a diagonal facing the audience seated around two sides of the stage, and dimly lit by a single spot on the diagonal. The stage brightened as the other characters filed in along the 'bridgeway' (*hashi-gakari*) to stand behind Hamlet and sit along the bridgeway. Like him, they wore modern kimono in sombre colours, mostly covered by a robe-like over-kimono that presented a less distinctively Japanese, more international appearance coordinating with the mixed hairstyles (Claudius, Polonius and Laertes all had contemporary-styled blond hair). Their acting was formal and restrained, while Hamlet remained seated, motionless, with eyes cast down. When Gertrude spoke to him he opened his eyes and looked up, but not at her, and delivered his ''Tis not alone my inky cloak of black' speech without moving his head, looking straight out over the audience.

Hamlet's immobility at first appeared to present his detachment from the court, as in Shakespeare. But as Horatio described his encounter with the Ghost, and Hamlet continued to act his role exclusively through his intense speech and facial

---

10 Dates refer to the first overseas tours of the productions, not the generally earlier Tokyo run.

11 See for example Tetsuo Kishi, 'Japanese Shakespeare and English Reviewers', in Sasayama Takashi, J. R. Mulryne and Margaret Shewring, eds., *Shakespeare and the Japanese Stage* (Cambridge, 1988), pp. 110–23. Different ways of reading Ninagawa's images of nature are discussed in Kennedy and Yong Li Lan, 'Why Shakespeare?' in *Shakespeare in Asia: Contemporary Performance.*

expressions without moving his head or body, remaining silent onstage in the same position during Laertes's farewell to Polonius and Ophelia that went on behind him, I kept feeling the pressure for him to move. When he spoke to the Ghost, who stood upstage on the bridgeway, without turning to face him it became clear that Hamlet's stillness was the pivotal device that not only defined his character but altered the kind of action taking place. To a spectator accustomed to relating to a realist Hamlet, this simple, striking device magnetized the action around Hamlet's consciousness, juxtaposing his consciousness against action in scenes where he is normally absent and erasing any distinction between his private and public selves which is usually a crucial point of dramatic tension. Instead, the actor's sustained immobility had the effect of suggesting that some part of Hamlet's reactions and feelings were continuously present but contained and unexpressed, while it also opened up the action to displaced embodied modes of presenting that action. As Hamlet and the Ghost spoke, three figures (adapted from *Karakuri Ningyo*, traditional Japanese mechanical dolls) who had been seated at the back of the stage rose to stand between them in a line of fixed, wooden, doll-like postures, creating a tableau that mimed the connection between Hamlet and his father's Ghost at a level distinct from the dialogue. At this moment, and throughout the performance at critical points, a repetitive, rhythmical western melody played by a live pianist built the momentum of the scene.

The production stayed close to Shakespeare's text, though it was heavily pruned, and a spectator familiar with *Hamlet* could follow the performance without difficulty. Hamlet did not physically engage the other characters except at one point when he turned to look at Ophelia standing immediately behind him: this appeared to present the moment when he appeared in her closet. The audience could not see his face, but her reaction in a scream prompted one to imagine what their exchange of looks communicated. This moment signalled that Hamlet's stillness could be broken, and heightened the tension of uncertainty as to when it might recur. Contrasted with the other characters' bodily movement and interaction, Hamlet's immobility resisted the empathetic identification with his character that his speech invited, and implied his theatrical mastery as the centre of the action, quite the opposite of the Shakespearian Hamlet's notorious passivity. Thus the verbal expressiveness that is central to Hamlet, and to Shakespeare's dramatic mode, was juxtaposed against the force of concentrated stillness used by *noh* drama. The two opposed modes were co-present in one body, each putting pressure on the other to break. The director Kurita Yoshihiro explains in an interview:

> I had come to feel a basic contradiction in the act of performing a play from a translated script that was not written originally in your native language. Even if you got the actors to use lines that had a natural sense of daily life, the historical background would still be missing and that in itself is enough to undermine the reality and make a production hopeless. But, with Shakespeare's plays there is a sense of un-reality or other-worldliness to the words to begin with, and that can make it all more poetic, musical and fanciful. You also have jesters and ghosts and nymphs and witches making appearances, so that it is in effect a world of the imagination from the outset.[12]

The Ryutopia Shakespeare Series aims to hybridize Shakespeare and *noh* to produce a unique third form. In the production of *Hamlet*, individual character and archetypal presentation, Shakespeare's dramatic expression of character in words, and *noh* drama's distillation of experience in form, were mutually altered and estranging.

It is thus inevitable that understanding the language should be crucial to the spectator's participation in the resolution of this tense pressure exerted by words and embodiment on each other. In the final duel, the acting of the remaining four characters – Claudius, Gertrude, Horatio and Laertes – closed the gap with Hamlet as they took positions

---

[12] Interview with Kensuke Yokouchi: 'Artist Interview: A meeting of Eastern and Western classics: The Noh-staged Shakespeare of Yoshihiro Kurita', ed. Tomoko Tajima, *Performing Arts Network Japan*, at http://www.performingarts.jp/E/art_interview/0503/1.html, accessed 10 December 2008.

in a straight processional line extending across the width of the stage, and spoke their lines while they walked very slowly from the back edge to the front, then turned and walked back. Meanwhile the doll actors mimed fight sequences narrated in voice-over while repetitive chords were heard on the piano. Hamlet had turned to face the audience squarely, but otherwise remained unmoving. At the climactic moment, he shouted, pressed his arms sharply against his knees and the other characters, now all at the front edge, dropped slowly down to kneel in a line (Horatio remained standing). I watched this performance on an un-subtitled video-recording of it and, without following the words, I was unclear of the function of the inter-polated narration, though the scene was differenti-ated from the rest of the action by a greater degree of formalization that shaded into ritualization. I later realised that the narration reprised the Pyrrhus speech, which had also been dramatized by the doll actors:

HORATIO   Treason! Treason!.
NARRATOR   *The city of Troy felt this fatal blow, through its senses, and collapsed in flames, and the crash captures Pyrrhus' attention.*
HAMLET   Now, you incestuous murderer, drink up this poison. Is your little pearl in there? Follow my mother. (*King dies*)[13]

The splicing of this reprise into the scene could be seen to juxtapose epic narration with the contained enactment of Noh and, by metatheatrical impli-cation, the final scene of confusion and misfired intrigue in Shakespeare's *Hamlet* here proceeded inevitably towards its climax in the same way as the death of Priam; both scenes, like Noh, perpetually restaged, re-enacted and folded over each other as cultural rituals.

Ninagawa's style and Ryutopia's *Hamlet* demon-strate opposite ends of the spectrum of staying faithful to Shakespeare's text while embodying it in different cultural, theatrical and/or aesthetic sys-tems. Whereas Ninagawa places sensory, spectacu-lar effects alongside Shakespeare's dialogue, Kurita removes realistic bodily behaviour from the ver-bal expression of Shakespeare's words. Although

it may seem self-evident, both strategies require English surtitles for the spectator to distinguish that the Japanese speech is translated from Shake-speare. Without the English, a spectator (whether Japanese-speaking, English-speaking or neither) is not faced with the tension between that speech and its presentation, and between the cultural and theatrical values they represent. Thus the spec-tatorial position that is the third point in the transaction can remain submerged. The perfor-mance of translation in surtitles, which is actually a counter-translation, makes explicit the first trans-lation (English to Japanese) that has taken place before the performance, by reflecting and corre-sponding to it.[14] In this way the stage action and audience reaction mirror each other in the distor-tions of their own reflections.

3. TRANSLATION IN CIRCULATION

If the practice of surtitling brings the audience into view, then its performative function is not to enable a foreign audience to enter into another culture but, rather, to introduce the spectator's relational position into what she is watching. In this section I shift from the embodiment of Shakespeare's text to new plays derived from Shakespeare's, and the more direct participation of translation and sur-titling in the stage action. The Ku Na'uka Theatre Company's *Nô Play of Spirit Othello*, directed by Miyagi Satoshi in 2005, and the Japan Asia Founda-tion Center's *LEAR*, directed by the Singaporean Ong Keng Sen in 1997, both presented the unquiet ghosts of Shakespeare's characters who relive and revise the course of events in Shakespeare's play; both treated language as a referent to Shakespeare. *Nô Play of Spirit Othello* adapts *Othello* to the *Mugen Noh* (fantasy *noh*) structure in two acts, with the

---

[13] Japanese script from the Ryutopia company translated into English by ACTC Translation Centre, Singapore.
[14] For a monolingual spectator listening to a new script in his/her own language, heterolingual address is at its minimal; whereas the non-aggregate community of English Shake-speare performances is ironically more plural, say, in Lon-don, where they play to audiences with different Englishes (as well as non-Anglophone tourists).

premise that a traveller to Cyprus meets the ghost of Desdemona, who tells him her story. The performance began with the traveller in European monk's habit introducing the beauty of Cyprus by re-imagining the night scene in the traditional Japanese garden of the Tokyo National Museum, where the open-air *noh* stage was mounted:

> Under the light from the setting sun the dense olive
> mountains on the left draw towards the shore.
> The deep blue Mediterranean sea is on the right.
> The two complement each other perfectly.
> The landscape of Botticelli's masterpiece must be like
> this,
> the crisp shadows of the trees captured
> in the ocean forever.[15]

Four women in peasant dress entered carrying jars on their heads, at which he marvelled that they should be singing a gondolier's song in Venetian, which he, a Venetian, recognized. These reflexive references to a doubly foreign language foregrounded the fiction of Japanese actors playing Venetians on Cyprus, where the ghost of Desdemona lingers. Costume was eclectic, including modernized plastic *kariginu* (commoner's clothes in pre-modern Japan), Asian masks and Western long dresses. A group of actors dressed uniformly in white was seated onstage throughout and doubled as chorus, musicians and additional performers.

Fragmented references to Shakespeare's lines ranged from direct quotes to adaptations spoken by the characters and the chorus. Recalling her marriage to Othello, Desdemona said, 'A bright sword, that spring eve', and broke off. The chorus responded by repeating the phrase with rising urgency until she completed the sentence, 'Passed through my body'. Key words and lines were also written on a small screen at the back as if by an invisible hand. Thus multiple modes of citing Shakespeare were presented simultaneously: as choric speaking, as a different Desdemona reliving her past life and as the writing and translating of Shakespeare's words into the Japanese script. The English subtitles on the DVD recording insert the location – or the language community – of non-Japanese spectators as a point

in the routing of repeated cultural estrangements and displacements: from Italy (via Cinthio) to London (where Shakespeare's *Othello* was performed), through Tokyo (where this production was conceived and played), back to Cyprus and Venice (imagined by Shakespeare and re-imagined here), and around the world (to New Delhi on tour). For a Japanese spectator at the Tokyo performance, the Japanese language and location may assume transparency, in the suspension of disbelief; but once translated, the imaginings and memories of race, culture and belonging redouble.

Verbal invocations of race and location were contrasted against the central moment at which Desdemona's ghost re-enacted her strangling by Othello wordlessly, through an extended dance sequence in which a large dark glove on her right hand represented the memory of the other. Performed as a visceral, unspeakable re-experiencing of that terrible end, which gradually dissolved almost imperceptibly into a transcendence of that memory in prayer, this climactic moment was capable of traversing cultural boundaries without language, through the concentrated expressive power of the actress's movements as she danced to the accompaniment of a rhythmic drum and the eerie sound of the flute. Its transmission through corporeal performance, however, was set in tension against the self-reflexive framework of re-playing, that paradoxically enabled it to emerge as a shared cultural memory of Shakespeare's play – out of time, place and language. It was the traveller who demands to hear her story, and to whom she appeals to pray for her release, who indexed the multiple displacements involved in the literal translation of languages and the figurative translation of cultures. A Japanese woman playing a Venetian man, in the role of a traveller disguised as a pilgrim, this unnamed figure to whom Desdemona's ghost told the story of *Othello* and who acted as mediator and representative for the audience, enacted the indeterminate subject position of intercultural Shakespeare on the move.

---

[15] English subtitles in the DVD recording from Ku Na'uka Theatre Company.

An extreme instance of the structural principle of translation is the Singaporean director Ong Keng Sen's intercultural strategy in his Shakespeare-based productions, where each character or group of characters was played in a different language and performance form. The first of his three productions was *LEAR* (1999), in which a *noh* actor played both the Old Man (Lear) and the Mother (the ghost of Lear's wife) in Japanese, a Beijing Opera actor played the Older Daughter (combining Goneril and Regan) in Chinese, and a Thai dancer played the Younger Daughter (Cordelia). The Retainer and the Loyal Retainer (Edmund and Kent respectively) spoke in Indonesian and acted in movements adapted from *puncak silat*, a regional, ceremonial martial arts form of Minangkabau in Sumatra. The music was interculturally matched, such that the Javanese gamelan orchestra or a modern pop ballad accompanied Umewaka's *noh* performance, and the *shakuhachi* (the Japanese wooden flute) accompanied Jiang's arias. The new script by the Japanese playwright Rio Kishida centred on the Older Daughter as the protagonist who kills her sister, lover and father at different stages in order to finally assume sole sovereignty. The performance was surtitled in the majority language of each venue on its tours through Hong Kong, Singapore, Jakarta, Perth, Berlin and Copenhagen.

Depending on the spectator's level of familiarity (if any) with Shakespeare's *King Lear*, *noh* drama, Beijing opera, and/or Thai *khon* dance, what she saw and how she reacted to it would differ, sometimes markedly, from what someone else noticed, found interesting, attractive or objectionable. As a Singaporean Shakespeare scholar, with a close knowledge of the text of *King Lear*, and some – but not extensive – knowledge of the Asian forms used, I have watched the video-recording of this performance, subtitled in English as was the Singapore performance, with several inter-cutting reactions: a) I am conscious that I half listen to the Mandarin and Malay that I partially follow, and half read the translation of these and the Japanese, thereby tracing a constant movement in comprehension closer to and further from the action; b) I register through the dialogue the echoes and points of departure from Shakespeare's text; c) I note details of the different costumes, gestures, vocal styles, both for how these re-create and resemble the roles of *King Lear* (I am quite secure in this identification), and where they depart from the conventions of the Asian forms (I am less sure of these); d) above all, I am acutely aware that the grand display of Asian forms defines and stages a unique presentation, equally unfamiliar in English Shakespeare or Asian performance traditions.

I thus watch this production from parallel inside/outside positions, at the unstable interstice of a passage that I make back and forth between Shakespeare's original and Asian theatre traditions. Neither *King Lear* nor any of the Asian forms is fully present on stage, but they are mentally invoked by the connections I make between them, and in the process I alternate between seeing each from the other side. This interstitial position would be different from one spectator to another, changing as the production toured to a different country. During the performance, I was aware of the margins of my own reaction, that those around me in the Singapore performance were watching and hearing with distinct differences from myself – the friend I attended the performance with, who was educated in Chinese rather than English like myself, found the Older Daughter very uncomfortable to listen to, as (he said) her expressions violated Chinese conventions of appropriateness. No doubt the gaps between how I reacted to what I saw and another spectator's reaction widened and proliferated with other audiences abroad, and I was conscious that, while these reactions were unavailable to me, they contextualized mine.

Verbal expression in *LEAR* concentrated on images that could attach to the visual, bodily images presented, and be transported with them across linguistic barriers – correspondingly, idiomatic distinctions capable of differentiating the multiple languages disappeared. The vocal style conventional to each form was heightened as the defining character of speech and culture. Without the evocation or inflexions of local reference specific to a cultural milieu, the languages did not signify places, but, rather, language communities. As such, each language virtualized belonging in a country of origin as competency in its language. These competencies are not specific to geographical location, but, as in Singapore, they have been dispersed through migration and the transnational mobility of globalized audiences. Language acted as a surrogate for, rather than as an embodiment of, locale. The several languages spoken concurrently on stage invoked access to, rather than being in, a location or culture, and thus drew attention to the performance of translation. Particularly since diction and syntax were kept fairly simple, the simultaneous languages related to an audience's partial bi- or tri-linguality. For instance, the Mandarin 'zhuren', Indonesian 'raja' and neutral enough English 'ruler' evoke vastly different histories, images and styles of command, yet in their simultaneous presence as spoken or read terms they acted as performative doubles of one another. The script was printed throughout in two languages, including a third set of lines with Arabic phoneticization of the Mandarin and Japanese kanji characters in the Chinese and Japanese portions. It was along what is usually understood as the margins of the performance, through the surtitles that translated the multilingual script into the predominant audience language at each location, that a spectator became conscious of her geographical location, and of belonging in or coming from outside that place. Since the action could be substantively followed through visual and aural cues, the surtitles drew attention to translation as an issue rather than a necessary function, as the performance of translation, where words are always read or heard as correlatives to other words, and thus no longer existed in the system of a language as such.

4. SCHOLARS, FANS AND INTERCULTURAL TIME

The simultaneous translation of a performance in written surtitles – or audio transmission over headphones (as in the Kabuki-za in Tokyo) – is an extension of the onstage performance made possible by modern technology, which thereby alters

that production's performativity. An appropriate coda to thinking about the triangulation of speech, embodiment and translation in live performance is the technological reproduction and circulation of Asian Shakespeare performance in digital media. The two examples sketched below focus on the agency of subtitling in the globalized distribution of digital performances. They highlight the mixed cooperative and interventionist roles that the medium of the Internet now plays, not as an interface between cultures that are thought of as discrete spaces of production and reception, source and target locations, but as a zone that both transforms and generates cultures conceived, in Anthony Pym's words, as 'a set of factors creating resistance to the movement of information; or more exactly, sets of factors that alter the status of information as it is moved'.[16]

My own role in the first example shifts from that of a spectator to a collaborator in an online archive of performance resources: the *Asian Shakespeare Intercultural Archive (ASIA)*, which is an intersection between practitioners, individual scholars and three Asian Shakespeare projects – the *MIT Shakespeare Project, Relocating Intercultural Theatre* (National University of Singapore) and *A Web Archive of Asian Shakespeare Productions* (JSPS Kaken/Gunma-Doho Universities). *ASIA* aims to bridge the language and access barriers that currently make it difficult for practitioners and scholars of Shakespeare performance in different Asian countries to interact with each other and the rest of the world, by assembling an online corpus of production footage accompanied by translated scripts, and by pooling local expertise in the creation of detailed data on each production, its forms, reception and references. The process of creating this archive has brought into view a number of broader considerations that bear upon this discussion.

First, the archive is itself an interculturalizing enterprise in that it transforms live performances into the globalized medium of digital materials, and

---

[16] Anthony Pym, 'Four Remarks on Translation Research and Multimedia', in Yves Gambier and Henrik Gottlieb, eds., *(Multi)media Translation* (Amsterdam, 2001), p. 278.

redistributes a performance's potential audience from a concrete location/locations to the virtual, indeterminately plural and indefinite temporality of access on the internet. Both these functions are extensions of theatre companies who make commercial DVDs of their productions. The difference that *ASIA* stands to make to the reproduction and distribution of live performance is in the archival aim of bringing materials together as a corpus, to be studied and compared across language and cultural communities through the translation of scripts and collation of data. To establish structures for sharing and organizing these materials, continuous negotiation between the specific cultural and institutional contexts of the collaborators that determine their priorities is needed, as well as between the differing kinds of knowledge brought by practitioners, audiences and academics interacting with those materials from distinct cultural positions.

Second, in formal terms, such an archive extends and alters the accessibility of audio-visual material through corresponding verbal understanding (translation) and information (data). The relationship of this verbal mode to the sensory impact of the performance footage is that of a discursive supplement to the processes of recording, editing and digitization by which the live performance is altered at different stages to produce a changed horizon of intersection between audiences and modes of reception. The structure of the data and the ways in which it facilitates searches for comparative studies, design layout decisions and priorities for translation all shape the discursive field of interaction with audio-visual modes of transmission. For instance, the translated script may relate to the video image in several ways: if subtitle text is superimposed over the image in the manner of film or television subtitles, the performance is approximated to those media and requires the least effort by the viewer to assimilate the translation; whereas if a text block is placed alongside the image and switches to the next block once the time code correlating to the last line is reached by the recording, the interactions represented by both making and using translations are distinguished as a separate activity from that of watching the image.

Different languages entail different orders of verbal knowledge. To translate diverse Asian productions into English alone would forego the lateral connections between cultures geographically and historically close to each other in favour of their vertical relation to the global language of English, placing them like the spokes of a wheel whose hub is English. Instead, multiple language translations into different Asian languages make the borders between the people and situations producing Shakespeare in Asian countries permeable to one another and enable an intercultural discourse to develop.

Thus, third, the construction of such an archive blurs the boundary between production and reception present in the initial act of theatrical production through its reproduction of the performance in a radically different format. For example, the Singapore team, which is responsible for translations, has commissioned an English translation of the Ryutopia *Hamlet* script for which the company has kindly given copyright permission to the archive along with its production footage. The company has reciprocally requested to use that translation in their tour and/or commercial DVD release of the production. That is, the reproducibility of the production (in digital streaming media) brings into play other modes of transmission (on the internet, subtitling) that create new circles of reception which may, in turn, interact with those modes of transmission and the original production.

My second example illustrates a related circuit which is looser, more informal and ad hoc than a scholarly archive, and has a much wider popular reach. From April to September 2007 the Japanese television station CBC aired an *anime* (Japanese animation) series *Romeo X Juliet* loosely based on Shakespeare's play, produced by *anime* studio Gonzo, in twenty-four half-hour episodes.[17] Each episode was subtitled in a variety of languages (English, Spanish, French, Italian, Greek, Israeli, Arab) by *anime* fan groups in an internet

---

[17] The official website address of *Romeo X Juliet* is http://anime. goo.ne.jp/special/gonzo/romejuli/. The English website address is http://romejuli.jp/english/

sub-culture known as 'fansubbing'. The subtitled files were available for viewing on YouTube as well as for download through the P2P protocol, and the series was closely followed and widely discussed on internet blogs, forums and chat sites.

The intersections that occurred in *Romeo X Juliet* between the iconicity of Shakespeare's quintessential star-crossed lovers, the cult appeal and icon formation of *anime* and fan cultures of participation must be understood through its serialized form, whereby the original play was elaborated over six months of weekly instalments – a 12-hour *Romeo and Juliet* would be inconceivable in any other genre and format! Fansubbing thus interacted with the complicated twists of the plot in a currency of demand and anticipation circulating over a virtual international network, often made explicit by individuals' requests on fan forums. The hybridization of Shakespeare with *anime* generates the frisson of unexpected conjunction between two very different genres and cultures of appreciation. A post on an American blog reads:

A Romeo and Juliet anime = a naked attempt to shove shakespeare down the throats of otakus [*anime* fans] who gagged on the original play and wouldn't be caught dead with it. And I was right. But I'm now captivated by the [sic] how they seem to be laughing in the face of Brit-Lit purists everywhere. Especially the characters being able to say 'Neo Verona' with a straight face. You start to love the plot twists and story until you realize . . . you know how it's supposed to end.[18]

The series attracted praise for its detailed drawing and high quality animation in a European period style, and features flying horses and the comic character of a playwright Willy who lives in the backstage quarters of the theatre where Juliet also grows up in secrecy. Juliet is the sole survivor of the Capulet line in a class-bound society ruled with an iron hand by Lord Montague, and is disguised as a boy by the surviving Capulet followers and not told her identity until she comes of age just after the story begins. Her character amalgamates the cross-dressing conventions of Shakespeare's comedies and of *anime* and *manga*, even as she also resembles a female Zorro in red cape, hat and mask in her self-appointed role as Red Whirlwind, a masked crusader for justice. The intercultural hybridization of the series is epitomized by its romantic theme song, whose melody is better known as the Irish song 'Danny Boy', here covered by Lena Park, a Korean-American R&B singer, in Japanese lyrics evocative of tragic, ideal love. It plays as a kind of signature-trailer at the start of every episode with karaoke-style subtitles that were translated into English with substantial divergences between the different fansub versions.

The community of fans, like that of scholars, positions itself in a relation of expertise to a specific site of cultural production. But fans carry out their role of supporter with a passionate attachment and desire to participate actively in the primary production. The subtitling of Japanese *anime* programmes originated in *anime* fan clubs in the 1990s as a way of sharing this otherwise difficult to obtain genre among local enthusiasts. The products are distributed free, initially on videotapes, and require only knowledge of Japanese and technical know-how in using the subtitling software. The agency of fansubs in adumbrating the original production is an explicitly translative one that manifests the foreign in language, locale and ownership – of both the original and the fansubbed versions – by crossing linguistic and media platforms. It occupies a legal and production grey zone: the fansub groups claim credit for the huge international popularization of *anime* over the last decade, and generally recognize a gentleman's code according to which fansubbing stops once the title is released for commercial distribution in their country.[19]

The participation of fansub groups in extending and multiplying the performance event of *Romeo X Juliet* differed strikingly from the careful distance foreign audiences normally maintain from Asian Shakespeare in the theatre, because the fans claim the foreign status of *anime* as their own; yet that

---

[18] Post #24 by 'Hope Renate', *Hop Step Jump*, http://anime.jefflawson.net/2007/04/07/romeo-x-juliet/

[19] Jorge Díaz Cintas and Pablo Muñoz Sánchez, 'Fansubs–Audiovisual Translation in an Amateur Environment', *JoS-Trans* 6 (2006), www.jostrans.org/issue06/art_diaz_munoz.php, accessed 10 December 2008.

participation also closed the circuit of competing and pluralized cultural positions enacted through Shakespeare. The majority of English posts situated the viewer's affiliation to and appreciation of Shakespeare and *anime*; everyone wanted to know if it would end the same way. So of course, long before it actually acquired the distribution rights to *Romeo X Juliet*, Funimation Entertainment issued a cease-and-desist request to the English group Shinsen Subs after episode 23 was aired, as a consequence of which all other groups fansubbing the series ground to an abrupt halt, and fans outside Japan were not able to access the last two episodes.

An online performance archive and the fansubbing of serialized *anime* together illustrate the extent to which linguistic translation is inseparable from technological conversions that not only extend the place of a performance, but also alter its 'real' time as an event. The reproducibility of Shakespeare in Asian performance gains its intercultural definition through the counter-translations that mirror the first translations of his plays out of English. This mirroring of translations brings into view the temporality of an intercultural relationship to Shakespeare, which is usually conceived in spatial terms. Translation manifests the old divide between language and the body, and draws a spectator's attention to her positionality in the orientalization of the one as western and the other as eastern. Self-reflexively incorporated into new plays based on Shakespeare's, translation foregrounds at once the circulation of Shakespeare and the mobility and virtuality with which we now imagine cultural locations in Asia – or indeed elsewhere. As an interstitial time zone that loops production and reception in a continuous circuit by means of digital technology, translation changes the synchronic and diachronic axes of the performance, and its status as event and artifact. Finally, the performativity of translation returns Asian Shakespeare to our continuing investments in the value of language for engaging the full range of receptions which can be optimal but not singular, objective or complete.

'THE SINGLE AND PECULIAR LIFE': HAMLET'S HEART AND THE EARLY MODERN SUBJECT

GRAHAM HOLDERNESS

... you would pluck out the heart of my mystery.[1]

Revisionist accounts of early modern subjectivity almost invariably begin with Hamlet's accusation. Elizabeth Hanson's fine book *Discovering the Subject* opens with the phrase as a paradigmatic statement, in which Hamlet assumes the position of the modern subject, endowed with an inner mystery, and resistant to its penetration and discovery.[2] In this model the subject *contains* something elusively called 'mystery'; the space of mystery is the interior of the subject's body, here symbolized by the heart; and other people are desperate to get access to that mystery, if necessary by tearing the heart out of the subject's body. Since this was physically accomplished in contemporary rituals of execution for crimes involving treason, especially at this time religious treason, the phrase seems to gesture towards the torture chamber, the scaffold and the whole dangerous recusant world of Catholic England and 'Secret Shakespeare'. Removing the heart from the chest was never a practical way of acquiring information, but here the torturer and the executioner merge into one, and the symbolic and literal are hard to prise apart. Torture was often a prelude to judicial killing, and methods of execution were refined to prolong physical torment. The removal of organs at execution could be seen as a grotesque literalization of the torturer's invasive inquiries, as suggested in *King Lear*: 'To know our enemies' minds, we rip their hearts.'[3]

Where Hamlet's phrase has been deployed in recent discussions of Renaissance subjectivity, it is generally without reference to its immediate dra-matic context. It appears after the play-within-the play, in Hamlet's speech to Guildenstern about the recorders. Hamlet is not, he protests, a musical instrument to be manipulated and played upon. But perversely he then proceeds to draw an elaborate parallel between man and recorder.

... you would play upon me! You would seem to know my stops, you would pluck out the heart of my mystery, you would sound me from my lowest note to the top of my compass.[4]

'Pluck out the heart' features here within a series of musical metaphors: to 'play upon', to 'know the stops', to 'sound' the human instrument through the whole of its acoustic range. But its contribution to that series is ambiguous. What is its musical content? If 'mystery' relates to 'mastery', profession, craft or skill, rather than to mystery as 'secret', then it could function as part of the man/instrument parallel. 'Mastery', however, should belong to the man, not the instrument. 'Pluck' is of course a musical action (Hamlet also uses the term 'fret'), but it would surely be a discordant reference, in this disquisition on woodwind, to a stringed instrument, such as a lute. Linguistically then the phrase

---

[1] Quoted from the 1604/5 second quarto, 3.2.357–8. *Hamlet*, ed. Ann Thompson and Neil Taylor (London, 2006).

[2] Elizabeth Hanson, *Discovering the Subject in Renaissance England* (Cambridge, 1998), p. 1.

[3] *King Lear*, 4.6.257–8.

[4] Quoted from the 1623 Folio, 3.2.354–7. *Hamlet, the Texts of 1603 and 1623*, ed. Ann Thompson and Neil Taylor (London, 2006).

presents some difficulty, and editors have had some difficulty explaining it.

The Folio and second quarto texts are virtually the same for this passage (the second quarto has 'my compass' instead of 'the top of my compass'). Quite different however is the first quarto:

You would seeme to know my stops, you would play
      upon mee,
You would search the very inward part of my hart,
And dive into the secreet of my soule.[5]

Here there is a logical transition from the instrument metaphor to the statement about the spies trying to gain access to the subject, a transition that precipitates the allegation: 'You would search the very inward part of my hart, / And dive into the secreet of my soule.' Though it is certainly less graphic than 'pluck out the heart', the physical nuance of 'search' could still echo the torture-chamber. Tortured Jesuit Thomas Cottam (younger brother of Stratford schoolmaster John Cottam) said of his rack-masters 'yow ar searchers of secrettes: for yow wolde needes knowe of me what penaunce I was enioined by my ghostlie father for my sinnes'.[6] Like Cottam, Hamlet is speaking here from the position of the tortured, and casting Rossencraft and Gilderstone (so named in the first quarto) in the role of torturers. Hence his emphasis is less on the violent dragging of truth out from the body, and more on the successive layers of defence located within the body and through which the searcher has to penetrate to find what he's after. The very inward part of the heart is a depth within the heart itself, a more removed ground of mystery, an inner sanctum. If we take 'dive' literally, then to get to the soul and its secrets the interrogator/spy would have to dive right in, swimming very deep into an interior psychological and spiritual sea, perhaps finding the sunken treasure of truth impossible to locate. By the same token the executioner might find himself holding his victim's heart in his hand, and yet, as far as secrets go, empty-handed.[7] The heart of a traitor may look much like anyone else's heart and may, as a sign, decline to declare the truth its excavation

is designed to elicit, the patient being no longer here.

Even more striking a contrast is provided by the fact that Hamlet's speech on the 'sponge' appears, in the first quarto, here next to the 'recorder' speech, whereas in the other two texts it is placed much later:

Zownds do you thinke I am easier to be pla'yd
On, then a pipe? Call mee what Instrument
You will, though you can frett mee, yet you can not
Play upon mee, besides to be demanded by a sponge.
    . . . a sponge, that sokes up the kings
Countenance, favours and rewardes, that makes
His liberalitie your store house . . .
                              (Tragicall Historie, p. 77)

The 'spunge' suggests the subject as open, porous, penetrable, fashioned and swayed by external influence. 'Men are sponges, which, to pour out, receive', said Donne.[8] Its pliable absorbency contrasts sharply with the recorder (which Hamlet is still holding) as a metaphor for the subject: a closed, hard exterior, with an enclosed and hidden inner space that can produce 'eloquent music' when some of its holes are stopped. Somewhere inside the instrument, the metaphor of 'diving' declares, there is also a hidden underground pool, a well of souls, into which you may, at your peril, attempt to 'dive'. But that is a liquid contained, pent up, inaccessible, while the sponge liberally sucks up and regurgitates whatever moisture it can find in the circumambient air. Hamlet of course says he is neither a sponge, nor an 'instrument', a pipe to be played on by others. He is not a

---

5   *The Tragicall Historie of Hamlet Prince of Denmarke*, ed. Graham Holderness and Bryan Loughrey (Hemel Hempstead, 1992), p. 77.
6   William Allen, *A True, Sincere and Modest Defence of English Catholiques that Suffer for their Faith* (Rheims, 1584), pp. 11–12.
7   John Aubrey recorded such evidence from the execution of Sir Everard Digby. ''Twas his ill fate to suffer in the Powderplott. When his heart was pluct out by the Executioner (who, *secundam formam*, cryed, Here is the heart of a Traytor!) it is credibly reported, he replied, Thou liest!'. John Aubrey, *Brief Lives*, ed. Oliver Lawson Dick (Ann Arbor, MI, 1962), p. 96.
8   'To Sir Henry Wotton', *Poems of John Donne*, vol. II, ed. E. K. Chambers (London, 1896), p. 8.

Foucauldian subject fashioned by external influences, like an Aeolian harp; nor, like his interrogators, a porous subject that has no intrinsic being, but merely soaks up external pressure like some magic dishcloth. He neither receives nor pours out: his being is inscrutable, veiled, hidden. 'I have that within which passes show' (Q2, 1.2.85); or in the first quarto, no 'outward semblance' is 'equall to the sorrow of my heart' (*Tragicall Historie*, p. 42). But he does, like the recorder, have an interior, albeit one that seems to be a hollow space, a thing of nothing: and from that interior emanates 'discourse', 'most delicate', 'most excellent music'. If that music be not produced by external influence and manipulation, from the breath and fingering of others, then where does it come from? What kind of recorder plays itself? What is the origin and nature of the subject?

The Q1 version of this classic observation ('You would search the very inward part of my hart,/And dive into the secreet of my soule') conveniently marks out the territory of the subjectivity debate as it has been woven around *Hamlet*. *Hamlet* was, as John Lee has shown, a test case for Cultural Materialism, and is a constant point of reference in histories of that movement.[9] Francis Barker in *The Tremulous Private Body* used *Hamlet* to demonstrate his contention that modern subjectivity did not exist before the later seventeenth century: 'At the centre of Hamlet, in the interior of his mystery, there is, in short, nothing.'[10]

Hamlet's sense of inwardness is 'anachronistic', wrote Barker, since 'bourgeois subjectivity' had not yet arrived, and in the play 'interiority remains gestural' (p. 163):

Pre-bourgeois subjection does not properly involve subjectivity at all, but a condition of dependent membership in which place and articulation are defined not by an interiorized self-recognition . . . but by incorporation in the body politic (p. 31).

Catherine Belsey followed this same line, quoting Barker on *Hamlet* with approval. The modern subject, 'the free unconstrained author of meaning and action, the origin of history',[11] was a later invention. The search for Hamlet's 'mystery', his

'authentic inner reality', is therefore a wild goose-chase: 'The quest is, of course, endless, because the object of it is not there' (p. 41).

To ascribe subjectivity to Renaissance characters is to posit an 'imaginary interiority', imported into reading of the drama by modern ideological habits. Jean Howard further endorsed this view, and claimed that the 'interiority and self-presence of the individual' belong to a later historical period.[12]

Other critics such as Jonathan Goldberg and Patricia Fumerton took different but compatible views. They argued that there clearly was a *perception* of interiority, and a rhetoric of inwardness, in the Early Modern period; but this was externally generated and externally oriented. 'The individual derived a sense of self', wrote Jonathan Goldberg, 'largely from external matrices'.[13] 'The private,' wrote Fumerton, 'could be sensed only through the public'; the "self" was void.'[14]

In this critical context, to imagine that Hamlet had an inner life, a sense of inwardness and interiority, that he could be the subject of his own sentence rather than 'subjected' to arrangements of knowledge and the ideological state apparatus, is to be helplessly under the sway of Barker's 'essential subjectivity' or Belsey's 'liberal humanism', and to be taken in by 'the idea of the autonomous, unified, self-generating subject'.[15]

The theoretical underpinning of these arguments derives of course from Althusser and Foucault, particularly Foucault (and possibly, it has

---

[9] John Lee, *Shakespeare's 'Hamlet' and the Controversies of the Self* (Oxford, 2000).

[10] Francis Barker, *The Tremulous Private Body* (London, 1984), pp. 163–4.

[11] Catherine Belsey, *The Subject of Tragedy* (London, 1985), p. 8.

[12] Jean Howard, 'The New Historicism of Renaissance Studies', *English Literary Renaissance*, 16 (1986), 15.

[13] Jonathan Goldberg, *James I and the Politics of Literature* (Baltimore, 1983), p. 86.

[14] Patricia Fumerton, *Cultural Aesthetics: Renaissance Literature and the Practice of Social Ornament* (Chicago, 1991), pp. 109 and 130.

[15] Jonathan Dollimore, *Radical Tragedy: Religion, Ideology and Power in the Drama of Shakespeare and his Contemporaries* (Brighton, 1984), p. 155.

been argued, an oversimplification of Foucault).[16] For Foucault interiority is produced by power, as in his discussion of 'confession' in *The History of Sexuality*:

Since the Middle Ages at least, Western societies have established the confession as one of the main rituals we rely on for the production of truth... One confesses – or is forced to confess. When it is not spontaneous or dictated by some internal imperative, the confession is wrung from a person by violence or threat; it is driven from its hiding place in the soul, or extracted from the body. Since the Middle Ages, torture has accompanied it like a shadow, and supported it when it could go no further: the dark twins.[17]

The impulse to confession now seems natural, as if 'truth, lodged in our most secret nature, "demands" only to surface' (p. 60). In fact such truth is 'the effect of a power that constrains us' (p. 60).

Foucault certainly did not say, as Barker and Belsey did appear to say, that there is 'nothing' inside Hamlet, or inside anyone else: 'It would be wrong to say that the soul is an illusion, or an ideological effect. On the contrary, it exists, it has a reality.'[18]

But this is manifestly not the 'Christian essentialism' diagnosed by Jonathan Dollimore, the person given unity and essence by the imputation of a 'metaphysically derived' soul (p. 155). The soul is, like all seemingly 'inner' truth, 'produced permanently around, on, within the body by the functioning of a power' (Foucault, p. 29). In later work, published posthumously, Foucault began to show more interest in the 'technologies of the self', 'how an individual acts upon himself'.[19] But in the 1980s it was his major published works with their anti-essentialist conception of subjectivity as the effect of power that underpinned Cultural Materialist thinking on the early modern subject.

A number of recent studies have reverted to these controversies and shown convincingly that the Foucauldian approach used by Barker and Belsey failed to account for the manifest superabundance of interiority in *Hamlet* and in early

modern culture in general. Katharine Eisaman Maus in *Inwardness and Theatre in the English Renaissance* shows that Hamlet's perception of an inner self, 'that within which passes show' 'would have been commonplace for his original audience'.[20] Everywhere in Renaissance writing and culture we find the fundamental difference named by St Augustine as the distinction between *homo interior* and *homo exterior* (a distinction actually used in *Hamlet*, by Claudius, between 'th'exterior' and the 'inward man').[21] In philosophy, ethics, politics, history, medicine and religion, writers continually allude to the split between 'that within' and 'actions that a man might play'. People in the Renaissance knew, amazingly enough, that 'a person's thoughts and passions, imagined as properties of the hidden interior, are not immediately accessible to other people' (Maus, p. 5). Jesuit Thomas Wright complained, perhaps regretfully, that 'we cannot enter into a man's heart, and view the passions or inclinations which there reside and lie hidden'; rather these are, as William Vaughan put it in 1600, 'concealed in a man's heart'.[22] When Campion, on the scaffold, continued to protest his innocence of treason, many wept: but that, says Anthony Munday, was because they were listening to his 'outward protestations', 'not entring into conceyte of his inward hypocrisie'.[23] Maus argues that ideas of interiority derive simply from 'the irreducible mysteriousness of human beings to one another' (p. 12). The gap between self-consciousness and

---

16 See Lee, *Controversies of the Self*, pp. 82–4.
17 Michel Foucault, *The History of Sexuality*, vol. 1, *The Will to Knowledge*, trans. Robert Hurley (London, 1998), pp. 58–9.
18 Michel Foucault, *Discipline and Punish: The Birth of the Prison*, trans. Alan Sheridan (New York, 1977), p. 29.
19 See Lee, *Controversies of the Self*, pp. 82–4.
20 Katharine Eisaman Maus, *Inwardness and Theater in the English Renaissance* (Chicago, 1995), p. 3.
21 Quoted from the 1623 Folio, 2.2.6. *Hamlet, the Texts of 1603 and 1623*, ed. Thompson and Taylor.
22 Thomas Wright, *The Passions of the Minde in generall*, ed. William Webster Newbold (New York, 1986), p. 165; William Vaughan, *The golden-grove, moralized in three books* (London, 1600), L4ʳ.
23 Anthony Munday, *A Discoverie of E. Campion and his Confederates, etc.* (London, 1582), G1ᵛ.

objective knowledge of others 'may seem so fundamental to social life that it cannot be the property of a particular historical moment', but must be part of the 'inescapable conditions of any human intercourse' (p. 12). The retort from Cultural Materialism would of course be that this appeal to universal human experience is nothing more than a capitulation to essentialist humanism.

By contrast Elizabeth Hanson in *Discovering the Subject* continues to operate within a broadly Foucauldian approach. Hanson differentiates her work from that of Maus:

I share with Maus the sense that inwardness was in fact a cultural obsession . . . I would stress, however, that the very ubiquitousness of the anxiety about inwardness which Maus so compellingly reveals actually supports the cultural materialist narrative of emergence (p. 51).

Hanson thus admits that the Renaissance had an 'obsession with the discovery of the heart's secrets' but sees this as 'symptom of an epistemic change, of a redrafting of the terms on which the subject relates to the world' (p. 2). Throughout her analysis we see subjectivity produced by external agency. 'As one man examined another, he confronted as in a mirror the idea of the subject, not merely as authority's subordinate but as the origin of discourse and action' (pp. 2–3). The idea of the subject as 'a cache of truth' emerges 'not at first as an oppositional strategy but as a disciplinary effect' (p. 4).

Hanson's argument, which focuses on subjectivity as constructed in the course of the Elizabethan state's efforts to understand and control religious dissent, is persuasive partly because the circumstances of the period (between the bull *Regnans in Excelsis* and the Gunpowder Plot) were so unusual, extraordinary and distinctive that they can reasonably be imagined as triggering a seismic shift in subjectivity. 'What is new and catastrophic,' she says, 'in the Renaissance is not, as Barker and Belsey assert, a sense of interiority, but the usually fearful, even paranoid recognition that interiority can give the subject leverage against his world' (p. 16). Interiority deep-

ened and withdrew, in other words, as the state sought to discover and manipulate religious and political convictions. Equivocation, predicated on a gap between interior and external utterance, was a distinctive feature of Catholic resistance in this period. Interrogatory torture was used extensively and unusually between 1570 and 1605, although it was never formally a part of English common law. 'In these circumstances, it is not surprising that the Crown made use of all those instruments that, de facto, were at its disposal for the discovery of its subjects who might attack or subvert it . . . These instruments . . . included torture.'[24] The objective of torture was that of 'discovering' information,[25] to 'discover the trothe' (p. 208), to secure the 'boultinge out of the truth' (p. 206) from its concealment in the subject's body. The torturer set out to 'wrest . . . the truth' (p. 210), to 'wring . . . the truth' (p. 211) out of their victims, threatening or applying 'terror' (p. 210) to effect the 'bulting out and opneynge of that which is requysite to be knowen' (p. 206). 'The structure of interrogatory torture,' says Hanson, 'posits a victim in possession of hidden information that the torturer must struggle to uncover, and therefore produces a narrative of discovery' (p. 25). This is not then about what is really in there, or even about what the interrogator wants to find (like most interrogators, he thinks he knows it already): it is much more about the process of torture as a means of demonstrating and enforcing, by eliciting, truth. The language of torture supposes that truth is an object that could literally be found in the body of the victim: 'wrested' from him, 'wrung' out of him, 'withdrawn' from his body.[26] Catholics complained that torturers exceeded their legitimate brief by 'attempting to discover matters that had to do, not with the alleged treasonable activities of

---

[24] James Heath, *Torture and English Law: An Administrative and Legal History from the Plantagenets to the Stuarts* (Westport, Conn., 1982), p. 109.

[25] 'Conciliar Records of Torture Warrants and of Letters Mentioning Acute Torture', in Heath, *Torture and English Law*, p. 210.

[26] Heath, *Torture*, pp. 206, 210.

the victims, but with their spiritual experience' (Hanson, p. 27). Campion said at his trial that his tormentors were not gathering evidence of treason, but probing the secrets of the confessional: 'these were the hidden matters, these were the secrets in concerning of which I so greatly rejoiced, to the revealing whereof I cannot, nor will not be brought, come Rack, come Rope'.[27] Thomas Cottam complained that the torturers tried to make him confess his sins.[28] 'The inviolable truth of conscience,' concludes Hanson, 'is a product of discovery' (p. 51).

Hanson, Maus, Lee and others have demonstrated convincingly what Hanson calls 'the absurdity of any account of the mental world of pre-Renaissance Europe that denies it the experience of interiority' (p. 16). There is on the other hand less consensus and less clarity on the sources of interiority. Was it, is it, an 'inescapable condition' (Maus's phrase) of human experience – something immanent, unchanging, a human essence? Or is it simply one of the effects produced by the operation of power on the human body and mind? Is 'truth' 'that which is susceptible to discovery,' asks Hanson, or 'that which is felt in resisting discovery'? (p. 27) 'It is difficult to know at this historical remove,' admits Maus, 'whether the aggressions of the state produced furtiveness in its enemies or supposed enemies as a defensive reflex, or whether the secretiveness of the heterodox necessitated the regime's attempt at surveillance' (p. 23). 'Direct evidence of Prince Hamlet's interiority . . . proves hard to find' (Lee, p. 90), perhaps because, as a reviewer of Lee's book argues, 'interiority as such is precisely what can never be exhibited on stage'.[29] We may grant the existence of inwardness, but still maintain that it is socially and ideologically produced.

It is my view that state interrogators and torturers discovered interiority in their victims because it was already there; and that it was there in such abundance because their victims believed what they professed. Katherine Maus suggests that Cultural Materialists denied the interiority of the subject because they themselves did not believe in its religious implications:

. . . as the idea of 'inward truth' in Early Modern England is intimately linked to transcendental religious claims, antagonism to those claims perhaps contributes to the recent tendency to underestimate the conceptual importance of personal inwardness in this period (p. 27).

I propose to argue more explicitly that the single biggest difficulty afflicting the study of subjectivity in the 1980s was a systematic blindness to the stubborn fact of religious faith, and that it is only by giving due regard to religious belief that we would be able to locate an authentic and integral early modern subject at all. This is not to pretend that we can avoid the difficulty that any attempt to describe the interior world of faith could also be taken for a description of the social and ideological world in which that faith happens to find itself. It follows hard upon: however fully described, the inner space of faith could still be, as Maus describes it, simply the 'inevitable result of religious oppression' (p. 16). But I want to suggest that it is rather more than that.

When veteran Cultural Materialist Alan Sinfield reviewed Ewan Fernie's *Spiritual Shakespeare* in *Textual Practice,* he attacked not only the book itself but any approach to cultural analysis that shares the religious faith of the culture under investigation.[30] Sinfield went into the business of criticism, he recalls, in order to 'undermine the hegemonic Anglicanism of mid-twentieth century literary criticism' (p. 161). Critics then were interested in early modern religion, but never taken in by it: 'many scholars proceeded to explore aspects of religion in the early modern period, and rarely in a way that presented it as transcending the conditions of its social and historical construction' (p. 163). 'On this topic,

---

27 'The Arraignment of Edmund Campion, Sherwin, Bosgrave, Cottam, Johnson, Bristow, Kirbie, and Orton for High Treason: 24 Eliz. A.D. 1581', *Cobbett's Complete Collection of State Trials* (London, 1809), vol. I, p. 1061.

28 Allen, *A Sincere and Modest Defence*, pp. 11–12.

29 Roger Starling, 'Review of John Lee, *Shakespeare's "Hamlet" and the Controversies of the Self*', *Early Modern Literary Studies*, 7.2 (September, 2001), 5.

30 Alan Sinfield, 'Turning on the Spiritual', *Textual Practice*, 20:1 (2006), 161–70.

everyone was a materialist' (p. 163). Now that consensus appears to have broken, with influential voices such as those of Derrida and Greenblatt setting the door to the spiritual even ever so slightly ajar. Sinfield dislikes Fernie's book because its spirituality seems syncretic, individualistic and quietist: it represents 'spirituality explicitly disconnected from institutional religion' (p. 167), divorced from 'allegiance to anything like a congregation' (p. 168) and with no 'project for furthering change in the world' (p. 168). Above all he rejects what he takes to be the premise of this book and any form of religious thought: that 'the spiritual may be accepted as an irreducible first principle'.[31] I would argue that for Christians the spiritual and the material are inextricably intertwined, from the creation of the world to the Incarnation, from the primacy of the Word to the Resurrection of the body. What is incontrovertible, however, is that for Cultural Materialists, then and now, matter is certainly the 'irreducible first principle' of the universe and of human existence. The Cultural Materialist is as much a scientific 'naturalist' as the evolutionary biologist and would agree with Richard Dawkins that: 'There is nothing beyond the natural, physical world, no supernatural creative intelligence lurking behind the observable universe, no soul that outlasts the body and no miracles – except in the sense of natural phenomena that we don't yet understand.'[32]

Religion, by contrast, presupposes subjectivity as a fundamental aspect of human existence, and Christian subjectivity was formalized early in the Christian era. It is often explicitly or tacitly assumed, as Foucault himself later acknowledged, that modern interiority can be said to begin with St Augustine, whose *Confessions* invented autobiography and perhaps the very notion of the subject. No-one before Augustine, says Karl Weintraub, had 'opened up their souls in the inwardness of genuine autobiography'.[33] In *De Fide Rerum Quae Non Videntur* Augustine points to the obvious fact that many things on which human beings depend are invisible: the minds of others, thoughts, intentions and so on. Nonetheless all these have to be inferred, and they are predicated on the

ground of belief. 'Lo, out of thine own heart, thou believest an heart not thine own.'[34] The subjectivity of another is grasped via the subject's own interior awareness of subjectivity. Human beings know that others have private spaces within, because we all have them ourselves. Hence Augustine's model of subjectivity is immediately different from the 'bourgeois subject', the 'liberal-humanist subject', the 'essential subject' of Cultural Materialism. It is not autonomous or independent or divorced from the human community. Augustine's interiority is a space in which human beings meet one another in reciprocal understanding and mutual love. Inwardness is the space of community.

Augustine's *Confessions* demonstrate that what you find at the centre of the human being is not nothing or a void or just the reflection of external things. What you find is God. 'I could not be then, O my God, could not be at all, wert thou not in me.'[35] God is both inside and outside, both the subject of the sentence that is the believer, and the external power to which he is subject. Augustine knows that God is inside him but still asks God to enter or re-enter him: 'Behold, Lord, my heart is before thee . . . *say unto my soul, I am thy salvation*' (p. 4). God is both self and other, both subject and object, both the agent and the object of the agent's desire. The form of *Confessions* is of course by self-definition a confessional autobiography, and the reader is placed in the ambivalent position of hearing and overhearing both Augustine's confession and the open secret of his life. We are listening to a man talking to God; but he is also addressing the reader, with a confessional invitation to share in

[31] Towards the end of the review Sinfield identifies any form of religious faith with belligerent fundamentalism: apparently there is little difference between a few Shakespearians with spiritual leanings and the warmongering zealotry of George Bush (p. 169).

[32] Richard Dawkins, *The God Delusion* (London, 2006), p. 14.

[33] Karl Weintraub, *The Value of the Individual: Self and Circumstance in Autobiography* (Chicago, 1978), p. 45.

[34] Augustine, 'Concerning Faith of Things Not Seen', trans. C. L. Cornish, in *Nicene and Post-Nicene Fathers of the Christian Church*, vol. 3 (Buffalo, NY, 1887), p. 338.

[35] Augustine, *Confessions*, trans. E. B. Pusey (London, 1907), p. 2.

an inner space into which God can also be invited. In this way the text generates a subjectivity-effect in the reader, but it is a subjectivity shared with the writer and with his audience.

The Confessions is, again by definition, all about opening the person to admit the divine: 'To thee therefore, O Lord, I am open, whatever I am' (p. 4). This is figured in intensely physical terms via the use of an anatomical vocabulary of inwardness, featuring the internal organs, the heart, the liver, the entrails. Augustine clearly had no sense of any qualitative distinction between the bodily organs and the thoughts and passions they supposedly housed. '*Venter interioris hominis conscientia cordis est*',[36] he assumed: 'the interior belly of man is the conscience of the heart'. The inward knowledge of a person possessed by God alone was a knowledge of the physical interior of the body, which contained the conscience and the moral being. God is, according to the *Book of Revelation*, '*scrutans corda et renes*': 'he which searcheth reines and hearts'.[37]

In *Shakespeare's Entrails* David Hillman demonstrates convincingly that in the early modern period the Cartesian separation of material body and immaterial mind had not yet supervened on human consciousness. On the contrary, human beings thought of themselves primarily in 'resolutely materialist' physical terms.[38] What we now think of as a metaphorical language of internal organs and processes – as in Hamlet's speeches to Guildenstern – was in practice perceived much more literally, with a 'fully embodied intensity' (p. 1). 'What we now call inwardness or interiority was inseparable from the interior of the body' (p. 2). The usefulness of this insight is that early modern notions of self, the subject and inwardness were not necessarily incompatible with a view of the person as fully engaged in the body with somatic others and with a carnally affiliated environment. What Yves Bonnefoy called the 'excarnation' of the world into body and spirit had yet to take place.[39]

For the pre-modern religious sensibility such as that found in St Augustine, the subject consisted of a solid, irrefutably material body which was sufficiently self-contained to house mind and spirit,

but which was also physically and spiritually open to the divine. Hence the assumption that the subject is inscrutable, invisible, inaccessible to immediate interpretation, is not in any sense incompatible with the apparently contrary assumption that the subject exists only in its openness to external influence. When the Jesuit Father Wright declared that 'hearts . . . be inscrutable', his qualification was that they are 'only open unto God'.[40] On the other side of the religious divide John Foxe said exactly the same thing:

For a man to pronounce assuredly upon the secret cogitation and intent either of man or woman, further than by utterance of speech is to him signified, passeth his capacity, and is to be left only to Him, who is 'scrutans corda et renes Deus'.[41]

'Shall not God search this out? for he knoweth the secrets of the heart' (Psalm 44.21); 'For the LORD searcheth all hearts, and understandeth all the imaginations of thoughts' (1 Chronicles, 28.9). And this language of the body as impervious to human vision, but opening to God, either by providing the divine with direct access into the interior, or by imagining the body as literally turned inside-out to disclose its interiority, became absolutely characteristic of Renaissance religious sensibilities. Here it is in the general confession of *The Book of Common Prayer*: 'ALMIGHTY God, unto whom al hartes be open, al desires knowe, and from whom no secretes are hyd . . .'[42]

---

[36] Augustine, quoted Ernst Robert Curtius, *European Literature and the Latin Middle Ages* (New York, 1953), p. 137.

[37] Revelation 2.23, *The Bible and Holy Scriptures Conteyned in the Olde and Newe Testament, translated according to the Ebru and Greke* (Geneva, 1560).

[38] David Hillman, *Shakespeare's Entrails: Belief, Scepticism and the Interior of the Body* (London, 2007), p. 2.

[39] Bonnefoy quoted in Hillman, *Entrails*, p. 4.

[40] Wright, *The Passions of the Mind*, p. 109.

[41] *The Acts and Monuments of John Foxe*, ed. Rev. Josiah Pratt, 4th edn (London, 1877), vol. 8, p. 238. '*Scrutans corda et renes Deus*': 'God who observes hearts and entrails' (see note 36).

[42] 'The Order for the Administration of the Lords Supper, or holy Communion', *The Booke of common praier and administration of the sacramentes and other rites and ceremonies in the Churche of Englande* (London, 1559).

Hence it is inevitable that there will be a doubleness or plurality about any description of Christian inwardness: and it is obviously tempting to read this as self-division, internal conflict, the effect of contested power relations such as those between the Elizabethan state and the Roman Catholic Church. But the point is that the interior of the Christian subject is a very crowded place. 'Narrow is the mansion of my soul', complained St Augustine (*Confessions*, p. 4), and that sense of spatial restriction is understandable given what he had to pack into it, including not only himself, but God, the world and humanity. 'What room is there within me, wherein my God may come?' (p. 5). The Christian subject typically feels internally divided from God who is both here and there, both 'within me and without' (p. 5). Augustine begs God to come to him, although God is already the ground of his being, because by his sin he has separated himself from God, and hence from himself. The territory of Christian interiority is a place of voices, the scene of dialogue and conversation, argument and debate.

. . . as there is a voice in writing as well as in speaking, according to *Aristotle* himselfe, so there is an internall voice, as well as an externall, and an internall speach as well as an externall, which speaketh, affirmeth, or denieth to the inwarde eares as well or better then the voice, or letter to the outward.[43]

This is Robert Persons defending the practice of Equivocation, so it is a statement that seems very much of its time and place. But the fact that the Christian conscience or soul is interpellated, speaking to and from different subject positions, accounting for itself before different tribunals, is neither unusual nor localized, but endemic to the experience of Christian faith, of Christian subjectivity.

Not every Christian hears that interior conversation in the same way. Augustine heard God speaking to him indirectly, through a child's song and a text of scripture. Joan of Arc heard St Michael and St Katherine speaking directly to her, and acted upon what they told her to do. This manifestation of 'aberrant agency' makes her for Donald E. Hall

an early example of 'proto-subjectivity'.[44] Joan's heart, we recall, according to legend, survived the consuming fire of her martyrdom.

Nowadays we are rightly suspicious of people who hear voices. But the inside of everyone's head is a buzz of conversation and, for the Christian, part of that is noise is the conversation of prayer. Few Christians (apart from Paris Hilton) think that God talks directly to them. But all Christians try to talk to God, to explain themselves, to get things straight, to apologise, to atone. God knows. Puritans John Dod and Robert Cleaver said 'God . . . searcheth into the heart and secret imaginations of the soule.'[45] Maus suggests that this 'presence of an omniscient spectator', 'seems so fundamental to the structure of human subjectivity that the fact of that subjectivity becomes part of the proof of God's existence' (p. 10).

William Perkins said no man or angel could ever really know 'what is in the heart of man'. But 'there is a substance, most wise, most powerful, most holy, that sees and bears record, and that is God himself.'[46]

Maus proposes that for someone like Perkins the individual exists as 'The object of a double scrutiny: of a human vision that is fallible, partial, and superficial, and of a divine vision that is infallible, complete and penetrating' (p. 11). 'Human inwardness' is created in the tension between these two perspectives: 'The inwardness of persons is constituted by the disparity between what a limited, fallible human observer can see and what is available to the hypostasized divine observer' (p. 11). This remains the case for a Christian (or indeed any religious) subjectivity, irrespective of whether there is external pressure on that subject to confess, conform or discover truth.

---

43 Robert Persons, *A Treatise Tending to Mitigation Towards Catholicke-Subiectes in England* (St Omer, 1607), p. 329.
44 Donald E. Hall, *Subjectivity* (London, 2004), p. 14.
45 John Dod and Robert Cleaver, *A Plaine and Familiar Exposition of the Ten Commandments*, revised edition (London, 1618), p. 32.
46 William Perkins *The whole treatise of the cases of conscience* (Cambridge, 1606), p. 211.

The Augustinian conception of subjectivity does not divide body from spirit or insist on spirit as an 'irreducible first principle'. David Hillman in *Shakespeare's Entrails* makes a distinction between belief and scepticism based not on gradations of spirituality but on differing conceptions of the body.

Scepticism . . . can be described as an attempt to deny the susceptibility of one's interior to external influence; faith as an attempt to deny one's exteriority or separateness.[47]

In belief there is an inside, but it is 'accessible or corresponds to the outside'. Faith is based on a willingness to accept the other into one's interior, and a conviction that 'the other is open to inhabitation by oneself'.

Belief seems to be inseparable from an acceptance of the interpenetrability of self and other, self and world, or self and God, an acknowledgement of the outer world or of the other akin to its incorporation or introjection into one's own bodily interior. (p. 28)

The sceptic by contrast 'experiences the world as if it were made up of insides and outsides radically opaque to one another'. Scepticism denies the inherence of inner in outer, and assumes a gap between inner truth and outer display. The sceptic assumes that outer display in others is probably misleading (actions that a man might play):

The sceptic's own interior matches this closure, refusing entry to the other and simultaneously refusing egress to his own deepest self. He will not take the other in, nor will he allow himself to be taken in . . . In this way, the sceptic in effect renders 'the inner' unknowable. (p. 28)

That within which passes show. What ties all this together in Christian belief is of course, uniquely, the Incarnation.

But Thomas one of the twelve, called Didymus, was not with them when Jesus came.
The other disciples therefore said unto him, We have seen the Lord. But he said unto them, Except I se in his hands the print of the nailes, and put my finger into the print of the nailes, and put mine hand into his side, I will not beleve it.
And eight days after againe his disciples were within, and Thomas with them. *Then* came Jesus, when the

dores were shut, and stood in the midst, and said, Peace *be* unto you.
After, said he to Thomas, Put thy finger here, and se mine hands, and put forthe thine hand, and put it into my side, and be not faithles, but faithful.
Then Thomas answered, and said unto him, *Thou art* my Lord, and my God.
Jesus said unto him, Thomas, because thou hast sene me, thou belevest; blessed *are* they that have not sene, and have beleved.[48]

The sceptic Thomas needs to pluck out the heart of Jesus's mystery before he will believe. Jesus offers his interior for penetration, and in the offering breaks down the barrier between himself and his doubting disciple. 'The stigmata and wound in his side,' says Hillman, 'literally puncture the boundary, the integument, separating him from the world' (p. 31). As Hillman points out here, the scripture doesn't actually say, notwithstanding the conventional representations of this scene, that Thomas does stick his fingers in. The offering is enough. 'It is rather the offer of access or the sense of being granted access, to the interior (to the divine object or to the human subject of faith) that constitutes faith' (Hillman, p. 32). Later in the seventeenth century the cult of the Sacred Heart founded by Sister Margaret Marie Alacoque gave the most graphic expression to this idea of corporeal openness and infinite generosity of grace. Devotion to the Sacred Heart did not appear, as Michael Neill says, 'first in baroque art': it was already well known to thirteenth-century monastics.[49] But it clearly came into its own with the Counter-Reformation.

The Protestant Reformation reconstituted the subject of faith as a disembodied spiritual subject in innumerable ways. Reinterpretation of the Eucharist diminished the literal incorporation of Christ into the body of the believer. Relics were suppressed; possession and exorcism treated with scepticism; stigmata denied; even the sacramental efficacy of unction rejected. All these reforms were disputes about the place of the body in worship, and

---

[47] Hillman, *Shakespeare's Entrails*, pp. 28–9.
[48] John 20. 24–9, *The Bible and Holy Scriptures* (Geneva, 1560).
[49] Michael Neill, *Issues of Death: Mortality and Identity in English Renaissance Tragedy* (Oxford, 1997), p. 158.

particularly about whether the body was open or closed to the external world and to the divine. After the Reformation, the body was relatively closed.

We are no longer surprised, notwithstanding, to find that early modern people had interiors. Nor should we be surprised to find those interiors complex, self-divided, cacophonous spaces of internal debate and dissension. We could assume, as the Cultural Materialists did, from that evidence that those interior spaces are produced by external cultural and ideological contradictions. But if we attend fully to the religious dimension, that conclusion does not necessarily follow.

Further, although those interior spaces display a dialectical interconnectivity with externality, this is not proof that externality is the primary driver of subjectivity. This seems to me particularly the case in Christianity (I cannot speak for other faiths), where the doctrine of the Incarnation establishes a synergy between the divine and the human that can never be disentangled. Christianity does not teach that the spiritual is an 'irreducible first principle'. It teaches the inextricable intertwining of spiritual and material, self and other, soul and world.

In the beginning was the Worde, and the Worde was
  with God, and that Worde was God.
This same was in the beginning with God.
All things were made by it, and without it was made
  nothing that was made.
In it was life, and the life was the light of men.
And that light shineth in the darkenes, and the darkenes
  comprehended it not.[50]

Subjectivity is constituted by, but not limited to, the spiritual. It was experienced in a common way by people throughout the Christian era because their life was very largely constituted by faith. It seems not to be there, or to be inexplicable, or to be merely an image in a mirror, to those who read with the eyes and ears of scepticism. It is accessible to the modern reader who reads with the eyes and ears of faith.

Religion, after all, was what the common life of those times was about; and it is curious that radicals, who are supposed to take popular consciousness seriously, should so often be found skipping embarrassedly over the religious rituals and beliefs which bulked so large in it. No ideology in human history has been more persuasive and persistent than religion, a symbolic form which links the minutiae of everyday conduct to the most ultimate of spiritual realities, and it is hard to see that any ideology ever will be. The radical's nervousness of religion is parochial as well as patronising; religion may not be the driving force in Middlesbrough, but it is in Dacca.[51]

In the poetic language of *Hamlet* we can see multiple possibilities of interiority, and the images deployed in the 'recorder' exchange function as different models for the subject. Man can be a pipe, or a sponge; an instrument played upon by others, or an 'organ' (Q2 and F) with its own individual voice. Hamlet characterizes Rossencraft and Gilderstone, his interrogators, as specimens of the 'spunge'. He can detect, concealed beneath the urbane drawl of their conversation, the sharp instruments of the torturer, eager to search out his secrets and pluck out the heart of his mystery. But as subjects they have no centre, no individual identity (they are of course in the theatre notoriously interchangeable), no intrinsic structure: they are porous, amorphous masses, permeated by the determinants of power:

> ... Such as you,
> Do the king, in the end, best servise;
> For he doth keep you as an Ape doth nuttes,
> In the corner of his Jaw, first mouthes you,
> Then swallowes you; so when hee hath need
> Of you, t'is but squeesing of you,
> And spunge, you shall be dry againe, you shall.
>
> (*Tragicall Historie*, p. 77)

Like the Cultural Materialists' pre-modern subject, the 'spunge' is an open site which offers no resistance to the networks of power that transect it. It is whatever the king wants it to be, and there is nothing inside it. In comparing himself to the recorder, Hamlet seems to invoke the ideology of the modern bourgeois subject, a resistant shell concealing what purports to be a mystery, though

---

50 John 1.1–5, *The Bible and Holy Scriptures* (Geneva, 1560).
51 Terry Eagleton, 'Foreword' to Jonathan Dollimore, *Radical Tragedy: Religion, Ideology and Power in the Drama of Shakespeare and his Contemporaries*, 3rd edn (London, 2003) xii.

when subjected to Cultural Materialist analysis invariably proving to be nothing at all. 'The single and peculiar life' can thus be thought of as 'bound / With all the strength and armour of the mind' (Q2, 3.3.11–12) and, as we have seen, Hamlet repudiates penetration, resists the passage of the breath that would make him something he is not, call his tune.

And yet, though the 'spunge' model of subjectivity does not seem a viable option for Hamlet, he cannot rest content with the closed exterior and hollow inwardness of the pipe. On the contrary, he is constantly seeking a somatic openness and permeability. He invites Gertrude to recognise herself as made of 'penitrable stuffe' (*Tragicall Historie*, p. 79), to see into the 'inmost part' (F reading) of herself: 'I'le make your eyes looke downe into your heart' (*Tragicall Historie*, p. 79).

He invites Horatio to dwell in his 'heart's core – ay, in my heart of heart' (3.2.69) (where 'core' is both 'heart', *cor*, and the heart's 'inward part'). The body, it seems, and the self from which it is indistinguishable, ought ideally to be open to affection, friendship, love; but the corrupt toxicity of the time forces it to close in upon itself, 'as if this flesh which walls about our life / Were brass impregnable'.[52] If the body is open to penetration by malice, as in Old Hamlet's murder, where poison flows in through the 'natural gates and alleys of the body', then like any biological organism it will close defensively against manifest danger. Norbert Elias labelled this newly 'bounded' individual '*homo clausus*', a being severed from all other people and things 'outside' by the 'wall' of the body.[53]

Poisoned by the world, but still open to the divine; closed to other people, but never to God. Hamlet's description of 'how ill all's here about my heart' lies close to his intuition that 'There is special providence in the fall of a sparrow'. Under this 'double scrutiny' (Maus, p. 11), presentiment and prophecy converge.[54] Hamlet's mystery is nothing less than the truth and reality of the soul, 'A thing of nothing', which yet given 'a little breath' could 'give most delicate musick' (*Tragicall Historie*, pp. 76–7). The rest is not, after all, silence: heart and soul remain together, in the First Quarto, till the very end, when the one survives the demise of the other:

> O my heart sinckes Horatio
> . . . heaven receive my soule.
> (*Tragicall Historie*, p. 99)

---

[52] *Richard II*, 3.2.163–4.

[53] Norbert Elias, *The Civilizing Process*, trans. Edmund Jephcott (Oxford, 1994).

[54] Q2, 5.2.190–1 and 197–8. See my discussion of the fall of the sparrow in 'Vanishing Point: Looking for *Hamlet*', *Shakespeare*, 1.2 (2005), 167–8.

MAPPING *KING LEAR*

ROBERT B. PIERCE

An older generation of critics frequently talked about the world of *King Lear* as a sort of framework within which the characters and events of the play exist.[1] By drawing on early modern conventions of constructing and using maps, John Gillies's commentary in *Shakespeare and the Geography of Difference*[2] offers a new vocabulary for talking about this creation of a space within which the tragedy is worked out. The sixteenth and seventeenth centuries were a great age of map-making, in part as they dealt with the discovery, exploration and colonization of the New World. Gillies argues that the Globe Theatre itself, in which *King Lear* had its early productions, was 'a kind of map: a quasi-cartographic product of the same type of cosmographic imagination which produced the world maps of Ortelius and Mercator'.[3] Gillies justifies calling the Globe a map by applying J. B. Harley's definition of maps as 'graphic representations that facilitate a spatial understanding of things, concepts, conditions, processes, or events in the human world'.[4] It is sometimes assumed that the movement toward new, more accurate modes of geographic representation in early modern map-making entailed a movement away from expressive representation, as in older maps, toward an objective, scientific kind of map; but Gillies argues persuasively that maps down even to the present remain full of expressive content, though precisely what is expressed may change in different maps with different social roles. What then is it that was mapped for an audience in 1607 or 2007 as they attended to *King Lear*? If the experience of seeing Shakespeare's tragedy in its early productions at

the Globe was in some ways analogous to that of reading a map of the world or of ancient Britain, how can approximating that experience affect our understanding of the play?[5] These are the questions that this article will consider.

---

1 See, for example, A. C. Bradley, *Shakespearean Tragedy* (New York, 1955); G. Wilson Knight, 'The *Lear* Universe', in *The Wheel of Fire: Interpretation of Shakespeare's Tragedy* (New York, 1957); Robert B. Heilman, *This Great Stage: Image and Structure in King Lear* (Baton Rouge, 1948); Richard Sewall, *The Vision of Tragedy* (New Haven, 1959); Maynard Mack, *King Lear in Our Time* (Berkeley, 1965). For a more recent reading of the playhouse as world, see Kent van den Berg, *Playhouse and Cosmos: Shakespeare's Theater as a Metaphor* (Newark, NJ, 1985).

2 (Cambridge, 1994). Gillies' emphasis is on how the mapping develops an antithesis of home and other, especially as it bears on character and society in a political reading of the play. I will be less centrally concerned with that antithesis and with character and politics as I adapt his concepts to my purposes. For a vigorous defence of the political focus characteristic of much contemporary criticism, see Terence Hawkes, 'Lear's Maps', in *Meaning by Shakespeare* (New York, 1992), pp. 121–40. I am grateful to Professor Richard Strier, the organizer, and my fellow members of the *King Lear* Seminar at the 2006 Shakespeare Association of America meeting for their stimulating discussions of the play.

3 Gillies, *Geography,* p. 70.

4 Gillies, *Geography,* p. 54. For the revolution in studying cartography on which Gillies draws, see J. B. Harley and David Woodward, *The History of Cartography,* vol. 1 (Chicago, 1987); further volumes emerging.

5 For evidence that mapping plays a role in creating the imagined human spaces of early modern drama including Shakespeare, see Peter Holland, 'Mapping Shakespeare's Britain', in Dermot Cavanagh, Stuart Hampton-Reeves and Stephen Longstaffe, eds., *Shakespeare's Histories and Counter-Histories* (Manchester, 2006), pp. 198–218.

Gillies himself goes on to explore the place of maps and mapping for *King Lear* in 'The Scene of Cartography in *King Lear*'.[6] He undertakes to 'ask whether Lear's map [in the opening scene] engages with the immense cultural and ideological authority of cartography in the period, and if so how it negotiates that authority'.[7] Thus his emphasis is on political significance, and he is inclined to see the map analogy as either present or absent by authorial design at given moments of the play, thus evoking 'the values and ideology of cartography' at different points, or not.[8] My aim is rather to ask whether a given element of the play suggests various elements of cartography and then to explore how responding to those elements with the map analogy in mind affects our overall response to the play. If using the older term 'world' pushes critics toward metaphysical readings of the play, I want to ask what potentialities, political, metaphysical and other, the map and its family of concepts and images might evoke. Returning to maps and mapping as models for making sense of a real or imagined space allows us to recapture something of the experience of seeing *King Lear* in 1605. That should enrich our twenty-first century response as we learn to see and hear the elements of the play under the aspect of cartography.[9]

How then do maps and mapping give shape to what we often call the world of *King Lear*? A play is primarily a temporal phenomenon, both experienced in and portraying a series of moments, but it also exists in and represents a space, an *oikumene* in the double sense of the Greek word, which is both a dwelling and a world. A map delineates a human space of dwelling bounded by spaces of difference, of the other.[10] What kind of human location does *King Lear* map out, with what kind of relationship between home and the other? An actual map plays a key role in the first scene, helping to create our perceived location, Lear's kingdom. When Lear makes use of a map of Britain to divide up his realm, the characters see portrayed on the map and hear powerfully evoked in his words a representation of their country, giving it a double presence on the stage. Lear enacts a change in the real country by lines drawn on the map; and this

division of the kingdom before their eyes and ours launches the action of the tragedy while creating for our imaginations the space within which that action occurs. Britain itself divides into three parts and then into two as they and we watch; and what the characters experience as their *oikumene* is irreversibly changed. My project is to explore the map that Shakespeare's play, imagined in its Globe setting, creates: to delineate its contours, to analyse by what dramatic and poetic means it is created, and finally to define as well as I can its imaginative role in the total economy of the play.[11]

The play begins with a rather ordinary conversation in an undefined space, though we quickly learn that Edmund is not quite part of that space, not really at home there. He may or may not hear what Gloucester and Kent are saying about him (depending on the staging), but in either case he can only respond with respectful conventionality to the one opening Gloucester gives him. So far we know little of his feelings about the situation, but we do know that his claim to belong in that space is tenuous: as Gloucester says, 'He hath been

---

[6] In Andrew Gordon and Bernhard Klein, eds., *Literature, Mapping, and the Politics of Space in Early Modern Britain* (Cambridge, 2001), pp. 109–37.

[7] Gillies, 'Scene', p. 118.

[8] Gillies, 'Scene', p. 119. For an essay arguing that the point of the play is the inadequacy of the map, its function being as mere rhetoric, see Bruce Avery, 'Gelded Continents and Plenteous Rivers: Cartography as Rhetoric in Shakespeare', in John Gillies and Virginia Mason Vaughan, eds., *Playing the Globe: Genre and Cartography in English Renaissance Drama* (Madison, NJ, 1998), pp. 46–62.

[9] Cf. how the modes of cognitive science and information technology help to shape our contemporary ways of making sense of all sorts of experiences. Ludwig Wittgenstein discusses this element of how we perceive under the concept of aspect: *Philosophical Investigations*, trans. G. E. M. Anscombe, 3rd edn (New York, 1968), II.xi, pp. 193–214. For a perceptive reading of the cartographic elements that builds toward an analogy between Lear's story and that of Noah, see F. T. Flahiff, 'Lear's Map', *Cahiers Elisabethains*, 30 (1986), 17–33.

[10] Gillies, *Geography*, pp. 4–25.

[11] For an ingenious, not to say remorseless, metaphoric exploration of the map and the spatial in *King Lear*, see Dan Brayton, 'Angling in the Lake of Darkness: Possession, Dispossession, and the Politics of Discovery in "King Lear"', *ELH* 70 (2003), 399–426.

out nine years, and away he shall again.'[12] However fond Gloucester may be of him, the bastard's only home is in that shadowy space out there, in the realm of the other.

The imaginative scope of the play expands with Lear's entrance and the opening up of the map, however the moment may be staged. Do we actually see Britain laid out before us in the map, as the characters presumably do? And, if so, is Britain recognizable in outline, as shown on a modern map, or is the map a visibly archaic approximation, covered with symbols and signs?[13] At any rate, the presence of the map facilitates our construction of an *oikumene* for the characters we see before us, their world as encompassed by that larger map that is the Globe Theatre itself or our modern equivalent of it.[14] And by stroke after stroke the play fills out and vivifies that dwelling place of human striving and suffering that is the world of *King Lear*.

If for a time we forget our moment-by-moment experience of the play and think of the place where we imagine the action occurring, a location in actual space rather than a series of events, what is that space like?[15] Let me start paradoxically with a sense of time imposed on the place, precisely what might seem to be left out in a map as spatial representation. It is true that we assemble pieces from the play into a single picture, the world of the play in that terminology, in which the castles and wild places, the storms and hot sun, the tiny room of the hovel and the vista down over the cliffs of Dover all exist simultaneously in our imagination of the play, like one huge panoramic canvas.[16] In any one scene the characters are normally in one place, though often that undefined place characteristic of the early modern stage, the *platea* descended from medieval stagecraft.[17] Is the opening scene in 'King Lear's palace', as editorial stage directions often have it?[18] Productions imagine the place in an endless variety of ways: a sort of Stonehenge in the Olivier filmed version, a post-Civil-War American country house in the Peter Ustinov version at Stratford, Ontario. Yet it is not quite true that temporal progression has no representation in the created space. Though *King Lear* is full of places, like Gloucester's castle and the hovel

on the heath and the battlefield near Dover, it is also full of journeys as characters go between the different places. Often the journeys occur offstage, between scenes, though we also see characters on the road: Lear, Gloucester, Edgar, etc. In an odd way the play is full of horses for these journeys, horses created verbally as they usually are on the early modern stage, so that it causes a delightful sense of dramatic as well as mannerly impropriety when Olivier's filmed Lear rides his horse into the hall as he demands his dinner at Albany's castle in 1.4. The unseen horses of the usual theatrical experience signify travel: motion through space and hence through time. One thinks of the

[12] 1.1.31–32. All references to the play are to *King Lear*, ed. R. A. Foakes, Arden Shakespeare, 3rd Series (Walton-on-Thames, 1997).

[13] Gillies speculates thoughtfully on how the map might be staged and on the implications of the episode, though his interest again is largely on the political meaning. 'Scene', pp. 109–18.

[14] 'Clearly, whatever use the prop is being put to, the real energy of the language here (its enduring tendency in performance) was invested in creating a virtual landscape.' Gillies, 'Scene', p. 118.

[15] Henry S. Turner brilliantly explicates the representation of space in the play in '*King Lear* Without: The Heath', *Renaissance Drama*, New Series 28 (1997), 161–93. I am not convinced by his vigorous contention that the play is a self-conscious investigation of place and space as categories of perception and thought, and at any rate I focus instead on what kind of dramatic experience the representations of place and space in *Lear* provide for an audience, not on the play as a philosophical discourse.

[16] The traditional New Criticism often reads Shakespeare's plays as spatial forms. The term 'spatial' suggests that the elements of the play – events, stage pictures, images, etc. – are simultaneously present to consciousness, the consciousness of one who has read the play and holds it in mind. Especially in performance-oriented criticism this view is rejected in favour of attending to the moment-by-moment progression of the theatrical experience. But surely neither mode of attention has ontological priority; we can attend to the play both ways in turn and allow each response to enrich the other.

[17] See Robert Weimann, *Shakespeare and the Popular Tradition in the Theater*, ed. Robert Schwartz (Baltimore, 1978), pp. 73–85.

[18] See, for example, David Bevington's note at the beginning of 1.1. in *The Complete Works of Shakespeare*, 5th edn (New York, 2004).

represented ship sailing through the ocean of many old maps.

The play incorporates another kind of temporal ambiguity, that is, the question of historical period. Holinshed's Lear belongs to the dim early days of British history, and elements of Shakespeare's play support that sense of a distant past, the legendary origins of early modern England. The Fool reminds us (in the Folio version) that Merlin has not been born yet, though of course this reference creates anachronism even while denying it. Shakespeare seems to make some effort to avoid the anachronistic references to Christianity common in his other pre-Christian plays. In some ways Lear's court evokes the ancient *comitatus* structure that Tacitus attributes to the Germanic peoples, with its emphasis on personal bonds and loyalty. The land we see is Britain, not England, with the former name's aura of distant origins; and there are passing references to Albion and even Camelot. Especially for an English audience the feeling generated must be of ancestral connection over a great distance, rather like the Augustan Romans looking back with Virgil to Aeneas and his band of Trojans. The effect is like seeing an old map of one's own country – both familiar and strange – or like reading of England as Fairyland in *The Faerie Queene*. But Lear's court is also recognizably a Renaissance place, not wholly unlike James's Whitehall. The 'gorgeous' dress that Lear attributes to Goneril suits a seventeenth-century environment, as does the decadent serving-man that Edgar as Poor Tom claims to have been and that Oswald embodies.

Like time, place is divided between the familiar and the strange, in this case primarily between the *oikumene* and the other, the alien, what is not home. Above all that contrast emerges in the scenes that alternate between Gloucester's castle and the heath. Home, the *oikumene*, is that place inside the walls and gates, the realm of family and protection, though of course in this play home often partakes of the qualities of the outside and vice versa. Insinuating himself within the walls, Edmund the Bastard feels no family loyalty though he can feign it with great skill, and the legitimate daughters Goneril and Regan are utterly without family love for their father and indeed for each other. Their cruelty to Lear culminates in Regan's order to Gloucester, 'Shut up your doors' (2.2.494, repeated by Cornwall at 498), an order that closes Lear out from everything that the *oikumene* signifies, including protection, love and loyalty. Of course Gloucester cannot be dissuaded from his loyalty to Lear, 'the King my old master' (3.3.17–18), but that loving impulse only renders him vulnerable to Edmund's treachery and Regan and Cornwall's cruelty.

The kingdom is to its subjects what the home is to the family. 'Land' refers both to the family estate, that which Edgar should inherit from Gloucester but which Edmund plans to steal, and to Britain itself, Lear's realm. If the estate is a piece cut off from wild nature and made home, like Gloucester's castle in the midst of the wilderness, so the land of Britain is a home bounded by the sea, with foreign lands as the other, the wilderness beyond the homeland. Rejecting Cordelia for her supposed lack of family love, Lear thinks of a foreign realm inhabited by 'the barbarous Scythian, / Or he that makes his generation messes / To gorge his appetite' (1.1.117–19). When his anger spreads from Cordelia to Kent, he sends Kent abroad to 'disasters of the world', misaligned stars, suggesting by 'disasters' (line 175, found only in the Folio; Q reads 'diseases') that malign astrological influence is one of the curses of that alien realm. But Kent imagines a foreign existence for himself in different terms: 'Thus Kent, O princes, bids you all adieu; / He'll shape his old course in a country new' (187–8). A new country, like the New World, offers opportunity as well as danger. And after all France is the most dramatically present of foreign lands. It is striking that Shakespeare consistently refers to the country thus anachronistically as France rather than Gallia, evoking for his audience the contemporary nation. In *Lear* France plays a role unusual for early modern drama. Its associations are largely favourable, being a sort of chivalrous rival, as in the sonnet of Sir Philip Sidney, who calls it 'that sweet enemy, France' (*Astrophel and Stella*, 41). Certainly the dichotomy of home and other in *King Lear* cannot be equated with good and evil. What lies beyond Britain is an intermediate place, as reflected

in Albany's ambivalent response to France's inva-
sion in defence of Lear's right (5.1.21–7).

Like the *oikumene* the wilderness embodies this
ambiguity.[19] Nothing in Shakespeare is more terrible than the storm-torn landscape that both echoes
Lear's mad anger and intensifies his suffering:

> Blow winds and crack your cheeks! Rage, blow!
> You cataracts and hurricanoes, spout
> Till you have drenched our steeples, drowned the
>   cocks!
> You sulphurous and thought-executing fires,
> Vaunt-couriers of oak-cleaving thunderbolts,
> Singe my white head! And thou, all-shaking thunder,
> Strike flat the thick rotundity o'the world,[20]
> Crack nature's moulds, all germens spill at once
> That make ingrateful man!   (3.2.1–9)

And yet that place is where the outcast Lear
finds loving companions and sympathetic witnesses. When his royalty has been brutally torn
from him inside the walls of human society, he can
touchingly find a crown of flowers in the wilderness. This comparatively benign nature has fore-
shadowings before the terrible storm scenes. We
see Lear return from hunting, from the wilderness
as a park for recreation. (One thinks of the Forest of Arden, where Duke Senior and his men can
hunt, feast and sing, even while Orlando and Adam
experience it as a hostile wilderness.) In a parallel
doubleness Edgar, who strips himself to confront a
brutal nature, 'The winds and persecutions of the
sky' (2.2.183), has found shelter from pursuit in
'the happy hollow of a tree' (line 173).

Britain is a geographical place, but as the definition of a map cited by Gillies suggests, the Britain
of *Lear*'s map is 'a human world', inhabited by
people who in their variety give it meaning. We
directly see and hear a considerable range of people: the two families of Lear and Gloucester, Lear's
nobles and knights, and a good number of servants and followers. The language of the play pop-
ulates the land even more fully. We hear of poor
pelting villages, madmen who wander from parish
to parish, archers, even dogs and demons. There
is little attempt to domesticate these linguistically
evoked inhabitants to the putative time of the play's

action, and so the effect is to connect the Britain
of the play's world with the immediate experience
of the Globe audience.

Finally, the Globe Theatre mapped more than
the Earth; it represented a whole cosmos. As
Gillies notes, the audience in its galleries within the
wooden O as cosmos could take the perspective of
gods looking on at the stage-earth;[21] but it was also
possible to imagine the stage-space in itself as the
cosmos, as symbolically indicated by the constel-
lations painted under the roof that jutted out over
the forestage. Filling out this vast imagined space,
King Lear powerfully creates a cosmic setting for its
action. From beginning to end characters populate its space with the gods they name, specifically
the classical gods, often praying to them and sometimes describing how they act on human beings.
Lear and Kent compete in swearing by Apollo, and
Kent asserts that Lear 'swear'st thy gods in vain'
(1.1.161–2). Lear wins the rhetorical battle with
Kent when he proclaims his kingly right to judge
by invoking Jupiter, Apollo's superior and king of
the gods (179–80). What reality are we to perceive behind these namings of the gods? Do they
embody a disposition toward justice in the cosmic
order? Albany seems to be persuaded of a supernatural foundation for justice, despite an initial doubt
expressed in an if clause (4.2.47–8). He sees justice
from the heavens in Cornwall's death:

> This shows you are above,
> You justicers, that these our nether crimes.
> So speedily can venge.   (4.2.79–81)

Gloucester in despair gives a darker picture of
divine involvement in the world:

---

[19] Flahiff argues that the imagined landscape is not really the
heath of editorial and critical tradition, which he points out
originates in Nahum Tate's Restoration rewriting of the play.
Shakespeare's wilderness space seems to be more like bogs
around Gloucester: 'Lear's Map', pp. 21–3.

[20] The image evokes those world maps that shape the world
into one or two circles, and it also suggests three-dimensional
images of the cosmos such as the one that Andrew Marvell
in 'A Definition of Love' imagines to be 'cramped into a
planisphere'.

[21] Gillies, *Geography*, pp. 77–9.

As flies are to wanton boys are we to the gods,
They kill us for their sport.   (4.1.38–9)

But both men and indeed most of the characters in *King Lear* habitually refer to the gods as they try to cope with the events of their dark world, even while their references and invocations form no single image of what the gods are and how they affect the human world. Like the allegorical figures pictured in maps, they are present in the play but of ambiguous reality. Again they are like those supernatural beings that watch over mapped spaces from places like the cartouches at the corners.

A sense of divine shaping behind the events of the play is created by the frequent references to astrological influence, which is after all interconnected with the classical gods. Those stars painted on the stage roof of the Globe include the gods and demigods of mythology.[22] Kent attributes Albany and Cornwall's high rank to 'their great stars' (3.1.22), and at 4.3.33–4 he claims directly, 'It is the stars, / The stars above us govern our conditions', attributing human qualities to astrological influence. Most expansively Gloucester appeals to astrology when he derives both Lear's rejection of Cordelia and Edgar's supposed unnaturalness from 'these late eclipses in the sun and moon' (1.2.103). Gloucester knows of the sceptics who see only natural cause and effect in eclipses, but he finds the uncanny power of prediction by eclipses to be evidence of their actually producing 'the sequent effects' (106), and he progresses in his thought to an image of human beings helplessly driven to their graves by great cosmic forces. One of the sceptics is standing beside him as he speaks: Edmund's following soliloquy mocks his father's human tendency to 'make guilty of our disasters the sun, the moon and the stars, as if we were villains on necessity, fools by heavenly compulsion, knaves, thieves and treachers by spherical predominance' (120–3). Is one or the other of them right in the perspective of the play as a whole? We never actually see the gods, though we hear the characters' constant addresses and references to them. In the literal Globe Theatre we would see a symbolic version of the stars, at least, but their putative influence on human life is by

definition invisible. If we see it as real, that reality is created by the behaviour of the human beings, as a mime creates an invisible wind for us by leaning into it, fighting its unseen impulsion.

Jupiter, whom Lear invokes as guarantor of his oath, is the Thunderer, and thunder and storm constitute one of the most powerful symbols in the play. In his madness Lear asks Edgar as Poor Tom, 'What is the cause of thunder?' (3.4.151). The question hangs unanswered. In theatrical experience the thunder of *King Lear* must have been as real as the resources of the early modern stage could make it, not only in the references to it by the characters but in the sound literally created as a stage effect, as is usual in modern productions. We hear the thunder; but whether or not it is Jupiter, or Jehovah, who is thundering – in short, the meaning of that phenomenon – is wrapped in mystery. The storm gathers during Lear's terrible encounters with Regan and then Goneril in 2.2, first in Lear's language, as he urges: 'You nimble lightnings, dart your blinding flames / Into her scornful eyes!' (354–5). Confronting Goneril herself, he for a moment swallows his rage: 'I do not bid the thunder-bearer shoot, / Nor tell tales of thee to high-judging Jove' (416–17), even as he teeters toward the mad belief that he can indeed summon up the storm with the fury of a wronged father and king. Then the storm physically appears at line 472 in the stage direction.[23] Surely one dramatic effect is that the storm echoes Lear's internal torment, but does it also represent divine anger at the cruelty of Goneril, Regan and Cornwall? Or is it perhaps a kind of divine sadism, adding to Lear's suffering? Is Nature indeed Edmund's goddess rather than

---

22 For an account of how the pagan gods were assimilated into astrological theory, see Jean Seznec, *The Survival of the Pagan Gods: The Mythological Tradition and Its Place in Renaissance Humanism and Art*, trans. Barbara F. Sessions (New York, 1961).

23 The stage direction, like the later stage directions about the storm, appears only in the Folio. In both versions references to storm in the characters' language make the occurrence of audible thunder throughout these scenes likely enough, though the simultaneity of the beginning of an audible storm with a peak of Lear's fury is explicit only in F.

Lear's? After all, the audible storm comes soon after Lear's prayer, 'You heavens, give me that patience, patience I need!' (460). And this juxtaposition of prayer and apparently indifferent or hostile answer is terribly like the later moment when Albany's prayer for protection of Cordelia, 'The gods defend her', seems to be answered by the stage direction, '*Enter LEAR with CORDELIA in his arms*' (5.3.254). The mad Lear is often wiser than the sane Lear, and perhaps his inability to name the cause of thunder is part of that wisdom, because thunder, immediately present to his and our experience, has no meaning that can be articulated by human intelligence.

Maps are not photographic equivalents of the places they map; they partake more of the presentational than of the representational. That is especially true of early modern maps with their symbolic winds at the corners, their gods and goddesses, their allegorical figures, etc. But even modern maps show roads as coloured lines that are as broad as the cities they link, show the cities as circles, put north at the top and draw a grid of lines that have no literal existence. Most of the world map that I grew up seeing was coloured pink, symbolizing the British Commonwealth. Certainly the map of Britain that *King Lear* draws for us is created mostly by presentational means. The thunder may sound more or less real, but at the Globe there was normally no lightning, no rain. We see people in locations that they name, see them pausing on the road, hear them refer to different cities, hear of horses that we never see; a whole society of people in their varied activity, their joys and pains, exists only in the words we hear. As the mime creates the wind that he leans into, so all these references and images come together to map the human, experienced space within which Lear and Gloucester and those around them act and suffer; or rather their words and gestures impel us as audience to draw the map in our imaginations.

So what is that mapped world like? How does it affect our experience of the terrible story that is the plot of *King Lear*? And do its qualities assert or help to imply any thematic ideas, any judgements about what if anything is natural to human beings, what impels them to act as they do, whether the cosmos

is sympathetic to their aspirations, whether kings and fathers act justly and deserve respect and submission? These are of course big questions about Shakespeare's tragedy, and the mapping of a world is just one of the means by which Shakespeare creates his thematic effects. I will close with some tentative conclusions that seem to me to follow from the qualities I have identified in the map that the play draws.

First, everyone has noticed the vast geographical and human scope of *King Lear*. Little touches throughout the language suggest extensions of reality far beyond the moments and places that we see. We are asked to picture people sitting around a lone candle that goes out, a dog barking at a beggar, all of humanity devouring itself, even the end of the world itself, 'the promised end', like a map torn to pieces or folded up. Characters' gestures and their speech are always creating something beyond what we see literally present on the stage. We even watch Lear simultaneously experiencing in his mind the torments of Hell and the bliss of Heaven, at the moment when he wakes in the restored presence of Cordelia. In particular the play evokes a whole world of people, high and low, familiar and strange, rejoicing and suffering, unaware of the events in their midst that absorb us as audience. Occasionally some of the bystanders are pulled into the vortex of events, as happens with the servants who witness Cornwall's blinding of Gloucester and with the old man who leads him and brings him clothes.

One result of this panoramic world is to give the play a sense of being exemplary, a kind of parable of human existence. The forces that impinge on the main characters extend outward like the grid lines of a map to imply how they operate on all of humanity. That is why the sensitive mind of Keats in 'On Sitting Down to Read *King Lear* Once Again' sees in the play so broad a theme as 'the fierce dispute / Betwixt damnation and impassion'd clay'. In two different ways Lear and Gloucester represent Everyman: Lear is humanity at the extreme: as a king, as a very old man near death, and as the ultimate of human passion; Gloucester is a more ordinary humanity. And in a sense the two Everymen inhabit different worlds, one remote, stylized, at the edge of human possibility, and the other more prosaic, mundane in its desires and limits. 'Land' is at stake in both worlds, but in Gloucester's world it is his estate, the property that Edmund plots to divert from Edgar's inheritance. In Lear's world it is the kingdom itself, what can be described only in Lear's grand period:

> Of all these bounds, even from this line to this,
> With shadowy forests and with champaigns riched,
> With plenteous rivers and wide-skirted meads,
> We make thee lady.   (1.1.63–66)

But both ordinariness and grandeur come crashing down when Gloucester and Lear are cast out from the *oikumene* into the chaotically inhuman world of the wilderness, a place where they come together in their sufferings. That world is phantasmagoric, filled with the shadows of Poor Tom's demons, the invisible dogs and cruel daughters that Lear sees in the hovel, the troops of bowmen that he imagines at his disposal. Most strangely of all, we see Gloucester on a bare stage that is also a level field and a steep path that ends in a dizzying fall down the cliffs at Dover. We know rationally that these phantasmagoric images are not real; but, in a world in which blind men see better for their blindness, men put on a disguise of nakedness, and fools and madmen are wiser than the sane, our trust in the boundaries between the real and the unreal is shaken.

One central quality of the world mapped out in *King Lear* is disorientation, the opposite of what maps usually provide. The characters are always on the road to somewhere or about to set out, but purpose and destination can be in doubt. As Gloucester says of Lear, 'He calls to horse, but will I know not whither' (2.2.487). And when the Old Man is reluctant to leave Gloucester himself alone and blinded on the heath, Gloucester replies, 'I have no way, and therefore want no eyes' (4.1.20). People have nowhere in particular to go. But at the same time elements of the play create a strong sense of impulsion. Dover, the site of the final battle between the forces supporting Lear and their enemies, is a leitmotif in the latter part of the play because the characters choose, or are driven, to

journey there. Dover is an end in the teleological sense as well as the geographical, though who precisely wills it as a purpose within the play is unclear. In one way the end at Dover is authorial or generic: for all the intricacy, even disorder, of *Lear*'s plot, it moves inexorably toward its tragic denouement around the battle near Dover.[24] This double sense of aimless flailing and accelerating movement toward an end fits the genre. After all, tragedy is about a figurative fall, and a literal fall combines both disorientation and destination: the helpless, chaotic feeling of being unable to act with purpose and the inevitability of being pulled to the bottom by gravity.

King Lear seems to be a play full of dualities and dichotomies, and surely that is not just a projection from our contemporary obsessions. Its very structure as a two-plot play (unique in Shakespearian tragedy and rare in tragedy generally) supports this double quality of chaotic disorder and obsessive shaping. When the closing speech is given to Edgar, as in the Folio, that voice from the Gloucester plot makes the final comment on the fate of Lear, resolving the two threads of the play into one authoritative commentary, albeit a cryptic, Euripidean one. One might think of Edgar's words as an inscription at the bottom of the map, one whose purport we cannot quite make out.

Does this world that Shakespeare maps out imply its own meaning? Just as Edgar through the play tries to find a stance, a personal perspective from which he can make sense of the world around him, so critics have been impelled to spell out what *King Lear* tells us about our world and ourselves, but Edgar's formulations are regularly mocked by the events they try to explain, and perhaps we as critics are not much more successful. Some negative conclusions do nevertheless seem clear from what we have seen of Shakespeare's map. For example, Lear's kingdom is not a simple place, to be explained by a few intellectual formulas. Thus it

---

[24] For a different reading of Dover as goal, see Jonathan Goldberg, 'Perspectives: Dover Cliff and the Conditions of Representation', in *Shakespeare's Tragedies*, ed. Susan Zimmerman (New York, 1998), pp. 155–66.

is not a realm defined by poetic justice, where the good are rewarded and the wicked punished. Nor is it a realm where human ideals are always only a mask for self-interest. It is not a place where a few sages (or even one) know the truths that all the fools around them fail to grasp and so fall to destruction. But the efforts of critics to find positive assertions implied or directly affirmed are stridently diverse.[25] It is suspicious that we critics tend to find *Lear* asserting what we already believe about the world. And that variety of interpretation may well be the point. As human beings we arrive at our deepest views when we try to make sense of the world around us. What we as critics do with *King Lear* is very like that. And the play stretches us to understand more than we did before, even while we fail to comprehend its mystery. Shakespeare's map is of course not the same as the world;

otherwise it would not be a map but an impossibly exact transcript. Still this strange, huge map does suggest much of the shape of our experience in all its complexity and ambiguity. Edgar speaks for us all, not just adopting a royal we, in his closing, and in doing so he repudiates any obligation to define the meaning of the play. We often feel more wisely than we speak, especially when our speaking comes out of a perceived duty to be definitive and our feelings come out of a sensitive response to the vastness and mysteriousness of our world.

---

[25] Two readings that are close to my sense of the mysteriousness of *King Lear* are William R. Elton's in *King Lear and the Gods* (San Marino, CA, 1966) and John Reibetanz's in *The* Lear *World: A Study of* King Lear *in Its Dramatic Context* (Toronto, 1977), esp. Chapter 5. One might say that my essay portrays a world much like the world they portray, seen under the aspect of cartography.

'LAST ON THE STAGE': THE PLACE OF SHAKESPEARE IN CHARLES DARWIN'S ETHOLOGY

REIKO OYA

I do not think any spectacle can be more interesting, than the first sight of Man in his primitive wildness.

(Darwin to J. S. Henslow, 11 April 1833)

THE BEAST AND THE SWAN

Along with 'the exquisite glorious delight' of tropical scenery, the encounter with the 'bona fide savages' of Tierra del Fuego marked the highlight of Charles Darwin's *Beagle* voyage (1831–6). Darwin was fascinated and repulsed in equal measure by 'the most curious and interesting spectacle' of Fuegians, whose attitudes and countenance were not only 'abject' but 'distrustful, surprised, and startled'.[1] The tribes inhabiting Wollaston Island were in particular 'the most abject and miserable creatures' Darwin ever saw: 'These poor wretches were stunted in their growth, their hideous faces bedaubed with white paint, their skins filthy and greasy, their hair entangled, their voices discordant, their gestures violent and without dignity.' Darwin could hardly believe them to be 'fellow-creatures, and inhabitants of the same world'.[2] The difference between a primitive and civilized man seemed 'greater than between a wild and domesticated animal, in as much as in man there is a greater power of improvement',[3] and, to Darwin, 'the cr[ie]s of domestic animals are far more intelligible' than the 'tones' and 'gesticulations' of Fuegians.[4]

While the disparity between Europeans and Fuegians, and the corresponding nearness of uncivilised humans and animals, would have unsettling implications relating to the beastly origins of human beings, the Swan of Avon would also have

a minor role to play in the controversy that Darwin's evolutionary theory occasioned. In the 'Great Debate' in Oxford following the publication of *On the Origin of Species* in 1859, Thomas Huxley reportedly defended the formation of biological complexity out of chance mutations against the staunch creationist Samuel Wilberforce, by arguing that, if an infinite number of monkeys keep hitting random keys on typewriters, the complete works of Shakespeare would eventually be bashed out. While this legend probably contained more fiction than fact (the concept of the typewriter being virtually unknown at that time),[5] John F. W. Herschel would certainly combine Shakespeare (and Newton) with a similar word-processing device

---

This essay is based on a seminar paper submitted to the 'Victorian Sages and Shakespearean Stages' session at the International Shakespeare Conference 2006, Stratford-upon-Avon.

[1] *Journal of Researches*, Part 1, in *The Works of Charles Darwin*, ed. Paul H. Barrett and R. B. Freeman, 29 vols. (London, 1986–9), vol. 2, pp. 178–9.

[2] *Journal of Researches*, Part 1, p. 184.

[3] *Journal of Researches*, Part 1, p. 179. Darwin recorded his memorable encounter with Fuegians repeatedly. See *Correspondence*, ed. Frederick Burkhardt and Sydney Smith, 16 vols. (to date) (Cambridge, 1985–), vol. 1, pp. 302–3 ('To Caroline Darwin', 30 March–12 April 1833), vol. 1, pp. 306–7 ('To J. S. Henslow', 11 April 1833), vol. 1, p. 316 ('To W. D. Fox', 23 May 1833); *The Diary of the Voyage of H. M. S. Beagle*, in *Works*, vol. 1, pp. 109–11; *The Descent of Man*, Part 2, in *Works*, vol. 22, p. 644.

[4] *Correspondence*, vol. 1, p. 397 ('To Charles Whitley', 23 July 1834).

[5] Nicholas Rescher, *Studies in the Philosophy of Science* (Frankfurt, 2007), p. 103 (note).

from Jonathan Swift's *Gulliver's Travels* in an additional footnote to the third edition of *The Physical Geography of the Globe* (1867). Herschel was however to refute the Darwinian hypothesis:

We can no more accept the principle of arbitrary and casual variation and natural selection as a sufficient account, *per se*, of the past and present organic world, than we can receive the Laputan method of composing books (pushed *à l'outrance*) as a sufficient one of Shakspeare and the *Principia*. Equally in either case, an intelligence, guided by a purpose, must be continually in action to bias the directions of the steps of change – to regulate their amount – to limit their divergence – and to continue them in a definite course.[6]

Even prior to the publication of the *Origin*, Darwin's evolutionary theory was causing an intellectual stir in the intimate circle of Victorian naturalists. After staying with the Darwins in April 1856, geologist Charles Lyell entered a flurry of notes in his journals to identify, and rationalize, the various stages of evolution, comparing infants with adults, the insane with the rational, animals with men, and 'men of humble capacity' with 'men of genius':

If there have been several (100?) millions of born & adult idiots & every gradation between them & men of every humble capacity & between the latter & men of genius, if there are every intermediate steps between the sensible or rational & the insane, why claim such dignity for Man as contrasted with the brutes. When does the sucking infant attain the rank of an intelligent dog? Has the child an hour before its birth a soul? or an hour after?[7]

Lyell also liked to include Shakespeare in the equation in the hope that a 'man of great genius born of parents of only ordinary, or even perhaps moderate & humble intellectual powers' should help explain the vast evolutionary potentials in both man and animals. A journal entry entitled 'Excelsior' (August 1856) traced Shakespeare's parentage to not just his father John but Adam and Eve:

If we could be assured that there were only 200 generations intervening between Shakespeare & two ancestors, or a pair as humble in intellect as the lowest of the human race ever known, being nevertheless of sound mind &

deserving to rank as rational & responsible beings, we should not think the fact as so extraordinary as to require as much evidence to substantiate its truth as a new creation in the common sense of the term.[8]

Following a similar reasoning, if 'a poet or philosopher of the greatest genius can be born of his ordinary commonplace parents, it lessens the wonder of a brute race producing a rude human savage race'.[9] Even within a single lifetime, if 'an unborn infant could in 30 or 40 years become author of Shakespeare's plays – the passage from the animal to the highest intellectual is rapid & from inferior to higher races of Man may be so'.[10] Lyell was certainly intrigued by the idea of 'the derivation of men like Bacon, Newton or Shakespeare, from parents far inferior to an average Negro, or Fuegian or Australian or Bushman',[11] but ultimately refrained from explaining 'the appearance of Man, last on the stage' in terms of Darwinian transmutation of species and natural selection.[12] As Thomas Huxley cogently put it, Lyell 'would have liked . . . to keep the name of creation for a natural process which he imagined to be incomprehensible'.[13]

While the issue of born genius would be taken up again in the eugenic treatises of Darwin's cousin

---

6 John F. W. Herschel, *The Physical Geography of the Globe*, 3rd edn (Edinburgh, 1867), p. 12. See also 'A Voyage to Laputa, etc.' (chapter 5) of *Gulliver's Travels*. For twentieth-century treatments of this so-called infinite monkey theorem, see Jorge Luis Borges, 'The Total Library', in *The Total Library: Non-Fiction 1922–1986*, ed. Eliot Weinberger, trans. by Esther Allen, Suzanne Jill Levine and Eliot Weinberger (London, 1999), pp. 214–16; Richard Dawkins, *The Blind Watchmaker* (Harlow, 1986), pp. 43–74.

7 Charles Lyell, *Scientific Journals on the Species Question*, ed. Leonard G. Wilson (New Haven, 1970), p. 86 ('Dignity of Man', 7 May 1856).

8 *Scientific Journals*, p. 153.

9 *Scientific Journals*, p. 102 ('Progressive Theory', 7 May [1856]).

10 *Scientific Journals*, p. 169 ('Development', [1858?]).

11 *Scientific Journals*, p. 153 ('Excelsior').

12 *Scientific Journals*, p. 121 ('From the Lower Mammalia to Man', [July 1856]).

13 'On the Reception of the *Origin of Species*', in Charles Darwin, *Life and Letters, Including an Autobiographical Chapter*, ed. Francis Darwin, 2 vols. (New York, 1896), vol. 1, p. 544.

and alleged follower Francis Galton,[14] Darwin himself refrained from discussing the evolution of humans in the *Origin*, in an apparent effort to downplay the heretical import of his hypothesis.[15] It was more than a decade after the publication of the *Origin* that he addressed the 'finest gradations' of bodily and mental properties that connect 'a savage who uses hardly any abstract terms' and 'a Newton or Shakspeare' in *The Descent of Man* (1871),[16] and went on to explore the 'gradual and natural origin' of emotional expression in its companion piece, *The Expression of the Emotions in Man and Animals* (1872), reusing, but also subtly revising, Lyell's coordinate of animals, the insane, infants, uncivilised men and 'men of genius'.

SHAKESPEARE THE NATURALIST

Being inspired by Charles Bell's *Anatomy and Philosophy of Expression as Connected with the Fine Arts* (1806; 3rd edn, 1844) and sharing its basic physiological premises, Darwin's *Expression* established its evolutionist stand by crucially refuting the predecessor's assertion that many human facial muscles are a 'special provision' for the expression of emotions.[17] Darwin then set out to compare the primordial expressions of infants, insane patients and preliterate people (or 'savages', as Victorians would call them) with those of higher animals. Unlike progressionist Lyell, Darwin's objective was to demonstrate the unity of human and animal expressions, and of human expressions across the races, rather than to differentiate the various stages of development. He had long observed the expression of himself, his family and animals in zoological gardens and, in January 1860, had sent out the following list of enquiries to one Thomas Bridges, a missionary working in Tierra del Fuego, directly associating the study of the emotions with his youthful experience aboard the *Beagle*:

Do the Fuegians or Patagonians, or both, nod their heads vertically to express assent, and shake their heads horizontally to express dissent?

Do they blush? and at what sort of things? Is it chiefly or most commonly in relation to personal appearance, or in relation to women?

Do they express astonishment by widely open eyes, uplifted eyebrows and open mouth?

Do they evince anger or fear by [the] same expression of countenance and actions as we do?

When out of spirits or dejected do they turn down the corners of the mouth?

Do they express contempt by the same gestures as we do, namely, by turning up nose and puffing out their breath or even by spitting?

Do they sneer, which is chiefly shown by turning up the corners of upper lip?

Do they frown when trying to understand anything or considering any difficulty?

Do they ever shrug their shoulders to show that they are incapable of doing or understanding anything?[18]

In 1867–8, Darwin went on to distribute a number of similar questionnaires to fellow naturalists, asylum keepers, and officers and missionaries stationed in North and South America, Australia, Asia and Africa.

Among the motley observations of primitive men and various mammals thus collected, Darwin cited nearly twenty passages and phrases from

---

[14] In *Hereditary Genius* (London, 1869), Galton failed to track down any significant talent in Shakespeare's family (pp. 225–36), and Henry Maudsley would later make a stand against Galton's eugenics by specifically citing Shakespeare 'as a supreme instance' of a genius with no apparent hereditary advantages (*Sociological Papers*, 1 (1905), 45–84; p. 54). See also Galton's use of the Shakespearian antithesis of 'nature' and 'nurture' in such eugenic studies as *English Men of Science: Their Nature and Their Nurture* (London, 1874), and 'The History of Twins, as a Criterion of the Relative Powers of Nature and Nurture', *Fraser's Magazine*, 12 (1875), 566–76.

[15] For Darwin's hesitation over the publication of his evolutionary theory especially of man, see Howard E. Gruber, 'A Psychological Study of Scientific Creativity', in *Darwin on Man: A Psychological Study of Scientific Creativity* (London, 1974), pp. 24–45.

[16] Part 1, in *Works*, vol. 21, p. 70.

[17] *The Expression of the Emotions in Man and Animals*, 3rd edn ed. Paul Ekman (New York, 1998), p. 17. For Darwin's disagreement with Bell's claims, see also pp. 144, 217 and 219.

[18] *Correspondence*, vol. 8, pp. 19–20. For later versions of this questionnaire, see R. B. Freeman and P. J. Gautrey, 'Charles Darwin's Queries about Expression', *Journal of the Society for the Bibliography of Natural History*, 7 (1975), 259–63.

Shakespeare's plays in the *Expression*.[19] These references were not a mere display of literary taste, as Darwin had long lost his youthful 'delight in Shakespeare, especially in the historical plays' and even 'found it so intolerably dull that it nauseated' him when he tried to read his plays.[20] To underwrite Darwin's own testimony, Gillian Beer's exhaustive survey of literary allusions in the *Origin* failed to track a single direct quotation from Shakespeare.[21]

Darwin's use of Shakespeare in the *Expression* was deliberate and strategic, and the idiosyncrasy of his citation stood in striking contrast with the example of Bell's treatise. As is clear from the title ('. . . *as Connected with the Fine Arts*'), Bell examined the expressive machinery of man and animals for the use of art students, firmly convinced that 'a knowledge of outward form, and the accuracy of drawing which is a consequence of it, are related to the interior structure and functions'.[22] Being a competent amateur painter himself, Bell treated Shakespeare, along with several other poets and prose writers, as a fellow artist and verbal painter. For instance, Bell's paragraph on 'jealousy' included a discussion about the artistic vehicles suitable for the emotion:

Jealousy is a fitful and unsteady passion: its chief character is in the rapid vicissitudes from love to hate; now absent, moody, and distressed; now courting love; now ferocious and revengeful: these changes make it a difficult subject for the painter; and it is only in poetry that it can be truly presented in the vivid colours of nature. Even among poets, Shakspeare alone seems to have been equal to the task.[23]

Likewise, Shakespeare's description of Gloucester's carcass (*2 Henry VI*, 3.2.168–78) was, to Bell, a 'picture' that is 'truly horrible from its truth and accuracy'.[24]

Darwin, on the other hand, regarded Shakespeare as a naturalist observer and informant. His paragraph on 'spitting' exemplifies his methodology. After stating that spitting 'seems an almost universal sign of contempt or disgust' that originated in 'the rejection of anything offensive from the mouth', Darwin produced various testimonials to that effect:

Shakespeare makes the Duke of Norfolk say, 'I spit at him – call him a slanderous coward and a villain'. So, again, Falstaff says, 'Tell thee what, Hal – if I tell thee a lie, spit in my face.' Leichhardt remarks that the Australians 'interrupted their speeches by spitting, and uttering a noise like pooh! pooh! apparently expressive of their disgust'. And Captain Burton speaks of certain negroes 'spitting with disgust upon the ground'. Captain Speedy informs me that this is likewise the case with the Abyssinians. Mr Geach says that with the Malays of Malacca the expression of disgust 'answers to spitting from the mouth'; and with the Fuegians, according to Mr Bridges, 'to spit at one is the highest mark of contempt'.[25]

Darwin gazed on the Duke of Norfolk and Falstaff with the same scientific eye through which he observed the aboriginal Australians, 'certain negroes', Abyssinians, Malays and Fuegians. In the appraisal of 'surprise' and 'astonishment', Darwin similarly quoted from *King John* ('I saw a smith stand with open mouth swallowing a tailor's news', 4.2.194–6) and *Winter's Tale* ('They seemed almost, with staring on one another, to tear the cases of

---

[19] Darwin's citations include: *Henry VIII*, 3.2.113–20; *Henry V*, 3.1.3–17; *Merchant*, 1.3.105–8; *King John*, 4.2.194–6; *Winter's Tale*, 5.2.11–15; *Caesar*, 4.2.333; *2 Henry VI*, 3.3.15; *Titus*, 2.4.28; *Romeo*, 2.1.127–9; *Hamlet*, 2.2.552–8. Short phrases on envy (3 examples), envy and jealousy (4), and spitting (2) are also quoted from Shakespeare. Darwin's other literary sources include Homer, Chaucer, Edmund Spenser, Milton, George Eliot, Dickens and the Bible. In this article, I cite Darwin's Shakespearian quotations as given in the *Expression*, with act, scene, line references to William Shakespeare, *The Complete Works*, ed. Stanley Wells, Gary Taylor, John Jowett and William Montgomery (Oxford, 1986).

[20] *The Autobiography of Charles Darwin 1809–1882*, ed. Nora Barlow (London, 1958), p. 138.

[21] Gillian Beer, 'Darwin's Reading and Fictions of Development', in David Kohn, ed., *The Darwinian Heritage* (Princeton, NJ, 1985), pp. 543–88. See also her *Open Fields: Science in Cultural Encounter* (Oxford, 1996), pp. 196–215; *Darwin's Plots: Evolutionary Narrative in Darwin, George Eliot and Nineteenth-Century Fiction*, 2nd edn (Cambridge, 2000), pp. 25–43.

[22] Charles Bell, *The Anatomy and Philosophy of Expression as Connected with the Fine Arts*, Bohn's Artists' Library (London, 1912), p. 2.

[23] *Anatomy*, p. 157.

[24] *Anatomy*, p. 170.

[25] *Expression*, p. 259.

their eyes; there was speech in their dumbness, language in their very gesture; they looked as they had heard of a world destroyed', 5.2.11–15), before bringing in the observations of the missionaries and explorers of faraway places: 'My informants answer with remarkable uniformity to the same effect, with respect to the various races of man; the above movements of the features being often accompanied by certain gestures and sounds, presently to be described'.[26] The discussion on the 'erection of the hair' was similarly oriented: with reference to Brutus's encounter with the ghost of Caesar 'that mak'st my blood cold, and my hair to stare' (*Caesar*, 4.2.333) and to the exclamation of Cardinal Beaufort after the murder of Gloucester ('Comb down his hair; look, look, it stands upright', *2 Henry VI*, 3.3.15), Darwin commented: 'As I did not feel sure whether writers of fiction might not have applied to man what they had often observed in animals, I begged for information from Dr Crichton Browne with respect to the insane.'[27] By persistently identifying Shakespeare with zoologists and asylum keepers, Darwin explored the lower limits of human expression and effectively campaigned for his theory of transmutation of species. In the discussion of 'rage', Darwin even made Shakespeare attest to man's beastly origin:

> In peace there's nothing so becomes a man,
> As modest stillness and humility;
> But when the blast of war blows in our ears,
> *Then imitate the action of the tiger.*
> Stiffen the sinews, summon up the blood,
> . . .
> Then lend the eye a terrible aspect;
> . . .
> Now set the teeth, and stretch the nostril wide,
> Hold hard the breath, and bend up every spirit
> To his full height! On, on, you noblest English.
> (*Henry V*, 3.1.3–17, my italics)[28]

Using the authority of Shakespeare's own words, Darwin related human rage to 'the action of the tiger' before shrewdly adding: 'The lips are sometimes protruded during rage in a manner, the meaning of which I do not understand, unless it depends on our descent from some ape-like animal.'[29]

Victorian naturalists liked to make literary allusions,[30] and the name of, and passages from, Shakespeare often graced their writings. In 1862, Mr Punch even felt obliged to issue a plea to 'Let the Swan Alone' in anticipation of a 'SHAKS-PEARE CYCLOPAEDIA . . . to be published in twenty parts', consisting 'of a classified summary of SHAKSPEARE's knowledge of the phenomena of nature, and of his allusions to zoology, botany, mineralogy, meteorology, medicine, agriculture, hunting, falconry, &c.', the first part of which would contain 'SHAKSPEARE'S Natural History of Man'.[31] While the story of the publication was apparently Mr Punch's fabrication, the age of Victoria certainly saw such naturalist tomes as Robert Patterson's *Letters on the Natural History of Insects Mentioned in Shakespeare's Plays* (1838), James Edmund Harting's *The Ornithology of Shakespeare* (1864), and Herbert West Seager's *Natural History in Shakespeare's Time* (1896). Reference to Shakespeare was particularly frequent in emotion studies, despite evolutionary psychologist Hiram Miner Stanley's misgivings expressed later in the century that 'to refer to Shakespeare or Goethe as psychological authorities, or in illustration or proof of psychological laws, is generally a doubtful procedure'.[32]

While Darwin was therefore not alone in conjuring the Bard in scientific discussion, his juxtaposition of Shakespeare's *dramatis personae* with the mentally underdeveloped subjects stood out for its lack of literary taste and sophistication. On the publication of the *Expression*, the *Edinburgh* reviewer Thomas Spencer Baynes attacked the 'illiterateness' or at least 'comparative

---

[26] *Expression*, p. 279.

[27] *Expression*, p. 295.

[28] *Expression*, p. 237.

[29] *Expression*, p. 238.

[30] For an analyses of the relationship between literary and scientific writings in the Victorian period, see Beer, *Open Fields*, pp. 196–215.

[31] 'Let the Swan Alone', *Punch*, 15 February 1862.

[32] *Studies in the Evolutionary Psychology of Feeling* (London, 1895), cited in Gesa Stedman, '"The Noblest Comment on the Human Heart": Shakespeare and the Theories of Emotion', *Shakespeare Jahrbuch*, 140 (2004), 115–29; p. 115.

indifference . . . to every culture except their own' of evolutionists in general, and Darwin's incompetent handling of Shakespearian materials in particular ('although he [Darwin] has derived a few graphic delineations from novelists and poets, especially from Shakspeare, this rich vein of illustration is left comparatively unworked'). Darwin attended almost exclusively to the physiological manifestations of rudimentary emotions, when 'great poets delight to exemplify the higher and nobler aspects of emotion which Mr. Darwin, as a rule, neglects'. Darwin's handling of literary materials was less than masterly and the reviewer was certainly right when he added this: 'Had he taken anything like an adequate view of the higher ranges of expression, the illustrative quotations from Shakspeare alone might have been multiplied ten-fold.'[33]

Moreover, Darwin was apparently not aware that description of emotional states in Shakespeare's plays was not necessarily based on the dramatist's personal observation of such passions. David Bevington has shown that Shakespeare inherited contemporary assumptions about emotions and their outward manifestations and made much use of them especially when his dramatic characters narrate the expressions and gestures of others. Such descriptions served as a useful shortcut to dramatic portrayal of specific affect states precisely by staying commonplace and idiomatic rather than personal. For instance, pallor and hair standing on end were traditional signs of fear deriving from Renaissance medical theory. They were 'so conventional and so unsuited for the theatre that they are employed only in reported scenes of offstage event' until actor David Garrick invented the fright wig in the mid-eighteenth century and actually made his Hamlet's hair stand on end in the second ghost scene.[34] In addition, Gail Kern Paster specifies the Galenic theory of four humours as crucially formative of the language of affect that Shakespeare and his contemporaries employed. This humourism presupposed the common possession of not only the bodily fluids but also their psychological consequences for humans and animals. Shakespeare's emotional expression and his abundant use of animal metaphor and simile should therefore be understood in the context of Galen and his Elizabethan exponents, not of Darwinian evolution.[35]

In the twentieth century, the *Expression* itself suffered blatant disregard, interspersed only with vicious attacks, from scientific communities, precisely because of Darwin's anthropomorphic ascription of human emotions to animals. In line with the behaviourist movement in psychology, twentieth-century scientists liked to talk about animals' behaviour and to keep silence as to whether it represented or expressed an emotion.[36] Darwin's neglect of the communicative value of emotional expression was also criticized, and his anecdotal, as opposed to systematic, collection of research data was censured. To make the situation worse, Darwin embraced the theory of inheritance of acquired characteristics (of which the best known proponent is Jean Baptiste de Lamarck), and believed that an organism passes on physiological changes that it acquired during its lifetime to its offspring. As this theory was common in the nineteenth century but is now known to be false, the whole of Darwin's observations and conclusions came to be discredited. Most crucial of all, the reigning dogma among the twentieth-century anthropologists and social scientists was cultural relativism and social constructionism, not universality, and Darwin's evolutionary explanation of the expression of emotions was not at all compatible with their assumptions.

If Darwin's ethological explorations were hopelessly clumsy and biased, and of limited value scientifically, his use of Shakespeare in the treatise was highly deliberate nonetheless. While the examples of infants, insane patients and savages cast light on the connection between humans and higher mammals, Shakespeare's references to spitting and to hair

---

[33] *Edinburgh Review* (April 1873), 492–528; p. 514.

[34] David Bevington, *Action Is Eloquence: Shakespeare's Language of Gesture* (Cambridge, MA, 1984), pp. 67–98; p. 82. Garrick's wig is mentioned on p. 210 (note).

[35] Gail Kern Paster, *Humoring the Body: Emotions and the Shakespearean Stage* (Chicago, 2004), pp. 135–88.

[36] See Paul Ekman's excellent survey of the twentieth-century dispute over Darwin's emotion theory in *Expression*, pp. xxix–xxxvi ('Introduction'), to which I owe the following summary.

standing on end also helped Darwin to confirm 'to a certain limited extent the conclusion that man is derived from some lower animal form' and 'the belief of the specific or sub-specific unity of the several races'.[37] Darwin achieved his own polemical goal with great success.

Darwin analysed expression of emotions in terms of three explanatory principles: 'serviceable associated habits', where useful muscular movements become fixed in the population through repetition and association; 'antithesis', where certain behavioural patterns emerge in opposition to other, more fundamental expression; and 'direct action of the nervous system' on the body.[38] In the concluding section of the *Expression*, however, Darwin problematically reversed the third principle and hinted at the ways in which bodily movement affects emotion:

The free expression by outward signs of an emotion intensifies it. On the other hand, the repression, as far as this is possible, of all outward signs softens our emotions. He who gives way to violent gestures will increase his rage; he who does not control the signs of fear will experience fear in a greater degree; and he who remains passive when overwhelmed with grief loses his best chance of recovering elasticity of mind.[39]

Darwin then moved a step further and suggested that '[e]ven the simulation of an emotion tends to arouse it in our minds'.[40] A notebook entry indicates that an anecdote about Tomasso Campanella in Edmund Burke's *On the Sublime and the Beautiful* (Part IV, section iv) informed Darwin's proposition:

[Campanella] had not only made very accurate observations on human faces, but was very expert in mimicking such, as were any way remarkable. When he had a mind to penetrate into the inclinations of those he had to deal with, he composed his face, his gesture, and his whole body, as nearly as he could into the exact similitude of the person he intended to examine; and then carefully observed what turn of mind he seemed to acquire by this change. So that . . . he was able to enter into the dispositions and thoughts of people, as effectually as if he had been changed into the very men.[41]

In *Hamburg Dramaturgy* (1767), Gotthold Ephraim Lessing made a similar observation in a theatrical

context and noted that the player can work up an emotion by performing the physical actions associated with the emotion.[42] In the *Expression*, however, Darwin illustrated the proposition with a passage from Shakespeare, 'who from his wonderful knowledge of the human mind ought to be an excellent judge' of emotional expression. While Burke and Lessing regarded bodily simulation as generative of internal emotion, Shakespeare's Hamlet supposes the actor's 'own conceit' to precede, and affect, both his emotion ('his soul') and expression ('visage', 'eyes', 'aspect', 'voice', and ultimately 'his whole function'):

> Is it not monstrous that this player here,
> But in a fiction, in a dream of passion,
> Could force his soul so to his own conceit,
> That, from her working, all his visage wann'd;
> Tears in his eyes, distraction in 's aspect,
> A broken voice, and his whole function suiting
> With forms to his conceit? And all for nothing!
> (2.2.553–9)

As a matter of fact, Hamlet's observation does not lead to the conclusion that Darwin was trying to draw, as its idealistic formulation of the actor's 'conceit' ultimately defies ethological explanations of human emotion and expression. The deviation of this final Shakespearian quotation from Darwin's overall discursive framework implicates the *Expression* further in a Victorian controversy over the art of acting.

MIMICKING AND TRAGIC ACTING

The *Expression* enjoyed a wide readership, selling '5267 copies . . . on the day of publication' alone.[43] Critical response, however, merely ranged

---

[37] *Expression*, p. 360.

[38] *Expression*, p. 34.

[39] *Expression*, pp. 359–60.

[40] *Expression*, p. 360.

[41] Darwin referred to this passage in *Notebooks, 1836–1844: Geology, Transmutation of Species, Metaphysical Enquiries*, ed. Paul H. Barrett *et al.* (Ithaca, NY, 1987), p. 566 n. 10.

[42] Cited in Joseph R. Roach, *The Player's Passion: Studies in the Science of Acting* (Newark, NJ, 1985), p. 181.

[43] Darwin, *Autobiography*, p. 132.

from the lenient to the virulent. What the reviewers unanimously regretted (or resented) was Darwin's neglect (or ignorance) of artistic expression of emotion. The hostile *Edinburgh Review* critic declared that 'Mr. Darwin apparently knows nothing of art, and certainly has no perception of its intimate relation to the subject he undertakes to expound',[44] while the *Athenaeum* reviewer inserted an apologetic reminder to the prospective reader: 'Although artists will be surprised at Mr. Darwin's statement that he has been disappointed in his hopes of obtaining much aid from paintings and sculptures in the study of his present subject, they will read his work with interest, and remember it with gratitude.'[45] Indeed, Darwin's discussion could have been much amplified by the lines of Homer and Virgil, who, 'in their descriptions of violent passions and emotion in man, were wont to institute comparisons with animals when similarly excited'.[46] Darwin did not make adequate use of these *loci classici*, either. Most crucially, his findings had direct bearings on the art of theatre: 'The whole charm of art lies in this expression, and no art is so powerful as the dramatic, in which words are interpreted by looks and gestures. Any one who has seen a great play well acted will know that even the most powerful words convey only half their meaning without a visible embodiment.'[47] However, dramatic expression was largely neglected in the publication, the only significant theatrical references being to the 'grief muscles' (*corrugator supercilii, orbicularis, pyramidalis nasi* and *frontalis*) of the queen of tragedy Sarah Siddons and her family, and to the 'the snarling muscles' (*ringentes*) and the canine tooth of actor George Frederick Cooke.[48]

Darwin's negligence notwithstanding, recent scholarship has revealed the far-reaching repercussions of his evolutionary and ethological theories especially in the field of performing arts. Alden T. Vaughan and Virginia Mason Vaughan trace the impact of Darwin's findings in the literary, visual and theatrical representations of Shakespeare's Caliban,[49] while Jane R. Goodall illuminates the colourful ways in which the major themes of Darwinism were performed on the popular stage in the formative years of evolutionary ideas

(1830–1900).[50] Darwin's treatise also triggered a paradigm shift in Victorian acting theory, exerting direct and indirect influences on G. H. Lewes's interest in 'animalism' in acting and on William Archer's hypothesis of 'innervation', or the actor's bodily preparation for the role.[51]

Researchers, however, have scarcely noted that the theme of tragic acting and mimicry crucially informed Darwin's ethology and that, precisely by excluding artistic and dramatic materials, the *Expression* itself directly participated in a theatrical debate that originated in David Garrick's virtuoso acting. Soon after the sensational debut in 1741, Garrick's lifelike portrayal of Shakespearian characters sparked a heated debate over theatrical emotion and expression that continued down to the nineteenth century. Do actors really feel the emotion they express on stage? What constitutes good acting, naturalness or artistry? G. H. Lewes's essay 'On Natural Acting' (collected in *Actors and the Art of Acting*, 1875) was a critique of an episode in Henry Fielding's *Tom Jones* (Book 16 chapter 5), where Garrick's tragic effusion as Hamlet called forth a sympathetic response in even that spectator (Mr Partridge) whose tastes were the least artistic. Lewes criticized the novelist's confusion over the 'naturalness' of Hamlet, Garrick and Mr Partridge, and advanced his own theory of theatrical decorum and artistry.[52] William Archer's *Masks or Faces?* (1888) was a rejoinder to Denis Diderot's *Paradoxe sur le comédien* (written 1773, published 1830), which in its turn was a response to Antoine-Fabio Sticotti's *Garrick ou les acteurs anglois* (1769).

---

44 *Edinburgh Review* (April 1873), 516.

45 *Athenaeum*, 9 November 1872.

46 *Journal of the Anthropological Institute of Great Britain and Ireland*, 2 (1872), 446.

47 *The Times*, 13 December 1872.

48 *Expression*, pp. 182–3, 246. Charles Bell had referred to both Cooke and the Kembles (*Anatomy*, p. 125).

49 *Shakespeare's Caliban : A Cultural History* (Cambridge, 1991).

50 *Performance and Evolution in the Age of Darwin: Out of the Natural Order* (London, 2002).

51 See Roach, *Player's Passion*, pp. 177–94.

52 George Henry Lewes, *On Actors and the Art of Acting* (New York, [1957]), pp. 100–2.

Diderot's anti-emotionalist acting theory was verified by a curious experiment:

Garrick will put his head between two folding-doors, and in the course of five or six seconds his expression will change successively from wild delight to temperate pleasure, from this to tranquillity, from tranquillity to surprise, from surprise to blank astonishment, from that to sorrow, from sorrow to the air of one overwhelmed, from that to fright, from fright to horror, from horror to despair, and thence he will go up again to the point from which he started. Can his soul have experienced all these feelings, and played this kind of scale in concert with his face? I don't believe it.[53]

Diderot's assumption is that an actor approaches perfection as he learns to detach his gesture and expression from his personal emotion and, to the *philosophe*, Garrick was clearly the greatest master of the game. Darwin's decision against using artistic materials in the *Expression* was closely related to this controversy in the theatre, to which a series of manuscript notes he jotted down after completing the *Beagle* voyage attest.

To observe expression of emotions had been Darwin's 'hobby horse' long before the publication of the 1872 treatise.[54] He states that his 'own observations . . . were commenced in the year 1838',[55] and that he 'commenced to make notes on the first dawn of the various expressions' in infancy as soon as his first child William was born on 27 December 1839.[56] He made use of these materials to write the *Expression* and allegedly 'arrived . . . at these three principles [of 'serviceable associated habits', 'antithesis' and 'direct action of the nervous system'] only at the close of my observations'.[57] Darwin emphasized in all these statements that the book was the result of careful observations and implicitly denied any theoretical speculations preceding them. However, even before William was born, Darwin had already formulated the three principles in two notebooks entitled 'Expression', covering the periods July to October 1838 (Notebook M, 'connected with Metaphysical Enquiries') and October 1838 to mid-1839 (Notebook N) respectively. It appears that, by downplaying these early theorizations, Darwin defended 'his unpopular views by suggesting that he had been driven to them by a mass of unassailable evidence, rather than the less acceptable reality that much of his evidence had been indeed patiently assembled, but only after his views were quite well developed'.[58]

A third group of documents from the same period (1838–9) 'about the moral sense & some metaphysical points', which Darwin would later label dismissively as 'Old and Useless Notes' (OUN), includes an important reference to Shakespeare and tragic acting, and helps explain why he excluded discussions of art from the 1872 treatise. According to the Introduction to the *Expression*, Darwin 'had hoped to derive much aid from the great masters in painting and sculpture' but 'with a few exceptions, have not thus profited'. Darwin explained the failure by loosely quoting from Lessing's *Laocoon*:

The reason no doubt is, that in works of art, beauty is the chief object; and strongly contracted facial muscles destroy beauty. The story of the composition is generally told with wonderful force and truth by skilfully given accessories.[59]

Darwin had already cited Lessing's *Laocoon* in the 'Old and Useless Notes',[60] along with another, equally celebrated, art theorist: Joshua Reynolds. Before the notes on Lessing, Darwin jotted down several fragments from Reynolds's *Discourses on Art*,[61] of which the most relevant to the *Expression* was the entry in OUN 11[v]:

---

53 *Paradox of Acting (Paradoxe sur le comédien)*, in Lee Strasberg, intro., *The Paradox of Acting* (by Denis Diderot) *and Masks or Faces?* (by William Archer), (New York, 1957), pp. 11–71; pp. 32–3.

54 Darwin used the phrase ('hobby horse') repeatedly to refer to his research on expression. See for instance *Correspondence*, vol. 10, p. 624 ('To J. D. Hooker', 24 December [1862]), vol. 15, p. 141('To A. R. Wallace', [12–17] March [1867]), vol. 15, p. 224 ('To Asa Gray', 15 April [1867]).

55 *Expression*, p. 25.

56 *Autobiography*, p. 131.

57 *Expression*, p. 33.

58 Gruber, 'A Psychological Study', p. 122.

59 *Expression*, pp. 21–2. See also Lecture 2 of Lessing's *Laocoon*.

60 *Notebooks*, p. 606 (OUN 22, 23, 24).

61 *Notebooks*, pp. 602–3 (OUN 10, 11, 11[v], 11b, 11b[v]).

How strange it [is], that Nature should have so little to do with art (p 128) R. compares a view taken by a camera obscura &c a Poussin. –

–

How are my ideas of a general notion of everything applicable to the high idea⟨(p.131)⟩in Tragic acting – [My idea. would make the mind have mysterious & *sublime* ideas independent of the senses & experience[62]

As Darwin's page references indicate, this fragmentary entry was a response to Reynolds's Discourse 13, where the painter distinguished between 'high' imaginative art and 'low' imitation of natural objects. The first half of the entry referred to Reynolds's distinction between art and nature as represented respectively by Nicolas Poussin and the *camera obscura*.[63] Reynolds's lofty aesthetic principle elicited a parenthetical comment from Darwin ('How strange it is, that Nature should have so little to do with art'), and presumably had a direct bearing on the scarcity of artistic materials, as well as on the ample use of photographic illustrations, in the *Expression*.[64]

The second half of the entry referred to the antithesis between artistic imagination and natural imitation as applied to theatrical art and to Fielding's rendition of Garrick's Hamlet in particular.[65] Anticipating Lewes's essay by many decades, Reynolds criticized Mr Partridge's sympathetic identification with Garrick's Hamlet in *Tom Jones*, arguing that 'the more low, illiterate, and vulgar' people are less disposed to accept theatrical conventions or to appreciate fine acting. These uncivilized folk are only capable of enjoying the realistic imitation of the 'lower kind of Comedy, or Farce', when high tragedy aims 'no more at imitation, so far as it belongs to any thing like deception' and is clearly beyond the appreciation of a Mr Partridge.[66]

While Reynolds's 'high idea . . . in Tragic acting' was premised on the sophisticated imagination of both the actor and the spectator, Darwin's ethology was deeply concerned with the 'lower' kind of imitation. During the *Beagle* voyage, Darwin was astonished by the Fuegians' 'excellent' mimicry: the savages imitated Europeans with astonishing astuteness:

as often as we coughed or yawned, or made any odd motion, they immediately imitated us. Some of our party began to squint and look awry; but one of the young Fuegians (whose whole face was painted black, excepting a white band across his eyes) succeeded in making far more *hideous grimaces*. They could repeat with perfect correctness, each word in any sentence we addressed them, and they remembered such words for some time.[67]

Nearly forty years later, Fuegians' 'hideous grimaces' were significantly transplanted to monkeys in the Introduction to the *Expression*. Crucially refuting Bell's 'special provision' for facial expression, Darwin pointed out that apes and humans actually share the same muscle system, noting that 'no one . . . would be inclined to admit that monkeys have been endowed with special muscles solely for exhibiting their *hideous grimaces*'.[68] The *Athenaeum* reviewer censured Darwin's inadvertent introduction of aesthetic judgement in the usage of 'hideous' ('we do not see what the hideousness of the grimaces has to do with a question which has no concern with beauty').[69] Darwin subsequently struck out the adjective in his copy of the *Expression* in deference to the criticism and thereby corroborated the inartistic nature of his discussion.[70]

Still, 'hideous grimaces' and undignified mimicking died hard in the *Expression*. Some of its illustrative photographs were supplied by the French physiologist G.-B. Duchenne, who modified the features of his subjects by galvanizing their faces, as

---

[62] See also *Notebooks*, p. 322 (C 269), where Darwin cited Reynolds's *Discourses* and Lessing's *Laocoon* alongside each other among the 'Books examined: with ref: to Species'.

[63] Joshua Reynolds, *Discourses on Art*, ed. Robert R. Wark (New Haven, 1997), p. 237.

[64] In fact, the *Expression* was one of the first scientific books with photographic illustrations ever published in Britain. See Philip Prodger, 'Photography and *The Expression of the Emotions*', 'Concordance of Illustrations', and Prodger and Paul Ekman, 'Note on the Orientation of the Plates', in *Expression*, pp. 399–415 (Appendix).

[65] Reynolds, *Discourses*, pp. 238–40.

[66] *Discourses*, p. 239.

[67] Italics mine, *Journal of Researches*, Part 1, pp. 179–80.

[68] Italics mine, *Expression*, p. 17. See also Francis Darwin's footnote.

[69] *Athenaeum*, 9 November 1872.

[70] *Expression*, p. 17 n.

a way to ascertain the particular muscles responsible for the several expressions. The expressions thus captured were artificial and vacant, as Duchenne relied 'only on my judgement and on my artistic feelings' in his experiments and was careful 'not to involve my subjects' feelings'.[71] Duchenne even created three portraits of Lady Macbeth (not cited by Darwin) simply by applying different voltages to the 'the muscle of aggression' (*m. procerus*) of a female subject.[72] Just as the Fuegians mimicked English gestures and words without understanding their emotional contents, Duchenne's Lady Macbeth was in fact devoid of the aggression that the galvanized features supposedly expressed. Duchenne's portraits cited in the *Expression* were disparaged as '*hideous*' in the *Edinburgh Review*.[73] Other photos supplied by Oscar Gustave Rejlander were also posed and lacked spontaneity, which prompted a criticism in the second *Athenaeum* notice: 'Now, we do not think that Mr. Rejlander, to judge by his photographs, is a first-rate actor, or a subtle director of actors . . . A man must be, indeed, a first-rate actor who could keep the intensity of an emotion displayed in his features while another person "took his likeness".'[74]

But what about tragedy? Where is *Hamlet* in all this? Tragic acting was not discussed in the *Expression* precisely because the usually materialistic Darwin recognized some 'mysterious & *sublime* ideas' behind the painted face of tragic actors ('My idea. would make the mind have mysterious & *sublime* ideas independent of the senses & experience'). Unlike the vacant mimicking of Fuegians and Duchenne's subjects, 'the high idea . . . in Tragic acting' is premised on a subtle interaction of the actor's emotion and expression. Neither Hamlet's 'conceit' nor the 'ideas' repeated many times in OUN 11[v] was reducible to 'the senses & experience' and therefore escaped Darwin's explanatory framework of 'serviceable associated habits', 'antithesis' and 'direct action of the nervous system'. In a paradoxical way, by keeping away from high tragedy and limiting itself to the 'hideous grimaces' of monkeys, Fuegians and galvanized subjects, Darwin's *Expression* let in the 'special provision' for human emotion and expression through the back door.

---

[71] G.-B. Duchenne de Boulogne, *The Mechanism of Human Facial Expression*, ed. and trans. R. Andrew Cuthbertson (Cambridge, 1990), p. 106.

[72] Duchenne, *Mechanism*, pp. 120–3 and plates 81–3. The scenes Duchenne illustrated were Lady Macbeth's invocation to evil spirits (1.7), her reflection on the resemblance of Duncan and her own father (2.2), and the off-stage scene where she returns the dagger to Duncan's bed-chamber (2.2).

[73] *Edinburgh Review*, April 1873, 513.

[74] *Athenaeum*, 16 November 1872.

SENSE/MEMORY/SENSE-MEMORY: READING NARRATIVES OF SHAKESPEARIAN REHEARSALS

CARY M. MAZER

1. 'I WANT TO SMELL THAT FEAR'

Rehearsals for a Christmas Eve pick-up production of Shakespeare's *Hamlet* have just begun in an insufficiently heated provincial village church in Kenneth Branagh's 1995 film, *In the Bleak Midwinter* (released in the United States as *A Midwinter's Tale*). Joe (Michael Maloney), a semi-employed actor who is directing, co-producing and starring in the production, is rehearsing his small ensemble of actors in the first scene. Carnforth (Gerald Horan), a bit-part character actor in provincial rep who routinely hides behind putty noses and crepe hair, is having trouble conveying Barnardo's fear in the play's first line, 'Who's there?' Joe instantly sees that Carnforth has no emotional connection to the material or the situation, and tells him, 'I want to see that fear – I want to smell that fear.' The actor repeats the line the same way. 'Let's take a little time out, here,' Joe then suggests, 'to ground this in some sort of reality. You tell me, Carnforth, when was the last time you were really terrified[?] Can you remember when that was or if there was such a time[?]'(p. 45).[1] Carnforth remembers that his hands shook when he once tried to change a punctured tyre on the motorway on his way to a birthday brunch for his mum. Joe asks him to try to recapture that fear, expecting him to bring the fear to the scene's given circumstances. But Carnforth misunderstands the exercise. He speaks the lines of the play, not as though he were on the battlements of Elsinore, but miming changing a tyre, as if he were on the shoulder of the motorway (illustration 56).

The immediate source of the comedy in this scene is Carnforth's cluelessness. He mistakes an exercise in imagination – remember the fear, imagine the given circumstances of the scene at hand, bring your earlier experience of fear in that real context to these imagined given circumstances of the play – for an exercise in white-face pantomime. Joe clearly wanted him to play Shakespeare's scene, not to mime a socket wrench while using Shakespeare's words.

But there is an irony, perhaps unintended, in the way the clueless Carnforth misinterprets Joe's imaginative exercise. For Carnforth has inadvertently employed a standard technique of mid-twentieth-century American 'Method' acting: the actor activates the emotions necessary for the scene by imaginatively re-experiencing an event from his or her past ('emotional memory'); this can often be accomplished by using an improvisation exercise to imaginatively re-experience the physical sensations of the past event ('sense memory') – the sight of breath condensing as you exhale, the sensation of the chill air on your cheek, the metallic feel of the four-way wheel-nut wrench in your hands, etc. – which generates the emotions the actor felt at that moment, just as tasting the madeleine generates in Proust's narrator Marcel the sensations and emotions of Combray; the actor then brings these emotions to the analogous given circumstances of the scene he or she is playing. A Method-based director or an acting coach might actually have

---

[1] Quotations are from the published version of the screenplay, *A Midwinter's Tale: The Shooting Script* (New York, 1996).

56. *In the Bleak Midwinter.* Carnforth/Bernardo (Gerald Horan) changes a tyre, as Joe (Michael Maloney) watches, centre.

asked Carnforth to improvise changing the tyre, in order to generate just the sense of genuine fear that Joe wanted, which the actor would then bring to Shakespeare's scene.

It may be significant that Branagh opted *not* to satirize Carnforth as an exemplar of American-style navel-gazing Method-acting self-indulgence, which he could easily have done by making Carnforth an American, thereby exploiting the persistent, if largely mythic, polarity drawn between British text- and verse-speaking-based acting on the one hand and stereotypically American emotionally based acting on the other – a distinction that still resonates in the popular imagination even if it has become less and less accurate in recent decades. Carnforth's inadvertent flirtation with sense-memory notwithstanding, the approach to acting exemplified by Joe's pick-up company of mismatched actors in *In the Bleak Midwinter* is consistently emotionally realist: the actors are asked to identify with their roles, to find points of biographical contiguity between themselves and their characters, to be genuinely, spontaneously emotionally authentic and 'in the moment'. Joe usually

doesn't inspire this in actors through touchy-feely acting exercises, but by painting verbal pictures of their scenes' given circumstances and the characters' emotional situations that are so vivid and evocative that the actors can't help but relive analogous moments from their own lives. During a rehearsal for the closet scene, for example, Terry (John Sessions), the one-time Panto Dame playing Gertrude in drag, breaks down as he/she cries out, 'Oh, Hamlet, thou hast cleft my heart in twain,' telling Joe, 'I'm sorry I can't go on' (p. 67). Joe, recognizing an emotional breakthrough, encourages Terry to continue by pushing him deeper into the context of Gertrude's situation: 'It's terrific. It's terrific. You must, you must. You're just avoiding confronting it as an actor that's all, you have to feel her guilt, you have to confess to our son –' Terry responds, 'I tried, I tried . . . he wouldn't listen,' and runs out of the rehearsal in tears. Terry later explains what was going on to his fellow-actor and room-mate Henry (Richard Briers): years before, he had met his adult biological son, backstage after a Christmas Pantomime, and his son had rejected him because of his homosexuality. Later,

Joe rehearses Nina (Julia Sawalha), the near-sighted accident-prone actress playing Ophelia, in the mad scene. He reminds her that the moment is all about death and loss, and then, remembering the story Nina had told him about her young fighter-pilot husband dying in a training exercise, apologizes to her. 'No, you're perfectly right, Joe,' she reassures him, 'We must imagine the reality of it. I'm fine' (p. 70). Then, as she sings 'Will he not come again', she breaks down and runs off.

These moments, and other aspects of Branagh's film, are characteristic of the genre of rehearsals-of-a-Shakespeare-production-within-a-film. There are three main tropes of the genre, common both to fiction films and documentaries, and, significantly, to several if not all non-fiction prose accounts of Shakespearean rehearsals, all of which are present, with laser-cut clarity, in *In the Bleak Midwinter*. The first trope is structural: these films almost invariably dramatize a rehearsal process approaching, and narrowly averting, catastrophic breakdown. Branagh mocks this in his film by playing Noel Coward's song 'Why Must the Show Go On?' ironically on the soundtrack; but then the plot neatly follows the pattern, when the company is threatened with eviction, and when Joe withdraws from the cast at the last minute to take a remunerative recurring role in a sci-fi film franchise, only to change his mind and return just in time for his first entrance.

The other two tropes are more thematic and functional. One is that Shakespeare is depicted as redemptive, for actors and audience alike. Invariably, characters (including several in Branagh's film) reminisce about the first time they saw a Shakespeare play, much as characters in a ballet film or memoir will talk about seeing *The Red Shoes* for the first time. By the end of Branagh's film, the actors who have gathered in the unheated church in the aptly named village of Hope each ultimately resolve their conflicts with estranged family members; they discover, from their newly forged relationships with one another, the true meaning of family; the villagers overcome their scepticism of Shakespeare and give the performance a standing ovation; and the film ends with the actors wishing one another 'Merry Christmas'.

The third trope of the genre – the one that we see at work in the break-through rehearsal scenes – is by far the most revealing about contemporary theatrical practices and the popular myths accruing to them: the actors must learn something about themselves in order to identify emotionally with the parts they are playing; and, having done so, they then learn something more about themselves from the very act of playing the part, of seeing the world through the character's eyes. The fictional (and, in non-fiction actor memoirs, the real-life) actor goes on a journey that arrives at the performance; and, in performance the journey that the character makes across the breadth of the play takes the actor playing that character along on that journey, from which the actor learns even more about him- or herself.

What is most remarkable about this trope is that it appears, at least, to fly in the face of most of the more advanced historicist scholarship on Shakespeare, theoretical writing on performance, and actual performance practice, which has, since the 1980s, either problematized or systematically rejected the entire notion of an 'emotional journey', as well of much of what had been the fundamental assumptions of theatrical mimesis. Literary and cultural scholars of early modern Britain have challenged as anachronistic such concepts as subjectivity, interiority and even the term 'character', which they claim date from much later in the seventeenth-century, and have dismissed our tendency to read psychology into a dramatis persona as the 'character effect'.[2] Books and articles (with apocalyptic titles such as *The Death*

[2] See Catherine Belsey, *The Subject of Tragedy* (London, 1985); Frances Barker, *The Tremulous Private Body* (London, 1984); Edward Burns, *Character: Acting and Being on the Pre-Modern Stage* (New York, 1990); and Christy Desmet, *Reading Shakespeare's Characters: Rhetoric, Ethics, and Identity* (Amherst, 1992). For a discussion of the 'character effect', see Alan Sinfield, 'When is a Character Not a Character: Desdemona, Olivia, Lady Macbeth, and Subjectivity', in *Faultlines: Cultural Materialism and the Politics of Dissident Reading* (Berkeley, 1992). The extremity of the argument about early modern subjectivity has been tempered considerably by more recent studies, such as Katherine Eisaman Maus, *Inwardness and Theater in the English Renaissance* (Chicago, 1995) and Gail Kern

of Character, The End of Humanism, The End of Acting, Unmaking Mimesis, The Death of the Actor, Acting (Re)Considered, etc.) have challenged the Stanislavskian acting paradigm that has prevailed since early in the twentieth century; have identified realism as sexist, heteronormative and ideologically retrograde; have defined identity (dramatic and real-life) as unstable and 'performative'; and have destabilized theatrical mimesis, even calling into question standard definitions of 'presence' and 'liveness'.[3] And theatrical productions, under the rubric of post-modernism, have experimented with pastiche and discontinuity, estranging the performer from the character, often through strategies of ironic distance or technological intervention.

But despite the noteworthy synergies – one might almost say collusion – between these three schools of history, theory and theatrical practice, the fact remains that most mainstream theatrical practice and most Shakespeare production, in the English-speaking world at least, is persistently mimetic in its language of representation and is resolutely Stanislavskian in its approach to character. Actor-training programmes still use the basic vocabulary of the Stanislavsky 'system' in their foundational courses. Actors, when speaking publicly about their roles, still consistently talk about the character's journey across the play, and about 'finding' and 'becoming' the character. And audiences still measure the actor's performance by the plausibility of the character's psychological make-up, the credibility of the actor's embodiment of the character, and the illusion of emotional actuality and apparent spontaneity of the actor's performance, as though the actor and the character were credibly feeling real things in the real time and real space of the performance. The continuing popularity of the rehearsal narrative as a genre, in popular theatre books, actor memoirs, and in backstage fictions, and the ways these narratives are crafted, are compelling evidence of the persistence of the Stanislavskian paradigm, in the popular consciousness at least.

Part of the dramatic impulse in crafting narratives of the rehearsal process comes from the desire shared by most theatre people to tell stories. M.K. Sinnett, in her recent dissertation on rehearsal narratives, identifies story-telling as one of the few ways that theatre artists acculturate themselves to the ways that professional rehearsals are meant to function; and it is how theatre people learn about what happens in the rehearsals of productions in which they are not participating.[4] Stories, she argues, are a mode of transmission by which the theatrical culture (in the anthropological sense) communicates the 'values and worldviews of its members'.[5] Sinnett seeks to identify, in first-person eye-witness narratives of rehearsal, the 'story maps' that these narratives make manifest. Surely one of the stories being mapped onto rehearsal narratives, and onto narratives of rehearsals of Shakespeare in particular, is the Stanislavskian paradigm, which provides both a diagnostic tool (what it was about the performance that makes it 'work' for its audiences) and a structuring drive (how the production became what it was), via the story of how the actor 'became' the character he or she is playing. And nowhere are these story maps more evident than in stories that are crafted, i.e. in the fictional, mass cultural, narratives found predominantly in film and television.[6] Films like *In the Bleak Midwinter,*

Paster, *Humoring the Body: Emotions and the Shakespearean Stage* (Chicago, 2004).

3 See Elinor Fuchs, *The Death of Character* (Bloomington, 1996); Richard Schechner, *The End of Humanism* (New York, 1982); Richard Hornby, *The End of Acting* (New York, 1992); Elin Diamond, *Unmaking Mimesis* (London, 1997); Martin Buzacott, *The Death of the Actor* (London, 1991); and Phillip B. Zarrilli, ed., *Acting (Re)Considered* (London, 1995). For 'performativity', see Judith Butler, *Gender Trouble* (New York: 1991) and subsequent books and essays. For a critique of presence and liveness, see Philip Auslander, *Liveness: Performance in a Mediatized Culture* (London, 1999).

4 'Rehearsal, A Story Map: A Critical Analysis of First-Person Narratives about Theatrical Rehearsals', Ph.D. Dissertation, University of Missouri-Columbia, 2003.

5 Sinnett, 'Rehearsal, A Story Map', p. 4.

6 Other films featuring Shakespearean rehearsals are *The Goodbye Girl, The Dead Poets Society, Shakespeare Wallah* and the documentary, *The Hobart Shakespeareans.* Examples of modern plays – a by no means and exhaustive list – that feature theatrical (though not necessarily Shakespearean) rehearsals,

television series such as *Slings and Arrows*, documentaries such as *Shakespeare Behind Bars*, and numerous exemplary non-fiction rehearsal memoirs, are the best evidence we have of the persistence of the Stanislavskian, emotional-realist paradigm in contemporary English-language Shakespeare performance, at least in the public consciousness. But while these dramatizations and narratives confirm the general public's fervent desire to believe in the Stanislavskian paradigm, they also document the public's anxieties about what the actors' emotional identification with the role might imply about their biographies, sexuality and self-control. Audience members, it appears, want to believe that the actors are being transcendently themselves, shedding real tears, resolutely present and 'in the moment'; but they find such identification, and such presence, oddly terrifying. The dramatizations and narratives about the rehearsal process navigate these roiled waters, skirting the contradictions (as Branagh does by satirizing Carnforth's opacity rather than his Method acting), or addressing the conundrum head-on.

2. 'IT *IS* THE CAUSE'

These anxieties are addressed directly in one of the first films of the genre, George Cukor's *A Double Life* (1947), with a screenplay by Ruth Gordon and Garson Kanin. Though neither are mentioned explicitly, the film brings together two strands only then coming to be represented in popular culture, several decades after their introduction to America: psychoanalysis and Stanislavskian acting.[7] Anthony John (Ronald Coleman, in his Academy Award-winning performance) is a successful Broadway actor coming to the end of yet another long run of a romantic society comedy. His producer suggests that he return to his long-dormant production scheme for *Othello*. All of the participants are wary, no one more than Tony's acting partner and ex-wife Brita (Signe Hasso). Tony's task is the task of every actor, 'Trying to make someone else's words you own, thoughts your own', which accounts for the film's title. But for Tony and the others the issue is not whether he can do that but the conse-

quences of his ability to do it so completely. Tony's regular director warns the producer about 'the way he has of becoming someone else every night, for just a few hours, so completely; now don't tell me that his whole system isn't affected by it'; and as Brita recalls, tracing the arc of their marriage, 'We were engaged doing Oscar Wilde, we broke it off doing O'Neill, we married doing Kaufman and Hart, and we divorced doing Chekhov.' No sooner does Tony start considering the role than he starts looking at his reflection in mirrors and shop windows, imagining himself in his moor's make-up; he notices travel posters for Venice; and he has dinner in a cheap Italian restaurant, the Venezia Cafe, where he meets a flirtatious waitress, Pat (Shelley Winters). His obsessive research, and obsessive submersion of himself into his role, start to generate auditory hallucinations, which turn the people around him into characters in the play, and lead him to suspect Brita of being in love with her press agent Bill (Edmond O'Brien) and, ultimately, to murder.

In many ways the film's title is a misnomer, for Tony has no double life, only the singular life of whatever role he's playing. And the play's invitation to psychoanalysis – that Tony is somehow acting out suppressed aggression towards his estranged wife – is a red herring, for Tony has no biography, no childhood trauma, no unresolved parental relationships and, finally, no free-standing identity of

---

are *Joan of Lorraine* (Maxwell Anderson), *Kiss Me Kate* (Sam and Bella Spewack), *The Rehearsal* (Jean Anouilh), *Moby Dick Rehearsed* (Orson Welles), *The Plebeians Rehearsing the Uprising* (Günter Grass), *The Dresser* (Ronald Harwood), *Inspecting Carol* (Daniel Sullivan), *I Hate Hamlet* (Paul Rudnick), *Book of Days* (Lanford Wilson), *It's All True* (Jason Sherman), *Orson's Shadow* (Austin Pendleton), *Anton in Show Business* ('Jane Martin') and *The Spanish Play* (Yasmina Reza).

7 Significantly, two early films explicitly representing psychoanalysis – *King's Row* (1942) and *Spellbound* (1945) – both feature pioneering Stanislavksian acting teachers in supporting roles: Maria Ouspenskaya (a veteran of the Moscow Art Theatre who co-founded, with Richard Boleslavsky, the American Laboratory Theatre, which served as the inspiration for the Group Theatre's pioneering work in the 'Method') in *King's Row*, and veteran acting teacher Michael Chekhov as a psychoanalyst in *Spellbound*.

his own. As he explains to his producing partners, 'I've had to tear myself apart, put myself together again and again, and the leftover pieces are all scattered, somewhere between here and a thousand one-night stands.' He is no more than who he appears to be to the people he's with: in the film's opening sequence, he encounters on the street in the theatre district two young actresses with whom he had evidently flirted, one of whom says of him, 'What a guy!', the other calling him a 'stinker.' As he says to Pat in her shabby apartment, when she asks him his name: 'Look, if I can find out that I'd be a happy man. Most people know who they are, or think they do, which is the same thing. It's simple for them. Want to know my name? Martin [the role he is currently playing]. Also Ernest, and Paul, and Hamlet, and Joe, and maybe Othello.'

Tony summarizes his actor process in a voice-over during a montage of the rehearsals. The actor, he explains, begins by identifying 'the key to the character' which for Othello is jealousy: 'You dig for it within ourself. . . . try to remember jealous moments in your own past. . . . Find it, hold it, live it, jealousy!' The actor must navigate between imagination and reality: 'Keep each in its place, that's the job, if you can do it.' The sequence ends with the final scene on the opening night of the finished production, with Tony acknowledging, in his voice-over, 'You're two men now, grappling for control, you, and Othello.' But the film's whole point is that Tony and Othello are now not two men but one, and the film is ultimately interested in the long-term effects of this fusion over the production's long run. After the 300th performance, Tony's jealousy of Brita has become so acute that she, and the other actors watching from the wings, are worried that he might actually strangle her (through the play-within-the-film's signature interpretive gimmick, the 'kiss of death'), and the actress playing Emilia must rescue Brita by jumping the cue for her off-stage knocking. At a tête-à-tête celebration in Brita's townhouse celebrating the second year of the run, Tony becomes so violent towards her that he flees, fearful that he will harm her, and sublimates his violent jealousy by murdering Pat with the kiss of death instead,

as stand-in both for Desdemona (she asks him, 'Ya wanna put out the light?') and for Brita.

On the surface, the film depicts, only a few years before the Method surfaced in the American popular consciousness, the nightmare of the Method actor's over-identification with a role, through an actor (both Anthony John and the movie star who plays him, Ronald Coleman) from whom we would least expect Method acting, or, for that matter, a performance of Othello.[8] But it is in Tony's final performance, in the final sequence, that the film provides – perhaps unintentionally – its most vivid representation of the Stanislavskian paradigm. We had already seen how, at the 300th performance, Tony lost control of the theatrical fiction in his near strangulation of Brita/Desdemona. Now, as the police close in on him, the cast and the police watch from the wings as Tony, guilt-wracked from having killed Pat, actually stabs himself as Othello. We're supposed to believe that his performance is falling apart: he flubs his lines and begins to have the same auditory hallucinations that plagued his off-stage relationship with Brita. But Tony/Coleman's performance of the character's final speech is more truthful and more compelling than any of the more polished performances we saw earlier in the film. The film's on-stage *Othello* sequences were staged under the supervision of the veteran Shakespearian actor Walter Hampden, and the performance of Othello, even making allowances for Anthony John's (and Ronald Coleman's) inadequacies, is inflated and orotund, even when the film asks us to find it acutely psychologically verisimilar. Even in 1947, the viewer, I suspect, would have had to take the performance's effectiveness on faith. But here, in what will be his last performance, Tony spontaneously changes the blocking and crosses to the bed to address Desdemona's corpse directly on 'loved not wisely but too well', as if apologizing to Brita in the voice of Othello apologizing to Desdemona.

There is, in Coleman/Tony/Othello's performance, a connection and a palpable truth,

---

[8] The screenwriters had originally conceived the role for Laurence Olivier.

57. *A Double Life*: Tony/Othello (Ronald Colman), perplexed in the extreme.

generated by the actor and the viewer's awareness of the off-stage realities affecting the on-stage dramatic actions. What the filmmakers might have intended as the breakdown of a performance resulting from the actor's over-identification with the role instead becomes a dramatized lesson in Method-acting: that substitution and affective memory can generate a performance that is more spontaneous and more perceivably 'real' than the norm.

Richard Eyre's *Stage Beauty* (2004), with a screenplay by Jeffrey Hatcher (based on his play, *The Compleat Stage Beauty*) reads the same Stanislavskian conundrum backward in history to the English Restoration theatre, and again uses rehearsals and performances of Shakespeare's *Othello* as its metatheatrical arena. Ned Kynaston (Billy Crudup) is the last of the male actors to play the great female roles on the English stage before King Charles II allows women to play the parts and, soon after, bans men from doing so; Maria (historically Margaret) Hughes (Claire Danes), here identified as Kynaston's dresser, becomes the first actress. Hatcher and Eyre (who, as one-time director of the National Theatre and author/host of a television series on theatre history, should know better) mark the change from cross-dressed actors to actresses as the crucial moment in the emergence of a new proto-Stanislavskian paradigm of acting. (It may not be a coincidence that Kynaston and Hughes,

the agents for this change, are played by American actors in an otherwise British cast.) In the first sequences, before women have appeared on stage, we see Kynaston as Desdemona; his performance is exquisitely beautiful, each hand gesture choreographed, as formal as kabuki. The new verisimilitude of the actress clearly calls out for something else, something that even Mrs Hughes, after the novelty of her debut, cannot provide, as she is only capable of doing a pale imitation of Kynaston's over-crafted choreography. Having lost faith in her own abilities, and losing ground to a host of new female competitors, Mrs Hughes rescues Kynaston from the molly-houses where he has been reduced to giving salacious drag performances, and brings him to a country inn where, she hopes, he can recover his health and teach her acting. He finds that he doesn't really know enough about 'real' acting to do so. He's always played women, he explains, because women do things, especially dying, beautifully; 'Men feel far too much. Feeling ruins the effect. Feeling makes it ugly.' He never got Desdemona right, he confesses, because he never allowed himself to feel: 'I couldn't let the beauty die.'

Kynaston learns what is missing from his own acting in a scene in which he explores his sexual identity, and both he and Maria explore their potential romantic and sexual relationship. Maria strips to her nightshirt and climbs into bed with the naked Kynaston, she for the first time with a man, and the homosexual Kynaston for the first time sleeping with a woman ('apart from myself', he adds). When she asks him how men have sex with other men, he demonstrates how the two men assume male and female roles. To illustrate, they change positions and take on sexual personae: first he acts the 'male' man and she acts the 'female' man, then he acts a heterosexual man and she, temptingly, plays herself. This unleashes heterosexual energies between them, and they discover their 'true' sexual, at the same time as their emotional, and potentially histrionic, selves.

In learning about themselves, and what it means to be 'real' – in their emotions, passions, feminist empowerment and (conveniently heterosexual)

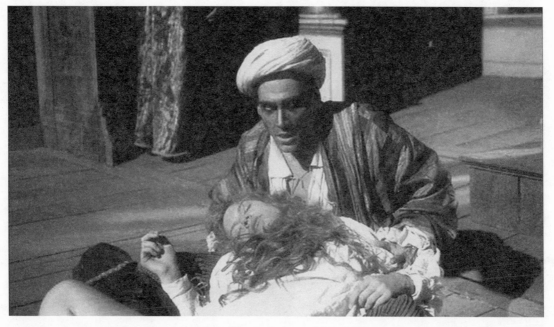

58. *Stage Beauty*: Kynaston/Othello (Billy Crudup) strangles Hughes/Desdemona (Claire Danes).

sexual identities – they are, despite their quarrel, now ready to reinvent English acting as Method acting 250 years *avant la lettre*. On short notice, Maria is scheduled to play Desdemona to Betterton's Othello (Hatcher, true to the genre, ups the tension by having the theatre's royal patent depend on that single performance's success), and Kynaston is recruited to coach her in the part. They rehearse the death scene onstage on the set, Kynaston forcing her into the new histrionic realism: he strips her of her fancy gown and makeup, continually reminds her that her organic reactions are as important as her speech and action, and teaches her how 'subtext' works (pointing out to her that, when she says 'Send for the man and ask him', she has a desire to speak Cassio's name countered by a mortal fear of doing so). They don't rehearse the actual murder: 'Save something for the moment,' Kynaston explains, 'Always do something different than you planned.'

Kynaston persuades Betterton to allow him to play Othello that night. The climactic performance

is freed from all of the kabuki-like choreography of its previous stagings, as the performers act and react to the emotions of what Kynaston had, in the rehearsal, called 'the moment'. As in *A Double Life*, both the audience and Othello's fellow actors are uncertain about whether the on-stage violence is real or theatrical. (And so are we: we have already seen Kynaston, at his dressing table, say to his image in the mirror, 'It is the cause . . . it *is* the cause.') And, as in *A Double Life*, this uncertainty redoubles what is already true about the language of acting being articulated for the first time in the performance of the play-within-the-film: the identity of actor and role, of biographically and given-circumstances-generated emotions, is so complete that the artifice of theatre is stripped away, and the correlation of life and art achieves complete equivalence.

Maria/Desdemona is genuinely worried for her life; the members of the audience (including King Charles, Pepys and Nell Gwynn) and Betterton in the wings gasp at the physical contact and

59. *Slings and Arrows*: Claire (Sabrina Grdevich) rehearses Ophelia, as Geoffrey (Paul Gross) and Ellen (Martha Burns) look on.

cringe in genuine fear for Maria/Desdemona's life; and the actress playing Emilia, genuinely uncertain about whether Maria is actually dead, also finds herself giving a transcendent performance. After the performance (which is greeted by rapturous applause, as per the genre), King Charles compliments Betterton for Kynaston and Maria's performances: 'That new ending – very, very real. Almost too much so.' Back onstage, by themselves, Maria tells Kynaston: 'You almost killed me!' He replies, 'I *did* kill you. You just didn't die.' They fall into each other's arms, kissing passionately. Echoing their sexual role-playing (and identity-revealing) games at the inn, she asks him, 'So, who [i.e. which gender and sexual role] are you now?' 'I don't know. I don't know,' he responds. And so the actors, having discovered enough about themselves to play their roles, are, by playing these roles, now freed to discover romance, sex and their 'true' selves, even – especially – in Kynaston's case, where the 'true' self he discovers embraces both his love and desire for Maria and his pansexuality.

3. 'HE'S MAKING IT HIS OWN. THAT'S HOW THEY DO IT IN AMERICA'

Geoffrey Tennant (Paul Gross), the one-time actor and one-time psychiatric patient who serendipitously becomes the artistic director of the New Burbage Shakespeare Festival in the three-season Canadian television mini-series *Slings and Arrows* (2003–6), is rehearsing Claire (Sabrina Grdevich), an ambitious but execrable actor, as Ophelia, in the mad scene.

Claire explains that she had smoked dope so that she could study what it felt like and use it in the role: 'I'm not mad . . . and I never have been. So I have to simulate it. . . . I'm using sense memory. I'm remembering what it was like being stoned.' But Geoffrey, who was only recently certifiably mad, explains that the feelings are in no way alike. Geoffrey bypasses Claire's sense-memory exercise, and uses instead what we have already learned is his favoured directorial technique: he describes the character's given circumstances, with a vivid emotional connection of his own. So vivid is Geoffrey's imagination that, as he describes them to the actors throughout the series, we often see, as though through his eyes, the stage world transformed into the world he is imagining.

As with *In the Bleak Midwinter* and other films of the genre, Shakespeare in *Slings and Arrows* is viewed as redemptive: many characters describe their *Red Shoes* moments of seeing a Shakespeare production for the first time (as does the Festival's philistine managing director, Richard Smith-Jones [co-writer Mark McKinney], remembering his first Broadway musical); and the writers have consciously structured the plays being produced at the festival in the series' three seasons (*Hamlet*, *Macbeth*, *King Lear*) to parallel Shakespeare's supposedly timeless wisdom about youth, maturity and old-age. Also, in keeping with the genre, the writers raise the tension and the dramatic stakes by putting obstacles in the path of the rehearsal process: *Hamlet* goes through three directors, is forced to open without any previews, and the actor playing the title role – Jack Crew (Luke Kirby), an American action-movie star – goes AWOL the day of the opening; an under-rehearsed understudy has to go on as Macbeth at short notice after the visiting star actor Henry Breedlove (Geraint Wyn Davies) is fired; and the opening night of *King Lear* is cancelled not once but twice, as Charles Kingman (William Hutt), the aging actor hired to play Lear in the series's third season, self-medicating his terminal cancer with heroin, slides deeper into dementia and (like Sir, the actor-manager modelled on Donald Wolfit, in Ronald Harwood's play and screenplay, *The Dresser*) ever closer to death.

But the series, like its generic predecessors, is most interested in the reciprocal process of discovery of the actor in the role and the role in the actor during the rehearsal process, what actor/co-writer Susan Coyne identifies (in an interview included in the DVD of the third season)[9] as the moment when an actor snuffs out a cigarette in the wings and strides onto the stage transformed into the character. The key-word in the series is 'transformation', which the three writers (Coyne, Bob Martin, and McKinney), through Geoffrey, use to describe both the actor's process of becoming the character and the effect the plays have on their audiences. The series continually addresses the conundrum of just how much, within the Stanislavskian paradigm, individual actors are capable of transforming themselves into characters different from themselves. Whatever the actor's strengths and weaknesses, the character is no more or less than the actor who plays it: when Geoffrey takes over as director of *Hamlet*, he tells the cast, after asking the actor playing Bernardo to speak his first line, 'Who's there?': 'Who's there indeed. Who are these people? Who is Hamlet and Ophelia? Well the answer is: whoever is playing them. Now I want this production to be about us.' Geoffrey doesn't give up on Jack, even as Jack struggles with Hamlet; as he tells the sympathetic board chair, 'I don't know who he is. I don't know what his "thing" is. I don't know what he's going to bring to the role. So I can't see the Hamlet, so I can't see the play.'

Like the actors, the festival's directors are only capable of making art consistent with their own temperaments. The Festival's long-time artistic director Oliver Welles (Stephen Ouimette) – who is killed at the end of the first episode and comes back to haunt Geoffrey, his former protégé and successor – goes for shallow but pretty stagey effects (at Oliver's memorial service, Geoffrey calls his work of recent years 'shit'); even before he is run over (by a truck carrying, appropriately, ham), he has become emotionally dead. At the other extreme is Darren Nichols (Don McKellar), fresh from guest gigs in Europe, whose work Geoffrey describes as 'post-modern, pseudo-Brechtian, leather-clad, school-boy thuggery'. (When Jack, the American movie-star, is trundled about the stage between the trapdoors, horses and open jets of flame by Darren during the Ghost scene, he remarks, 'I had no idea that the theatre was so much like the movies.') The theatre made by Darren is overly schematic and emotionally lifeless because he is an emotionally self-denying poseur; and he awakens as a director (while directing *Romeo and Juliet* in Season Two) only when he awakens as

---

9 Acorn Media.

a human being – when Geoffrey tricks him into acknowledging his humanity and embracing the memory of his idealistic youth.

Geoffrey occupies the aesthetic, and moral, centre of the spectrum: the theatre is actor-centred, emotionally truthful, and at all times 'honest', both in terms of the actors' performances and their biographies and temperaments. His theatre is on the edge because he, too, is psychopathologically on the edge: 'My reason may very well be hanging by a thread,' he tells the *Hamlet* cast, on taking over from Darren, 'Well, my friends, it is my belief that the best stuff happens just before the thread snaps.' Geoffrey is intolerant of Claire's putative sense-memory exercise, not because it is Stanislavskian, but because being stoned and being insane – particularly being insane because of personal loss – are simply not equivalent. Similarly, Geoffrey is impatient with Jack's persistent paraphrasing of the lines. (While Jack is paraphrasing, Frank (Michael Polley), a slightly deaf and rather opaque elderly gay actor, asks the smarter and more cynical Cyril (Graham Harley), his stage and romantic partner and fellow choric figure, 'Why is he allowed to do that?' Cyril responds, 'It's the Method, isn't it, duckie. He's making it his own. That's how they do it in America.')[10] Geoffrey doesn't reject Jack's desire to make the words, and the role, 'his own'; but he sees the actor's prolonged dependence on paraphrasing as a Hamlet-like evasion of his truly committing himself. They begin to rehearse 3.1, and Geoffrey forces Jack to choose between the options of the given circumstances during 'To be or not to be' – that Hamlet knows that Claudius and Polonius are spying on him, or that he doesn't – and to use the language of the script: 'You have to do it. You have to do it right now. And you have to do it with the text.'[11]

Jack must recognize the Hamlet-like qualities in himself – the very qualities that kept him from committing to his words and his actor choices – in order to play Hamlet. The afternoon that Jack disappears, Kate (Rachel McAdams), the young actress who is now playing Ophelia and has become Jack's lover, finds him and listens to him describe his double-bind about returning to the theatre in time for the opening-night performance; she tells him, sympathetically, 'So you're afraid to do it but you know you have to and if you don't you won't be able to live with yourself... Well, I think you can use that on stage.' When Jack throws up before going on that night, Geoffrey says, simply, 'Use it.'

By contrast, Geoffrey's own Hamlet years before, and the nervous breakdown it precipitated in the middle of the third (and prematurely last) performance, illustrates the outer limit of actors using their lives in their art. We already know through dreams and flashbacks that Geoffrey had fallen in love with his Ophelia, Ellen Fanshaw (played by Martha Burns, Paul Gross's real-world wife) – who is still the temperamental leading lady of the company – and had decided on opening night to get married; and we also know that their relationship was shattered after Geoffrey learned that the otherwise homosexual Oliver had slept with Ellen as part of some manipulative directorial ploy. What we learn only when Geoffrey and Ellen finally walk through the events of the fateful night of the third performance (as they must, before they can

---

10 It is significant that the writers make Jack American; Keanu Reeves, whose 1995 Hamlet in Winnipeg clearly inspired this plot line, is Canadian.

11 *Slings and Arrows* doesn't fetishize Shakespeare's language, or beautiful Shakespearian speaking. In a scene cut from the first season (and included as a special feature on the DVD), Jack responds to the mockery of his castmates by launching into Lear's storm speeches, in impeccable, but emotionally empty, verse-speaking. When, in the second season, Sarah and Patrick, the actors playing Romeo and Juliet, come to Geoffrey in his office to complain about Darren's lifeless directing, Sarah wails, 'I love this play. I've seen in millions of times. And finally I get to say these beautiful words, but without character or story these words are just... they're air.' And, in the first season, Geoffrey teaches a workshop for business executives which Oliver used to teach as a seminar on management skills, and turns it into an impromptu scene-study workshop instead. The sequence culminates when an accountant, Terry (played, significantly, by Bob Martin, the only one of the three co-writers not to have a continuing role in the series), takes in Geoffrey's characteristic emotionally rich description of the given circumstances, and recites Macbeth's 'Tomorrow' speech with an admirable emotional groundedness that exceeds both his verse-speaking ability and his acting talents.

rekindle their romance) is that the moment of Geoffrey's psychotic break, during the graveyard scene, came when he saw Ellen watching in the wings, and found himself addressing his lines ('I loved Ophelia . . . ') directly to her. Art draws on life; but when life intrudes too deeply into the art of acting, art, and life, shatter.

If Season One had explored how the actor can learn to be 'honest' and 'real' in the role, Season Two pursues the more ontological question of who the actor actually is: how people who take on different identities to make their living – who, as numerous characters point out, cannot compartmentalize their professional life and the personal lives – nevertheless have a core identity that makes them able, or unable, to 'be' certain characters.[12] More centrally, the second season explores what it means to be 'in the moment', the cornerstone of Stanislavskian emotional-realism. Geoffrey had been slavishly following Oliver's long-germinating production scheme for *Macbeth* (and arguing with Oliver's ghost every step along the way). At the same time, he is coaching Patrick and Sarah (David Alpay and Joanne Kelly), the young actors playing Romeo and Juliet, behind Darren's back, making them run around the parking lot so that they do the balcony scene completely breathless, their defences down, aware only of their own and one another's bodies. (As Geoffrey no doubt planned, Patrick and Sarah succumb to the rising sexual temperature between them and become lovers, even though Patrick is gay.) Patrick and Sarah's breakthrough teaches Geoffrey what had been missing in the *Macbeth* rehearsal. He marches into the rehearsal room and announces a new direction. The journey of the title role is not, as Oliver had conceived it, an exploration of innate evil, but (like his own life, he admits in private) a slide into near madness; and he wants to pick up the pace of the Macbeth and Lady Macbeth scenes: 'I would like them to be breathless', i.e. as alive and as unself-consciously in-the-moment as the actors he has just rehearsed in *Romeo and Juliet*.

Backstage in Jerry's dressing room before he is set to go on as understudy, Geoffrey tells Jerry (Oliver Dennis), the understudy, 'Look . . . all you

really have to do is connect . . . with the other actors. And don't worry about anything else. You're going to be living moment to moment. That's exactly how Macbeth is living. So just ride with it.' As Geoffrey watches Jerry and Ellen in 1.7 from the booth, he mutters to Maria (Catherine Fitch) the stage manager, 'That's the play.' Jerry's performance is thrilling because the circumstances of the moment have made him live, spontaneously, in the moment, in the emotional reality of his own life and circumstances.[13] What Jerry brings to the role that night is terror: of losing his lines, of forgetting his blocking, of getting clobbered in the swordfights, and above all of his own inadequacy. And the result is a degree of connectedness, an emotionally reality, that the production had not previously achieved.

Once Geoffrey rehires Henry Breedlove to play Macbeth, he must inject into the star actor's performance the same breathless spontaneity and moment-by-moment improvisatory reality that

---

[12] This issue is addressed in two of the subplots of the second season: when Ellen is audited by Canada Revenue (and tries to claim a bra as a business expense on her income taxes); and when a playwright, Lionel (Jonathan Crombie), whose new play is being workshopped, cannibalizes the private life of the Festival's associate managing director Anna (co-writer Coyne), for a character in the play ('I . . . I love that you're real,' he tells her, lamenting that he doesn't know any real people, only theatre folk, 'pretending to be someone they're not'). Ellen, having played the character in the script-in-hand without realizing that it was based on Anna, tells her, tactlessly, 'Your work and your personal life are separated, that's why you're happy. Your life is simple. I envy you,' and asks Anna, 'Do you think I'm miserable because who I am or what I do?'. For actors, these are, inescapably, the same thing; recognizing that enables them to make their art.

[13] Spontaneity and improvisation are motifs in several of the subplots of the second season: when Richard discovers that Sanjay (Colm Feore), the high-powered new-age marketing consultant he had hired to 'rebrand' the festival, is an impostor and a con man, he realizes that 'He made up the whole campaign as he was going along!'. When Sarah and Patrick have sex, she asks him what it was like to make love with a woman for the first time; he answers, 'I was just making it up as I went along', to which she responds, admiringly, 'You've got strong improvisational skills then.' And Ellen tells an auditor for Canada Revenue (whom she increasing uses as a therapist), 'I don't plan, I just react.'

60. *Slings and Arrows*: Henry/Macbeth (Geraint Wyn Davies) in true terror.

on or off the stage, and even whether Young Siward will stay dead.

'This isn't theatre,' he cries, terrified, after finally finding his way offstage, after his first scene, 'this is improvisation!', to which Geoffrey responds, 'Still, that's a kind of theatre, isn't it? Very alive, very exciting.' And when he comes off, after the standing ovation, he shouts at Geoffrey, 'I am Henry Breedlove. I am a great actor. I do not need this shit! I don't want to feel that kind of terror ever again.' But of course, within the aesthetic paradigm embodied by Geoffrey and endorsed axiomatically by the series, he does, and will. 'Theatre is dynamic,' Geoffrey churlishly tells a BBC interviewer at the beginning of the third season, on hearing that one critic has called the *Macbeth* production, which has transferred to Broadway, 'perfect': 'It is constantly in change, from performance to performance, so the concept of perfection is meaningless.'

The parallels between life and art are comparatively neat in the third season of *Slings and Arrows*: Charles Kingman, his heroin and pain medications in constant flux, alternates, like Lear, between patriarchal tyranny and complete disorientation, reduced at one point (somewhat predictably) to wandering about the town of New Burbage in a downpour, with Geoffrey, Fool-like, trying to bring him into the shelter of a phone booth. But unlike *A Double Life*, the fact that the actor has become his role does not in any way call into question the paradigm of histrionic emotional identification on which this process of transformation (and the series as a whole) is based. Charles makes life hell for everyone in the company, not because he brings too much of his life to his acting, but because, with his body and mind failing, he has no choice but to do so. 'He's not playing Lear, he's living Lear,' Ellen complains to Geoffrey, and adds, 'That's the problem.'

After his failed body and mind force the cancellation of two opening nights and of the production itself, Charles ultimately succeeds magnificently in the role when it is remounted for a single performance in an off-site venue, not just because he has adjusted his medications, but because he – like all

Jerry had brought to the role. Henry has played *Macbeth* three times before, and describes himself as a 'creature of habit', content to be who he is without risking losing himself in his role. He grudgingly acknowledges that Geoffrey's Hamlet years before may have been (in Ellen's word) 'incandescent', but says that that was possible only because there were only three performances; over a longer run, the actor must protect himself or, like Geoffrey, he runs the risk of 'going over the edge'. And he admits that Jerry was able to be real in his one performance as Macbeth: 'I mean of course, if you put a man on stage unprepared, he's going to create some sort of energy; you feel his fear.' It is now Geoffrey's goal to push Henry towards, and over, the edge, to make what he brings to the role as real as Jerry's fear had been. And so, on opening night, he conspires with the stage manager and the rest of the company to change the set and the blocking, leaving Henry continually uncertain about where people will be on stage, where he'll be able to get of the other leading actors in all three of the series' seasons – has gone on a journey and has arrived at a new understanding of himself and of his character. That Charles is in the process of dying while he is rehearsing the role, both Charles and Geoffrey learn, is not enough; he must also acquire a functional understanding of what it means to approach death. In one of the rare moments when Charles's performance catches fire in rehearsal, he begins to attack Ellen/Regan on 'Reason not the need'; 'Dying,' he explains to Geoffrey afterward, 'doesn't make you compassionate; it pisses you off.' It is not until the production is cancelled, and Charles is in a momentary remission before what he knows will be his imminent death, that he has a final insight about himself that unlocks the role. Even at the beginning of the play, Lear doesn't really want to crawl, unburdened, towards death; he says it, Charles tells Geoffrey, 'but he doesn't mean it, of course. . . . He doesn't really think he's going to die. No one does. I don't. That's the real insanity of it.' If, in Season Two, the thing that could strike the most terror into Jerry, Henry and Macbeth's heart was theatre itself, the most terrifying thing here is death. Charles can finally play Lear, not because he is resigned to his death, but because, like Lear, he cannot accept it.[14]

4. 'IT'S ONLY THIS MOMENT'

That the redemptiveness of Shakespeare, and the reciprocal journey that the actor embarks upon in becoming, and learning from, the character, are foregrounded in Hank Rogerson's 2005 documentary, *Shakespeare Behind Bars*, is not surprising, as both of these are the therapeutic goals of the programme the film is documenting: inmates in a medium-security penitentiary in Kentucky rehearsing *The Tempest*. These tropes, along with the dramatic device common to virtually all dramatizations of Shakespeare rehearsal – imminent disaster – are explicitly invoked in the first three talking-head interviews in the film's first five minutes. The inmate-actor who is to play Prospero says that the play is meaningful to himself and the other actors because of its 'theme of forgiveness'; the

prison warden credits Shakespeare's cultural transcendence for the programme's rehabilitative function; and another inmate-actor promises that the nearly year-long rehearsal process will have its own suspense: 'A couple of unexpected things will happen. Somebody might go to the hole, somebody might get transferred, some things are going to happen that are going to throw things off, and every year we've had to deal with something like that. We just can't help it.'

With the encouragement of the theatre professional who volunteers his time as director of the production and the programme, the inmates constantly, and ostentatiously, relate the theme of the play to their individual and collective lives: the prison is like an island; forgiveness redeems both the forgiver and the forgiven; revenge (as in *Titus Andronicus*, the previous year's project) is never the answer, etc. And the director constantly asks the actors to bring aspects of their lives to their scene-work: egged on by the director and his fellow-actors, the inmate playing Miranda, on asking Prospero 'Are you not my father?', shares the uncertainty he had about parentage when he was being raised by his single mother, and recalls that when, after his mother's death, he asked his grandmother who his father was, he was fifteen, precisely the age Miranda is in the play. The filmmaker cunningly lets us learn about the inmates' crimes (mostly murder), sentences, chances of parole, and varying degrees of rehabilitation in ways that force us to see the parallels they are (or are not) finding in their roles. One particularly eloquent inmate (serving a 50-year sentence for an unspecified crime) has more to say about Prospero and forgiveness than he does about his character, Antonio. Soon after, we see him in solitary confinement. Once again, he talks about forgiveness, and the redemption he's been seeking since 1994: 'All of us need to be redeemed for something we've done . . . and I grant you, the degree that I need to be redeemed is

---

[14] In one final parallel between art and life, William Hutt, who played Charles, died of leukemia at 87 on 27 June 2007, ten months after the final episode of the series first aired in Canada.

61. *Shakespeare Behind Bars*: Leonard/Antonio struggles to name his crimes.

much greater than the average person.' He says he wants to complete treatment, to live honorably and make amends, 'to redeem my life, so that I am not remembered for the very worst thing that I have done.' When asked what crime he had committed, he pauses for an excruciating length of time, and then tells the interviewer: he abused seven girls.

Soon after, the other inmates/actors learn that he has been transferred to a higher-security prison, and that his role will need to be recast. No official reason has been given, but the rumour the prisoners are circulating is that he was caught looking at inappropriate websites in the prison's computer lab. The actor who replaces him is a young and sassy ne'er-do-well, who wants to try the Shakespeare Behind Bars programme because, he says, he has never finished anything in his life. Only a few days before the performance, he, too, must be replaced, since he has gone to the hole for getting a tattoo. Only incorrigibles, it seems, can play (or, finally, not play) the unrepentant Antonio.

The inmates talk incessantly about the biographical determinants of their criminal acts, and these almost always revolve around missing or

abusive parents, creating, or at least contributing to, their various addictions and anger-management problems, and leaving them without the tools they needed to cope with their wives and girl friends, whom they ended up killing. And these explanations – honed no doubt through years of various rehabilitative therapies and activities ('Shakespeare Behind Bars' being only one) – are invoked again and again as the performance date nears, and the actors begin to lose patience with the project and one another: the inmate playing Prospero and the inmate playing Miranda testily accuse each other of acting out unresolved real-life family issues in their father-daughter scenes with one another.

Perhaps the most interesting and eloquent equation of art and life – and specifically between art and prison life – comes, not from a facile equation of the play's themes and rehabilitation or of the inmates' lives and their characters, but from a point that the stage director makes about making theatre, at one pivotal rehearsal session two-thirds of the way through the film, at what might be, in a fictional film, the end of the 'second act' of a traditional three-act structure. Move on from bad days in rehearsals, he tells them, and don't dwell on the past:

Now the ball is in your court, for the noble attempt, at this moment, in this rehearsal, to create the most truthful moment that you can. And if it isn't truthful, you move to the next moment and attempt it there. You can't change the past, the past is gone, that moment in time is gone. It's only this moment, and in this moment it creates the future: how are you going to live this moment in time, 'cause that's what you have. The next moment may be gone.

'All right, let's go,' he concludes, and they resume rehearsal. Not only is the Stanislavskian paradigm – the reciprocal discovery of the self in the role and the role in the self – a therapeutic tool in the prisoners' process of rehabilitation; but the cornerstone of the Stanislavsky system – living spontaneously 'in the moment' – becomes, much more than the play's theme of forgiveness, a metaphor for the process of rehabilitation itself.

5. 'THEY ARE PART OF US'

Antony Sher, in Johannesburg, South Africa, to rehearse the title role in *Titus Andronicus* at the Market Theatre under the direction of his partner Gregory Doran, is taking a side trip to his home town of Cape Town, accompanied by one of the South African actors, who is visiting his girlfriend, and is on an airplane for only the third time in his life. In his co-authored rehearsal journal, *Woza Shakespeare!*,[15] Sher describes watching his fellow-actor's delight as the plane makes its descent:

It isn't only Oscar's joy that touches me. As the character Titus slowly grows, there's more and more of Dad in him – I'm moving like Dad, sounding like him, *being* him – and there's a profound connection between Dad and the airport, D. F. Malan, which we're about to reach... (p. 130, emphasis and ellipses in the original)

Sher then begins a long digression about his father's death two years before: his parents, who had been visiting him in England, flew at short notice to Israel to attend a nephew's funeral, where the father died in a hotel room. Doran and Sher flew to Israel, and then accompanied Sher's mother and his father's coffin to Cape Town, where they landed here, at D. F. Malan Airport. Arriving at this airport reminds Sher of arriving, the year before, with the coffin of his father, the father who is increasingly, to Sher's surprise, serving as the model for the character he is building in rehearsal.

Woza Shakespeare! purports to be an actual journal (or pair of journals: entries from Sher's journal alternate with entries from Doran's) and, if that is true, it is quite possible that Sher did indeed write at length about his father's death in his actual journal, the night that his plane landed in Cape Town. But Sher is also a novelist and prose-stylist (as well as an accomplished painter), capable of introducing thematic elements and shaping a narrative arc; and so the story of his father's death, which had arisen in his mind as the plane descended into Cape Town, may have been a much later addition, designed to fill the reader in on an important component in the unfolding story. Either way, it is certainly, in the resulting book, an artful and effective literary device, a way of charging place (South Africa, Cape Town, the airport), relationships (his father), biography (exile and return) and identity (as a South African, a middle-class Jew, an expatriate, a homosexual) with narrative significance in relation to the narrative arc of the rehearsals of the production they are preparing. Sher, as author, is bringing place, relationships, biography and identity into his narrative in much the same way that Sher, as an actor, brought place, relationships, biography and identity into his work in preparing to play his character in *Titus Andronicus*. The airport in Cape Town serves as a sense memory both for Sher's memories of his father's death, and for playing his role in a Shakespeare play.

Woza Shakespeare! is just one of more than a dozen book-length eye-witness narratives of Shakespearian rehearsals, which, along with the dozens of eye-witness narratives of other theatre productions, have become so numerous that they constitute a distinctive literary genre, with its own distinctive features. The books encompass a wide range of purposes (academic monograph, journalistic profile, promotional tool for the theatre, etc.), a wide range of positions the narrator can occupy in the rehearsal process (lead actor, supporting actor, understudy, director, dramaturg, outside journalist, in-house publicist, etc.), and a wide range in tone and literary artfulness.[16] These rehearsal

---

[15] Antony Sher and Gregory Doran, *Woza Shakespeare! 'Titus Andronicus' in South Africa* (London, 1997). All subsequent references will be given in parentheses in the text.

[16] Leading actor and director accounts include Antony Sher, *Year of the King* (London, 1985); Michael Bogdanov and Michael Pennington, *The English Shakespeare Company* (London, 1990); Brian Cox, *The Lear Diaries* (London, 1992); and Oliver Ford Davies, *Playing Lear* (London, 2003). Supporting actor accounts include Richard L. Sterne, *John Gielgud Directs Richard Burton in Hamlet* (New York, 1967) and William Redfield, *Letters from an Actor* (New York, 1967). Understudy accounts include Maurice Good, *Every Inch a Lear* (Victoria, 1982). Assistant director and dramaturg accounts include: Charles Marowitz, 'Lear Log', *Tulane Drama Review*, 8 (1963), 103–21; Richard Pettengill, 'Peter Sellars's Merchant of Venice', *Theatre Research International*, 31 (2006), 298–314; and Geoffrey Proehl, *Toward A Dramaturgical Sensibility* (Madison, 2008). Scholarly eye-witnesses include Kristina Bedford, *Coriolanus at the National*

narratives share a sense of temporality, with events unfolding in sequence, as if in real time, with each day's rehearsal building on the previous day's work, and pointing towards the next and towards the approaching run-throughs, technical rehearsals, previews, openings nights, tours (in some cases) and closing nights. This narrative linearity replicates the theatre's temporality, its continual sense of unfolding as though in the present tense. And so the journey of the artistic collaborators across the span of rehearsals resembles the journey of the characters over the span of the play's unfolding action in performance, a resemblance which is occasionally exploited in the narratives just as, as we have seen, it is frequently invoked in the cinematic depictions of rehearsals, where the off-stage relationships among the actors replicate, in plot and theme, the situation, plot and theme of the play being rehearsed.[17]

Moreover, these rehearsal narratives are, inescapably, memoirs. This is true both of personal narratives, like Sher and Doran's, and journalistic and scholarly rehearsal narratives, whose goal is more explicitly documentary and analytical. In both cases, the events being witnessed are subject to the perspective of the person witnessing.[18] And so the resulting narratives represent not one but three overlapping and often congruent journeys: the characters over the arc of the play; the artists, artisans and technicians building the production in rehearsal, and the narrators over the span of the events they are narrating, and synecdochically over their lifetimes. Whether the narrator is the star actor or a freelance writer jobbed in by management to produce a book for the theatre bookshop in time for opening night, the narrator both draws upon his or her biography and sensibilities and allows these sensibilities, and occasionally even his or her life, to be transformed by the experience of rehearsals and performance.[19]

This makes the eye-witness rehearsal narrative as potent a source for documenting the persistence of the Stanislavskian paradigm in contemporary theatre practice as the more obviously manufactured and manipulated fictions of mainstream backstage movies and television series. Just as actors discover things in themselves in order to play the role, and,

having 'found' the character, then discovers things about themselves from playing them, so too do the narrators bring themselves to rehearsals and are fundamentally changed by them.

In this, *Woza Shakespeare!* is exemplary, a telling document of the persistence of the Stanislavskian emotionalist paradigm in the popular imagination, in part because Sher is such an experienced memoirist and a craftsman of prose fictions, in part because he is a professed adherent of emotionalist acting, and in part because questions of identity, ethnicity and community (and questions of Sher's identity) are crucial to the theatre piece that Sher and Doran are creating. Conceived when the

---

(Selinsgrove, 1992) and Tirza Lowen, *Peter Hall Directs Antony and Cleopatra* (New York, 1991). Journalist eye-witnesses include David Selbourne, *The Making of 'A Midsummer Night's Dream'* (London, 1982). And observers writing on behalf of the company include Jonathan Croall, *Hamlet Observed* (London, 2001); Peter Reynolds and Lee White, *Henry V at the National* (London, 2003); and Bella Merlin, *With the Rogue's Company* (London, 2005).

[17] The illusion – and actuality – of contemporaneity accounts for the very recent genre of rehearsal blogs, which appear in real time: Peter Reynolds and Lee White on Nicholas Hytner's 2003 National Theatre *Henry V*, and Barrie Rutter's blogs of Northern Broadsides's *The Merchant of Venice* and *Richard III*, appeared at www.Stagework.com, where they are archived, as is actor Nick Asbury's blog of rehearsals and performances of the Royal Shakespeare Company's 2008 history cycles, at www.rsc.org.uk. General Director Antoni Cimolino's blogs of current productions at the Stratford Shakespeare Festival in Canada appear on the Festival's website (www.stratford-festival.on.ca) until the productions' runs are over.

[18] This is true even in cases where the narrator tries to erase his or her presence and efface their own identities: thus Richard Sterne's account of John Gielgud's 1964 *Hamlet* with Richard Burton, in which, playing A Gentleman, he secretly tape-recorded the rehearsals, and at one point concealed himself underneath a stage riser to tape a closed rehearsal session; and yet the personality and perspective of the writer (in the case of Sterne, his idolization of Gielgud) is readily apparent throughout.

[19] See, for example, David Selbourne's account of the rehearsals of Peter Brook's milestone Royal Shakespeare Company *A Midsummer Night's Dream* in 1970: he is, throughout, sceptical, puzzled, bored, dispirited and sometimes actively hostile to what he witnesses of the rehearsal process; and yet he is transformatively redeemed by the preview performance that ends his narrative.

two were part of a Royal National Theatre Studio workshop on Shakespeare's language for local actors in Johannesburg, the impetus for the production was, like the workshops themselves, anti-colonialist: the actors should draw upon themselves, with their own cultures and their own accents (the accent that Sher taught himself to lose when he left for England twenty-six years before). Their production aspired to reflect contemporary post-apartheid South Africa, a multi-racial society, with a history of violence and a legacy of revenge, sinking into crime; and the various families, clans and nations in the play were mapped across South Africa's communities and apartheid-era categories: Afrikaaner, Anglo, Black and 'Coloured', etc.[20]

As narrated in *Woza Shakespeare!*, the political agenda of the production and the lives of the narrators (and the other actors) are interwoven. Doran records that 'My brain's antennae get so tuned in to a play at this stage, before rehearsals start, that every conversation, every newspaper article, *everything* seems to be on the right wavelength' (p. 46). During the London workshops, Doran asks each member of the group to recount a personal experience of violence; one actor confesses that she keeps with her photos of a member of her family who was raped and murdered. Sher asks her about it, and she replies, 'They are part of *us* . . . my family . . . part of our history' (p. 73, ellipses in the original). In a later rehearsal, remembering one actor's story about a friend who mutilated herself, Sher has Titus carve the names of Lavinia's rapists into his own flesh. When the cast is shown a documentary about the My Lai massacre by US troops during the Vietnam War they remain relatively untouched; but one image from a documentary about violence in the South African townships – of a man being stabbed whose mind takes longer to realize than does his body that he is dying – becomes a keynote of the production. The violence, Sher observes, 'belongs to them' (p. 93). Before the opening-night performance, Sher notices that Jennifer Woodburne, the actress playing Lavinia, has plastered her dressing-room mirror with photos of mutilated victims of violence: ' "I can hardly see myself." She giggles. Then, without

a smile, she adds, "How am I going to do justice to all these people?" ' (p. 199).

Sher makes the connection between his own emotional method as an actor and the lives of his fellow actors explicit:

When I started out as an actor, my heroes were, as I've said, the great character actors: Olivier and Sellers, or Alec Guinness in the Ealing films. But now I've become as interested in another side of acting, what the Americans call Method Acting . . . actually, I've never quite understood what it is . . . but what I mean is a kind of acting where you invest – personally, passionately – in the part and the play, and use emotional recall to make the moments of sorrow, joy, fear, etc. completely real. Instead of Method Acting, it could just be called good acting. (p. 164, ellipses in the original)

Sher complains that, 'perhaps because of a degree of reserve in the British character, actors in the UK don't always do this kind of acting and audiences are forced to sit through endless scenes where the emotion is presented at arm's length, rather than experienced' (p. 164). By contrast, 'I think Market Theatre actors have more immediate access to their feelings. The shows born of apartheid (which I've heard some whites sneeringly dismiss as *protest theatre*), shows like *Woza Albert!* and *Sizwe Bansi*, were always too close to one to hold at arm's length' (p. 166, Sher's emphasis).

Doran, meanwhile, observes Sher at work:

I watch Tony turning into Titus. Sometimes it's like watching his father, Mannie, shuffling around the stage, stooped and tired, with his hands slapped behind his back. Tony soaks up direction like a sponge, always ready to try something new. The key, I discover, is not to explain an idea too much, but just to suggest it, pour it in and leave it to percolate.

At these moments of deepest grief, I see Tony trawling through recent events of his life for a sense memory to draw upon. It's a painful process, painful in its honesty. Where do you look to find a recollection which can qualify?

---

[20] Doran and Sher's mapping of South African ethnic and racial identity on the play has not escaped criticism; see Adele Seeff, '*Titus Andronicus*: South Africa's Shakespeare', *Borrowers and Lenders*, 4.1 (2008).

It is not until months after Mannie's death that I saw Tony cry for his father, crumpling at the waist, reaching out to clutch me, gulping with sobs. That's what Titus does now. I recognise it. But never let on. He has filed away the physical memory of that experience and calls it up now. (pp. 150–1)

While the others actor explore themselves and their community, Sher explores his family and his nationality, keenly aware, as he speaks them at the first rehearsal and at the Johannesburg opening, of Titus's first lines, in which the character comes 'To re-salute his country with tears'; and he feels these lines in a new way as he leaves South Africa when the production moves to Britain: 'I can't bear this... I'm still leaving home, still seeking home... I feel as young and vulnerable as I did three decades ago... and there's something else today as well – I feel completely bloody bruised. What the hell happened to my triumphant home-coming? It was exactly like Titus's. Just one shock after another' (p. 243, ellipses in the original). When the production plays a week in Leeds, even Doran is made aware of his own ancestry in York-shire. And Sher realizes that 'the country which I'm now thinking as *mine*, and which I'm re-saluting with my "tears of true joy" – with this produc-tion – is England' (p. 254). Sher finishes mourning his father (and another father figure: the Market Theatre's founding director Barney Simon, who dies suddenly when the production is on the last leg of its tour in Spain); and Sher, Doran and the production simultaneously reach the end of their journey.

6. 'THE CONNECTION BETWEEN HIS OWN SUFFERING AND THE SUFFERING OF OTHERS'

As with the fictional and documentary dramati-zations of the rehearsal process, Sher and Doran's rehearsal narrative/dual memoir *Woza Shakespeare!* rests on the twin narrative tropes of the genre: that the actors learn about themselves for and through the characters they are playing; and that the result-ing theatre event is somehow redemptive both for the actors and for the audiences who come to witness and experience the resulting performance. Indeed, Doran's production of *Titus Andronicus* relies upon the dynamic interplay of these two tropes. In his portions of the memoir, Sher nar-rates a journey of the self: he returns to the land of his birth and rediscovers his roots and his man-ifold identities in order to rehearse the role of an aging warrior returning to the land of his birth; he finds that he can play a father only when he begins to see his father's face looking back at him in the mirror. So, too, the resulting production itself is a journey of selves: Doran has cast the actors, not only for their talents, but for who they are, within the complex codes of racial and ethnic identity in apartheid and post-apartheid South Africa. The post-apartheid audience is being invited to under-stand their own community by watching actors who, like Titus carving the names of his daughter's rapists into his own flesh, have inscribed their per-sonal and social identities onto their skins. These identities are ultimately communal as well as indi-vidual. The actress playing Lavinia, in her dressing room, gazes both at her own face and at the faces of the mutilated victims she has taped to the mirror. The production is redemptive *because* the actors have embarked upon, and ultimately arrive at, a journey into their individual and social selves.

It is, admittedly, difficult to get beyond the retrograde invocation of familiar myths about Shakespeare's redemptiveness in many of these dramatizations and factual narratives of Shakespear-ian rehearsal: the 'Merry Christmas' wishes in the Dickensian ending of *In the Bleak Midwin-ter* after the standing ovations for *Hamlet*, or the language of therapeutic rehabilitation employed by prison wardens and inmates alike in *Shake-speare Behind Bars*. Even *Slings and Arrows* pan-ders to this myth: as Charles Kingman observes, 'You can go right through the ages of man with Shakespeare', reiterating the youth/maturity/old age triptych of the plays (*Hamlet, Macbeth, King Lear*) being rehearsed in the three seasons. The putative 'universal truths' of Shakespeare here rep-resent, as always, an exploitation of Shakespeare as cultural capital.

62. *Slings and Arrows*: Patrick/Romeo (David Alpay) and Sarah/Juliet (Joanne Kelly) play the balcony scene, as Geoffrey and Ellen watch from the wings.

And yet, the concluding episode in the second season of *Slings and Arrows* demonstrates that there is, as in *Woza Shakespeare!*, something more integral, and Stanislavskian, to the trope of Shakespearian redemptiveness. Darren has abandoned his anti-Stanislavskian post-modernism ('Why can't you understand this?!,' he had harangued his actors, 'Romeo and Juliet are not real people, or characters, they are signifiers'), and the production of *Romeo and Juliet*, newly liberated into emotional reality, the actors literally uncaged from their chess-piece costumes, plays before its opening-night audience. Before the performance begins, the CEO of the season's corporate sponsor, accepting a special citation from the stage, speaks with touching awkwardness about his own special relation to the play: he and his wife have never missed a production of *Romeo and Juliet* at the festival, and the play always reminds him of why and how they were able to stay together through a long, sometimes rocky, marriage. During the performance, Ellen and Geoffrey, haunted by the CEO's speech,

watch the balcony scene from the wings, struggling to resist the emotional identification with the play and with the roles that Sarah and Patrick's ardent, emotionally filled performances inspire.

'I hate this play,' Ellen whispers to Geoffrey; 'You watch it and you feel miserable because you don't have that kind of passion in your life. Nobody does. It's a fantasy. It's irresponsible.' But we know that Ellen is whistling in the dark, that the actors and the characters and the play are forcing both of them to acknowledge in themselves what we and everyone in their world (even Ellen's boy-toy lover from Season One, who has just seen the production and meets them in the bar afterwards) already know about their inescapable and abiding love for one another.

It is here that we see a fusion between two of the tropes of the genre of rehearsal narrative: that actors reciprocally find their roles in themselves and learn about themselves in their roles; and that theatre – and Shakespeare in particular – is transformative. For the CEO, and for Ellen and Geoffrey, spectatorship is transformative *because* Sarah and Patrick have succeeded in emotionally and biographically becoming their roles. In both cases, transformation is effected by an act of empathy: of one character for another ('He makes the connection between his own suffering and the suffering of others,' Charles Kingman says of Lear's prayer, 'Poor naked wretches', before the hovel, which convinces Geoffrey to cast him in the role), of actor for character and, finally, of the audience for the characters. Spectatorship is irresistibly transformative because the actors have transformed themselves.

The 'story maps' of these fictional dramatizations and factual narratives of Shakespearian rehearsal, then, have as much to do with the phenomenological act of observation as with the craft of acting. The ultimate Stanislavskian argument of these story maps is not only about the journey of the actor to the role, and of the role across the duration of the play, but of the audience towards an understanding of itself. The journeys being dramatized and narrated may be politically retrograde; they may reify tacit assumptions about cultural value and supposedly universal and transhistorical human values; they may reinscribe what W. B. Worthen has identified as the multiple myths of Shakespearian 'authority';[21] they may be based on assumptions about character, acting and theatrical mimesis that are neither those embedded in the scripts in the sixteenth and seventeenth centuries, nor those being reformulated in the more advanced theatrical work of the twenty-first century. But these journeys constitute the stories that mainstream theatre people tell one another, and that mainstream audiences want and expect to hear about how the performances they have come to see were made, which can explain why and how these performances are able to generate the empathic emotional effects that have brought them to the theatre, and to Shakespeare, in the first place.

---

[21] W. B. Worthen, *Shakespeare and the Authority of Performance* (Cambridge, 1997).

SHAKESPEARE PERFORMANCES IN ENGLAND (AND WALES), 2008

CAROL CHILLINGTON RUTTER

New Year's Day, 2008. Under a louring sky, Stratford-upon-Avon woke up to find (nine months after it officially closed) 'The Greatest Dramatist', 'The Essential Year', the RSC's 'Complete Works Festival' still somehow staggering on, not least in company press releases reluctant to kick the 'essential year's' addictive publicity habits. More bingeing was promised: a 'Once in a lifetime opportunity to see Shakespeare's complete History Cycle performed by one ensemble company of actors' (on the matter of the 'ensemble company', more anon). Reading that, some spectators may have felt a weary sense of déjà vu. Four of these eight histories had already been revived once, in 2006, recycled from original productions back in 2000, to pass muster as RSC Artistic Director Michael Boyd's contribution to the 'Complete Works Festival'. Now, just when these veteran campaigners might have been thought honourably discharged and demobbed, here they were again, hauled back into active service, re-rehearsed one more time, and shoved up the front line of the new year's offerings. (It was, by the way, the prospect of taking up this 'once in a lifetime opportunity' that finally killed off *Survey*'s last reviewer – see *Shakespeare Survey 61*.) But what I chiefly remember of New Year's Day was taking a late morning walk on the south bank of the Avon to shake off the last of the hangover – and being instantly sobered up by the sight that hit me, a sight you couldn't see on the town side of the river, where it was hidden behind a long stretch of hoardings plastered with giant-sized full-colour blow-ups of recent RSC 'greats' (Harriet Walter as Cleopatra, Chuk Iwuji as Henry VI).

From the south bank, the naked back-side of the Royal Shakespeare Theatre looked like the film set of war-wrecked Warsaw in Roman Polanski's *The Pianist*. Two storeys of the Elizabeth Scott-designed front of house foyer and circle bar from 1932 were still standing, bizarrely intact. So, ironically, was the picture frame structure of the proscenium arch (its exposed girders seeming to hold up two insulting fingers to its legions of detractors): fall guy for so much of what, in production terms, had gone wrong for the past seventy-five years in a theatre built to the specifications of a pre-war cinema which, since the 1960s at least, had been trying to confound its architecture and make itself over as a thrust-stage playhouse. But for the rest, it looked like a bomb site. What had been the auditorium was a wasteland of brick and concrete rubble. Half-way up demolished walls, bits of dressing rooms hung suspended in space and lavatories were forlornly exposed to the sky. Stairwells ended in thin air. More dismal still, now that the exterior wall was sliced away, a corridor that once had connected backstage to front of house was open to the skies – a hallway wallpapered with theatre posters going back decades (among them Peter Brook's *Titus Andronicus*). Now the famous faces, titles, lists of players, memories ran with rain. With the RST a demolition site, the Swan closed, and The Other Place turned into the foyer for the Courtyard Theatre (the single stand-in while the RSC is, as the publicity eupeptically puts it, 'Transforming Our Theatres'), the company, on New Year's Day, looked as though it had hunkered down with the builders for a long siege.

Poor old 'unhoused' Shakespeare: how much of *him* would Stratford audiences be seeing in the new year? Meanwhile, in London, Shakespeare was the hottest ticket in town – and audiences couldn't get enough of him. *Othello* was sold out at the Donmar (thanks to Ewan McGregor); *Macbeth* was sold out at the Gielgud (thanks to Patrick Stewart); *Much Ado About Nothing* was sold out at the National (thanks to Zoë Wanamaker and Simon Russell Beale). As the year progressed, ideas that struck me on that grey morning as the big challenges facing Shakespeare performance in 2008 continued to preoccupy producers, actors, directors, designers, spectators: ideas about theatre space, 'star turns', the acting ensemble, the role of the audience. By summer, however, roles were reversed: the Shakespeare razzmatazz had rolled out of the metropolis into the provinces where the sell-outs were at the Tobacco Factory and the Courtyard. Unless you pulled strings or went onto the black market, you couldn't get a ticket for *Hamlet* in Stratford – or in Bristol.

HISTORIES

I'll begin by clearing the decks of stowaways, productions I inherited from my predecessor, the RSC's second tetralogy histories that opened between July and October 2007. By rights, then, they should have been reviewed in last year's *Survey*: *Richard II*, *1 Henry IV* and *Henry V* (directed by Michael Boyd) and *2 Henry IV* (by his associate director, Richard Twyman). These productions showed Boyd taking on the challenge of the Courtyard, the theatre that aims to serve as the working prototype for the new RST, figuring out how the stage 'acts', what actors can do on its deep, open platform that every which way exposes them, and, perhaps more unpredictably, discovering how the auditorium 'acts', how spectators behave put eyeball to eyeball with actors, shoved right up against the action and wrapped around the story.

These productions likewise showed Boyd walking the tightrope any director stretches out for himself – or knots into a noose – when he attempts a cycle. How do you balance the part with the whole? How do you make sense of the individual play (complete in itself, its own thing) wherever it comes in the series (not least for the spectator who's seeing it singly) while keeping the arc of the full cycle in view, hearing cross-play echoes, reiterations; seeing doubles, subsequence, re-visions that (should) build cumulatively into something of 'great constancy' (not least for the spectator who's signed on for a four- or eight-play viewing marathon)?

Boyd wasn't new to the Courtyard. He'd opened it back in 2006 with his *Henry VI* trilogy. But those *Henry*s were themselves revivals – in effect, straight transfers from the Swan, the 'baby' prototype for the Courtyard's larger dimensions. Even recast, they felt like Xerox copies. (Weirdly, they even put black and white actors into the same roles Boyd originally cast black and white.) As such, they offered no original thinking for the new space. *Richard II*, then, was Boyd's opportunity to begin that thinking.

A version of medievalized period dress and a permanent set (designed by Tom Piper) served all the histories: a copper-clad wall or rusty 'O' with barrel gates, set centre, that could slide open to reveal, behind, 'news' or a spectacle – or a return from the past. Above, galleries were connected by spiral stairways that put me in mind as much of open industrial lift shafts as of medieval turrets. Lit, the copper shone like gold; unlit, it looked like the dull dead hide of some slough-skinned beast. Beaten – with swords, fists, women's tears – it produced a terrible acoustic, background noise to a world savaging itself. Piper's fixed set achieved unity-with-difference (and vice versa). Play by play, it could be swiftly localized. In *Richard*, stairs were thrust out for the king to mount to watch the trial by combat; a cushion-lined pit opened up for the king's favourites, not so much caterpillars of the kingdom as lounge lizards, to loll in; a watering can made the space a garden. But across the tetralogy, the local registered as a universal: 'everywhere again'. At the top of each play, spectators were brought back to the impassive face of the copper-clad façade. We weren't getting anywhere. Location

was a place of perpetual return and history, a journey that jumped its tracks to circle round to its first
beginnings. These plays figure time as both linear
and cyclical, secular and divine, mortal and eternal:
experienced as tragedy by individuals running out
of life – and black comedy by spectators watching
political systems rotate on well-oiled axes. Piper's
set instantiated these ideas.

Equally insistent as a strategy for finding unity-
in-difference by making bold, local performance
claims that assert themselves as precedents in a pattern is Boyd's use of invented ceremonials: penitence rituals at the openings of *1* and *2 Henry IV*;
a fealty rite to open *Richard II* that had the massed
court, formally arranged and facing out, performing a ceremony that was half court dance, half secular worship as Richard approached, awesomely
alone, through the audience, and mounted the
stage before turning to display to spectators the full
effect of his gorgeousness. For Boyd, the invented
ritual appears to be a way of announcing gravitas,
portentousness, a way of locating spectators from
the off in a meaning-full world of coded significance: Richard's entrance figured not just ostenta-
tion but heightened relationship, all that could be
taken for granted between gilded king and subjects. But the rituals also code an attitude to time,
for ritual sustains the illusion of time suspended in
an unchanging present while actions are timelessly
re-enacted. Boyd is fascinated by recapitulation,
the way the past continually repeats itself, the way
history is prophecy and 'what's [historically] past is
[politically] prologue'. In his productions, the dead
return not just to haunt the living but, by strategic
doubling, to people the present, their past actions
in one role seeping into their subsequent futures in
another.

This sort of thing is intriguing – though of
course it works to deny political immediacy, any
sense that the politics of the moment speak to
England *now* (our now, their now, *any* now). And
for spectators coming cold to the single production, it's frequently frankly bewildering. Take that
opening sequence in *Richard*. As the king passed
through, the ranks of courtiers parted, revealing a
bloody body sprawled in his path which Richard,

simply oblivious, stepped over, and courtiers, for
the rest of the scene, ignored. So: a 'symbolic'
corpse. But who was it? (That's the trouble with
hauntings: for them to signify, you need to recognize the dead.) Answer #1: Thomas Woodstock. But to know that, spectators had to read the
programme where a note informed them about
Richard's uncle – and about a contemporary play
of his name that might have made him topical for
Shakespeare's audience – whose unsolved murder
fuels the accusations in the opening scene (where,
unhelpfully for Boyd's audience, he's not 'Woodstock' but the 'Duke of Gloucester'). Answer #2:
Chuk Iwuji. But for *that* to mean anything, spectators had to be veterans of Boyd's first tetralogy
where Iwuji was last seen as his own ghost haunt-
ing hunchback Richard and before that, in roughly
the same position, dead, as Henry VI, murdered by
the actor now playing Richard II.

Even more mystifying, when Jonathan Slinger
turned to face his spectators, he presented a
Richard bizarrely got up to look like an over-
stuffed Elizabeth I: in wicked stepmother crown
perched on red curled wig, white lead face paint,
carmined lips and cheeks, high court shoes and
round hose that padded out his flanks to the 'feminine' dimensions of Ursula the Pig Woman. Why?
Answer (again) in the programme where a note
cites Elizabeth's conversation with Lambarde (and
reporting it, makes a complete hash of 'real' history). But it's one thing for Elizabeth, post hoc,
to observe 'I am Richard II. Know ye not that?'
Quite another for Richard to anticipate 'I am Elizabeth I. Deal with it.' What was Boyd doing? Fix-
ing an arresting image onto his opening, lifting,
magpie-like, from Frank McGuinness's *Speaking
Like Magpies* (RSC, 2005) its stunning initial conceit which saw James, still only King of Scotland, sleeping aspirationally in 'Aunt' Elizabeth's
clothes? Suggesting, as he finished rehearsing the
first tetralogy and circled round from the end of
Richard III to start work directing *Richard II*, that (by
some curious switch-back of thinking) the Tudors
didn't *end* the political crisis begun six reigns earlier
but somehow participated in it, that, far from 'fix-
ing' England, they showed us that we still had

63. *Richard II*, 1.1, RSC, Courtyard Theatre, directed by Michael Boyd. Left to right: Bagot (Forbes Masson), Duchess of York (Maureen Beattie), York (Richard Cordery), Richard (Jonathan Slinger), Bushy (Nicholas Asbury), Gaunt (Roger Watkins), Queen Isabel (Hannah Barrie), foreground corpse of Gloucester (Chuk Iwuji).

a lot to learn about the human ruler cast in quasi-divine rule? Or more cheaply, twinning Richard with Elizabeth, was Boyd putting on view the clichéd theatrical idea of the last Plantagenet as the 'girly king', and worse, the king as queen as quean?

Slinger's performance never recovered from this disastrous original decision. He minced, he preened; a pantomime dame fancying himself principal boy whose mannered vocal style, swooping and diving like a strangled diva (or doing a dreadful impression of Simon Russell Beale) but mostly hitting a single note of petulance, was evidently instructed by hunchback Richard (Slinger's other big part this season) who'd taught him how to 'Murder' his 'breath in middle of a word . . . then again begin, and stop again'. There were so many

pauses, breaks, cues for smirks and camp twitches between every word that you never heard the full story a line might be telling – for instance, the witty, deep rhetorical resonance of so simple a line as 'He is our cousin, cousin.'

Perhaps to cover how seriously o'erparted Slinger was in the role, daft things were introduced to distract the eye: a hovering harpsichord was flown into 2.2, a vintage lawnmower pushed into 3.4 (turning the gardeners into rustic simpletons, this into the clown scene Shakespeare forgot to write, while the cheap laughs raised by spraying spectators in the front row with water discovered just how sophisticated Boyd was inviting the new relationship between stage and 'pit' to be). For the joust scene, there were horses: stylized beasts, metal saddles and stirrups fixed to industrial cable from the flies, positioned far down the thrust facing each other across the width of the stage, that, as the Marshal ordered the combat, Bolingbroke and Mowbray mounted to be winched backwards, like cocked triggers or pendulums aimed at head-on collision. Then Richard threw down his warder, the cocked triggers never fired, and I was left wondering how much the whole, over-elaborate business had cost for a two-minute damp squib of a theatrical effect that didn't begin to simulate in performance the dangerous political and physical contradictions Shakespeare writes into this showdown. Anyway, the RSC doesn't 'do' danger any more: Health and Safety has seen to that. Spectators watch actors helping each other into safety harnesses as casually (and visibly) as into coats. So why fake danger that, to all eyes, has been gelded? And my crack about cost wasn't just niggardly carping. This was the year ACE – Arts Council England – cut grants to the arts by 35 per cent and axed funding from some 200 organizations, 37 of them theatre companies, among them Northcott Theatre in Exeter, the National Student Drama Festival, English Touring Theatre, Bristol Old Vic, Derby Playhouse. While regional theatre scrabbled around for small change to keep going, the RSC defended the Arts Council's in-line-with-inflation increased subsidy to them as acknowledging their national importance. But you've sometimes got to quibble with the RSC's hyped-up sense of self. This year, the company didn't win a single Olivier award. In this belt-tightening world, what looks like conspicuous waste sticks in the craw. And King Lear's lines come to mind, about 'pomp' taking 'physic' and shaking the 'superflux' to others.

But at least in 2.1 spectators knew what was going on. Not so at the end of 4.1. The abdication left Richard not conveyed to the Tower but (unaccountably) alone on stage to step centre into a circle of light as, from the flies, a stream of sand fell onto his bowed head – a long 'wow' moment theatrically that took spectators goggle-eyed into the ruined king's farewell to his Queen. But what did it signify? A ritual of penitence, emblematic of sack cloth and ashes? A retrospective, remembering the streams of red feathers that fell in *Henry VI*

(for spectators who were there)? A prolepsis, accessible to spectators-in-the-textual-know, anticipating and performing York's narration in the following scene that remembers Richard's London entry, when 'rude misgoverned hands' threw 'dust and rubbish' on the 'sacred' head, or indeed suggesting the sands of an hourglass running out, anticipating Richard's reflection, four scenes later that he 'wasted time'? Or was the stage image just a 'wow', spectators who didn't know what was coming faced with a bold visual statement that must mean something – like the bloody corpse in the opening scene – if they only knew what: designer dumb show, and so much empty visual rhetoric?

Even at its most poignant, Slinger's was a performance that stood at a distance from the part, that never got beneath its skin. Calling for a mirror in 4.1 he furiously clawed at his make-up and snatched off his fright wig – a 'manly' gesture, but one that (paradoxically) refused to acknowledge him male, rather reinstating him as 'girly' king by linking him to Cleopatras from Helen Mirren to Mark Rylance to Harriet Walter. His grey polled pate and smeared lipstick were genuinely shocking – and shocked *him* as he silently gazed at himself, but (once he'd recovered speech, once he began interrogating his gaze – 'Was this face the face . . . ? . . . Was this the face . . . ?' – adopting again his standard arch petulance) only as a Wildean dandy might be shocked to detect in his 'flattering glass' 'wrinkles' that spoiled the cosmetic effect.

For all Slinger's giddy faults, this was still a one-man show, partly because Clive Wood's wooden Bolingbroke, old enough to be this Richard's father (but making nothing political out of the generational tensions) and with a vocal range that aspired to monotony, offered no more inducement to regime change than the dead certainty that he was the kind of man who would strip out of the court Richard's flame-coloured taffeta soft furnishings and cover every surface instead in turd-brown canvas, and partly because this Richard's self-absorbed narcissism allowed for no investigation of relationship. So we got no sense of these cousins as political doubles or psychic twins or even relatives sharing family history – or of a restless, virile rival knowing he can make a better fist of government than a feckless self-styled Phaeton. And no sense of the intricate, mind-game politics they were negotiating, either in soliloquy ('My brain I'll prove the female to my soul . . .') or dialogue ('Here, cousin, seize the crown'), where this astonishingly poised text requires them to manoeuvre each step of the story across iambic pentameter like cats walking on barbed wire, conducting a usurpation that is *not quite* a usurpation, an abdication that is *not exactly* an abdication ('Ay, no; no ay'). They failed to find either the throat-choking laughs in Richard's tragedy – or the black comedy in Bolingbroke's (disingenuous?) attempts to achieve high political seriousness in staged moments, like the reinvestigation of Woodstock's murder (4.1) or the abdication (4.1), that are sabotaged by farce. Neither were they helped by some bizarre emendations Boyd made to the script. In 5.5, 'thoughts of things divine' 'intermix'd / With scruples' that 'do set the word itself / Against the word' was changed – Boyd evidently mistrusting the audience's understanding even though the lines demonstrate themselves rhetorically by setting 'thoughts' against 'scruples', and even though Shakespeare has Richard immediately gloss his hard 'thoughts' with explanation, 'As thus . . .'. Incomprehensibly, 'Set the word . . . / Against the word' became 'set the *faith* . . . against the *faith*', introducing faith-war nonsense while cutting Richard's poised articulation – for him, an astonished revelation – of the trope that's been structuring this play from the beginning. Setting 'the word' against 'the word': that's the core activity of *Richard II*. It's Bolingbroke v. Mowbray, Northumberland v. Carlisle, York v. his Duchess, king v. subject, history v. prophecy, cousin v. cousin.

In the end, the discoveries Slinger's Richard made weren't tragic recognitions hammered out in prison; they were ironies delivered upon him there. The humble groom who entered his cell, telling of a detour he'd taken from his journey towards York to see his 'sometimes royal master's face': he was the messenger who'd brought waves of bad news from Ravenspurgh, the under-gardener who'd seen a kingdom choked with weeds – and the corpse of Woodstock. Moments later, when Richard looked up to see his murderer, he recognized an old crony (even though his one-time minion was now dressed head to foot in Bolingbroke-black). He called him by name: 'Bagot'.

Like *Richard II*, *I Henry IV* opened with a ritual. But whereas there spectators were paparazzi rubber-necking a player king's royal show, here we were voyeurs, peeping through a crack into one man's private closet drama. On an almost bare stage in half-light, behind him, rusty, metal-clad walls, a man, booted, in (those signature) black breeches and plain white shirt under (something new) a golden linen gown, stood at a high table set with candles, poured water from a ewer into a basin, and slowly, methodically washed his hands. Pilate. Judas. Any number of killers caught red-handed. Secret guilt performing secret penance – or destroying the evidence. Over and over and over. The stain he silently worked on was both imagined and ingrained.

Then a switch flipped. The lights came up. Interiority snapped on a public face as Clive Wood's bullet-headed King Henry, speaking a rhetorical version of magical thinking, willed personal executive control over history. 'NO MORE,' he roared, pounding the table, 'the thirsty entrance . . . of this soil / Shall daub her lips with her own children's blood. / NO MORE . . . .' Everything that failed this actor as Bolingbroke made his Henry riveting. Wood can't dazzle, can't electrify, can't do wit or even deep-revolving thought. But he can do the bull, head down, backed into a corner, doomed and dangerous. Ironically, of course (and this Henry knew it), the hounds that were worrying him were some of those children whose future he wanted saved, a couple of pups, a pair of Harries.

On the evidence of Wood's Bolingbroke in *Richard II*, I could understand his son going AWOL to Eastcheap – and could imagine Geoffrey Streatfeild's Hal slamming doors on his way out, wailing 'I never asked to be Prince of Wales.' At the top of *1 Henry IV* my sympathies swung. Wood was a Dad who deserved better. And if only he could have cut a deal with some cradle-snatching fairies, he could have had Lex Shrapnel's Hotspur for a son. But I doubt the changeling would have made him happier. This Hotspur was a bristling youth to out-Bolingbroke Bolingbroke – a fact that infuriated the king. For Hotspur wasn't just a better Hal. He was a better *Henry*. Out-facing the king in the first Council scene (1.3), set simply as a circle of chairs, Shrapnel's Hotspur in his full-length black leather coat and tangled hair trumped Henry's rhetoric with physical evidence. He wore the bruises of battle on his face. Stung by Henry's sarcasm ('shall our coffers then / Be emptied to redeem a traitor home?') Hotspur launched himself out of his seat, only to meet the king's jabbing finger, prodding him in the chest and back into his place – and worse, wagging while he 'tut-tutted' at him. The emotion that would fuel the rest of Hotspur's life was born in that moment, a rage against geriatric authority – not just the king's, but his father's, uncle's, Glendower's – that registered in a spasmodically clenching fist.

The son the king was missing finally turned up. In bed. With – as the huge heap of heaving, knotted, none-too-clean sheets revealed – Falstaff. (In one of the many strong staging moments this production produced, father and son actually appeared to confront each other, though in separate worlds, the bed retreating into the open doors upstage as the king strode past it into the Council scene.) First time around, I couldn't make sense of Streatfeild's Hal. It wasn't just that he was cold and snide, his rejection of Falstaff a done deal in their first exchange. It was that he didn't seem to be inside the play. He mugged the audience, gurning and grimacing as though he were playing melodrama or pantomime. Later in the season, he'd moved Hal's performance out of the refrigerator and reined in the semaphoring, and I got the point of the staging. The bed with its tangled sheets and later the Boar's Head, established by the introduction of a false proscenium flown in, a valance and traverse of heavy, red velvet draperies like moth-eaten matinee idol cinema curtains that could tease open for entrances: these places were theatres. This Hal (like Hotspur making every horse a throne) made every space a stage. He lived in a play-house, was playing for us. But he hadn't worked out the plot. 'I know

you all' at the end of 1.2, delivered propped up against the grubby pillows, was improvised, made up on the trot by a smart aleck kid who thought it would work. Playing the Courtyard audience as his world of spectators, Streatfeild managed also to fail to convince us.

David Warner's Falstaff never did convince me. Back at the RSC for the first time since his decade-defining work in the 1960s (when he invented the role of Henry VI in Hall and Barton's 1963 *Wars of the Roses* and in 1965 played the most iconic Hamlet of his generation, the *Hamlet* that had Stones and Beatles fans queuing down Waterside for tickets), he wasn't just a thin man bulked out in a poorly padded fat suit (that kept the dent when prodded). He was a Falstaff already waning, dwindling, falling off. It wasn't his lard that needed levers to lift it, but his wit: a morose Falstaff whose stringy hair turned him into a dilapidated water spaniel, who needed time to think up his next answer; who applied gags to the surface of his performance (whoever thought the Groucho Marx nose-and-glasses 'disguise' was a good idea for the Gadshill caper?); who, in a Dad's Army tin helmet and in another misjudged attempt to employ the 'groundlings', forced shuffling, hapless spectators in the front row to play his scarecrow recruits. Only in 2.4 did he give me a sense of another Falstaff, one whose corpulence might dance, whose imagination was a feathered Mercury. In his voluminous red velvet slops and sweat-yellowed shirt, collapsed in the massive red leather chair in front of the tavern's red velvet curtains, he held the Boar's Head captive with his story of the (not) captive pilgrims, rising to every raising of the narrative ante, his toes wiggling in his boots as, with astonishing delicacy, his fingers drummed his belly. Playing the king, making Hal practise an answer, the old ruffian was a surprisingly severe interrogator before capitulating craftily to blackmail when the watch at the door interrupted play with the Sheriff's world-shattering banging. But later, this energy fizzled out. Soldier-Falstaff could have used a Zimmer frame; the 'Honour' speech was so much geriatric wingeing and, worse, its climax was wrecked by the interpolation of a textual footnote after a half-beat pause

64. *Henry IV Part I*, 1.2, RSC, Courtyard Theatre, directed by Michael Boyd. Geoffrey Streatfeild as Prince Hal, David Warner as Falstaff.

(as if weighing up the uncomprehending dopes in the audience) to explain 'scutcheon': 'an epitaph,' intoned Falstaff, 'on a coffin' (What?). Casting Warner, it wouldn't have been the first time the RSC had used Falstaff to rehabilitate a delinquent veteran, old rogue or dimmed star. (Think back to Robert Stephens in Adrian Noble's 1991 *Henry IV*s.) But it was a decision that queered the 'new', USP (Unique Selling Point) image that the RSC is putting out of itself, of an 'ensemble'. (Of course the ensemble isn't a new idea; it's a return, post the company-wrecking innovations of Adrian Noble in the 1990s, to the original idealism of Peter Hall in the 1960s.) By 2008, the Histories Company – as RSC PR endlessly publicized – had worked together for more than two years, an 'ensemble' grooming talent while establishing the kind of immediacy (on the model of Shakespeare's original company) that allows actors to share a common rehearsal and performance vocabulary. So what happens to this idea of the 'ensemble' when a star is brought in, six plays into the season, to play a lead? And what happens to the talent, the actorly

ambitions this 'ensemble' is notionally developing? I can't have been the only spectator who, watching him develop from Duke Humphrey to Buckingham, expected the big man of the first tetralogy, Richard Cordery, to play Falstaff – and felt cheated that he didn't.

The great moments in this production were between father and son (3.2) and between rival Harries (5.4). Clive Wood's Henry met Streatfeild's Hal in a cold blast of white light. Remembering the past, imagining the future, he gave the kid a merciless drubbing, the word-work like a heavyweight boxer's jabs landing 'God', 'doom', 'punish', 'low', 'lewd', 'Bolingbroke', 'Richard', 'Percy' on Hal's chin before slamming him up against the wall with the knock-out: 'degenerate'. Hal took it. He was already on his way out of adolescence: he'd ripped off the Christmas cracker paper crown he'd worn drunkenly in 2.4, messing about with the drawers, when the joke on Francis finally disgusted him, and, at the end of that scene, finding Falstaff snoring behind the arras, after rifling his pockets and outrageously mocking his 'monstrous' buttery bill, he'd gently tucked a blanket around him. The party was over. He'd sobered up and was 'to the court in the morning'. But when he got there, yet again, he failed to convince. 'Thou shalt have charge' was sarcastic, a test. Any 'reconciliation' was on hold, a promise, not a performance – and left plenty of work for this Hal to do later.

His encounter with Hotspur came on the back of as thrilling a piece of theatre as I've seen at the RSC in a decade, the barrel doors opening in the upstage metal-clad walls as, in a surreal smoke-filled half-light to a percussion underscore, nine shadow warrior kings, seemingly the size of war horses, moved out in slow motion, swords swinging, performing a martial arts choreography of doom. The nightmare erupted into real time, full-on battle, the melee producing cross-firing, bodies bloodied, mistaken deaths, confusion that finally cleared, and the two Harries were facing each other. Not even the lumbering of Falstaff into view and his spectacular 'death', his blood spurting like a geyser, upstaged this fight to the death. Earlier, we'd heard Lady Percy (Ann Ogbama), at home on the battlements, Cassandra-like foreseeing, bloodcurdlingly crying out 'My lord! My lord!' as, in Percy's camp, a messenger arrived with letters, echoing 'My lord', telling him to retreat, letters that Hotspur had no time to read. Now Hotspur's death was heartbreaking. The wound, the pain astonished him, Hal standing stock still, aghast, as the youth who should have been his brother, not his foe, pitched forward onto his belly, crawled toward him, sword arm groping, and died. In Hal's reaction, a (now) grown man close to tears, awesomely respectful, recognizing the waste of war, we saw Harry V in the making in an England, in the final wrap-up moments of this production, where the slack guy ropes that the rebel soldiers had used to swing into action were being converted from military junk into apparatus for civil peace: knotted into nooses.

Part II opened with Bagot. Last seen hauling the coffin of the king he'd murdered into Bolingbroke's view at the end of *Richard II*, he returned now, still dragging that death, the damned exile, the eternal remembrancer of the original dynastic sin, struggling across a Beckettian wasteland where the heavens were hung with nooses. And he would, like Chuk Iwuji's messenger in *Richard*, keep returning, playing every Messenger part in this play, doom's proxy. Here, though, as in the distance plainsong was chanted, he lifted off the coffin lid, kissed the corpse's hand, watched Richard rise in a robe stained with dried blood and exit, and began, 'Open your ears': Bagot-as-Rumour. (All of this perhaps finally made some sort of retrospective sense to the uninitiated spectator when the Archbishop's great 'sick commonwealth' speech kicked in at 1.3.)

Part I haunted *Part II*. Hal's bed returned (2.2) – but Streatfeild's 'play' with Kieran Hill's open-faced, frank-hearted Poins was weary, edgy. The Boar's Head returned – with its stagey curtains and tawdry theatricality, but we were looking at this theatre in the punishing glare of broad daylight. Despite Maureen Beattie playing a deliciously feisty, bodice-breakingly indignant Mrs Quickly, the Eastcheap crowd (what with Pistol's (Nicholas Asbury) wild west swaggering and drink-dulled Falstaff's fumbling at Doll Tearsheet (Alexia Healy) on his knee) were going through old routines. Even the gag – 'anon, anon, sir' – played by Hal and Poins as drawers in false moustaches and leather jerkins, was one everyone had heard before. When the knock came on the door – again – and Rumour-as-Messenger entered to summon Hal to Westminster, it was with a real sense of self-loathing 'so idly to profane the precious time' that Hal tore off his disguise and exited *running*. Behind him, the Boar's Head fell apart: the curtains collapsed, the furniture vanished, the revels were over, even Falstaff, called to duty, shuffled off, resolved to 'leave the sweetest morsel of the night' 'unpicked' – and only just capitulated to delinquency, off-stage, summoning Doll.

Picking at morsels, even ones gone cold on trenchers, old men in this play were latching on to life while they stared at a skull they recognized as themselves. Clive Wood's insomniac King Henry, pushed into view in 3.1, sat on those same stairs Richard had so long ago occupied. Pasty-faced, hollow voiced, as weary remembering the past as Falstaff, remembering the jokes, this king's feet were bandaged (gout? leprosy?), his white jersey under his nightgown stained (with blood?), the suppurating wounds on his chest looking like stigmata, or evidence of self-harming, mimicking Richard's wounds. He wore his crown, but removed it, as though it instantiated the weight of memory ('uneasy lies the head . . . .'). There were flashes of anger in his reminiscence ('This Percy was the man nearest my soul'), the habits of testosterone – like the habits of 'foining' – dying hard in these dying men. But even here, in agonised confession, the politics of regime change remained opaque: 'I had no such intent . . . *necessity* . . . I and greatness were *compell'd* to kiss'). As he turned to exit, still yearning for a guilt-assuaging pilgrimage (but why guilty if 'compell'd'?) 'unto the Holy Land', a door opened on the balcony above him. Dead Richard stood there in his blood-dried smock. The two kings gazed at each other – as sand began to spill down on Henry's head.

The feeling that I'd tagged on to the end of a conga line in a slow Dance of Death played by the terminally ill was only just relieved during, of all things, the interval, which Matt Costain as Davy setting up Gloucestershire filled with a hilarious 'turn' that involved a ladder, two folding chairs, several lengths of bunting – and a genre shift onto a different emotional planet. There, Geoffrey Freshwater's genially approximate Shallow (who'd clearly dressed to the nines in best quilted doublet to meet the toffs from the metropolis) and Sandy Neilson's sober, sober-suited, half-speed Slender offered the antidote to Eastcheap and Westminster. Two old geezers sitting simply side by side on a bench talking about bullocks and death showed where the heart of England lay. The musters were a parade of disability that produced brilliant comic cameos: an over-strung Shadow (Anthony Shuster) who kept fainting, a crab-like Wart (Rob Carroll), a Bullcalf (Luke Neal) who looked like Rasputin, and a parenthesis-shaped (and cross-dressed) little Feeble (Katy Stephens) who proved the best man of the lot. I couldn't help but think that, were the 'wisdom' of backwater Gloucestershire adopted as government policy in Henry's rebellion-wrecked

land – Davy's notion in 5.1 that 'once or twice in a quarter' a 'knave should have some countenance at his friend's request' – England would be all the better for it.

The final sequence of *Part II* offered no easy solutions. Wheelchair-bound, death's rattle in his chest, Wood's Henry went into a convulsive fit and staggered to the bed that Rumour-as-Messenger solicitously wheeled out after he'd delivered not a 'packet' of news (4.4) but Northumberland's head, dumped at the king's feet. Sitting in that same wheelchair, watching his father sleeping, it was as if Hal were feeling under his haunches the real shape of the throne before he inherited the ceremony-padded version. He was stunned to see the feather on the king's lips not stirring. And it was only after a long pause that he finally picked up the crown, slowly placed it on his head, and exited, eyes big with terror, but a voice grown to manhood and confirmed in inheritance: 'This from *thee* . . . to *me*'. So when a huge rasp from the bowels brought the king back to life, groping for his property, staggering out of bed, falling, railing, bellowing, clawing at his son (when, mortified, he returned) and clutching at the crown, a covetous miser, when *it* returned, not just the audience was stunned. We'd been here before. And so had Hal. At Shrewsbury. Only this death, unlike Falstaff's, though delayed, was for real. But also for real was the reconciliation reached in these final urgent exchanges, through rage, desperation, a need to tell on both sides. These last words settled the crown in *two* hands, recalling Bolingbroke and Richard ('here cousin, seize . . .'), but now registered father and son holding England together before Henry released the crown (and England) into Harry's grasp, and they finally embraced.

If that embrace concluded the story this production told of delinquent sons and care-full fathers (or was it vice versa?), Streatfeild's entrance as King Harry signalled the political story of the nation to come. The player prince of the Boar's Head was dead. Wearing the strange 'garment, majesty' he was not in theatrical costume but a new skin. Neither was the crown he wore some holiday favour but a plain thing for a jobbing king. Later,

65. *Henry IV Part II*, 4.5, RSC, Courtyard Theatre, directed by Richard Twyman. Clive Wood as King Henry IV, Geoffrey Streatfeild as Prince Hal.

white confetti rained gracefully from the sky on his head – not sand – as he entered through the audience, in white, for his coronation, towards the massed crowds facing him, some who'd ridden from as far away as Gloucestershire. As he announced the banishment of 'fool-born' Hal – 'I have turn'd away my former self' – more banishments were proceeding. A black cage was lowering over 'the rest of my misleaders'. The lights, fading, captured a political emblem: on the forestage, an exchange between Justice and Brotherhood; behind, Riot contained, its several faces arrested behind iron bars.

This production was billed as directed by Richard Twyman, Boyd's assistant. But because he was locked into so many decisions previously made – everything from cast and design to choreography, stage effects and hauntings – it's hard to see his autograph here. A look at a 'genuine' Twyman article awaits another day. *Henry V* (which opened in November 2007, four months behind the *Henry IV*s) brought Boyd back. But this final production looked tired of history (or maybe just exhausted of ideas), so instead of investigation it

gave us theatrical tricks, some of them, I want to say, stunners.

The ensemble was in fine shape. Streatfeild – though in some of the big speeches there was still too much of a tendency to saw the air and illustrate each rhetorical image so that he seemed both to be speaking and signing the speech for deaf spectators – had matured into a pensive, serious king, one capable of sustaining the contradictions Shakespeare writes into the role, both hero and sceptical anti-hero. At Harfleur he pulled no punches telling the walled city what he intended ('mowing like grass / Your fresh fair virgins and your flowering infants'), but then quietly instructed Exeter 'use mercy to them all'. Before Agincourt, concealed in Erpingham's cloak and taking on the common soldier's disillusion with war as 'royal occupation' (Williams, played by Lex Shrapnel), he was a close listener and tough interrogator of the tongue-clacking squaddies, of 'ceremony', of inheritance – but ultimately, a tough interrogator of himself. After the slaughter of the baggage boys, he was a man staggering under the weight of the body he bore – but staggered also by rage.

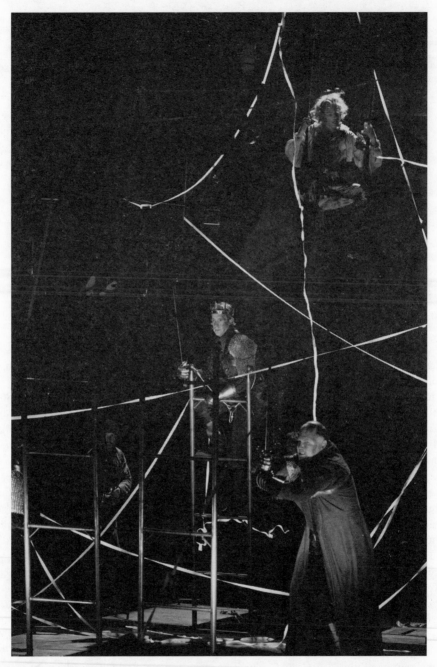

66. *Henry V*, RSC Courtyard Theatre directed by Michael Boyd. Left to right: Lex Shrapnel as Michael Williams, Geoffrey Streatfeild as Henry V, Chris McGill as Duke of Bedford, Tom Hodgkins as Westmoreland; above, John Mackay as the Dauphin.

With Katherine (Alexia Healy), he was a scrubbed up but gormless wooer, tongue tied in French knots – but also a canny imperialist who intended to have the *whole* body of France (not least, those parts Kate had so prettily learned to name in English).

There were fine performances by Forbes Masson and Maureen Beattie. He (Bagot-turned-Murderer-turned-Rumour-turned-Chorus, the edgy menace of his earlier incarnations dropped) gave us, now, history told by a non-combatant, a *story* teller, whose claim was also that, through the serious act of imagination he was requiring from us, his auditors, something serious was being made in this theatre we were sharing. She (Quickly) gave an account of the death of Falstaff that left me thinking that 'Nothing in his life / Became him like the leaving it'. Jonathan Slinger's pedantic, purse-lipped and taciturn but somehow also garrulous Fluellen, a brilliant blend of Welsh chapel and Caesar's *Wars*, all buttoned up military correctness citing 'the disciplines of the wars, the Roman wars' and constantly tugging at a tunic that threatened to retract like a roller blind over his (non-military) portliness, brought into view, this time comically, the contradictions that throbbed, too, in Harry's brain: war as magnificent 'occupation'; war as mess, and muddle, brutality, craven fear, and comrades-turned-looters; war as waste, child-killing.

This production occasionally faltered. It was moronic to allow textual emendations – like Julius D'Silva's Bardolph re-citing 'greyhound in the slips' as 'with the squits'. It was a worse idea to put the French in 3.7 in Barbie doll wigs doing contortionist routines on trapezes. Effete the French may be as Shakespeare writes them, but they aren't lassy-lads auditioning for 'the daring young girl' in the Music Hall song – and if they were, it would be no miracle, as it is in the play, for the English to defeat them, even at the appalling odds of five to one.

More often, Boyd produced striking theatrical images. The Dauphin's tennis balls, exploding by the dozen out of a chest and rolling around the floor, turned Harry's court into ludicrous 3-D human pinball. A golden picture frame, lowered from the heavens, first brought French Katherine (like French Margaret, eight plays back, in *1 Henry VI*) into view. Clearly, spectacular airmail was the preferred Gallic mode for delivering English kings their royal packages. Later, the Anglo-Franco wooing was conducted on a platform set on a foundation of French coffins. Earlier, the war was ignited, literally, by Chorus, cued by his own lines about 'the nimble gunner' that 'With linstock now the devilish cannon touches'. As he set touch paper to fuse, the ground around him exploded as though shelled: all six of the stage's trapdoors slammed open simultaneously and the English surged up and out, 'Once more unto the breach . . .'. Agincourt spectacularly mimicked the English bowmen's celebrated historic contribution to the day's work – and seemingly did the impossible by quoting, on stage, those classic shots in Olivier's 1944 film that watch the English loose their flights of arrows. White paper streamers fired in all directions across the stage knotted into a terrible cat's cradle that tangled the French and strung them up to die.

These days, images like that one need time to settle their after-shocks in my spectatorly brain. Not for me, then, a quick cup of tea and back to the stalls for the next leg of a four-day viewing marathon: I declined the RSC's 'once in a lifetime opportunity' to see all eight histories on the trot. But I know someone who grabbed the chance. And described the experience as 'invested viewing'. I take that as an understatement.

COMEDIES

On, then, to this year's work, which I'll treat, as is *Survey*'s custom, generically, beginning with the most glorious *Much Ado About Nothing* since Terry Hands's at the RSC (1982**)**.

In Nicholas Hytner's National Theatre production, the announcement of Don Pedro's imminent arrival interrupted breakfast in Leonato's household. It was taken *al fresco* on a terrazzo shaded by slatted woodwork that filtered the hot morning sun (and that later would let in surveillance), overlooked by Sicilian façades, white-washed plaster, little balconies, shutters thrown back from windows blowing with lace curtains: space that inscribed 'noting' on its domestic surfaces. A leisurely gathering by ones and twos around a grape-laden table established a prosperous *borghesia contadina* – lovely Hero (Susannah Fielding) practically undistinguishable from the family servants in rustic skirts and aprons, clothes that could have put them in the twentieth, nineteenth *or* sixteenth century, Leonato (Oliver Ford Davies), trousers stuffed into boots, the genial padrone at the head of the table, Beatrice (Zoë Wanamaker) only marked apart by the way she eventually turned her chair and back on the chat and, coffee in hand, absorbed herself in a book.

The design by Vicki Mortimer was canny: set on a revolve, scenes turned to register different takes (inside, outside) on the household, views that were framed or boxed or squeezed through slatted apertures, giving a sense of always seeing *through* something, seeing this *and* that simultaneously. (Eavesdropping, we would discover, provided this Sicilia's regular messaging service.) Performance detail produced the same effect of double vision. Mocking the messenger ('is Signor Mountanto returned . . . ?'), Wanamaker's control was fixed by the arch set of her ever-so-slightly raised chin (as though she were offering to take one on that chin, if anyone *dared*) – but undone by her hands in her lap spasmodically tugging at her napkin as though she were choking chickens. When Simon Russell Beale's Benedick turned up, carrying a flower and a parcel of books tied up with string, we saw a match. But a match missing its chances, killed in the crossfire of barbed wit hitting its targets. The books weren't delivered. Nor the rose. (But maybe we'd misread the signs. Maybe the portable library wasn't a gift. Maybe bookish Benedick, the regimental square-eyes, rusticated to hicks-ville, had brought it along determined to stave off boredom swotting up his Cicero. And Caesar. And Ovid.)

These two were a pair of love's losers. Past middle age, thick in the waist and lumpy with emotional scar tissue, they'd been damaged by life – and each other. Her wisecrack about hearts won with false dice spoke some past misery that still bruised her voice. Thinking of her, *his* voice couldn't even climb out of his throat. 'There's her cousin,' he began, pouring the cold water of comparison on Claudio's sudden ardour for Hero. Then stopped. The rueful laugh that broke his silence told a whole bitter history mingled with something like sorrow. For this Beatrice and Benedick, their 'merry war' was more a doomed siege of Stalingrad than a dashing charge of the Light Brigade.

That said, there was plenty of laughter here. The paired gulling scenes that led the two 'curst' 'bears' by the nose into love's yoke were hilarious – involving collapsing garden chairs, posts that couldn't have concealed Benedick's shadow never mind his girth, a sunhat the size of a picnic umbrella, and a garden pool. But they drew blood. These bears were baited by tormentors who enjoyed the sport. When Benedick cannon-balled into the pool to avoid discovery, Don Pedro and the rest hung around the side, savouring his fix. How long could he hold his breath? How long before his lungs would explode or he'd blow his cover, coming up for air? When Beatrice (playing deck-swabbing mop maid to get close to the gossip) in the borrowed hat (that fooled no one) accidentally dropped her bucket into the pool, Hero fixed such a killing gaze on the cack-handed 'servant' that she had miserably to slide into the water to retrieve it. Between them, Wanamaker and Russell Beale have four of the most loud-talking eyes in the business. When she heard Hero's censure ('She cannot love'), hers widened and froze, written on them, self-'noting' that was heart-stopping. When he heard Leonato's gossip ('Beatrice . . . in love'), his shot out like chapel hat pegs, alarm headlined there in capitals ('Is't possible?'). Surfacing from the pool, bobbing, his goggle-eyed astonishment (which registered in a line reading that was pure Russell Beale: 'Love *me*? WHY?') made Benedick a giant frog who'd just discovered he was indeed a prince and was finally willing to offer himself to the kiss that would settle the metamorphosis.

The real triumph of this production, however, wasn't the way it staged the discovery that Beatrice and Benedick were in each other's books. It was the way it interrogated the deeply serious crisis in masculinity this play brings to book: here showing, despite the age difference, that it's Benedick and *Claudio* who make a pair, male doubles, the one capitulating to loving as instantly as the other capitulates to loathing and both (despite this Benedick literally dripping puddles as he preened before his 'lady') expecting their discoveries to be taken seriously. Daniel Hawksford's bristling but deeply adolescent Claudio had clearly spent most of his time on the last campaign growing his moustache. Injury – this Claudio hated being mocked – ran across his body in muscle spasms. It never occurred to him that, while he'd just duped Benedick into believing Beatrice loved him, he himself might have been duped into believing Hero betrayed him.

The scene in the church (set up simply with a few chairs in rows and a cloth-covered altar) showed men at their ugliest, hanging around the back, egging each other on. Claudio wept, but still savaged Hero and threw her, violently, the 'rotten orange', to the ground; Don Pedro apologized, but laddishly took the lad's part; Ford Davies's suddenly monstrous Leonato turned on his child as though they'd both slid, sickeningly, into *King Lear.* In the aftermath, with only Beatrice and Benedick left behind to pick up the pieces of the wrecked wedding, it was pure genius to play the scene with him talking to her back – 'Lady Beatrice, have you wept all this while?' – and moving without so much as taking a breath (as though even inhaling might destroy the delicate poise of the moment) into 'I love you' while she stared stonily ahead. When she faced him on 'Kill Claudio', his answer was a real laugh, 'Ha!', an instant 'not for the wide world' that left him groping after her as she made to go, then recoiling as she battered him with her righteous anger for her cousin, and finally felled, dropping thuddingly onto his knees. You could see the man's knowledge system in ruins. Moments earlier this Benedick's world had been staggered by the suggestion that women were faithless. Now it was devastated by the certainty that men were wrong.

Fortunately for this production, rehabilitating masculinity (starting with himself, levity drained from lines like 'Serve God, love me and mend') wasn't left to Benedick alone. While Benedick was challenging the delinquent toffs, Mark Addy's ample Dogberry (who could have stood in as Benedick's body double) and Trevor Peacock's gloriously maundering geriatric Verges (predicting young Claudio's inability to string sentences together later) were taking witness statements from the villain's down-market side-kicks. Frequently tedious in the extreme, here the Watch scenes were comic gems because these beetle-browed incompetents, who dismantled their activity in the very act of constructing it, took themselves entirely seriously. They were to the business of neighbourhood watching what Quince & Co. are to the business of play-making. When Dogberry squared off with Borachio (Daniel Poyser), then, two mutually informing categories of men 'behaving badly' came into glorious collision – and put that behaviour squarely in the socially recuperative space of the ludicrous.

Hytner's production ended with a foot-stomping dance. It spilled off the revolve as the scene turned, leaving us – eavesdroppers – looking through the slatted wall into the heaving party. Two figures scuttled furtively around the corner. Escapees. Collapsing on chairs side by side, they started talking. Talking. Talking! That's the last we saw of Beatrice and Benedick as the lights went down. No more 'war war'. 'Jaw jaw'. It was going to be a great marriage.

You can learn a lot from the final 'shot' a production gives you. And you can learn a lot from a curtain call. Looking at Michelle Gomez, hatchet-faced and grim, taking her call at the end of the RSC's latest *Taming of the Shrew* I reckoned she'd had the same kind of night in the theatre playing in Conall Morrison's production as I'd had, watching it. Gomez was trapped in a coarse, crude, adolescent 'in-yer-face' *Shrew*, the kind of thing you might expect from undergraduates who've just discovered Marber and Ravenhill. And she looked like she knew it. Recently, the reviewer John Peter enlisted the cockney spiv 'Flash Harry' from the St Trinian films to put a name to the 'self admiring' director who, wanting 'more than anything else, to show off his virtuosity', turns Shakespeare's plays 'into big-time showbiz playgrounds'. Conall Morrison is a wannabe Flash Harry. But also a Derivative Dan, plagiarizing (the word, remember, means 'kidnapping') previous RSC *Shrews* from Nunn to Bogdanov to Miller to Daniels to Doran (via Marowitz) by nicking ideas that had integrity in their original locations but here, stuck together any old which way, operated as lazy collage aimed at shocking the grown-ups. (Who weren't – because they'd seen the real stuff.)

Worse, he's a Cynical Sid. This was a production that literally made no sense of the story it was telling – and Morrison was evidently counting on audiences not noticing. See if you can follow this, his 20-minute opening 'induction'. Set on the Courtyard stage: a free-standing grunge-grey structure, perhaps a Blackpool (read: down-at-heels) porn shop offering X-rated videos. Enter: 'Worker'. Tight bum-warmer skirt. Thigh boots. Plastic jacket, fake fur collar. Face like a wet Thursday. Enter: 'Manager'. Classy dame. Gold velvet fitted suit. Gestures. 'Worker' (we read: 'sex worker') hands over metal money box. 'Manager' examines contents, pouts, extends hand. 'Worker' removes thick wad of cash from bra. 'Manager' smiles, exits. Enter: Mayhem. Disco music, strobe lights, load of lager louts doing a stag night, one fondling a blow-up doll with watermelon tits. Enter: various junior 'Workers', a pole dancer. When one of the guys tries to touch her up, 'Worker' head-butts him. Scuffle. Enter: 'Bouncer', throws 'Drunk' through video shop window. 'Worker' steps up, delivers 'Drunk' (unconscious in street) swift kick to crotch, mouthful of spit, straightens collar, retires to balcony, conducts noisy mobile phone conversation with 'Manager'. Enter: 'Men In Flat Caps': Barbour jackets; shotguns (in downtown Blackpool?) Enter: 'Manager'. To confer (oh, I get it: she's Shakespeare's 'Lord') about 'Drunk' now deposited in wheelie bin. Sound cue: theatrical furnishers moving van backs into view, tail-gate flourishing 'Comical Tragical Historical Pastoral' and 'XME K8' licence plates. Disgorges contents. Players. All-male troupe of mock-RSC 'luvvy thesps', flouncing, posturing, led by Donald Wolfit-style

actor manager. 'Manager'/Lord arranges performance. Re-enter: 'Drunk' – duh! Christopher Sly – wheeled in on red-plush day bed: weasel-faced urban trash with the kind of nasally Birmingham accent that makes your sinuses spasm, still playing jack-the-lad on the wrong side of 50, addicted to cheap booze, cheaper gags ('Dost though love hawking?' asks servant as he hawks up a gob-full of phlegm), rough sex. To wit: hysterically laughing 'Lady Wife' rolls in looking like pornographer's transvestite fantasy. Sly mimes masturbation ('it stands so') with bottle of brown ale; launches at 'her' crotch for oral sex that 'she' repels by sinking 'her' teeth into his equipment – leaving him resigned to 'tarry in despite of... the blood', and, as displacement activity, to watch a play, the text of which, in the latest Penguin edition, the 'Manager' hands him.

Got it? The 'taming' play activated as tart's revenge upon stag night yob? But hang on. Wasn't the ball-breaking kick and spectacular gobbing sufficient revenge? Dealing with louts: isn't that all in a night's work for the professional 'Worker'? That stuff on the mobile: wasn't this lady protesting just a teeny-weeny bit too much? Well, never mind. If the lasses are over-reacting, the laddies in the all-male troupe are on hand, and they'll sort out masculinity since, for once, it looks like the taming play is going to be – as it was on Shakespeare's stage – *all about men* and their anxieties. (Remember, men, what we women know: after the Hostess exits at line 10, there are no more women in Shakespeare's *Shrew*. So: a 'taming play' that pits male myth against male fantasy, the misogynist nightmare of the woman-as-shrew against the supremacist dream of patriarchal correction, with men playing all the parts? Bring it on, I say!)

Except that Morrison doesn't. When the actors return in joke-Tudor dress and cod-regional accents (the video shop revolving to show a cartoon Paduan townhouse, the doublets part-constructed of Fair Isle knitwear), they have unaccountably acquired new recruits, those hard-working girls from Blackpool! Look, the pink tart is Bianca, corseted so tight that she's the double of the blow-up doll; and (wait for it), the 'Worker', now in

Elizabethan dress, is – of course – Kate. So the next move follows (*pace* Bogdanov et al.): Sly is Petruchio. After the first play scene, he chucks away his Penguin, leaps upon his 'Lady', only to be hauled off by the 'Manager'/Lord who returns the book, pushes him centre stage and points at the lines, where he makes a hash of it until the Lord slaps him smartly across the face, the recoil taking him instantly into RP (Received Pronunciation) and Petruchio. (Gosh! A clout round the ears! Instant 'method'!)

Depressingly, what we'd seen so far predicted the rest: on the one hand, the inset taming play reduced to an un-funny but oh-so-hilarious send-up of *commedia*; on the other, the shrew story put into the scrawny hands (and gnat's brain) of Stephen Boxer's 'meacock wretch' of a Sly, a jumped-up loser with a permanent hard-on that the slap transformed into a Sadean psychopath. The 'wooing' was a series of nasty physical jokes where all the choreography showed (like bad stage fights: 'one, two, three, hit'). There were kicks to the groin, mimed sodomizing, childishly crude gestures, and a long look under Kate's skirt to confirm, presumably from her blood-stained (Elizabethan) knickers, that she's 'curst'. So why at the end of it, did this Kate give her father a satisfied little nod, and exit smiling?

She hadn't seen what we had: this 'wooing' pre-played between Petruchio and Grumio (Will Beck), the abused servant standing in for the future abused wife. Here, Grumio was half Caliban, half Smike. He endured Petruchio smashing his head against Hortensio's door ('Knock me here'), throttling him, using him as a chair, flogging him into the wedding scene – his 'horse' – so that he rolled over like a dying beast and spewed. But nobody took any notice, because they were staring at the apparition that was Petruchio, who arrived looking like the victim of a charivari. (There'd been a sequence just before that, nicked from Zeffirelli's *Shrew* film, that had Padua marking time, waiting for the groom from sunrise and eager anticipation to noon, wilting in the heat, and on to sunset and total boredom: stop frame pictures composed between blackouts.) Petruchio wasn't just an 'eye-

67. *The Taming of the Shrew*, 3.2, RSC, Courtyard Theatre, directed by Conall Morrison. Stephen Boxer as Petruchio, William Beck as Grumio.

sore' to Padua's 'solemn festival'. He was a monster. Cross-dressed in a filthy, blood-streaked wedding dress and veil held in place by stag's antlers (the latter registering the groom's inevitable destiny and remembering the stag night – get it?; the former, marital violence and the husband's revenge) he countered Padua's objections by lifting his skirts and flashing his naked cock before dragging Kate off to church. But wait a second: how was it that, when he returned from the wedding, the horns and dress had disappeared and Petruchio was back in mock-Tudor mufti? And later:

how was it that Kate, arriving home for her sister's wedding stripped down to her filthy Elizabethan smock, entered the final scene dolled up in chic modern sheathe dress and high heels with state-of-the-art 'fascinator' on her head? For that matter, why was Bianca's wedding set in the present?

The 'invention' Morrison achieved was perverse. Keir Charles's Tranio was an embarrassing take on Ali G. Larrington Walker's Pedant of Mantua, who came on speaking the Queen's English, was transformed into a cringe-worthy racist self-parody, 'disguised' by suddenly adopting 'comic' Jamaican patois. At Baptista's, the Bianca/Lucentio (Amara Karan/Patrick Moy) tutorial was played as though the text they were reading was not Ovid (even his *Amores*) but the Kamasutra, bonking frontal, oral, anal, frenzied blow jobs, multiple orgasms. At Petruchio's, Grumio was abusively schooled to play the master's part. Climaxing the fandango over the meat and the mustard in 4.3, he meaningfully thrust at Kate from behind ('or else you get no *beef* of Grumio'). Meekly, Kate raised her skirts, willing to be sodomized. (Oh – I get it. Neo-Marowitz, with the woman as collusive victim. But come on Kate – you only left Daddy's on Sunday. How many meals have you missed that you're transformed into self-humiliating abject?)

The final scene rumbled with male noise, rancid with male jokes. Could Boxer's Petruchio be *serious*, all straight-faced and pious, proposing that Kate's new-found 'obedience' 'bodes peace', bodes 'love'? What planet was he on? And Kate – beaten, an automaton (thanks again, Marowitz) – recovered (wow!) to deliver her 'submission' speech like she really, really meant it. *Then* reverted to glaze-eyed dummy, dragged off 'to bed'. But that wasn't the final exit. Almost immediately, Petruchio returned with her limp in his arms, laid her out on her back, was opening his belt and trousers when the 'Manager'-as-Lord-as-Widow-now-Wife-to-Hortensio tackled him. The play was done. The actors regrouped. They stripped Petruchio of his costume. Former-Kate dumped on him a carrier bag full of Sly clothes – and a final gobful of spit. They climbed into the lorry.

They drove off. Pathetic little Sly in his boxer shorts stood staring at the audience. Silence. Blackout.

What was the point of this *Shrew*? Those costumes that moved from cod-Elizabethan to contemporary: were they meant to mark this as a timeless tale of mindless misogyny – and obnoxious, whenever, wherever? That won't wash. Both the mindlessness and the misogyny (along with the homophobia and racism) that this production found, it planted. So was it meant to explore the limits of representation, 'play' as social engineering or aversion therapy? (Handy-dandy: which was the doctor, which the patient?) Was 'Kate' an actor? Was her pain fake? Was the laugh on Sly – the 'real' victim here? That's where this show left us. But hang on, why would any actor subject herself to perform in a fiction where her opposite number was playing it for real? Why would any actor put up with this garbage? Come to think of it, why would Michelle Gomez put up with this *Shrew*? She was one of this season's RSC 'star turns', cast from a TV sit-com where she's a stroppy hospital administrator whose glare can shrivel scrotums and freeze testosterone, a reputation that Morrison surely recruited to his *Shrew* – and, on the nasty evidence of a production which enacted upon his actors the very abuses it purported to be exposing in the narrative, a reputation he just as surely 'Kated'. We know that one story any production tells is the story of its rehearsal. The mind boggles, imagining the conditions Morrison created in his rehearsal room that produced the choices we saw on stage. Hey ho. Shakespeare will survive Morrison. But Morrison would be advised to direct something more suited to his tacky talents. Like video nasties.

That said, I'd guess RSC actors cast in both shows were banging on the door and clamouring to get into Morrison's rehearsals after putting up with Tim Carroll directing the season's opener, *The Merchant of Venice*. Carroll's shtick as director is to profess not directing – that's what he told a post-show audience (more than one of whom legitimately wondered whether a director who doesn't direct still takes a fee). Carroll doesn't like 'interpretations' that 'reduce the interpretations of the play'.

His plan is 'simply to give everyone in the play a fair crack of the whip – to go in to bat for what they believe in and let the audience sort it out'. But *The Merchant* isn't cricket; the issues the play deals with – race, religion, marriage, money, law, discrimination, good and bad choosing, just for starters – can't be reduced to 'boy's own' metaphors, and an audience isn't on call to 'sort out' what a director can't be bothered to think through.

What kind of performances do actors give if they haven't spent rehearsals rehearsing? On the evidence of this production, they retreat as far upstage as possible, shove hands deep into pockets, and lounge around pretending to be elsewhere. (It's a fascinating word, 'rehearse'; etymologically, it comes from the verb, 'to harrow'. Think: chain-linked spikes dragged over ploughed fields. Think: Last Judgement, the harrowing of hell. Now examine carefully the photographs that these days appear in RSC programmes showing whatever company in whichever rehearsal . . .)

Eventually, however, self-preservation kicks in: by the time I saw this *Merchant* a second time mid-season, a fair amount of acting was going on and some of it was terrific, particularly Georgina Rich's Portia. But even on first viewing, the disingenuousness of Carroll's pose was evident. He'd done plenty of pre-interpretational interpreting. Like deciding there would be 'no Venice' in *Venice* – the city was nowhere, just a blank, purple wall. Like deciding that 'sunny' Belmont was somewhere Siberian: a cave thick with stalactites (bizarrely, decorated with a ring of what looked like champagne glasses doubling as musical instruments played by disembodied hands) where the caskets were blocks of ice (that shattered when Bassanio, Jack Laskey, broke the code). Like deciding everybody would speak every line, prose *or* iambic pentameter, as though they were bouncing a ball. Like deciding that Antonio (James Garnon) and the rest of the city types would behave like recent releases from long sentences in public school – affecting 'cool' grunge and parrot-headed hair styles. Like deciding that the parade of naff suitors – 'Neapolitan Prince . . . County Palatine' – mocked by Portia and Nerissa would be picked out of the audience. Like deciding that this modern-design production would begin and end with an Elizabethan jig. These last two are giveaways: Carroll came to the RSC from the Globe where patronising the 'groundlings' and simulating 'original practices' are standard practice to jolly spectators into themselves simulating 'nut-cracking Elizabethans'. But he can't be held responsible for the way the RSC is borrowing this hokey stuff because it arrived on the Courtyard stage – *vide* the histories – before Carroll got into town. That the RSC is giving these 'practices' houseroom in Stratford is perhaps a sign of provincial panic at the Globe's spectacular success as a tourist destination – and one senses that industrial spies are being planted to discover the Globe's secret. But what (sort-of) works in the broad open air of the Globe's wooden-O, falls thuddingly flat inside the interiorized Courtyard. Take note, RSC foxes: some raids on the chicken coop just leave you with egg on your face.

Equally, however, left to their wits (and once they'd elbowed aside their ineffectual director and recovered from rehearsal room paralysis), actors made some brilliant choices that at least began to crack open the heart of this play. Angus Wright's Shylock – a man no older than Bassanio and Antonio, but a zillion times more serious as a human being – let the Christian dogs dance around him, yapping themselves into a lather as he calmly entered the 3,000 ducat debt into his ledger and snapped it shut; let them, in the trial scene, foam at the mouth while he silently calibrated his scales, getting the balance precise; shocked them by leaping upon the table where he'd laid out Antonio's body, to straddle his victim, knife poised; then shocked them even further by baring his own chest, wanting death. 'Hath not a Jew eyes?' was not a humanist manifesto but a sober casting up of racial accounts that reached the bottom line like a total in arithmetic: 'revenge'. At Belmont, Georgina Rich's bright, smart, savvy Portia stood to attention as each suitor tried the caskets – veiled, and in her wedding dress. In the trial, she was improvising, sometimes bungling, wrong-footed by arcane legal etiquette, but stopped in her tracks, powerfully impressed with Shylock's dignity and therefore passionate in needing him to change his mind. In that parlour game we play, doing a better job of matchmaking Shakespeare's characters than he did (Beatrice should marry Hamlet: that would shape him up), it had never occurred to me – as this production demonstrated – that Shylock and Portia are made for each other. But it was too late. Getting her ring back, Rich's Portia knew she was a loser. And we knew it even more profoundly: I've never seen the little exchange between Antonio and Bassanio ('Let . . . my love . . . / Be valued 'gainst your wife's commandment') played with such twisted calculation. 'Love' was not what this play had learned, not what trumped law and 'commandment. It was a poisoned euphemism for something unnamed between these two men. Rich's final scene, coming home to Belmont, to sunrise, to the world-without-end bargain of married life ahead, was exquisitely poised between comedy – flummoxing the men, stewing them in their own hot sexual juices – and something altogether darker, warier: a Portia who'd caught a slight chill.

I'd rather come out of the theatre fuming than dulled. At least rage makes me think. But best of all is to come out feeling slightly out of body, tugged out of my normal shape by an experience that has either wrenched me – Shakespeare that puts me on the rack – or produced that precious sense of wonder that gets right into the sinews and the bones on its way to the heart, restoring me to 'childness', the genuine Shakespearian article: magic. Gregory Doran's RSC *A Midsummer Night's Dream* revived from 2005 (see *Shakespeare Survey 59*) was magic – but also, as a theatre experience, disconcerting. First, the magic. Transferred from the RST's proscenium arch stage, the production showed Doran – making his debut at the Courtyard – getting the measure of the new thrust stage. The original design, Stig of the Dump via Arthur Rackham, gave way to a blank polished surface fixed behind the action that, playing off the black mirror floor, made everything 'seem double'. Acoustically, we travelled from the opening bars of Mendelssohn to weird atonality in Titania's lullaby to ravishing pure-voiced harmony in

Peter de Jersey's (Oberon) final sung blessing ('gentle *im*mortal, sing again!') that sent spectators home smiling loopily and humming the tune. Visually, moments of wit-made-beautiful delighted the eye – Mark Hadfield's Puck, tossing off the line about amusing Oberon, flicked a hand heavenward, and a whole constellation of lights twinkled like a shower of meteors. The assured stagecraft made you think Doran had been working in this space for years: the Mechanicals came on from every direction, pushing a falafel wagon, a mobile tailor's outfit, carrying a carpenter's horse, riding a bicycle, using every bit of the thrust. Haunted, they fled, first slow motion then double time, helter-skelter, pursued by fairies who transformed the familiar tools of their trades into monsters: Snug's horse a chomping beast with a clacking teapot for a head; Quince's bicycle chasing him, levitating then bursting into parts, handlebar changed into horns, wheels into giant eyes; Starveling's newspaper flapped after him, then reappeared, remade by supernatural origami into a full-sized paper giant stalking him.

From the moment Hadfield's Puck appeared out from under a pile of rubbish and entertained Mariah Gale's First Fairy by yanking the head off her doll (instantly transforming her from fey-voiced soprano to bass-toned harridan clomping off in wilted tulle and high dudgeon), the worker fairies were the stars of this production: Zoe Thorne (Moth), Samuel Dutton (Mustardseed), David Ajala (Cobweb), Mariah Gale (Peaseblossom), reinforced by recruits from the mortal world, Robert Curtis (doubling Theseus), Riann Steele (Hipployta), Sam Alexander (Philostrate) and Keith Osborn (Egeus). This small army of busy meddlers were like full-grown three-year-olds (their toys, the kind of plastic, devil-eyed dolls that 'nice' children aren't allowed to play with). Sartorially anarchic (striped stockings, bovver boots, fish-net face masks, ballet skirts, cycling shorts, punk hair), they were ubiquitous (though unseen in Athens in the first Mechanicals' scene), curious (rifling the absurd collection of 'essential' suitcases, hatboxes, vanity cases Hermia had loaded on Lysander as they made their getaway, turning knickers and bras dancing on coat hangers into bushes and bears and loathsome insects that the lovers had to fight past), and genuinely perplexed by these mortals, thrashing and banging around in their woods. (Helena's abjection, Demetrius's brutality shocked them as so, so, well, so *human*.) Attentive, their faces constantly reacting, they were onlookers always behind the action, or under it – used as pillows. They were instrumental to its workings, human climbing frames blocking the runaways' progress, apparatus enacting Hermia's 'never so weary' frustration, lifting her, as she plodded exhaustedly forwards, and carrying her backwards to the place she'd just left. They organized the fairy court as well, principally serving as kindergarten for the beloved Indian boy, here an articulated puppet, pot-bellied, chubby-cheeked, a brown toddler who, under their helping hands, wandered and wondered, chasing a balloon that lifted him into the sky, plonking himself down and wailing when the grown-ups quarrelled. In the final moments of this production, as grace was distributed and bride beds blessed, these fairies showed me something I had never seen in Shakespeare's *Dream*. The boy, cradled in Peter de Jersey's arms, was the spitting image of this Oberon. His DAD? Suddenly, the story of a mortal votaress and some other stories of a gallivanting Fairy King slipped into place.

Faced by such a deal of wonder, then, why did I find this production disconcerting? Simply, because I'd seen these performances before. Three years earlier, given by other actors. Except for Joe Dixon (Oberon in 2005, Bottom in this revival), this cast was all new to the *Dream*. They rehearsed – RSC standard practice – for six or so weeks. But at the end, they gave us *Dream 05* – an exact copy of characterisation, choreography, delivery, gags, even detailed stage business, the original property of the 05 company. I didn't see Dixon playing Bottom. I saw Dixon playing Malcolm Storry playing Bottom. So while I left the theatre humming Oberon's tune, I also left pondering the role of the revival in today's Shakespeare theatre. The art of rehearsal at the RSC is supposed to be that of 'making discoveries', of 'new-minting Shakespeare' and 'owning texts': that's the official company line anyway. So

what's the state of this art in an age of Mechanicals' re-production?

Magic of a different order was on offer in Footsbarn's *Dream*. An international touring company that has been on the road since 1971, Footsbarn arrives 'in a field near you' (a rugby ground at Warwick University, when I saw them), pitches their big-top tent, and invites you into a *Dream*-world populated by oriental puppets, masked grotesques from Grimms' fairy tales, carnivalesque *commedia* zanies stepped out of Renaissance genre painting, and circus clowns improvising local gags; an acoustic world of weird and wonderful sounds made on percussion, strings and fourth-world woodwinds; a world that speaks both to children and to 'childness' in adults. Seven actors – a couple of them founder members of the troupe, men in their sixties – played all the parts, which meant cross-dressing in masks and doubling roles that conventional performance keeps miles apart: Joseph Cunningham played Oberon and Flute, Paddy Hayter, Lysander and Bottom. Puck (Mas Soegeng) looked and moved like a lion dancer from Chinese opera so that, metamorphosed into Snug-playing-Lion, he was simply more himself. Lysander and Demetrius, in slashed tunics, arrived like flapping Renaissance birds of prey. Muriel Piquart's Peaseblossom (behind a fairy-tale crone's mask) shrank herself to a three-foot-tall dwarf in hoop skirt and bounced like a wonky dodgem across the stage, doing a roaring trade in magic mushrooms. The Mechanicals here looked like they belonged inside their job-worn clothes: shirts tallow-yellow with decades of honest sweat, goofy artisan bonnets over rubbery ears and prosthetic noses, thick-soled shoes, slack socks, belts and braces, work-stained craftsman's aprons.

Coming out of a tradition of European clowning (and beautifully observed as case studies in physical theatre), their gags had the childish delight of the cartoon strip and the comic timing of the circus stunt. Bottom (like Caesar refusing the crown he's itching to wear) flirted with the sword that Quince offered him as a prop for Pyramus. Fingers fluttering, he still, primly, pushed it aside, *twice*, before grabbing it with both hands and instantly transforming himself before his colleagues' eyes into weapon-flourishing Bruce Lee hardman. Changed into the Ass, he was unmistakeable. We knew him by the buck teeth protruding from the donkey's overbite. Put to bed with the Fairy Queen, he disappeared into a giant lotus flower that had spread its petals like chastity shyly opening – then snapped shut around them like a famished Venus flytrap.

This is an ensemble Molière would recognise – and Michael Boyd only dream of. They're committed story-tellers (Akemi Yamauchi's Titania conjured up the images in the 'forgeries of jealousy' speech with her dancing fan) for whom bodies are as expressive as words, who celebrate play as performance and performance as play. This was a *Dream* that fused wonder with delight. The sombre and beautiful but also austere Giacomettiesque life-sized puppets in purples and oranges raised high on dressed poles who stood in (literally) for Theseus's court were oriental onlookers watching a gloriously daft English village show that, as Philostrate predicted, brought tears to spectators' eyes. Even better for me, though, were the looks it brought onto the upturned faces of the dozens of children in Footsbarn's audience. Mesmerised. Rapt. Translated.

Two *Dreams* running in tandem in a single season are scarcely remarkable. But when you've waited fifteen years for a decent *Love's Labour's Lost* (Dominic Dromgoole's at the Globe last year doesn't qualify, see *Shakespeare Survey 61*), and then two come along in convoy, you'd be excused for making a joke about the proverbial 58 bus. I'll resist the temptation, only observing that if these two productions *were* vehicles, they'd be improved by cut-and-shut welding, each of them giving just about half of a knock-out show.

At the Rose Theatre in Kingston, just outside London, fifty-two years on from his first production of the play at the RSC, Peter Hall's *Love's Labour's Lost* was a handsome, sophisticated investigation of adolescence, where the particular vice that needed exposing was precisely the virtue that Navarre (Dan Fredenburgh) had set up his 'little academe' to celebrate. He and his 'fellow scholars'

were like college freshmen the world over who reject the world (for at least twenty minutes) to dedicate themselves strictly to study. Not for them real life and straight talking. Their aim was 'living art', which meant cultivating an absurdly sophistical language (able to self-persuade these earnest twits of any amount of nonsense) as the rhetorical expression of that artful 'living'. The irony was that, would-be ascetics, they were gluttons for sophistry *and* punishment.

The Rose offered a hospitable platform for staging what this play both indulges and critiques: elaborate word games and eloquence-as-smokescreen. Open since only January 2008, the auditorium is a blend of early modern design and early and post-modern materials: a metal frame roof hangs over the wooden stage. It's modelled on (and constructed to the dimensions of) Philip Henslowe's 1587 Rose, the original Bankside playhouse, home to Christopher Marlowe's greatest hits and some of William Shakespeare's first efforts. Circular, with three galleries and a space for 'groundlings' (who, sitting on the floor, are regularly addressed directly from the stage and treated as intelligent collaborators in the shared business of making the play), the new Rose's best feature is its open stage, not a thrust (like the Globe's and Courtyard's) but a wide and rather shallow platform tapering toward the audience that puts all the spectators out front – where they can see and hear everything. Christopher Woods's elegantly minimalist design and Elizabethan costumes focused action on the actors, suggesting (rather than furnishing) a world. At the beginning, off-stage sounds of hunting horns cut out and high, wrought iron gates set in the back wall clanged shut. A solitary lectern stood stage left, spiral iron ladders, left and right, led above to a gallery, a place for eavesdropping. Our eyes undistracted by stuff, our ears were allowed to tune in to this knottiest of Shakespeare scripts, which Hall's company delivered so that we heard the ducking and diving, the weaving and unravelling of its poetry: iambic pentameter side-stepping into rhyming couplets, then arcing into prose, and back into verse. We heard sonnets made – and mocked. We heard brain-crunching argument conducted via paradox and antithesis, repetition and wordplay. We heard sets of wit well played – and smashed into silence.

But there was something flat-footed about it all. Finbar Lynch's Berowne was far too circumspect (and middle-aged) ever to have signed up to Navarre's daft project, and the King, Dumaine (Nick Barber) and Longaville (Nicholas Bishop) were performance anorexics. They simply didn't find characters big enough to serve their parts' extravagant linguistic appetites. The women (Rachel Pickup, a lovely, intelligent Princess of France) felt under-directed. It's their indictment of the men's easy oath-making (and just as easy perjury) that calls masculinity's bluff in this play, and their argument ('You nickname virtue'; 'Nor God nor I delights in perjured men') needs to be heard. Where this production did strike gold was in the parallel plot, where pedant and curate offered, by hilarious, brow-furrowing and tedious demonstration, the play's internal critique of Navarre's affected dedication to life-long learning. William Chubb's Holofernes was a young fogey – scarily, Navarre's near contemporary. Smelling 'false Latin', he became the face-crumpling Grinch contemplating Christmas. Kevin Trainor's big-boy Moth was dopily pert (and rhetorically acute) as Armado's sidekick. Greg Haiste's shock-headed Costard (his vertical hair, like a row of exclamation marks, balancing his horizontal grin) encountered language ('remuneration'; 'guerdon') with the astonished delight of Adam on the first day of creation.

By contrast, Greg Doran's RSC *Love's Labour's Lost* was full of distractions: a stunningly ugly tree that squatted up-stage (inspired, evidently, by IKEA, its leaves made of shards of plastic strung together like a giant mobile), a dancing bear and puppet owl, a village clog dance, a masturbated milk churn (that upstaged Riann Steele's poor Jacquenetta). There were gorgeous Elizabethan costumes (by Katrina Lindsay) – but their period authenticity, entirely disconnected from the resolutely modern behaviours acted inside them, left them operating as just so much fancy dress. There were loads of over-heated testicle jokes, complete with frantic fanning, speeches performed as gangsta rap, an Armado (Joe Dixon) who played every scene at half speed, milking every (limp) gag for twice its worth, a Moth who, weirdly knowing (the part was played cross-dressed by the diminutive Zoe Thorne), gave an impression of the 'acute juvenal' that put me in mind of the bizarre crossovers of effect you get when an animal in human clothes performs – say, an organ-grinder's monkey. To cap it all, at the climactic moment, there was a rugby scrum over Jacquenetta's dishclout, here produced as a blood-stained early modern sanitary towel. Bewildered? Consult the relevant line gloss in the RSC's *Complete Works*. Above, I thought it was mildly aberrational that the RSC should start performing editorial footnotes (see Warner's Falstaff). But at least those footnotes were ones we would credit. Here, where the 'historical' footnote is crack-brained, the stage business it 'authorised' was historically (and gynaecologically) nonsensical and the precedent insane. It appears that no actors were damaged making the RSC's *Complete Works* – leastwise, none were named among the small army of graduate students employed to do its editorial donkey-work. But actors will be, if the RSC actually starts taking direction from the theatrically wrong-headed edition that bears its name.

Despite the distractions (which showed Doran uncharacteristically at sea with Shakespeare's writing – and there's a lot of it in *Love's Labour's Lost*), some of this wondrous play happened anyway. Arraigning the men for their new-fangled 'proof' of faith-as-faithlessness in 5.2, then, dumb with grief at the news Mercade brings and stunned into incomprehension ('I understand you not') by the men's ham-fisted persistence with their adolescent suits, Mariah Gale's Princess was magnificently adult. By contrast, the Lords (Edward Bennett, Navarre; Sam Alexander, Dumaine; Tom Davey, Longaville) were so many Peter Pans frankly bewildered that Wendy wanted them to grow up: beamingly smug as they were piling on the restrictive vows, then earnestly gormless when they were outed as lovers by a paper trail of bad verse that caught them red-handed. Would they pass the year-long test the women set them at the end? Even

68. *Love's Labour's Lost*, 4.3, RSC, Courtyard Theatre, directed by Gregory Doran. David Tennant as Berowne, Edward Bennett, King of Navarre.

David Tennant's Berowne (who could have been next casting for either Mercutio *or* Benedick) didn't inspire confidence. Marked off from the others by his blue doublet and his (native) Scots accent that droned like a whining bagpipe under-score to the romantic witterings of his fellows, Tennant's Berowne was a comic tour de force. Aghast, bug-eyed at what they'd vowed ('Who devised *this* penalty? . . . *WHY*?'), baffled by his own capitulation to 'Dan Cupid' and his inability to answer his own questions ('*I* love, *I* sue, I seek *a WIFE*?') which he offered to the air with anxious flourishes of his hands, puffings of cheeks and sceptical twists of lips and eyebrows, he ultimately legitimated the men's perjury with heart-stopping sincerity in his paean to 'love, first learned in a lady's eyes', a speech that made book burning and vow-breaking sound

sacred. When he came to that line about 'Love's feeling' being 'more soft and sensible / Than are the tender horns of cockled snails', you could feel the theatre holding its collective breath, *seeing* the image. This was comic playing at its triumphant best – and not least because this Berowne, at the end, sustained scepticism, turned such 'sensible' feelings on their heads and cast resolution all in doubt. When he observed, cynically, of the year's trial, 'That's too long for a play', he meant it – the remark of a man you couldn't be sure would be kept waiting.

While directors in Stratford and Kingston were experimenting with putting Shakespeare on bare neo-Elizabethan platform stages, directors at Shakespeare's Globe were, perversely, going the opposite way, seemingly intent on loading the stage that got everybody thinking about original practices with scenic effects on a scale just short of Beerbohm Tree. Directing *The Merry Wives of Windsor* as Elizabethan sit-com-costume-drama, Christopher Luscombe not only mocked up a timber-frame house front as permanent on-stage set (designed by Janet Bird); he extended the stage with a *second* stage, an island built out over the yard, connected to the main stage by cute rustic bridges and pathways, serving first as Mrs Page's (wholly inauthentic) Elizabethan garden (where modern hybrids grew next to lavender), then (flipped over) to present the stump of Herne's oak. The effect: the groundlings so necessary to open air daylight performance at the Globe were elbowed out of their space and (even more disastrously) their role as play-makers, the main stage was largely abandoned, and the focus was on pretty pictures. Indeed, prettiness was the signature of a production that never got close to prodding the play's unsavoury bloat, its images of 'wicked lust' melting in its 'own grease', its leering (and hilarious) predation upon female flesh as purse restorative. Christopher Benjamin's Falstaff, in velvet doublet and purple cloak, then (drying out after the humiliations of Datchet) resplendent in branched gown and furred ruff, was simply too well-heeled to need to 'cony-catch' or 'shift'. Lacking the itch of greed and need, his double-barrelled attack on his neighbours' pockets via their wives' plackets lacked menace – so the wives' 'revenge' was mere merriment, Sarah Woodward's Mrs Ford and Serena Evans's Mrs Page spending a great deal of time laughing at their own jokes. (And looking at all the onstage clutter, I couldn't help but think back to the Globe's 1996 'Prologue' season when the austerely bare stage – and the rigorous performance theories that underpinned its reconstruction – were brand spanking new and fiercely, not to say fascistically, defended. Northern Broadsides, there for one performance of *A Midsummer Night's Dream*, asked stage management for a ladder to prop against the stage for an entrance from the yard. A flurry of consultation followed. Ladders and yard entrances: could they be authenticated from original documents? The site architect thought not; to introduce either would compromise the reconstruction. So: no ladder.)

The stink of lechery I never got a whiff of on the 1590s streets of Luscombe's (evidently) power-hosed Windsor hung like low-level fog over the 1890s Vienna of Phillip Breen's intense and searching *Measure for Measure* at Clwyd Theatr Cymru. The culture on view was a culture that took itself seriously – a culture who wore black, played Chopin études and, for kicks, dressed its whores in Kaiser helmets; a culture whose physical geography inscribed on its surfaces hypocrisies (or perhaps just confusions of purpose) that it simultaneously exposed and repressed, an urban geography shared by the licit and illicit. The brooding set, brilliantly designed by Max Jones for Clwyd's studio space, was both public and secret, promiscuous and claustrophobic, indoor and outside. High black walls of what felt like a courtroom (perhaps) or a railway station or a cloister reached up to one single opening, a high-set rose window filled with clear glass that let into the gloom the only natural light. The elegantly tiled floor spoke of pattern, order, social intricacy. But its central space was inset with a metal grill – like a lid on lavatories or police cells buried underground – that oozed smoke. Lit from below, it suffused the space with the shadows of expressionist nightmare. Along the back wall, an iron stairway trundled pedestrians up and down –

perhaps to prison, or to knee-tremblers against damp surfaces. For openers, as Chopin played, there was a leather hat-box on stage, a couple of suitcases, and a single, formally dressed flunkey. Waiting. Clasped hands occasionally tensing. Waiting. Another figure appeared. Then another. Each time, the noise of the entrance made those waiting tense. Each time, the courtier entering took up a formal position. And waited. So did Angelo (Paul Amos), whose frock coat and little beard made him young Freud, but whose burning eyes, the eyes of a firebrand, turned him into young Marx. Waiting.

The time this took, the tension it built, showed a director taking risks and pulling them off. When Vincentio (David Fielder) finally entered, lank grey hair grazing his overcoat, looking like a pettifogging lawyer pursuing Jarndyce v. Jarndyce, wearing his failure stale about him and itching to get out of town, the scene slammed into top gear, and the pace never let up. Scenes overlapped with scenes, but constantly got held up in the crossover, making me aware how much of this play is about interrupted exits, exits called back, new entrances wrong-footed on the brink of things. Except for a disappointing Duke, Breen's ensemble were right on the money, their finely judged portraits of Vienna's would-be saints and has-been slummers constantly reversing understanding of who, precisely, the city's monsters were. Steven Elliott's rouge-lipped playboy Lucio went everywhere in wilted evening dress and champagne haze, but his wit was as lacerating as the ebony cane he whipped out to illustrate it. Richard Elis's beefy Pompey in brown bowler, soiled rag neckerchief and waistcoat losing the fight to cover his paunch might have been a drover calling prices in Smithfield meat market. His Welsh voice, moving caressingly over all the r's in a line like 'Groping for trouts, in a peculiar river', delivered something like aural sex – though his bug-eyed amazement at each instalment of the news he was delivering made him the perpetual innocent, or at least gave the impression of someone surprised by sleaze. Effete, bent like an apology, screwing his defence before the law out of pinched fingers, Guy Lewis's Froth in spats and cutaway coat was a toff's Uriah Heep

69. *Measure for Measure*, 2.1, Clwyd Theatr Cymru, Emlyn Williams Theatre, directed by Phillip Breen. Guy Lewis as Froth, Richard Elis as Pompey.

with an ice cream cone quiff. Grahame Fox's skin-head Abhorson was terrifying – not because of his blood-stiff leather apron and cradled meat axe, but because of his absolute stillness, the menace of the cobra just before it strikes. The one bright moth flapping around this darkness was Rachel Lumberg's Mrs Overdone: her cheeks as livid as plague sores, her yellow curls screwed to her scalp, her abundant avoirdupois spilling out of her velvet gown, and her washer-woman right arm capable of slinging her girls downstairs without their feet so much as touching the ground. Low-life Vienna was not so much *Under Milk Wood* as under Cardiff docks.

At the centre of this production, Leila Crerar's Isabella and Amos's Angelo really were innocents: her face shining under her short veil; his face twisting as new thoughts knotted in his brain. Her first 'YES!' ('Yes: I do think you might pardon him') came out so loud it shocked her. His voice, picking his way across the tortured debates Shakespeare writes, line by line, into *Measure*'s impacted utter-

ance, lifted up each contradiction, each rhetorical shift and turn to inspection. She followed the argument, physically leaning into the contours of the persuasion. Here, the cerebral was erotic; the words they exchanged, arousal. When she touched him ('Go to your bosom / Knock there, and ask your heart . . .') it was as though she had slammed 10,000 volts through his nervous system. When he scrambled inexpertly to grope her ('Be that you are / . . . a woman') and almost by accident yanked off her veil, the violation felt like rape.

Finally, though, it was Mariana – the incandescent Louise Collins – who saved the life of this *Measure* for comedy: who simply wouldn't be silenced by the Duke's (as it happens, wrong) judgements ('we are definitive'; 'Away with him to death'; 'Against all sense you do importune'). A tiny Welsh terrier worrying away at blind authority, she performed the miracle of making Vincentio think again. Making him remember a prisoner. When Jordan Bernarde's prison-wrecked, shuffling Claudio, unhooded, blinking in the light, fell into his sister's arms and Angelo, wonderingly, embraced Mariana, the heart-breaking love story this play tells felt complete.

TRAGEDIES

This is the year that will be popularly remembered in Stratford as 'Dr Who meets Jean-Luc Picard at Elsinore-on-Avon'; the year when crash barriers had to be set up at the stage door to keep screaming teenagers from mobbing Hamlet; when tickets to Shakespeare were trading on eBay for £600. Each. But before Greg Doran's hugely hyped production starring David Tennant and Patrick Stewart opened at the Courtyard, Jonathan Miller's low-key *Hamlet* played to sell-out crowds in Bristol.

So what if the Tobacco Factory Theatre seats only 300? So what if Miller made a bit of a prat of himself in the national media slagging off the opposition and moaning in Harry Enfield mode 'Life's not *fair*!' when he failed to get his production a London transfer (for which he didn't fight very hard)? And so what if this bread-and-butter, near full text Elizabethan-dress production didn't stretch director, designer or space very far? There were things in this *Hamlet* to cherish. Principally, Jamie Ballard's Prince.

During the first court scene (three church pews facing each other on three sides of the postage stamp-sized playing space made up the production's permanent set) Ballard's only-just-grown-up Hamlet in black doublet sat quietly, knotting the handkerchief that went nowhere near the tears sliding unregarded down his taut face. This was a Prince who was grieving, deeply *grieving*, for his father, one whose facial reactions showed he couldn't make literal sense of the insane questions he was being asked ('Why seems it so particular with thee?'), whose answers came through half smiles as almost comic quips to people who somehow couldn't see the gaping hole in his chest where his heart had once lodged. (It was perhaps the experience of living in this 'reasonable' madhouse that gave him the idea to imitate its 'antic disposition' later.) As his uncle's gaudy court swept out he reached a hand to Laertes (Oliver Le Sueur). The only man in Elsinore who might have begun to understand him impatiently daffed him aside.

No other actor of his generation can take spectators so deep – with so little fuss – into sorrow. (Remember Ballard's show-stopping appearances as Thisby mourning Pyramus, 2005, and *King John*'s Count Melun, coming on to die, 2006, both RSC productions.) But what made his Hamlet so fine was that the emotion was without sentiment. The human contact he couldn't make with his father's Ghost – arms outstretched and straining – found other release: in thought (soliloquies spoken as noise – 'Ooooh . . .' – wrung from the soul, each idea *felt*); in plot (listening, totally captivated by the Player remembering Hecuba, unconsciously handing him his dagger when the 'rugged Pyrrhus' needed it, then using 'O what a rogue . . .' not to beat his breast but to work out how to use the players); in other contacts (the betrayal by Annabel Scholey's Ophelia doubled him up in rage as though wounded then exploded him in tears of despair; the dead body of Polonius was food for banter even as he dragged it off). His patter chat with the skull confirmed him as Yorick's functional replacement – and the pair, posed cheek by jowl, bizarrely, as twins. The final duel (choreographed thrillingly by Kate Waters) staged the most vicious fight-to-the-death I've even seen in *Hamlet* and as, in the breathing-space, it had Ballard wryly tut-tutting at Laertes as he exchanged weapons and examined the unbuttoned foil, so it finally left him smiling – that same wry smile from the opening scene – at his own death. 'I'm dead, Horatio' was a comic discovery, spoken bolt upright, before the knowledge felled him. I don't often weep for Hamlet. Ballard's Hamlet made me laugh. But then I wailed.

There was a moment in Greg Doran's production when Penny Downie's Gertrude had the same reaction to *her* Hamlet. It came at the end of the closet scene. They'd just been through hell together. Now, on his way out, he tossed over his shoulder 'G'night mother!' as though he were Christopher Robin climbing the stairs to bed, not her killer son lugging Polonius's guts into the

70. *Hamlet*, 3.2, RSC, Courtyard Theatre, directed by Gregory Doran. David Tennant as Hamlet, Peter de Jersey as Horatio.

neighbour room. A great bark of laughter escaped from Gertrude – that turned into heaving sobs. That moment captured the essence of this fine production, where hilarity and tears swivelled on a single axle.

Older than Ballard's Prince, yet much more of a loose-cannon kid, Tennant's was a modern dress Hamlet, a Hamlet on a frequently empty stage. (The design, by Robert Jones, was the near double of Doran's *Dream* stage: polished black surfaces, floor and back wall, giving off mirror images.) Quirky, mercurial, gawky, he was a clown whose hitched-up eyebrows and wide eyes could mock incredulously or harden, deadpan, his wisecracking mouth tightening into ugly meanness. He certainly knew how to rattle the grown-ups. He arrived at the court entertainment he'd arranged in black tie – and bare feet. He'd sponsored a show of outrageous impropriety: the dumbshow, a noisy, sleazy cross-dressed burlesque in garish mock-tudor costume that had the 'king' (Samuel Dutton) in monkey ears; the stupendously bulging, bald-headed and flat-chested 'queen' (Jim Hooper) bare-breasted,

tweaking 'her' own nipples; and the 'poisoner' (David Ajala) with a sequined, flame-coloured codpiece that ejaculated a coiled spring penis – a delicious sight that silenced the widow's tears. Hamlet ended the more decorous spoken play following on from this disturbing travesty when he leaped forward, snatched the Player King's crown, jammed it drunkenly on his own head, and jigged around the space, tongue lolling like the village idiot or innocence itself, cocking a 'come-and-get-me' snook at Claudius.

This was a Prince whose standard dress was blue jeans and a tatty red T-shirt and whose standard take on life in Elsinore was parody: he mimicked the old buffer Polonius (Oliver Ford Davies) to his maundering face ('Buzz, buzz!'), scorned his university chums, Rosencrantz (Sam Alexander) and Guildenstern (Tom Davey), by picking up the patronising cadence of their (genuine) concern ('You were *sent for* . . . I *know*'); brought Claudius to meltdown playing back to him the exact sound of his absurd bluster ('WHERE'S POLONIUS?' 'ATTT SUPPPPERRR!'). He was an anarchist whom Horatio (the excellent Peter de Jersey) found hysterically funny. His double act with Osric (Ryan Gage), a time-pleaser whose ostentatiously ornate rhetoric was squeezed through a grin that could have sold toothpaste, left Horatio creased with laughter as the out-worded 'water-fly' floundered in sarcasm he couldn't quite decode ('The concernancy, sir . . . ?', 'Sir?').

But Tennant's Hamlet was also a deeply angry young man. In the first glittering court scene (where Stewart's Claudius presided, polished as a billiard ball in white tie and tails – and medals) Hamlet was completely missable. He looked like a court flunkey, head bowed, unmoving, and didn't react when the King conspicuously snubbed him – looking straight at Hamlet to ask, 'And now Laertes . . . ?' There was anguish in his first crushed soliloquy; there was self-mockery ('but no more like my father / Than I to Hercules') and astonished incomprehension at his mother ('Why she . . . *married*!'). But it wasn't until he met the Ghost on the battlements that he was galvanized into dangerous plotter, cunning risk-taker. The father whom Ballard's Hamlet yearned to touch and couldn't, here (doubled by Stewart, a fiercely material ghost) was violently hands-on. He grabbed his son and shook him by the throat as though beating into him the mortal rage he still felt – then clutched him in a suffocating grapple.

The immediate consequence of this paternal exchange was felt by Ophelia (Mariah Gale): for once, an Ophelia clearly as smart as her Hamlet and someone he clearly adored, he briefly finding her hand, squeezing it, as she exited the first court scene. She was a girl who (when the formal dress was off) wore capris, listened, eyes rolling, to her sensible brother's homily on chastity (Edward Bennett), then outed him, finding in the suitcase she was helping him pack for Paris a package of condoms. But she was also, ultimately, the dutiful daughter. Her primness, handing back to Hamlet her 'remembrances', was immediate disclosure. There was no sense of intimacy betrayed in this 'nunnery' scene – in contrast to Ballard's Hamlet who ran to Ophelia, knelt and held her by the waist, his face buried against her as she caressed his

hair, so that Polonius had to step out of hiding to wave an angry hand, motioning her to get on with it. Tennant's Hamlet savaged Ophelia openly, contemptuously, dumping on her the hideous Ghost-roused rage he felt against his mother. He exited ('Farewell'), returned with more of a beating ('If thou dost marry . . . .'), exited ('Farewell'), and returned to begin it all again ('I have heard of your paintings . . . '). By the final 'To a nunnery, go!', she was pulped – a mind disintegrating as she picked up the letters, speaking 'O, what a noble mind is here o'erthrown!' as though its images were strung along a highwire across a bottomless pit. Such cruelty Hamlet only partly redeemed at her funeral, played for once as shockingly written, with Laertes leaping into the grave, catching up his sister and raising her to view in his embrace, a hideous *revenant*. But he dropped her to grapple with Hamlet beside the grave, then stood back, watching horrified – the rest of the cortege gasping, averting eyes – as Hamlet threw himself full length across the grave, like a lover coming down upon his bride to consummate marriage in his wedding bed, as he howled, 'I loved Ophelia'.

Terrific as Tennant was, this wasn't a one-man show. It was a real ensemble that played every scene with total concentration, yielding strong performances across the entire casting from Mark Hadfield's slack-cardiganed Gravedigger – giving nothing away to nosey parkers – to John Woodvine's magnificent Player King to Riann Steele's silent Lady in Waiting. Stewart's sleek Claudius moved from genial court 'host', new to the job of king and needing prompting from his wife ('Wittenberg', she cued him), to cool-nerved killer. Rising in the play scene, he walked across the space, calmly ordered 'Give me some lights', looked unflinching into Hamlet's face, slowly shook his head, then just as calmly ordered, 'Away'. At the end, he reached for the chalice Hamlet shoved toward him – he'd lived too long – and knocked it back. Oliver Ford Davies played a Polonius slipping into senile aphasia, speech running down like an old gramophone ('What was I about to say?'). His scene with Reynaldo (David Ajala, new to the RSC, an actor I couldn't take my eyes off) was a miracle of comic acting as high seriousness. But in 1.3, when 'What is't, Ophelia, he hath said to you?' meandered, seemingly harmlessly, up to the surface of his mind, she was instantly alert. Her Dad might be endearingly vague, his discourse hit-or-miss, but the iron grip of this patriarch – senility had not eased that. And he was about to spring a steel trap around his daughter's heart.

So: an embarrassment of actorly riches. But for my money, the gold-standard performance of this production was Penny Downie's Gertrude. Vivacious, gracious, beautiful in her ice-blue satin gown in the first court scene, she was a veteran royal expertly managing a tricky occasion when both a war and a wedding were under consideration. She had, of course, been Queen of Denmark for thirty years. Her new husband was the novice. She stuck to his side (where she could cover his gaffes: 'Wittenberg'). But she was hyper-attuned to Hamlet's every muscle flex, visibly stung by Claudius's insult as he looked straight at Hamlet to ask Laertes 'And now, Laertes, what's the news with you?' Later (2.2), learning from Polonius about a boy in love whom she didn't know, she took Hamlet's confiscated letter, his violated poetry, scanning it with both eyes and fingers, wonderingly, pained. Meeting the daughter she'd winced to hear Polonius plotting to 'loose . . . to' her son as bait, she spoke her name – 'Ophelia?' – as if for the first time. At the play, she was the one who saw the bare feet, registered the dumbshow's impropriety as powerplay, read Hamlet's loutish behaviour ('look you how cheerfully my mother looks') as testing her loyalty and his idiotic synposis – ''A poisons him i'th' garden . . . The story is extant' – as provocation too far.

Waiting in pyjamas in her bedroom for their post-show showdown, she paced, livid, dragged on a fag, raked off her wig, silently rehearsed the 'corrective' speech she had in mind, then nearly shrieked – 'FEAR ME NOT!' – when meddling Polonius appeared. Her speech to Hamlet didn't go to plan. He grabbed her, threw her on the bed; when she screamed, he knocked out the light, grabbed a pistol from the bedside table, shot through the mirror door that splin-

tered and slowly opened under Polonius's dead weight. Death cleared the way for straight talking: Gertrude defied her son's sick accusations, but quailed at the evidence. The 'counterfeit presentment of two brothers' were newspaper front pages, the death notice, the coronation issue both still on her dressing-table. She laughed wearily at youth's arrogance ('You cannot call it love, for at *your age* / The heyday in the blood is *tame*, it's *humble*') before covering her head to keep out those 'words like daggers'. Hamlet's abuse of Ophelia had been the merest of warm-ups for this scene, and he kept bludgeoning his mother, until the wall opened. His father appeared. A ghost. He sat next to his wife, who passed a hand across her hair as though someone had touched her, and calmed his son: a strange royal portrait, the Denmarks at home. This interruption produced resolution ('Confess yourself'; 'Let' not 'the bloat King tempt you'), and recollection ('I must to England'; 'Alack, I had forgot'), and a strange calm when Hamlet, a child again, knelt at his mother's feet, head in her lap, and clutched her as she stroked his hair. Such a difficult boy! So dazzling! So damaged! So adored! Touch recovered sanity, restored relationship, restored love to this 'child-changed' pair. No wonder that 'G'night Mother' produced laughter, then sobs, which ended in a heart-stopping gasp when Claudius walked in, silently, behind, and touched her shoulder.

From this sequence onward, we saw a Gertrude progressively alienated. She was punished with Ophelia's madness. The filthy body, sick mind, bundle of weeds, savage dance and animal ferocity drove Gertrude back when she attempted to cover the girl's nakedness. She was at fault for telling her death. (Claudius's only response was a rebuke: 'How much I had to do to calm his rage! *Now* . . .') At the funeral, she was bereft of the daughter she might have had – 'Sweets to the sweet, farewell' – and the son who'd gone beyond her maternal knowledge. When Claudius coldly instructed her, 'set some watch over your son', and exited, she gazed around wildly at the funeral crowd. They turned away – turned their backs on a disowned queen. So in the duel scene, when

Claudius ordered 'do not drink', for Downie's Gertrude every penny had already dropped. She gave a little laugh of final recognition. And drank.

This was astonishing work by an actor at the peak of her inventive and technical powers. Girl-groupies who came to this *Hamlet* to see a Time Lord up close, how lucky they were to get the unimaginable bonus of this lady's Queen. I know whose performance I hope they (also) took away.

Looking at Terry Hands's *Macbeth*, you could see how indebted Doran's *Hamlet* was to the master who first trained him up at the RSC. Hands has spent the past ten years as Artistic Director of Clwyd Theatr Cymru, first saving this regional theatre from closure, then establishing it as the (unofficial) National Theatre of Wales. This *Macbeth* was his third complete re-think of the play, his second with Owen Teale and Vivien Parry in the title roles. It showed him on top form, delivering a production on the wide open Anthony Hopkins stage that was both poetic and harrowing, domestic and epic, empty – and crowded with shadows seemingly cast by images seeping from damaged imaginations. Hands doesn't just direct actors. He directs light – indeed, he lights every production he directs, using lighting to write a spatial poetry around actors that suspends them in space, locates their speech elementally, and finds the correlative to utterance not in objects but in atmosphere. Here, light palpably thickened on a near bare black stage (designed by Timothy O'Brien) where a single torch set in a wall sconce burned throughout. Theatre images leaped into shocking relief under sudden harsh illumination: Macbeth materialized out of black mist cut by shafts of light. In this light, you could see fear travelling down soldiers' spines (even Banquo's, played by Josh Richards as the kind of warrior who, counting on his nervous system being cauterized, was stunned to find it wasn't) while the fearless – children – were broken, crushed. Beauty was terror's outward face.

After a huge thunder clap and plunge into total darkness, the lights came up on an image that, we'd realise retrospectively, contained the whole future tragedy. A gigantic warrior – he would turn out to be the Bloody Captain – greatcoat curl-

ing around him, in slow motion, broadsword in both hands, scythed the air, turning, reeling, aiming hurtless blows at an invisible enemy. Around him the witches (Jenny Livsey, Victoria Pugh, Catrin Aaron), their faces caught half-way through a monstrous Ovidian metamorphosis that figured them man-savaging harpies, took turns swooping down, attacking: 'When shall we three . . . ?' Finally, exhausted, he fell, rolled onto the forestage and into Duncan's view (John Atterbury) to gasp the story of the battle. In this *Macbeth*, the mortal world was evil's adventure playground – and no hero was too big to be exempted from its games.

In Teale's *Macbeth* evil targeted prime manhood. Massive, powerful in trenchcoat and breeches that were neither period nor modern, a boyish grin creasing his weather-hardened face, this Macbeth was perplexed by the feminine: the weird things who'd marked his future on the heath, the wife who filled his hungry arms at home, as hungry as he. The electricity between them crackled. Parry was both sensual and brittle, a ruthless Lady M who calculated (correctly) the effect that 'I have given suck' would have upon her husband – who turned away, staggered by the shared memory. But she had no arithmetic to begin to calculate what her child substitute, Ambition, coaxed into male birth, might produce in him. Later, surrounded by wide-awake thanes, she stood, eyes bulging at what only she saw, memory hideously replaying itself as, for the second time that night, she watched Macbeth emerge red-handed from the murder chamber, this time, calmly wiping on his handkerchief the blood of the grooms he'd just slain. At the banquet, more man than he, she taunted his 'unmann'd . . . folly' by sitting coolly on Banquo's 'stool' – then found herself yanked off her feet, weightless as a rag doll, throttled, taken by him for Banquo's ghost. Stumbling free, she fled to a chair, pressed hands hard over ears, and crouched there whimpering in terror as her husband – a stranger lost to her – wailed, 'We are yet BUT YOUNG IN DEED'. It was the self-shattered sound of a soul sliding into hell. Sleepwalking in a white muslin shift, her long plait hanging down her back, she was shrunken, a child whose brain had been laid open, one terrified of

71. *Macbeth*, 5.7, Clwyd Theatr Cymru, Anthony Hopkins Theatre, directed by Terry Hands. Owen Teale as Macbeth.

the dark. 'Give me your hand' was a lost child wanting safety.

Meanwhile, Teale's Macbeth was learning to kill children. At Macduff's, the murderers enacted Lady's Macbeth's imagination. They plucked the infant from the mother's arms, swung it by the legs through the air, and smashed its skull against the stones. Meeting young Siward – cast here as just a boy (Rupert Hands), David to Goliath – Macbeth easily disarmed him, wrapped him in a bear hug, then twisted his neck – another 'pretty chicken' gone – as he cooed admonishingly over the corpse, 'Thou wast born of woman'. The bluff soldier who'd been surprised by thought before he murdered Duncan ('If it were done when 'tis done') was maddened to discover himself booby-trapped by that murder: 'To be thus IS NOTH-ING!' At the end, *he* was the Bloody Captain. Much the stronger warrior, he was moving in for

the kill on Macduff (Nicholas Beveney) when the witch-harpies attacked, spinning him off balance, smearing him with blood, wrecking his sword arm as it scythed hurtless blows at invisible enemies in the empty air. Malcolm (Oliver Ryan) whispered the death of his 'fiendlike queen' into the deaf ear of the 'dead butcher'; Macduff stolidly (stupidly?) proclaimed 'The time is free'. But as a final silent tableau composed itself in a light nothing like day, and Fleance (Francois Pandolfo) entered to stand gazing at the new King Malcolm, the witches were there in the woods, shadowing the survivors.

This ending was rather too neat, too 'signifi-cant'. It took us back to a beginning and told us tragedy was cyclical when we knew we'd never see the likes of this Macbeth again. Much more characteristic of Hands's direction was an earlier scene, 2.4. As Ross (Simon Armstrong, a kind of Odysseus figure, a traveller, observer, thinker) stood motionless downstage centre, the Old Man (Robert Page) entered (upstage right) and trudged his slow way across the bleak grey wasteland, remembering 'Threescore years and ten . . .' while Ross, choric counterpoint, worried over today. Macduff then entered (stage left) and just as slowly, his heavy broadsword weighing on his shoulder, cut an upstage arc past Ross, thinking about home, about Fife. These histories met, crossed, vanished out of sight, words dispersed on the wind. Sheer brilliance.

At the Globe, I missed Dominic Dromgoole's *King Lear*, by most accounts, except for David Calder's Lear, undercast and under-rehearsed (a complaint aimed at the Globe's Artistic Director with worrying frequency). But I did see Lucy Bailey's over-produced *Timon of Athens*. In the 2006 Globe season, directing *Titus Andronicus*, Bailey and her designer, William Dudley, wrapped the theatre in black and hung over its empty 'O' a semi-translucent black awning that transformed the space into something that felt 'a little like being in the arena before the lions arrive' (*Shakespeare Survey 60*, p. 308). Now, their predator of choice was Hitchcock's birds. Dudley stretched netting across the 'O', trapping spectators inside an aviary where, above our heads, half a dozen big, black-clad birds of prey – extras menacingly helmeted and padded up, their sleeves cut like feathers – knew the ropes and patrolled the space: bouncing, swinging, tumbling across the netting like vultures trained by Jacques Lecoq, waiting to swoop down on Timon's Athens. And he extended the stage with a semi-circular lip and a trough that made it one gigantic dining table, scene of Timon's squandered largesse and homosocial feeding frenzies where the food served up was first jewels then creditors' bills. On paper, the design must have looked sensational. In practice, it replaced most of the acting – and certainly, the aerial parallel play pulled focus from anything happening on stage where the story seemed to have been kicked into the corner and forgotten. *Timon* has flashes of the kind of writing that works on the imagination like Nitromors on paintwork – writing by Shakespeare *and* Middleton: 'Hold up, you sluts, / Your aprons mountant'; 'Paint till a

horse may mire upon your face'; 'Will the cold brook, / Candied with ice, caudle thy morning taste / To cure thy o'er-night's surfeit?' The problem with Bailey's production was that no-one rose to the demands of speech that requires actors to out-Thersites Thersites, least of all Simon Paisley Day's thin-voiced, tortured, anguished and introverted Timon. Dressed in white robes and slippers in the first half (like some oriental satrap) and in filthy loincloth in the second (making him improbably Christ-like), Day gave a Timon out of Lee Strasberg rather than the Timon we needed for these stunned times of credit crunch, market meltdown and global economic disaster when profligacy well and truly has come home to roost in empty coffers, a Timon imagined by Hieronymus Bosch.

If Northern Broadsides' *Romeo and Juliet* (a play they first staged in 1996) broke no new ground for this touring company, it showed them doing what they do best. Broadsides tell a tale at speed, making the tragedy as urgent as today's news. They place the action in space that foregrounds the text's imperatives (here, a raised wooden platform with beautiful marquetry inlay, suggesting 'households alike in dignity', that made plenty of noise when street brawlers smacked weapons on it but coded intimacy, set as Juliet's bed). And they create full-company performance sequences that rise joyously to the occasion of Shakespeare's big production numbers. Capulet's ball, scored by Conrad Nelson as dixieland song-and-dance on the theme of 'More Lights!', was splendidly riotous – dropping down to near whisper for the first breath-stopping meeting between Romeo (Benedict Fogarty, fresh out of drama school, wonderfully gangling and gauche) and Juliet (Sarah Ridgeway, hardly appearing to be fourteen until, betrayed by the Nurse – Sue McCormick – she transformed, even as the Nurse continued to pet and infantilise her, from schoolgirl to adult). The sequence of Juliet's marriage-morning 'death' was shattering. It had Capulet (Barrie Rutter) roaring over her body as, from a distance, the wedding music that Paris had commissioned approached – a gorgeous aubade scored for voices, hand bells

72. *Romeo and Juliet*, 1.5, Northern Broadsides, Viaduct Theatre, directed by Barrie Rutter. Full Company.

and string band by Nelson again – its harmonies colliding in the air with the ugly sounds of grief.

I know what I'm doing, saving the best for last and putting it in this section. Bleak, beautiful, iconoclastic, sexually mischievous, desperately funny and painful beyond belief, Cheek by Jowl's *Troilus and Cressida* was, for me, this year's most memorable Shakespeare: a *Troilus and Cressida* that was very definitely *The Tragedy*.

Working, as always, as a team with the director Declan Donnellan, Nick Ormerod designed a dull-gold world. The stage was set traverse, constructed upon the much bigger Barbican stage, with raked bleacher seating for about 350 that effectively divided spectators into two camps, them and us, and the space between, into a no-man's land, a middle ground of indecision, irresolution, fatal contradiction. Down its length ran five canvas

runways, like chariot lanes or athletic tracks. They coded action, urgency, entrances on the run. But also posturing, preening: warriors here spent more time as male models on show than combatants. At one end, the canvas ran up the wall and curled back over into a pavilion; at the other, three hangings stretched ceiling to floor. Lit one way, the mottled canvas suggested rain or shifting sand, 'the stones of Troy' 'worn' by 'waterdrops', or the city 'swallow'd . . . up' by 'blind oblivion'. Lit another way, its stains looked like blood that had seeped into the pavement and dyed the city's fabric. On this 'field', four boxes were set: the only furniture.

Still in the foyer, spectators must have had an inkling what kind of show they were in for. The production poster gave an image of war, a helmeted squaddie in camouflage gear, not unlike the lads we saw nightly on TV, on their way to Iraq – but this

73. *Troilus and Cressida*, 3.1, Cheek by Jowl, Barbican Theatre, directed by Declan Donnellan. Gabriel Fleary as Helenus, Oliver Coleman as Paris, Marianne Oldham as Helen, Alex Waldman as Troilus.

one was in grinning white clown mask, his black skin showing through skull-sized eye sockets that looked like they were weeping; a red nose stuck on the front. So: war advertised as black joke, as killing comic turn.

In their seats, spectators could have been in no doubt: Helen (Marianne Oldham) appeared in brilliant, figure-hugging white tulle gown and elbow-length gloves, posed languidly against the hangings, then strolled the length of the runway – for her, the athlete's track was a catwalk – as she began, 'In Troy! There lies the scene!' This was *her* war. *She* was its Prologue-herald. And she was *loving* it. A file of Darth Vaders marched in ('fresh and yet unbruised Greeks') and froze mid-action like futuristic versions of warriors on an Attic vase while she, 'expectation', wafted among them, 'tickling skittish spirits'. She tested muscles, probed sword points with a delicate gloved finger,

flashed her celebrity smile – and summoned up the horrors to come in lines she spoke like seduction. Later, 3.1 was staged as an 'Exclusive!' photo-shoot for *Hello!* magazine, Helen decorating her dim hunk, Paris (Oliver Coleman), as he posed first in black tie, then in uniform, while David Collings's fussy old queen Pandarus in his double-breasted linen suit dodged popping flashbulbs. He'd brought along his wind-up Victrola, so when Helen 'tickled' him into a song, it provided the accompaniment for a nostalgic Piaf-inspired ballad, 'Love, love, nothing but love': the first airing of a theme tune that *both* camps knew, that kept returning. This time, it ended in tears, with Helen first joining in ('shaft . . . wounds . . . tickles . . . die!') then cutting out – sobbing. This was her war. And she wasn't loving it. (In one of those wonderfully iconoclastic moves that mark his directorly signature, Donnellan had Helen double Cassandra.

'Placket', prophet, pretext, see-er of endings: these were all one woman. Just as 'raper' Paris and 'cuckold' Menelaus were both one man: doubled by Coleman.)

Trojans were in white: singlets and the kind of body armour (on external show) that cricketers wear. Greeks wore black. But there were no good guys – or bad – in this war. Indeed, the way Donnellan cut scenes together, creating narrative overlaps and visual superimpositions showed us a world not of opposites but of bizarre doubles. David Caves's lean, decent Hector was his baby brother's mentor, and the closest thing either side could offer as a hero. But he was also, if not a hypocrite, a dope. In the Trojan council scene – Priam (Paul Brennen, in another ironic double, also played Achilles) was so feeble that he had to be carried on in Helenus's arms – Hector won the argument about 'worth', 'cost', 'value' hands down: 'Let Helen go'. Logic, moral force, economic sense were all behind him. He could have ended the war. But he brushed aside 'truth' to indulge his 'spritely brethren'. The boys wanted a scrap? He'd roll out the big guns. (Were meetings like this one happening even now, in the Oval Office and on Downing Street? Was 'Helen' just a code name for the original weapon of mass destruction?) The old-school 'dignities' Hector touted were just a refined form of vanity – that finally killed him. When he pointed out to Achilles in their last combat that he was 'unarmed', Brennen's bandy-legged and bald Greek, laughed, and loosed the Myrmidons.

In the Greek camp, things were no different. Nobody knew they were supposed to be heroes. Menelaus was on the sauce. Ryan Kiggell's Ulysses – a daring debunking of this role as the play's wise man or moral compass – was a small-time bureaucrat from the War Office: buttoned up, blinking behind wire-rim specs, hesitating to offer his analysis of their failure, a nervous academic lecture on 'degree'. But when asked 'What . . . remedy?', he whipped out a file and, eager, giggling, laid out compromising photos of Achilles and Patroclus that outed himself: a voyeur, a nasty little boy's mind in a grown man's body. For sure, ten years' warring for a 'weight' of 'contaminated carrion' had screwed up all these men. Mark Holgate's Diomedes was a hyper-sexed misogynist who treated all women like meat. (His 'seduction' of Cressida used the full length of the traverse, horizontal yo-yo.) David Ononokpono's Patroclus was a testosterone drop-out, a beautiful boy – so, meat for Achilles, who was desired, too, by Richard Cant's Thersites, this production's most outrageous – and heartbreaking – manifestation of Shakespeare's play as eulogy for those trapped in the middle. For this Thersites was man-as-woman, a fast-talking Lily Savage transvestite in henna-red wig, cinch-waisted military jumpsuit and pearls. Camp skivvy, camp commentator, 'she' went everywhere in pink Marigolds, spraying disinfectant on surfaces she scrubbed ferociously, even as she sprayed over them her own corruscating bile. (But the wisecracking: was its desperation envy – or a tragic love language turned rancid?) At Achilles's all-night party for Hector on the eve of battle, she came on dolled up to the nines in figure-hugging gown and elbow-length gloves, a Dietrich-esque chanteuse singing 'Love, love, nothing but love'. Entertainment for the troops. But equally a show that put this warrior caste's fatal contradictions on stunning display. For Thersites wasn't Marlene. He was Helen. Hector approached. Awkwardly, held out his hand. Asked 'her' to dance. Tomorrow, back in uniform, Thersites would compère the battle down a microphone like a bingo caller shouting numbers. Tonight, though, he waltzed in Hector's arms. And astonishingly, the others fell in: Greeks and Trojans all in each others' manly embrace, woodenly dancing to 'nothing but love'.

What chance did 'real' love have in this world? None. Alex Waldman's baby-faced Troilus and Lucy Briggs-Owen's girl-next-door Cressida were totally clueless, both achingly young, both set up (in a culture that gave them no other models) as 'wannabes': 'wannabe Hector' (but six sizes too small), 'wannabe Helen' (but dressed down in white jeans and sneakers). Was Troilus a hysterical idealist? Was Cressida a faithless 'tamed piece', 'sluttish spoils of opportunity'? Were their vows 'five-finger-tied' knots just as easily 'slipp'd' as 'tied'? No, they were just kids pretending to be grown-ups. With no other 'nurse' than leering Pandarus. The opening scene had Cressida appearing – almost the materialization of love's pain – while Troilus sighed and Pandarus minced, then diva-like flounced out, while she, silent, as though watching action in the far distance, walked the full lenth of Helen's catwalk. The 'morning after' scene, 4.2, was played as a noisy kid's game of tag, the naked lovers, wrapped in bed sheets, running and shrieking from a 'shocked' Pandarus, then turning to flash him.

What Cheek by Jowl's production gave us then was a world in ruins: the end of heroism, certainly, but, far more devastating, the failure of love. Our last sight of Cressida had her caught between two ends of the traverse. Like Helen, like Thersites-as-Helen, Cressida-as-Helen played out, in a man's world, the only part for women: the divided self. This was theatre at its best: no star turns, but an ensemble at work on top form, making a live connection between actors in the space that jumps over the audience like an electric shock.

Ending my maiden review of Shakespeare performed, I want to recount an anecdote from real life. The Courtyard Theatre had emptied. A last spectator remained sitting in the stalls. An usherette approached. 'It's over,' she said. 'It's time to go home.' A woman looked up as from a trance. 'It's my birthday,' she said. 'I'm eighty-five today. I've never been to the theatre. But I'm a Dr Who fan, so my friends got together and bought me a ticket to *Hamlet*. Tell me, is theatre always like that? Have I been missing that *my whole life?*' Unknown Birthday Girl: no, theatre is not always 'like that'. But it's 'like that' often enough for those of us who believe that theatre is prime cultural space for making us human to keep on taking our seats in the stalls – or circle or gallery. So wherever you are in the coming year, I hope you spend some part of it in the theatre, making up for lost time.

PROFESSIONAL SHAKESPEARE PRODUCTIONS IN THE BRITISH ISLES, JANUARY–DECEMBER 2007

JAMES SHAW

Most of the productions listed are by professional companies, but some amateur productions are included. The information is taken from *Touchstone* (www.touchstone.bham.ac.uk), a Shakespeare resource maintained by the Shakespeare Institute Library. Touchstone includes a monthly list of current and forthcoming UK Shakespeare productions from listings information. The websites provided for theatre companies were accurate at the time of going to press.

ANTONY AND CLEOPATRA

Royal Shakespeare Company. Novello Theatre, London, 15 January–17 February.
www.rsc.org.uk
Director: Gregory Doran

AS YOU LIKE IT

Sheffield Theatres. Crucible Theatre, Sheffield, 7–24 February; Swan Theatre, Stratford-upon-Avon, 6–10 March.
www.sheffieldtheatres.co.uk
Director: Samuel West
Rosalind: Eve Best

Derby Playhouse Company. Derby Playhouse, 26 May–23 June.
www.derbyplayhouse.co.uk
Director: David Freeman

THE COMEDY OF ERRORS

Royal Shakespeare Company. UK tour 19 October–8 December.

www.rsc.org.uk
Director: Nancy Meckler

Theatre Set-Up. Tour 9 June–27 August.
www.ts-u.co.uk

Ludlow Castle, 25 June–7 July.
Director: Glen Walford

Oddsocks Theatre Company. Tour 1 July–27 August.
www.oddsocks.co.uk

CORIOLANUS

Royal Shakespeare Company. Royal Shakespeare Theatre, Stratford-upon-Avon, 6–31 March.
www.rsc.org.uk
Director: Gregory Doran
Coriolanus: William Houston
Volumnia: Janet Suzman
The last production before the refurbishment of the Royal Shakespeare Theatre.

Ninagawa Company. Barbican, London, 25–29 April.
Director: Yukio Ninagawa
Samurai-themed production in Japanese.

Mercury Theatre Company. Mercury Theatre, Colchester, 22 October–3 November.
www.mercurytheatre.co.uk
Director: Tina Packer

CYMBELINE

Cheek by Jowl. Barbican Theatre, London, 29 May–23 June and on tour.
www.cheekbyjowl.com
Director: Declan Donnellan
Posthumus/Cloten doubled.

Marlowe Dramatic Society. Cambridge Arts Theatre, 1–6 October.
www.societies.cam.ac.uk/marlowe
Director: Trevor Nunn

Adaptation
Kneehigh Theatre. Lyric Hammersmith, London, 17 January–4 February; Birmingham Repertory Theatre, Birmingham, 4–10 February.
www.kneehigh.co.uk
Director: Emma Rice
Adaptor: Carl Grose

HAMLET

Creation Theatre Company. Oxford Castle, Oxford, 1 June–28 July.
www.creationtheatre.co.uk
Director: Gari Jones

Citizens' Theatre. Glasgow, 21 September–13 October.
www.citz.co.uk
Director: Guy Hollands
Hamlet: Andrew Clarke

Adaptation
Gertrude, Queen of Denmark
Act Provocateur. Lion and Unicorn Theatre Club, London, 2–21 October.
www.actprovocateur.net
Playwright: Sarah Lawson
Adaptation from the point of view of Gertrude and includes an older sister for Hamlet and a wife for Polonius.

The Hamlet Project
Chameleon's Dish Theatre Company. Arcola Theatre, London, 31 July–18 August.

Adaptor and Director: Hannah Kaye
Hamlet played by two actors.

Rosencrantz and Guildenstern Are Dead
Library Theatre, Manchester, 2 February–10 March.
www.librarytheatre.com
Director: Chris Honer
Playwright: Tom Stoppard

Ballet
Elsinore
Bolshoi Ballet. London Coliseum, 13–14 August; Sadler's Wells, 19–23 August.
Choreography: Christopher Wheeldon
Loosely based on *Hamlet*, part of a triple bill.

HENRY IV, PART I

Royal Shakespeare Company. Courtyard Theatre, Stratford-upon-Avon, 16 August–14 March 2008.
www.rsc.org.uk
Director: Michael Boyd
Henry IV: Clive Wood
Falstaff: David Warner

HENRY IV, PART 2

Royal Shakespeare Company. Courtyard Theatre, Stratford-upon-Avon, 16 August–14 March 2008.
Director: Michael Boyd
Henry IV: Clive Wood
Falstaff: David Warner

HENRY V

Compagnia Pippo Delbono and ERT-Emilia Romagna Teatro. Swan Theatre, Stratford-upon-Avon, 1–3 February.
Director: Pippo Delbono

Royal Exchange Theatre, Manchester, 10 September–20 October.
www.royalexchangetheatre.co.uk
Director: Jonathan Munby
Henry V: Elliot Cowan

Royal Shakespeare Company. Courtyard Theatre, Stratford-upon-Avon, 6 November–14 March 2008.
www.rsc.org.uk
Director: Michael Boyd
Henry V: Geoffrey Streatfeild

JULIUS CAESAR

Liverpool Everyman and Playhouse Youth Theatre. Ilkley Playhouse, Ilkley, 29 October–10 November.
www.everymanplayhouse.com
Director: Dan Meigh

Mercury Theatre Company. Mercury Theatre, Colchester, 7–24 November.
www.mercurytheatre.co.uk
Director: Dee Evans
All female production.

LOVE'S LABOUR'S LOST

Shakespeare's Globe. 11 July–7 October.
www.shakespeares-globe.org
Director: Dominic Dromgoole

KING LEAR

Royal Shakespeare Company. Courtyard Theatre, Stratford-upon-Avon, 31 May–21 June and tour.
www.rsc.org.uk
Director: Trevor Nunn
King Lear: Ian McKellen

Adaptation
I, Lear
The Black Sheep. Trafalgar Studios, London, 21 July–16 August and tour.
www.blacksheepcomedy.co.uk
Director: Cal McCrystal
Two-handed comedy.

MACBETH

West Yorkshire Playhouse Quarry, Leeds, 28 February–24 March.
www.wyplayhouse.com
Director: Ian Brown

Macbeth: David Westhead
Lady Macbeth: Michelle Fairley

Royal Shakespeare Company. Swan Theatre, Stratford-upon-Avon, 17 April–21 July.
www.rsc.org.uk
Director: Connall Morrison
Macbeth: Patrick O'Kane
Lady Macbeth: Derbhle Crotty
Scheduled to play in rep with Ionesco's *Macbett*.

Dancing Shadows Theatre Company. Pleasance Theatre, Edinburgh, 15 May–3 June.
www.dancingshadowstheatre.com
Director: Samuel Miller

Chichester Festival. Minerva Theatre, Chichester, 1 June–1 September; Gielgud Theatre, London, 26 September–1 December.
www.cft.org.uk
Director: Rupert Goold
Macbeth: Patrick Stewart
Lady Macbeth: Kate Fleetwood

New Shakespeare Company. Regent's Park Open Air Theatre, London, 4 June–16 August.
http://openairtheatre.org
Director: Edward Kemp
Macbeth: Antony Byrne
Lady Macbeth: Sarah Woodward

Northcott Theatre Company. Northcott Theatre, Exeter, 13 July–11 August.
www.exeternorthcott.co.uk
Director: Ben Crocker

Replay Productions. Belfast Festival, Crumlin Road Gaol, Belfast, 17 October–3 November.
www.replayproductions.org
Director: Richard Croxford

Pentameters Theatre Club. Hampstead, London, 23 October–11 November.

Adaptation
Macbeth Kill Bill Shakespeare
South Hill Park in association with The Wales Theatre Company. Aberystwyth Arts Centre, tour September–October.

www.walestheatrecompany.com
Director: Malachi Bogdanov

Macbeth – the Prologue
Dakh Centre for Performance Arts. Pit, London,
31 January–10 February.
www.dax.com.ua/en
Director: Vladislav Troitsky
Ukrainian company. Loose adaptation created
in the aftermath of the Orange Revolution.
Despite the title, not obviously linked to a *Macbeth* prequel.

Macbett
Royal Shakespeare Company. Swan Theatre,
Stratford-upon-Avon, 30 May–21 July.
www.rsc.org.uk
Playwright: Eugene Ionesco
Translator: Tanya Ronder
Director: Silviu Purcarete

Lunchbox Productions. Bridewell Theatre, London, 9–19 January.
www.bridewelltheatre.org
Director: Joanna Turner
Part of the Bard at the Bridewell Shakespeare
Series. 45-minute production.

Opera
Macbeth
Glyndebourne Festival Opera. Lewes, East Sussex,
19 May–26 August and tour.
www.glyndebourne.com
Composer: Giuseppe Verdi

MEASURE FOR MEASURE

Adaptation
Lunchbox Productions. Bridewell Theatre,
London, 20 February–2 March.
www.bridewelltheatre.org
Director: Joanna Turner
Part of the Bard at the Bridewell Shakespeare
Series. 45-minute lunchtime production.

THE MERCHANT OF VENICE

Theatre for a New Audience. Swan Theatre,
Stratford-upon-Avon, 27–31 March.
www.tfana.org
Director: Darko Tresnajak
Shylock: F. Murray Abraham
Modernized production, substituting laptops for
caskets.

Shakespeare's Globe, London, 28 June–6 October.
www.shakespeares-globe.org
Director: Rebecca Gatward
Shylock: John McEnery
Portia: Kirsty Besterman

Heartbreak Productions. Tour 10 July–26 August.
www.heartbreakproductions.co.uk

Pascal Theatre Company. Arcola Theatre, London,
14 September–13 October.
www.pascal-theatre.com
Adaptor and Director: Julia Pascal
Tagline: 'What happens when someone who
escaped the Warsaw Ghetto goes to the Venice
Ghetto today and meets a group of performers
about to play *The Merchant of Venice*?'

THE MERRY WIVES OF WINDSOR

Adaptation
Merry Wives: The Musical
Royal Shakespeare Company. Royal Shakespeare
Theatre, 12 December 2006–10 February.
www.rsc.org.uk
Adaptor/Director: Gregory Doran
Lyrics: Ranjit Bolt
Music: Paul Englishby
Falstaff: Simon Callow
Mistress Quickly: Judi Dench

Opera
Falstaff
Opera North. Grand Theatre & Opera House,
Leeds, 27 September–9 November and tour.
www.operanorth.co.uk
Composer: Giuseppe Verdi

A MIDSUMMER NIGHT'S DREAM

Dash Theatre Arts. Roundhouse, London, 13 March–21 April.
www.dasharts.org.uk
Director: Tim Supple
Revival of production at Royal Shakespeare Theatre, June 2006.

New Shakespeare Company. Regent's Park Open Air Theatre, London, 8 June–18 August.
http://openairtheatre.org
Director: Christopher Luscombe

Shakespeare at the George. George Hotel, Huntingdon, Cambridgeshire, 26 June–7 July.
www.atthegeorge.co.uk
Director: Richard Brown

Glasgow Repertory Company. Botanic Gardens, Glasgow, 28 June–14 July.
www.bardinthebotanics.org
Director: Gordon Barr
Cast of five.

Oxford Shakespeare Company. Kensington Palace Gardens, London, 8–17 August and tour.
www.oxfordshakespearecompany.co.uk
Director: Jilly Bond

Kaos Theatre. New Theatre Royal, Portsmouth, 1–2 October and tour.
www.kaostheatre.com
Adaptor and Director: Xavier Leret

Ballet
A Midsummer Night's Dream
Northern Ballet. West Yorkshire Playhouse, Leeds, 6 September–1 November and tour.
www.northernballettheatre.co.uk
Composer: Felix Mendelssohn
Director: David Nixon

Opera
The Fairy Queen
Armonico Consort Productions. Harrogate Theatre, 27 June and tour.
www.armonico.org.uk

Composer: Henry Purcell
Set inside a mental institution.

MUCH ADO ABOUT NOTHING

Lyric Theatre, Belfast, 31 January–24 February.
www.lyrictheatre.co.uk
Director: Rachel O'Riordan
Beatrice doubled with Claudio; Benedick doubled with Hero.

Globe Education and Shakespeare's Globe Theatre. Globe Theatre, Bankside, 5–8 March.
www.shakespeares-globe.org
Director: Joanne Howarth

Shakespeare at the Tobacco Factory. Tobacco Factory, Bristol, 23 March–28 April.
www.sattf.org.uk
Director: Andrew Hilton

Liverpool Everyman and Playhouse, Liverpool, 17 April–5 May.
www.everymanplayhouse.com
Director: Phil Wilmott

Royal Shakespeare Company. Swan Theatre, Stratford-upon-Avon, 18 May–12 October; Novello Theatre, London, 13 December–6 January 2007.
www.rsc.org.uk
Director: Marianne Elliott
Benedick: Joseph Millson
Beatrice: Tamsin Greig
Set in 1950s Cuba.

Illyria Theatre Company. Tour 2 June–28 August.
www.illyria.uk.com

Red Shift Theatre Company. Greenwich Theatre, London, 6–10 November.
www.redshifttheatreco.co.uk
Director: Jonathan Holloway
Benedick/Borachio: Dean Lepley
Beatrice/Margaret: Rebecca Pownall
90-minute version set in war-torn Sarajevo.

The National Theatre. Olivier Theatre, London, 18 December–29 March 2008.
www.nationaltheatre.org.uk
Director: Nicholas Hytner
Benedick: Simon Russell Beale
Beatrice: Zoë Wanamaker

Adaptation
Days of Significance
Royal Shakespeare Company. The Swan Theatre, Stratford-upon-Avon, 10–20 January.
www.rsc.org.uk
Playwright: Ron Williams
Director: Maria Aberg
A response to *Much Ado About Nothing*.

Lunchbox Productions. Bridewell Theatre, London, 24 April–4 May.
www.bridewelltheatre.org
Director: Alex Summers
Part of the Bard at the Bridewell Shakespeare Series. 45-minute lunchtime production.

OTHELLO

Shakespeare at the Tobacco Factory. Tobacco Factory, Bristol, 9 February–17 March.
www.sattf.org.uk
Director: Andrew Hilton
Othello: Leo Wringer
Iago: Chris Donnelly

Shakespeare's Globe, London, 24 May–19 August.
www.shakespeares-globe.org
Director: Wilson Milam
Othello: Eamonn Walker
Iago: Tim McInnerny

Glasgow Repertory Company. Botanic Gardens, Glasgow, 19 July–4 August.
www.bardinthebotanics.org
Director: Gordon Barr
Cast of six.

Birmingham Stage Company. Old Rep Theatre, Birmingham, 18 September–13 October.
www.birminghamstage.net
Director: John Harrison

Salisbury Playhouse. Salisbury Playhouse, Salisbury, 1–24 November.
www.salisburyplayhouse.com
Director: Raz Shaw

Donmar Warehouse, London, 30 November–23 February 2008.
www.donmarwarehouse.com
Director: Michael Grandage
Othello: Ejiofor Chiwetel
Iago: Ewan McGregor

Ballet
Othello
Scottish Ballet. Festival Theatre, Edinburgh, April.
Revival of Peter Darrell's ballet set to Liszt's Faust Symphony. One of four works performed.

PERICLES

Royal Shakespeare Company. Swan Theatre, Stratford-upon-Avon.
15 November–6 January 2007.
www.rsc.org.uk
Director: Dominic Cooke
Pericles: Lucian Msamati
Promenade production.

RICHARD II

Royal Shakespeare Company. Courtyard Theatre, Stratford-upon-Avon, 16 August–13 March 2008.
www.rsc.org.uk
Director: Michael Boyd
Richard II: Jonathan Slinger
Bolingbroke: Clive Wood

RICHARD III

Royal Shakespeare Company. Courtyard Theatre, Stratford-upon-Avon, 11 January–17 February.
www.rsc.org.uk
Director: Michael Boyd
Richard: Jonathan Slinger

Southwark Playhouse and Tangram Theatre. Southwark Playhouse, London, 27 September–20 October.
Directors: Daniel Goldman and Donnacadh Daniel
90-minute version combining live actors and puppets.

Adaptation
Richard III: An Arab Tragedy
Sulayman Al-Bassam Theatre. Swan Theatre, Stratford-upon-Avon, 13–17 February.
www.albassamtheatre.com
Adaptor and Director: Sulayman Al-Bassam
Emir Gloucester (later Richard III): Fayez Kazak
Modern-dress adaptation with Middle East parallels.

ROMEO AND JULIET

Lord Chamberlain's Men. Tour May–September.
www.tlcm.co.uk
Director: Lucy Pitman-Wallace

Globe Theatre Company, touring production, 17 June–2 September.
www.shakespeares-globe.org
Director: Edward Dick

Studio 1, BAC, 12 July–12 August.
Director: Polly Findlay
Winner of the 2007 JMK award for promising directors.

Honest Hands Theatre Company. Greenwich Playhouse, 25 September–21 October.
Director: Linnie Reedman

The Troika Collective. New Wimbledon Theatre, 31 October–17 November.
www.tcollective.com/aboutus.php
Director: Mhairi Grealis

Adaptation
Noughts & Crosses
Royal Shakespeare Company. Civic Hall, Stratford-upon-Avon, 29 November–2 February 2008 and tour.
www.rsc.org.uk

Director: Dominic Cooke
Adapted from the novel by Malorie Blackman.

Romeo and Juliet: A Rock and Roll Love Story
Western Connecticut State University at the Edinburgh Fringe Festival. Gilded Balloon Teviot Debating Hall, Edinburgh, 3–26 August.
Director and Composer: Sal Trapani
A musical.

Romeo in the City
Theatre Centre Company. Tour September–November.
www.theatre-centre.co.uk
Playwright: Amber Lone
Director: Michael Judge
Loose adaption set in modern Britain.

Ballet
Romeo and Juliet, On Motifs of Shakespeare
Mark Morris Dance Group. Barbican, London, 5–8 November.
markmorrisdancegroup.org
Composer: Sergei Prokofiev

Romeo and Juliet
Bolshoi Ballet/Moscow City Ballet. UK Tour January–March

Romeo and Juliet
Northern Ballet Theatre. Tour 18 September–10 May.
www.northernballettheatre.co.uk
Director: Christopher Gable

Opera
I Capuleti e i Montecchi
Pimlico Opera. Tour 18 September–27 October.
Composer: Vincenzo Bellini

Romeo and Juliet
Bampton Classical Opera. Buxton Opera House 12, 15 July and tour.
www.bamptonopera.org
Composer: Georg Benda

Romeo and Juliet
Royal Opera House, London, 16 October–25 November.
Choreography: Kenneth MacMillan

THE TAMING OF THE SHREW

Propeller Theatre Company & The Watermill Theatre. Old Vic, London, 5 January–17 February, UK and international tour.
www.propeller.org.uk
Director: Edward Hall
All-male cast.

Wilton's Music Hall, London, 22 March–28 April.
www.wiltons.org.uk
Director: Nick Hutchinson

Stamford Shakespeare Company. Rutland Open Air Theatre, Tolethorpe Hall, Little Casterton, 4 June–25 August.
www.stamfordshakespeare.co.uk

Creation Theatre Company. Oxford Castle, 24 July–25 August.
www.creationtheatre.co.uk
Director: Heather Davies

Adaptation
Lunchbox Productions. Bridewell Theatre, London, 20 March–5 April.
www.bridewelltheatre.org
Director: Mark Leipacher
Part of the Bard at the Bridewell Shakespeare Series. 45-minute lunchtime production.

TEMPEST

Royal Shakespeare Company. Novello Theatre, London, 28 February–24 March. Revival of 2006 production.
www.rsc.org.uk
Director: Rupert Goold
Prospero: Patrick Stewart

Northern Broadsides. New Vic Theatre, Newcastle-under-Lyme, 1–17 March and tour.
www.northern-broadsides.co.uk

Director and Prospero: Barrie Rutter

Royal Exchange Theatre, Manchester, 29 May–7 July.
www.royalexchangetheatre.co.uk
Director: Greg Hersov
Prospero: Pete Postlethwaite

Maddermarket Theatre Company. Maddermarket Theatre, Norwich, 18–27 October.
www.maddermarket.co.uk
Director: Peter Sowerbutts

Love and Madness. Tour 30 October–30 November.
www.loveandmadness.org
Director: Jack Shepherd

Tara Arts. Tara Studio, London, 25 September–14 October.
Director: Jatinda Verma

Adaptation
Bush Theatre Company. Bush Theatre, London, 16 October–10 November.
www.bushtheatre.co.uk
Playwright: Ian McHugh
Director: Josie Rourke
Shakespeare's island translated to modern Great Yarmouth.

Opera
The Tempest
Royal Opera House, London, 12–26 March.
www.royaloperahouse.org
Composer: Thomas Adès
Director: Tom Cairns

TIMON OF ATHENS

Instant Classics. Camden People's Theatre, London, 8–24 August.
Director: David Cottis
Relocated to 40s Hollywood.

TWELFTH NIGHT

Propeller Acting Company. Old Vic, London, 17 January–17 February and international tour.
www.propeller.org.uk
Director: Edward Hall
All-male production.

Oddsocks Productions. Tour 2–26 January.
www.oddsocks.co.uk

Royal and Demgate at the Royal Theatre, Northampton, 30 January–17 February.
Director: Lauris Sansom

Cheek by Jowl. Swan Theatre, Stratford-upon-Avon, 28 February–3 March.
www.cheekbyjowl.com
Director: Declan Donnellan
All-male production, in Russian with English surtitles.

Heartbreak Productions. Tour 10 July–26 August.
www.heartbreakproductions.co.uk

Chichester Festival Theatre, 20 July–31 August.
www.cft.org.uk
Director: Phillip Franks
Malvolio: Patrick Stewart
Feste: Michael Feast
Post-WWI setting.

The Royal Shakespeare Company. Courtyard Theatre, Stratford-upon-Avon, 5 September–6 October.
www.rsc.org.uk
Director: Neil Bartlett
Viola: Chris New
Malvolio: John Lithgow
Cross-gender casting with Sir Toby, Sir Andrew and Fabian played by women.

THE TWO GENTLEMEN OF VERONA

Brave New World Theatre. Theatro Technis, London, 3–24 February.
www.theatrotechnis.com
Director: Kim Durham

Barnard Castle Players. Bowes Museum, Barnard Castle 4–7 July
www.castleplayers.org.uk
Director: Simon Pell

THE WINTER'S TALE

Royal Shakespeare Company. Swan Theatre, Stratford-upon-Avon, 15 November 2006–6 January 2008.
www.rsc.org.uk
Director: Dominic Cooke
Leontes: Anton Lesser
Hermione: Kate Fleetwood
Promenade production.

Royal Lyceum Theatre Company. Royal Lyceum, Edinburgh 21 September–20 October.
www.lyceum.org.uk
Director: Mark Thompson

Steam Industry. Courtyard Theatre, London, 20 December–27 January 2008.
www.finboroughtheatre.co.uk
Director: Phil Willmott

POEMS AND APOCRYPHA

Nothing Like The Sun: The Sonnet Project
Royal Shakespeare Company and Opera North. Courtyard Theatre, Stratford. 24–25 February and tour.
www.rsc.org.uk
Curator: Gavin Bryars
Film Director: Pippa Nelson
Musical settings for 13 sonnets.

Venus and Adonis
Royal Shakespeare Company and Little Angel Theatre. Little Angel Theatre, London, 26 March–28 April.
www.rsc.org.uk
Director: Gregory Doran
Narrator: Harriet Walter
Revival of 2004 production for the Complete Works Festival.

MISCELLANEOUS

The Big Secret Live. 'I am Shakespeare'. Webcam day-time chat-room show.
Chichester Festival Theatre, 31 August–8 September and tour.
www.cft.org.uk
Director: Matthew Warchus
Playwright: Mark Rylance
Discussion of the authorship question.

Kean
Yvonne Arnaud Theatre. Tour, 30 May–18 August.
www.yvonne-arnaud.co.uk
Director: Adrian Noble

Love Labours Won
Rogue Shakespeare Company. Gilded Balloon, Edinburgh, 1–27 August. First shown in Edinburgh 2006.
www.lovelabourswon.com

Playwright: Ryan Smith
A blank verse play using pastiches of Shakespeare to explore the theme of fidelity.

Shakes vs Shav
Orange Tree Theatre, 8–23 June.
www.orangetreetheatre.co.uk
Playwright: George Bernard Shaw
Director: Henry Bell
Part of a *Director's Showcase* season.

Sinful Shaxxxspeare
1623 Theatre Company. Derby Silk Mill, Derby, 20 October and tour.
www.1623theatre.co.uk
Directed: Ben Spiller
Compilation of sinful scenes in Shakespeare.

Sweet William
Little Angel Theatre, 21–26 August and tour.
Writer/solo performer: Michael Pennington
Personal reminiscences about Shakespeare.

THE YEAR'S CONTRIBUTION TO
SHAKESPEARE STUDIES

1. CRITICAL STUDIES
reviewed by JULIE SANDERS

Shakespeare in the Classroom

There is sometimes a perceived divide between the scholarly monograph and the textbook, at least in the minds of the academic community and its funding bodies. Certainly this is the case in the UK's all-consuming Research Assessment Exercise – the method by which all Higher Education Institutions are vetted and rated for their 'research quality' by the funding arm of the British government – the influence of which on this year's output of critical studies is palpable in terms of monographs by UK academics (many of which I will come to in the last section of this article). Only the 'scholarly', 'full-length' monograph is usually deemed suitable for submission as part of an individual academic's publishing and research profile. And yet, as a host of publications this year demonstrate, some fine work is published in the textbook domain, and is frequently fed directly by cutting-edge research. The shorter, pithier book may do its intellectual work more efficiently and with a potentially broader reading audience than some over-stretched 'full-length' rivals. One of the interesting themes to emerge, then, amongst this year's batch of books is a deep concern with Shakespeare in the classroom, how we deploy his works, the manner and context of our teaching of Shakespeare, but also how we encourage students to do their own things with those works. Two collections of essays are notable in this regard: G. B. Shand's *Teaching Shakespeare:*

Passing it On and Laurie Maguire's *How to Do Things with Shakespeare.*

Maguire's *How to Do Things with Shakespeare* offers what its subtitle implies are 'New Approaches' to studying Shakespeare, with the undergraduate and postgraduate student very much in mind. Maguire's aim is to empower these students to find their own things to 'do' with these plays and poems, despite the centuries of footfall over their pages and related stages. In practice these struck me as new angles on somewhat age-old approaches. The sections are divided under headings such as 'How to Do Things with Sources' which is in essence an attempt to breathe new life into the somewhat tired domain of source studies, not least through the theoretical framework of intertextuality and adaptation studies. Other sections such as 'How to Do Things with History' or 'How to Do Things with Text' are not exactly 'new approaches' though they do offer fresh insight on existent practices such as historicism, archival research, performance studies, and editorial transmission. Maguire herself offers suitably pithy and engaging introductions to each of the sections and sets out very clearly at the start of the volume the remit she gave her contributors, which was to provide 'rationales' for why they do what they do in the essays that follow in an attempt to persuade students to be self-reflexive about their own potential engagements with Shakespeare.

It struck me that this was a sound idea – to think about offering students a series of paradigms for how they themselves might conduct research in the inevitably daunting world of Shakespeare studies – but the practical and pragmatic soul in me ended up wishing that there had been a more hard and fast sense of the methodologies adopted by each scholar in carrying out their specific analysis. Admittedly, Maguire stresses that this was not her intention but, in terms of the practical application I can put a volume like this to in the classroom, this felt like a somewhat self-limiting and constraining decision. If the essays in 'How to Do Things with Sources' offer us 'new and flexible ways of thinking about questions of influence' (p. 8), what are the practical skills required – languages? The skills of close reading and analysis (what used to come under the heading of 'practical criticism')? A background in genetic criticism or the history of the book? Learning how to 'do' things with Shakespeare requires learning what skills need to be developed and honed and, while the contributors here have those skills in abundance, there was less of a sense of 'passing it on' (to borrow the subtitle of Shand's essay collection) than there might have been.

That is not, however, to dismiss out-of-hand some very well-conceived and achieved essays. Julie Maxwell offers a fascinating essay on the 'art' of biblical misquotation in Shakespeare's plays, arguing that we should not read misquoting of the kind enacted by Falstaff and others as a key to judging their character or ability as somehow failed or lacking. Misquoting, she suggests, was an embedded, indeed honourable, practice in early modern society, stemming partly from the widespread use of commonplace books and nuanced understandings of the practice of the arts of memory in which invention remained key to the process of transmission. In the section on the use of history, Chris R. Kyle, a historian by trade rather than a literary scholar, offers a contextualized reading of *Henry VIII* that sits happily alongside other recent readings of that play in the context of the post-Reformation landscape, including Gordon McMullan's seminal Arden 3 edition

(2000), as well as his co-edited collection with David Matthews, *Reading the Medieval in Early Modern England*, Peter Lake's forthcoming arguments, and Anita Gilman Sherman's exemplary chapter on the play in her books on *Skepticism in Shakespeare and Donne* reviewed later in this essay.[1] Building on this emergent interest in the post-Reformation positioning of Shakespeare's responses to both past and present, Gillian Woods offers a persuasive reading of *Love's Labour's Lost* that interrogates what she evocatively describes as the 'Catholic symbolic residue embedded' in that 'insistently topical' play (p. 121).

Laurie Maguire introduces the section on 'How to Do Things with Text' with a description that many scholars involved in producing major new editions at present will recognize all too well: 'Pioneering textual work takes place in rare book rooms over many years; it strains the eyes, taxes one's patience, and sabotages one's social life.' As a result, she rightly asks the question how undergraduate students usually with papers and assignments to produce in a single semester can even begin to engage with this world. Certainly, Maguire has chosen fine exponents of this kind of painstaking scholarship to convey to readers the importance and excitement of this kind of research, but whether they provide any practical models for undergraduates to try and 'do' any of this for themselves is more questionable. Nevertheless, in Tiffany Stern's contribution, 'Watching as Reading: The Audience and Written Text in Shakespeare's Playhouse', Maguire has enabled a typically dazzling performance by this brilliant early modern scholar. In a carefully achieved argument that connects in very interesting ways with Julie Maxwell's earlier contribution, Stern explores the practice of 'reading critically' in the early modern theatre, suggesting that the effects and practices of commonplace book culture can be seen in the audience as well as in specific examples of characterization and dialogue in the play-texts themselves. The early modern practice of reading books out loud meant

---

[1] Gordon McMullan and David Matthews, eds., *Reading the Medieval in Early Modern England* (Cambridge, 2007).

that reading at this time was a highly 'social activity' (p. 137) and commonplace book culture meant that the garnering of quotations from plays, both as examples of good and bad writing, was a common response to the activity of playgoing. Manuscript books were also sold and distributed at playhouses, so there are manifold ways in which 'textual presences' can be recorded and accounted for at these sites of performance. Stern goes so far as to register this sense of 'textual presence' in the title boards and signboards used in open-air amphitheatrical productions.

Maguire's volume closes with a challenging article on performance criticism by Emma Smith, a scholar who has done more than most in recent years to revivify Shakespeare as a classroom text. While I share her sense of the value of speculative imaginings of performance as a means of access into the text-worlds of Shakespeare plays, I wasn't wholly convinced by the way in which this essay seemed to make the case for this kind of free-play in the seminar room at the expense of theatre history. It seems to me that the two practices can sit excitingly alongside each other, more phenomenologically based responses building on or enlightening theatre archaeology of a more traditional kind.

G. B. Shand's *Teaching Shakespeare* is an equally intriguing essay collection, a blend of autobiographical reflection, case studies of particular student bodies and classrooms, and examinations of particular means and modes of teaching Shakespeare, from the edited text, to performance, to Shakespeare on screen. Jean Howard heads up the volume with what is more a general, albeit impassioned, essay on mentoring postgraduate research students from an eminent Shakespearian and Richard Dutton offers a transatlantic comparison of UK and US university teaching from his unique perspective. Carol Chillington Rutter ends the volume with a heartfelt account of the great teaching that inspired her to study Shakespeare and that she aims to pass on to her own students. As someone who has had the pleasure of being one of those students, watching Carol's dynamic presence light up a lecture hall on cold, rainy English winter mornings, it was a pleasure to read her firsthand

account of why she does what she does and the deep pleasure she derives from it.

This diverse gathering of accounts and explorations also includes occasional devil's advocate approaches, such as Russ MacDonald's plea for a recuperation of authority in the classroom and the old-fashioned lecture. While that idea of 'Teaching Shakespeare' is perhaps the baton I felt least inclined to take up, there were some fascinating examples from experience offered by major figures in Shakespearian studies including David Bevington and Kathleen McLuskie. Bevington's beautifully achieved essay makes a case for the use of editorial technique and practice in the classroom, stressing that it operates as a particularly vivid and engaged form of close reading. The specific examples he offers from *King Lear* of this idea in action are extremely persuasive as he charts a seminar group's attention to the question of stage directions when Kent is placed in the stocks. Allowing students to discover for themselves that there is no formal stage direction to account for the moment of Kent's exit, or the extraction of a major item of property from the stage, Bevington is able to raise the idea of juxtaposition and the ebb and flow of performance on the early modern stage, as he suggests the visual and emblematic power of a decision to leave Kent visible in the stocks on stage when the persecuted and hunted Edgar appears from the hollow of a tree in which he has been hiding. Bevington's fine work is complemented in this volume by Anthony B. Dawson's, which thinks about performance-led criticism as opposed to textually driven scholarship in an essay entitled 'Teaching the Script'.

Theoretical approaches are represented here in the assured hands of Ramona Wray (on gender studies) and Ania Loomba (on concepts of race and ethnicity). Kathleen McLuskie's essay is a typically trenchant and important contribution to the debate about Shakespeare's role in the classroom of the future. Using the suggestive contrast between a 'thinker' and a 'dancer' (a binary derived from Samuel Beckett's *Waiting for Godot*, specifically from a speech by Pozzo), she asks whether in our rush to make Shakespeare available and accessible to the widest possible community of readers and per-formers, there is the danger of loss of detail and depth. Are we, she asks, just dancing on the glit-tering surface of the iconic Shakespearian canon, and is there any way back once this becomes a default position? There is a danger that McLuskie could be read as being oddly conservative and resis-tant to change and evolution in this stance – is she pleading for a return to 'old-style' scholarship and is there kinship with Russ McDonald in this regard? – but this is a contribution that provokes and demands response. Only this year in the UK, a change was wrought in the school GCSE English examination that will see students still required to study Shakespeare but only in extract form. Since often these extracts are studied via the prism of dif-ferent cinematic interpretations, how should uni-versity lecturers respond to an incoming under-graduate community which thinks of Shakespeare in fragments and through the cinematic medium first and foremost? As a proponent and practi-tioner of adaptation studies myself I do not want to argue against these updated means of teach-ing Shakespeare but there is a danger – and it is one that McLuskie rightly sounds the warning bell for in this essay – that this becomes a monolithic approach in itself and we need to be alert to the need for maintenance of nuance, textual complex-ity and a sense of historical difference in a teaching context if we are to do full justice to the remark-able body of work that remains the Shakespearian oeuvre.

A number of the contributions to *Teaching Shakespeare* – for example, those of Frances Teague and Miriam Gilbert – comment, not necessarily negatively, on the persistent tendency of students to want to discuss character in the plays, both as a first and a last resort. A series that has decided to con-front this pedagogic conundrum head-on is Con-tinuum's 'Character Studies' series, one which does not focus exclusively on Shakespeare but which has already published volumes on *Othello* and *Twelfth Night*. The latest addition to the list is a fine study of *Hamlet* by Michael Davies, which actually turned out to be one of my favourite reads of this year's large batch of critical studies.

Davies hooks the reader from the opening page with an inspired opening gambit that deploys the parodic figure of Hamlet the footman from Jonson, Chapman et al.'s *Eastward Ho!* to indicate that almost as soon as the character of Hamlet trod the boards (supposedly at the Globe in 1601 though we only have tantalizing suggestions rather than firm records of that fact as Ann Thompson and Neil Taylor's recent Arden 3 edition of the play reminded us) he was a subject for parody, allusion and spoof. What the 1605 *Eastward Ho!* example also indicates is that early modern responses to the character may be rather different from the contem-plative philosopher fashioned by Romantic theory and twentieth-century psychoanalytic frameworks, since what seems to be the essence of Hamlet's character here is his endless activity, his seeming inability to rest still on the stage. From the out-set then Davies establishes in the reader's mind the need for a historicized and nuanced understanding of character that will be his watchword through-out. In a striking chapter entitled 'The Man in Black' Davies also asks us to think anew about the first encounter with Hamlet on the stage as one which takes place through the prism of sight rather than the 'words, words, words' for which he is so renowned. Hamlet's 'inky cloak' in 1.2 of the play is, says Davies,' 'arguably . . . the single most important factor for us to consider when address-ing how Shakespeare initially presents him' (pp. 33–4). In this way Davies invites his undergradu-ate audience – for this is undoubtedly the target population of this text and the series in which it appears – to think in new ways, both historically informed and aesthetically engaged, about the stage type of the melancholic and the practical elements of the play's staging, including costume but also 'the stage properties that orbit Hamlet's person' (p. 37). This well-written and imaginatively conceived study also finds exciting ways to analyse the verse-drama of the play by suggesting that evidence of the ways in which Hamlet as a character plays with the stage type of the melancholic or malcontent can be found at the level of the line, and in partic-ular the tendency to hypermetricality identifiable in the soliloquies. If I wanted more of anything it would have been a sense of the ways in which space and embodiment of space also contribute to the creation of character on the stage, but Davies achieves a tremendous amount in his own restricted page-space. It is a volume that I have already recommended to my own students and which will find many friends.

One of the great strengths of Davies's approach, apart from his engaging style and smart selection of angles for focus, is his emphasis throughout on *Hamlet* as a performed text and in a similar vein another student-aimed publication, this time in the Palgrave-Macmillan 'Shakespeare Handbooks' series, on *Henry IV, Parts I and II*, James Loehlin manages to bring its focus plays alive on the page for tutors and students alike. Loehlin has long been a writer whose style I have greatly admired and he demonstrates here his impressive ability to engage both the familiar and unfamiliar reader with a play-text. This volume has a specific emphasis on performance but in the process of providing a scene-by-scene commentary, which admirably opens up rather than closes down performative possibilities, Loehlin also conveys the linguistic and geographical range of these paired history plays. He made me want to look afresh at often easily dismissed and frequently cut scenes such as 2.1 of Part I where we see the 'two carriers, . . . lanterns in their hands, create – through their sleepy manner, distinctive speech, and road-stained garments – a very, precise image of an inn-yard in the early morning' (p. 8). In this moment the world of early modern travel and the cultural and spatial significance of inns was reiterated for this reader and the significance of the tavern space in the plays more generally given added depth and energy. Loehlin, like Davies, can move deftly between the over-arching dramaturgy of a play to effects at the level of the line. Describing the linguistic register of these two unnamed carriers (who have not been seen before and will not be seen again, as Loehlin informs us, while at the same time stressing their importance to the overall effect), he informs us that 'The earthy images and simple, monosyllabic words create the smell of the stables' (p. 8). In fact, like me, Loehlin seems particularly fascinated by Shakespeare's deployment of

monosyllables at particular moments and for particular characters, and scholars of stylistics, who sometimes suggest that they have a monopoly on the capacity to study dramatic discourse and its cognitive and linguistic effects, would find much of interest and resonance in this study. Loehlin's great skill though is to weave these linguistic sensibilities with an understanding of the practical dimensions and operations of the early modern playhouse and the cultural dimensions of the same. The tavern scene in *Part I* in which Hal and Falstaff famously 'perform' the role of king is thereby compared to the performance of monarchy in early modern procession and pageantry, and the narrative and spatial dynamic of the knocking on the door that propels this scene, and the play, forward draws us back to the material conditions of the theatre itself.

Loehlin makes the mechanics of stage blocking say something pertinent in the context of this study; arguing for Shakespearian theatre as a 'theatre of physical presence', he makes the case that the dynamics of these two plays is in many respects about the 'forming and breaking of physical groupings' (p. 15). We seem almost to move into the adaptational domain of ballet and choreography and, perhaps as a result, we can begin to understand why creative artists such as Gustav Holst saw the potential for opera in these plays in the twentieth century. In this short but packed volume Loehlin not only provides a summary of the plays that allows students to consider alternative stagings and possibilities for many of the central moments, but also chapters on sources and cultural contexts and the stage and screen histories of the plays and their critical assessment over time. It is a volume that wears its learning lightly but every point is carefully researched and considered and the real achievement is the manner in which it both makes the plays available for interpretation and gives undergraduate readers the confidence to carry out those acts of interpretation for themselves.

Gabriel Egan's *Shakespeare* is one of a multitude of books on the shelves now that offer undergraduate students a guide to Shakespeare's works as a whole; here ostensibly the plays, discussed via a series of case-studies shaped by the notion of genre. But it is a welcome addition to an albeit already crowded stage. What Egan manages to do in the course of extended analyses of sample plays, including *Measure for Measure, Macbeth, Hamlet, Othello, Much Ado About Nothing,* and *A Midsummer Night's Dream,* is to offer the student-user an admirably inclusive account of several important current debates in Shakespeare scholarship, not least the perceived tension between those who subscribe to a performance-based understanding of his plays and those who buy into Lukas Erne's influential thesis about Shakespeare as a literary dramatist. Egan deftly links a discussion of both approaches into his introductory chapter and while individual readers may not always agree with specific readings or suggestions, it is part of the generous spirit of the study that it will allow students to find their own critical view and voice amidst its pages (surely the mark of the best textbook?). A particularly fine example of this comes in Chapter 6 on *Macbeth* (part of the volume's second section comprised of 'Critical Approaches'). This performance-led chapter manages to embrace the notion of the collaborative production of early modern drama and include Middleton's participation and intervention in the text and its performance history in impressive detail (a similar thing is achieved with *Measure for Measure* in the preceding chapter), alongside a detailed and vivid exploration of practical aspects of the play in performance such as exits and entrances, and the use of different stage levels in the performance. A typically subtle response to the notion of doubling in early modern theatre companies is Egan's consideration of the common doubling of Duncan and the Porter in the context of the alternate effects of their exits and entrances through different or the same portals onto the stage. If the Porter enters through the same door which the audience has only moments earlier been asked to perceive as the entrance to Duncan's chamber, Egan notes, there is a 'brief moment of cognitive dissonance which is resolved once the actor begins speaking' (p. 194).

It is a measure of Egan's achievement that I have already put this volume to use in my own undergraduate seminar rooms, as indeed I have Lukas Erne's *Shakespeare's Modern Collaborators,* a volume in the increasingly intriguing and provocative 'Shakespeare Now' series, which in its own words seeks to represent on the page 'ideas still heating in the mind'. Erne's short monograph (or 'minigraph' to borrow the general editors Ewan Fernie and Simon Palfrey's term) was not necessarily conceived as student 'textbook' in the manner of Egan's and yet it constitutes a taut and suggestive introduction to the role of editors and the question of editorial transmission of play-texts that will help to turn new students of Shakespeare onto what might otherwise seem the slightly arcane world of editing and collation. Just as Bevington's essay in *Teaching Shakespeare* argued for the value of teaching editorial practice as another form of close reading, so Erne finds traces of editorial presence in all areas of the textual life of Shakespeare, from the world of the book to the playhouse, but resists a negative or proprietorial response to this idea, celebrating instead the role of the editor as an additional collaboration in the historical production of meaning. There is a particularly fine chapter on 'Editing Stage Action' which will be of interest to hardened editors, actors and students alike.

SHAKESPEARE COLLECTED

A number of volumes this year collect previously published articles by a single author under one title: the two most significant of these are by Catherine Belsey and Marjorie Garber. Garber's cleverly titled *Profiling Shakespeare* draws on contemporary notions of profiling in the disciplines of psychology and criminology but also aims to offer its readers a rather different version of 'Shakespeare' to that found in conventional biographies. Garber describes her method as 'the obverse of biographical investigation', pursuing instead traces, repetitions and 'odd emphases' for evidence (p. 1). She is, of course, also concerned with Shakespeare as an 'effect' not least in postmodern culture. The collection offers up a series of provocative and informing arguments which in a sense revisit some of the shaping concerns of Garber's academic career thus far; so we get the 'authorship controversy' reworked in 'Shakespeare's Ghost Writers' and ideas of the ghost as a 'cultural marker of absence', memory or trace in '*Hamlet*: Giving Up the Ghost', as well as questions as to why Shakespeare is so central to the canon. There is no effort to iron out differences or inconsistencies in these arguments, which have been produced across time and in different circumstances, but there is much to be gained from reading them alongside, in juxtaposition, indeed in dialogue, with each other. Garber takes issue with a number of recent critical 'fetishes' and fads in the process, not least what she describes as the recent 'infatuation with history' among literary scholars which in her view has led to a 'certain overestimation of the object' (p. 195). While I am not sure I share her sense that the 'historical turn' was necessarily a disavowal of the prior 'linguistic turn' she nevertheless invites us at all stages to examine our own practices and assumptions. The examination of the social and cultural function and effect of Shakespearian quotation in the final essay in the collection embodies the very best of Garber's work. It is incisive, challenging, playful, and above all it is a source of the very pleasure that she herself regards as so key to the ongoing experience of Shakespeare.

Catherine Belsey's *Shakespeare in Theory and Practice* is, similarly, a collection of essays written and published over a long period. Interestingly, she has chosen to arrange them (with very little retrospective editing) not in date order but according to Shakespeare's own chronology. All of the essays attest to Belsey's career-long commitment to theory and its ability to deliver new ways of reading. Like many of the volumes discussed in the first section of this article, Belsey is committed to education in theory and in practice: 'Interpretation,' she says, 'is only to a degree intuitive: we can learn to do it in new ways' (p. 1). In her introduction she pays tribute to those figures who most influenced and shaped her own thinking, from Roland Barthes to Jacques Lacan, dismissing other critical schools of thought with fairly short shrift in the process: 'I was never a new historicist . . .', she declares, 'Too bland' (p. 8). Yet, as she herself acknowledges, several of the essays here are concerned with a kind of Cultural Materialism or embeddedness which would seem to share at least something with the new historical enterprise. Several of the contributions focus on her long-term interest in patterns and strategies of love and desire as they can be located in the Shakespearian text. Her innovative reading of the *Sonnets* alongside Barthes's *A Lover's Discourse: Fragments* has been very influential and it is good to see it reissued in print here. Her attention in this collection to materiality and wordplay is indicative of her considerable skills as a close reader, for all her championing of theory's ability to think in the abstract. Another essay on love and psychoanalysis (as applied to the particular example of *A Midsummer Night's Dream*) commences with the eminently quotable line, 'Love is inevitably citational . . . ' (p. 94). Elsewhere we get a potent reading of John of Gaunt's 'This sceptred isle' speech freshly relocated in its context in *Richard II* where we can once more appreciate it as a speech of 'reproach' rather than eulogy, an essay on Hamlet and conscience, and an impressive analysis of 'Iago the Essayist' which places the anti-hero of *Othello* in the context of Renaissance essayists and sceptics, such as Montaigne, rather than the more traditional theatrical legacy of the medieval Vice. In an archetypal neat move, Belsey closes on the matter of style, on the surface Iago's, but for this reader a sense of her own inimitable style as critic and theorist inevitably rose to the surface.

Michele Marrapodi's edited collection *Italian Culture in the Drama of Shakespeare and his Contemporaries: Rewriting, Remaking, Refashioning* commences with a learned critical overview of its own field, suggesting its prime concerns are with 'The aesthetics of intertextuality . . . interdiscursivity . . . and interlexicality' (pp. 5–6). Many of its rather traditional essays are interested in the cultural and discursive exchanges between Italian culture and the Shakespearian stage. Some familiar fields are revisited in the process, including the importance of *commedia dell'arte* to Shakespeare's plays (this topic is raised in essays by Louise George Clubb, Frances K. Barasch, and Robert Henke). Florio and Castiglione are re-examined as part of Shakespeare's and early modern London's inheritance and understanding of Italian political and linguistic culture in essays by Keir Elam and Adam Max Cohen respectively.

Marrapodi's introduction stresses the need for 'a reassessment of the dramatist's art of documentation in representing historical as well as imaginary urban realities, social settings and city-states' (p. 8). This kind of work is certainly visible in the contributions of J. R. Mulryne and John Drakakis, who both look at Shakespeare's representation of Venice in plays such as *The Merchant of Venice* and *Othello* as a rich hybrid of the mythic and imaginative associations of 'La Serenissima' and a form of documentary realism. Mulryne goes so far in his essay 'Between Myth and Fact' as to style *The Merchant of Venice* as a proleptic form of 'docu-drama' in the way that its evoked world resembles the genuine festive and ritual culture of Venice. Mulryne takes as his prime case-study the celebrations to welcome the French king Henri III in the sixteenth century, also referred to in Jonson's Venetian play, *Volpone*, some years later. In his complementary essay on 'Shakespeare and Venice' Drakakis asks us to consider the 'semiotic complexity of Venice as a geographical location' for Shakespeare and his contemporaries, suggesting that the plays are as much a critique as an invocation of myths accruing around the city-state in the early modern period. But for all this interest in the interaction between real and imagined geographies in this collection, it is surprisingly light on what has been a very rich field of theoretical studies in this area, with work being conducted in literature and performance studies and complementary disciplines such as cultural and historical geography. Similarly, the deference paid to linguistic analysis in this European-authored collection is admirable and welcome, but there remains a more ambitious collection to be produced that would bring into play current studies on creativity and interdiscursivity by practitioners of language and linguistics with this more recognizable form of comparative, intercultural analysis.

My discussions are necessarily limited largely to those essays on Shakespeare in volumes which range wider than just the Shakespearian canon, but it is worth adding that it is something of an irony that in some ways the most innovative and challenging essay in this collection (which, incidentally claims on its cover to include work on Richard Brome, another interesting deployer of Venetian settings for his drama, but fails to deliver on this – Brome does not even appear in the index) is on Middleton not Shakespeare. Perhaps inevitably in a year when Middleton publishing has taken off in the wake of the Gary Taylor Oxford University Press edition we are now beginning to see publication of much of the fruits of many years' labour by Taylor and fellow Middletonians in the archive. Celia Daileader's 'The Courtesan Revisited' in this collection, which makes a case for Middleton as a great sympathizer with the female position in early modern society, is a great essay, marred only for this reader by its insistence on reinscribing Jonsonian representations of female characters to the same kind of constrictive critical cage from which it seeks to liberate Middleton.

Perhaps the most cohesive and fully achieved collection of essays on Shakespeare this year is *Shakespeare and Childhood*, co-edited by the venture tripartite of Kate Chedgzoy, Susanne Greenhalgh and Robert Shaughnessy. Shaughnessy provides a thoughtful introduction and overview to the volume, hampered only by the fact that he makes detailed discussion of the book's cover image which will in many library copies already have been removed by the time readers encounter his references to the striking photograph of an amateur production of *A Midsummer Night's Dream*; perhaps the publisher should have been persuaded to repeat the image inside the covers of the collection as well? Chedgzoy and Greenhalgh introduce the two sections on 'Shakespeare's Children' and 'Children's Shakespeare' respectively. Chedgzoy, one of the more subtle theorists of early modern childhood in current practice, achieves a rather neat comparison between the fictional Miranda of *The Tempest* and her participation in the 'household' theatricals and island spectacles of her father in that play and the real-life actor, director and playwright Rachel Fane who as a teenager in the

1620s produced masques and entertainments in the context of her Northamptonshire aristocratic residence. What Chedgzoy is able to bring into view in the process is the complex world of 'imaginary and imaginative play' in the life of children, early modern or otherwise. This in turn sets the scene for the various essays on specific plays in this section which includes one by Catherine Belsey on the royal children of, in particular, the histories, but also the doomed Mamillius of *The Winter's Tale*, a collaborative piece by Hattie Fletcher and Marianne Novy on father–child relations, and an excellent and well-informed essay by Lucy Munro that considers *Coriolanus*'s obsession with the figure of the boy in the light of the success and impact, not least on Shakespearian dramaturgy, of the children's companies in the early modern commercial playhouses. In introducing the second section Susanne Greenhalgh brings more recent youthful engagements with Shakespeare into the frame, considering both the nineteenth century's highly particular constructions and manipulations of childhood experience and more recent encounters in the field of children's literature. Essays in this section include some very detailed studies (the value of the archive and new attentions to the archival domain is omnipresent in this volume), including Kathryn Prince on Victorian children's periodicals, Pascale Aebischer on theatrical family memoirs, and Chedgzoy herself on children's novels that deploy Shakespearian characters, tropes and themes. The volume is generous in its provision of a very full bibliography on its chosen topic as well as an appendix that identifies child characters in Shakespearian plays. This is a collection of frequently groundbreaking research but it is also impeccably conceived as a whole, presenting the very best example of what an essay collection should be and 'do'.

SHAKESPEARE IN THE MONOGRAPH

Despite my spirited defence at the start of this article of the value of work published under the aus-

pices of textbooks and student guides, it should be stressed that this year has seen the publication of some especially fine monograph studies of Shakespeare. Emily C. Bartels has provided an important and subtly argued study in the form of *Speaking the Moor: From 'Alcazar' to 'Othello'* which, as its title suggests, looks at Moorish characters on the early modern stage. This is no basic survey of that field, however. Building on the work of Michael Neill in particular, Bartels considers the complex sociocultural contexts from which those stage characters emerged. In an impressively argued book, she deftly interweaves chapters on actual and textual engagements with the Mediterranean world picture. Her focus is on a particular cultural moment, when in her own words 'the Moor seems to have captured England's imagination newly and urgently' (p. 19). Bartels is alert to her own innate desire to discover a form of early modern drama that is 'more radical' than it really is (p. 19), but in the process she provides impressive new analyses of the cultural impact of Richard Hakluyt's published accounts of his navigational enterprises and of the considerable pamphlet culture that grew up around accounts of the Barbary Coast. It would be wrong for this reviewer only to focus on those sections of the book concerned with Shakespeare since Bartels's case – and it is most persuasively made – is that *Othello* is just one piece in a complicated cultural jigsaw of imagined geographies, actual cultural encounter and practice, and the complex history of literary representation.

One chapter for example investigates with a new sense of context and urgency, Elizabeth I's repeated letters to the Lord Mayor of London, dating from 1596 onwards, ordering the deportation of 'divers blackamoors brought into this realme' (p. 100). We are very familiar with a cultural anxiety about 'strangers' in early modern London and how this played out within the diegetic worlds of much early modern drama, but Bartels stresses that this correspondence is a very specific instance of that and we would do well to think about Moorish characters who appeared on the commercial stages at this time in a new light as a result. Her reading of *Othello* is highly pertinent in this context. She moves consciously against more engrained readings of the play that see Othello as a 'stranger' in Venice, in a manner akin to the 'blackmoors' of Elizabeth I's epistles. Suggesting instead that Othello is distinctly located within Venetian society, in his 'lodging' or residence, which would have required some status within the city, then as now, Bartels explores the manner in which Othello only gradually descends 'into stereotype' as Iago's plot progresses. Reading *Othello* alongside texts both fictional and documentary from the period but also in the context of Shakespeare's evolving engagement with the figure of the Moor, Bartels finds a particularly vivid sense of intertheatricality at play: 'There can be no greater irony in *Othello* than that the figure of Iago is himself fashioned on a Moor (Aaron – in Shakespeare and Peele's *Titus Andronicus,* subject of an earlier chapter in this study, as, indeed, is Peele's own *Battle of Alcazar*), who is fashioned on a Jew (Barabas – in Marlowe's *The Jew of Malta*), who resembles a Turk (Ithamore)' (pp. 189–90). Bartels's scholarship throughout is an impressive combination of rigorous history combined with a theoretical verve and subtlety that for me was lacking from some of the other historically inspired analyses of Shakespeare plays this year.

Other stand-out contributions, however, include two studies that are designed around a comparative analysis of Shakespeare and Donne. Nancy Selleck's *The Interpersonal Idiom in Shakespeare, Donne, and Early Modern Culture* offers a kind of 'pre-history' of ideas of selfhood and identity that are usually only regarded as fully emerged by the later seventeenth century. In a linguistically sensitive and scientifically informed study – she invokes, in particular, recent developments in neuroscience and the identification of the relationship between neural networks and interpersonal experiences – Selleck offers what she describes as a 'field-based understanding' of Renaissance subjecthood (p. 15). Building on innovative work by Mary Thomas Crane and others on cognitive processing, as well as studies by Lynne Magnusson and fellow linguists on speech-act theory she explores the 'variety of kinds of selfhood available in the early modern period' (p. 7).[2] In the process,

she offers some intricate and convincing readings of plays such as *Hamlet* which have frequently been read in the context of ideas of subjectivity and selfhood but rarely with this attention to detail in terms of linguistic dynamic: 'Identity in *Hamlet*,' argues Selleck, 'is not just a question of the inwardness... of its protagonist, but of how inwardness is *socially deployed or interrogated*' (p. 16). As well as paying renewed attention to the significance of the humoural body and the language of humouralism in Shakespeare, Donne, and, inevitably, almost necessarily, Jonson, Selleck locates a body of work that is about sensory perception rather than abstract beauty and relates this both to developments in the new discipline of anatomy as a well as what she terms the 'ecological' self, which entails a 'sense of the self's embeddedness in a dynamic context' (p. 60). This seems to me an exciting new development in terms of analysing early modern theatre in practice and enables us to find links with other movements and research in performance studies more generally.[3] In the process invigorating studies are offered of *Hamlet, Every Man Out of His Humour* and Donne's verse and sermons. Perhaps it is indicative of my own leanings as a scholar, but Selleck's study seemed evidence of my overall sense that the most ambitious studies this year – those that advanced our thinking and practice in Shakespeare scholarship – tended to be those in which Shakespeare was not seen in isolation but as part of the theatre ecology of early modern society.

Another excellent example of just such an embedded study of Shakespearian drama is Anita Gilman Sherman's *Skepticism and Memory in Shakespeare and Donne.* Sherman's understandings of scepticism are heavily inflected by the work of

---

[2] See, for example, Mary Thomas Crane, *Shakespeare's Brain: Reading with Cognitive Theory* (Princeton, NJ, 2001) and Lynne Magnusson, *Shakespeare and Social Dialogue: Dramatic Language and Elizabethan Letters* (Cambridge, 1999). On speech-act theory, see also David Schalkwyk, *Speech and Performance in Shakespeare's Sonnets and Plays* (Cambridge, 2008).

[3] I am thinking in particular of Baz Kershaw's thought-provoking *Theater Ecology* (Cambridge, 2007).

Stanley Cavell (as the study openly acknowledges) and she is interested throughout the book in the way in which what she terms 'collective memory' often functions as a consolation for those beliefs and practices which scepticism itself would seem to undo. Her study is an informed and thoughtful engagement with the current very vibrant field of memory studies both in early modern scholarship and adjacent disciplines. She invokes postmodern ideas of countermonument and forgetting to provide a material focus for memory and nostalgia as practices and processes in the early modern era (and there are kinships in this materiality between her project and Selleck's in this regard). Fascinated by the hidden or subterranean, Sherman is eager to make readers aware of the 'disnarrated and the unnarrated' in her subjects' oeuvres. In the case of Shakespeare, she provides extended analyses of *The Winter's Tale* and *Henry VIII, or All is True* alongside Donne's sermons and the *Anniversaries*. The chapter on *Henry VIII* is particularly memorable itself. Sherman explores the ways in which Shakespeare and Fletcher excite 'different modalities of experience' in audiences for this play in order to explore the phenomenon of scepticism, unsettling in the process received history via the mobilization of 'collective memory'. The 'collective memory' that the play-text is mobilizing is of course that of a pre-Reformation Catholic England and in this way Sherman continues work by historians on the particular resonances and residues of this play mentioned earlier in the discussion of specific contributions to *How to Do Things with Shakespeare*. '*All is True*,' states Sherman, 'exposes the state's appropriation of religious memory' (p. 135). What informs both Selleck and Sherman's studies as well as Bartels' is exactly the kind of informed and developed theoretical thinking that I was bemoaning the lack of in some of the more conventional essay collections released this year. Sherman is able to bring into play both a developed understanding of historical and theological context (thinking through the Blackfriars theatre itself as a site of memory and resonance for this play) and a highly ambitious set of theoretical frameworks derived from anthropology and history as well as literary studies.

This is also a study alert to experiential and phenomenological responses in ways that I think will contribute to a new shaping of the field of theatre history and archaeology over the next few years.

Sherman's study as a whole is a demonstration of the rich readings that can be produced by an encounter between literary study and philosophy as disciplines and David Bevington's *Shakespeare's Ideas: More Things in Heaven and Earth* might be seen as a parallel contribution to this interdisciplinary domain. His book purports to be about the philosophical, political and cultural issues that concern the plays. However, I have to confess that the chapters that inspired me most were actually those where Bevington, surely one of the greatest editors of early modern drama, gets back to the material conditions of the playhouses and the plays. While for me the more theoretical chapters on ideas of acting and on religious controversy and issues of faith (which were oddly anaemic, displaying none of the vivid sense of context and urgency that Sherman's work achieved on related matters and texts) fell somewhat flat, the book came alive on the subject of witchcraft, because it got back to the physical conditions of staging and representation. Bevington's prose seems to catch fire again once he gets back into the theatre, describing how and where the witches in *Macbeth* could have risen up onto the stage, as well as how and where the 'fiends' who enter to Joan la Pucelle in *Henry VI* would have entered the scene. There is an unmistakeable Christian undertow to what Bevington writes here, and he himself makes that explicit in the closing section. It left me feeling a little uncomfortable as a reader, as if a problematic melding were taking place between personal belief and practice and a critical account of the plays. It is to the David Bevington who lights up the page and the seminar room and who is so clearly visible in his essay in *Teaching Shakespeare* that I will be more tempted to return and to direct my own students in future.

Joan Fitzpatrick's *Food in Shakespeare* is described as 'the first detailed study of food and feeding in Shakespeare's plays', though it clearly complements work by Robert Appelbaum and others, and in the process it is a volume that engages with medicine and the body as well as wider social structures.[4] The humours again resurface here as a crucial informing framework for early modern belief. Interestingly, for Fitzpatrick, food and drink are a key point of access to the study of character that so exercised the student subjects of many of the teaching textbooks discussed above. This is a well-written book and there is much illuminating detail on early modern diet (as applied to Sir John Oldcastle and the Falstaff plays). I did feel it was a volume that would have greatly benefited from some illustrative material and in these cash-strapped times it would still behove publishers to see the value in visual material on the page. The associations between foodstuffs and regional and national identities are mapped in the second chapter on *Henry V* and *Macbeth* and a rather more unexpected account of vegetarianism and the stage type of the melancholic is proffered in the chapter on *As You Like It* and *The Winter's Tale*. Other chapters look at famine and dearth, looking in particular at *Thomas More*, *Pericles* and *Coriolanus*, and what Fitzpatrick terms 'profane consumption' in *Titus Andronicus*, *Timon of Athens* and *Hamlet*. There is evidence of careful study here but the closet social and cultural historian in me wanted more on the world of receipts, cookbooks and kitchens in the period.

In her book, Fitzpatrick, like critics before her, reads the witches' cauldron in *Macbeth* as an inversion of domestic norms. The most stunning exposition of this idea, however, is to be found in another study this year. Chris Laoutaris's *Shakespeare's Maternities: Crises of Conception in Early Modern England* was, for me at least, a book not really helped by its title, which suggests a focused study of conception and birth in the early modern period, a topic which one would imagine would have fairly strict parameters. A quick glance through the book's generously illustrated pages (and in this respect it is the opposite of Fitzpatrick's text-only study of food – proof, were it needed, that some publishers at least are willing still to invest in the visual apparatus of understanding early modern culture) would appear to confirm this as we confront images of the womb, of dissections of dead pregnant women, Italian christening plates and so

on. But taken in the round this book is much more than the delimited (albeit valid) study I would seem to be describing. What I found as I read on was a densely argued, archivally rich, but also sociologically complex account of responses to the female body and gendered corporeality in the early modern period. Laoutaris's study moves out from the archives of the Barber-Surgeons' Hall in London (a still much under-used archive, although Laurie Maguire, a scholar whose work is evoked in several places in this article, is one of the key practitioners working with this material at present) and an account of a now familiar sense of the increasing medicalization and masculinization of the birthing chamber in this period to embrace a whole range of 'materials of evidence' including textual and iconographic traces as well as actual artifacts and remains (p. 17).

In the course of the book, Laoutaris has recourse to anatomical broadsides, pornographic plates, *Wunderkammers*, fountains and clothing, amongst many other sources of knowledge. This is a study which is ambitious in its interdisciplinary methods and approaches as well as intellectually erudite in its production of meaning. I had not been expecting in a study of 'Shakespearean maternities', for example, a detailed study of the vogue for fountains and grottoes, often featuring the female form, in the late sixteenth and early seventeenth century, and alongside Shakespeare's texts Laoutaris's work sheds light on much related material in Jacobean court masques and household entertainments. Fundamental to his work on these sites and their attendant statuary is a recuperation of the 'language of wonder' and a brilliant reading of *The Tempest* is produced out of this historical and architectural evidence base. As Laoutaris puts it, 'Shakespeare's *Tempest* transports its audiences to an artificial island, a world of grotto-like spaces, rocky pools, fertile inlets, streams, underground conduits and groves. At its centre is a cave-dwelling monster – a prodigy of nature' (p. 121). As well as shedding

---

4 See Robert Appelbaum, *Aguecheek's Beef, Belch's Hiccup and other Gastronomic Interjections: Literature, Culture and Food in among the Early Moderns* (Chicago, 2006).

light on the play's deployment of automata and special effects, however, he produces a persuasive reading of the play that builds out from the sense of wonder associated with early modern voyages and exhibitions (and exhibited after the fact in spaces such as John Tradescant's 'Cabinet of Curiosities') to suggest that one of the things Caliban also represents in this play is 'geological and hydrological knowledge' (p. 137), despite Prospero's concerted efforts to define him as 'a product rather than a knowledgeable surveyor of these spaces' (p. 138). This is an inspirational response to the play that manages to harness evidential material from natural history, the writing and performance of Elizabethan exploration, and the semiotics of portraiture and maps. The study continues in the same impressive vein when Laoutaris turns to the topic of witchcraft, a well-trodden field in which he is able to find something new to say. Starting with a fascinating account of a series of objects and artifacts found in a house in Highgate Hill, London in 1961 during building work, which appear to be physical testimony to early modern practices of warding off evil or *maleficium*, Laoutaris develops outwards from an account of the archaeological location of these objects clustered around thresholds, doors, entries and portals to households, to the suggestion that 'The materials of magic were often the very stuff of routine labour in the household economy' (p. 158). He then applies these observations to the specific textual and performative example of *Macbeth*, revivifying the study of witchcraft as phenomenon and practice in this play as a result. Stressing the importance and persistence of the 'paraphernalia of witchcraft' in the play (p. 176), items such as pots, chalices, cauldrons, and animal and human remains, it is argued that the play at its heart is concerned with a 'threat to the integrity of the body and the household'. Any future director of the Scottish play surely could not help but be inspired to a newly informed staging of the text on reading about the ways in which the play makes manifest the circulation of familiar objects in newly alienated contexts, how the playworld appropriates objects and invests them with demonic meaning (p. 176). Other chapters look

at the monumental culture adhering to women in death and funereal ritual in the early modern period as well as the textual traces of mothers' legacies. This is a learned study which succeeds in mobilizing ideas of space, medicine, archaeology and cultural practice with considerable ease and lucidity. It is a very fine book and should reach a far wider audience than its slightly lacklustre title might seem to identify.

Patrick Cheney's *Shakespeare's Literary Authorship* is in many respects a companion volume to his earlier *Shakespeare National Poet-Playwright*.[5] His interest is less in the performance-based collaborative creative force that seems to have risen to the surface in so many other works this year and more in the published poet. In this context Cheney revisits some key works from the vantage point of established literary and generic categories in Shakespeare's own time, applying them in innovative ways to the canon. Exploring both *The Rape of Lucrece* and *Troilus and Cressida*, for example, he asks 'What would a study of epic look like if approached through works lying outside epic's formal boundaries?' (p. 53). From this position, *Hamlet* becomes for Cheney 'a play about the death of epic as a Western literary form' (p. 61). It is 'post-epic' because it is 'bent on eliminating heroic values' (p. 61). This vein of argument is one exemplary instance of points in the study where I wanted a more comparative account of early modern writing to come into play, to see Shakespeare in a wider and therefore more nuanced context than his own canon. Where does this category of 'post-epic', after all, leave Milton's *Paradise Lost* which in so many ways appears to effect its own poetic and literary engagement with the world of practical theatre? The 'bookish' quality of plays such as *Titus Andronicus* is certainly well established and Cheney pays welcome attention to the extensive presence of lyric poetry in plays as diverse as *As You Like It*, *Henry V* and *The Tempest*. I was fascinated by the specific sense of geography which Cheney ascribed to these 'lyric' moments in the

---

[5] Patrick Cheney, *Shakespeare: National Poet-Playwright* (Cambridge, 2004).

plays: 'If poet-figures produce lyrics,' he says, 'they do so in specific geographic locales . . . most memorably the countryside with pastoral, as in *As You Like It* . . . and the city with epic and romance, as in *Antony and Cleopatra*' (pp. 100–1). These arguments seem persuasive enough on the page but brought into play with a whole other body of work that has sought to examine the particular local and geographic specifics of Shakespeare and early modern drama they can seem too broad, too sweeping to be entirely satisfactory. Cheney is surely right to suggest that Shakespeare 'uses the stage to associate theatrical space with [specific] poetic genres' (p. 101) but this cannot be the only means of reading or understanding those spaces. Cheney himself appears to admit as much when he explores those impulses in the plays to break free of what he terms 'the literary', where characters break out of blank verse. These moments when Cheney leads us into the actual point of impact of language in the theatre are when the argument of the book seems most keen and alive. Cheney is a superb close reader and while in many respects I felt myself at odds with the major premises of this densely written study, itching to get back to the practical and material conditions of the early modern playhouse, I still found myself enchanted by the attention to poetry that he compels us to have.

In another linguistically alert study, Laurie Maguire's *Shakespeare's Names* seeks to interrogate language's relation to material objects and entities in Shakespeare's plays. It is interested in the 'lexical and the local' stresses of the author (p. 4). Maguire is explicit from the outset about her 'formalist methodology' and looks at the historical debates around nomenclature. As well as considering rituals and ceremonies of naming she also considers the potential causal effect. Do names create identity? This is an intriguing way to come at established ideas of language and power in the Shakespearian canon. Perhaps inevitably, she starts out with a detailed consideration of that play in which names seem to *do* so much, culturally and in terms of plot and action, that is *Romeo and Juliet*. Maguire sees this as a play of and about clash, not least at the level of language (p. 55) and she builds on this

via some fascinating digressions into the worlds of translation and adaptation. The following chapters consider in turn 'the mythological name', looking in particular at Helen of Troy, and the manifold narratives in which her story and name circulated, and then at various deployments of the diminutive 'Kate' in Shakespeare's plays. Maguire makes recourse at various turns to specific performance examples in an unusual and ambitious book. Her final recourse is to place-names, concentrating on Ephesus in *The Comedy of Errors* and suggesting that even at the level of place-name the play embodies 'duality, polarity, antithesis, symbiosis, fusion, binary oppositions' (p. 153). There is, as ever, much interesting and challenging suggestion in the work that Maguire presents here. I was never entirely convinced that the book had fully exhausted its own subject of focus and suspected that there might have been an even deeper, more cohesive study to emerge had greater time and space been available.

By contrast to this seeming plea for additional pages and length, the shorter form than the traditional monograph of volumes in the Continuum 'Shakespeare Now' series has already been mentioned, but the innovative approach of this series (already highlighted in the discussion above of Lukas Erne's *Shakespeare's Modern Collaborators*) doesn't just reside at the level of the conceptualizing of the study, but in some volumes in the print history of the text itself. Henry S. Turner's *Shakespeare's Double Helix* is a fascinating and sometimes infuriating text that is essentially two books in one. On the left-hand-side pages there is a more conventional study of *A Midsummer Night's Dream* that encompasses topics such as myth, nature, magic and magical phenomena, mimesis and translation. The second 'book', to be found on the right-hand-side pages of the volume, is less closely tied to a Shakespearian text though it uses both the phenomenon of Shakespeare and some of the specific events of *Dream* as its starting point. This second volume is ostensibly a consideration of science and particular branches of the field such as genetic engineering and biotechnology as a form of poetics (see, for example, p. 7). En route, Turner looks at subjects as diverse as the act of scientific nomenclature, olfactory sciences (brilliantly connected through the damask rose to the dialogue and action of *A Midsummer Night's Dream*), and biomimetics from the standpoint of a literary scholar. Turner himself suggests that the two embedded and entwined studies in the volume can be read simultaneously but I found that virtually impossible, fast proceeding to a state of cognitive meltdown when I attempted it. I read the left-hand first and the right-hand second and actually found that once I had got to the end of the second it was well worth my while returning to the first and rereading it. I found it a whole lot more stimulating second time around and could see the (scientific as well as artistic) premise behind many of its topics and organizational sections far more clearly as a result. So by the end I was fully won over to the complicated structure, which Turner himself describes as modelling both the intertwining of the DNA double helix model of Crick and Watson and Titania's woodbine or honeysuckle from the play. This is a difficult but eventually worthwhile attempt to bring the poetic and the scientific use of metaphor and action together and is worth the patience of the slightly resistant reader.

At the other end of the scale, perhaps, from the 'Shakespeare Now' volumes' attempts at concision, stands Gordon McMullan's major publication this year on *Shakespeare and the Idea of Late Writing*. In the course of its nearly 400 pages, McMullan attempts to take on the concept of 'lateness' and its role in the construction of career trajectories for canonical authors (and composers – it is a mark of this book's interdisciplinary credentials that it finds the most trenchant work on 'lateness' in the field of musicology and reapplies that to Shakespeare and the early modern scholarship with considerable skill). McMullan is, self-confessedly, establishing the concept of 'lateness' in his study only to deconstruct and challenge it. He describes this as a conscious act of 'critical iconoclasm', since he seeks to demonstrate that 'late style' is an 'elite concept' developed to shore up a certain aspect of canon formation and protection (p. 11). Comparing constructions of late Shakespeare to analogous careers such as Milton's, Mozart's and Beethoven's as well

as novelist Henry James's fashioning of his own late style in the shadow of an idea of the Shakespearian, McMullan's wide-ranging and challenging study asks us to rethink the particular position of plays such as *The Tempest* both in the Shakespearian canon per se and in the wider field of the discipline. The notion of a 'conscious writerly trajectory' (p. 25), the idea of a career having an identifiable beginning, middle and end, sits rather uncomfortably for McMullan in the version of collaborative, sometimes happenstance, early modern cultural and specifically theatrical production that his own academic career has to date been influential in conveying. Chapter 4 of this study is the one which focuses in most clearly on this topic and is for me the backbone of the whole argument. Via a careful comparison of the Shakespearian career with other contemporaries, not least Webster and Jonson, but also within the context of recent repertory studies which have recuperated for us the active idea of a 'company style' in this period, McMullan builds his case in detailed, step-by-step arguments. From this point of achievement, he can then return to the canon afresh to reconsider the significance of *The Tempest* and *King Lear* to the twentieth century, on both stage and screen, as a product of a philosophical concern with lateness, death and the achieved career, authorial or otherwise. Like many of the other finer monograph studies on Shakespeare this year, McMullan's benefits from his ability to meld the archival discipline of the literary historian with the conceptual imagination of the theorist. The particular theoretical voice who 'haunts' this volume is, by McMullan's own admission, Theodor Adorno, returning us to the world of musicology which I have already argued is central to McMullan's purpose, and which, I would suggest, is part of a wider engagement between the disciplines of music and literature in the field of early modern studies which is just beginning to bear fruit in publication terms.

I want to make an ending, though, with an account of two of the finest monographs published this year – and I suspect in any – both, incidentally, written by professors at the University of St Andrews which may or may not say something about the elixir of Scottish waters. Lorna Hutson has long been one of the finest minds in early modern scholarship and her new book confirms this status. *The Invention of Suspicion: Law and Mimesis in Shakespeare and Renaissance Drama* is a heavyweight publication in all senses of the term. Hutson limns her personal intellectual project in terms of tracking the 'important changes [which] took place in the rhetoric of dramatic narrative . . . in late sixteenth-century England' and the ways in which they 'corresponded closely to developments in popular legal culture' (p. 1). For Hutson the training in grammar provided by early modern educational institutions was also an apprenticeship in ideas and methods of providing proof and evidence. She uncovers, as a result, in much early modern drama a proleptic performance of what would come to be described as forensic science; and it is perhaps unsurprising that the play-text of *Hamlet* proves particularly central to her argument. This is, as its title suggests, a study that invokes far more than just Shakespeare in the making of its case and is, I would claim, also one of the more important works to be published on Ben Jonson in recent years. In Hutson's capable hands we see a Jonson who is not only a celebrant of theatrical practice and possibility, but someone whose reputation for closed and controlling endings to his plays begins now to look like a fundamental misreading (Hutson persuasively argues that *Volpone* is the exception rather than the rule – and even there the epilogue has always been an invitation to theatre audiences to question the closure, legal and ethical, supposedly achieved in the final act). In the course of the book Hutson asks us to consider such complex ideas as 'evidential uncertainty' (p. 17) at the level of plot. She casts fresh light on the well-worn topic of revenge drama by thinking about the 'forensic rhetoric of the plot' and recasting Hamlet himself as a would-be amateur detective. Throughout she skilfully weaves a deep attention to the nuances of performance and dramaturgy with an unparalleled comprehension of legal and jurisdictional practice in the period. Often easily dismissed 'recognition plots' (such as Jonson's *The Case is Altered* or Shakespeare's *The Comedy of Errors*) become newly per-

tinent within this framework and make us aware again of the Inns of Court presence in the audiences for these plays as a shaping force. As well as giving impressive accounts of the evolving role of local officials in the administration of justice in the early seventeenth century and early modern drama's complicated response to this phenomenon not least through a series of plays featuring Justices of the Peace, what Hutson provides is an exemplary analysis of dramatic technique. She is an attentive historian, a fine close-reader, and an exemplary theorist and this monograph is a considerable achievement that will impact upon the way in which many of us write about legal presences and practices in early modern drama.

Andrew Murphy's equally impressive *Shakespeare for the People: Working-Class Readers, 1800–1900* shares some of its archival territory with the previously discussed collection *Shakespeare and Childhood* in that it is concerned with the nineteenth-century engagement, some might say obsession, with Shakespeare. Murphy's focus is on the printed form in which Shakespeare captivated working-class lives and imaginations and in this respect he is building on the considerable achievements of historians of the nineteenth century including John Burnett, Jonathan Rose, David Vincent and David Mayall (all generously acknowledged in the introduction to this book). What Murphy is able to offer in the process is a detailed and considered account of nineteenth-century working-class culture, not least in the context of educational developments (the rise of day schools for the poor, for example) and the emergence of social movements such as the working men's clubs and mechanics institutes that were a prime social and cultural facilitator in many major cities and towns throughout that century. The central evidence base for these considerations is a set of nineteenth-century autobiographies and in his introduction Murphy offers up a calm, rational discussion and justification of his sample, acknowledging the limited female presence as well as the self-selecting approach of looking for references to Shakespeare. The product of this painstaking research and selection process is, though, a deeply revealing, often moving, study. In chapters on 'The Educational Context', 'The Publishing Context', 'Reading' and 'Political Shakespeare' we are able to map broader social movements – the effects of cheap, easily available editions of Shakespeare on wider efforts to educate the poor, for example – through the vivid individual story or anecdote. The second chapter introduces us to innovations such as circulating libraries and one particularly moving story of a North Durham shepherd who exchanged reading with his fellow field-workers via the use of sheep walls (recounted in the autobiography of Robert Skeen, p. 72). Andy Goldsworthy, the British environmental artist who has done much of late to draw our attention to structures in the landscape such as sheep walls and penfolds as art may be moved to realize the kind of continuity of practice this represents. There are equally inspiring tales of workers who shared wages to be able to purchase particular anthologies or collections in which the poetry of Shakespeare, often in the form of extracts from the plays themselves, frequently loomed large.

Murphy demonstrates, with considerable sensitivity towards his subjects, the ways in which the thirst for learning and for the very particular act of reading Shakespeare were sometimes thwarted by the everyday nature of working-class life; long working hours and poor lighting in the evening often militating against the obtainment of private reading space required. The importance of access becomes the main undertow to the social and cultural history offered throughout. In a year when this particular scholar's office shelves were groaning under the weight of all the new publications in Shakespeare studies and at those times when their spines seemed more a reproach than a pleasure, it was chastening to read about Charles Shaw, a potter in Tunstall, Staffordshire, who derived almost immeasurable pleasure from being able to establish in his latter years a study of sorts, a room of his own, which he furnished with an iron stove, a small desk and two small bookshelves (p. 95). 'I don't know what a university atmosphere is,' he writes, 'I have dreamt of it, but I knew when I entered this little room at night I was in another

world' (p. 95). Reading in his room, Shaw felt he was 'as a giant refreshed with new wine' and there can be no better description, even for the most hardened of academics, of the ongoing excitement of the kind of inspirational research and engagement that Murphy's monograph undoubtedly represents.

If there is any quibble that I have with this volume it comes with the 'afterword', which, like too many Shakespeare publications I saw this year, felt obliged to make a gesture, however cursory, to the contemporary moment, a need to 'make Shakespeare relevant'. I am not sure if the drive comes from the publishing companies themselves but it can create a surprisingly flat closure to important scholarly works, which seems to me counterproductive. The chapter in which Murphy recounts the twentieth-century shift towards a different formulation of popular working-class culture than that he has been delineating in the nineteenth century, as represented by figures such as Richard Hoggart and Raymond Williams, is useful; it is the brief 'afterword' that tries to come right up to the present day that feels somewhat more cursory and arbitrary in the context of an otherwise scholarly and highly achieved study. To return to those sub-Beckettian categories of thinking and dancing that Kathleen McLuskie outlined for us in her essay in *Teaching Shakespeare*, I would argue that Murphy's is the text of a thinker and there is no need to perform the kind of dancing with Shakespearian surfaces that McLuskie has asked us to be aware of and concerned about for the future. The value of Shakespeare and all these books were clear enough to Charles Shaw in his Tunstall study and that is good enough for me.

WORKS REVIEWED

Bartels, Emily C., *Speaking the Moor: From 'Alcazar' to 'Othello'* (Philedlphia, 2008)

Belsey, Catherine, *Shakespeare in Theory and Practice* (Edinburgh, 2008)

Bevington, David, *Shakespeare's Ideas: More Things in Heaven and Earth* (Oxford, 2008)

Chedgzoy, Kate, Susanne Greenhalgh and Robert Shaughnessy, eds., *Shakespeare and Childhood* (Cambridge, 2007)

Cheney, Patrick, *Shakespeare's Literary Authorship* (Cambridge, 2008)

Davies, Michael, *Hamlet* (London and New York, 2008)

Egan, Gabriel, *Shakespeare* (Edinburgh, 2007)

Erne, Lukas, *Shakespeare's Modern Collaborators* (London and New York, 2008)

Fitzpatrick, Joan, *Food in Shakespeare: Early Modern Dietaries and the Plays* (Aldershot, 2007)

Garber, Marjorie, *Profiling Shakespeare* (London, 2008)

Hutson, Lorna, *The Invention of Suspicion: Law and Mimesis in Shakespeare and Renaissance Drama* (Oxford, 2007)

Laoutaris, Chris, *Shakespearean Maternities: Crises of Conception in Early Modern England* (Edinburgh, 2008)

Loehlin, James N., *Henry IV Parts I and II: A Guide to the Texts and their Theatrical Lives* (London and New York, 2008)

McMullan, Gordon, *Shakespeare and the Idea of Late Writing: Authorship in the Proximity of Death* (Cambridge, 2007)

Maguire, Laurie, ed., *How to Do Things with Shakespeare* (Oxford, 2008)

Maguire, Laurie, *Shakespeare's Names* (Oxford, 2007)

Marrapodi, Michele, ed., *Italian Culture in the Drama of Shakespeare and his Contemporaries* (Aldershot and Burlington, VT, 2007)

Murphy, Andrew, *Shakespeare for the People: Working-Class Readers, 1800–1900* (Cambridge, 2008)

Selleck, Nancy, *The Interpersonal Idiom in Shakespeare, Donne, and Early Modern Culture* (London and New York, 2008)

Shand, G.B., ed., *Teaching Shakespeare: Passing it On* (Oxford, 2009)

Sherman, Anita Gilman, *Skepticism and Memory in Shakespeare and Donne* (London and New York, 2008)

Turner, Henry S., *Shakespeare's Double Helix* (London and New York, 2007)

2. SHAKESPEARE IN PERFORMANCE
reviewed by EMMA SMITH

Two books, particularly significant in that they will stimulate and enable new work, locate performance authority in two different agents. John Russell Brown's *The Routledge Companion to Directors' Shakespeare* gathers thirty-one contributors each writing on a single director judged to be innovative in his (usually – on this more later) own time, to have a canon of work spanning some years to show development or change, and to have influenced other directors. Some of the figures highlighted are expected: it is good to have Maria Shevtsova's account of Peter Brook's working methods, and to read Matthew Wilson Smith's reconstruction of the political and technical genesis of Orson Welles's Harlem *Macbeth*. I for one was less familiar with some of the European directors selected: the work of Roger Planchon, including a prominent *Henry IV* in Lyons, or the importance of Giorgio Strehler to Italian dramatizations of Shakespeare with his *commedia dell'arte* Trinculo and Stephano (a relief from their so often being Scottish) and

Brechtian *Coriolanus*. Some contributors have the knack of bringing productions into visual life – Carol Rutter on Deborah Warner's *Titus Andronicus*, for example – although the understandable pragmatic decision not to include photographs does mean that a number of the productions cited remain very two-dimensional. The choice of subjects fills in some mid-century gaps with Guthrie, Byam Shaw, Iden Payne and Granville Barker all getting proper attention to their impact. Some directors are more familiar to English-speaking readers in relation to specific performances, and here the narrative accounts helpfully situate, say, Peter Zadek's challenging *Othello* as a 'Shakespeare-negro, not a real one' in the context of a longer career of engagement with Shakespeare's plays in Hamburg, Berlin and Vienna. Directors known largely for Shakespeare films – Zeffirelli, Welles, Taymor – have their familiar and accessible cinema work revealingly reinstated alongside past theatrical explorations. Occasionally the chapters drift towards PR puffs for particular directors or seem to draw heavily on self-assessments rather than other forms of evidence. Christian M. Billing's summary of Barrie Rutter's career reads like an Arts Council pitch or honorary degree citation, whereas Lesley Wade Soule's account of Joan Littlewood's influence seems ultimately to lack confidence in her subject. Implicit in Russell Brown's project is the idea that the director is a, or perhaps the, dominant creative presence in twentieth-century theatre and, for the most part, his contributors stay within that brief. Bridget Escolme's characteristically precise and suggestive analysis of Mark Rylance, self-proclaimed 'actor-manager' at the new Globe, allows both her subject and her essay to challenge the paradigm, since what she argues about Rylance's importance is his innovative implication of the audience in the production of theatrical meaning. Her account of the Globe's *Julius Caesar*, in which a potentially disruptive audience is both contained and exploited as the Roman crowd, is particularly acute to the riskiness of this kind of derogation of theatrical responsibility.

In *Performing Shakespeare's Tragedies Today*, a revealing account of productions of *King Lear*, *Hamlet*, *Othello* and *Macbeth*, Michael Dobson's articulate interviewees address an audience more directly through print than their theatres tend to encourage in performance. Like the *Players of Shakespeare* series that provides Dobson's model, these accounts combine clichéd – and knowing – thespian solipsism with real insight into the plays (or, at least, it's easier to identify the actors' brand of solipsism as such, unlike that of the academic register we more usually adopt). So Greg Hicks, playing Ghost, Player and Gravedigger in Boyd's 2004 *Hamlet* discusses getting his 'inner psyche into a raw place' and talks lucidly and intelligently through ideas about the emotional impact of the Ghost as a 'withered, pallid, tormented, dead thing who was horribly there but also horribly wasn't', and about experimenting with other-worldy percussive rhythms of speech and movement. Imogen Stubbs is thoughtful and provocative on the patrilinear tendency of *Hamlet* in production, on Trevor Nunn's paternal relationship with his young

Hamlet at the Old Vic (2004), and on the ways in which this dynamic can exclude women from the world of the theatre as well as that of the play. Her Gertrude 'cherished a celebrity-magazine idea of glamour around herself', but the challenges of this 'very strange underwritten part' from Stubbs's perspective include the problematic account of Ophelia's death. Stubbs's account of this speech, with its 'mildly obscene botany' and the questions begged about why Gertrude doesn't try to help Ophelia brings out its tilt towards bathos (Claudius and Laertes 'did sometimes get terrible giggles'), and is a model of the strengths of the book in combining rehearsal anecdote, literary criticism and personal insight. Elsewhere Antony Sher talks about playing Iago, Sam West Hamlet, Simon Russell Beale Macbeth, Sian Thomas Lady Macbeth, David Warner King Lear, John Normington Lear's Fool, Nonso Anozie Othello and Amanda Harris Emilia.

Despite their editors' best efforts, both of these books reflect a Shakespearian performance world dominated by men. One apparent riposte to this worldview is in the title of David Mann's *Shakespeare's Women: Performance and Conception* – but on closer inspection, it isn't. Mann's emphasis on performer over role means that his analysis of the transvestite early modern theatre uncovers, as it were, a thoroughly male world. Interestingly, Mann's tabulation of female roles in early modern plays sees a remarkable statistical continuity across the adult and children's companies, and between the Elizabethan/Jacobean period and the Restoration stage, leading him to argue that women's roles are limited not for logistical but for ideological reasons: they're just not that interesting to male playwrights and audiences. Mann suggests that female characters should be seen less as psychological studies (although that might also be said for male characters) and more as '(often incidental) male dramatic constructs', and argues that female roles were probably taken by experienced experts, rather than pre-pubescent juveniles, who nevertheless played male roles in those plays with little demand for their cross-dressed specialism. Biographical evidence identifies the Duchess and Cariola in the revival of *The Duchess of Malfi* as played by actors around twenty and seventeen years old respectively; although Alexander Gough was only twelve when playing Caenis in Massinger's *The Roman Actor*. Mann's emphasis throughout is on collating and reassessing available evidence, and this identifies trends and debunks assumptions in numerous enlightening ways. But sometimes evidence is less fun and less suggestive than criticism ought to be, and sometimes Mann's own literary criticism is a little wooden. Summarizing *Edward II* as demonstrative of 'an uncompromising moral on the dangers of sodomy' doesn't seem to read the nuances of either the play and its critical reception or the word 'sodomy' with sufficient delicacy; suggesting that Valerie Traub's subtle argument – Mann's adjective 'elaborate' does not commend it – about same-sex female eroticism in Renaissance culture 'was not perceived as such by an Elizabethan dramatist and his audience, and the proof of this lies in the detail of the lines' (of Heywood's *The Golden Age*) substitutes for Traub's densely associative interpretation a historically cautious but critically bathetic reading. There's much positive to be said about this disciplined book as a revision of recent critical excitation about a queer theatre, but still a slight sense of disappointment about its reinstitution of gender playing as rather unplayful.

By contrast, the contributors to James C. Bulman's edited collection *Shakespeare Re-Dressed: Cross-Gender Casting in Contemporary Performance* are *very* playful, addressing what the fantasy of Shakespearian gender play has enabled for modern dramaturges, actors and audiences. Bulman's introduction charges (presumably other) scholars with perpetuating 'a conservatism endemic to Shakespeare studies' because of their preference for arguing over the ineffable historical performances 'they can only imagine', rather than discussing contemporary performances 'for which they have all the material evidence necessary to do a thorough cultural analysis'. The point is striking in its simplicity: history is conservative, contemporary is radical; the past is irretrievable, the present is here around us. Putting the Cheek by Jowl all-male *As You Like It* alongside public responses to AIDS and the British government's homophobic Section 28

legislation (forbidding local government organizations from 'promoting' homosexuality, thankfully repealed in 2003), Bulman waves the flag for the young Turks, as do other essays taking much of their methodology about gender and performance from Judith Butler's anti-essentialist *Gender Trouble*. The essays which most usefully unsettle Bulman's faux-naïve distinction between historical and contemporary are those considering performance at the rebuilt Globe theatre on London's South Bank. Quite different interpretations emerge when Robert Conkie discusses Mark Rylance's *Antony and Cleopatra* with Rylance as Cleopatra, when Elizabeth Klett analyses the all-female productions at the Globe, and when Judith Rose and Bulman each consider the Globe's *Twelfth Night*. For Conkie, the Globe's version of historical playing conditions corroborates stereotypical femininity, constructed from a male perspective. Rylance's own understanding of Cleopatra's own predilection for play-acting is seen, in the context of his cross-gendered performance, to be less her own particular characteristic and more an apparently universal insight into female identity: the modern performance does not challenge but confirms gender stereotypes, and the erasure of female actors constitutes an erasure of female subjectivity. Klett's entertaining reading of Janet McTeer as a crudely charismatic Petruchio, and her description of cuts to the all-female *Richard III* designed to minimize homoerotic potential, suggests that all-female casting does not in fact 're-dress the balance', serving more often to downplay gender's significance rather than highlight its fluidity. For Rose, the cross-dressed male Viola is a challenge to heteronormativity, and Tim Carroll's production constructs gender as 'a dance, a performance staged at every moment of our lives'; for Bulman the production eschewed the homoeroticism many cross-cast performances have found in, say, the relationship between Sebastian and Antonio but still 'pervasively queered the audience'. Cross-dressing clearly speaks to us as scholars and as audiences, but its message is an ambivalent one, caught between an ideal of gender playfulness and a culture, both Elizabethan and modern, still invested in gender stereotypes and in women's unequal access to many resources, including theatre itself. Elizabeth Schafer's readable biography of Lilian Baylis documents and contests this bias, with some great Shakespearian vignettes including a sketch of Baylis speaking to the playwright by telephone in a Shakespeare's Birthday revue for 1925.

Segueing, perhaps via Bergman's distinction between the cinema as mistress and the theatre as wife, to performances on screen in Samuel Crowl's *Shakespeare and Film: A Norton Guide*, Crowl focuses on the use of Shakespearian film in the classroom, reminding students that 'the best Shakespeare films are rarely those that cling to a fidelity model'. His is above all a useful book, but its arrangement by director in the first section and by technical or formal theme in the second, rather than by play, may not dovetail without some predigestion into 'Shakespeare on Film' courses. Crowl takes up Jack Jorgens's tried and tested taxonomy of theatrical, realist and filmic, abjures the often proposed 'adaptation' and instead introduces a different fourth category of 'hybrid' – films 'that find their inspiration as much from other, conventional Hollywood films and film genres as they do from their Shakespearean source material', citing from the 1990s boom as examples. Crowl often references the period between the fall of the Berlin Wall and the attack on the World Trade Center as a 'golden period of revival' when Hollywood turned from spy thrillers to Shakespeare. The historical survey is lucid and brisk, peppered with occasional vivid detail, for example that the blue colour of the Thames in the opening of Olivier's *Henry V* was achieved with motor oil. The second half of the book is more suggestive and less usual, brimming with provocative points that could easily spark off seminar discussion, such as the camera in Branagh's *Hamlet* as 'omniscient narrator', on the relevance of the soundtrack to Luhrmann's *Romeo + Juliet*, on the tracking rhythms of Welles's *Othello*. A very useful glossary of terms concludes an excellent pedagogic resource, though Crowl tends to refer to students in the third person and so may be addressing an audience of their teachers.

Crowl's chapter on Shakespeare on television is adept in bringing out the differences between productions for the big and small screen – but these mostly identify things that television is not good at. A collection of essays in honour of Michèle Willems opens by asking the question 'Is there still such a thing as "Television Shakespeare"?' and proceeds on the next page to reassure us that 'there is still such a thing as Television Shakespeare after all'. Whether this is a good thing or even a 'Good Thing' is not so clear. That Television Shakespeare is broadly defined is clear from the cover – a still from Luhrmann's memorable news-anchor Prologue against the graphic 'star-crossed lovers': Dominique Goy-Blanquet's essay discusses television as an image of surveillance and media spin in modern productions, including the sly glimpse of George W. Bush on screen in Cheek by Jowl's *Measure for Measure*. Michael Hattaway discusses *Richard II*, Anthony Davies *King Lear*, and Florence Cabaret gives a reflective account of Tim Supple's *Twelfth Night* (2003). The most tautly argued piece is Ruth Morse's on the *Shakespeare Retold* series, which situates the three comedies expertly amid institutional debates about public sector broadcasting as well as the ongoing socio-cultural ones about gender roles. Elsewhere the tone is enthusiastic rather than pointedly critical: Bernice W. Kliman ends her piece on televisual *Romeo and Juliet*s by urging directors on stage or screen 'to send a burst of joy into our hearts and minds', despite, or perhaps because of, having conveniently watched the films she discusses on a corner of her laptop screen with 'a word processing program open below it to capture my notes simultaneously'. Peter Holland's characteristically cool conclusion discusses YouTube postings without condescension, imagines watching Shakespeare in the future on an even smaller mobile phone screen, and wonders whether the BBC's announcement of a new canon of televised plays under the direction of Sam Mendes isn't a rather retrograde step.

The same editors, Hatchuel and Vienne-Guerrin, have also brought out another volume in their 'Shakespeare on Screen' series, this year devoted to *The Henriad*. The heroic, epic implications of this critical terminology are not explored, although almost all the contributors address the ways in which film versions of individual plays need to gesture towards the other plays, or at least the story of the other plays. Anthony Davies's sensitive essay 'Falstaff's shadow' shows how versions of the *Henry IV* plays are particularly dependent on what goes before and after; both Warren Chernaik and David Margolies discuss elegiac flashback moments in films of *Henry V*. Charles Forker sounds a sceptical note: 'it is interesting to speculate whether the ancient subject matter [of the history plays] and modern cinematic freedoms are even potentially compatible', and although his account of John Farrell's cinematic version of a guerrilla *Richard II* (2001) makes it sound very interesting, he judges it 'largely a failure'. Michael Hattaway is much more impressed by the televised version of Deborah Warner's production with Fiona Shaw, arguing for the relative unimportance of Richard's gender – 'difference becomes invisible after about ten minutes of good theatrical experience' – and instead for the emotional qualities of the performance. His essay sometimes wanders between the stage and screen, however, and the statement that Warner finds 'televisual conventions' to enhance rather than compromise the stage production is not closely argued. Elsewhere, Mariangela Tempera gathers a likeable range of references to these histories in other films, from Jed Bartlet taking his staffers to a five-hour version of *War of the Roses* in *The West Wing* to a modern dress *Henry V* at the end of Carrie Preson's *29th and Gay* (2005) in which the film's gay wannabe actor spoofs American militarism and the attempts of the Bush White House, like the Bartlet one, to connect its president with Shakespeare's play. As ever, there is an invaluably extensive 'annotated filmo-bibliography' by José Ramón Diaz Fernández.

Carol Rutter begins her suggestive and original *Shakespeare and Child's Play: Performing Lost Boys on Stage and Screen* with a brisk dismissal of previous forays into the topic. Stone, Ariès, Fumerton and Garber are 'quite simply, wrong'; there are in fact scores of children's roles in Shakespeare's texts and productions, from the Princes in the Tower to the child witnessing Noble's film of *A Midsummer Night's Dream*, from that lost child of Lady Macbeth to the infant's first age of man. In discussing children in the texts and in the recent history of their reproduction, Rutter is able to combine cultural anthropology, literary criticism and theatre history, juxtaposing these diverse methods of enquiry to considerable effect. Reading Mamilius as a repository for patriarchal nostalgia in *The Winter's Tale*, Rutter considers early modern herbals to understand his putative role to recuperate adult sicknesses, and discusses productions which focus on him, particularly at the play's conclusion, as a counter to its effortful attempts at a happy ending. Ed Hall's 2005 production, shaped by a pyjama-clad Mamilius scarcely revivified by doubling as Perdita, ended with father and dead son grimly facing each other; the Maly Theatre in 1999 had Mamilius, led by Time, enter into the final scene of family reunion, reminding us of what the fairy-tale can never repair. On *Macbeth*, Rutter is able to combine ideas about lineal succession and King James I's ideas about the education of princes with recent productions' excavation of an infant death as the unspoken wound in the Macbeth marriage. Throughout, her book is exemplary in integrating performance with other vectors to produce a multi-dimensional critical praxis, and this book is strongly recommended, not least for all those perplexed by that scene with the toy soldiers, the ketchup and the paper-bag mask at the beginning of Taymor's *Titus*.

Julie Sanders's *Shakespeare and Music* is erudite and quick – covering jazz, musical theatre, opera, symphonic and hybrid film scores, classical music, and Shakespeare references in popular music. She seems equally at home with Rufus Wainwright's adaptation of Sonnet 29 as with Dvořák's overture on *Othello*, and her take on the musicality of *A Midsummer Night's Dream* can encompass Mendelssohn's ballet, Purcell's *Fairy Queen*, Duke Ellington's *Such Sweet Thunder* and the Beatles playing 'Pyramus and Thisbe', shaped by a real familiarity with the play's own critical responses. Drawing on a lexicon informed by studies of adaptation on film, Sanders also shares that field's inclusivity. Brief accounts of hiphop versions of *Comedy of Errors* as *Da Boyz* (via *The Boys from Syracuse*) and *Bomb-itty of Errors* are non-evaluative, although she is severe on the failure of Branagh's *Love's Labour's Lost* – not, it must be said, for its aesthetic of whimsical amateurism identified by most film critics but for its deployment of a fascist context that is decorative rather than politically interrogative. Throughout, her emphasis is on 'deep contextualisation' – understanding the musical adaptations and responses in their own cultural and historical terms, as well as in relation to the Shakespearian host. Some less familiar material is brought into the mainstream, including a number of responses to tragedies, although Sanders is particularly suggestive on the absence of non-diegetic music in Brook's film of *King Lear* and in the Namibian Dogme adaptation *The King is Alive*. Again, Sanders shows herself a critic of rare, unshowy range: the book is highly recommended as a companion, as she herself hopes, to David Lindley's historical *Shakespeare and Music* (2006).

The range of publishers in this field seems to have narrowed, with Cambridge University Press taking the lion's share of Shakespeare criticism, and Ashgate most prominent in early modern drama. Four books in Ashgate's series 'Studies in Performance and Early Modern Drama' expand historical investigations of the Renaissance stage. The title of Michelle Ephraim's *Reading the Jewish Woman on the Elizabethan Stage* seems like the setup for the rejoinder 'short book?': in fact it takes us far beyond Jessica into a dense argument about the ways in which Elizabeth is inscribed in figures of Old Testament women, particularly Deborah. Lisa Hopkins's account of *The Cultural Uses of Caesars on the English Renaissance Stage* brings together a range of dramatic Roman material to discuss the layering of Catholicism and papal authority onto fictions of ancient Rome, the movement eastwards of the power and title of Caesar, and the deployment of the Brutus myth to corroborate Stuart monarchical authority, including a suggestive analysis of *Cymbeline*. Shakespeare's late plays also feature strongly in the contributions to Kathryn Moncrief and Kathryn McPherson's *Performing Maternity in Early Modern England*, and essays play interestingly on the dynamics of revelation and concealment in dramatic representations of pregnancy. Representations of transnational dialogue (between characters of different nationalities or languages, for example) and dramatic enactments of such dialogue (touring acting troupes and translation) are the focus of contributors to *Transnational Exchange in Early Modern Theater*, edited by Robert Henke and Eric Nicholson. In his study of *Laughter and Weeping in Early Modern Theatres*, Matthew Steggle traces inscriptions of affect in play-texts and argues for a close correlation between staged and audience emotion with particular attention to the acoustic textures of playgoing.

Ashgate also offer the most substantial work on cross-cultural Shakespeare in Dionne and Kapadia's collection *Native Shakespeares: Indigenous Appropriations on a Global Stage*. The book has two epigraphs – one a familiar line from *The Tempest* where Caliban asserts that without his books Prospero's 'but a sot as I am', the other a more challenging line from the Indian writer Kalyan Ray: 'Reflect on that Willybaba! This is my turn.' Between citation and revision, then, both quotations identify a power that can be wrested from the colonial text, a book that can be possessed, a voice that can make itself heard. As a model for the 'native' appropriations discussed here, the dynamic of citation and revision is apposite: contributors find Shakespeare defiantly reworked to articulate conflicts in Arab nationalism, as unlikely parts of Caribbean ritual, as standard-bearer for the New Zealand language *te reo*, as Bollywood gangster warfare. The editors collect these diverse examples under the heading of repossession: the cultural process by which native cultures and local traditions bear and reinterpret the imprint of contact with colonial authority. Whereas previous essay collections on global Shakespeares have focused on theatre and performance as the primary sites for the generation of postcolonial meanings, Dionne and Kapadia's contributors take a wider view, involving a range of cultural and institutional productions, from Salman Rushdie's short story 'Yorick' to the documentary *Shakespeare Behind Bars*, from the Sudanese novel *Season of Migration to the North*, by Tayeb Salih, to an Aboriginal *As You Like It*. The results are enlightening, if inevitably uneven, with a dispiriting tendency to outline a rather flat critical apparatus in the early paragraphs of the essay followed by an exciting and challenging description of the work – almost always unfamiliar to most readers – under question.

Some final edited collections to mention in conclusion: Paul Yachnin and Patricia Badir gather contributions on *Shakespeare and the Cultures of Performance*. 'Performance' in the first part of the book, subtitled 'early modern cultures of performance', seems less distinct from other textual manifestations and manoeuvres than it does in the second half on 'modern cultures', in which stages, theatrical, cinematic and more broadly cultural, are foregrounded. Coppélia Kahn's piece on Shakespeare and blackface minstrelsy explores the controversial 1844 rewriting of *Othello* as *Otello, A Burlesque Opera*, and the ways in which it translated the play's racial transgression into the familiar world of its mid-nineteenth-century audiences. Kahn is adept at acknowledging the discomfort of her argument, in which blackface at once denaturalizes racial essentialism but also draws on highly racialized mores and laws for its legibility. Gordon McMullan's careful account of recent Prosperos shows how they draw on the simultaneous myths of Dowden-style autobiography and of anti-Stratfordianism. Gretchen E. Minton cleverly weaves problems of *Troilus and Cressida* on stage with its own sexualized inscription of 'literary belatedness' under the nice heading of 'performance anxiety'. In Michael Cordner and Peter Holland's valuable collection *Players, Playwrights, Playhouses: Investigating Performance, 1660–1800*, a range of star contributors on the long eighteenth century investigate the literary, economic, cultural, regulatory and geographical states of playing, beginning with Robert D. Hume's brisk acknowledgement that theatre history is much practised but seldom theorized. His robust essay, acknowledging 'postpositivism', 'the limits of evidence' and 'enforced omission' as significant challenges

to theatre history methodology, is strongly recommended. Although not focusing specifically on Shakespeare, the essays have much of interest, not least their consciousness of methodology, and, unusually in a genre much enamoured of the prefix 're-', their genuine commitment to the revisionary challenge of that series title 'Redefining British Theatre History'.

Last of all is another essay collection, Peter Holland's *Shakespeare, Memory and Performance*. Holland and his contributors probe the paradox of memory as an inevitable compound of its corollary, forgetting, the sometimes unconscious allure of invented memories, and the ways in which memories remembered within the plays move into the memories *of* the plays, by actors and their audiences. Performance studies is a field at once potentially hampered by, but also crucially dependent on, the fallibility of memory, as Bruce Smith brilliantly anatomizes in his apparently conversational depiction of the processes of his writing the first section of the essay, in which memory, his freshman notes in the Signet *King Lear* and his own theatre archive are deployed to show the contingency of what we actually think we remember of things we have read or seen. Barbara Hodgdon's work on the RSC's costume archive sees how memories and performance cohere in the visual, and, in reflecting on the status of the photographs used to illustrate the chapter, intersects with the concerns of other contributors in discussing technologies of memory, from writing tablets to phonographs to cinema. A trio of essays by W. B. Worthen, Robert Shaughnessy and Dennis Kennedy take the digital age as the site of modern memory, distinguishing between professional and recreational consumers of these information sources. Kennedy's essay ends challengingly with an amnesiac fantasy: 'I would like to forget *Hamlet*,' while acknowledging 'I am not a spectator, I am a museum of *Hamlet*.' In their engagement with the affect of theatre and the detail of Shakespeare's texts, with a range of disciplinary perspectives on memory and an attentiveness to different types of material evidence, and a self-consciousness that eschews critical narcissism to provoke and stimulate, Holland's team have produced a work of exemplary scholarship. Performance studies and theatre history converge to present those fallible, forgetful, suggestible spectators, and their professional academic counterparts, as the ultimate location of interpretative authority.

WORKS REVIEWED

Brown, John Russell, ed., *The Routledge Companion to Directors' Shakespeare* (London and New York, 2008)

Bulman, James C., ed., *Shakespeare Re-Dressed: Cross-Gender Casting in Contemporary Performance* (Madison, 2008)

Cordner, Michael, and Peter Holland, eds., *Players, Playwrights, Playhouses: Investigating Performance, 1660–1800* (Basingstoke and New York, 2007)

Crowl, Samuel, *Shakespeare and Film: A Norton Guide* (New York and London, 2008)

Dionne, Craig, and Parmita Kapadia, eds., *Native Shakespeares: Indigenous Appropriations on a Global Stage* (Aldershot, 2008)

Dobson, Michael, ed., *Performing Shakespeare's Tragedies Today: The Actor's Perspective* (Cambridge, 2006)

Ephraim, Michelle. *Reading the Jewish Woman on the Elizabethan Stage* (Aldershot, 2008)

Hatchuel, Sarah, and Nathalie Vienne-Guerrin, *Television Shakespeare: Essays in Honour of Michèle Willems* (Rouen, 2008)

Holland, Peter, ed., *Shakespeare, Memory and Performance* (Cambridge, 2006)

Hopkins, Lisa, *The Cultural Uses of the Caesars on the English Renaissance Stage* (Aldershot, 2008)

Mann, David, *Shakespeare's Women: Performance and Conception* (Cambridge, 2008)

Moncrief, Kathryn M., and Kathryn R. McPherson, *Performing Maternity in Early Modern England* (Aldershot, 2008)

Rutter, Carol Chillington, *Shakespeare and Child's Play: Performing Lost Boys on Stage and Screen* (London, 2007)

Sanders, Julie, *Shakespeare and Music: Afterlives and Borrowings* (Cambridge, 2007)

Schafer, Elizabeth, *Lilian Baylis: A Biography* (Hatfield, 2006)

Steggle, Matthew, *Laughing and Weeping in Early Modern Theatres* (Aldershot, 2008)

Yachnin, Paul, and Patricia Badir, *Shakespeare and the Cultures of Performance* (Aldershot, 2008)

3a. EDITIONS AND TEXTUAL STUDIES
reviewed by ERIC RASMUSSEN

I. EDITIONS

The programme note is an undervalued genre. Although the programmes sold in the lobbies at major Shakespearian productions often include superbly incisive accounts of the play and its reception history, usually written by a prominent figure in the profession, they are virtually never cited in scholarly discourse. So it comes as a pleasant surprise to find programme notes given pride of place in Roger Warren's new Oxford edition of *The Two Gentlemen of Verona*. Warren begins his introductory essay by quoting at length from Hilary Spurling's description of the world of the play in her programme note for a 1970 RSC production. The next section of the introduction similarly opens by citing Anne Barton's programme note for her

husband's 1981 production, in which she defines the central topic of the play as 'how to bring love and friendship into a constructive and mutually enhancing relationship'.

Warren's unconventional use of programme notes is one of the features that distinguishes this edition as the work of a man of the theatre. Whereas the 'stage history' in many editions can be a tired distillation of previous reviewers' accounts, Warren's descriptions of productions over the last forty-odd years draw extensively on his firsthand experience. Warren does not suffer bad acting gladly. He witheringly characterizes the

With thanks, as always, to Arthur Evenchik, Trey Jansen, and James Mardock.

BBC Television version of the play as a 'vilely spoken' production in which 'few of the actors know how to speak verse – the main fault is to stress personal pronouns when the text doesn't'. When Warren's recollection of a given production differs from that in a published review, he attempts to adjudicate the discrepancy by tracking down the original players. In reviewing Robin Phillips's 1970 production of the play, Robert Smallwood reported seeing 'a little enigmatic flicker of a smile' on the face of the actor playing Proteus, Finbar Lynch, before he began to speak his crucial lines in the final scene. Warren, however, 'recalled a clenching of the mouth that spoke of inner tension, even resentment', and so asked Lynch 'to cast his mind back fifteen years to that moment'. Lynch reported that 'both he and his director believed that Proteus' repentance was genuine'.

Although Warren's edition is not especially concerned with textual issues (perhaps uniquely among critical editions of Shakespeare, the word 'compositor' does not appear therein), its text of the play is letter-perfect. The only slips in the textual notes are minor ones: at 3.1.56 'tenor' probably ought to have been recorded as Theobald's emendation of F1's 'tenure' (although one could argue that this is modernization rather than emendation); at 3.1.278 'master's ship' should have been recorded as Theobald's emendation of 'Mastership'.

Tipping the scales at 450 pages, Anthony B. Dawson and Gretchen E. Minton's Arden 3 *Timon of Athens* includes an ambitious introductory essay (divided into twenty-nine sections) as well as seven appendices. It is impossible to comment on all of this material, but I do want to draw attention to innovations that ought to be emulated by future editors. For example, Dawson and Minton provide a tremendously useful appendix that lists 'Notable performances of *Timon of Athens* in the past century' in tabular form, each with its date, venue, director, actor playing Timon, brief accounts of 'setting/style/concept', and 'notable features'. This is such a good idea that one could imagine doing away with the standard narrative stage history altogether. Given the space limitations of the table, one can forgive some of the minor omissions, such as

the fact that the young Benjamin Britten wrote the incidental music for Nugent Monck's 1935 production. (The omission of the name of 'midget actor' who played Apemantus in the 1978 Ashland, Oregon production is perhaps less forgivable.)

In reviewing Dawson's Cambridge edition of *Troilus and Cressida* several years back, I enthused over the brief guide he provided to help users understand collations. He and Minton have prepared a similar guide for their Arden 3 *Timon*, providing several examples of textual notes along with explanations of their meanings. I once again applaud this important innovation; it is naïve to assume that even advanced students will understand the arcane conventions of textual collations, but editors rarely give much guidance in this regard. Many readers would no doubt be baffled by a collation that reads 'window-bars] *Steevens (Johnson); window Barne F*' and will be grateful for Dawson and Minton's explanation: 'this note indicates that we print "window-bars", following George Steevens's 1773 emendation, which itself derives from a conjecture of Samuel Johnson's (the parentheses indicate a conjectural reading)'.

Overall, this is a beautiful edition, splendidly illustrated with Wyndham Lewis's Vorticist designs for a planned edition that never appeared, Byam Shaw's art nouveau illustrations for the Chiswick Shakespeare (1902), and a Dürer woodcut of a man afflicted with syphilis. Dawson and Minton clearly take textual matters seriously: I have not found a single substantive error in their text of the play. I am puzzled, however, by their handling of elisions. Despite a prefatory remark that 'in verse speeches, marks of elision are retained where they are necessary guides to the scansion and pronunciation of the line', several Folio elisions are *not* retained, and their expansion results in verse lines with extra metrical feet: at 1.1.55 for 'slippery' read 'slipp'ry', 2.2.171 for 'showers' read 'show'rs', 4.2.6 for 'fallen' read 'fall'n', 4.3.457 for 'desperate' read 'desp'rate', 5.1.68 for 'shower' read 'show'r', and 5.5.25 for 'towers' read 'tow'rs'. There is some confusion at 3.7.112, where F reads '2' and the editors follow Capell's emended speech-prefix '3 LORD' but accidentally state in the textual note that

F reads '3'. The speech-prefix '3 SERVANT' at 3.3.5 ought to have been accompanied by a note that the Folio reads simply 'Ser.'; oddly, the numeral is dropped in the speech-heading for the next speech by the same character (3.3.28), where he becomes simply 'SERVANT'. In the quotation from 2.1.21 on page 79, for 'me' read 'mine'. The emendation at 2.2.102 of 'sad' for 'sadly' is not original to this edition but should properly be attributed to Chalmers; similarly, the emendation at 4.3.348 was anticipated by Knight. There are a handful of slips in the collations.[1]

Keir Elam's introduction to his Arden 3 *Twelfth Night* is a model of critical (sometimes highly critical) synthesis punctuated by original contributions. After discussing the many prurient critics who seem 'infected' by Aguecheek's desire to understand and Malvolio's 'will to knowledge' in their forced readings of 'c, u, t, and p's' as 'the symbolic gelding of the boy actor' playing a 'feminized, ridiculed, castrated' Malvolio, Elam proposes that 'the idea of watching Olivia pee is not so much an erotic fantasy as a dream of social equality, since only her husband, the "count" (a title achieved with the addition of another letter) has the right to do so'. After ranging over the many critical accounts of Viola's cross-dressing, Elam extends the analysis to Malvolio's cross-garters, an instance of 'cross-class-dressing' that is 'in some ways a negative image of Viola's . . . as disastrous as hers is all too successful'.

With the exception of John Dover Wilson – who famously placed Hamlet's mid-scene entry in 2.2 eight lines earlier (so that he could overhear Polonius's plot) – editors tend to preserve the copy-text placement of entrance directions, save for those instances in which they are manifestly misplaced. And yet, Elam relocates quite a number of Folio mid-scene entrance directions (1.3.40, 1.5.27, 3.4.136, 4.2.9, and 4.3.21). In this edition, Sir Andrew enters before Sir Toby announces 'here comes Sir Andrew Aguecheek' (1.3.41) rather than immediately after, Olivia enters before Maria's 'here comes my lady' (1.5.28), and the like. But Elam nowhere provides an explanation for these changes. He takes an even less defensible liberty in

deleting the Folio's direction for '*Musicke*' at 2.4.50; surely the fact that 'no contemporary musical setting survives for this song' cannot be offered as a rationale for removing the direction from an edited text.

I have complained repeatedly in this space about editors who use '*this edn*' as shorthand for 'I'm too busy to look it up'. Unfortunately, the practice persists in Elam's *Twelfth Night*, where readings that have appeared in many previous editions are unaccountably flagged as unique to this one. The '*aside*' at 3.1.88, first added by Dyce and used in Mowat and Werstine's Folger edition as well, can hardly be said to have been 'adopted for the first time' in this Arden 3 edition. Similarly, the emendation at 3.1.144 appears in both Delius and Craig; that at 4.2.14–15 was anticipated by Wright, Penguin, and the Riverside; and it's impossible to see how 'Aha!' at 4.2.126 is original to Elam's text when Oxford reads 'Aha'. In one instance in which Elam makes a textual change with a legitimate claim to uniqueness, the result is a subtle difference in meaning: Where the Folio reads 'More longing, wavering, sooner lost and worn' (2.4.34), Elam suggests that 'More longing' is best understood as an intensifier qualifying an adjective and emends to 'longing wavering', which he glosses as 'yearningly indecisive'.

There is one error in Elam's text of the play (at 2.3.124 for 'when man's a-hungry' read 'when a man's a-hungry') and two minor errors in the collations (in the textual note at 3.4.274–5 for 'Pacified' read 'pacified'; 4.2.119–20 for 'gone' read 'goue'). The Folio text occasionally mixes 't' and 'r' types; one of these instances is noted (at 3.3.8) but several others are not.[2] The claim that *TN*

---

[1] In the textual note at 1.1.21 for 'Lord' read 'Lord.'; 1.1.62 for 'himself' read 'himselfe'; 1.2.38–9 for 'me:' read 'me:' 2.2.168 for '*Timon:*' read '*Timon:*' (twice); 3.6.59 for '(2)' read '(2. *Sen.*)'; 5.1.42 for 'serves' read 'serues'; 5.2.105 for 'four' read 'foure'. 'He's' at 3.3.14 should have a textual note recording that the F reading is 'Has' (as is done in the identical instance at 4.3.445).

[2] In the textual note at 1.4.14 for 'the' read 'rhe'; 2.5.87 for 'her' read 'het'; 3.4.168 for 'for't' read 'fot't'; 5.1.367 for 'Lord' read 'Lotd'.

is 'unique among Shakespeare's plays in having received a contemporary review [in Manningham's *Diary*] after a performance by the Lord Chamberlain's men' would appear to overlook Thomas Platter's account of a performance of *Caesar* in 1599. Quite a few printers' devils seem to have been at work in the production of this edition: stray underlining oddly links all of the collations on page 171; the caption to Figure 17 includes what appears to be the remnant of a direction to a copy-editor, 'see List of Ills' (where the List of Illustrations provides only an identical caption); there's an unindented paragraph on page 359, and the indents on pages 380–1 are twice the size of those elsewhere in the text.

II. TEXTUAL STUDIES

Shakespeare's Book: Essays in Reading, Writing and Reception, edited by Richard Meek, Jane Rickard and Richard Wilson, extends recent work by Lukas Erne and others on Shakespeare as a literary dramatist – although he is here reclassified, by Patrick Cheney, as an early modern author, 'a *literary poet-playwright*'. The book's evocative title finds its origin in an inventory, compiled by the sister of printer Richard Field, of items that had fallen 'deceitfully' into the grasp of another Stratford widow on 20 July 1595: 'Mr Shaxpere one book'. The editors' introduction is a reading of the apparent allusion to Richard Field in *Cymbeline*, 'Richard du Champ' (4.2.379): 'Field' is a near anagram of the name 'Fidele', and the lines that follow – 'Thy name well fits thy faith, thy faith thy name' (4.2.383) – could be taken, the editors suggest, as a hint that Field was the only printer Shakespeare trusted, the printer he would have chosen to produce his collected works. A slight irony attends this discussion of faithful printing: the editors get the name of Field's sister wrong (for 'Margery' read 'Margaret').

More significantly, the editors of *Shakespeare's Book* do not seem fully informed about the current state of Shakespearian textual studies. For instance, all recent editions of *Cymbeline* (Oxford,

Cambridge, RSC), including the one that the editors are using (Norton), put an end to the tradition of reproducing the erroneous 'Imogen' and have restored 'Innogen'. And yet, the editors open their introduction with an allusion to 'the boy Fidele played by Imogen'. It's a minor point, to be sure, but certainly germane to a speculative analysis about whether Field would have been a better printer for the Folio than Jaggard; one wonders whether Field's more careful compositors would have made the original mistake of 'Imogen' for 'Innogen', or whether his more assiduous readers of proof might have caught it if they did.

Of greater significance still, the editors of *Shakespeare's Book* perpetuate the discredited notion that the 1619 Pavier collection was 'unauthorized' ('Introduction', p. 11), as does one of the contributors to the volume, Duncan Salkeld, who, after correctly pointing out that the 'publishing rights' to *Henry V* 'were transferred from Millington and Busby to Thomas Pavier', unaccountably goes on to assert that when Pavier printed the 1619 quarto of this play *to which he owned the rights*, it was 'surreptitiously produced'. As Thomas Berger wryly observes in an essay in the *Concise Companion to Shakespeare and the Text* (reviewed below), the old ideas about 'corruption and foul play' behind the Pavier quartos ('textual historians being no less paranoid than the average citizen') have now been supplanted by Sonia Massai's suggestion that the 1619 quartos, also printed by Jaggard, should be viewed not as an unauthorized collection but as a 'marketing device to whet the play-reading public's hunger for the larger collection that would appear in 1623'.

There are compensatory aspects of *Shakespeare's Book*, particularly Lukas Erne's 'Afterword', in which he ruminates about 'when and where Shakespeare first encountered a book that was clearly marked as his, with his name on the title-page'. In revisiting an earlier essay on false starts, E. A. J. Honigmann puckishly wonders whether 'passages that are, quite simply, less brilliant than we might expect' throughout Shakespeare should be viewed as 'intended deletions' that 'can be removed without damaging the play'. When a distinguished textual critic makes such a suggestion, one wonders how long it will be before we see a return to Pope's practice of 'degrading' passages that he found 'excessively bad' to the foot of the page in his edited text.

George Donaldson finely observes that whereas the largest capitals on the title-page of Jonson's Folio are used for *Workes*, the largest capitals on the title-page in Shakespeare's Folio are used for Shakespeare's surname. To Donaldson, this difference illustrates a larger contrast between the two folios, 'one overseen by its living author and one commemorating its dead author, with Jonson's emphasis on his writings and Heminge's and Condell's repeated emphasis on the writer'. Donaldson sees the First Folio as a 'collective effort of remembrance and of contending views of how Shakespeare is to be remembered'. The contention is neatly articulated in the prefatory poems as one between private and public – between Ben Jonson's 'my Shakespeare' and Leonard Digges's 'our Shakespeare'.

Jane Rickard notes that little critical attention has been given to the *Workes* of the patron of Shakespeare's playing company, King James, published in folio in 'the same year' as the 1616 Jonson Folio. Although she is right about the lack of critical interest in James's *Workes*, the king's folio was not actually published until the spring of 1617. Thus, the folios that Rickard refers to throughout as 'the two 1616 collections' are not as co-temporal as she thinks.

The essays in *A Concise Companion to Shakespeare and the Text*, edited by Andrew Murphy, engage some of the same issues as *Shakespeare's Book*, but in ways that are more informed and often more stimulating. Commenting on the recent fascination in textual studies with the gradual appearance of Shakespeare's name on the title-pages of play quartos, Peter Stallybrass and Roger Chartier ask 'to what extent was this an attempt to associate the plays with what was *still* Shakespeare's bestselling work: *Venus and Adonis*?' Stallybrass and Chartier point to the shift in the printed format of the narrative poems, which were first published in quarto but later reprinted exclusively in octavo.

The purpose of the change, these critics suggest, was to 'avoid the ephemeral status of the quarto' by making it possible 'to bind the later editions of all three volumes of Shakespeare's poetry (including the 1599 octavo of *The Passionate Pilgrim*)'.

Stallybrass and Chartier also note that fragments of Shakespeare's plays and poems began to circulate in printed commonplace books alongside the words of Spenser and Sidney. 'Shakespeare thus emerges as a canonical English poet in a bound volume neither through poems nor through his plays but rather through individual "sentences" (of 10 or 20 syllables) extracted from his works.'

Andrew Murphy offers a concise history of editing, drawing particular attention to the fact that in the eighteenth century and for most of the nineteenth, no editor of Shakespeare was formally attached to an institution of learning. 'A considerable change would come in the 1860s when a group of scholars based at Trinity College, Cambridge was commissioned to produce a new edition', a development that 'signaled the professionalization of Shakespeare studies generally and of Shakespeare editing more particularly'. Paul Werstine's essay deconstructs 'the illusion of consensus' among New Bibliographers that is presented 'most comprehensively and very persuasively' in Greg's 1955 *Shakespeare First Folio*, the source that most editors working over the last several decades have relied upon for information regarding foul papers and bad quartos. David Bevington provides a pleasantly personal narrative about being assigned to edit *1H6* just as he was leaving Harvard for his first job at the University of Virginia:

Wonderful! I said to myself. I can study textual theory with him [Fredson Bowers], and thus learn what I need to know in editing *1H6*. It was an important factor in my deciding to go to Virginia. (We had choices in those palmy days.) I had not studied textual scholarship at Harvard: the department officially looked down its critical nose at the field as technical and non-literary. Fredson Bowers would be my teacher.

In the event, however, Bevington is disappointed to find that the advice Bowers provided for deciding between variant readings often boiled down to 'you pays your money and you takes your choice'. Sonia Massai's essay on 'Differential Readings' offers an account of the vigorous debate over the two texts of *Lear* that dominated late twentieth-century discourse about the play and looks back to the quieter, simpler time when W. J. Craig could remark on his conflation of Q1 and F1 in the first Arden Shakespeare *Lear* (1901): 'I do but follow the example of my predecessors, and my readers must therefore not expect to find in my text any very noticeable differences from that generally received; the ground has been too exhaustively worked by preceding editors to admit of any new discoveries of importance.' Anthony James West provides a companionable account of the reception history of the First Folio, drawn from his two published volumes on the topic. But West should have updated his discussion of 'the copy now in the Dr Williams Library in London', since that copy was sold at Sotheby's on 13 July 2006.

Leah Marcus writes about her experience editing *Merchant* for the Norton Critical Edition (2006), focusing on how she dealt with Q1's variant speech prefixes '*Iew*' and '*Shy*'. She writes that since the two do not alternate 'with anything approaching predictable regularity', she decided to preserve the variation in her edited text. Marcus's contention about the absence of 'predictable regularity' is called into question, however, by Richard Kennedy's work. Kennedy discerned a pattern in the speech prefixes that revealed a distinct compositorial preference for '*Iew*': '*Shy*' occurs only when supplies of italic '*I*' type apparently ran low.[3] In the 'Afterword' to *Shakespeare and the Text*, John Drakakis echoes Kennedy's conclusions, writing that 'depleted supplies of italic . . . seriously affected the setting of speech prefixes throughout a large part of the quarto'. Drakakis plans to preserve the variant *Jew* and *Shylock* speech prefixes in his forthcoming Arden 3. By the time that volume appears, however, I hope he will abandon his claim that 'no edition yet has been prepared to follow the instability of Q1 and F1 in representing *both*'. Since Marcus's Norton edition does exactly that, Drakakis's assertion – like all too many claims to editorial precedence – does not withstand scrutiny.

WORKS REVIEWED

Berger, Thomas L., 'Shakespeare Writ Small: Early Single Editions of Shakespeare's Plays', in Murphy, *Shakespeare and the Text*, pp. 57–70

Bevington, David, 'Working with the Text: Editing in Practice', in Murphy, *Shakespeare and the Text*, pp. 165–84

Donaldson, George, 'The First Folio: "My Shakespeare"/"Our Shakespeare": whose Shakespeare?', in Meek, Rickard and Wilson, *Shakespeare's Book*, pp. 187–206

Drakakis, John, 'Afterword', in Murphy, *Shakespeare and the Text*, pp. 221–38

Erne, Lukas, 'Afterword', in Meek, Rickard and Wilson, *Shakespeare's Book*, pp. 255–66

Marcus, Leah S., 'Editing Shakespeare in a Postmodern Age', in Murphy, *Shakespeare and the Text*, pp. 128–44

Massai, Sonia, 'Working with the Texts: Differential Readings', in Murphy, *Shakespeare and the Text*, pp. 185–203

Meek, Richard, Jane Rickard and Richard Wilson, '"Th'world's volume": Printer, Page and the Literary Field', in Meek, Rickard, and Wilson, *Shakespeare's Book*, pp. 1–28

Meek, Richard, Jane Rickard and Richard Wilson, eds., *Shakespeare's Book: Essays in Reading, Writing, and Reception* (Manchester, 2008)

Murphy, Andrew, 'The Birth of the Editor', in Murphy, *Shakespeare and the Text*, pp. 93–108

Murphy, Andrew, ed., *A Concise Companion to Shakespeare and the Text* (Oxford, 2007)

Rickard, Jane, 'The "First" Folio in Context: The Folio Collections of Shakespeare, Jonson, and King James', in Meek, Rickard and Wilson, *Shakespeare's Book*, pp. 207–32

Salkeld, Duncan, '"As sharp as a pen": *Henry V* and its Texts', in Meek, Rickard and Wilson, *Shakespeare's Book*, pp. 140–64

Shakespeare, William, *Twelfth Night, or What You Will*, ed. Keir Elam, Arden 3 (London, 2008)

    The Two Gentlemen of Verona, ed. Roger Warren, Oxford Shakespeare (Oxford, 2008)

Shakespeare, William, and Thomas Middleton, *Timon of Athens*, ed. Anthony B. Dawson and Gretchen E. Minton, Arden 3 (London, 2008)

---

[3] See 'Speech Prefixes in Some Shakespearean Quartos', *Papers of the Bibliographical Society of America*, 92 (1998), 177–209.

Smith, Helen, 'The Publishing Trade in Shakespeare's Time', in Murphy, *Shakespeare and the Text*, pp. 17–34

Stallybrass, Peter, and Roger Chartier, 'Reading and Authorship: The Circulation of Shakespeare 1590–1619', in Murphy, *Shakespeare and the Text*, pp. 35–56

Werstine, Paul, 'The Science of Editing', in Murphy, *Shakespeare and the Text*, pp. 109–27

West, Anthony James, 'The Life of the First Folio in the Seventeenth and Eighteenth Centuries', in Murphy, *Shakespeare and the Text*, pp. 71–90

3b. EDITIONS AND TEXTUAL STUDIES
reviewed by PETER HOLLAND

In reviewing *The RSC Shakespeare*, Jonathan Bate and Eric Rasmussen's edition of the *Complete Works* (2007), in the *TLS* (17 August 2007), I complained that 'the RSC-ness of *The RSC Shakespeare* is an invisible element', for, apart from the title-page, a one-page foreword by the RSC's Artistic Director, Michael Boyd, and a single insert of some photographs from RSC productions, there was no sign of the RSC's work informing the edition. Now, with the appearance in 2008 of the first five volumes of individual plays in the series, there has been a distinct turn for the better.

Chosen in part to match the RSC's 2008 repertory, the editions of (in F1 order) *The Tempest*, *Love's Labour's Lost*, *A Midsummer Night's Dream*, *Richard III* and *Hamlet* use the introductions, texts, commentary and collations from the *Complete Works*, unaltered as far as I have checked. But they add to them brief but deft 'Overviews' of each play's stage-history by Jan Sewell, a more extended and well-researched examination of the play in performance at the RSC by Karin Brown and, probably most significantly, interviews with and, in some cases, an essay by actors, directors and designers who have been involved in productions, mostly, though not always, at the RSC. *Richard III*, for instance, has interviews with the actor Simon Russell Beale (Richard in 1992), the director Bill Alexander (1984) and the designer Tom Piper (2006) and an essay by Richard Eyre reflecting on his National Theatre production (1990), while *Hamlet* has interviews with Ron Daniels (RSC 1984 and 1989), John Caird (NT 2000) and Michael Boyd (RSC 2004).

Conducted separately but with the same questions asked so that the answers can be spliced together, the interview materials are often perceptive and thoughtful: Terry Hands on his *Love's Labour's Lost* and Tim Supple on *Dream* are sharp on the ways their reading of the play informed the particularities of their productions; the contrasts between the approaches of Peter Brook (Bouffes du Nord 1990), Sam Mendes (1993) and Rupert Goold (2006) to *The Tempest* are intriguing. Brook, for instance, describes how his casting of Ariel 'tried to avoid the clichés of a lighter-than-air dancer', resisting what he calls 'illustration': 'instead we had an African actor, Bakary Sangary, with the physique of a rugby player, but with such a lightness of spirit, wit and fantasy that he suggested Arielness more than any illustration could do'.

Beale is fascinating on Richard's decision to eliminate Buckingham, a consequence in his production (directed by Mendes) of Richard's falling over his coronation robes as he moved to the throne in the elaborately staged coronation:

> The person he reached for was Buckingham, and quite precisely, because he had to rely on Buckingham to help him up, that meant he had to go. This was the immediate psychological reaction to having been humiliated in front of everybody – that he would have to get rid of the man who helped him. (p. 191)

The extra-textual act of falling becomes then the 'mini-version' of why Richard would have to rid himself of the individual who had helped him throughout the play. As an example of how a production or actor seeks a local cause for a larger one it works perfectly. Throughout, the theatre workers' comments serve to reveal process and move from text to performance.

But, inevitably, there is a disjunction between the new materials in these editions and the format of the text and commentary, a gap that cannot be effectively bridged. However useful, provocative or engaging the interviews and stage histories may be, they cannot integrate into the previously prepared and rather less performance-conscious text and commentary. As such, these additions to *The RSC Shakespeare* face the same kinds of problems that other performance-oriented editions confront and are signs of a continuing and far from resolved dilemma over what exactly the status and function of performance evidence could or should be. Three other series engage differently but no less problematically with the difficulties of function and integration, to some extent, as with these new examples, defined by the target audiences and in part by the nature of their conception of what kind of edition each seeks to be. Since *Survey* has not given them attention, I want here to note them very briefly in order to suggest the configuration of editions within which *The RSC Shakespeare* might be placed.

The dozen or so volumes in Jacky Bratton and Julie Hankey's series 'Shakespeare in Production' for Cambridge University Press, originally begun for Junction Books and then continued briefly with Bristol Classical Press, are superb scholarly achievements; the lengthy introductions chart the chronological history while the annotation on the line tracks single-mindedly what happened at each moment in dozens of productions. As resources for scholars and graduate students and, for certain kinds of performance courses, even for undergraduates they are outstanding. But, in an odd way, it is the text of the play that is least relevant, for users do not turn to them in order to read Shakespeare but to read the editors' work. The text is no more than a finding aid for the commentary. The depth of the series' archival work is in direct proportion to the narrowness of its conception; there is no need here for glossing, for textual analysis or for innovation in emendation (the texts are taken from the New Cambridge Shakespeare without its apparatus), for such concerns have no place beside the specification of, say, how productions have cut the play, how an actor moved or what s/he was wearing.

The Applause Shakespeare Library, edited by John Russell Brown, has sought to be innovative in providing a sustained commentary, usually written by an actor or director, sometimes in collaboration with an academic (Janet Suzman for *Antony and Cleopatra*, John Hirsch and Leslie Thomson for *A Midsummer Night's Dream*, Brown alone for *Macbeth*). The commentary does not refer to specific productions, even though, inevitably, an actor's or director's comments are profoundly shaped by the experience of involvement in a particular production. Instead it seeks to follow through the line by line possibilities that open up, the choices one might make and the consequences across the rest of the play of making those choices. It develops the interiority of characters, within conventional late twentieth-century parameters of how that interiority might be constructed, and sets that inside against an abstracted visual dimension of movement and blocking. If, as Brown argues in his general introduction, reviews of production most often mark what is 'unusual . . . rather than the opportunities offered to actors in any production of the play' – what he calls 'the text's enduring theatrical vitality' – then the need to outline that middle ground is fully justified. As Brown puts it,

Everything that happens on stage comes within the notice of this commentary. A reader can 'feel' what the play would be like in action . . . With this text in hand, the play can be produced in the theatre of the mind, creating a performance suitable to the moment and responsive to individual imaginations.[1]

Plagued by weak distribution, this series has not had the impact it deserves. Yet, the separation of the thinking-through of the play as performable from the evidence of performance is as problematic in its way as the narrowness of the

---

[1] John Russell Brown, 'Introduction' to *A Midsummer Night's Dream*, ed. Brown (New York, 1996), p. vi.

series' conception of what performance might be, restricted, in effect, to an imagination firmly and at times constrictingly grounded in late twentieth-century assumptions, denied precisely that sense of history, development and tradition that is so strongly present in the 'Shakespeare in Production' volumes.

Finally in my group, there is *The Sourcebooks Shakespeare*, for which I must acknowledge my being an occasional advisor. A trade publication aimed at a broad readership, this series makes no pretensions to textual scholarship. With superb accounts of each play's presence in popular culture by Douglas Lanier and with an account of one recent major production, it is not the print that is most striking, for the series' main innovation is the accompanying audio CD with extracts from numbers of productions linked by narrative read by Derek Jacobi, with most extracts represented in two or more different versions. The *King Lear* CD, for instance, has, impressively, Olivier, Wolfit, Gielgud, Scofield and Trevor Peacock as Lear. In a culture in which neither general readers nor students are used to listening to Shakespeare (for all their familiarity with film versions in which language is subordinate to visuals), *Sourcebooks Shakespeare* is a brave undertaking in seeking a different audience, rather than spectatorship, for Shakespeare. Again,

though ambitious, the volumes are not fully coherent, since, for instance, Lanier's marvellous range of examples does not resonate with the rest of what the volume seeks to create.

The RSC Shakespeare paperback editions are, then, another stage in the prolonged and sustained current impasse between the ambitions of performance-aware analysis and pedagogy, publishers' targets for the slice of the market an edition might reach, and the differing and apparently incompatible elements that all editions, not only these four series, provide. Good though it is to hear the voices of the directors and other theatre workers in these RSC volumes, I still await a more innovative form that might bring what is best in these series together. Perhaps, though, that is not to be achieved in print at all but only in a web-space or similar transformation of the ways in which we read Shakespeare.

WORKS REVIEWED

Bate, Jonathan, and Eric Rasmussen, eds., *Hamlet* (Houndmills, Basingstoke, 2008)
Love's Labour's Lost (Houndmills, Basingstoke, 2008)
A Midsummer Night's Dream (Houndmills, Basingstoke, 2008)
Richard III (Houndmills, Basingstoke, 2008)
The Tempest (Houndmills, Basingstoke, 2008)

INDEX

NOTE: locators in italics denote illustrations.

INDEX

INDEX

INDEX

INDEX

INDEX